PHYSICAL ANTHROPOLOGY

PHYSICAL ANTHROPOLOGY
SIXTH EDITION

PHILIP L. STEIN
Los Angeles Pierce College

BRUCE M. ROWE
Los Angeles Pierce College

The McGraw-Hill Companies, Inc.
New York   St. Louis   San Francisco   Auckland   Bogotá   Caracas
Lisbon   London   Madrid   Mexico City   Milan   Montreal
New Delhi   San Juan   Singapore   Sydney   Tokyo   Toronto

McGraw-Hill

A Division of The **McGraw·Hill** *Companies*

To our families and in memory of
Eleanor Frances Blumenthal Rowe Michael
and Barbara Stein Akerman

PHYSICAL ANTHROPOLOGY

1 2 3 4 5 6 7 8 9 0   DOW   DOW   9 0 9 8 7 6 5

ISBN 0-07-061252-8

This book was set in Trump Medieval by York Graphic Services, Inc.
The editors were Jill S. Gordon and Peggy Rehberger;
the production supervisor was Elizabeth J. Strange.
The cover was designed by Karen K. Quigley.
The photo editor was Kathy Bendo;
the photo researcher was Barbara Salz.
New drawings were done by Fine Line Illustrations, Inc.
R. R. Donnelley & Sons Company was printer and binder.

Cover photo: Chauvet/Le Seuil-Sygma

Library of Congress Cataloging-in-Publication Data
Stein, Philip L.
    Physical anthropology / Philip L. Stein, Bruce M. Rowe.—6th ed.
        p.   cm.
    Includes bibliographical references and index.
    ISBN 0-07-061252-8
    1. Physical anthropology.   I. Rowe, Bruce M.   II. Title.
    GN60.S72   1996
    573—dc20   95-39797

CONTENTS

IN BRIEF

v

CONTENTS

PREFACE

The story of evolution is the story of change through time. This story is told by physical anthropologists as they have reconstructed it through the discovery of evidence, often subtle and fragmentary, and the development of hypotheses to explain the evidence. Theodosius Dobzhansky wrote: "Evolution is change. Mankind has evolved; it is evolving; if it endures, it will continue to evolve. Human evolution has biological and cultural components. Man's biological evolution changes his nature; cultural evolution changes its nurture."[1]

The story of human endeavors is also a story of change through time. The first edition of *Physical Anthropology* appeared 22 years ago, in 1974. On the occasion of the appearance of the sixth edition, in 1996, it is instructional to look back and observe the changes that have occurred during these past 22 years.

While in 1974 physical anthropologists postulated that fossils ancestral to modern humans existed as long as $5\frac{1}{2}$ million years ago, the evidence was very fragmentary. The earliest credible evidence dated back an estimated 3 million years. In the 1990s fossil hunters uncovered the fragmentary bones of our earliest ancestors in Ethiopia. Dated at more than 4 million years old, these bones suggest that they are close to the common ancestor of humans and the apes. Looking at the more recent origins of anatomically

---

[1]T. Dobzhansky, *Mankind Evolution* (New Haven: Yale University Press, 1962), 23. Reprinted in P. L. Stein and B. M. Rowe, *Physical Anthropology*, 1st ed. (New York: McGraw-Hill, 1974), 295.

modern humans, new discoveries in Israel and South Africa, coupled with new dating methodologies, have brought to the forefront new discussions on the origins of modern *Homo sapiens*. Analysis of genetic material has provided further fuel that has fired discussions and controversies regarding the origins of modern peoples.

In 1995, contemporary humans entered the cave named Grotte Chauvet, located near the town of Vallon-Pont-d'Arc, France, for the first time in 30,000 years. Over 300 paintings and engravings created by *Homo sapiens* living at that distant time provide us with new and exciting glimpses of the lifestyles of these ancient people.

Equally exciting discoveries have been made in the areas of genetics and molecular biology. Scientists, working in many countries, are rapidly working out the complete genetic code for humankind. This endeavor is called the Human Genome Project. Still others are collecting and analyzing the genetic material from samples being collected from peoples living in many different regions of the world—the controversial Human Genome Diversity Project. Other efforts are leading to new medical techniques only dreamed of a short time ago. The analysis of the genetic material, DNA, also played a major role in human public affairs, as in the 1995 O. J. Simpson trial in Los Angeles.

Human knowledge is not divided into neat domains, each the property of a specific group of scholars. This is especially true in the study of human biology and human evolution. Many endeavors, both in the laboratory and field, draw from a variety of disciplines or include a multidisciplinary team. Working with anthropologists are evolutionary biologists, geneticists, molecular biologists, geologists, paleontologists, physicians, zoologists, chemists, psychologists, and many more. This volume is a tribute to these scholars who are constantly expanding the envelope of human knowledge and understanding.

This text has been written from the viewpoint of anthropology. The authors are anthropologists and the text is designed to be used in anthropology courses, although it is certainly useful in a variety of classes, such as human biology. The anthropological orientation has influenced the choice of topics and the organization of the book.

In this book we attempt to accomplish three major things. First, we present to the beginning student the basic concepts of anthropology in general, and physical anthropology in particular. Second, since a dominant theme of physical anthropology is human evolution, the book emphasizes a discussion of evolutionary theory and reviews our current knowledge about the evolution of the human species and its close biological relatives. Finally, this book embodies a philosophical concern with the biological nature of humans and the relationship of humans to the environment—what may be thought of as environmental issues from an anthropological perspective.

The first two chapters of this text deal with basic concepts necessary for a proper understanding of evolutionary theory. Next follow chapters on human genetics and population genetics, evolutionary theory, the human ability to adjust to differing environments, growth and development, human adaptations, and human social and biological variation.

The next series of chapters addresses the study of primatology. We focus on humankind's relationship with the animal world, especially with our closest living relatives, the nonhuman primates. Through comparative studies of these forms—prosimians, tarsiers, monkeys, and apes—anthropology attempts to reconstruct many aspects of human evolution.

The final group of chapters discusses paleoanthropology, the study of the fossil and archaeological record, and the physical remains of human evolutionary history. The text concludes with a consideration of our evolutionary present and future.

The study of human biology and human evolution is of great interest, especially because it is the study of ourselves. Physical anthropology, however, provides a fresh approach to the study of our present ecological crises. Traditionally, the people of Western culture view humanity as the center of a universe created for humanity to occupy, utilize, and control. Reports of overpopulation, drought and starvation, pollution, depletion of the ozone layer, destruction of the tropical rain forest, and social unrest strongly imply that humans are not beyond the influence of nature.

People are an integral part of the natural scheme. Their survival, like that of all other living organisms, depends upon maintaining a balance with supporting environments; actually because of past abuse, it may depend upon *reestablishing* the balances that have been disrupted. Humans are dependent upon the natural world, and when people ignore this dependence, survival itself is threatened.

Through its unique viewpoint—the holistic approach—anthropology provides insights into the dynamic interrelationships of the biological, environmental, cultural, and social aspects of human existence. Humans as biological beings cannot be studied apart from humans as cultural and social beings. By examining our biological limitations and potentials, we can gain a fuller understanding of how cultural innovations affect biology and environment. By discovering our relationships to the rest of the animal world, and by reconstructing our evolutionary history, we can appreciate more clearly our place in nature and the requirements for survival.

We would like to conclude this Preface by pointing out some of the features that can be found in this sixth edition. Each chapter begins with a chapter outline that will provide the student with an overview of the chapter. Many new illustrations and tables, including six sets of color photographs, will aid the student in understanding the data and concepts discussed. Basic information on the anatomy of the skeleton and the brain is found in the Appendix, permitting this material to be used with any of the several chapters that require this knowledge. Over fifty information boxes present material of unusual or special interest. Each chapter has summary sections following each main topic, two to three per chapter, and the many headings permit the student to organize the information in an outline form. Each chapter ends with study questions that act as another type of summary to test the student's understanding of the topics presented. An annotated Suggested Readings is also provided.

The text is supplemented by a *Study Guide*. It contains sample tests and short exercises designed to help the student remember and understand the terminology and concepts presented in each chapter of the text.

A book does not develop in a vacuum. We wish to acknowledge those who have counseled, encouraged, and aided us in the tasks of reviewing, editing, typing, and illustrating. Over the years many individuals read all or portions of manuscript of the six editions of this book, and we would like to offer them our greatest appreciation. These people are listed in the acknowledgments section that follows the preface.

We would like to pay tribute to the memory of the late Ronald D. Kissack, the editor of the first edition, in deep appreciation of his faith and encouragement. We also wish to thank Jill Gordon, Peggy Rehberger, Karen Quigley, Elizabeth Strange, and Kathy Bendo of McGraw-Hill for their assistance on this sixth edition.

And finally, a special appreciation to our families and wives, Carol Stein and Christine L. Rowe, for their encouragement and help over these past twenty-two years.

Philip L. Stein
Bruce M. Rowe

ACKNOWLEDGMENTS

David Abrams, Sacramento City College
Leslie Aiello, University College, London
Clifton Amsbury
James Baker, Okanagan College
Robert L. Blakely, Georgia State University
Rita Castellano, Los Angeles Pierce College
Russell L. Ciochon, University of Iowa
Glenn C. Conroy, Washington University School of
    Medicine
Mildred Dickerman
Daniel Evett, Cornell University
Marc Feldsman, Portland State University
Robin Franck, Southwestern College
Everett L. Frost, Eastern New Mexico University
Janet O. Frost, Eastern New Mexico University
Douglas R. Givens, St. Louis Community College
Glenn A. Gorelick, Citrus College
Philip G. Grant
Joseph Guillotte III, University of New Orleans
Van K. Hainline, Citrus College
Mark E. Harlan
L. Lewis Johnson, Vassar College
Gail Kennedy, University of California, Los Angeles
Karen Kovac
Leonard Lieberman, Central Michigan University
Mary Jean Livingston, Wayne County Community
    College
James H. Mielke, University of Kansas
Edward E. Myers
Robert L. Pence, Los Angeles Pierce College
Louanna Pettay, California State University,
    Sacramento, retired
Gary D. Richards, University of California, Berkeley
Peter S. Rodman, University of California, Davis
Irwin Rovner, North Carolina State University
Paul W. Sciulli, Ohio State University
J. Richard Shenkel, University of New Orleans
Paul E. Simonds, University of Oregon
Sandra L. Snyder
Soheir Stolba, American River College
Mayl L. Walek, North Carolina State University
Tim White, University of California, Berkeley

PHYSICAL ANTHROPOLOGY

It is dangerous to show man too clearly how much he resembles the beast without at the same time showing him his greatness. It is also dangerous to allow him too clear a vision of his greatness without his baseness. It is even more dangerous to leave him in ignorance of both. But it is very profitable to show him both.

Blaise Pascal (1623–1662)

CHAPTER

1

INVESTIGATING THE NATURE OF HUMANKIND

What is it to be human? This question has been satisfactorily answered for some, has puzzled others, and has tormented many. Plato defined people as "bipeds without feathers," an amusing image but also an early attempt at classifying people as animals. Mark Twain observed, "Man is the only animal that blushes—or needs to." He recognized the human social consciousness, the ability to be embarrassed. An anonymous author wrote, "Man is the only animal that eats when he is not hungry, drinks when he is not thirsty, and makes love at all seasons."

Physical anthropology is concerned with several fundamental questions which include: What is it to be human? How did humans evolve? What is the relationship of humans to the rest of the animal kingdom? What is the nature of humankind? The attempt to solve these puzzles throws light on the even more intriguing question: What am I?

THE WORLD OF PHYSICAL ANTHROPOLOGY

Welcome to the study of anthropology! What is anthropology? The word **anthropology** derives from the Greek *anthropos*, meaning "man," and *logos*, meaning "study." Therefore, anthropology is the study of people.

This text considers one of the major branches of anthropology, **physical anthropology**, which studies the biological nature and evolution of humankind. This is a formidable task, for the field of physical anthropology, also called biological anthropology, concerns itself with many issues.

Much of the excitement in physical anthropology comes from the fact that it is a constantly changing field. New discoveries and new interpretations are constantly bringing about new insights. The work of many physical anthropologists relates to many controversies and issues in today's world. Also, much of the subject matter of physical anthropology is simply exciting and unusual. Other than satisfying a requirement, a course in physical anthropology will better equip you to understand and evaluate many issues of our time. What follows is a sampling of some topics and issues that are found between the covers of this textbook.

Many major advances in modern medicine are in the area of medical genetics. Anthropologists are especially interested in the distribution of genetic traits, including medical abnormalities, among different peoples of the world. The Human Genome Project is attempting to decipher the entire human genetic code. The Human Genome Diversity Project is taking samples of genetic material from populations throughout the world for comparative genetic study.

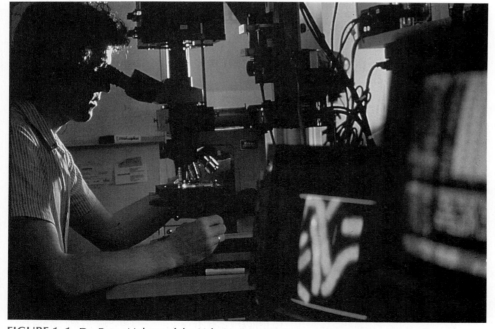

FIGURE 1–1 Dr. Peter Lichter of the Yale University Human Genome Project is shown mapping a cloned DNA fragment to human chromosome 11.

The airplane has brought together larger numbers of people from many parts of the world as tourists and immigrants. People whose appearance and behavior are different from that of the majority resident population are often misunderstood. Policies designed to limit the rights of such peoples are often given "scientific" validity. For example, the idea that people of certain "races" are less intelligent than members of other races is a theme of *The Bell Curve*, published in 1994. Physical anthropologists study human variation and the classification of populations into categories. They examine the nature of this variability. We will see how popular writers, pollsters, and many science writers misuse the idea of race.

FIGURE 1–2   Novelist and Princeton University Professor Toni Morrison receives the 1993 Nobel Prize in Literature from King Carl Gustaf of Sweden.

Acquired immunodeficiency syndrome (AIDS) has become a major health problem. How people perceive and deal with AIDS, however, varies from place to place. Physical anthropologists are interested in the relationship between human behavior and health and disease. They have identified behaviors that actually act to spread disease. For example, AIDS was initially found in the United States in homosexual male populations and among people using intravenous drugs.

Government activities at that time were directed toward the behaviors of these populations. On the other hand, in central Africa AIDS was found concentrated among heterosexual female prostitutes. Many men with several wives are not able to adequately support them because of the poor economic situation in this part of the world. Some wives have had to resort to prostitution in order to provide money for necessities such as health services for themselves and their children.

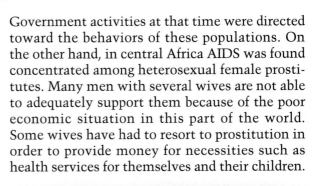

FIGURE 1–3   Sign on car uses the motto "Zero Grazing" to encourage sexual fidelity as part of Uganda's AIDS Control Program.

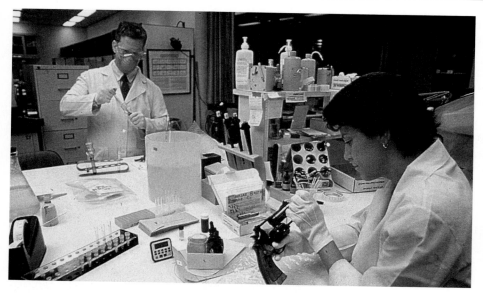

FIGURE 1–4 Technician tests gun for blood samples to be used for DNA fingerprinting in the F.B.I. crime lab.

Identifying a murderer from a bloody glove may seem quite distant from the normal concerns of physical anthropologists. Yet the analysis of genetic material, DNA and RNA, provides important clues as to our evolutionary history. For example, DNA analysis reveals the genetic relationship between animals. Such analysis has shown that genetically speaking humans and chimpanzees are very closely related.

Several anthropologists have distinguished themselves for their studies of the great apes in the wild. Jane Goodall has studied wild chimpanzees for over 35 years. Dian Fossey was murdered while studying the endangered mountain gorilla. And, for almost 30 years, Biruté Galdikas has investigated the elusive orangutans of Borneo. Many other primatologists are observing monkeys, apes, and other primates in the wild, attempting to understand their biology and behavior. Recently much of Goodall's time has been spent raising funds to save wild chimpanzees and other wild animals and their tropical habitats from human encroachment.

FIGURE 1–5 Primatologist Dian Fossey discusses the fine points of photography with some of her subjects. Her life is recounted in the movie *Gorillas in the Mist.*

The editors of *Time* listed newly discovered fossils from Aramis, Ethiopia, as one of the most important scientific discoveries of the year.[1] These fossils, about 4.4 million years old, belong to the line that split off from the chimpanzees and ultimately gave rise to modern humans. According to many physical anthropologists, they are not much younger than the common ancestor of the human and chimpanzee lineages. People are fascinated by the fossil and archaeological evidence of our beginnings. Slowly, through the painstaking work of a legion of anthropologists, new fossils and cultural remains are clarifying the story of human evolution.

[1]Editors of *Time*, "The Best Science of 1994," *Time* 144 (December 26, 1994–January 2, 1995), 138.

FIGURE 1–6   In 1995 paleoanthropologists introduced this fragment of fossil jaw discovered at the site of Aramis, Ethiopia. Thought to be about 4.4 million years old, this and other fossils from Aramis are near the common ancestor of the ape and human line.

Other Branches of Anthropology

When you tell someone that you are an anthropologist, a usual reply is, "Have you dug up any bones lately?" Anthropology is not all old bones. There are four main branches in the study of people: sociocultural anthropology, archaeology, linguistics, and physical anthropology (Figure 1–7). Many anthropologists see applied anthropology as a distinct fifth field.

It is the aim of **sociocultural anthropology** to understand human social organization and culture. **Archaeologists** study material remains of human activity in order to reconstruct how different cultures adjust to varying situations through time and to explain stability and change. The **anthropological linguist** examines the history, function, structure, and physiology of one of a people's most definitive characteristics—language. **Applied anthropology** is concerned with the application of anthropological ideas to current human problems. For example, some physical anthropologists who specialize in the study of skeletal anatomy have become

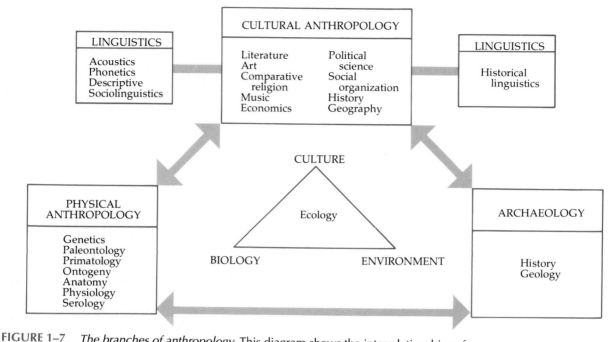

FIGURE 1–7   *The branches of anthropology.* This diagram shows the interrelationships of the branches of anthropology with some of their major areas of interest and related fields. Applied anthropology is the practical application of knowledge gained from any of the branches of anthropology.

forensic anthropologists employed in the identification of crime victims and other information vital to the criminal justice system.

Traditionally anthropologists have been trained in all five fields and see anthropology as a holistic discipline. The concept of **holism** asserts that all aspects of human existence, be it biological, social, ideological, and so forth, are tightly interrelated and should be studied as an integrated whole. In recent years anthropology has become more diverse and specialized and many new anthropologists are given minimal training outside their own specializations. This has become very much the case in physical anthropology.

Some Characteristics of Humankind

Physical anthropologists study the characteristics that define us as human. Biologically, people are not as different from other animals, especially other primates, as many would like to believe. Humans share some characteristics with all animals, more with all vertebrates, and even more with all mammals. It is not surprising that people are quite similar to their primate relatives.

Humans are very similar to the chimpanzee. The anatomical differences between people and chimpanzees are, to a degree, matters of size and proportion. Not only do chimpanzees have the same bone and muscle structure as humans, but most of these structures are located in the same places and serve the same or similar functions. The internal organs of both animals are similar, and the body fluids, such as blood, are alike. Even the genetic material in chimpanzees is remarkably close to that in humans.

Nevertheless, every organism displays some differences from all others. Biological idiosyncrasies exist, but even these are mostly matters of *degree* rather than kind. Some of the characteristics that define people are discussed below.

THE DEPENDENCE ON CULTURE   An important characteristic of humans is the development of the brain in a way that provides the biological potential for cultural behavior. **Culture** is one of those words that everyone uses but almost everyone uses differently. A person may say, "Those people belong to the Art Society; they certainly are cultured." To the anthropologist there is one thing culture is not, and that is a level of sophistication or formal education. Culture is not something that one person has and another does not.

Anthropologists have defined culture in hundreds of ways. Fortunately, most definitions have points in common, and these points are included in our definition. Culture is learned, nonrandom, systematic behavior and knowledge that is transmitted from person to person and from generation to generation. Culture changes through time and is a main contributor to human adaptability.

Culture is learned; it is not biologically determined, coded by the hereditary material. A baby abandoned at birth has *no* chance of surviving by itself. In fact, most 6- or 7-year-olds would probably perish if left to their own resources. Survival strategies, and other behaviors and thoughts, are learned from parents, other relatives, teachers, peers, friends, and so on.

Culture is nonrandom behavior and knowledge; that is, specific actions or thoughts are usually the same in similar situations. For example, people in Western societies usually shake hands when they meet. A specific behavior pattern, such as shaking hands, in a particular situation, such as two people meeting, is called a **norm.** A norm is the most frequent behavior that the members of a group show in a given situation.

Culture is patterned in the sense that it is systematic; that is, one aspect of behavior or thought is related to all others. Taken together, they form a **system.** A system is a collection of parts that are interrelated so that a change in any one part brings about specifiable changes in the others. In eastern Europe, for example, the change from a socialistic to a capitalistic economy has repercussions for educational, political, moral, and other elements of society. In addition, a group's cultural traditions and the way in which its members relate to each other reflect certain underlying principles about the basic characteristics of people and nature.

Culture is transmittable; it spreads. Information is learned, stored in the cortex of the brain, interpreted, and then transmitted to other people. Knowledge builds on information from past generations. In societies with writing, each generation can continue to influence future generations indefinitely. A particular culture is the result, therefore, of its history as well as its present state. In other words, culture forms a pool of shared information. Although there is evidence that certain nonhuman animals also possess some ability to pass on acquired behavior, in none of these has the ability evolved to the same degree as it has with humans.

THE HUMAN BRAIN AND ITS ABILITY TO SYMBOLIZE   One thing that makes the human brain a revolutionary instrument is the potential for speech. Other animals can create and respond to a limited number of **signs** and, in some cases, **symbols.** Humans can teach chimpanzees to communicate to a limited degree in systems similar to language. Yet the human cortex has the greatest ability to organize symbols into an effective system that can relate and create experiences and ideas. Note, however, that this is a matter of degree; the great potential to use symbols is but one way to accomplish the task of survival and has nothing to do with "superiority."

A symbol is anything, whether it be visual, oral, tactile, or olfactory, that represents something else that is distant in time and space. A word, for instance, is a symbol of the object to which it refers. In order to understand the meaning of the symbol, the thing that it refers to need not be present. Such things as stop signs, trademarks, Morse code, and braille are all symbolic. At a higher level of abstraction, a symbol can be mentally substituted for the thing that it represents. For example, a flag represents a country, and some people consider an attack on a nation's flag to be an attack on the country or on its people.

The symbol itself is arbitrary; that is, there is no intrinsic relationship between the symbol and the thing it represents. For instance, the word *pen* denotes the object it refers to only because in English it has been designated to do so. To an Italian, a Navaho, or another non-English speaker, the sound "pen" might have a different meaning or no meaning at all. Since each culture codes its unique complex of knowledge and experience into its own set of symbols, its conception of itself and the world that surrounds it differs from the conceptions of others. This is one main reason for the different configurations that culture takes.

BIPEDALISM   Habitual bipedalism, the ability to walk consistently on two legs, is another human trait, although some other animals are bipedal. An examination of human bipedalism provides a good example of the relationship between culture and biology. The locomotor patterns of many animals are exclusively the result of inborn reflexes. Although human anatomy is adapted for bipedal locomotion, the neural control needed to walk bipedally is learned behavior. This is shown by the fact that "the congenitally blind child never spontaneously attempts to stand or walk but must be carefully taught."[2] The learned aspect of human bipedalism and other movements is also displayed by the great variety shown by different cultures in styles of walking, standing, sitting, and dancing.

Bipedalism has several advantages. It frees the hands for use in activities other than movement.

For example, in times of danger the adult can carry a baby to safety. Humans are also able to carry large quantities of food back to their camps; food need not be carried in the mouth or eaten where it is found. This allows people to protect their food from scavengers that could otherwise steal it from their larger-brained but weaker neighbors. It also means that people can transport their food to a home base and share it with those who were not along during the search. People who are unable to hunt or gather can be supported by others. Another activity made possible by the human's dangling arms and grasping hands is the ability to throw weapons. This arm-hand combination also aids in unparalleled manipulation of the environment.

Birds walk on two legs, yet their upper limbs have been modified into wings and are useless for manipulating objects. A kangaroo moves on three "legs"; its tail acts as an efficient balancing device. Bears, dogs, monkeys, and apes, among others, often rear up on their hind legs and can even walk short distances on them. People are habitually bipedal, and their upper limbs are highly efficient structures for grasping, holding, and manipulating objects (Figure 1–8).

Another advantage of bipedalism is that it increases the range of the visual field because of the elevation of the eyes. A crocodile's eyes are only a short distance off the ground. Although some quadrupeds, such as giraffes, have eyes well above the ground, many animals cannot see above fields of grass or clumps of bushes. Human habitual two-legged posture allows people to see over these bushes and grasses. This is significant because it enables humans to sight predators from a distance.

Advantages in one area often mean disadvantages in others. Because of the development of human bipedalism, certain structural weaknesses occur. For example, humans cannot run as fast as many other animals. In addition, the upright position of the human body is related to a weakening of the back and abdomen, problems in circulation, and a loss of flexibility of the toes. Finally, changes in the anatomy related to effective erect bipedalism result in a restricted birth canal and

---

[2]V. T. Inman et al., *Human Walking* (Baltimore: Williams & Wilkins, 1981), 1.

Ostrich   Kangaroo   Human

FIGURE 1–8 *Bipedal animals.* Although many animals are bipedal, human posture is structured for more efficient use of the arms and hands than is found in other animals.

difficult childbirth when compared with childbirth in the monkeys and apes.

HUMAN REPRODUCTION   In nonhuman mammals, the female is usually sexually receptive to males only during certain times of the year. Because of this, for most mammals births peak within specific seasons, such as the onset of spring or the beginning of the rainy season.

On the other hand, human females are sexually receptive throughout the year, although their ability to produce offspring is based on variable ovulatory patterns. Most people recognize this distinction between sexual receptivity and ovulatory patterns. It was therefore quite a surprise to early explorers to discover that births among the Yurok Indians of California occurred predominantly in one season. The explorers thought that they had found a biologically primitive people whose mating behavior was closer to that of the apes than of humans. What was actually occurring was a cultural phenomenon. The explorers did not realize that the Yuroks' ideas of marriage and cohabitation were completely different from those of the Europeans. For reasons seeded in tradition, the Yurok men spent most of the year living together, apart from their wives, in a men's sweathouse and clubhouse. It was there that they kept all their possessions. Only during the summer did the couples sleep together outside. Nine months later babies abounded.

Not only are humans biologically able to breed in all seasons, but their **reproductive risk** is low. Reproductive risk is the number of fertilized eggs required from a mating pair to produce two offspring that will in turn reproduce. The fewer fertilized eggs needed, the lower the reproductive risk. Fish produce a phenomenal number of eggs. Because of the harshness of the marine environment, the hazards of external fertilization and development, and the always present predators, a single codfish must generate 30 million eggs, of which 50,000 might hatch and only 2 might reach maturity. More than two offspring per female might overpopulate and lead to degeneration of the environment; fewer would eventually shrink the population to a level at which extinction would be probable. An average of two offspring reaching reproductive maturity per two adults is the magic number for animal populations that are in equilibrium with their environments. The greater the hazards of birth and life, the greater the number of eggs that are

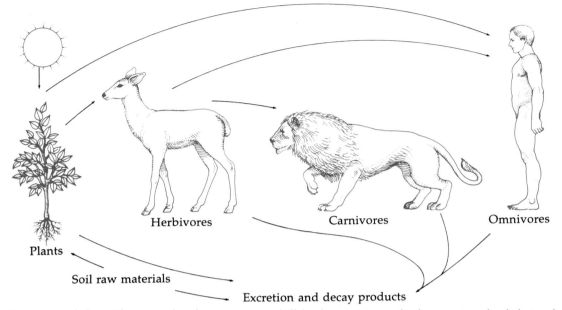

FIGURE 1–9   *Food chain.* The sun is the ultimate source of all food energy. From this base various food chains develop.

needed to ensure that two offspring will survive to reproduce.

As we progress from fish to amphibians to reptiles and finally to mammals, the number of eggs needed to ensure two surviving offspring diminishes. Human reproduction is one of the lower-risk systems; on average, every five births results in two individuals who will eventually reproduce. This represents the number of reproductive individuals for nonindustrial societies. Today, in countries with advanced medical procedures and relatively stable food supplies, the ratio of live births to reproductive individuals is closer to 1:1.

This low risk is due to the fact that in humans, as in most mammals, fertilization and development occur within a controlled environment, the mother's body. The mother fish is long gone when the baby fish hatch, whereas the mammalian progeny is nourished and protected by its mother even after it is born.

In humans the mother-child relationship is extended in two ways. First, other relatives and friends can aid directly in the child's survival. Second, the period of dependence is prolonged; in fact, a child may remain at least partially dependent on kin for life. On the other hand, protective parents might eventually become dependent

on their offspring. This type of relationship is unknown in the rest of the animal world.

In humans, cultural factors, such as providing adequate shelter, food, and general care, help lower reproductive risk. However, since the efficiency of these cultural factors depends on what the physical environment can provide and on the acquired knowledge of the specific group, reproductive risk varies from culture to culture.

People and Nature

People are biological entities. With the development of the biological potential for culture, people began to interact consciously with the natural environment. Culture became a method of adjustment. Through culture humans could enter new areas by fashioning raw materials into protective and manipulative devices that would allow them to survive in environments to which they were not suited biologically. This did not place people above nature; rather, it thrust them into a different relationship with it.

Human beings, like all organisms, are dependent upon nature. People, for example, are part of **food chains** (Figure 1–9). A food chain is a sequence of sources of energy, each source being

FIGURE 1–10 *Oil spill.* An oil-soaked cormorant on the shore of the Persian Gulf, a casualty of the Persian Gulf War.

dependent on another source. The sun is the major source of energy for plants, plants provide energy for herbivores (plant eaters), and herbivores are eaten by carnivores (meat eaters) and omnivores (plant and meat eaters).

The relationship among organisms in a food chain is seen clearly in the effect of oil spills (Figure 1–10). Such spills kill or poison fish and birds that may then be eaten by carnivores such as bears; the bears then become sick and die. The oceans are becoming increasingly polluted, and if they "die," which is a possibility, all animal life, including humans, will probably become extinct. Seventy-one percent of the earth's surface is covered with water. This oceanic environment contains a large percentage of green plants which contribute oxygen to our environment. If all the aquatic plants were to pass out of existence, so would all animal life.

Plants are at the bottom of most food chains. All animals ultimately depend on them, not only for oxygen but also for sustenance. That hamburger you had for lunch could not have existed without the grass, corn, or other plant material that the cow ate. The amount of plant material available determines the number of cows and, hence, the amount of beef available for people. As the human population increases, it is becoming increasingly difficult to feed everyone. Since there is little reason to believe that the problem can be solved technologically, population control appears to be the ultimate answer.

Myths about Humankind

We have been discussing several essential features of human beings, but many things about humans that are believed to be true are actually myths.

THE MYTHS ABOUT HUMAN ANTIQUITY

Many people believe that humans were created last, after the stage had been set for them. According to the Bible, humanity was created on the sixth day and commanded to "subdue" the natural environment and the other living things. People who have had limited contact with evolutionary theory also believe that human beings were the last organisms to evolve. They assume that they were the end product of previous mistakes and experiments in nature. These ideas are incorrect. Many kinds of animals and plants evolved after the first *Homo sapiens.* In fact, in the last 5000 years, human domestication of animals has produced many new breeds. In addition, people alive today have an ancestry as long as that of any other contemporary animal species; all animals ultimately derived from cells that originated billions of years ago. Also, the group of animals to which humans belong, the primates, has been around longer than many other kinds of mammals, such as rodents. Finally, humans are not an end product in that, like all organisms, they are still evolving.

If you were in a sarcastic mood, you might suggest that the chimpanzee on the television screen is your friend's relative. A common misconception is that people evolved from living apes. In reality, the chimpanzees are our collateral relatives; they have a common ancestor with us in the past. They are *not* our direct ancestors; one cannot evolve from a contemporary. These two species took separate paths from a common ancestor more than 5 million years ago. As the human line developed, it diverged from that of the apes.

THE MYTH OF TECHNOLOGY

In the last century people have accomplished almost unbelievable technological feats. From the invention of the steamship to the development of the spaceship, humankind's mechanical genius has been displayed. When a phone is picked up, conversation reaches people around the block or thousands of miles away through a thin, plastic-coated wire. Television creates images on a glass screen, and through holography (the projection of three-dimensional images by laser beams) a screen is not even needed. Artificial heart valves and human-made joints, as well as genetically engineered alterations, are becoming increasingly important in medicine. Technology appears to be able to solve any and every problem that the environment presents. All that is needed is enough time, effort, money, and know-how.

Humans have the ability to think about objects and principles that do not exist. However, not everything that people dream about is possible. For example, unaided humans in their present form cannot run a mile in a minute or anywhere near it. That is believed to be biologically impossible.

Just as some things are biologically impossible, others are technologically infeasible or improbable. It is not likely that we will solve the world's food problem through technology. Even with great advances in methods of food production, more people are starving today than ever before. This is partly because population size is increasing faster than research and technology can be applied and partly because the costs of modern technology are enormous. It is also because cultural traditions often hamper progress, such as the prestige that comes from having many children in some societies.

A major negative aspect of modern technology is that it cannot be "unlearned." For example, many people would like all humanity to forget how to make atomic weapons, but this is not possible. Even if all nuclear arsenals were destroyed, the potential for making new weapons would remain. The reduction or elimination of nuclear weapons would eliminate the threat of an "accidental" nuclear war and could also reduce the chance of a major nuclear catastrophe, but it would not prevent any group of people from acquiring the technology needed to make new nuclear bombs.

Technology, for most people, is not the solution to loneliness or despair, nor will it alleviate hatred or prejudice. It can be a tool but not a cure. In fact, modern technology may ultimately end our existence. If technological "progress" is not accompanied by appropriate social change and ecological responsibility, people may drown in the poisons of their own industrial wastes.

THE MYTH OF PLENTY   This leads us to the third myth, the idea that people can continue to increase in number forever. This is not true for two main reasons. First, the resources that life depends on are limited. For example, green plants, the ultimate source of all animal food, receive only a finite amount of solar energy. This limits the potential number of green plants, which in turn imposes an absolute limit on the size of the population of any animal species, including humans, for a particular environment (Figure 1–11).

The second reason that people cannot continue to increase in number indefinitely is simply the lack of space. People cannot occupy every inch of the earth's surface without cutting off their food and water supplies. That wide-open land in the American Midwest must remain wide open. It is from there and from similar places that the more than 260 million people in the United States obtain most of their food. Wheat could not be grown in a coast-to-coast Manhattan.

THE MYTH OF HUMAN SUPERIORITY   It was once thought that the sun revolved around the earth, that the earth was the center of the universe, and that humans were the highest form of life on earth. This **anthropocentricity,** which is comforting but scientifically useless, embodies the fourth myth. It is true that, compared with other animals, humans are capable of more conscious activities that can modify the environment, yet this is only one of many criteria for superiority. For instance, termites have been around longer than humans. Evolution has brought innate solutions to their problems of starvation, internal conflict, and division of labor. Termite societies are highly organized and extremely efficient. These insects, which often

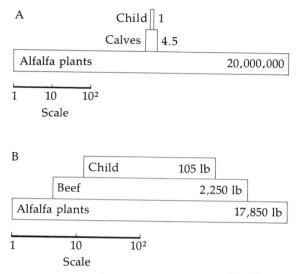

FIGURE 1–11   *Food pyramids.* Pyramid A shows the number of plants required to support the number of calves needed to support one child in a hypothetical situation. Pyramid B shows the relationship in terms of total weight.

are considered so lowly, also greatly outnumber us. Any of these characteristics could be taken as a measure of *their* superiority. Of course, the point is that superiority is relative to the criteria being used. If human beings are superior, it is only because they define themselves as such.

HOW FREE ARE PEOPLE?   Growing out of the idea of human superiority is the belief that people control their own destiny, that they possess "free will." Certainly, more variation of behavior exists among human groups and individuals than among other animals, because of the great diversity of learned behavioral patterns among humans. However, there are limitations to behavior. Free will is not so much "free" as it is confined. Every action that we take depends on our biological makeup, our culture, and the environment that surrounds us at the moment. On the biological level, for example, some people simply are not equipped to be heavyweight boxing champions or mathematical geniuses. On the cultural level, patterned, learned behavior creates habitual ways of thinking that incline people to analyze experiences according to the particular customs of their culture. In other words, the choices that we make are conditioned or caused by previous events. The environment also limits what people can and cannot do—you cannot go skiing in the middle of the Sahara Desert.

The following chapters will provide more explanations of these and other myths. The proper understanding of humanity not only involves learning what people are but also requires comprehending what they are not.

Summary

Physical anthropology is the branch of anthropology that studies the biological nature and evolution of humankind. People are not biologically divergent from the rest of the animal kingdom. However, there are certain traits that have evolved to their greatest degree in humans. We must realize that it is a complex of various traits that defines humanity. Each species has its own complex of characteristics.

One feature of humans is the genetic potential for cultural behavior. Most animals adapt to their environments in terms of changes in their bodies and innate behavior, although for some, such as the chimpanzees, learning plays an important role. For humans, however, learned, patterned, transmittable behavior and knowledge, defined as culture, are the main way of adjusting to environments.

The main way that cultural knowledge is transmitted is through the neural potential for language. Other human characteristics are habitual bipedalism and low reproductive risk. Humans, like all animals and plants, are a part of food chains, and for this reason people cannot ignore their relationship with other organisms. Humans have great antiquity, and today they represent one of the most widely dispersed species.

There are many things that people are not. Humans are not capable of totally controlling nature through technology. Indeed, much of our technology may be more destructive than constructive in the long run. The human population cannot continue to grow indefinitely. It is also incorrect to consider humans as being superior to all other creatures. All organisms have a specific complex of adaptations that serve them. Nor is it correct to think that human will is totally free. Humans, like all animals, have biological limitations. Although the human mind frees people's actions from most innate behavior, it also locks them into habitual, patterned behavior called *culture*.

Conclusion

The purpose of this book is to provide a basic understanding of humans, their evolution, and their place in nature. We cannot promise that all your questions about people will be answered; in fact, we can promise that they will not. A great deal has been learned about human nature over the centuries, especially in the last 130 years, yet anthropology today is a dynamic subject. With each publication of a research project, it is probable that new information will be added to our knowledge of humanity. In other words, data needed to answer crucial questions about the human species are still being uncovered.

Anthropology provides empirical knowledge about the human condition. On one level, this simply serves to feed our curiosity about ourselves. However, anthropological studies also provide data useful to the fields of medicine, environmental maintenance, urban planning, education, and so forth. Anthropology also attempts to provide a profile of human potentials and limitations. We will attempt to give, in each part of this text, a more complete statement of the relevance of anthropology.

STUDY QUESTIONS

1. From this introductory chapter and from looking through the table of contents, how would you define the focus of physical anthropology?
2. Humans are animals, yet humans are different from other animals. What, in your opinion, uniquely characterizes human beings?
3. What are some of the myths that are commonly held about humans?

SUGGESTED READINGS

The readings listed for Chapter 1 are general in nature. References to information on specific topics mentioned in this introductory chapter are given in the chapters that discuss these topics in more detail.

Barash, D. P. *The Hare and the Tortoise: Culture, Biology, and Human Nature.* New York: Penguin, 1987. This is a well-written popularized book on the relationship between human biology and culture.

Brown, D. E. *Human Universals.* New York: McGraw-Hill, 1991. Professor Brown concludes that there are human universals. He describes many universals and analyzes the reasons for their universality.

Eddy, E. M., and W. L. Partridge (eds.). *Applied Anthropology in America,* 2d ed. New York: Columbia University Press, 1987. This book contains twenty-two essays on applied anthropology.

Honigmann, J. J. *The Development of Anthropological Ideas.* Homewood, Ill.: Dorsey, 1976. Here we see a detailed look at the development of cultural anthropology.

In addition to books, the journals and magazines listed below consistently have materials useful to physical anthropology students.

The following are popular magazines:

American Scientist
Archaeology
BioScience
Discover
Earth
National Geographic
Natural History
Science News
Scientific American
Smithsonian

The following are scientific journals:

American Anthropologist
American Journal of Human Biology
American Journal of Physical Anthropology
Current Anthropology
Evolutionary Anthropology
Human Biology
Human Evolution
Journal of Animal Behavior
Journal of Forensic Science
Journal of Human Evolution
Journal of Primatology
Nature
Science

Charles Darwin's study at Down House.

We have now seen that man is variable in body and mind; and that the variations are induced, either directly or indirectly, by the same general causes, and obey the same general laws, as with the lower animals. Man has spread widely over the face of the earth, and must have been exposed, during his incessant migrations, to the most diversified conditions.[1]

Charles Darwin (1809–1882)

[1]C. Darwin, *The Descent of Man*, 2d rev. ed. (London: J. Murray, 1874), 47.

CHAPTER

2

PREREQUISITES TO THE DEVELOPMENT OF AN EVOLUTIONARY THEORY

The ideas embodied in the above quotation, taken from *The Descent of Man* by Charles Darwin, were revolutionary for their time. This statement contradicts a literal interpretation of the Bible in many ways. The point of Darwin's message is that humans are animals who were not specially created and that human characteristics arise from the actions of the same natural forces that affect all animals.

Darwin is thought to have been a great discoverer of new facts and ideas, and indeed he was. On the other hand, Darwin's ideas, like all ideas, were formed, nurtured, and brought to maturity in the context of a particular intellectual background. The things we think, the relationships we see, and the very process of creativity are, in part, determined by our cultural environment. The knowledge that a person has at any one time represents the accumulation of information and ideas from his or her whole lifetime. Therefore, the theory of evolution was not developed by one person. It was part of a chain of intellectual events, each link being necessary to the continuity of that chain.

This chapter will show some of the developments that led to modern biological theory. It will also discuss the method scientists use to collect and analyze data.

EARLY VIEWS ON THE ESSENCE OF HUMANS, NATURE, AND TIME

Although there were many variations in the early ideas about the universe, they were often the opposite of those embodied in present evolutionary theory. These old ideas had to be challenged before a new concept of reality could arise.

First among the early views was the idea of human superiority, or **anthropocentricity.** This belief was that the earth is the center of the universe and that all the celestial bodies revolve around it. Humans placed themselves on a pedestal, believing that God provided the animals and plants for people's use and fancy. The similarities that people observed between humans and animals and among various animal species were seen as reflecting the design of the Creator. Many people believed that certain shapes and forms were pleasing to God and that God therefore used them as models for all creations.

People of that era, as well as many people today whose beliefs are based upon a literal interpretation of the Bible, thought that life had been formed from nonlife at the will of the Creator. Some believed that this process of creation continued even after the original 6 days of Genesis; this concept is known as **spontaneous generation.** People also believed that once a type of organism is created, its descendants will remain **immutable,** in the same form as the original, from generation to generation.

The original creation, as described in Genesis, supposedly took place a few thousand years before the Greek and Roman empires. In fact, in 1636 Archbishop James Ussher of Armagh, Ireland, used the generations named in the Bible to calculate that the earth's creation took place in 4004 B.C. Another theologian, the Reverend Dr. John Lightfoot of Cambridge University, asserted that this event had taken place at exactly 9 A.M. on October 23!

The idea of a spontaneously created and static life, a life brought into being only 6000 years ago, is directly counter to modern evolutionary theory. The development of evolutionary theory depended upon an increasing disbelief in these old ideas.

Questioning the Old Ideas

What a shock it must have been to European scholars of the sixteenth century when Nicolaus Copernicus (1473–1543) showed conclusively that the earth was not the center of the universe and was not even the center of the solar system! This was but one of a series of revelations that were to bombard the old ideas (see Box 2–1).

A tired, lost sea captain, who was fearful that he was going to fall off the edge of the earth, might have been both elated and confused at the greeting he received from an exotic people living on a shore that he thought could not possibly exist. The Age of Exploration, which began in the late 1400s with the voyages of explorers such as Christopher Columbus, revealed variations of life not dreamed of before. By 1758, 4235 species of animals had been cataloged. Today about 1,032,000 species are known. During the Age of Exploration, strange animals never mentioned in the Bible were seen by Europeans for the first time. Naturalists were overwhelmed by the quantity of new discoveries and the problems of organizing this rapidly growing wealth of data.

WHAT IS THE RELATIONSHIP BETWEEN LIVING THINGS?   Although all cultures classify plants and animals into some kind of scheme, it was not until the seventeenth and eighteenth centuries that comprehensive written classifications were made. The Swedish naturalist Carolus Linnaeus (1707–1778) succeeded in classifying every animal and plant known to him into a system of categories. This type of classification is absolutely necessary for a scientific understanding of the relationship of one plant or animal to the next. Yet at first it reinforced traditional ideas. Linnaeus saw each category as fixed and immutable, the result of divine creation (Chapter 9).

Linnaeus's scheme became important to modern biological sciences for many reasons. First, it imposed order upon nature's infinite variation. Linnaeus saw that the analysis of anatomical structures could be used to group plants and animals into categories. The most specific groups included organisms that were very much alike, whereas the more general levels encompassed

BOX 2-1

SCIENCE, RELIGION, AND POLITICAL INTRIGUE—THE TRIAL OF GALILEO

In 1633 the Roman Inquisition found Galileo Galilei (1564–1642), at the age of 69, guilty of supporting the Copernican view that the sun, not the earth, is at the center of the universe. In 1616 the Catholic Church had condemned this sun-centered (**heliocentric**) view of the universe as "false and opposed by the Holy Scripture." In 1600, even before this official condemnation, Giordano Bruno had been burned at the stake for his support of the Copernican view. Galileo was saved from that fate and was instead put under "house arrest" for the last 9 years of his life.

Pietro Redondi, an Italian historian of science, has proposed a new account of the trial of Galileo. He believes he has uncovered an ancient case of plea bargaining.

Redondi believes that a Jesuit named Orazio Grassi wrote the note indirectly accusing Galileo of heresy. In 1623 Galileo had pro-fessed his belief that all matter consists of small, unchangeable atomic particles. The letter suggested that this view contradicted the idea that the bread and wine of communion could be transformed into the body and blood of Christ. It would have been extreme heresy to suggest such a thing.

Pope Urban VIII, a personal friend of Galileo, had given Galileo permission to publish his ideas on Copernicanism. In 1632 the Copernican idea was not as controversial as it had been in 1600 and 1616, but the Jesuits, who wished to control the Vatican, knew that the atomic theory was a much more profound contradiction of church doctrine. They continued to place pressure on the Pope by attempting to discredit his friend Galileo. In 1624 nothing was done about the Jesuit attack on Galileo; the Jesuits did not have enough influence at that time. However, de-velopments in the European Thirty Years' War had made Pope Urban VIII more politically vulnerable, and so in the 1630s the Jesuits attempted to reopen their attack. For political reasons, the Pope now had to pay attention to the Jesuits or be discredited himself.

The Pope defused the situation by allowing Galileo to plead guilty to supporting the Copernican theory. In return, the Inquisition would not charge him for promoting the atomic theory. Galileo agreed to cooperate. In this way Galileo was saved from being burned at the stake, and the Pope showed he still had control. In 1984 Galileo was given a full pardon by the Catholic Church.

Reference: D. Dickson, "Was Galileo Saved by a Plea Bargain?" *Science,* 233 (1986), 612–613; and L. S. Lerner and E. A. Gosselin, "Galileo and the Spector of Bruno," *Scientific American,* 255 (November 1986), 126–133.

the specific groups, thereby representing a wider range of variation. Linnaeus wrote that the first order of science is to distinguish one thing from the other; his classification helped do just that.

Second, although Linnaeus considered organisms to be immutable, paradoxically his classification provided a means for "seeing" changes and possible ancestral relationships. Scientists wondered if similar organisms were related by common ancestry. If two or more types had a common origin but were now somewhat different, it followed that evolution must have occurred. Linnaeus, who had been so emphatic about the idea of unchanging species, began in later life to question this concept of fixity. He had observed new types of plants resulting from crossbreeding, and he had decided that perhaps all living things were not immutable.

Third, Linnaeus included people in his classification. Although he did not contend that humans are related to other animals, his placement of humans in this scheme was sure to raise the question.

COULD NATURE BE DYNAMIC? Many people of the eighteenth century were intrigued with the rapidly increasing information brought to the fore by exploration (see Box 2–2). Not only were new varieties of plants and animals being discovered, but so were new people. Who were the American Indians, the Polynesians, the Africans? Were they human, or were they part human and

BOX 2–2

THE DISCOVERY OF THE GORILLA

The nineteenth century was an age of exploration as Europeans learned of new lands, plants, animals, and peoples. These discoveries provided fresh data for the scientists of the time who were developing new ideas to explain the natural world, a world suddenly made more complex. One of these ideas was that of evolution. Throughout the nineteenth century reports reached Europe of new species of monkeys and apes that provided important clues to the mystery of human origins.

The gorilla was the last of the apes to be discovered by Europeans. Although the largest of the great apes may have been seen by early explorers, "as an object of scientific study this ape simply did not exist at the beginning of the nineteenth century, and it was not until the middle of the century that it was definitely described and generally accepted as a new genus of anthropoid ape."[1]

The first scientific account of the gorilla was an article by Thomas Savage in 1847. The creature was named after the "hairy people" or "gorillae" described in the fifth century B.C. by the Carthaginian, Hanno, who had sailed along the western coast of Africa. (In all probability, however, Hanno's "gorillae" were monkeys.) Additional studies of the animal followed as bones and preserved specimens were sent to Europe. The first living gorilla seen in Europe was exhibited in England in 1855.

The early accounts of gorilla behavior were based upon rumors and stories that were more fanciful than factual. Little was known about the behavior of gorillas in the wild, and this ignorance enabled storytellers to create images of gorillas as large, terrifying beasts, as exemplified in the movie *King Kong*. As Robert Yerkes wrote in 1929:

> Creature of mystery, the gorilla long played hide and seek in the reports of hunters and naturalists. Even now the name holds peculiar fascination because imaginative descriptions abound. Relatively rare, inaccessible, powerful, reputedly dangerous, difficult to capture, and untamable, it has yielded slowly to human curiosity. For centuries rumors of the existence of such a huge anthropoid, native superstitions, and alarming tales stirred popular and scientific interest.[2]

Today we have a very different understanding of the natural history and behavior of the gorilla through the studies of several primatalogists including George Schaller and Dian Fossey. Our comprehension of the gorilla has changed considerably as a result of these investigations. In contrast to the image of King Kong, George Schaller writes: "The gorilla is by nature reserved and shy and, whenever it can possibly do so, it avoids contact with its human neighbors."[3] Dian Fossey's book *Gorillas in the Mist* and the movie of the same name show gorillas as gentle vegetarians characterized by only rare acts of aggression.

[1]R. M. Yerkes, *The Great Apes* (New Haven: Yale University Press, 1929), 31.
[2]Ibid., 381.
[3]G. B. Schaller, *The Year of the Gorilla* (Chicago: University of Chicago Press, 1964), 101–102.

part ape? Credible answers to these and other questions could not be supplied by traditional explanations.

The effect of exploration in guiding people to new realities was intensified by the great revolutions of the eighteenth and nineteenth centuries. These revolutions included technological changes in the industrial age as well as political upheavals, such as the American and French revolutions. Technological and political developments that brought about major social changes created an atmosphere in which the idea of immutability could be questioned. If people could change their social systems so rapidly and if human life could be so dynamic, then perhaps so was nature. It was in the late eighteenth century that the first modern theories of organic evolution emerged.

Early Evolutionary Ideas

Comte Georges-Louis Leclerc de Buffon (1707–1788), a contemporary of Linnaeus, proposed many major points that Darwin would later include in *On the Origin of Species.* Buffon recognized the tendency of populations to increase at a faster rate than their food supply, hence the struggle for survival. He noted the variations within species and speculated on methods of inheritance. He questioned spontaneous creation. He also challenged the Church's dating of the earth, proposing that the earth is much older than 6000 years. Buffon's importance was diminished by his lack of conciseness, but he might have been vague and apologetic about his thoughts for fear of being considered a heretic.

Although Buffon and others of the era implied evolution in their writings, it was left to Jean-Baptiste de Lamarck (1744–1829) to articulate a systematic theory of evolution as an explanation of organic diversity. Lamarck used the previous nonevolutionary idea that organisms could be ranked in a progressive order, with humans at the top. He envisioned evolution as a constant striving toward perfection and believed deviations were due to local adaptations to specific environments.

Lamarck is remembered by many for his explanation of the cause of these deviations. He again used an idea that had been around for centuries. He proposed that an organism acquired new characteristics in its lifetime by virtue of using or not using different parts of its body and that these newly acquired characteristics could then be inherited by the individual's offspring. For instance, if an animal constantly had to stretch its neck to reach food in the branches of a tree, its neck would get longer. If the trees grew taller, the animal would then have to stretch more, and its neck would get longer still. This was Lamarck's explanation of the giraffe. He believed that a trait, once acquired, was passed on to the next generation. This concept is known as the **theory of acquired characteristics.**

Lamarck's importance lies in his proposal that life is dynamic and that there is a mechanism in nature that promotes ongoing change. The method of change he suggested, however, is incorrect. Acquired characteristics are not transmitted to offspring. A person who is very muscular as a result of lifting weights will not be more likely to have a muscle-bound child (Figure 2–1).

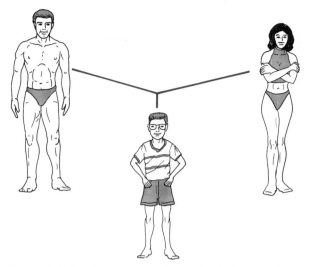

FIGURE 2–1 *Inheritance of acquired characteristics.* Today biologists do not believe that the increase or decrease in the size or strength of parts of the body due to use or disuse is transmitted to offspring. For example, if a couple lift weights and become muscular, their newly acquired physical condition will not be passed on *genetically* to their offspring.

Lamarck, like so many famous people of science, was a synthesizer. He combined previously existing notions (such as Linnaean classification and the idea of acquired characteristics) into a new system with new meaning. Although the details of his ideas are incorrect, his emphasis on change gave support to the thoughts of those investigators who would ultimately discover accurate explanations for the changes he proposed.

The work of Lamarck and other early evolutionists, along with increasing evidence that changes had occurred in the living world, prompted thinkers to attempt to reconcile the traditional view of a divinely created changeless world with new evidence and ideas. The French scholar Georges Cuvier (1769–1832) is known for developing the idea of **catastrophism.** Cuvier recognized the fact that as we dig down into the earth, we see different assemblages of plants and animals. In many cases, specific layers of flora and fauna seem to have been almost totally replaced by new types overlying them. Cuvier believed that the living organisms represented in each layer were destroyed by a catastrophic event and that the next set of plants and animals represented a new creation event. The last catastrophic event was thought by some to have been the biblical flood.

According to the proponents of catastrophism, not all plants and animals need be destroyed by a cataclysmic event. For instance, the animals that were collected by Noah survived the flood. Also, Cuvier believed that catastrophes could be localized. Organisms that survived in an area not affected by the cataclysm could then migrate into the areas left vacant by the catastrophe.

Today, evolutionists reject the ideas of divinely created organisms and divinely orchestrated catastrophes. However, just as Linnaeus's classification, originally conceived to explain traditional religious concepts, has become a major tool for modern biologists, some of Cuvier's ideas are still present in the work of some modern evolutionary theorists. Like Linnaeus's beliefs, Cuvier's ideas have been expanded upon and reinterpreted in nonreligious terms. For instance, some modern researchers see catastrophic events, such as the effects of meteorites that hit the earth (see Box 14–3), as the catalysts of major evolutionary events such as mass extinctions of plants and animals and ensuing rapid evolutionary changes in some of the surviving populations. However, other evolutionists do not view catastrophic events as primary causes of evolutionary change. They see large-scale evolution as a result of the gradual accumulation of small changes over time. This idea of gradual modification of a species is the basic thesis of Darwin's model of evolution. Before we discuss Darwin, however, we turn to a scientist who directly influenced him.

What Is the Age of the Earth?

By the early nineteenth century, masses of new data had been gathered that threw doubt on traditional interpretations. Charles Lyell (1797–1875) synthesized this new information in a textbook, *Principles of Geology*, the first of three volumes being published in 1830 (Figure 2–2). In it he popularized the theory of **uniformitarianism,** which was a main prerequisite for the develop-

FIGURE 2–2 *Charles Lyell (1797–1875).*

ment of a credible evolutionary theory. The principle of uniformitarianism states that physical forces, such as wind, rain, heat, cold, moving water, volcanism, and earthquakes, that are at work today altering the earth were also in force, working in the same way, in former times. Therefore, "the present is the key to the past."

Lyell also realized that, as they operate today, the processes resulting in physical alteration of the earth would have required very long periods of time to form the layers of the earth known as **strata** (Figure 2–3). Therefore, it could be inferred that the large number and often great thickness of strata formed in the past must have taken a long time to develop. This inference also challenged biblical chronology because it showed that the earth's age was many times greater than previously thought. In developing the theory of uniformitarianism, Lyell was also setting the stage for a theory of the evolution of the inorganic world.

FIGURE 2–3 *Stratigraphy*. The Grand Canyon shows the various strata that have accumulated over millennia.

Lyell also studied fossil plants and animals that were embedded in the various strata. These and other similar investigations suggested that the earth is extremely old and that life has existed in various forms, some now extinct, for hundreds of centuries. Lyell, himself, did not become convinced of the antiquity of living things until later in his life when, in his text *The Antiquity of Man* (1863), he supported Charles Darwin's theory of natural selection.

HUMANS BEFORE ADAM AND EVE?   Fossils of extinct forms of plants and animals had been known long before Lyell's time, and many valid interpretations had been made. However, as often happens, the evidence was more frequently viewed in terms of predispositions and the special interests of the observer; it was not analyzed critically. For instance, early proponents of catastrophism believed that extinct animals were creatures "who did not make the Ark." After Lyell's systematic investigation, some scientists began at last to speculate on the idea of a more dynamic world. Yet the notion of prehistoric people was still heresy. Were not all people descendants of Adam and Eve?

In the early 1800s Jacques Boucher de Crèvecoeur de Perthes (1788–1868) made a systematic

By the time of Darwin, the notions of anthropocentrism, immutability, and a date of 4004 B.C. for the earth's origin had been altered or reversed. For most of the scientific community, the final discrediting of spontaneous creation would have to wait until the time of the French chemist Louis Pasteur (1822–1895). Pasteur, who had developed the pasteurization process and vaccinations against anthrax and rabies, also disproved spontaneous creation.

How Do Populations Change over Time?

It was Charles Darwin (1809–1882) who proposed a compelling theory for the mechanism of organic evolution which accurately synthesized the available evidence (Figure 2–5). At the age of 22, Darwin was invited to serve as naturalist on the HMS *Beagle*. On December 27, 1831, the *Beagle* sailed from Plymouth, England, on what was to be a 5-year voyage of discovery (Figure 2–6). Darwin spent much of the 5 years confined

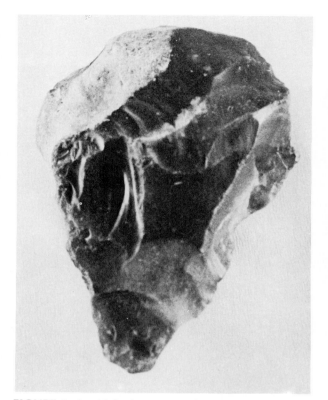

FIGURE 2–4 *Lightning stone.* This is an example of a hand ax from the Lower Paleolithic of southwestern France.

FIGURE 2–5 *Charles Darwin (1809–1882).*

attempt to demonstrate the existence of a prehistoric period. While digging on the banks of the Somme River in southwestern France, he discovered that many stones were not made of the same material as the walls of the pit in which they were uncovered. In addition, the stones had obviously been shaped into specific forms. Other people had also observed these types of rocks. They considered them to be "figured stones" of an unknown origin or "lightning stones," petrified lightning cast to the earth by God during thunderstorms. Boucher de Crèvecoeur de Perthes was convinced that they were made by ancient people (Figure 2–4). To back up this conviction, he collected what he thought was an immense amount of evidence to support his case. He submitted his report in 1838 to various scientific societies where it was rejected. Not until 20 years later, a year before the publication of Darwin's *On the Origin of Species*, were his conclusions accepted.

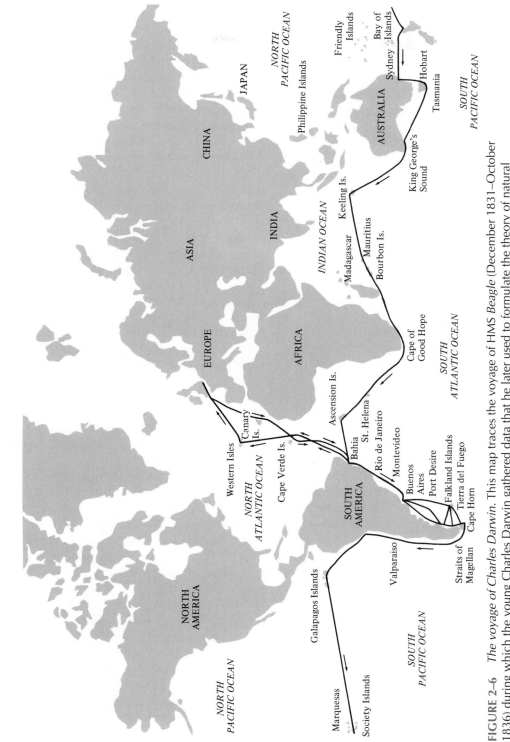

FIGURE 2–6 *The voyage of Charles Darwin.* This map traces the voyage of HMS *Beagle* (December 1831–October 1836) during which the young Charles Darwin gathered data that he later used to formulate the theory of natural selection.

25

on the small ship, which measured 90 feet in length and less than 25 feet at the widest point. He was one of seventy-four aboard.

The purpose of the voyage was to chart the coast of South America and to calculate an accurate fixing of longitude around the world. It was the role the voyage played in Darwin's life, however, that made it one of the most famous journeys in history. On this voyage, Darwin gained new insights into the origin of coral reefs, described fauna and flora in detail, and studied fossilized animals.

In the Andes, Darwin found seashells in rocks at 3962 meters (13,000 feet), and in Valdivia, Chile, he personally experienced a devastating earthquake that elevated the shore by several feet. These and other experiences showed how dynamic the earth is. He realized that the tops of mountains had once been under the sea and that coastlines could be altered by earthquakes.

Throughout his trip, Darwin witnessed the great diversity in nature. His 5-week visit to the Galápagos Islands, a volcanic group of islands some 965 kilometers (600 miles) west of Ecuador, possibly provided a major stimulus for his most famous contribution to science: the concept of natural selection. It was there that he observed giant tortoises, seagoing lizards, ground finches, and other animals that showed variations related to differences in the different island habitats. Ultimately he hypothesized that environmental forces had acted to weed out those individuals whose characteristics were not as well suited to a particular situation. One example he used was the different bill shapes of finches.

Finches are songbirds that belong to the same family as sparrows and canaries. Darwin noted several species of finches that exhibited similarities in body plumage and song to South American finches, but they also showed some features that were unique to the Galápagos Islands. Within this group of birds were several variations in beak size (Figure 6–12). Darwin further observed that the various types of birds generally ate different foods. The finches with powerful beaks could break open hard seeds that other finches could not. One variety of finch had a short, thick beak; its diet consisted mainly of

leaves, buds, blossoms, and fruits. Another finch had a long, straight beak; it subsisted mainly on nectar from the prickly pear cactus.

Having evolved these different bill shapes, the different varieties of finches were able to take advantage of different foods. Darwin believed that competition led to diversity in animal and plant types. For example, the small-beaked birds could not compete for hard seeds with the birds that had more powerful beaks. Unless the birds with smaller beaks possessed characteristics that allowed them to exploit a different segment of the habitat, they might become extinct.

Darwin was impressed by the fact that animals on the Galápagos Islands had "cousins" on the South American mainland, as well as by the variations on different islands. Darwin postulated that since these volcanic islands were younger than the mainland, the animals must have originated on the mainland. He then reasoned that as members of the original population became isolated from each other, they evolved differently, depending on the local environment. Hence, lizards on different islands evolved different colorations, tortoises different-shaped shells, and, as we have seen, finches different-sized and -shaped bills. Darwin saw in these facts proof that life is not immutable. He saw this as evidence of evolution.

Darwin was not the only person who was developing a theory of evolution based on species adaptation to the environment. As often happens in science, two people came up with basically the same conclusion simultaneously. In the summer of 1858, Darwin must have gotten quite a jolt when he received an essay from Alfred Russell Wallace (1823–1913), another famous naturalist, with whom he had been corresponding (Figure 2–7). Wallace had come up with basically the same ideas that Darwin had been working on for two decades. Both men received credit for their work at a meeting of the Linnaean Society in 1858. Because Darwin was the first to publish his work, in the book *On the Origin of Species* in 1859, he has since received most of the credit for modern evolutionary theory. Wallace certainly deserves more credit than he is usually given.

FIGURE 2–7 Alfred Russell Wallace (1823–1913).

Both men had read *Essay on the Principles of Population* by Thomas R. Malthus (1766–1834). Malthus wrote that the world population was growing at a faster rate than food production (remember, Buffon had also asserted this) and implanted the idea that famine and economic chaos would result as the population grew and food resources dwindled. Darwin and Wallace both saw natural selection as the process by which those individuals within a population that are best suited to the environment are more likely to survive and leave behind the most offspring. They saw this process as being applicable to all life. The development of the theory of natural selection was Darwin's and Wallace's great contribu-

tion to the theory of organic evolution, which had been emerging from the work and ideas of many individuals.

Evolution Versus Creationism

On departing from Plymouth in 1831, the captain of the *Beagle,* Robert Fitzroy, presented Charles Darwin with a gift. That gift, a copy of the newly published *Principles of Geology* by Charles Lyell, influenced the development of Darwin's ideas and was the source of some heated debates between Darwin and Fitzroy, a religious fundamentalist. Had Fitzroy read the book, he may never have given it to Darwin.

After the voyage, Lyell became Darwin's friend. In 1859 Lyell recommended that a partial disclaimer of sorts be added to *On the Origin of Species,* one that would recognize the role of the "Creator" in evolution. The book was first published on November 24, 1859, with no disclaimer; it sold out its first printing that same day. *On the Origin of Species* became the focus of a controversy between those who believed in the divine creation of life (creationists) and those who believed in a natural origin of life (evolutionists).

THE SCOPES TRIAL   By the 1920s, many Western theologians, as well as much of the public, had reconciled the concept of natural selection and organic evolution with their religious beliefs. Yet, in some quarters, there was still strong opposition to Darwinism. This opposition had its most dramatic airing in the summer of 1925 in a public spectacle called the "Scopes trial."

John T. Scopes was a high school teacher in Dayton, Tennessee, who decided to challenge that state's new law, the Butler Act, which prohibited the teaching of evolution. After teaching evolution in the classroom, Scopes was arrested. The trial focused national attention on the controversy. Clarence Darrow helped defend Scopes; William Jennings Bryan, the Democratic nominee for president in 1896, 1904, and 1908, worked for the prosecution (Figure 2–8).

FIGURE 2–8 *The Scopes trial.* Clarence Darrow (left circle) defends high school science teacher John T. Scopes (right circle) in 1925 for teaching evolution in the state of Tennessee.

Darrow argued the case on the basis that Scopes's academic freedom had been violated and that Scopes also had the constitutional guarantee of separation of church and state. Bryan, an old man by 1925, did not argue well and was severely embarrassed by the defense. Yet Scopes *had* broken the state law and was fined $100. The conviction was later overturned on a technicality. It was not the conviction that was important but the fact that the publicity over the trial acted to increase public acceptance of evolution and to discourage many states from enacting so-called monkey laws.

"CREATION-SCIENCE" The year 1925 did not mark the end of the story. In fact, the Tennessee law was not repealed until 1967. However, as Darrow's argument of academic freedom and separation of church and state took firmer hold, the creationists modified an old strategy. They called the concept of the divine creation of life a scientific view, and the term **creation-science** was born. Even creationists of the nineteenth century had used the argument that the biblical account of creation could be scientifically proved. Creation-science advocates began to sue teachers and school districts to force them to teach creation-science alongside evolutionary theory. They also put pressure on publishers to deemphasize evolution in biology textbooks.

Under such pressure, several states passed balanced-treatment acts, which required that teachers present "scientific" evidence for creation concurrent with the teaching of evolution. Because it ultimately came before the U.S. Supreme Court, the 1981 Balanced Treatment Act of Louisiana became one of the most important of these acts. On June 19, 1987, the Supreme Court, by a vote of 7 to 2, ended the argument by declaring the Louisiana act, and therefore all others like it, unconstitutional on the same grounds that Darrow had argued 62 years before. The Court agreed that the act

> advanced a religious doctrine by requiring either the banishment of the theory of evolution from public classrooms or the presentation of a religious viewpoint that rejects evolution in it entirely.[2]

The Court ruled that the Louisiana act violated the First Amendment's prohibition of the state's promotion of religious beliefs. Although creation-science advocates were dealt a blow in their legal battle to establish laws that prohibit or cripple the teaching of evolution, they have developed another strategy. For some time, creationists have been lobbying school districts to choose textbooks that eliminate or minimize mention of evolution and other subjects that are not in line with fundamental Christian beliefs. One agency that monitors censorship in the national schools has reported a 117 percent increase in censorship between 1982 and 1986.[3] This type of censorship may also be in trouble. In 1990, the Board of Education in Texas approved biology textbooks for grades 1 through 12 that "teach the theory of evolution unimpeded by creationist views."[4] The California Department of Education has enacted similar policies. Perhaps this is the beginning of a new trend to insist that science be presented in science books and religion be prominent in theology (and history, philosophy, humanity, and art) books.

Evolutionary theory is controversial in ways other than those described above. Some people use evolutionary principles to describe human social change. The application of evolutionary theory to social phenomena has had significant political consequences, some of which are discussed in Box 2–3.

Evolutionary Theory after Darwin: The Synthetic Theory

The basic concepts of Darwin's theory of evolution remain the cornerstone of modern evolutionary theory, yet much has been added to this base. Darwin, Wallace, and other naturalists of their day did not have an accurate picture of inheritance. They therefore were not sure of how characteristics were passed on from generation to generation or how new characteristics might arise. Progress in this area began to be made by Gregor Mendel, who will be discussed in the next chapter. Mendel discovered the basic laws of heredity, which he published in 1866.

Mendel's work began to answer basic questions about inheritance. Since Mendel's time, our knowledge of genetics has grown enormously. In the 1930s, population geneticists began to explain, in mathematical and statistical terms, how evolution could be seen as a change in the genetic composition of populations (Chapter 5). From the 1970s through the 1980s, dramatic new discoveries about the genetic material (DNA and RNA) have allowed us to see evolutionary processes that occur at the molecular level (Chapter 13). In addition, advances in the study of embryology, paleontology (Chapters 14 to 19), animal behavior (Chapter 11), and other disciplines have all contributed to a modern understanding of evolution. Because this understanding is based on a synthesis of information from diverse fields, it is sometimes called the **synthetic theory of evolution.**

---

[2]C. Norman, "Supreme Court Strikes Down 'Creation-Science' Law as Promotion of Religion," *Science,* 236 (1987), 1620.

[3]C. Holden, "Textbook Controversy Intensifies Nationwide," *Science,* 235 (1987), 19.

[4]C. Shulman, "Texas Votes for Evolution," *Nature,* 348 (1990), 271.

BOX 2–3

SOCIAL DARWINISM

What famous person who lived in the nineteenth century coined the phrase "survival of the fittest"? When asked, many students assertively answer: Charles Darwin. Actually the phrase was coined by the English philosopher Herbert Spencer (1820–1903), who was greatly influenced by Darwin's ideas. In many of his works, including *First Principles* (1862) and *Principles of Ethics* (1879–1893), Spencer attempted to apply his own and Darwin's notions of biological evolution to psychology, sociology, and other social sciences. The application of the principles of biological evolution to explain topics such as social inequalities became known as **social Darwinism.**

Spencer and other proponents of social Darwinism viewed social life as a competitive struggle for power, wealth, and general well-being among individuals and nations. Using this concept, Europeans of the nineteenth century could argue that their dominant position in the world was the result of natural superiority that resulted from natural selection. The Asian,

African, Polynesian, and other peoples that Europeans ruled or subdued at the time were seen as belonging to earlier and more primitive stages of evolution. Likewise, the social inequalities among individuals within European society were thought to be variations on which natural selection acted. The prosperous were seen as being "fit," while the poor and powerless were seen as "unfit" individuals that natural selection would select against.

Spencer and other social Darwinists, including the American sociologist William Graham Sumner (1840–1910), believed that government should do nothing to aid the poor or sick. Modern social Darwinists assert that programs such as food stamps, Aid to Families with Dependent Children, and free public health clinics interfere with the natural weeding out of unfit people and thereby weaken society. Or, said in reverse, a laissez-faire approach to social inequalities would lead to a natural cleansing of a population and hence would lead to a society and

a world better adapted to environmental pressures. In the United States and Europe, social Darwinism has been used to justify discriminatory actions against women, nonwhites, and various ethnic groups. It must be noted, however, that Charles Darwin was not a social Darwinist; at least, he avoided any discussion of the social implications of his ideas.

Scientific studies on human populations have not supported the tenets of social Darwinism. It appears that it is discrimination and the ideas of superiority, as well as differential access to natural resources, that produce most inequalities. The fact that some societies are more powerful than others and that some individuals within a society do not have equal access to necessities and luxuries is due to social history. When populations or classes of people within societies are freed from discriminatory practices, they can reach the same levels of wealth, power, and education as those groups who traditionally define themselves as superior.

Summary

Evolutionary theory has been shown to be a valid and reliable explanation of basic questions about life. Modern evolutionary theory grew out of a European intellectual climate. Before the nineteenth century most Europeans saw humans as the superior center of a world populated by spontaneously created organisms that did not change once created. Each of these ideas fell in light of new knowledge gathered by hundreds of schol-

ars, including Copernicus, Linnaeus, Buffon, Lamarck, Lyell, Boucher de Crèvecoeur de Perthes, Darwin, Wallace, Mendel, and Pasteur. Darwin's concept of natural selection has fused with Mendel's concept of genetics; to this mixture new ingredients continue to be added, including concepts about the genetics of populations. Also, ideas of what embryos, fossils, and animal behavior can tell us about the past have become part of what is called the synthetic theory of evolution.

THE NATURE OF SCIENCE

The physicist investigating the relationship between time and space, the chemist exploring the properties of a new substance, the biologist probing the mysteries of the continuity of life, and the anthropologist searching for human origins share a common trait—curiosity. This is not to say that nonscientists are not curious; most people possess curiosity. The scientist, however, uses scientific reasoning as a specific method for delving into enigmatic problems.

Unfortunately, science often is misunderstood. The multiplication of our knowledge in medicine and technology has led to the idea that science can cure all and explain all and that only enough time, money, and intelligence are needed. In truth, science cannot provide all the answers. In fact, many phenomena are not even subject to scientific explanations.

Science has also been attacked as a cause of most contemporary problems. It is said to be responsible for depersonalizing the individual, for stripping creativity from human behavior, and for creating massive threats to the species through the development of nuclear power, insecticides, and polluting machinery. If we analyze the situation, we can see that the people who developed computers did not intend to debase humankind, nor did those who introduced mass production wish to crush creativity. It is what society, policymakers especially, does with scientific achievements that makes them social or antisocial. There is nothing inherently good or bad about science.

The Many Aspects of Science

Just what is **science?** This is where the dictionary fails, for science is not something that can be easily defined. It is an activity, a search, and a method of discovery that results in a body of knowledge.

Science is the activity of seeking out **reliable** explanations for phenomena. *Reliable* here means "predictable." *Predictability* does not mean "assurance"; it simply indicates the percentage of cases in which, under a given set of conditions, a particular event will occur.

Science is also a search for order. Nature does not categorize; people do. Through classifications, such as that of Linnaeus, systematic similarities and differences can be found. This display of ordered relationships allows for discoveries that might otherwise never be made.

SCIENTIFIC THINKING   The precise mental steps taken in thinking scientifically about a problem vary depending on the nature of the problem being studied. For instance, because of the different nature of the variables involved, scientific inquiry in the physical sciences differs significantly from that in the social sciences.

The first step in scientific studies is identifying the variables to be studied. A **variable** is any property that may be displayed in different forms. For example, the volume of the brain case, the part of the skull that houses the brain, is a variable; it may measure 400 cubic centimeters in one animal and 1600 cubic centimeters in another. In order for a variable to be the subject of a scientific study, we must be able to measure it precisely. Different people measuring the same variable should arrive at the same size.

The second step in scientific studies is proposing a hypothesis. A **hypothesis** is an educated guess about the relationship of one variable to another. Is one variable independent of the other variable, or does one variable cause another variable to occur? For example, one might hypothesize that among the ancestors of modern humans as the average volume of the brain case increases, so does the ability of the population to manufacture tools. Brain case size is one variable, and the manufacturing of tools is a second variable. The hypothesis proposes a direct relationship between the two variables: as one increases, so does the other. While this particular hypothesis proposes a relationship between two variables, it does not propose that one variable causes the other to occur.

Once proposed, the hypothesis must be tested against reality. In the above example, we could measure brain case size in fossil skulls and count the number of stone tools found in association with each skull. If, upon analysis, we find that as the average size of the brain case increases, so does the number of tools, then we have identified one line of evidence that supports the validity of the hypothesis.

Evidence is not necessarily absolute proof. There can be unknown factors responsible for the observed correlation of the variables. For instance, an increase in the population density at a series of sites might influence the number of stone tools found. Perhaps some habitats are more easily exploited with simpler technologies than are others. In other words, the relationship between the variables in the hypothesis may turn out to be accidental or to be the result of a variable or variables not identified in the original hypothesis.

After a number of studies exploring the relationships of all the variables have been completed, we might develop some generalizations. We might suggest that an increase in the volume of the brain case is correlated with a whole range of behaviors that differentiate earlier humanlike organisms from later ones. Each of these new hypotheses would then have to be tested by some research design. Each test might reveal hidden variables that either disprove or modify the original and related hypotheses. This hypothesis-test-hypothesis-test cycle is a self-corrective feature of science. Scientists realize that results are never final.

Science is cumulative. After many tests have been conducted on a set of similar hypotheses with confirming results, a **theory** may be proposed. For example, the testing of thousands of hypotheses on the reasons for progressive change in anatomy and behavior has led to great confidence in the theory of evolution.

There are more components to scientific thinking than we can discuss in this book. The main point is that scientific thinking is a way to test one's ideas against the real world in a disciplined way. Each step in the process must be made clear so that the procedure can be repeated and yield the same results.

Science as a Creative Process

Science is a creative process. The scientist must be a keen observer, possess a questioning mind, and ask unique, nonstereotyped questions. The scientist must be clever in suggesting possible answers to his or her own queries. Above all, the scientist must be innovative in designing experiments that will test the validity of the hypothesis. However, it is a mistake to believe that intuition and passion are absent from science. A hunch, along with persistence, has more than once led to a revolutionary discovery. This happened when Mary Leakey and her husband, L. S. B. Leakey, found evidence of early humans in an area that they had been combing for 28 years (Chapter 16).

The passion involved in the search for a new truth or simply a new fact can be as intense as that of an artist attempting to create a masterpiece. From Copernicus's calculations to modern methods of charting the entire human genetic system, the scientist displays an ability to see unique solutions to problems that most people do not even recognize as problems.

Applying Scientific Thinking to Anthropological Problems

In many instances it is difficult to apply the methods scientists use to the investigation of humans. For one thing, physical scientists, such as physicists and chemists, can design experiments that can be repeated—in many cases, as many times as desired. The physical anthropologist is often limited in the degree and manner in which the phenomena being studied can be repeated for the sake of experimentation. For instance, how does one repeat the past in an attempt to test hypotheses about early human ancestors? Anthropologists who deal with living people are faced with ethical problems strictly limiting the ability to experiment directly on their subjects. They must often rely on "after-the-fact" observations. In other words, anthropologists do not have as much control over the phenomena being studied, or over the variables that affect the phenomena, as physical scientists do.

Another major problem faced by the anthropologist is that the subjects of anthropological study, humans, are more complex than anything dealt with by the physical scientist. The latter may find a single element that explains the subject under study. This is a **monocausal explanation.** Water turns to ice at sea level when the temperature is 0°C (32°F), and that's that. Anthropologists are much less likely to find a single cause for anything they study; their explanations are usually **multicausal.** All things about humans are due to an interplay of factors at different levels of being. After all, a human is a physical entity and a chemical substance, as well as a biological organism and a social and cultural being. Human behavior, evolution, variation, growth and development, and so on, are subject to explanations on all these levels (Figure 2–9). The realization of multicausality is reflected in the holistic approach employed by anthropologists (Chapter 1).

Because of the complexity of the subject matter, anthropology approaches its hypotheses from numerous angles. For example, the general theory of evolution has been validated not only by the study of the fossil record (Chapters 14 to 19) but also through comparative anatomy (Chapter 13), comparative growth and development (Chapter 10), molecular biology, and cytogenetics (Chapter 13). The confidence in any hypothesis is increased when several lines of evidence all point to the same conclusion. In the case of evolutionary theory, they all do point to the same thing—a dynamic, changeable world.

Anthropology is a newer discipline than physics and chemistry, and its subject matter is more complex. It is thus understandable that the methods and techniques of anthropology are still in a formative stage. Yet, because of its holistic approach and commitment to the scientific exploration of human nature, anthropology perhaps offers us the greatest chance at attaining a general "theory of humanity."

Science and Religion

The theologian deeply involved in an interpretation of scriptures, the bereaved individual looking to prayer to explain death, and the shaman dancing for rain are putting their trust in traditional doctrines that, for the most part, they do not question. In contrast, the biologist examining cell structure, the anthropologist studying death rituals, and the meteorologist investigating the weather rely on methods and techniques that are aimed at producing new information and validating or correcting old explanations. Thus they build a body of knowledge from which accurate predictions about natural occurrences can be made.

Science is the process of testing questions about the nature of empirical observations. An **empirical** observation is an observation based upon information received through the senses (seeing, touching, smelling, hearing, tasting). The information can be received directly through the senses or indirectly through an instrument that enhances the senses, such as a microscope or telescope. The credibility of scientific conclusions is based on the concepts of accuracy, validity, and reliability; belief in religious doctrines is based on faith.

Scientists can attempt to answer only some questions; others cannot be subjected to scientific inquiry and are therefore not in the domain of empirical or objective research. For example, science cannot deal with the question of the existence of an omnipotent force. In order for an experiment to be carried out, a **control,** a situation that differs from the situation being tested, must be possible. If a phenomenon is present always and everywhere, how can its absence be tested?

Scientists do not claim that their conclusions are final. They realize that their statements are only as good as the data they have and that new information may alter their concepts. A religious belief can change in response to personal interpretation and public opinion, but such an interpretation or new information is not necessarily linked to new empirical facts. To a believer, his or her religious belief or faith is taken as being absolutely true, whereas at no time is a scientific statement considered totally and irrefutably correct.

The scientific approach has been consciously and consistently used in Western societies since the 1600s; however, it is not just the industrial societies that practice science. All people make conclusions on the basis of experimenting with observations. The phenomena that they can treat in this way make up their objective knowledge; the more mysterious facets of life are treated re-

Level of biological organization		Constituents	Features characteristic of each level
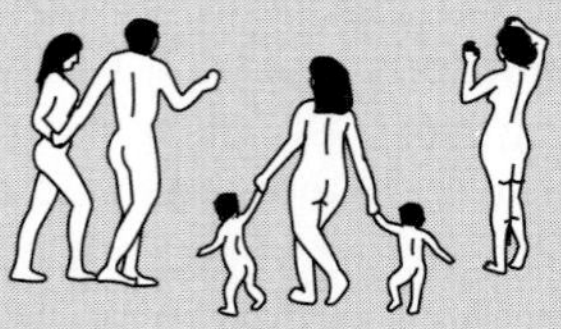	POPULATION	individual organisms	Mating patterns, migration, birth and death rates, growth rates, density.
	INDIVIDUAL ORGANISM	cells	Behavior: feeding, mating fighting, growth and development, reproduction, maintenance of physiological states.
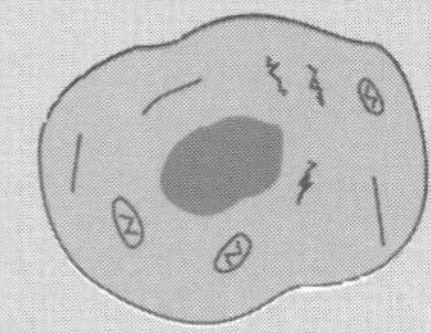	CELL	organelles: e.g., mitochondria, ribosomes, chromosomes	Grows, develops and reproduces, obtains energy from food, orchestrates protein production, maintains internal states.
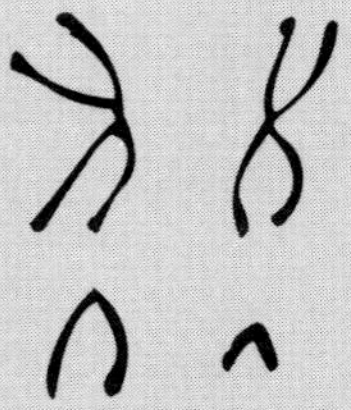	CHROMOSOME	molecule (DNA & protein) genes (segments of DNA)	Organizes and "packages" DNA, reproduces, exchanges material with other chromosomes, regulates gene action.
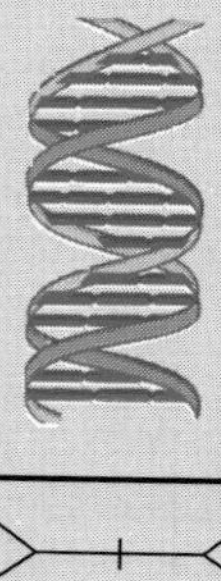	DNA MOLECULE	sugars, phosphates, bases	Contains instructions which influence the development of cell and organism from conception to death.
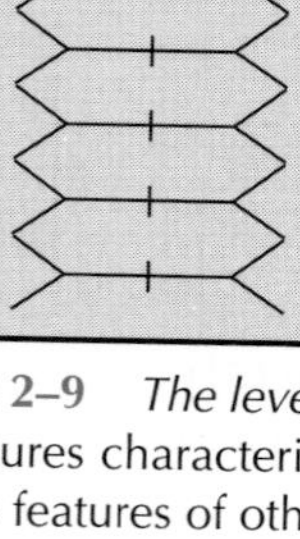	GENE: Segment of DNA molecule	sugars, phosphates, bases	Genes may contain instructions to: 1.) make proteins which serve functions in cells and tissues 2.) affect growth rates of body parts 3.) activate or inhibit other genes 4.) coordinate cell and tissue differentiation.

FIGURE 2–9 *The levels of biological organization.* Humans can be studied at many levels. The features characteristic at any given level are distinct, and while certainly interrelated with the features of other levels, they cannot predict the characteristics of the other levels.

ligiously or magically. For example, the Trobriand Islanders of the Pacific do two types of fishing: one in the shallow coastal pools and the other far out at sea. The first type is safe and is undertaken by men, women, and children; the second, filled with the unknown, is dangerous and is considered a male activity. Since shallow fishing is undertaken with regularity, time is spent making observations of fish behavior and experiments are performed on how best to catch the prey. Nothing is done religiously or magically to protect the fishing party or to ensure a catch. The story is different with deep-sea fishing. Men occasionally do not return from the expeditions, and so elaborate rituals are performed in order to appease or appeal to the gods of the unpredictable seas.

In conclusion, a scientific statement asserts the natural causality of phenomena. One thing happens because of the preceding events that led up to it. Things happen and conditions exist because of the physical, chemical, biological, behavioral, and/or cultural characteristics of the thing in question and the context in which it is found. Religious or magical statements assert causality beyond the natural; when natural causality cannot be determined or is not sought, spiritual causality is often assumed.

Summary

Science is the activity of seeking out reliable explanations for phenomena. Science is also the search for order and a method for discovery. The result of the activity of science is a body of empirical knowledge that can be used to understand the universe better and to predict the processes, structure, form, and function of natural occurrences. Scientific thinking provides a systematic way of investigation, including the identification of variables, hypothesis formation, and tests of the validity of the hypothesis, and of postulating theories. All scientific statements are tentative. It is because new evidence is always possible that a scientific statement can never be completely proved.

Science is not a mere mechanical pursuit of knowledge but involves creativity and the passion of discovery and accomplishment. Many breakthroughs, as well as more mundane discoveries, have resulted from a hunch followed by long years of persistent examination.

The scientist and the theologian are both interested in giving answers. However, the scientist proceeds by testing questions about the nature of empirical observation, whereas the theologian consults the philosophy of his or her particular religion and interprets the meaning of that philosophy for a particular situation. Scientific statements are never considered absolute, but at any one time religious doctrine often is. All people have a body of scientific knowledge, but for the things they fear or cannot understand in an empirical way, religion and magic provide a measure of comfort and assurance.

STUDY QUESTIONS

1. The development of the evolutionary concept was part of the general changes that were occurring in Western society from the fifteenth through nineteenth centuries. How were such historical events as the discovery of North America and the American Revolution related to the development of the theory of evolution?
2. What were some of the concepts about human nature and the relationship between humans and nature that had to change before an evolutionary concept could develop?
3. How does the idea of catastrophism differ from Darwin's concept of natural selection?
4. Who were some of the scholars who contributed to the development of evolutionary ideas? What did each contribute to that development?
5. Darwin, Wallace, and other naturalists of the nineteenth century did not have an accurate notion of one aspect of modern evolutionary theory. What element of modern theory was missing from their writings? Who began to provide accurate analyses of this missing element?
6. What is meant by the phrase "the synthetic theory of evolution"?
7. Many antievolutionists believe that since science does not have answers for all questions, scientific conclusions are not necessarily correct. This attitude reflects a failure to under-

stand the nature of science. What is the general nature of scientific thinking? In what way is science self-correcting?

8. In what way does a scientific statement differ from a doctrine?

SUGGESTED READINGS

Alland, A., Jr. *Human Nature: Darwin's View.* New York: Columbia University Press, 1985. This is a fascinating glimpse of Darwin's sometimes contradictory ideas on human nature. Alland has excerpted materials from three of Darwin's famous works.

Bowler, P. J. *Theories of Human Evolution: A Century of Debate.* Baltimore: Johns Hopkins, 1986. This book deals with the development of theories of human evolution and the controversy surrounding these theories.

Darwin, C. *On the Origin of Species by Means of Natural Selection, or the Preservation of Favored Races in the Struggle for Life.* London: J. Murray, 1859. Many editions have been produced of this classic, including a 1967 facsimile of the first edition.

Desmond, A., and J. Moore. *Darwin: The Life of a Tormented Evolutionist.* New York: Warner, 1991. This recent biography of Darwin makes use of newly available sources and places Darwin and his ideas in the context of Victorian science and society.

Edey, M., and D. C. Johanson. *Blueprints: Solving the Mystery of Evolution.* New York: Penguin, 1989. This volume is a fascinating survey of the "evolution" of the theory of evolution. It gives interesting biographical portraits of the main figures in the development of evolutionary theory.

Giere, R. N. *Understanding Scientific Reasoning,* 4th ed. Fort Worth: Holt, Rinehart and Winston, 1996.

This book explains scientific thinking using examples of scientific discoveries and everyday events.

Gould, S. J. *Time's Arrow Time's Cycle.* Cambridge, Mass.: Harvard University Press, 1987. The author describes the historical development of the concept of deep time in geology, including a discussion of Charles Lyell's contributions.

Hoover, K. R. *The Elements of Social Scientific Thinking,* 6th ed. New York: St. Martin's Press, 1995. This is a highly readable book dealing with scientific thinking as applied to the social sciences.

Lyell, C. *Principles of Geology,* 3 vols. London: J. Murray, 1830–1833. New York: Johnson Reprint, 1969. This was the first geology "textbook," and it influenced Darwin's perceptions of nature.

Mayr, E. *The Growth of Biological Thought: Diversity, Evolution, and Inheritance.* Cambridge, Mass.: Harvard University Press, 1985. This is an award-winning book on the history and development of modern biology.

Milner, R. *The Encyclopedia of Evolution.* New York: Facts on File, 1990. This is a very useful encyclopedia with entries on important people and concepts.

Scientific Genius and Creativity: Readings from Scientific American. San Francisco: Freeman, 1987. This book includes biographies of ten great scientists and explores the role of genius and creativity in scientific discoveries.

Simpson, G. G. (ed.). *The Book of Darwin.* New York: Washington Square Press, 1982. The great biologist George Gaylord Simpson presents selections from the writings of Charles Darwin with insightful commentary.

Young, D. *The Discovery of Evolution.* Cambridge, England: Cambridge University Press, 1991. Richly illustrated by many historical photographs and drawings, this volume traces the development of evolutionary theory. It is an excellent introduction to evolution for the new student.

Albino among the Hopi Indians of the American Southwest.

Charles Darwin, not knowing of Gregor Mendel's work, was making some experiments of his own, which led him within an ace of obtaining results paralleling Mendel's. Whether or not he would have analyzed the results as masterfully as Mendel did is a moot point.[1]

Theodozius Dobzhansky (1900–1975)

[1]T. Dobzhansky, "Mendelism, Darwinism, and Evolution," *Proceedings of the American Philosophical Society,* 109 (August 1965), 205.

CHAPTER

3

HUMAN GENETICS

Charles Darwin's concept of natural selection helped explain why variants within a population increased or decreased in number over generations. Although Darwin recognized the relationship between the processes of inheritance and natural selection, he was never able to define the rules of heredity. He did not discover how new variants, the raw material of natural selection, arose. Nor could he figure out how characteristics were transmitted from generation to generation.

Gregor Mendel is credited with the discovery of the basic principles of heredity. Since Mendel's time, **genetics,** the study of the mechanisms of heredity and biological variation, has become the foundation of the modern theory of evolution. The diversity of form, function, and, often, behavior that Darwin observed is attained by changes that occur to the genetic material.

Genetics plays a major role in many areas of human interest. Many human diseases and abnormalities are of genetic origin, and genetic studies have provided clues to the treatment and management of some of these problems. An understanding of genetics provides the background necessary for intelligent discussion in many areas of social concern, such as therapeutic abortion and social integration of the handicapped in our society. Genetics also helps us comprehend the nature of individual and group differences. Because human differences are, in part, genetic, an accurate perception of human variation calls for unemotional, empirical knowledge of the genetic nature of people and the mechanisms of differentiation. The misunderstanding of the nature of this variation has created much human suffering.

This is the first of three chapters devoted to genetics. After a discussion of Mendel's contributions to genetics, this chapter will consider the genetic knowledge we have gained since Mendel's day and the influence of that knowledge on medical science.

NINETEENTH-CENTURY STUDIES OF HEREDITY

Almost everyone would agree with the statement that children resemble their parents; peculiarities in physical traits often characterize family lines. Moving from a simple and obvious statement about family likenesses to an actual determination of the genetic mechanisms involved is a long jump.

One early attempt at explaining family similarities was the **blending theory.** This theory maintained that hereditary units merged or mixed as one might mix two colors of paint. However, if such were the case, traits would be irreversibly changed from generation to generation and would not persist. For example, red paint mixed with white paint yields pink; both the red and the white colors cease to exist. Neither the red nor the white color can be reconstituted from the pink. This theory implied that a child was a human alloy, a blend of traits from both parents, with the parental characteristics being homogenized in the offspring. As we will see shortly, this simplistic notion is far from the truth.

Although Charles Darwin recognized some examples of nonblending, he never came to a correct understanding of genetics. He believed that particles present in the body were influenced by activities of the organism. These particles traveled to the reproductive cells through the circulatory system. They modified the sex cells in such a way that the acquired characteristics of the individual organism could now be passed on to the next generation. This concept of heredity, called **pangenesis,** was wrong. Because of poor methodology, inappropriate materials, and incorrect hypotheses, many of Darwin's contemporaries went equally astray in their quest for an explanation of the transmission and differentiation of life.

Problems in the Study of Human Genetics

Much of the nineteenth-century interest in genetics revolved around the study of human characteristics. However, the study of human heredity is many times more difficult than the study of heredity in other organisms. This is perhaps the main reason so many biologists failed to discover the underlying principles of genetics.

The experimental method requires control over the object of experimentation, yet no scientist can control human matings. The study of human genetics must accept matings that have already occurred. In addition, human families tend to be very small. Many basic genetic principles were developed from the statistical examination of large numbers of progeny, possible only with certain organisms. Also, the length of the human generation is much too great to allow one investigator to follow the inheritance of a particular trait for more than a few generations.

Another major problem in the study of genetics is the selection of the trait to be studied, as many traits are difficult to measure and quantify. Until quite recently, when sophisticated instruments came into use, skin color was difficult to measure accurately. Also, many traits such as skin color and stature are greatly affected by the environment: skin color by sunlight, and stature by diet and childhood disease. A further complicating factor is that the inheritance of many traits is complex; it involves more than one genetic factor. Hence, it is not surprising that the breakthrough in the understanding of hereditary principles took place outside the arena of human genetics. During the nineteenth century, many scientists turned their attention to small animals, such as mice, and to the plant world. In the mid-nineteenth century a monk by the name of Gregor Mendel (1822–1884), while working with the common pea plant, first determined many of the principles of heredity.[2]

---

[2] G. Mendel, "Versuche über Pflanzen-Hybriden," *Verhandlungen des Naturforschenden Vereins Brünn,* 4 (1866), 3–37. Translation in C. Stern and E. R. Sherwood (eds.), *The Origins of Genetics* (San Francisco: Freeman, 1966), 1–48.

The Work of Gregor Mendel

Gregor Mendel realized that the best traits for genetic study are those that are either obviously present or completely absent, rather than those that have intermediate values and must be measured on some type of scale. Mendel chose seven contrasting pairs of characteristics of the common pea plant: flower color (violet or white), stature (tall or dwarf), shape of the ripe seed (smooth or wrinkled), and four others.

Mendel chose the edible pea only after several years of experimentation with many different plants. Using as large a sample as possible to eliminate chance error, he observed each pea plant separately and kept the different generations apart. The results were quantified and expressed as ratios.

In the first series of experiments, Mendel started with **true-breeding** plants. These are plants that have been bred only with plants of the same kind and show the same traits over many generations. Mendel cross-pollinated true-breeding plants that produced only violet flowers with true-breeding plants that produced only white flowers. These plants made up the parental, or P_1, generation. The plants grown from the seeds produced by these parental plants made up the next generation, called the first filial, or F_1, generation. Mendel noted that plants of the F_1 generation produced only violet flowers; he observed no white flowers or flowers of intermediate color, such as pink. These plants are termed **hybrids.** The hybrid plant produced violet flowers, as did one of the parental plants. (The hybrid plant differed from the true-breeding parents in having one parent that produced flowers unlike its own, in this case white.)

Mendel then allowed the hybrids to self-pollinate to produce the next generation, called F_2. In this generation, he found that some plants showed violet flowers while others showed white flowers. When he counted the number of plants showing each trait, he found that approximately three-fourths of the plants bore violet flowers, while one-fourth bore white flowers—a ratio of 3:1.

The F_1 hybrid plants bore only violet flowers, although these plants had parents with white flowers. When the F_1 generation was self-pollinated, some plants with white flowers were produced. The trait that is seen in the hybrid is termed **dominant.** The trait that is not seen and yet can be passed on in a later cross is termed **recessive.** Mendel noted that violet flowers, tallness, and smooth seeds were dominant features, while white flowers, dwarfness, and wrinkled seeds were recessive.

The fact that the F_1 generation produced *only* violet flowers and the F_2 generation produced violet *and* white flowers showed that the blending theory was erroneous. No plant with pink flowers appeared in the F_1 generation, and in the F_2 generation white flowers reappeared. This confirmed the fact that the genetic unit for white flower color had not blended but had persisted without having been altered in any way.

A MODEL OF GENETIC EVENTS   A **model** is a representation of an object or an ideal. Models help us test hypotheses, make predictions, and see relationships. The model may be a diagrammatic representation of some phenomenon, a statistical description, or a mathematical formula. For precise predictions to be made, models must be phrased in mathematical terms. For instance, the formula $A = \pi r^2$ allows us to predict exactly how a change in the radius of a circle affects the area of that circle. Models act as summaries of the known characteristics of a phenomenon. They provide a means of testing hypotheses about the phenomenon by measuring the effect of one element (variable) of the model on other elements. Gregor Mendel was not aware of the physical or chemical realities of the hereditary mechanism, but he did develop a model to explain what he had observed.

PRINCIPLE OF SEGREGATION   Mendel believed that in every plant the hereditary factors are particulate; that is, they maintain their individuality by not blending with one another. They also exist as pairs.

In the formation of the sex cells of plants—pollen and ova—the paired hereditary factors separate, forming sex cells that contain either one or the other factor. For example, they may contain the factor for violet or white flower

BOX 3–1

MENDEL AND THE CREATIVE INTERPRETATION OF DATA

We are shocked when we learn that a medical researcher has made up data to support a hypothesis on how to treat a serious illness. We may be angry that he or she did this to advance in academic rank or to gain fame or fortune. Serious instances of this type of fraud have been reported in recent years.[1]

In 1936 statistician R. A. Fisher published an analysis of Mendel's work. From the standpoint of statistics, Fisher thought that Mendel's results for crosses between hybrid peas were too close to the expected results considering the sample size and other statistical factors.[2] The numerical results of Mendel's crosses of two F_1 plants are shown in the accompanying table.

Current evaluation of Fisher's own analysis and more recent re-analysis of Mendel's experiments have shown that it was Fisher who was incorrect. Mendel's ratios come closer to the expected because of situations having to do with germination in the pea plant,

not because of Mendel's conscious "adjusting" of the data. Still, Mendel may have done other things that would not be acceptable today.[3]

Mendel's observations of nature and his knowledge of statistics led him to believe that two genetic units must exist for each characteristic. He concluded that a specific ratio would be shown in matings between plants with specific combinations of dominant or recessive units. He *expected* certain results. When his results were close to the expected but not precisely so, he possibly assumed that it was his ability to discriminate between variations in characteristics, not the purity of the concept, that was at fault. For instance, some peas are smooth (round), while others are wrinkled. Mendel expected to find three smooth peas (they are dominant) for each wrinkled one (recessive) in crosses of hybrid pea plants. Yet some seeds are not clearly smooth or wrinkled. Mendel counted the results of his

experiments, and then he may have placed the intermediate cases in whichever group made the ratios approximate the ideal.

To Mendel, this was not cheating. He knew that there was bias in his observational abilities, but he believed in the validity of his hypothesis. To him, the only logical place for the intermediate forms was in the category that maximized agreement with his expected ratios. There "is subjectivity in the process of inventing categories for comprehending nature and there is subjectivity in assigning objects to these categories."[4] Not only is science a creative process, but the standards for designing experiments, the way in which evidence is interpreted, and the data that are accepted as proof change with time.[5] What cannot be denied is that after decades of experimentation, Mendel's basic principles of segregation and independent assortment stand as the valid foundations of modern genetics.

Form of seed	5474 round	1850 wrinkled	2.96 to 1
Color of albumen	6022 yellow	2001 green	3.01 to 1
Color of seed coats	705 gray*	224 white*	3.15 to 1
Form of pod	882 inflated	299 constricted	2.95 to 1
Color of unripe pods	428 green	152 yellow	2.82 to 1
Position of flowers	651 axial	207 terminal	3.14 to 1
Length of stem	787 long	277 short	2.84 to 1
Average			2.98 to 1

*Gray seed coats are associated with violet flowers, while white seed coats are associated with white flowers.

[1] J. Horgan (ed.), "Science and the Citizen: Doctored Data," *Scientific American,* 256 (April 1987), 68–69; D. E. Koshland, Jr., "Fraud in Science," *Science,* 235 (1987), 141.
[2] R. A. Fisher, "Has Mendel's Work Been Rediscovered?" *Annals of Science,* 1 (1936), 121.
[3] J. A. Miller, "A Matter of Genius or of Guile?" *Science News,* 125 (1984), 108–109.
[4] R. S. Root-Bernstein, *History of Science,* 21 (1983), 275.
[5] D. E. Chubin, "Research Malpractice," *BioScience,* 35 (1985), 80–89.

color, but not both. This is the principle of **segregation.** Thus, in the parental generation, the violet-flowered plant produces sex cells that carry the factor for violet flowers only, while the

white-flowered plant produces sex cells that carry the factor for white flowers only. The hybrid develops from the union of two sex cells, one carrying the unit for violet color and one carrying the unit for white color. The hybrid therefore contains a pair of units—one is for violet color, and the other is for white. Since the unit for violet color is dominant, the flowers blooming on the hybrid plant are all violet (Figure 3–1).

When the hybrid produces sex cells, the two units segregate, producing sex cells of two types. Half the sex cells carry the unit for violet flowers, while the other half carry the unit for white flowers. When fertilization takes place, three different combinations may occur in the new plants. Some F_2 plants may inherit two units for violet flowers; others may inherit two units for white flowers; and still others may inherit one unit for violet flowers and one unit for white flowers (this last combination can occur in one of two ways: violet-white or white-violet). Since the violet-violet, violet-white, and white-violet combinations all produce violet flowers, three

FIGURE 3–2 *Back cross.* The hybrid violet-flowered plant is crossed with the true-breeding white-flowered parent.

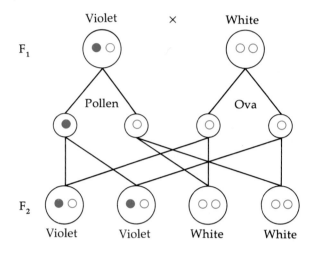

out of every four plants yield violet flowers. Only the white-white combination (one out of every four plants) produces white flowers.

To test his hypothesis, Mendel planned another experiment. He predicted the results before beginning, and he managed to predict them correctly. He crossed an F_1 hybrid with a true-breeding, white-flowered plant. This is called a **back cross.** Figure 3–2 shows the result of this experiment.

FIGURE 3–1 *Segregation.* In the formation of sex cells, the hereditary factors separate, forming sex cells that contain either one or the other factor. Individual sex cells combine at fertilization, producing new combinations of hereditary units.

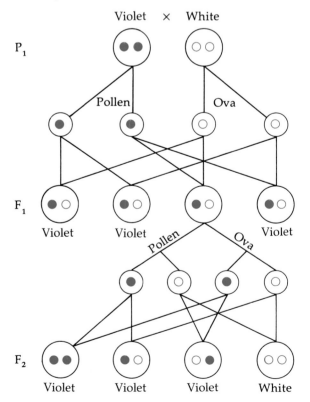

PRINCIPLE OF INDEPENDENT ASSORTMENT   Mendel next studied the simultaneous inheritance of more than one trait. For example, he crossed a normal-stature (tall) plant bearing violet flowers with a dwarf plant bearing white flowers. The F_1 hybrid was a tall plant with violet flowers. When the F_1 hybrids were crossed, four distinct types of offspring resulted: tall plants with violet flowers, tall plants with white flowers, dwarf plants with violet flowers, and dwarf plants with white flowers, with the frequencies of $\frac{9}{16}$, $\frac{3}{16}$, $\frac{3}{16}$, and $\frac{1}{16}$, respectively. The explanation for these results is seen in Figure 3–3.

From these data Mendel formulated the principle of **independent assortment,** which states that the inheritance patterns of differing traits are independent of one another. Whether a plant is tall or dwarf is unrelated to whether that plant bears violet or white flowers.

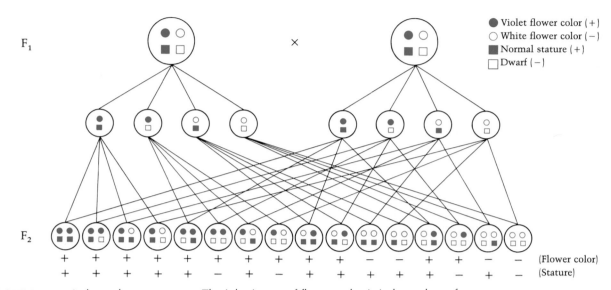

FIGURE 3–3 *Independent assortment.* The inheritance of flower color is independent of the inheritance of stature.

Summary

Because of the lack of control over matings, the small size of families, the long generation span, the difficulties in determining what part of a trait is genetic as opposed to environmental, and problems of measurement and quantification, human beings have not been easy subjects for genetic research. The basic principles of heredity were worked out using nonhuman organisms.

Through careful experimentation with the common pea plant, Gregor Mendel was the first scientist to discover the principles of heredity. From his data he formulated two principles based upon a model of genetic events. The principle of segregation states that in the formation of sex cells, the hereditary factors separate, forming sex cells that contain either one or the other of the paired factors. The principle of independent assortment states that the inheritance patterns of differing traits are independent of one another. These principles are universal among all living organisms, including the human species.

THE STUDY OF HUMAN GENETICS

Gregor Mendel published his study in 1866, but his work did not become generally known until 1900, sixteen years after his death. In that year three scientists, Hugo de Vries of Holland, Karl Correns of Germany, and Erich Tschermack of Austria, independently rediscovered Mendel's principles. In the next year, it was shown that Mendel's principles of genetics applied to human heredity. The basic rules of genetics were universal.

We have already seen that the study of heredity in humans is extremely difficult. Yet, despite all the problems, since we ourselves are humans, the study of human genetics has become a major concern of biology, medicine, and anthropology. In this section we will explore the problems of genetics in people.

What Is a Trait?

A person's observable or measurable characteristics make up his or her **phenotype.** The phenotype includes, among other things, the physical appearance, internal anatomy, and physiology of an individual.

In describing the phenotype of one individual, we can observe certain features such as skin color, eye color, hair color and texture, and general body build. We can also measure such traits as stature, head circumference, nose width, and arm length. Such studies of the measurements of the human body make up the field of **anthropometry** (Figure 3–4, Box 3–2). Various physiological traits, such as the rate of glucose metabolism, can also be analyzed. Even personality and intelligence can be investigated. The result of these examinations is a profile of the individual's total phenotype.

A **trait** is but one aspect of that phenotype—a particular hair texture, an allergy, a blood type. The phenotype results from the interaction of the individual's **genotype,** that is, the specific genetic constitution, and the environment. A trait can be the result of the interaction of many genetic and environmental factors.

The Effects of the Environment upon the Phenotype

If genetic mechanisms are to be understood, we must know the degree to which traits are determined genetically. One of the most difficult tasks of the geneticist is to discover the role of the environment in the development of a particular trait.

Many traits are determined genetically. Other traits are determined almost exclusively by the environment—a broken leg or a dyed head of hair. Most features, however, are influenced by both genetic and environmental factors. It is the task of the investigator to determine the relative influence of genetic and environmental factors in the development of specific traits.

TWIN STUDIES   One method of estimating the environmental influence on a particular trait is studying twins. Identical, or **monozygotic,** twins, which are derived from a single fertilized egg, or **zygote,** share identical genotypes. On the other hand, fraternal, or **dizygotic,** twins are derived from separate zygotes; they have genotypes that differ to the same extent as those of brothers and sisters who are not twins. Monozygotic twins are always of the same sex, while dizygotic twins can be of the same sex or different sexes.

Since monozygotic twins share the same heredity, it follows that differences in their phenotypes are due entirely to the effects of the environment. On the other hand, differences between dizygotic-twin partners are due to both genetic and environmental factors. Therefore, we can use twin data to estimate the importance of genetic versus environmental factors with respect to a given trait.

Several methods exist for making such an estimate. One is to locate one twin with a particular trait and see if the other twin also has that trait. In one study, both twins had cardiovascular disease in 19.6 percent of the monozygotic twins and 15.5 percent of same-sex dizygotic twins. One could conclude from these data that the genetic factor in the development of cardiovascular disease is relatively unimportant. With respect to schizophrenia, the percentages were 46 percent for monozygotic twins and 14 percent for dizygotic twins. This leads us to the conclusion that there is a strong genetic factor in the development of schizophrenia; but since both twins had the trait in only 46 percent of the monozygotic twins, and not in 100 percent, we

FIGURE 3–4   *Anthropometry.* Taking anthropometric measurements of the Efe Pygmies of the Ituri Forest, Zaire.

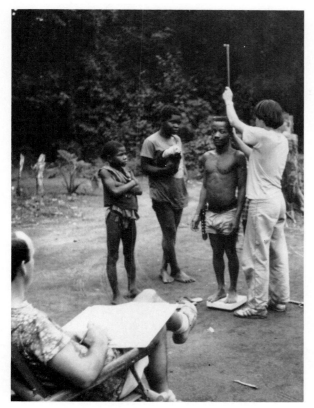

BOX 3–2

MAKING THINGS FIT

In the past most people spent their waking hours hunting, gathering food, or farming. In the eighteenth century, because of the Industrial Revolution, increasing numbers of people began to work inside factories, shops, and offices. Today, many people spend long hours behind a desk. In response to problems that have arisen from changes in the cultural environment, a group of scientists known as **ergonomists** or **human factors researchers** attempt to apply scientific information about the human body to problems of design.

Improperly designed elements of the environment can cause numerous physical problems. For instance, badly designed chairs can cause general musculoskeletal strain, swelling of the lower legs, varicose veins, bad circulation, and even elevated blood pressure.

One of the main tools ergonomists use is anthropometric data. These data provide statistical information on the size and shape of various parts of the body; they include such factors as strength and flexibility. These data are used to produce computer workstations and keyboards, cockpits, bathtubs, control panels, and so on, designed for comfort, effectiveness, and efficiency. Because of differences in body size and proportion, people from different areas of the world, men and women, young and old, require different designs for many of the things they use.

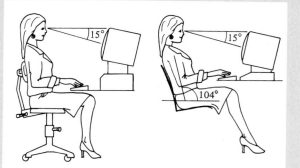

Working posture at the visual display terminal.

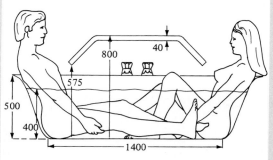

The ergonomically designed bath. (All measurements in these illustrations are in millimeters.)

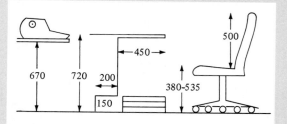

Dimensions for office furniture.

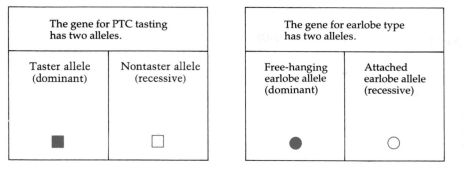

The gene for PTC tasting has two alleles.	
Taster allele (dominant)	Nontaster allele (recessive)
■	□

The gene for earlobe type has two alleles.	
Free-hanging earlobe allele (dominant)	Attached earlobe allele (recessive)
●	○

FIGURE 3–5 *Alleles.* Gregor Mendel determined that each genetically controlled trait is determined minimally by two units of one gene, one unit from each parent. A gene can have different forms, and these different forms of a gene are called alleles.

must conclude that there still is a very strong environmental factor.[3]

Twin studies give indications of the relationship between heredity and environment, but these studies present problems. For instance, monozygotic twins are treated more similarly by parents, friends, and teachers than are dizygotic twins. Therefore, a similarity in the behavior of a set of monozygotic twins might be due to their parallel treatment rather than to their genetics. Also, the results of twin studies are valid only for the population from which the twins come. The results of studies of the same characteristics vary in different populations.

Similarly, an estimate of the relationship between the genetic and environmental effects of a trait is valid only for the specific environment the estimate is made for. If the environment changes, this relationship may also change. For example, if monozygotic twins are both raised in the same environment, their stature will be similar. However, if one of a set of such twins is deprived of adequate vitamin D while the other is not, the former's stature may be reduced because of bone deformations that might occur.

Mendelian Inheritance in Humans

There are a small number of human characteristics that are inherited in a simple Mendelian manner. One of these is the ability to taste the organic chemical **phenylthiocarbamide (PTC).**

This ability is tested by having people chew a piece of paper soaked in a concentrated PTC solution. Most people experience a definite bitter taste, but about 30 percent of North American whites and 3 percent of blacks find the paper has no taste.[4]

The ability to taste PTC is an ideal trait for genetic study, since it is extremely easy to determine a person's phenotype—just give that person a piece of treated paper to taste. Because only two phenotypes exist for concentrated solutions, taster and nontaster, there are no problems of quantification and measurement. Also, it appears that the ability to taste is not affected by the environment.

Genealogical studies show that a mating between a taster and either another taster or a nontaster may produce both taster and nontaster children but that a mating between two nontasters produces nontaster children only. The explanation for the observed data is as follows: The genetic unit for a particular trait is called a **gene,** and alternate forms of a gene are termed **alleles.** The gene for PTC tasting occurs in two forms: the allele for tasting is dominant, and the allele for nontasting is recessive. The dominant allele is indicated by a capital letter, in this case *T,* and the recessive allele by a lowercase letter, in this case *t* (Figure 3–5).

A person with a pair of alleles for tasting (genotype *TT*) is a taster, while a person with a pair of alleles for nontasting (genotype *tt*) is a

---

[3]S. E. Nicol and I. I. Gottesman, "Clues to the Genetics and Neurobiology of Schizophrenia," *American Scientist,* 71 (1983), 398–404.

[4]A. C. Allison and B. S. Blumberg, "Ability to Taste Phenylthiocarbamide among Alaska Eskimos and Other Populations," *Human Biology,* 31 (1959), 352–359.

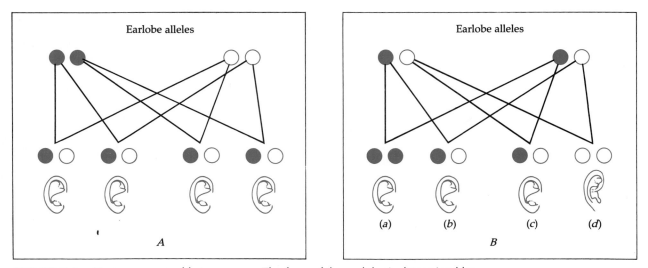

FIGURE 3–6 *Homozygous and heterozygous.* The form of the earlobe is determined by two alleles, one for free-hanging (dominant) and the other for attached (recessive) lobes. *(A)* All of the offspring of a homozygous dominant and a homozygous recessive parent are heterozygous. *(B)* The offspring of two heterozygous parents can be *(a)* homozygous dominant (two dominant alleles), *(b)* and *(c)* heterozygous (one dominant and one recessive allele), or *(d)* homozygous recessive (two recessive alleles).

nontaster. These people are said to be **homozygous,** which means that they have two alleles of the same kind. The former is **homozygous dominant;** the latter is **homozygous recessive.** An individual with the genotype Tt is said to be **heterozygous,** which means that he or she has two different alleles. Since the allele for tasting *(T)* is dominant, it is expressed in the phenotype, whereas the recessive allele *(t)* is not. The heterozygous individual is therefore a taster (Figure 3–6).

While tasters and nontasters cannot be mated in the same way as mice of various colors, couples of certain phenotypes can be located and their children can be studied. Three basic types of matings would be found: taster × taster, taster × nontaster, and nontaster × nontaster. Tasters can be either homozygous *(TT)* or heterozygous *(Tt).* Table 3–1 shows all the possible matings in terms of genotype and the expected probabilities of possible offspring.

INDEPENDENT ASSORTMENT IN HUMANS
There are several other traits that show Mendelian inheritance in humans. Some individuals have earlobes characterized by the attachment of the lower part directly to the head. Other people have a free-hanging earlobe, which is genetically dominant. The attached earlobe is recessive.

PTC tasting and the shape of earlobes can serve to illustrate independent assortment in people. We will examine the results of a mating between two individuals who are heterozygous for both traits. Using the letter E to represent the

TABLE 3–1

POSSIBLE COMBINATIONS AND OFFSPRING FOR A TRAIT WITH TWO ALLELES

MATING TYPE	OFFSPRING		
	TT	*Tt*	*tt*
TT × *TT*	1	0	0
TT × *tt*	0	1	0
TT × *Tt*	½	½	0
Tt × *TT*	½	½	0
Tt × *Tt*	¼	½	¼
Tt × *tt*	0	½	½
tt × *TT*	0	1	0
tt × *Tt*	0	½	½
tt × *tt*	0	0	1

TABLE 3–2

INDEPENDENT ASSORTMENT: POSSIBLE GENOTYPES AND PHENOTYPES FROM A MATING BETWEEN TWO INDIVIDUALS HETEROZYGOUS FOR TWO TRAITS, PTC TASTING AND EARLOBE TYPE*

	OFFSPRING			
	TE	*Te*	*tE*	*te*
TE	*TTEE* taster–free-hanging lobe	*TTEe* taster–free-hanging lobe	*TtEE* taster–free-hanging lobe	*TtEe* taster–free-hanging lobe
Te	*TTEe* taster–free-hanging lobe	*TTee* taster–attached lobe	*TtEe* taster–free-hanging lobe	*Ttee* taster–attached lobe
tE	*TtEE* taster–free-hanging lobe	*TtEe* taster–free-hanging lobe	*ttEE* nontaster–free-hanging lobe	*ttEe* nontaster–free-hanging lobe
te	*TtEe* taster–free-hanging lobe	*Ttee* taster–attached lobe	*ttEe* nontaster–free-hanging lobe	*ttee* nontaster–attached lobe

Summary of phenotypes	Probability of phenotypes
9 taster–free-hanging lobe	9/16
3 taster–attached lobe	3/16
3 nontaster–free-hanging lobe	3/16
1 nontaster–attached lobe	1/16

*The mating can be written in terms of their genotypes, *TtEe* × *TtEe*. Each individual will produce four types of gametes, *TE, Te, tE, te*, in equal frequency.

---

earlobe gene, we can express the mating as *TtEe* × *TtEe*.

In the production of sex cells, the *T* and *t* segregate, as do the *E* and *e*. The segregation of the *T* and the *t* is totally independent of the segregation of the *E* and the *e*. Therefore, four kinds of sex cells will result. Some will carry the *T* and the *E*; others will carry the *T* and the *e*, or the *t* and the *E*, or the *t* and the *e*. The male sex cells, the **sperm**, and the female sex cells, the **ova**, combine at random. A *TE* sperm may fertilize a *TE, Te, tE*, or *te* ovum, or a *Te* sperm may fertilize a *TE, Te, tE*, or *te* ovum. The same is true for the other two types of sperm. Table 3–2 shows the sixteen different combinations that can occur. Four different phenotypes are observed: taster–free hanging, taster–attached, nontaster–free hanging, and nontaster–attached. These occur in frequencies of 9/16, 3/16, 3/16, and 1/16, respectively.

Inherited Medical Abnormalities

In 1966 Victor A. McKusick's first edition of *Mendelian Inheritance in Man* listed 1487 in-

herited human traits. By 1994 the number of known inherited characteristics had reached 6678.[5] Because of recent advances in determining the genetic nature of traits, our knowledge of genetics is exploding, with new genetic traits being discovered almost daily. Early in the twenty-first century molecular biologists expect to complete a map of all human genes (Chapter 4). Still, the known number of genetically influenced or controlled traits represents only a small percentage of the number of genes that have been estimated to exist in humans. Since genetic research is costly, most studies of human genes have focused on inherited abnormalities and have been motivated by the hope that cures or treatment can be found. As a result, most of the known inherited traits are abnormalities.

The majority of genetic abnormalities are caused by the interaction of genes and the environment. Although the role of the environment

---

[5]V. McKusick, *Mendelian Inheritance in Man: Catalogs of Autosomal Dominant, Autosomal Recessive, and X-Linked Phenotypes*, 11th ed. (Baltimore: Johns Hopkins, 1994), xvii.

TABLE 3–3

SOME HUMAN GENETIC ABNORMALITIES

ABNORMALITY	SYMPTOMS	INHERITANCE	INCIDENCE*	
Cystic fibrosis	Excessive mucus production, digestive and respiratory failure, reduced life expectancy.	Recessive	1/2500	(Caucasians, U.S.)
Albinism	Little or no pigment in skin, hair, eyes.	Recessive	1/200	(Hopi Indians)
Tay-Sachs disease	Buildup of fatty deposits in brain, blindness, motor and mental impairment, death in early childhood.	Recessive	1/3600	(Ashkenazi Jews)
Thalassemia	Anemia due to abnormal red blood cells, bone and spleen enlargement.	Recessive	1/10	(some Italian populations)
Sickle-cell anemia	Sickling of red blood cells, anemia, jaundice; fatal.	Codominant	1/625	(African Americans)
Achondroplastic dwarfism	Heterozygotes display long bones that do not grow properly, short stature, other structural abnormalities; homozygotes stillborn or die shortly after birth.	Dominant	1/9100	(Denmark)
Familial hypercholesterolemia	High levels of cholesterol, early heart attacks.	Dominant	1/500	(general U.S. population)
Huntington's disease	Progressive mental and neurological damage leading to disturbance of speech, dementia, and death.	Dominant	1/2941	(Tasmania)

*In a population with a high incidence of disease.

in these situations is difficult to determine, many abnormalities are primarily the result of the action of the genotype. Some of the better known ones, listed in Table 3–3, are a result of the inheritance of a simple dominant or recessive allele. Note that some are structural abnormalities, such as dwarfism, while others are errors in metabolism, such as phenylketonuria and Tay-Sachs disease. Some of these defects can be medically managed so that the affected individual may expect to live a reasonably normal life. Others cause serious mental and physical handicaps, and some are **lethals,** causing premature death. The incidences of some selected genetic abnormalities are given in Table 3–3.

SOME EXAMPLES OF INHERITED ABNORMALITIES
Many inherited abnormalities involve errors in metabolism. One of the best known of these is **phenylketonuria (PKU),** an abnormality inherited as a recessive. PKU involves

an error in the enzyme phenylalanine hydroxylase, which is responsible for the conversion of the amino acid phenylalanine to tyrosine.

A child with PKU is unable to convert phenylalanine into tyrosine. Not only does this result in an inadequate supply of tyrosine, but the levels of phenylalanine build up in the blood. As this buildup progresses, the excess phenylalanine is broken down into toxic by-products. These by-products usually cause, among other things, severe brain damage and mental retardation. This defect occurs in about 1 out of 100,000 live births among northern Europeans and in lower frequencies in most other populations. PKU accounts for about 1 percent of all admissions to mental institutions.[6]

---

[6]R. Koch et al., "Phenylalaninemia and Phenylketonuria," in W. L. Nyham (ed.), *Heritable Disorders of Amino Acid Metabolism: Patterns of Clinical Expression and Genetic Variation* (New York: Wiley, 1974), 109–140.

Another type of genetic abnormality is one that leads to an anatomical problem; an example is **chondrodystrophic dwarfism.** A chondrodystrophic dwarf is a person whose head and trunk are of normal size but whose limbs are quite short. In contrast with PKU, this abnormality results from the inheritance of a dominant allele. A person who is heterozygous (*Dd*) for this gene is a dwarf. A homozygous dominant (*DD*) individual is usually stillborn or dies shortly after birth; a normal person is homozygous recessive (*dd*).

STUDIES OF PEDIGREES   Studies of human genetics are after-the-fact studies; that is, after a child with PKU has been born, an attempt is made to reconstruct the matings that have already occurred. Such a reconstruction is called a **pedigree.** In the pedigree in Figure 3–7 the males are indicated by squares, the females by circles. Matings are indicated by horizontal lines, while descent is shown by vertical lines. Individuals with the trait in question are in solid color. As you examine the pedigree in Figure 3–7, note that the trait is infrequent. In every case the parents of PKU children are normal, since a PKU individual generally does not reproduce. Therefore, it can be assumed that the parents are heterozygous for the trait while the affected individual is homozygous recessive.

Now let us compare this pedigree for a recessive trait with that for a dominant trait. Figure 3–8 shows a pedigree for chondrodystrophic dwarfism. Note that all dwarf children have at least one parent who is also a dwarf. Since the abnormality is the result of a dominant allele, it

FIGURE 3–7   *Pedigree of PKU.* Phenylketonuria is inherited as a recessive trait. Individual with PKU is shown in color. Note that neither of his parents has the disease; they are both carriers.

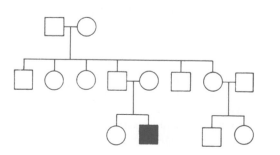

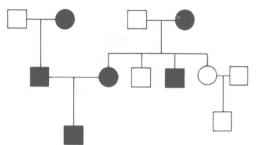

FIGURE 3–8   *Pedigree of dwarfism.* This type of dwarfism is inherited as a dominant trait. Dwarfs are shown in color.

is expressed in the heterozygous individual. A mating between two nondwarfs produces nondwarf children only.

You might think that a good way to identify the mode of inheritance from a pedigree is to look for the characteristic Mendelian proportions, but such proportions are rarely found. The size of families is too small to provide a large enough sample. Although the data from several families can be pooled, this requires specific mathematical procedures.

Mendel and Darwin and the Concept of Variation

Charles Darwin explained how natural selection worked upon the phenotype, but he was unable to account for new phenotypes in a population. Mendel showed that some phenotypic variation comes from the "reservoir" of recessive alleles in the genotype of a population. Recessive alleles are expressed in some generations and not in others, and so each generation possesses phenotypes that were not present in the previous generation. This is because some individuals have combinations of alleles that express recessive traits not previously present.

Neither Darwin nor Mendel knew of a second way that variation occurs in populations. The idea of **mutation,** the sudden change in an allele with the potential to modify the phenotype, was popularized in 1901 by Hugo de Vries in his book *Die Mutationstheorie.* Mutations, which produce new alleles, will be discussed in Chapters 4 and 5.

Deviations from the Mendelian Principles

The basic principles of genetics as worked out by Gregor Mendel are seen in all living organisms. However, inheritance of many traits does not follow these basic patterns. In fact, because the actual modes of inheritance are usually more complex, traits inherited in the basic Mendelian pattern are the exception rather than the rule.

Problems frequently arise in the interpretation of the inheritance pattern of a trait when it appears to be inherited differently in different families. This is often caused by the occurrence of different genes in each family line, although these genes act in a similar way.

Many genes often affect the same characteristic. For example, the inheritance of stature is **polygenic,** that is, the result of the interaction of several genes—the exact number is not known. For our example, we will assume that the inheritance of stature is due to the interaction of just three genes (it is probably more than that). All three genes will have the same phenotypic effect, and each will occur in two allelic forms. An extremely tall individual might have the genotype $A^1A^1B^1B^1C^1C^1$, while an extremely short person might be $A^2A^2B^2B^2C^2C^2$. If they mate and produce an offspring, that offspring will have the genotype $A^1A^2B^1B^2C^1C^2$ and will be intermediate in stature. The genotypes $A^1A^2B^1B^1C^1C^1$ and $A^1A^2B^1B^2C^2C^2$ will show still different statures.

Another complication is **intermediate expression,** in which a heterozygous genotype is associated with a phenotype intermediate between two homozygous genotypes. For example, male tenor and bass singing voices result from homozygous genotypes; the heterozygous individual is intermediate, a baritone. Another situation is **codominance,** in which both alleles are expressed in the heterozygous person. For example, the **hemoglobin** molecule, which serves to transport oxygen in the red blood cell, exists in several forms. One allele is responsible for the production of a normal form of hemoglobin, hemoglobin A. The other codes for the production of an abnormal hemoglobin, hemoglobin S. A person homozygous for A produces hemoglobin A, while a person homozygous for S produces hemoglobin S; a person who is heterozygous produces both hemoglobins.

All the genes we have discussed so far have had two alternate forms, or alleles. Any individual has only two alleles for any gene, one inherited from the person's mother and the other inherited from the person's father. The two alleles may be the same, resulting in a homozygous genotype, or they may be different, resulting in a heterozygous genotype. However, within a population, more than two alleles may exist for the same gene.

A collection of three or more alleles for a specific gene is a **multiple-allele series.** The rare dominant abnormality **familial hypercholesterolemia** is controlled by at least four alleles. The disease is caused by a defective protein that can result in extremely high levels of cholesterol in the blood. One allele codes for a completely defective protein; a second allele codes for a protein that has about 10 percent normal activity. A third allele in this system codes for a protein that is able to carry out one of the functions of a normal protein but not a second function. The fourth allele codes for the normal protein.

Multiple-allele systems outnumber systems with only two alleles. For instance, the factors responsible for tissue rejection in heart, liver, and kidney transplants are controlled by many genes, each with multiple alleles. This is why suitable organ donors are often difficult to find. The best known multiple-allele system is the ABO blood-type system, which is discussed in the next chapter.

The expression of an allele may be variable for several reasons, one of which is the existence of a **modifying gene.** This is a second gene that alters the expression of the first. In some pedigrees, **cataracts** (opacity of the eye lens) are inherited as a dominant, yet the type of cataract may vary according to which alleles of a second gene are present.

Whereas modifier genes affect the expression of other genes, **regulatory genes** initiate or block the activity of other genes. They are important in controlling the amount and timing of the production of various molecules of the body.

A particular allele may be **incompletely penetrant,** which means that it is not always expressed in an individual possessing it. **Penetrance** may have a genetic basis in that the expression of the allele can be altered by a modifying gene, but the environment also may play a role. For example, **diabetes** has a genetic basis, but whether or not an individual has the disease may depend upon other factors, such as diet.

The expression of many genes is influenced by the sex of the person. A **sex-limited trait** is one that is expressed in only one sex. For example, the genes controlling the development of a beard are found in both males and females, but they are usually expressed only in the male. A **sex-controlled trait** is one that is expressed differently in males and females. **Gout,** for example, is found in both sexes and appears to have a genetic basis, but the trait is incompletely penetrant. When the allele is present, it is expressed about 80 percent of the time in males but only about 12 percent of the time in females. This is why the disease is usually associated with males.[7]

Recent studies have suggested that the sex of the parent who contributes an allele may influence how that allele is expressed. In ways not yet understood, an allele may be marked as coming from either the mother or the father; that allele may then have a different effect on the offspring depending on the sex of the contributing parent. This phenomenon, known as **genome imprinting,** has been described only for some rare genetic diseases. However, many investigators believe that it might be a more widespread and highly significant genetic characteristic. Another form of genetic inheritance that is dependent upon the sex of the parent is the inheritance of mitochondrial DNA from the mother; this will be discussed in Chapter 4.

Finally, a single allele may affect an entire series of traits. This is called **pleiotropy.** For example, the allele for **sickle-cell anemia** in the homozygous condition results in such abnormalities as anemia, poor physical development, kidney damage, lung damage, and heart damage. Such a complex of associated features is known as a **syndrome.**

[7]C. Stern, *Principles of Human Genetics,* 3d ed. (San Francisco: Freeman, 1973), 404.

Genetics and Human Affairs

The study of human genetics is not just a theoretical study. Genetic problems profoundly affect human lives, and an understanding of the principles of inheritance is essential in understanding these problems. Because a significant number of medical problems are genetically based, this chapter has emphasized those medical abnormalities that are determined by heredity in a fairly clear-cut fashion. Many medical problems, however, are influenced by both heredity and environment.

Today much research is in progress involving the identification, treatment, and ultimate prevention of genetic disease. Only under rare occasions are genetic diseases curable, although some are manageable. For example, if PKU is detected in a newborn soon after birth, the results of the disease, such as severe mental retardation, may be prevented by a special diet. A blood test to identify such infants is mandated by law in many states.

TAY-SACHS DISEASE   **Tay-Sachs disease,** like phenylketonuria, is a metabolic abnormality caused by an abnormal enzyme. In this case, the enzyme is hexaminidase A, which occurs within the brain cells. Absence of the normal enzyme permits the buildup of lipid material in the brain cell, leading to cell death. Appearing normal at birth, the child develops symptoms at about 6 months of age, and death occurs a few years later. Ashkenazi Jews (Jews of central and eastern European origin) show a high carrier rate for Tay-Sachs disease. A **carrier** is a person who possesses a recessive allele in the heterozygous condition.

When a disease occurs at a high frequency in a specific population, an agency may conduct an educational screening program. Screening is especially effective for Tay-Sachs disease because the test is very accurate and relatively inexpensive. Screening programs have helped reduce the incidence of Tay-Sachs disease by 10,000 percent among Ashkenazi Jews.

How does screening reduce the frequency of a genetic disease? In order for a child to have Tay-Sachs disease, both parents must be carriers. If screening shows that both are carriers, several

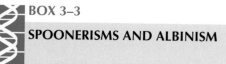

BOX 3–3

SPOONERISMS AND ALBINISM

> You hissed my mystery lecture, you hissed all my mystery lectures! You tasted the whole worm!!

This strange reprimand was uttered by the famous eighteenth-century classicist Reverend Dr. W. A. Spooner. Garbled speech, in which sounds are unintentionally interchanged, has come to be known as spoonerisms. Reverend Spooner meant to admonish an often absent student by saying:

> You missed my history lecture, you missed all my history lectures! You wasted the whole term!!

What does this have to do with genetics? It appears that **albinism** —a simple recessive abnormality that leads to little or no production of skin pigment—may be associated with spoonerisms. The allele that causes albinism also affects vision. Albinos often display a neurological problem in which the eyeballs move spasmodically. This condition may have caused Rev. Spooner, an albino, to transpose letters when he read. These experiences may then have affected his speech pattern. Thus, a behavioral characteristic that most people assumed was due to Spooner's level of excitement or anger may have been influenced by inheritance.

References: A. G. Levinthal, D. J. Vitek, and D. S. Creel, "Abnormal Visual Pathways in Normally Pigmented Cats That Are Heterozygous for Albinism," *Science,* 229 (1985), 1395; and J. B. Jenkins, *Human Genetics,* 2d ed. (New York: Harper & Row, 1990), 79.

---

options are open. The parents may choose to have no children; they may try to adopt children; or if the woman does become pregnant, she may choose to undergo amniocentesis (to be discussed shortly). In the last-mentioned case, if it is determined that she is carrying an affected child, the parents can elect to abort the fetus.

Unfortunately, because most people do not know of Tay-Sachs disease or falsely believe that it is exclusively a Jewish disease, they do not seek testing. As a result, most of the recent cases of Tay-Sachs disease have been among non-Jews. The carrier rate for Ashkenazi Jews is about 1 in 30, but it is about 1 in 150 in the general population, which is still an appreciable rate.

PROBABILITIES OF A SPECIFIC GENETIC DISEASE   If both members of a couple are carriers of Tay-Sachs disease, what is the probability of their having an affected child? A carrier has one normal allele and one abnormal one, and so each parent in our example has the genotype Tt. The mating is represented as $Tt \times Tt$. Since the disease is caused by a recessive allele, the affected individual has the genotype tt (homozygous recessive). Because the alleles T and t each have an equal chance of being included in any sex cell,

half the father's sperm carries the t allele, as does half the mother's ova.

The probability of the couple's producing a tt genotype is $\frac{1}{2} \times \frac{1}{2}$, or $\frac{1}{4}$. This calculation is based upon the statistical principle that the probability of the occurrence of two independent, random events is the product of the events' separate probabilities. As with the tt combination, the probability of a TT combination's occurring is $\frac{1}{2} \times \frac{1}{2}$, or $\frac{1}{4}$. The probability of a carrier's occurring is $\frac{1}{2}$. This is because there are two ways that the alleles can combine to produce a carrier: either the father's allele is normal and the mother's allele is abnormal, or the father's allele is abnormal and the mother's allele is normal. The probability of each separate case is $\frac{1}{4}$; the probability of both cases is the sum of the separate cases. Thus, $\frac{1}{2} \times \frac{1}{2} + \frac{1}{2} \times \frac{1}{2}$ (or $\frac{1}{4} + \frac{1}{4}$) equals $\frac{1}{2}$. The probability of all combinations must equal 1 ($\frac{1}{4}$ $TT + \frac{1}{2} Tt + \frac{1}{4} tt = 1$).

When we take population data and individual mating probabilities into consideration, we can calculate the overall probability of having a Tay-Sachs child. In the Ashkenazi Jewish population, the incidence of carriers is $\frac{1}{30}$. The chance that two carriers will mate is $\frac{1}{30} \times \frac{1}{30}$, or $\frac{1}{900}$. Since the probability of two carriers' producing a Tay-

Sachs child is ¼, the probability of a Tay-Sachs child for anyone from this population is ¹⁄₉₀₀ × ¼, or ¹⁄₃₆₀₀. Until recently, this was the actual rate of such births; but as mentioned earlier, because of screening programs, the percentage is much lower today.

There are no tests for most genetic abnormalities. However, genetic researchers are making progress in the detection of carriers. As of 1993, 80 percent of carriers of cystic fibrosis can be detected by testing. One out of every 25 white Americans is a carrier of this recessive genetic disease, the most common fatal genetic disease of young Americans.

GENETIC COUNSELING   When a person suspects that he or she or a relative has a genetic disease or abnormality, that person might seek genetic counseling. A **genetic counselor** is someone who advises prospective parents or an affected individual of the probability of having a child with a genetic problem.

Often, a couple has already conceived a child with an abnormality. They go to a genetic counselor to seek information about the probability of their conceiving another child with a genetic defect.

In other cases, members of a specific cultural or ethnic group that is characterized by a high frequency of some inherited disease might wish to know what the chances are that they are carrying the abnormal allele. This is the case for Tay-Sachs disease among Ashkenazi Jews. As further examples, African Americans and certain other people show a high frequency of the blood disorder sickle-cell anemia (Chapter 4); Mediterranean peoples display a high frequency of another blood disorder, beta thalassemia; the general northern European population has a high rate of cystic fibrosis (a respiratory disease); and Eskimos have a high frequency of kushokwin (a protein disease).

For many diseases the inheritance pattern is more complex than in Tay-Sachs or cystic fibrosis. In these cases a genetic counselor must construct a pedigree to determine the probability of a concerned individual's being a carrier or having an allele or alleles for a specific genetic problem. A genetic counselor can work out probabilities

only for genetic disorders with a known mode of inheritance, and the validity of a probability calculation is dependent on how much information is known about the client's relatives.

Genetic counseling has grown as a profession along with the enormous growth in the genetic knowledge gained in the last couple of decades. As more diseases are found to have a genetic basis and as the inheritance patterns of more genetic diseases are learned, the job of the genetic counselor will become increasingly complex. Society will benefit from the ability to treat or manage more genetic diseases successfully.

IDENTIFYING PROBLEMS IN A FETUS   Another approach to genetic problems is the identification of genetic and nongenetic abnormalities in the fetus. If the fetus is found to be defective, a therapeutic abortion may be performed if the parents so decide. Abnormalities in the fetus can be detected by ultrasound, amniocentesis, chorionic villus biopsy, and a blood test. **Ultrasound** is a diagnostic method that uses sound waves to take a picture or **sonogram** of the fetus (Figure 3–9). In **amniocentesis,** a sample of **amniotic fluid,** the fluid surrounding the fetus, is taken. The cells in the fluid are of fetal origin, and they can be grown in the laboratory and tested for a variety of enzyme deficiencies. The genetic material itself can also be examined for defects. More than eighty metabolic disorders, including Tay-Sachs disease, and several abnormalities of other types can be detected in this manner.

The method of **chorionic villus biopsy** involves analysis of the tissue surrounding the developing embryo. It can provide answers faster than is possible with amniocentesis, but this technique is not generally available and its relative safety has not yet been determined. Also, the blood of the mother can be tested for high levels of **alpha-feto protein (AFP),** which enters the mother's blood through the placenta. Excessive amounts of AFP may indicate neural tube defects or other fetal abnormalities.

Summary

A trait is one specific, observable, or measurable characteristic of an individual. *Trait* is synony-

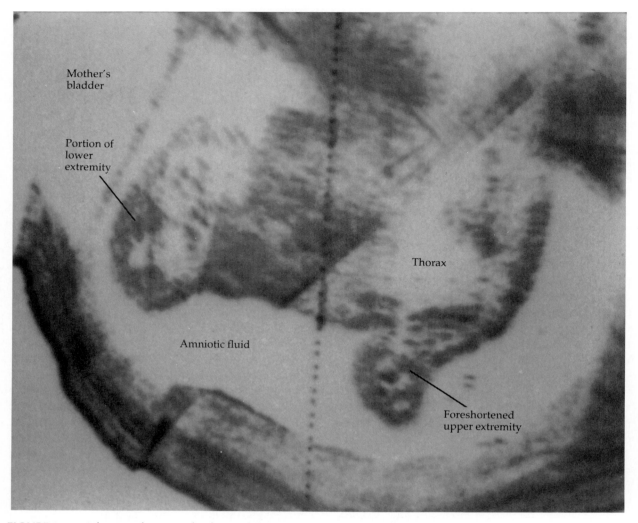

FIGURE 3–9 *Ultrasound.* Longitudinal transabdominal sonogram showing a portion of a dwarf human fetus with a foreshortened upper extremity.

mous with one meaning of the word *phenotype,* but *phenotype* can also mean "the sum of all traits." The environment can affect the phenotype. Studies of twins are one means of measuring how much of a trait is genetically determined and how much is environmentally determined.

A gene is the hereditary unit that controls or contributes to the control of a specific trait, such as eye color and the ability to taste PTC. Each trait, however, can have different aspects, and each aspect is controlled by an alternate form of the gene, called an allele. The types of alleles that an individual possesses for a specific gene is

that individual's genotype. The term *genotype* can also apply to the totality of allelic pairs of an organism.

Many medical abnormalities are inherited or have a genetic component. Much of the research in human genetics today revolves around the identification and treatment of genetic disease. Although very few genetic problems can be cured, techniques have been developed for early detection and treatment, identification of carriers, and identification of abnormal fetuses through amniocentesis, ultrasound, chorionic villus biopsy, and blood tests.

STUDY QUESTIONS

1. Describe the concepts of segregation and independent assortment. In what ways do these concepts differ?
2. Many people take the term *dominant* to mean that an allele is common. However, dominance and recessiveness have nothing to do with frequency. What, precisely, do these two terms signify?
3. Why have the major breakthroughs in the understanding of the mechanisms of heredity been made with bacteria, plants, and nonhuman animals, such as fruit flies and mice, rather than with humans?
4. An individual's phenotype results from the interaction of the genotype and the environment. How does a geneticist proceed to demonstrate the relative importance of these two factors?
5. What are some of the ways in which culture influences an individual's phenotype?
6. Mendel dealt with traits that are inherited as a dominant or as a recessive and are controlled by one gene with two alleles. What are some of the more complex patterns of inheritance that we know of today?
7. What is a pedigree as used in genetic studies? Why do geneticists construct pedigrees?
8. What does a genetic counselor do?

SUGGESTED READINGS

Fraser, C. F., and J. J. Nora. *Genetics of Man*, 2d ed. Philadelphia: Lea & Febiger, 1986. This is an excellent introduction to human genetics, with several chapters on medical genetics.

Jenkins, J. B. *Human Genetics*, 2d ed. New York: Harper & Row, 1990. This is a basic introductory text for courses in human genetics.

Lewin, B. *Genes*, 5th ed. Oxford: Oxford University Press, 1993. This is a popular introductory text on general genetics. It presents an encyclopedic treatment of genetics and as such is an excellent reference book.

Olby, R. *Origins of Mendelism*, 2d ed. Chicago: University of Chicago Press, 1985. This book summarizes genetic research before Mendel, Mendel's work, and the rediscovery of Mendel's research.

Orel, V. *Mendel.* New York: Oxford University Press, 1984. This is a short introduction to Mendel's life and work.

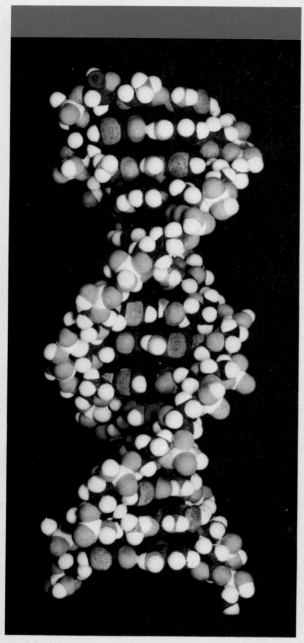

Model of the molecule deoxyribonucleic acid, the hereditary material.

Determining the structure of DNA (the genetic material) has been described as the most important event in twentieth century biology, as profound in its implications as Charles Darwin's theory of natural selection a century earlier.[1]

Neil A. Campbell

[1]A. Campbell, "Discovery of the Double Helix," *BioScience*, 36 (December 1986), 728.

4

CHAPTER
CYTOGENETICS AND MOLECULAR GENETICS

When Gregor Mendel first worked out the basic principles of inheritance, he was not aware of the actual physical and chemical nature of the genetic mechanism. Around 1900 scientists began to examine the processes within the cell that determine the genotype of the organism. This research gave us knowledge of the physical and chemical realities of heredity.

The hereditary material is located within the cell in bodies known as chromosomes. Studies of the behavior of chromosomes during cell division provide a partial explanation for the Mendelian rules of heredity. Going a step further, scientists have learned that the genetic material itself is the large molecule deoxyribonucleic acid (DNA). Modern studies of chromosomes and of the DNA molecule are leading to a clearer understanding of the mechanisms of heredity.

CYTOGENETICS

Cytology is the branch of science that specializes in the biology of the cell. This term is derived from *cyto,* meaning "cell." The study of the heredity mechanisms within the cell is called **cytogenetics.**

The Cell

The **cell** is the basic unit of all life. In fact, cells are the smallest units that perform all the functions that are collectively labeled "life." These include taking in energy and excreting waste; using and storing energy; combining nutrients into substances for growth, repair, and development; adapting to new situations; and, perhaps the most important of all, reproducing new cells. Early geneticists probed the cell for the secrets of heredity and the location of the units of inheritance, the genes.

The great variety of cells all share several structural characteristics. A cell is bounded by a **plasma membrane** which allows for the entry and exit of certain substances and maintains the cell's integrity. A **nucleus** in the cell is contained within its own **nuclear membrane.** The material between the nuclear membrane and the cell membrane is called the **cytoplasm** (Figure 4–A of the color insert).

The Chromosomes

When a cell begins to divide, long ropelike structures become visible within the nucleus. Because these structures stain very dark purple, they are called **chromosomes**—*chroma* means "color," and *soma* means "body." Viewed under the microscope, a single chromosome is seen to consist of two strands—the **chromatids.** These chromatids are held together by a structure called the **centromere.**

Figure 4–B of the color insert is a photograph of chromosomes prepared from a human blood sample. They have been stained and dispersed over a large area so that individual chromosomes can be identified.

Much information can be obtained from a photograph of chromosomes. First, the chromosomes can be counted. Different organisms are characterized by specific chromosome numbers per cell. For example, the Indian fern has the highest number, with 1260 chromosomes; the roundworm has only 2. More typical numbers of chromosomes are found in humans (46), chimpanzees (48), boa constrictors (36), and garden peas (14).

Second, not all chromosomes are alike; they differ in relative size and in the position of the centromere. In some, the centromere is centered, and so the "arms" of the chromosomes are equal; in others, the centromere is off-center, and so the arms are unequal. Thus, it is possible to classify and identify chromosomes. Each chromosome in a photograph can be cut out and arranged in a standardized representation known as a **karyotype** (Figure 4–1).

Looking at the karyotypes in Figure 4–1, we can see that all the chromosomes, with one exception, exist as pairs. The chromosomes that make up a pair are called **homologous chromosomes.** Homologous chromosomes have the same shape and are of the same size. They also carry the same genes, but they may carry different alleles for specific genes. The **sex chromosomes** of the male, however, are not homologous. The normal female possesses two homologous sex chromosomes, the **X chromosomes,** but the male has only one X chromosome which pairs with a different type, the **Y chromosome.** In both sexes there are twenty-two pairs of nonsex chromosomes, referred to as **autosomes.** These autosomal pairs are numbered from 1 to 22. In addition, all chromosomes are classified into seven major groups, A through G, on the basis of relative size and the position of the centromere.

Cell Division

The physical basis of Mendelian genetics becomes clear when we observe the movement of chromosomes during cell division. There are two basic forms of cell division, mitosis and meiosis. **Mitosis** is the process by which a one-celled organism divides into two new individuals. In a multicellular organism, mitosis results in the growth and replacement of body cells. **Meiosis,** on the other hand, is specialized cell division that results in the production of sex cells, or **gametes.**

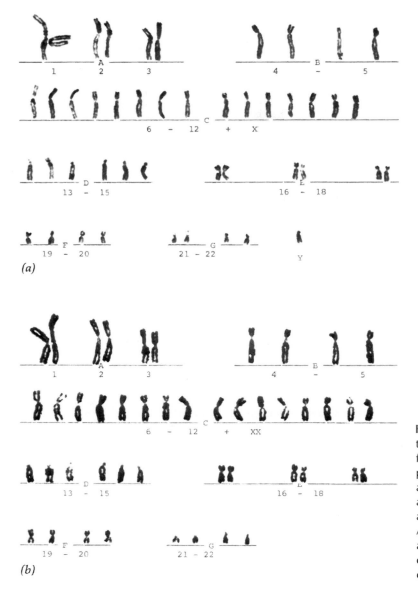

(a)

(b)

FIGURE 4–1 *Human karyotypes.* Karyotypes of *(a)* a normal male and *(b)* a normal female. In both sexes there are twenty-two pairs of nonsex chromosomes or autosomes and a pair of sex chromosomes. The autosomal pairs are numbered from 1 to 22 and are classified into seven major groups, A through G, on the basis of relative size and the position of the centromere. The X chromosome belongs to group C, and the Y chromosome belongs to group G.

MITOSIS   The events of mitosis follow each other in a continuous fashion. Various studies show that it takes 30 to 90 minutes for one complete mitotic division in humans, depending on the type of cell. Some cells, such as skin cells, are constantly being replaced, and so they divide often. On the other hand, nerve cells stop dividing at birth or shortly thereafter. In order to make the events of this process clear, mitosis is divided into several arbitrary phases defined by specific landmark events. These phases are illustrated in Figure 4–2.

MEIOSIS   Meiosis differs from mitosis in many ways. Meiosis takes place only in specialized tissue in the testes of the male and in the ovaries of the female. Meiotic division results in the production of gametes, which are the sperm in the male and the ova in the female.

Meiosis consists of two cycles of division. In the male a complete meiotic cycle takes approximately 74 hours. A significant feature of meiosis is the reduction in chromosome number. If a sperm and an ovum each contained 46 chromosomes, the cell resulting from the fertilization

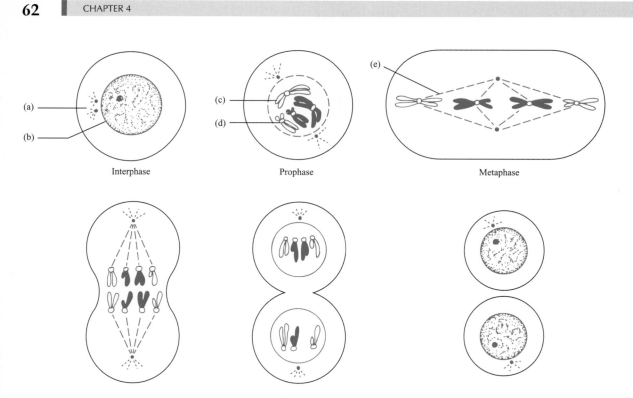

Interphase   Prophase   Metaphase

FIGURE 4–2 *Diagram of the events of mitosis in a hypothetical animal cell with four chromosomes.* Features include *(a)* centrioles, *(b)* nuclear membrane, *(c)* chromatid, *(d)* centromere, and *(e)* spindle. One member of each chromosome pair is white; the other, colored. To make the events clear, mitosis can be divided into a number of arbitrary phases. *Interphase* is the period between successive mitotic divisions, not an actual step in cell division. No visible change occurs during interphase, but the cell processes associated with growth and preparation for mitosis are occurring. Chromosomes appear as an undifferentiated mass. *Prophase* is the first stage of mitosis. The chromosomes first become visible as threadlike structures and then become shorter and thicker. At this point, each chromosome is made up of two strands called chromatids. Two centrioles are now at opposite sides (poles) of the nucleus. The nuclear membrane begins to break down, and during *metaphase* it disappears completely. The centromere of each chromosome attaches to a spindle-shaped structure by way of spindle fibers. The chromosomes align themselves on a plane midway between the centrioles. In *anaphase* the chromatids of each chromosome separate at the centromere and move away from each other toward different poles of the cell. Each chromosome at each pole of the cell consists of only one chromatid. During *telophase* the two sets of chromatids revert to the interphase condition, and a nuclear membrane reappears. The cytoplasm divides (cytokinesis) between the two developing cells. After a time in *interphase,* chromatids may be replicated in preparation for another cycle of division. If the chromatids are replicated, then mitosis may occur again.

would have 92 chromosomes. In the next generation there would be 184 chromosomes, and so on. Instead, meiosis in humans produces gametes with 23 chromosomes each. When fertilization takes place, the number of chromosomes remains constant at 46. The events of meiosis are illustrated in Figure 4–3.

SPERM AND OVA PRODUCTION **Spermatogenesis,** or sperm production, begins in the average American male at 12 to 13 years of age and usually continues throughout life. However, the onset of spermatogenesis is variable, not only among individuals but also among the averages for different populations. The male normally pro-

Oogenesis

Spermatogenesis

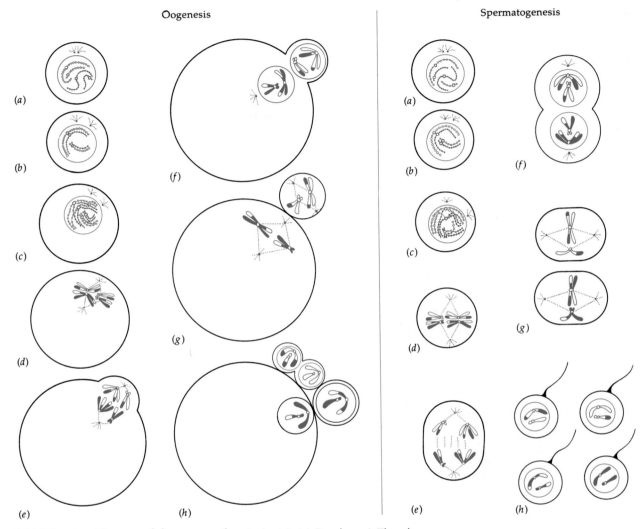

FIGURE 4–3 *Diagram of the events of meiosis. (a)–(c) Prophase I:* The chromosomes become visible as they contract and thicken. Homologous chromosomes (members of a pair) come together, and crossing-over may occur. *(d) Metaphase I:* Paired chromosomes line up along the equatorial plane. *(e) Anaphase I:* Chromosomes separate and are pulled to opposite poles by spindle fibers. *(f) Telophase I:* A nuclear membrane forms, and the cell divides. Note the uneven division of cytoplasm in oogenesis and the production of a polar body. The second meiotic division is very much like mitosis except that it starts with half the number of chromosomes found in body cells. *(g) Metaphase II:* Chromatids line up on the equatorial plane. *(h)* At the end of meiosis we see four sperm as the end products of spermatogenesis, and one ovum and three polar bodies as the end products of oogenesis.

duces millions of sperm at any one time.

Oogenesis, or ova production, is different. The beginnings of the first division of meiosis occur within the ovaries during fetal development, between the fifth and seventh month after concep-

tion. These cells remain in metaphase I until they are stimulated, beginning at puberty, by certain hormones to complete their development.

The first meiotic division is different in the female than in the male. In the female the spindle does not form across the center of the cell; instead, it forms off to one side. During cell division, one nucleus carries the bulk of cytoplasm. This is also true of the second meiotic division. Thus, a single large ovum and three very small cells, the **polar bodies,** are produced from the one original cell. The large ovum contains enough nutrients to supply the embryo until the embryo implants itself in the wall of the uterus.

Oogenesis is cyclical. While the length of the cycle is often given as 28 days, it is actually highly variable. It varies not only within the female population but also in the same female at different times of her reproductive life. The median length of the cycle among American women between the ages of 20 and 40 ranges from 26.2 days to 27.9 days. Ninety percent of the cycle lengths range from a low of 21.8 days to a high of 38.4 days.[2]

The reproductive cycle itself is under hormonal control. At the midpoint of the cycle the mature ovum breaks through the wall of the ovary. This event is known as **ovulation.** In contrast to the great quantity of sperm produced by the male, only one ovum is usually produced during each cycle by the average human female.

Fertilization must take place soon after ovulation. In nonhuman mammals, sexual receptivity is related to the ovarian cycle. The female comes into **estrus,** the period of sexual receptivity, at about the time of ovulation. Unlike the case with other mammals, sexual receptivity in the human female is not linked to the periodic occurrence of estrus (Chapter 12).

Chromosomal Abnormalities

The processes of mitosis and meiosis are precise, yet errors do occur. Any alteration of the genetic material is called a **mutation,** whether the alteration occurs on the molecular or on the chromosomal level. Alterations on the latter level are termed **chromosomal aberrations;** they consist of two types: abnormal chromosome number and abnormal chromosome structure.

ABNORMAL CHROMOSOME NUMBER   A common error of meiosis is **nondisjunction.** It leads to abnormal chromosome numbers in the second-generation cells. When two members of a chromosome pair move together to the same pole instead of to opposite poles, nondisjunction has occurred. Thus, two second-generation cells are formed: one contains twenty-two chromosomes, and the other has twenty-four. The union of a gamete having the normal complement of twenty-three chromosomes with a gamete having an abnormal number of chromosomes produces a zygote with either extra or missing chromosomes. For example, if a sperm with twenty-four chromosomes fertilizes an ovum with twenty-three, the zygote will have forty-seven chromosomes.

What phenotype is found in an individual developing from a zygote with an abnormal karyotype? Figure 4–4a shows a karyotype of an individual with forty-seven chromosomes, one too many. Since the extra chromosome is a number 21, a fairly small chromosome, a relatively small number of genes are involved. Figure 4–4b shows a child with this karyotype; the condition is called **Down's syndrome.**

Down's syndrome is characterized by a peculiarity in the eyefolds (which some seem to think resembles the Mongoloid eye, although it is different), short stature with stubby hands and feet, and congenital malformations of the heart and other organs. Perhaps the most significant feature is mental retardation.

Down's syndrome is not rare. The risk of giving birth to a Down's syndrome child increases with the age of the mother and perhaps the father. Women who are 20 years of age have a 1 in 2000 chance of having a child with Down's syndrome, but for a 30-year-old woman the risk is 1 in 300, and for a 42-year-old woman, 1 in 20.[3] Although it was once thought that Down's syndrome was due exclusively to nondisjunction in the ova, it is now thought that in about 5 percent of all Down's syndrome children, the disease is the result of defective sperm.[4]

---

[2]A. E. Treloar et al., "Variations of the Human Menstrual Cycle through Reproductive Life," *International Journal of Fertility,* 12 (1967), 77–126.

[3]L. Holmes, "How Fathers Can Cause the Down's Syndrome," *Human Nature,* 1 (October 1978), 71.
[4]C. Ezzell, "New Clues to the Origin of Down's Syndrome," *Science News,* 139 (1991), 292.

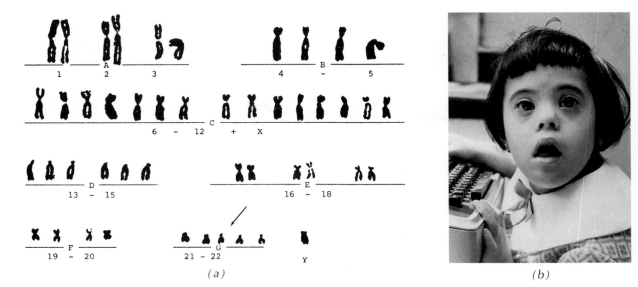

(a)   (b)

FIGURE 4–4 *Down's syndrome. (a)* Karyotype of a male with Down's syndrome. Note the extra chromosome 21. *(b)* Girl with Down's syndrome. Down's syndrome is characterized by a peculiarity in the eyefolds, short stature with stubby hands and feet, congenital malformations of the heart and other organs, and significant mental retardation.

More common than nondisjunctions of autosomes are extra or missing sex chromosomes. Among these are such abnormal sex chromosome counts as X− **(Turner's syndrome)**, XXY **(Klinefelter's syndrome)**, XXX, and XYY (Table 4–1). While these individuals have a higher survival rate than do infants with extra or missing autosomes, possessors of abnormal sex chromosome numbers often show abnormal sex organs and abnormal secondary sexual characteristics, sterility, and, sometimes, mental retardation.

STRUCTURAL ABERRATIONS OF CHROMOSOMES In addition to abnormal numbers of chromosomes due to nondisjunction, several types of structural abnormalities can occur. Structural abnormalities are the result of breaks in the chromosome (Figure 4–5).

Deletion occurs when a chromosome itself breaks and a segment of it that is not attached to the spindle fails to be included in the second-generation cell. The genetic material on the deleted section is "lost." **Duplication** is the process whereby chromosome parts are repeated; that is, a section of a chromosome is repeated. **Inversion** occurs when parts of a chromosome break and

reunite in reversed order. No genetic material is lost or gained, but the position of the alleles involved is changed. **Translocation** is the process whereby segments of chromosomes become detached and then reattached to other nonhomologous chromosomes. The causes of chromosome mutations will be discussed later in Chapter 5.

Abnormal chromosome numbers and structural aberrations account for a significant number of defects in newborns and a large number of spontaneous abortions (miscarriages). About 50 percent of the miscarriages in the United States are due to chromosomal abnormalities. Approximately 1 in 160 live births is accompanied by a chromosomal abnormality.[5] One way of preventing what is very often a tragedy is to identify the abnormality before birth through amniocentesis (Chapter 3). Karyotypes can be made from the fetal cells found in the amniotic fluid; if chromosomal abnormalities are seen, the early fetus can be aborted. Amniocentesis is now routine in many hospitals in special situations. For

[5]R. H. Tamarin, *Principles of Genetics*, 2d ed. (Boston: Prindle, Weber, Schmidt, 1986) 246–247.

TABLE 4–1

SOME EXAMPLES OF ABNORMAL CHROMOSOME NUMBERS

TYPE	INCIDENCE	PHENOTYPE
AUTOSOMAL ABNORMALITIES		
Trisomy*13 (Patau syndrome)	1/15,000	Severely malformed. Small head, sloping forehead, cardiac and other defects.
Trisomy 18 (Edward's syndrome)	1/7500	Growth and developmental retardation, death usually before 6 months.
Trisomy 21 (Down's syndrome)	1/700	See text for description.
SEX-CHROMOSOME ABNORMALITIES		
47, XXY (Klinefelter's syndrome)	1/850 males	Phenotypically male. Sterile, small penis, breast enlargement in 40% of cases, average IQ scores.
45, X− (Turner's syndrome)	1/5000 females	Phenotypically female. Variable characteristics. Short stature, relatively normal IQ scores, small chin, webbing of neck in 50% of cases, shield-shaped chest, cardiovascular disease in 35% of cases, affectionate, sterile.
47, XYY (XYY syndrome)	1/900 males	Phenotypically male, fertile. Tendency for delayed language development, cognitive problems, suggested tendency toward aggressive and generally antisocial behavior.
47, XXX (XXX syndrome)	1/1250 females	Phenotypically female. Some impairment of intellectual development in about two-thirds of cases, suggested increase in risk for schizophrenia, sometimes menstrual disorders and early menopause.

*Trisomy refers to three of a given chromosome; an individual with trisomy 13 has forty-seven chromosomes with three chromosome 13s. *Data from*: Clark F. Fraser and James J. Nora, *Genetics of Man,* 2d ed. (Philadelphia: Lea & Febiger, 1986), 31–68.

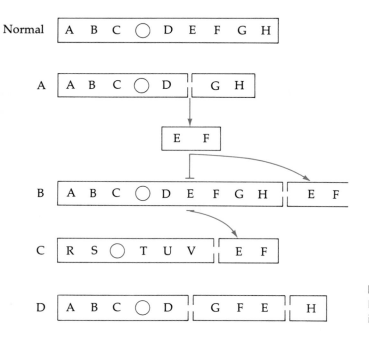

FIGURE 4–5 *Chromosomal aberrations. (A)* Deletion, *(B)* duplication, *(C)* translocation, *(D)* inversion.

example, the procedure is recommended for all mothers over 35 years of age as a means of identifying fetuses having Down's syndrome or other chromosomal abnormalities.

Reexamining Mendelian Genetics

The details of cell division can help us understand Mendelian genetics. Mitosis is merely a copying of the genetic material, but in meiosis the physical reality of Mendel's principles of segregation and independent assortment can be observed.

Each individual cell contains twenty-three pairs of chromosomes. One member of each pair is obtained from the mother and one from the father. When the individual then produces gametes, the paired chromosomes separate during the first meiotic division; this is segregation. Therefore, each gamete contains only one of each pair and, hence, only the alleles on these particular chromosomes.

As one meiotic division follows another, gamete after gamete is produced, yet each individual gamete is unique, consisting of a particular set of chromosomes. One mechanism of meiosis that is responsible for the uniqueness of each gamete is **recombination.** As the twenty-three chromosomes line up in metaphase, they can recombine into several configurations, following the principle of independent assortment.

Let us assume that in Figure 4–6 the chromosomes with dominant alleles are inherited from the mother *(A, B)* and those with the recessive alleles are inherited from the father *(a, b).* When you are looking at two pairs, they can be oriented in two basic patterns: both paternal chromosomes can lie on one side and the maternal chromosomes on the other, or one of each can lie on each side. From this, four types of gametes are produced, as shown in Figure 4–6. When all twenty-three chromosome pairs are considered, there are 8,324,608 possible combinations.

A child born from the union of a sperm with an ovum has four grandparents. The sperm contains the father's chromosomes, which were inherited from the father's parents, and the same is true of the ovum with respect to the mother's parents. The child usually is considered to be de-

scended equally from each of the four grandparents. If one grandparent shows a special characteristic, the child is said to be one-quarter of whatever that characteristic happens to be.

An examination of the process of meiosis shows that this is not necessarily true. When the chromosomes derived from the father's parents line up in metaphase of meiosis, they may line up so that the sperm contains more chromosomes from the father's mother than from the father's father. For example, of the twenty-three chromosomes inherited from the father, eleven may have come from the father's father but twelve may have been from the father's mother. Thus, more genes are inherited from the grandmother than from the grandfather.

FIGURE 4–6 *Recombination.* The chromosomes can orient themselves in two different ways, resulting in four distinct combinations of alleles.

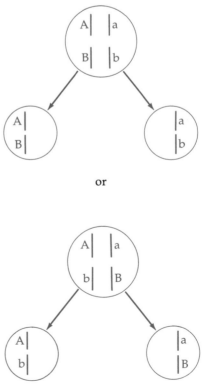

In addition, the chromosomes inherited from a parent are not always exactly the same as they were when they existed in the parent. During meiosis, genetic material is often exchanged between homologous chromosomes inherited from the parent's father and mother; this event is called **crossing-over.** As a result, each individual chromosome within each gamete may contain genetic material from both parents (Figure 4–7). Variation among gametes is the rule. The variations that result among living individuals form the basic raw material for the operation of natural selection (Chapters 5 and 6).

Linkage

Early studies of inheritance revealed that Mendel's principle of independent assortment does not always work. Traits determined by genes carried on different chromosomes do behave in the way he described, but if different genes are on the same chromosome, they tend to remain together in the formation of gametes. Interestingly, some of the seven traits Mendel studied in the pea plant are located on the same chromosome, but in his experiments demonstrating independent assortment he by chance chose pairs of traits located on separate chromosomes.

Genes on the same chromosome are said to be linked, and the phenomenon is called **linkage.** Theoretically, if two genes are linked, only two types of gametes are produced instead of the four predicted by the principle of independent assortment. In reality, crossing-over can occur whereby alleles from homologous chromosomes are exchanged (Figure 4–8). The farther apart two genes are on a chromosome, the greater the chance that they will cross over. According to one theory, this is because there are more points between genes at which the chromosome can break and then reunite.

SEX LINKAGE   The X and Y chromosomes are not homologous; each has genes unique to it. Genes on the Y chromosome are said to be **Y-linked,** whereas genes on the X chromosome are said to be **X-linked.** Because of this nonhomogeneity, inheritance of traits carried on the X and Y chromosomes does not follow the simple Mendelian pattern.

The Y chromosome is small and probably carries few genes. Since male progeny inherit the Y chromosome, all males inherit the Y-linked gene. Y linkage, however, is difficult to distinguish from a sex-limited gene. Although such genes behave as if they were on the Y chromosome, they are actually carried on an autosome but are expressed only in the male.

So far, the only gene discovered on the Y chromosome appears to be one that determines the male sex. This gene accounts for about a thousandth of a percent of the DNA in the Y chro-

FIGURE 4–7 *Crossing-over.* Crossing-over is a source of genetic variation. *(a)* Two homologous chromosomes come together during prophase I of meiosis (see Figure 4–3). *(b)* Crossing-over occurs as parts of chromatids are exchanged. *(c)* Crossing-over now completed, the homologous chromosomes separate in anaphase I. *(d)* At the conclusion of anaphase II the chromosomes of the resulting gametes are genetically different from those of the parents. More distant genes (genes *A* and *B*) cross over more frequently than genes nearer to each other (genes *B* and *C*).

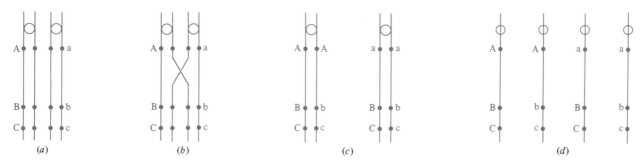

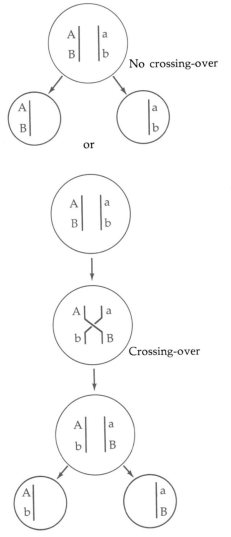

FIGURE 4–8 *Linkage.* Genes located on the same chromosome are inherited as a unit except when crossing-over occurs.

mosome; when it is "switched on," an embryo that would have become a female becomes instead a male. The gene causes undifferentiated embryonic sex organs to develop into male sex organs. The testes then produce testosterone, which helps direct the development of other masculine characteristics. If this does not occur, the embryo develops into a female.

X LINKAGE The story is different with the X chromosome. About 120 genes are known to lie on it, and more is known about the X chromosome than any of the other chromosomes. The inheritance of X-linked genes differs from classical Mendelian inheritance in one important way. Males inherit X-linked genes only from their mothers. One such gene, the one responsible for hemophilia, will be used as an example.

Hemophilia is a recessive X-linked trait characterized by excessive bleeding due to a defect in the clotting mechanism of the blood. Although treatment is now available that reduces the fatality of the disease, in the past hemophiliacs rarely lived past their early twenties.

Early studies of the disease noted that males were the only apparent victims, and we now know that this is because the allele for hemophilia is carried on the X chromosome but not on the Y. Since the trait is recessive, a female would have to be homozygous for the recessive allele in order to have the disease. Because a male has only one X chromosome and a Y chromosome that does not carry the trait, he need have only one recessive allele for defective clotting to result (Figure 4–9).

Since a male child receives his Y chromosome from his father, his mother is the only parent who can transmit the disease to him. The statistical probability that a normal male, X^HY, will mate with a carrier female, X^HX^h, and have a hemophiliac son is ½. This is because all sons inherit the Y chromosome from the father, but they have an equal chance of inheriting either the normal or the abnormal allele from the mother. All daughters are statistically expected to be normal since they receive the normal X from the father, but 50 percent of them can be expected to be carriers because half of the mother's X chromosomes carry the abnormal allele.

Can a woman be a hemophiliac? Until the early 1950s, no female hemophiliacs had been identified. The assumption was that X^hX^h individuals either died before birth or were phenotypically normal and hence not distinguishable from X^HX^H or X^HX^h individuals. However, female hemophiliacs have now been found (Figure 4–10), but their existence is rare because of the low probability that X^hY and X^HX^h individuals will mate.

BOX 4–1

GENDER, SEX, AND ATHLETICS

Gender represents a person's social identity as a male or a female. Most of us accept the fact that people are born either as female or male—that's all there is to it. While sex and gender are simple matters for most people, it is a complex issue for some. In order to understand the problem, we have to distinguish among phenotypic sex (a person's sex organs and secondary sexual characteristics), chromosomal sex (the number of X and Y chromosomes), and genetic sex (the presence of genes that determine sex).

A human embryo develops a set of generalized organs and tubes that will eventually turn into the sex organs. A gene, usually found on the Y chromosome, controls which set of organs, male or female, develops. Between the fifth and seventh week of development, this gene, if present, produces a chemical that influences the undifferentiated gonad to become a testis. Once the testis begins to develop, it produces secretions that turn the other structures into the male sex organs. If this does not occur by the thirteenth week, the gonad begins to develop into an ovary, and under the influence of ovarian secretions, the undifferentiated organs develop into female structures.

How can a person with two X chromosomes become a male? If the male-producing gene breaks off of a Y chromosome in the father's sperm and attaches to an X chromosome, a translocation, the male-producing gene will still operate even though it is on the X chromosome.

Can an XY individual be a female? This can happen if the male-producing gene is not operating (a mutation) or if the receptor sites on the undifferentiated organs do not respond to the presence of the hormone. In addition to these examples, other problems result in ambiguous phenotypic sex.

One area of human endeavor where this has become a major issue is athletic competition, especially the Olympics. Fearing that a phenotypic female who is a genetic or chromosomal male will have an unfair advantage, all phenotypic female athletes have been forced to undergo testing. Female athletes are put through this demeaning process in spite of the fact that several decades of testing have demonstrated that the few phenotypic females who, for example, carry an X and a Y chromosome, do not have any particular athletic advantage.

The Spanish hurdler, Maria Patino, is a phenotypic female, yet carries an X and a Y chromosome in her cells. Because of an androgen insensitivity syndrome, there are no masculinizing effects and she has no advantage over other female athletes in terms of speed and strength. Women with this syndrome have breasts and vaginas and are socialized as females, but lack a uterus and ovaries and have testes located within their bodies. Patino made her case public, and after several years has been certified a female by the International Olympic Committee.

A total of 2406 female athletes competing in the 1992 Barcelona Olympics were tested for the presence of the male-sex producing gene. Five athletes, about 1 in 500, "failed" the test. Four athletes that agreed to a follow-up physical exam exhibited physical abnormalities. The International Olympic Committee has not revealed whether or not these women were allowed to compete. Many geneticists have called for an end to genetic screening for athletes.

Reference: J. Diamon, "Turning a Man," *Discover* (June 1992), 71–77; and D. Grady, "Sex Test of Champions," *Discover* (June 1992), 78–82.

Before the development of new medical procedures for treating hemophilia, matings between people with the above genotypes were severely limited because so few hemophiliac males lived to reproductive age. Recent treatment of hemophiliacs allows them to live somewhat normal lives. Since the disease is simply controlled but the defective allele is not "repaired," two concerns may be relevant in the future.

First, there might be a general increase in the frequency of the X^h allele; second, there might be an increase in the number of homozygous recessive females.

AN EXAMPLE OF THE INHERITANCE OF HEMOPHILIA   During the nineteenth and twentieth centuries, hemophilia occurred with some frequency in the royal houses of Europe. The dis-

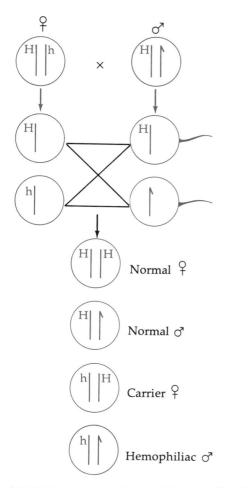

FIGURE 4–9 *Inheritance of hemophilia.* The gene for hemophilia is located on the X chromosome but not on the Y. Hemophilia, as well as all other genes on the X chromosome, displays the X-linked pattern of inheritance.

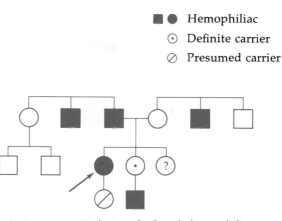

FIGURE 4–10 *Pedigree of a female hemophiliac.*

ease probably originated with Queen Victoria of England because all the people involved are descended from her. None of her ancestors had the disease, but of Queen Victoria's nine children, two daughters were carriers, three daughters were possible carriers, and one son (Leopold) had the disease. These people brought the disease into the royal families of England, Spain, Russia, and probably Germany (Figure 4–11).

A famous case of the relationship of hemophilia to history involved Alix, granddaughter of Victoria, who married the future czar of Russia, Nicholas II, and became known in Russia as Alexandra. She had four daughters and one son, Alexis, who was a hemophiliac. Historians have suggested that the preoccupation of Nicholas and Alexandra with their son's disease brought them under the control of Rasputin and hastened the overthrow of their government.

Linkage Maps

Because of the distinctive inheritance pattern of X-linked traits, geneticists have identified several genes that reside on the X chromosome. Hemophilia is perhaps the best known of these X-linked traits. Other genes known to be on the X chromosome include red-green color blindness, congenital night blindness, Xg blood type, vitamin D-resistant rickets, glucose-6-phosphate dehydrogenase deficiency, and one form of muscular dystrophy.

In the 1950s geneticists identified the first human autosomal genes associated on the same chromosome. Such sets of genes are called **linkage groups.** Genes located close together on the same chromosome tend to be inherited together unless crossing-over occurs between them. Genes located far apart on large chromosomes, however, behave as if they are on separate chromosomes; they recombine according to the principle of independent assortment.

Crossing-over data can be used to determine the linear order of genes in a linkage group. Since the frequency of crossing-over is proportional to

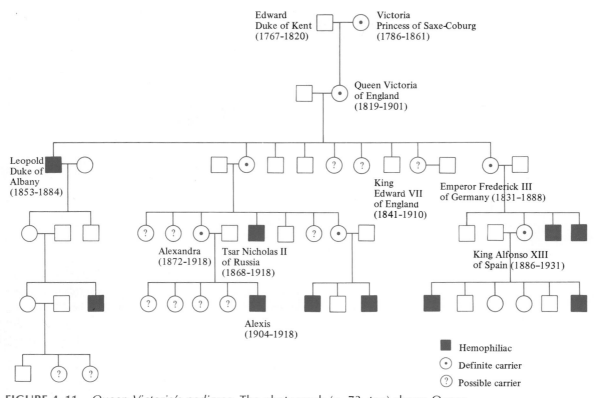

FIGURE 4–11 *Queen Victoria's pedigree.* The photograph (p. 73, top) shows Queen Victoria and some of her descendants: Princess Alix (Alexandra) of Hesse (left), Queen Victoria (center), Princess Irene of Prussia (right).

the distance between genes on a chromatid, genes that are farther apart cross over more frequently.

Let us assume that there are three genes, *A*, *B*, and *C*, linked on the same chromosome (Figure 4–12). *A* and *B* cross over in 2 percent of cell divisions, while *B* and *C* cross over 8 percent of the time. Therefore, *B* and *C* are farther apart from each other than *A* and *B* are. We can predict that *A* and *C* will cross over either 6 or 10 percent of the time (8 − 2 or 8 + 2). This method gives the linear order of genes on a chromosome. The relative distance between individual genes is measured in **centiMorgans (cM),** named after Henry Hunt Morgan, a pioneer in the study of genetics. One centiMorgan represents a crossing-over rate of 1 percent.

The next step is to associate linkage groups with specific chromosomes. Small chromosomal

aberrations are often associated with unusual inheritance patterns. These can be used to determine the location of specific autosomes on a specific chromosome. Today we know that cystic fibrosis is located on chromosome 7, sickle-cell anemia on chromosome 11, phenylketonuria on chromosome 12, and Tay-Sachs disease on chromosome 15.

Summary

Stimulated by Mendel's work, early geneticists began to search for the physical reality of the gene. Their work led them to the cell and to those small bodies within the nucleus of the cell, the chromosomes.

By means of special techniques, chromosomes can now be routinely observed through the microscope. Each chromosome consists of two

strands, the chromatids, held together by the centromere. For a particular species there is usually a characteristic chromosome number, but abnormalities in number and structure occur.

There are two basic forms of cell division. Mitosis is the division of body cells, while meiosis is the production of gametes—sperm and ova—in special body tissues. Detailed studies of the behavior of the chromosomes during cell division have provided a physical explanation for Mendelian genetics.

Deeper probing of the mechanisms of inheritance has shown that Mendel's principles do not always work. This is not because they are wrong but simply because the real hereditary mechanisms are very complex. For example, some traits are inherited on the sex chromosomes, and so their pattern on inheritance differs from the patterns seen by Mendel.

Careful study of linkage groups is used to determine the location of specific genes on spe-

FIGURE 4–12 *Calculating gene distances.* This diagram shows possible arrangements of three genes on a chromosome. In this example, genes *A* and *C* cross over in 2 percent of the cell divisions, and genes *B* and *C* cross over 8 percent of the time. In order to learn whether *A* or *B* is first in this sequence of three genes, the number of crossovers between *A* and *C* must be determined. If *A* and *C* cross over 10 percent of the time (8% + 2%), the gene sequence will then be *A-B-C (a)*. If *A* and *C* cross over 6 percent of the time (8% − 2%), the gene sequence will be *B-A-C (b)*.

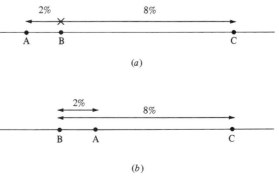

cific chromosomes. Crossing-over data are used to determine the sequence of genes within a linkage group and their location on the chromosome.

THE MOLECULAR BASIS OF HEREDITY

The previous section focused on the behavior of chromosomes as a means of explaining and expanding the observations of Mendel. However, the chromosome is not the gene itself. What is the gene, and how does it operate? To answer this question and others, we must turn to an examination of the chemical nature of the hereditary material.

All substances are composed of **atoms,** the basic building blocks of matter. Of the ninety-two kinds of atoms that occur in nature, four are found in great quantity in living organisms: carbon, hydrogen, oxygen, and nitrogen. Others that play extremely important roles, but are less common, include calcium, phosphorus, sulfur, chlorine, sodium, magnesium, iron, and potassium (Table 4–2).

Atoms can be joined to form **molecules,** which can vary tremendously in size depending on the number of atoms involved. The molecules found in living organisms are usually of great size because carbon atoms form long chains that can consist of hundreds or thousands of atoms and often include rings of five or six carbon atoms. Other kinds of atoms are attached to the carbon backbone.

TABLE 4–2
COMMON ELEMENTS IN LIVING ORGANISMS

ELEMENT	APPROXIMATE COMPOSITION OF HUMAN BODY, BY WEIGHT (%)
Oxygen	65.0
Carbon	18.5
Hydrogen	9.5
Nitrogen	3.3
Calcium	1.5
Phosphorus	1.0
Others	1.2

Molecules of Life

Most of the molecules found in living organisms fall into four categories: carbohydrates, lipids, proteins, and nucleic acids. **Carbohydrates** include the sugars and starches. **Lipids** include the fats, oils, and waxes.

Some of the most important molecules of the body are **proteins.** An understanding of the protein molecule is essential in comprehending the action of the genes. Proteins are long chains of basic units known as **amino acids.** All twenty basic amino acids share a common subunit which contains carbon, oxygen, hydrogen, and nitrogen. Attached to this subunit are various units ranging from a single hydrogen atom to a very complicated unit containing several carbon atoms. The end of one amino acid can link up with the end of another, forming a **peptide bond.** Short chains of amino acids are called **polypeptides.** A protein forms when several polypeptide chains join together.

In addition to simple chains of amino acids, many proteins are further complicated by other bonds. These bonds can involve sulfur and hydrogen and can lead to a folding, looping, or coiling of the protein molecule. The three-dimensional structure of proteins is important in determining how they function.

The Nucleic Acids

The largest molecules found in living organisms are the **nucleic acids.** The hereditary material that was discussed earlier is a nucleic acid.

Like the proteins, the nucleic acids are long chains of basic units. In this case the basic unit is a **nucleotide.** The nucleotide itself is fairly complex, consisting of three lesser units: a five-carbon sugar, either **ribose** or **deoxyribose;** a **phosphate unit;** and a **base.** The bases fall into two categories, **purines** and **pyrimidines,** both containing nitrogen. The purine consists of two connected rings of carbon and nitrogen atoms; the pyrimidine consists of a single ring.

The nucleic acid based upon the sugar ribose is called **ribonucleic acid (RNA).** The nucleotides that make up the RNA contain the following bases: the purines **adenine** (A) and **guanine** (G) and the pyrimidines **uracil** (U) and **cytosine** (C). The nucleic acid based upon the sugar deoxyribose is called **deoxyribonucleic acid (DNA).** DNA also contains adenine, guanine, and cytosine, but in place of uracil is found the pyrimidine **thymine** (T) (Figure 4–13).

THE DNA MOLECULE   As in proteins, the three-dimensional structure of the nucleic acids can be critical in understanding how the molecule works. The basic structure of DNA consists of a pair of extremely long polynucleotide chains composed of many nucleotide units lying parallel to one another. The units are linked in such a way that a backbone of sugar and phosphate units is formed with the bases sticking out. The chains are connected by attractions between the hydrogen atoms of the two bases. Since the distance between the two chains must be constant, one of the two bases must be a pyrimidine and the other a purine. Two pyrimidines would be too narrow, and two purines too wide. In addition, because of the nature of the bonding, it can take place only between an adenine and a thymine and between a cytosine and a guanine. These are said to be **complementary pairs.** In 1953 J. D. Watson and F. H. C. Crick proposed a model for the three-dimensional structure of DNA.[6] DNA consists of two long chains wound around each other, forming a double helix, with a complete turn taking ten nucleotide units (Figure 4–14 and Figure 4–D in the color insert).

REPLICATION OF DNA   At the end of mitosis and meiosis, each chromosome is composed of a single chromatid that will eventually replicate itself to become double-stranded again. A chromatid is basically a single DNA molecule. In molecular terms, the DNA molecule has the ability to replicate itself to become two identical molecules.

In replication, the bonds holding the complementary pairs together are broken and the molecules come apart, with the bases sticking out

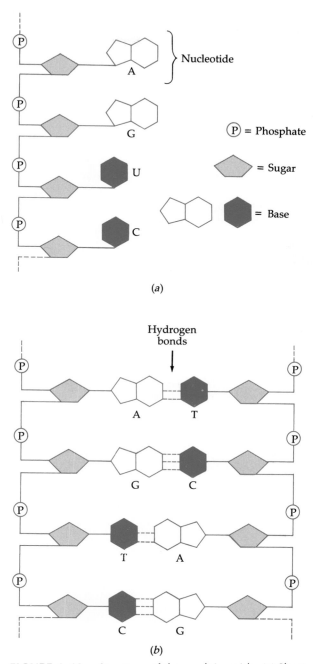

(a)

(b)

FIGURE 4–13 *Structure of the nucleic acids. (a)* Short segment of mRNA molecule. Note the presence of the base uracil and the absence of thymine. *(b)* Short segment of DNA showing four varieties of bases. Each base is joined to a deoxyribose molecule, and each deoxyribose is held in the chain by phosphate molecules.

[6]J. D. Watson and F. H. C. Crick, "Molecular Structure of Nucleic Acids: A Structure for Deoxyribose Nucleic Acid," *Nature,* 171 (1953), 737–738.

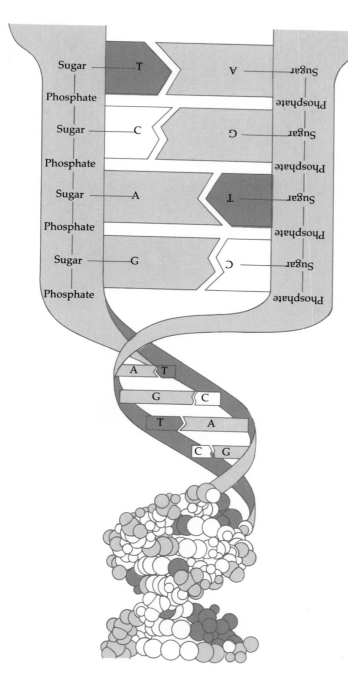

FIGURE 4–14 *The DNA molecule.*

from the sugar-phosphate backbone. Individual nucleotides of the four types (ultimately obtained from the digestion of food) are found in the nucleus, and the bases of these nucleotides become attracted to the exposed bases on the chain. Thus, a nucleotide with an adenine be-

comes attracted to a thymine, and so on. When the nucleotides are in place, they bond to one another (Figure 4–15).

THE GENETIC CODE   In order for the DNA molecule to function as the hereditary material,

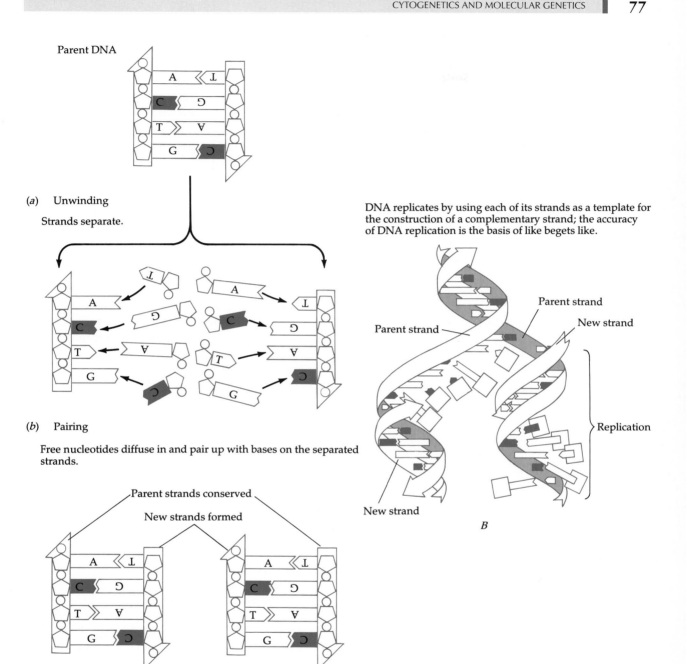

Parent DNA

(a) Unwinding

Strands separate.

(b) Pairing

Free nucleotides diffuse in and pair up with bases on the separated strands.

Parent strands conserved

New strands formed

(c) Joining

Each new row of bases is linked into a continuous strand.

A

DNA replicates by using each of its strands as a template for the construction of a complementary strand; the accuracy of DNA replication is the basis of like begets like.

Parent strand

New strand

Parent strand

Replication

New strand

B

FIGURE 4–15 *Replication of the DNA molecule.*

there must be a method by which information is stored in the molecule. Remember, there are four bases that can be arranged in several ways. In the following hypothetical example, the DNA back- bone of sugar and phosphate units is indicated by a single line, the bases by letters on the line:

C T C G G A C A A A T A

TABLE 4–3

THE GENETIC CODE

AMINO ACID	CODONS*
Alanine	CGA, CGG, CGT, CGC
Arginine	GCA, GCG, GCT, GCC, TCT, TCC
Asparagine	TTA, TTG
Aspartic acid	CTA, CTG
Cysteine	ACA, ACG
Glutamic acid	CTT, CTC
Glutamine	GTT, GTC
Glycine	CCA, CCG, CCT, CCC
Histidine	GTA, GTG
Isoleucine	TAA, TAG, TAT
Leucine	AAT, AAC, GAA, GAG, GAT, GAC
Lysine	TTT, TTC
Methionine	TAC
Phenylalanine	AAA, AAG
Proline	GGA, GGG, GGT, GGC
Serine	AGA, AGG, AGT, AGC, TCA, TCG
Threonine	TGA, TGG, TGT, TGC
Tryptophan	ACC
Tyrosine	ATA, ATG
Valine	CAA, CAG, CAT, CAC

*The code is given in terms of the nucleotide sequence in the DNA molecule. In addition, there are specific codons signaling the beginning and end of a sequence.

The above sequence codes for amino acids. Each amino acid is determined by specific three-base units called **codons.** This code has been broken: CTC on the DNA molecule is the codon for glutamic acid, and GGA is proline (Table 4–3).

MITOCHONDRIAL DNA   In the early 1960s a different type of DNA was discovered in the cells of plants and animals. This DNA is not found in the nucleus but in bodies that occur in the cytoplasm; these bodies are known as **mitochondria.** Mitochondria convert the energy in the chemical bonds of food (organic molecules) into **adenosine triphosphate (ATP).** ATP is the main fuel of cells.

Mitochondrial DNA (mtDNA) is a double-stranded loop of DNA (Figure 4–16). There can be one or many mitochondria per cell. Each mitochondrion possesses between four and ten mtDNA loops. Cells with high energy demands, such as muscle cells, have high numbers of mitochondria.

Human mitochondrial DNA contains the codes for only thirteen proteins, whereas **nuclear DNA (nDNA)** codes for as many as 100,000 proteins. Viewed another way, nDNA contains about 3 trillion base pairs, whereas mtDNA has only 16,569 base pairs.

Until the 1970s the function of mtDNA was a complete mystery. Slowly, some of the roles of mtDNA have been revealed. It is now suspected that mutations of different segments of mtDNA cause or contribute to several rare diseases. Mitochondrial DNA also has been linked to Parkinson's disease. Some researchers believe that as mutations accumulate in the mtDNA, the body ages. Perhaps therapy aimed at counteracting mtDNA mutations can slow aging. Research along these lines is currently being conducted.

The inheritance of the genes in mtDNA does not follow Mendelian principles. Mitochondrial DNA is inherited only from one's mother. The mitochondria of the zygote are supplied by the cytoplasm of the ovum; the sperm does not contribute mitochondria.

Protein Synthesis

The blueprint for a specific protein is located in the DNA molecule within the nucleus of the cell or the mitochondria. The actual production of proteins by the joining of specific amino acids in a specific sequence takes place within the mitochondria for genes encoded by mtDNA. For genes encoded by nDNA, protein production takes place outside the nucleus. An electron microscope reveals many structures in the cytoplasm, including extremely small, spherical bodies known as **ribosomes.** The ribosomes provide one area for protein synthesis. How is the information transmitted from the nDNA to the ribosomes?

The carrier of the information is **messenger RNA (mRNA).** This molecule copies the sequence of base pairs from the nDNA molecule. A segment of DNA that contains the code for a particular polypeptide chain unwinds, leaving a series of bases on the DNA chain exposed. Nucleotide units of RNA, which are found in the nucleus, are attracted to the complementary bases on the nDNA chain; the adenine of the RNA is attracted to the thymine on the nDNA, the guanine to the cytosine, the cytosine to the guanine, and the uracil of RNA (remember, uracil replaces thymine) to the adenine on the nDNA.

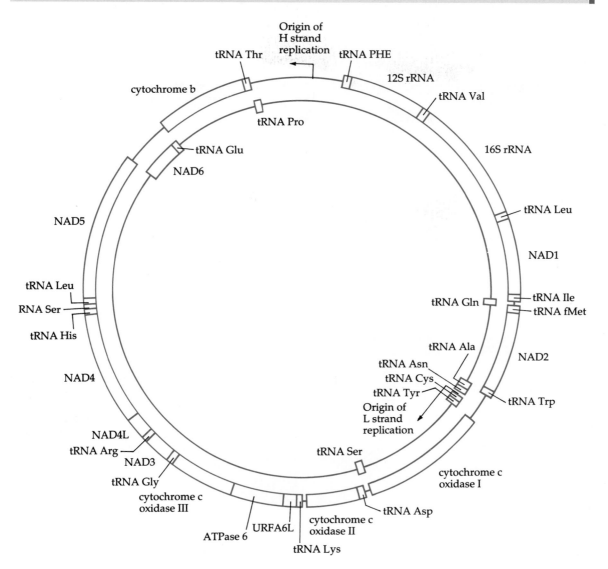

FIGURE 4–16 *Mitochondrial DNA.* The continuous double-stranded loop of mitochondrial DNA encodes thirteen proteins and twenty-four RNA molecules.

After the nucleotide units are in place, they link together and the newly formed messenger RNA leaves the nDNA molecule as a unit. This chain of nucleotide units is called messenger RNA. A molecule of mRNA is considerably shorter than a molecule of nDNA since the mRNA contains the code of a single polypeptide chain.

In the ribosome is another form of RNA, called **transfer RNA (tRNA).** The tRNA is extremely short, consisting in part of a series of three nucleotide units. The three bases form an anticode for a particular amino acid; that is, if

the code on the mRNA is ACG, then the code on the tRNA consists of the complementary bases, UGC. Attached to the tRNA is the amino acid being coded.

The tRNA moves in and lines up opposite the appropriate codon on the mRNA molecule. For example, GUA is the code for valine on the mRNA, and so the tRNA that carries the amino acid valine has the base sequence CAU. After the amino acids are brought into their proper positions, they link together by means of peptide bonds and the polypeptide chain moves away from the mRNA and tRNA (Figure 4–17).

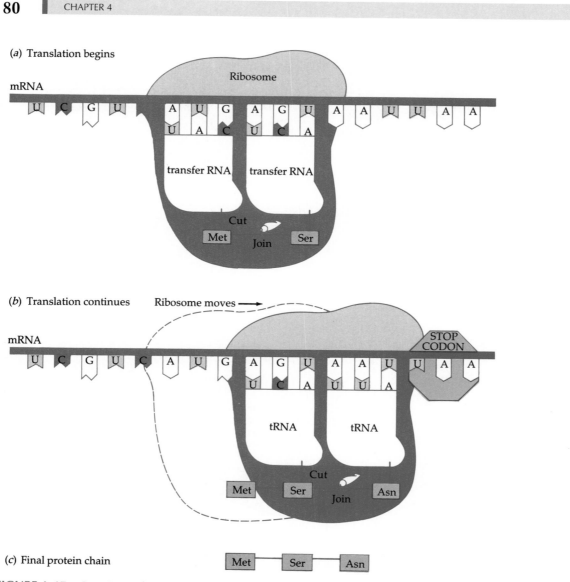

(a) Translation begins

mRNA

Ribosome

transfer RNA   transfer RNA

Cut

Met   Join   Ser

(b) Translation continues   Ribosome moves →

mRNA

STOP CODON

tRNA   tRNA

Cut

Met   Ser   Join   Asn

(c) Final protein chain   Met   Ser   Asn

FIGURE 4–17 *Protein synthesis in the ribosome.*

Genetic Abnormalities as Mistakes in Proteins

Many genetic abnormalities result from abnormal protein molecules. Since the blueprints for proteins are located in the DNA molecule, it follows that these abnormal proteins are the result of an incorrect sequence of nucleotides in the DNA molecule itself. This can be demonstrated with respect to sickle-cell anemia.

THE MOLECULAR STRUCTURE OF HEMOGLOBIN   Blood is a very complex material composed of a liquid and a solid portion. The solid por-

tion consists of the **erythrocytes (red blood cells)**, the **leukocytes (white blood cells)**, and the **platelets.** The liquid portion is the **plasma.** The term **serum** refers to plasma after the clotting material has settled out. Dissolved in the plasma are a wide variety of materials including salts, sugars, fats, amino acids, and hormones, along with the important plasma proteins.

Packed into the erythrocytes are millions of molecules of the red pigment **hemoglobin A (HbA).** The major constituent of the molecule is a larger **globin** unit to which are attached four **heme** groups. The latter are small, iron-containing molecular units. The globin unit consists of four chains, two **alpha** and two **beta.** Each alpha chain consists of 141 amino acids, and each beta chain consists of 146.

Several other hemoglobins are known. **Hemoglobin A₂** is found in small amounts in adult human blood. **Fetal hemoglobin (HbF)** is found in the fetus but usually disappears within the first year after birth. These three hemoglobins differ somewhat in their ability to carry oxygen.

ABNORMAL HEMOGLOBINS   Perhaps the best known of all the hemoglobin abnormalities is **hemoglobin S (HbS),** which is responsible for **sickle-cell anemia.** This disease is characterized by periodic sickling episodes during which the red blood cells become distorted and rigid (Figure 4–18). These abnormal cells clog the minute capillaries by forming small clots. Cells located beyond the clots are deprived of oxygen and die. Depending upon the location of the clots, they may cause heart failure, stroke, blindness, kidney damage, and other serious physical injuries.

The genetics of sickle-cell anemia is quite simple. The individual homozygous for HbA is normal, while the person homozygous for HbS has abnormal hemoglobin and the potential of developing the disease sickle-cell anemia. The heterozygous individual has a mixture of normal and abnormal hemoglobin but very rarely has symptoms related to HbS. Such an individual is said to have the **sickle-cell trait.** This is an example of codominance (Chapter 3).

Identification of the individual heterozygous for sickle-cell anemia is relatively simple, and many methods now exist, including the use of **electrophoresis.** In this method a hemoglobin sample is placed in a solution containing atoms that carry electric charges. These, in turn, cause the proteins to develop electric charges of their own. The sample is then placed in an electric field, and the proteins migrate to one of the poles. The speed of travel depends on the weight of the molecule and the strength of the charge. The proteins are stopped before they reach the poles and can be identified by their relative positions. Figure 4–19 shows the result of such a procedure.

The precise molecular structure of HbS has been worked out. The hemoglobin molecule consists of four heme units and a globin. The globin, in turn, consists of a pair of alpha and a pair of beta chains. In HbS the alpha chains are normal; the defect is found in the beta chains. Out of the

FIGURE 4–18 *Normal and sickled erythrocytes.* The electron microscope reveals the distinctive shape of *(a)* the normal erythrocyte and *(b)* the sickled erythrocyte.

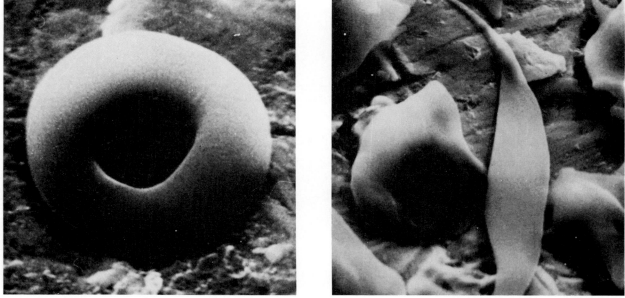

(a)   *(b)*

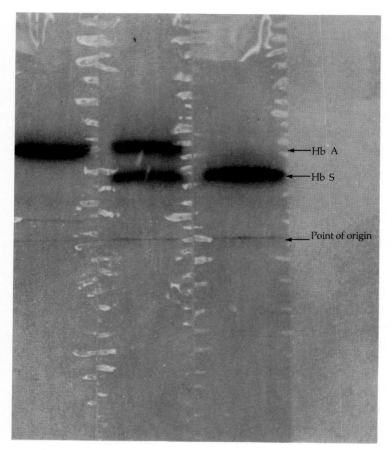

Hb A

Hb S

Point of origin

FIGURE 4–19 *Electrophoresis.* Charged hemoglobin molecules, placed initially at the point of origin, migrate differentially in an electric field.

146 amino acids in each of the beta chains, the sixth from one end is incorrect: instead of glutamic acid, which is found in HbA, the amino acid valine is present in HbS. The rest of the chain is the same. The codons that code for glutamic acid and valine differ in only one base pair. One code for glutamic acid is CTT, while one code for valine is CAT. There are 146 amino acids in the chain; a mistake in only one, brought about by a single mistake in the code, produces an abnormal hemoglobin with drastic consequences.

Many other abnormal hemoglobins are known. More than thirty of them are caused by defects on the alpha chain, and more than fifty involve the beta chain. They all result from a substitution of one amino acid for another at some point in the polypeptide chain. The substitution, in turn, results from some alteration of the genetic code, following which the inheritance of the altered code conforms to rules of normal Mendelian inheritance.

What Is a Gene?

We can examine this question in the light of studies of the structure and function of the hereditary material, the DNA molecule. The concept of the gene was originally developed as part of a model to explain the mechanisms of heredity when the actual physical and chemical nature of the hereditary material was unknown.

A gene is a biological unit of inheritance; it is a section of DNA that has a specific function. That function could be the coding of a particular protein, a polypeptide chain; or it could be a regulatory function, that is, controlling the activity of other genes. In the first situation, the 438 nucleotides that code for the structure of the hemoglobin beta chain can be thought of as a gene.

SEQUENCING DNA AND GENE MAPPING

We saw earlier how analyses of inheritance patterns permit geneticists to develop linkage maps.

BOX 4–2

DNA IN THE NEWS

In the 1880s Sir Francis Galton, cousin of Charles Darwin, reported that no two people could have exactly the same fingerprint pattern. Since that time the use of fingerprint analysis has played a central role in criminal investigation. A century later another powerful identification tool was developed—DNA fingerprinting. DNA fingerprinting played a major role during the 1995 O. J. Simpson trial.

This method relies on analysis of the genetic material. Except for identical twins, each person's genetic code is unique. DNA analysis can be done using blood, skin,

hair, saliva, or semen left at a crime scene. In this way an individual can be either identified or excluded as the culprit.

The method involves the use of enzymes to break up the DNA recovered at the crime scene and the DNA obtained from the suspect. The DNA fragments are then separated in an electric field, producing a specific pattern. These patterns are the "fingerprints" that can then be compared.

The area of controversy in the courtroom today revolves around the probability that any particular fingerprint is unique. Since foren-

sic scientists do not analyze the entire genome of an individual, it is theoretically possible for two people to show the same pattern. The probability of this occurring with today's methods varies from 1 in 100,000 to 1 in 100 million. More complex methods being developed will reduce this probability to about zero.

References: K. C. McElfresh, D. Vining-Forde, and I. Balazs, "DNA-based Identity Testing in Forensic Science," *BioScience,* 43 (1993), 149–157; and R. Nowak, "Forensic DNA Goes to Court with O. J.," *Science* 265 (1994), 1352–1354.

The next stage is the development of a physical map. A physical map includes specific features of the chromosome and the banding patterns

FIGURE 4–20 *Physical map of chromosome 18.*

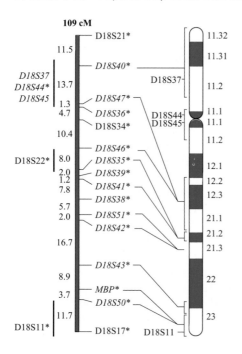

that develop when the chromosome is treated with certain dyes. These features are then associated with specific genes and DNA sequences called gene markers. The first physical maps were published in 1992. By 1993 simple physical maps had been produced for all human chromosomes. Figure 4–20 is a physical map of chromosome 18, a middle-sized chromosome, being 109 centiMorgans long. (Chromosome 1, the longest chromosome, is 390 centiMorgans long, while chromosome 21 is only 67 centiMorgans long.)

The next step is determination of the genetic code. Less than 25 years after the structure of the DNA molecule was described in 1953, it became possible to determine the sequence (linear order) of actual nucleotide bases on a chromosome. In a method first used in 1977, a single-stranded DNA molecule was chemically cut (cleaved) by enzymes into individual nucleotides that were then separated in an electric field. Each base was identified in the order in which it was cleaved. By 1987 scientists were working out plans to determine the entire human genetic code (see Box 4–3).

Genes are made up of sequences of nucleotides. DNA sequences, however, show only the

BOX 4–3

THE GENETIC RECIPE FOR HUMANKIND

We are living in an age of communication. Through computers and other advanced technologies information moves around the world at the speed of light, complex problems are analyzed in seconds instead of lifetimes, and vital information is readily available to a wide audience. Yet as data move through wires, optic fibers, or as electromagnetic waves through the atmosphere, we must remember that we are basically dealing with very simple codes, such as the presence or absence of an electric charge.

The genetic material, DNA, communicates through a code. Computer scientists as well as biologists appreciate the elegance of the DNA code. Some futurists envision computer storage devices based on codes at the molecular level. The words in this text, maintained on a hard disk in the authors' office, might some day be actually coded in the computer of the future by artificial DNA or a molecule like it.

Geneticists today are actively studying the genetic code in order to understand how it works. In 1977 researchers developed the first efficient methodology for determining the sequence of nucleotides or base pairs in a strand of DNA. Almost immediately biologists began to ponder the possibility of determining the base-pair sequence for all human genes. Although in 1977 such a dream appeared technologically light-years away, by the second half of the 1980s molecular biologists were beginning to think that such a project was feasible.

It is estimated that the entire human genome contains about 3 billion base pairs or nucleotides. In the mid-1980s biologists estimated that one technician could sequence 100,000 base pairs a year, which meant that it would take 30,000 person-years to sequence the entire human genome. The cost was established at $3 billion. Out of this early interest came the Human Genome Project. In 1988 the National Center for Human Genome Research was established by the National Institutes of Health. The first director, from 1988 through 1992, was James Watson, who, with F. H. C. Crick, had first determined the structure of DNA in 1953. The project formally began in 1990 and was seen as a 15-year project, although new technologies are speeding up the process. Other governments have established similar problems that work cooperatively with the American effort.

The Human Genome Project is not without controversy. Some people ask if we should undertake the task of mapping the human genome. What would be the consequences? A complete human gene map would lead to improved diagnosis of hereditary diseases and the development of new drugs for genetic abnormalities. The mapping of the human genome could also lead to ethical dilemmas and abuses. Whose genome should be taken as prototypically human? Would only the rich be able to take advantage of the health benefits gained from the new technology? And who would control the technology? Control of the human genome could lead to the engineering of specific types of humans, and it could create an elitist society. Yet work continues on the project with the proponents believing that the benefits of its success will far outweigh any problems it creates.

---

linear order of nucleotides on a chromatid. They do not indicate what parts of the sequence correspond to the specific functional units that we have called genes. By the end of the century we may know the location of the estimated 50,000 to 100,000 human genes.

Regulation of Gene Action

Genes do things. They control the production of a product such as a polypeptide chain or they control the action of other genes.

Not all genes in a particular type of cell operate in that cell. Although the gene for the production of melanin (a pigment) is present in all cells, melanin is produced only in skin, hair, and eye cells. Also, of the genes that do function in a particular cell, not all of them function all the time.

Knowledge of the way in which genes are activated or suppressed was first gained from studies of bacteria. Bacteria and other simple organisms are called **prokaryotes.** These organisms lack well-defined nuclei in their cells, and their

BOX 4–4

THE HUMAN GENOME DIVERSITY PROJECT

The first-year medical student is often pictured bent over a human cadaver learning the size, shape, location, and name of all parts of the human body. Today human anatomy is entering the computer age. One recent project involves taking cadavers of anatomically average individuals, one male and one female, and cutting them into thin sections. The sections are then scanned into a computer. Using this data the computer can then present a cross section of the human body at any level and can electronically combine the data to represent three-dimensional images for study.

If the software developers are taking a single human male and a single human female as the model for the computer images, how is the selection being made? What is the age of the cadavers selected? What is their height and weight? What is their "race"? In other words, what do we mean by "typical" or "average"?

The same issue has arisen in the Human Genome Project. The investigators are working out the genetic code of the human genome. However, since every individual, except for identical twins, is genetically different, whose code will be selected as the standard? Many geneticists are concerned that the genome being analyzed is essentially "Caucasian."

Geneticist Luca Cavalli-Sforza and his colleagues have been instrumental in the development of the Human Genome Diversity Project. They plan to collect samples of blood, hair, and saliva from which DNA can be extracted for study. The samples are to be collected from anonymous donors in different populations throughout the world. Initially a small series of DNA sequences will be determined for these DNA samples to study the variation that occurs among different human populations. This data will then be used for studies of the relationships among human groups. The data will also be used to test how much individuals from different populations differ from the sequence being uncovered by the Human Genome Project.

The proposed project has not been met with enthusiasm by all. Some peoples see the taking of blood samples as desecrating the body. Others believe that these genetic studies will support negative eugenic studies. The major concern is that these studies may lead to new definitions of race based on genetic data and that these studies are basically racist. The researchers are quick to point out, however, that the project is a weapon against racism. Since the major work on the human genome is using "Caucasian" genes, the diverse DNA in the database will provide a means of including all peoples in the benefits that the genome project will bring. In addition, anthropologists note that genetic data may also demonstrate the nonexistence of races in the human species (see Chapter 8).

genetics is simpler than that of more advanced organisms called **eukaryotes.**

In prokaryotes, a group of genes, arranged in linear order and all concerned with the same product, is called an **operon** (Figure 4–21). The first gene in the series, called the **operator,** initiates the action of the entire group of structural genes. These genes code for specific proteins.

Another gene, called the **regulatory gene** (Chapter 3), acts as a switch, activating or suppressing the operator. It may be located on the same chromosome as the structural gene it controls or on a different chromosome. The regulatory gene controls the production of a **repressor protein.** This protein inhibits the action of an operator gene by chemically binding with the operator. This is the "off" position of the switch. However, an **effector** molecule, which is usually an enzyme produced by one of the structural genes, can also bind with the repressor. When it does, the repressor is prevented from binding to the operator. This is the "on" position of the switch. By artificially adding or removing repressor or effector molecules, scientists can switch protein synthesis on and off in some prokaryotes (see Box 4–5).

In eukaryotes, gene regulation is more complex. In addition to the regulator and operator, there are other regions on the same chromosome as the operon that influence its action. One re-

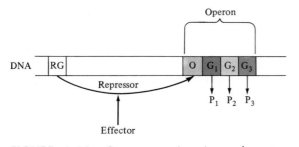

FIGURE 4–21 *Gene operation in prokaryotes.* A regulatory gene (RG) controls the rate of synthesis of three structural genes: G_1, G_2, G_3. The regulator gene controls the production of a repressor protein that acts on an operator gene (O). The operator gene "turns off" the synthesis of proteins 1, 2, and 3 (P_1, P_2, P_3) by binding with the repressor. An effector protein "turns on" synthesis by binding with the repressor.

gion is thirty base pairs from the operon, another is eighty pairs away, and still others are farther away. The function of these regions is not completely understood.

Another complexity of eukaryotic genetics is that interspersed among the base pairs that code for a protein are base-pair sequences that are not represented in the protein. The sequences that code for the amino acid sequences of corresponding proteins are called **exons,** and those that do not code for amino acid sequences in the protein are called **introns.** The function of the introns is basically unknown, but in some cases they seem to act as a type of punctuation. They may separate exons that code for parts of a protein molecule that have different functions. For example, the globin molecule has parts that function in two ways: one part surrounds the heme, and the other parts wrap around the hemoglobin molecule and stabilize it. The globin molecule is coded by three exons separated by two introns. The middle exon codes for the part of the molecule that surrounds the heme; the other two exons code for the stabilizing parts of the hemoglobin molecule.

Like regulators, introns might function to activate or suppress other genes for certain activities such as cell differentiation. "Introns may also be important in evolutionary dynamics, since their presence increases the rate at which the exons will be shuffled and reassorted to make new combinations. The farther apart regions of the molecule are, the more chance for recombination and new arrangements to 'try out' evolutionarily."[7]

Blood-Type Systems

A large number of proteins are found in blood. Some of them, such as hemoglobins, are essential to the body: alterations of these molecules lead to abnormalities and death. Other proteins are not as critical; some people may have them, others may not. Since they often occur in several alternate forms, these proteins are said to be **polymorphic,** from *poly,* meaning "many," and *morph,* meaning "structure." Polymorphism refers to the presence of distinct forms within a population. The polymorphic situation makes these proteins very valuable in the study of evolution and human variability.

Through blood transfusion and occasional mixing of maternal and fetal blood at birth, proteins can be introduced into the blood of a person whose blood naturally lacks them. The body reacts to these foreign proteins by producing or mobilizing **antibodies,** whose role is to destroy or neutralize foreign substances that have entered the body. A protein that triggers the action of antibodies is known as an **antigen.** Antigen-antibody reactions are of great medical significance and help define differences in blood proteins that exist in humans.

THE ABO BLOOD-TYPE SYSTEM   The best known set of blood antigens is the **ABO blood-type system.** This system consists of two basic antigens, which are simply called antigens A and B. Other antigens do exist in the system, and the actual situation is more complex than is presented here.

There are four phenotypes in the ABO system, depending on which antigens are present. Type A indicates the presence of antigen A, while type B shows the presence of antigen B. Type AB indicates the presence of both antigens, and type O indicates the absence of both antigens. The anti-

[7]C. F. Fraser and J. J. Nora, *Genetics of Man,* 2d ed. (Philadelphia: Lea & Febiger, 1986), 73.

BOX 4–5

THE CONTROL OF HUMAN BIOLOGICAL EVOLUTION

. . . Like other creatures, man evolves, but unlike other creatures, man knows that he evolves. The control of this biological evolution is therefore the change from reproductive success caused by natural selection to reproductive success caused by human choice.[1]

Techniques for improving the human gene pool are referred to as **eugenic methods.** The simplest eugenic methods involve the control of breeding. **Negative eugenics** is any procedure whereby some people that some group or government labels undesirable are prevented from mating. The converse is **positive eugenic** methods for encouraging certain people to mate. Adolf Hitler practiced both positive and negative eugenics. He encouraged and sometimes forced people he called "members of the superrace" to mate with each other in breeding camps. He discouraged others from mating in the most extreme way possible—he had them killed. These practices bestowed a sinister connotation upon the word *eugenics.*

Today new eugenic methods aim first to eliminate deleterious genes and eventually to alter the human genome. Methods now on the horizon will go well beyond changing the frequency of alleles in a population by controlling conceptions and matings. The hope of most eugenic researchers is the actual altering of the genetic material to produce a healthier person. The industrial or experimental technology to do this is called **genetic engineering.** A few of the things that may be applied to human genetic engineering in the near future are listed below:

1. *The control of regulatory genes:* Genetic diseases that result from the faulty action of a regulatory gene may be managed by treatment that leads to adjusting that activity. As we discover what materials affect what genes, regulation may be controlled. For instance, it is believed that aging is controlled by regulatory genes and that the aging process could be arrested if the cytoplasmic products that influence the aging regulatory genes could be controlled.

2. *Recombinant DNA:* In 1973 scientists discovered that certain types of enzymes, called **restriction enzymes,** could be used to "cut" the DNA at specific sites. This has enabled scientists to cut out specific genes, which can then be spliced into a different organism. For instance, the human gene for insulin has been spliced into the genetic system of a bacterium. The resulting bacterial progeny produced human insulin, which is marketed under the name Humulin. In the future, it may be possible to replace defective genes with normal ones.

3. *Artificial genes:* In 1976 it was announced that a completely **artificial gene,** used to replace a defective gene in a virus, had been synthesized. Will we be able to manufacture genes that will make us have more endurance, be resistant to disease, and be more intelligent? Perhaps these "designer genes" will be the wave of the future.

4. *Cloning:* Humulin was made possible, in part, by cloning. **Cloning** is the process of producing a group of genes, cells, or whole organisms that have the same genetic constitution. Once the human gene for adrenalin was introduced into bacteria by recombinant DNA techniques, repeated mitosis in the bacteria continued to produce the same gene over and over again. The gene originated from a body (somatic) cell, not from a sex cell.

Whole organisms can be cloned. In fact, a type of cloning has been done with plants for years. If humans were to be cloned, then any number of genetically identical people could be produced.

Only the imagination limits what genetic-engineering feats could be accomplished by combining techniques involving the control of regulator genes, recombinant DNA, artificial genes, and cloning. Other aspects of genetic engineering may also become applicable to humans in the future. You are referred to the suggested readings for more information on this subject.

The new genetic techniques are exciting to some, but others consider them extremely dangerous. Many of those who see danger think of Aldous Huxley's *Brave New World,* in which classes of people were genetically created to serve an elitist race of rulers.[2] The potential for this type of world is only one of the problems that may greet the generations of the future. Some of the other problems will be discussed in Chapters 6 and 19.

---

[1] M. W. Strickberger, *Genetics,* 3d ed. (New York: Macmillan, 1985), 782.
[2] A. Huxley, *Brave New World* (New York: Harper & Row, 1946).

gens themselves are large protein molecules found on the surface of the red blood cells.

The inheritance of ABO blood types involves three alleles (I^A, I^B, and i). Two of these alleles are dominant with respect to i: I^A results in the production of the A antigen, and I^B in the production of the B antigen. In relationship to each other, alleles I^A and I^B are said to be codominant in that an $I^A I^B$ individual produces both antigens. The allele i is recessive and does not result in antigen production. The various genotypes and phenotypes are summarized in Table 4–4.

The ABO system is unusual in that the antibodies are present before exposure to the antigen. Thus, type A individuals have anti-B in their plasma and type B individuals have anti-A. Furthermore, an AB individual has neither antibody, while an O individual has both.

Because of the presence of antibodies in the blood, blood transfusions can be risky if the blood is not accurately typed and administrated. If, for example, type A blood is given to a type O individual, the anti-A present in the recipient's blood will agglutinate all the type A cells entering the recipient's body. **Agglutination** refers to a clumping together of red cells, forming small clots that may block blood vessels.

Table 4–5 shows the consequences of various types of blood transfusions. An individual with blood type O is often referred to as a universal donor because the entering O cells lack antigens of this system and therefore cannot be agglutinated. However, type O blood does contain anti-A and anti-B, which can cause damage in an A, B, or AB recipient. Although such damage is minimal, since the introduced antibodies become diluted and are rapidly absorbed by the

TABLE 4–5

RESULTS OF BLOOD TRANSFUSIONS*

RECIPIENT	DONOR			
	A	B	O	AB
A	−	+	(+)	+
B	+	−	(+)	+
O	+	+	−	+
AB	(+)	(+)	(+)	−

*+ indicates heavy agglutination of donor's cells. (+) indicates no agglutination of donor's cells, but antibodies in donor's blood may cause some agglutination of recipient's cells. − indicates no agglutination of donor's cells.

body tissues, the safest transfusions are between people of the same blood type.

THE RH SYSTEM   Another major blood-type system, which is a great deal more complex than the ABO system, is the **Rh blood-type system.** This blood-type system is polygenic and has multiple alleles, resulting in many antigens. In the United States and Europe a problem arises with respect to one of these antigens (Rh_0). About 15 percent of the people in this population lack this antigen; these people, who are homozygous recessive, are Rh-negative (Rh−).

Although Rh compatibility can cause problems in transfusion, it is of greater interest as the cause of **erythroblastosis fetalis,** a **hemolytic** (blood cell-destroying) disease affecting 1 out of every 150 to 200 newborns. The problem occurs when an Rh-negative mother carries an Rh-positive fetus. At birth Rh antigens in the fetal blood can mix with the maternal blood, causing the production of the antibody anti-Rh in the mother's blood. Although the first few pregnancies usually do not present any danger to the fetus, eventually the anti-Rh levels in the mother's blood become fairly high. At this point, if the anti-Rh comes into contact with the fetal bloodstream, it can cause destruction of the fetal blood cells (Figure 4–22).

The Rh problem can be handled by an interesting medical technique. Very shortly after each birth of an Rh-positive child to an Rh-negative mother, the mother is given an injection of synthetic anti-Rh, which suppresses her own pro-

TABLE 4–4

PHENOTYPES AND GENOTYPES OF THE ABO BLOOD-TYPE SYSTEM

TYPE	ANTIGEN	ANTIBODY	GENOTYPE
A	A	Anti-B	$I^A I^A$, $I^A i$
B	B	Anti-A	$I^B I^B$, $I^B i$
O	—	Anti-A, Anti-B	ii
AB	A, B	—	$I^A I^B$

Rh⁻ mother   Rh⁻ mother   Rh⁻ mother

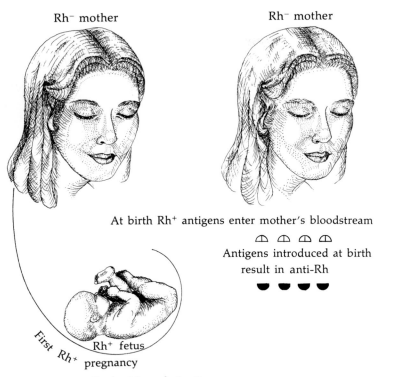

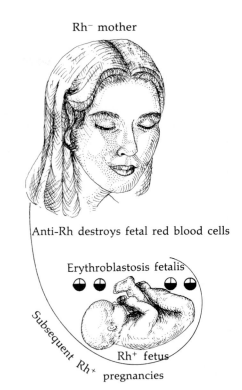

At birth Rh⁺ antigens enter mother's bloodstream

Antigens introduced at birth result in anti-Rh

Anti-Rh destroys fetal red blood cells

Erythroblastosis fetalis

First Rh⁺ pregnancy

Rh⁺ fetus

Subsequent Rh⁺ pregnancies

Rh⁺ fetus

FIGURE 4–22 *Erythroblastosis fetalis.*

duction of the antibodies. Soon the injected antibodies disappear, leaving the mother's blood free of any anti-Rh and, therefore, safe for future pregnancies. It is now also possible to transfuse the fetus while it is still in the uterus.

OTHER BLOOD-TYPE SYSTEMS   There are many other blood-type systems that are known for human blood, including the MNSs, Diego, P, Lutheran, Kell, Lewis, Duffy, Kidd, Auberger, Sutter, and Xg. Because each of these systems consists of many diverse antigens, the probability of two persons' having an identical combination of antigens is small. Also, research indicates that certain antigens and frequencies of antigens tend to be found in particular geographical regions. This will be discussed in Chapter 8.

Summary

Processes like inheritance can be understood on many levels. In the years after Mendel proposed his model for inheritance, scientists began in-

vestigating the chemical nature of genetic transmission. Their examinations have revealed that the genetic material is a nucleic acid, DNA. DNA controls cell activities and hence determines inherited physical characteristics. DNA, which has the ability to replicate itself, is also the mechanism through which one generation passes its characteristics on to the next. The information contained in the DNA molecule is coded by the arrangement of base pairs, and small errors in any of the base pairs can have extreme consequences. The information on the nuclear DNA molecule is transmitted by messenger RNA to the ribosome, the site of protein manufacture, where transfer RNA functions to bring the appropriate amino acids into position.

On the molecular level, a gene is a segment of the DNA molecule that codes for a particular functioning protein or segment of a protein. Mutations arise when a random change occurs in this code, and they increase genotypic variation by creating "new" alleles. The various alleles of a particular gene are simply slight variants in the code itself.

Blood studies have traditionally been important to anthropology because they provide a relatively easy way to study genetically controlled variability in human populations. A number of proteins in blood are present in some people and absent in others. The study of blood types and other biological systems has further expanded Mendelian genetics by, for instance, providing examples of traits with more than two alleles.

STUDY QUESTIONS

1. How does the process of meiosis tend to confirm Mendel's observations of segregation and independent assortment? Is independent assortment an unbroken rule, or are there exceptions?
2. Could life exist without meiosis? If so, how would it differ from present life? If not, why not?
3. In what ways does oogenesis differ from spermatogenesis? Because of these differences, does the mother's genetic contribution differ from that of the father? In what way?
4. An important feature of meiosis is the reduction in chromosome number. What is the significance of this reduction?
5. In terms of the chemical structure of DNA, what is a gene? Is the concept of a gene a valid one?
6. What is mitochondrial DNA? How does it differ from nuclear DNA? What is known about the function of mtDNA genes?
7. Why are studies of the genetics of blood types of more use to anthropologists than studies of IQ or skin color?

SUGGESTED READINGS

Drlica, K. *Understanding DNA and Gene Cloning: A Guide for the Curious.* New York: Wiley, 1984. Written for people with little background in chemistry, this book describes the chemical processes and molecular structures of DNA. Cloning is also explained.

Kevles, D. J. *In the Name of Eugenics.* Berkeley: University of California Press, 1986. This book outlines the history of eugenics in the United States and Great Britain.

Lewin, B. *Genes,* 5th ed. Oxford: Oxford University Press, 1993. This is a popular introductory text on general genetics. It presents an encyclopedic treatment of genetics and as such is an excellent reference book.

Watson, J. D., et al. *Molecular Biology of the Gene,* 4th ed. Menlo Park, Calif.: Benjamin/Cummings, 1987. This two-volume set, written by five researchers and teachers, including one of the discoverers of the structure of DNA, gives a detailed discussion of DNA and gene structure.

GENETICS: FROM CELLS TO DNA

Cell   Nucleus

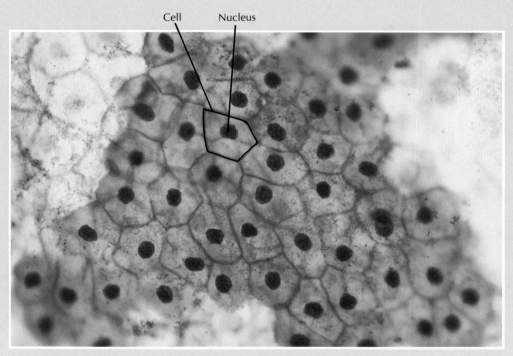

FIGURE 4-A Most living organisms are either single cells or are made up of cells. Here is a picture of human skin cells as they appear under a microscope. The nuclei appear dark because they have been stained with a purple dye. The chromosomes, which contain the genetic material, are found within the nuclei.

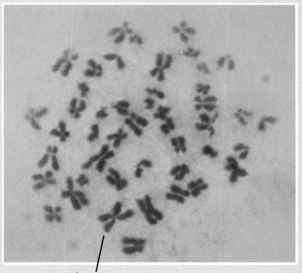

FIGURE 4-B The genetic material is contained within bodies known as chromosomes. Pictured here is a complete set of 46 chromosomes obtained from a white blood cell from a normal human female.

A chromosome

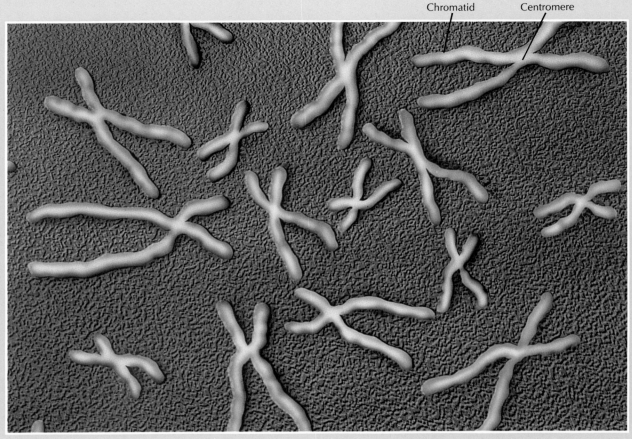

Chromatid   Centromere

FIGURE 4-C The structure of the chromosome can be clearly seen in this photograph of chromosomes obtained from a white blood cell from a normal human female. Each chromosome consists of two strands, or chromatids, connected by a structure called a centromere. Note that chromosomes differ in size and in the position of the centromere.

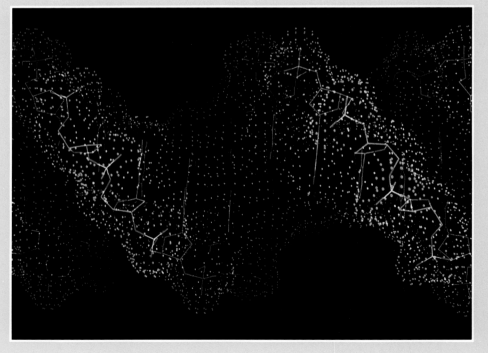

FIGURE 4-D The genetic information is coded in the DNA molecule, located within the chromosome. This molecule, the largest molecule in living organisms, is composed of units that form a double helix. The three-dimensional structure of DNA is seen in this model.

Mennonites from Lancaster County, Pennsylvania, an example of a reproductive population.

The object is to combine certain ideas derived from a consideration of . . . a population of organisms, with the concepts of the factorial scheme of inheritance, so as to state the principle of Natural Selection in the form of a rigorous mathematical theorem.[1]

R. A. Fisher (1890–1962)

[1]R. A. Fisher, *The Genetical Theory of Natural Selection* (Oxford: Clarendon Press, 1930).

CHAPTER
5

POPULATION GENETICS

In 1930 R. A. Fisher published a book that evaluated Darwin's theory in terms of mathematics and statistics. In *The Genetical Theory of Natural Selection,* Fisher described equations that showed how genetic diversity within populations allows more possibilities for adapting to environments.

The individual is not the unit of evolution, although a person does change over time. An individual gets taller and heavier, and perhaps his or her hair changes color; other changes occur that are variously labeled "growth," "development," and "decline." Yet although an individual today is not the same individual he or she will be tomorrow, that person is not evolving. Likewise, evolution is not occurring when people produce offspring different from themselves. For no two individuals, whether contemporaries or living at different times or whether related or unrelated, are exactly alike. Variation is not evolution. Evolution is change that can lead to the development of new kinds of populations, and the population is the unit of evolutionary change.

Up to this point we have been mainly concerned with the mechanisms of heredity in the individual and in family groups. This chapter focuses on the dynamics of populations and various mathematical principles that measure genetic changes in populations.

A MODEL OF POPULATION GENETICS

Populations

A population is a group of genetically related individuals. The unit of evolution is the **reproductive population.** The reproductive population can be defined as a group of organisms potentially capable of successful reproduction.

Successful reproduction requires sexual behavior culminating in copulation, fertilization, normal development of the fetus, and production of offspring that are normal and healthy and capable of reproducing in turn. A number of conditions can prevent closely related populations from exchanging genes by preventing successful reproduction. One way in which this occurs is if the sexual behavior of the male, such as the mating dance of birds, fails to stimulate the female of a closely related population. Several types of reproductive isolating mechanisms are discussed in Chapter 6.

Of course, successful reproduction of a population requires a rate of reproduction sufficient to sustain the population. The number of individuals produced each generation must be great enough to compensate for deaths due to accident, predation, disease, and so on. However, the rate of reproduction cannot be so great that the population will increase to the point at which it can no longer be supported by its food sources or other elements in the environment. In other words, a successful reproductive rate is one that maintains a balance between population size and the potentials and limitations of the environment.

The largest reproductive population is the **species.** The members of a species are potentially capable of successful reproduction among themselves but not with members of other species. Species can be broken down into smaller reproductive populations, which are to some degree and often temporarily isolated from one another (Chapter 6).

PHENOTYPE OF A POPULATION   Just as one can speak of the phenotype of an individual, one can also speak of the phenotype of a population. Since a population is made up of varied individuals, such a description must be handled statistically. For example, one can calculate the average stature for a population and the variation from that average. It is also possible to calculate the percentage of blood-type O, blue eyes, red hair, and so on, and emerge with a statistical profile.

As stated earlier, no two individuals are ever alike; the number of possible combinations of alleles is staggering. Nevertheless, the frequency of alleles in a population may remain relatively constant over many generations. What we have are individuals being formed out of a pool of genes that can be combined in an almost infinite number of ways. New combinations do not necessarily change the frequency of any gene in the next generation (Figure 5–1).

GENOTYPE OF A POPULATION   The sum of all alleles carried by the members of a population is known as the **gene pool.** The frequency of alleles in the gene pool can be calculated with formulas that will be discussed in a moment. Since each body cell has the same genetic components, each individual can be thought of as contributing one of these cells to the gene pool. From these cells the genes can be extracted and tallied.

For example, if the alleles for PTC tasting in a population are tallied, the result may be that 41.3 percent of them are dominant (T) and 58.7 percent are recessive (t). Further examination may reveal that 17.1 percent of the genotypes that emerge from the gene pool of PTC alleles are homozygous dominant, whereas 48.4 percent are heterozygous and 34.5 percent are homozygous recessive. A complete statistical description of the genotype of a population would require that we know the frequency of every allele in the gene pool.

Genetic Equilibrium

Before we discuss the mechanisms of evolution, evolution must first be defined. **Biological evolution** can be defined as a change in the gene pool of a population. So, for example, if the frequency of the allele T changes from 41.3 percent to 44.1 percent, we can say that the population has evolved.

Gene pools   Genotypes

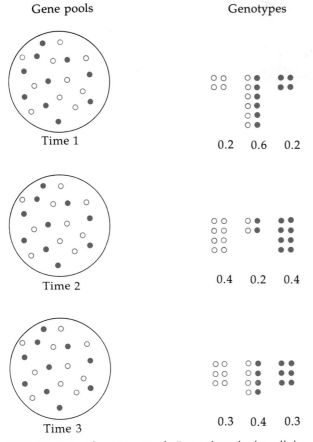

Time 1   0.2   0.6   0.2

Time 2   0.4   0.2   0.4

Time 3   0.3   0.4   0.3

FIGURE 5–1 *The gene pool.* Even though the allele frequencies remain constant, the genotype frequencies can differ through time.

A population is evolving if the frequencies of its alleles are changing. It is not evolving if these frequencies remain constant, a situation termed **genetic equilibrium.** Since several factors can bring about frequency changes, it is best to begin with a consideration of genetic equilibrium and then to follow with a separate consideration of each factor that brings about change.

A MODEL OF GENETIC EQUILIBRIUM   In building a model of genetic equilibrium, we can simplify things by considering only one gene. This gene occurs in two allelic forms, *A* and *a*, each with a frequency of ½. The symbol *f* will be used to indicate "relative frequency of." Therefore, $f(A) = ½$, and $f(a) = ½$. If these are the only

alleles for this gene, the relative frequencies must add up to 1, or unity:

$$f(A) + f(a) = ½ + ½ = 1$$

This model presents a hypothetical situation of no change, but the fact that populations *do* change is what makes the model important. By being able to specify under what conditions a static situation would exist, we can see, measure, and analyze change.

Certain conditions must be assumed for a population to remain in genetic equilibrium. Mutation must not be taking place. The population must be infinitely large so that change does not occur by chance. There must not be any **gene flow;** that is, individuals from other groups must not introduce alleles into the population. Mating must take place at random, that is, without any design or propensity of one kind for another. These matings must be equally fertile; that is, they must produce the same number of viable offspring. Deviation from equilibrium shows that one or a combination of these conditions is not being met.

If the relative frequencies of the alleles are each ½, what are the relative frequencies of the different individual genotypes? If $f(A) = ½$, it follows that $f(AA) = ½ × ½ = ¼$. So, one-fourth of the population is homozygous dominant. Similarly, $f(Aa) = 2 × ½ × ½ = ½$. Why the number 2? Because we are including two separate cases, *Aa* and *aA*. While the origin of the alleles differs in each, the genotype is the same. Therefore, one-half the population is heterozygous. Finally $f(aa) = ½ × ½ = ¼$; one-fourth of the population is homozygous recessive.

Now let the individuals within this population mate at random. The possible matings are $AA × AA$, $AA × Aa$, $AA × aa$, $Aa × Aa$, $Aa × aa$, and $aa × aa$. Three of the six matings can be accomplished in two ways; for example, $AA × Aa$ can also be $Aa × AA$. To simplify matters in each of these three cases, the two situations will be combined as one mating.

How frequent is each of the mating types? To find out, we multiply the frequencies of each genotype. For example, the frequency of the first type, $AA × AA$, is $¼ × ¼ = 1/16$. In the case in which mating types can be accomplished in two ways, the number 2 must be included. The relative frequencies of the mating types are shown in Table 5–1; note that the frequencies add up to 1.

The next step is to calculate the frequency of progeny produced. We are interested in seeing how the relative frequencies of the alleles change between generations. Table 5–2 presents a series of calculations showing the contribution of each mating type to the next generation. The first case, $AA \times AA$, occurs one-sixteenth of the time and therefore produces one-sixteenth of all the offspring. Since all these offspring are AA, we can say that this mating type contributes one-sixteenth AA children to the next generation, as shown in the AA column in Table 5–2.

The second case, $AA \times Aa$, which accounts for one-fourth of all matings, produces one-fourth of all the offspring. Of these offspring, one-half are AA and one-half are Aa. Since ½ of ¼ is ⅛, ⅛ is placed in the AA column and in the Aa column. The same procedure is followed for calculating the contributions of the other mating types. When each column is added up, we see that one-fourth of the offspring are AA, one-half Aa, and one-fourth aa. In other words, the relative frequencies of the varying genotypes have remained unchanged from the previous generation. The population is therefore in genetic equilibrium.

THE HARDY-WEINBERG EQUILIBRIUM   The above calculations were first made independently by Godfrey Hardy and Wilhelm Weinberg in 1908 and are known as the **Hardy-Weinberg equilibrium.** This equilibrium, described above using

TABLE 5–1

FREQUENCIES OF MATING TYPES

MATING TYPE	FREQUENCY
$AA \times AA$	¼ × ¼ = ¹⁄₁₆
$AA \times Aa$	2 × ¼ × ½ = ¼
$AA \times aa$	2 × ¼ × ¼ = ⅛
$Aa \times Aa$	½ × ½ = ¼
$Aa \times aa$	2 × ½ × ¼ = ¼
$aa \times aa$	¼ × ¼ = ¹⁄₁₆
Total	1

TABLE 5–2

CONTRIBUTIONS OF MATING TYPES TO THE NEXT GENERATION

MATING TYPE	FREQUENCY	OFFSPRING AA	Aa	aa
$AA \times AA$	¹⁄₁₆	¹⁄₁₆		
$AA \times Aa$	¼	⅛	⅛	
$AA \times aa$	⅛		⅛	
$Aa \times Aa$	¼	¹⁄₁₆	⅛	¹⁄₁₆
$Aa \times aa$	¼		⅛	⅛
$aa \times aa$	¹⁄₁₆			¹⁄₁₆
Total		¼	½	¼

a specific case, can also be developed algebraically (Table 5–3). This results in the following general formula for the Hardy-Weinberg equilibrium:

$$p^2 + 2pq + q^2 = 1$$

where $p = f(A)$ and $q = f(a)$, from which it follows that

$$f(AA) = p^2 \qquad f(Aa) = 2pq \qquad f(aa) = q^2$$

The assumptions necessary for this formula have already been listed: no mutation, infinite population size, no gene flow, random mating, and equal fertility. Since these conditions can never hold true for any population, the Hardy-Weinberg formula defines a model that can be used to test hypotheses about gene pools and the evolutionary forces that work on them.

Using the Genetic-Equilibrium Model

While no population is actually in genetic equilibrium, some do come close. For the sake of illustration, we will first look at a hypothetical population that is large; we will focus on a trait that does not play a role in mate selection and does not influence fertility or survival to any appreciable degree. That trait is PTC tasting, which was discussed in Chapter 3.

TABLE 5–3

ALGEBRAIC DERIVATION OF HARDY-WEINBERG EQUILIBRIUM

ALLELE	FREQUENCY	GENOTYPE	FREQUENCY OF GENOTYPE IN POPULATION
A	p	AA	p^2
a	q	Aa	$2pq$
		aa	q^2

OFFSPRING RESULTING FROM RANDOM MATINGS

PARENTS	FREQUENCY OF MATING TYPES	FREQUENCY OF OFFSPRING		
		AA	Aa	aa
AA × AA	$p^2 \times p^2 = p^4$	p^4	—	—
AA × Aa	$2 \times p^2 \times 2pq = 4p^3q$	$2p^3q$	$2p^3q$	—
AA × aa	$2 \times p^2 \times q^2 = 2p^2q^2$	—	$2p^2q^2$	—
Aa × Aa	$2pq \times 2pq = 4p^2q^2$	p^2q^2	$2p^2q^2$	p^2q^2
Aa × aa	$2 \times 2pq \times q^2 = 4pq^3$	—	$2pq^3$	$2pq^3$
aa × aa	$q^2 \times q^2 = q^4$	—	—	q^4

$$f(AA) = p^4 + 2p^3q + p^2q^2 = p^2(p^2 + 2pq + q^2) = p^2(1) = p^2$$
$$f(Aa) = 2p^3q + 2p^2q^2 + 2p^2q^2 + 2pq^3 = 2pq(p^2 + pq + pq + q^2) = 2pq(1) = 2pq$$
$$f(aa) = p^2q^2 + 2pq^3 + q^4 = q^2(p^2 + 2pq + q^2) = q^2(1) = q^2$$

PTC TASTING   In taking a random survey of a hypothetical population, we find that out of 1000 individuals tested, 640 are tasters and 360 are nontasters. What are the relative frequencies of the alleles T and t, and how many tasters are carriers of the recessive allele?

Since 360 out of 1000 individuals are nontasters, and hence tt, we can set up the equation $q^2 = 0.36$, where q^2 is the proportion of homozygous recessive individuals and 0.36 is the decimal equivalent of $^{360}\!/_{1000}$. If $q^2 = 0.36$, then $q = 0.6$ (0.6 being the square root of 0.36). If $q = 0.6$, then p must equal 0.4 (since $p + q = 1$). Therefore, 40 percent of the alleles in the gene pool are dominant T, while 60 percent are recessive t. This may be surprising at first since the majority of the individuals are tasters, yet the majority of the alleles are for nontasting. This means that most of the recessive alleles must be found in the heterozygous condition and are therefore not phenotypically expressed.

What proportion of the population consists of heterozygous tasters (carriers)? The answer is $2pq$, or 48 percent ($2 \times 0.4 \times 0.6$). Only 16 percent ($p^2 = 0.4 \times 0.4$) are homozygous dominant tasters, and 36 percent are nontasters.

PHENYLKETONURIA   In England, approximately 1 out of every 40,000 children is born with the metabolic abnormality PKU.[2] Several questions may be asked: How frequent is the defective allele in the gene pool? What is the probability that an individual in the population will be a carrier? What is the probability that two normal individuals mating at random will have a child with PKU? This is not a case of genetic equilibrium since the assumptions for genetic equilibrium are not being met. For example, until very recently, children with PKU did not grow up and reproduce. However, we can assume genetic equilibrium and use the Hardy-Weinberg formula to estimate the answers to these questions.

---

[2]The incidence of PKU in England ranges between 2 and 6 per 100,000; 1/40000 falls within this range. See T. A. Munro, "Phenylketonuria: Data of 47 British Families," *Annals of Eugenics*, 14 (1947), 60–88.

BOX 5–1

POPULATION GENETICS: EXERCISES

These exercises are meant to check on your understanding of the basic mathematical principles of the genetic equilibrium formula. All data in these exercises are hypothetical.

SITUATION 1

The MN blood-type system is one in which the heterogeneous genotype shows codominance. On a small island, the results of blood group testing for the MN blood group yield the following data: M, 12 islanders; MN, 24 islanders; N, 12 islanders. What is the gene frequency of the M and N alleles in this population? Is this population in genetic equilibrium?

SOLUTION

There are two ways that allelic frequencies can be calculated. The first starts out as a simple counting exercise. There are 48 people on the island, representing 96 alleles (2 alleles per cell). We know that each person who is blood-type M has two M alleles, and so the 12 people who are M represent 24 M

alleles. The 24 islanders who are MN have 24 M alleles (and 24 N alleles). So the total number of M alleles on the island is 24 + 24, or 48. The relative frequency of M [abbreviated as $f(M)$] is $^{48}/_{96}$ or 0.5. The 96 is 2 times 48 islanders. Each islander contributes two alleles per cell to the MN system. Since $f(M) + f(N)$ equals 1, $f(N) = 1 - 0.5$, or 0.5.

The second way of achieving the same result is based on knowledge of the relative genotypic frequencies. We know the following:

$$f(MM) = {}^{12}/_{48} = 0.25$$

$$f(MN) = {}^{24}/_{48} = 0.5$$

$$f(NN) = {}^{12}/_{48} = 0.25$$

Therefore,

$$f(M) = f(MM) + \tfrac{1}{2}f(MN)$$
$$= 0.25 + \tfrac{1}{2}(0.5)$$
$$= 0.25 + 0.25 = 0.5$$

$$f(N) = \tfrac{1}{2}f(MN) + f(NN)$$
$$= \tfrac{1}{2}(0.5) + 0.25$$
$$= 0.25 + 0.25 = \underline{0.5}$$
$$1.0$$

To determine if the population is in genetic equilibrium, we compare the observed genotypic frequencies (or number of individuals with each genotype) with what would be expected if the formula $p^2 + 2pq + q^2 = 1$ were applied.

	MM	MN	NN
Observed number of islanders	12	24	12 = 48
Observed frequency	0.25	0.50	0.25 = 1
Expected frequency	p^2	$2pq$	q^2
	$(0.5)^2$	$2(0.5 \times 0.5)$	$(0.5)^2$
	0.25	0.50	0.25
Expected number of islanders	0.25×48	0.50×48	0.25×48
	12	24	12

If the rate of abnormality is 1 child out of 40,000, then the relative frequency of the trait is $^{1}/_{40000}$, or 0.000025 (0.0025 percent). Therefore, $f(kk) = q^2 = 0.000025$, and so $q = 0.005$. This means that 0.5 percent of the gene pool is k, while 99.5 percent ($p = 0.995$) is the normal allele K.

What is the probability of being a carrier? The answer is $2pq$, which equals 0.00995 ($2 \times 0.995 \times 0.005$) and is rounded off to 0.01. Therefore, approximately 1 percent of the members of the population are carriers, which is 1 out of 100 in-

dividuals. This is a large number, especially when we realize that only 1 out of 40,000 actually has the disease.

What is the probability that two persons mating at random will have a PKU child? The probability of being a carrier is 0.01, and so the probability of two persons being carriers is 0.01 × 0.01, or 0.0001. If both are carriers, 1 out of every 4 of their children will be expected to have the defect. When 0.0001 (the probability that both will be carriers) is multiplied by ¼ (the probability that two carriers will have a PKU child), the

Since the expected frequencies (and number of islanders) match the observed, the population is in genetic equilibrium.

SITUATION 2

On a second island, the following results were obtained: M, 12 islanders; MN, 12 islanders; and N, 24 islanders. What are the frequencies of M and N?

SOLUTION

The number of M alleles in the population, again counting the content of one cell, is $f(M) = 2(12) + 12 = 36$. Likewise, the number of N alleles in the population is $f(N) = 12 + 2(24) = 60$. The total number of alleles for this trait is 2×48, or 96, and so the frequency of M and N is

$$f(M) = \tfrac{36}{96} = 0.375$$

$$f(N) = \tfrac{60}{96} = 0.625$$

The population is not in genetic equilibrium because of the following facts:

The observed number of islanders is as follows: MM, 12; MN, 12; NN, 24. The expected number of islanders, if the population were in equilibrium, would be 6.72 MM, 22.58 MN, and 18.72 NN, as shown below (answers have been rounded off):

$$p^2 = (0.375)^2 = 0.14$$
$$0.14 \times 48 = 6.72$$

$$2pq = 2(0.375 \times 0.625) = 0.47$$
$$0.47 \times 48 = 22.58$$

$$q^2 = (0.625)^2 = 0.39$$
$$0.39 \times 48 = 18.72$$

ADDITIONAL PROBLEMS

What are the relative gene frequencies in the following two populations? Which of the two populations is in genetic equilibrium? The number under each genotype refers to the number of islanders who possess each genotype.

	MM	MN	NN
Population 1	32	16	2
Population 2	10	10	10

ANSWERS

(1) 0.8 M, 0.2 N; population is in genetic equilibrium.
(2) 0.5 M, 0.5 N; population is not in genetic equilibrium.

answer is 0.000025, or ¼0000. (For further problems, see Box 5–1.)

It is obvious from the above that populations contain large reservoirs of deleterious alleles hidden in the heterozygous condition. In fact, estimates show that every one carries an average of three to five recessive alleles that in a homozygous condition would lead to death or disablement. The term **genetic load** refers to the totality of deleterious alleles in a population. The expression of this genetic load is responsible for certain natural abortions and abnormal conditions such as PKU.

DEMONSTRATING GENETIC EQUILIBRIUM

The Hardy-Weinberg formula can also be used to show if a population is in genetic equilibrium with respect to a particular trait. With this information, we can gain some idea of the impact of the forces of evolutionary change upon the population. We can take as an example a hypothetical population with the following genotypic frequencies: $f(AA) = 0.34$, $f(Aa) = 0.46$, and $f(aa) = 0.20$. To find the frequency of A, we add the frequency of the AA individuals, who contribute only A alleles to the gene pool, and one-half the frequency of the Aa individuals since only one-half of their alleles are *A*. Therefore, $f(A) = p = f(AA) + \frac{1}{2}f(Aa) = 0.34 + 0.23 = 0.57$. Since $p = 0.57$, $q = 0.43$.

To determine whether this population is in genetic equilibrium with respect to this gene, we take the calculated allele frequencies and compute the expected frequencies of the genotypes. Thus, the expected frequencies are

$$f(AA) = p^2 = (0.57)^2 = 0.325$$

$$f(Aa) = 2pq = 2 \times 0.57 \times 0.43 = 0.490$$

and

$$f(aa) = q^2 = (0.43)^2 = 0.185$$

When these figures are compared with the observed frequencies, they do not agree. The amount of disagreement between the expected and observed frequencies may or may not be statistically significant. (Methods exist for determining significance, but they will not be discussed here.) Therefore, our population is not in genetic equilibrium with respect to this gene.

Summary

The unit of evolution is the reproductive population. Such a population is described, in statistical terms, as having both a phenotype and a genotype. The genotype of a population is referred to as the gene pool. The gene pool is composed of all the alleles carried by the members of a population. As the frequencies of alleles within the gene pool change, the population evolves. Conversely, if the allele frequencies remain constant, the population does not evolve; it is said to be in a state of genetic equilibrium. Genetic equilibrium, however, can be only a hypothetical state because the evolutionary forces of mutation, finite population size, gene flow, nonrandom mating, and unequal fertility are always present and lead to change.

Using the Hardy-Weinberg formula, we can measure the strength of evolutionary forces by making comparisons between the hypothetical situation of no change and observed situations of change. Also, the formula can be used to calculate the frequencies of specific alleles and specific genotypes, such as carriers, within a population.

MECHANISMS OF EVOLUTIONARY CHANGE

In the model of a population in genetic equilibrium, the frequencies of the alleles in the gene pool remain constant. Such a population is not evolving. However, in order to have genetic equilibrium, five requirements must be met: (1) no mutation, (2) infinite population size, (3) absence of gene flow, (4) random mating, and (5) equal fertility. Since no natural population meets these requirements, it follows that all populations must be evolving. The mechanisms of evolutionary change are mutation, small population size, gene flow, nonrandom mating, and differential fertility rates. Proposing the conditions under which no evolution will occur allows us to measure the degree to which evolution is occurring.

Mutations

A **mutation** is any alteration in the genetic material, such as a change at a particular point on the DNA molecule (**point mutation**) or an aberration of the chromosome (Chapter 4). These changes are chance changes. A point mutation, for example, is a chance alteration of a single base in the DNA molecule.

Mutations do not arise to fulfill a need; they are chance alterations. Organisms do not sense a change or potential change in the environment and then "decide to" mutate; nor are there innate mechanisms that can provide predictions of what future environmental conditions will be like. Mutations arise with no design, no predetermined reason or purpose; in other words, they are random. However, mutation is the ultimate source of all variation within the gene pool. It creates variability rather than directly bringing about evolutionary change.

What is the probability that a chance alteration of the genetic code will be advantageous to the organism? Imagine that a Shakespearean sonnet is being transcribed into Morse code. Suppose that in the process a dot is selected at random and replaced with a dash. What is the probability that this change will improve the poem? Probably it will result in a misspelled word; it might even change the word and, hence, the meaning.

Likewise, the probability that a chance alteration in the genetic code will bring about an improvement is very low. In fact, mutations are usually deleterious to individual organisms. An individual who has a mutation that is expressed in the phenotype is often less fit than other members of the population and produces fewer offspring. Mutations that are advantageous, or at least neutral, are usually very subtle and are difficult to notice in the phenotype.

Whereas mutations are generally deleterious to an individual, they provide genotypic variation for a population. The environment that a population is adapted to at one time may not be the same at another time. Mutations within a population represent a potential for meeting new conditions as they arise. Put another way, mutations are often not fit for the environments they originate in, but they might provide the genotypic variation needed to survive in a new environment. Mutations provide one mechanism to keep the population viable.

HOW DO MUTATIONS OCCUR?   A mutation may occur **spontaneously,** that is, in response to the usual conditions within the body or environment, or it may be **induced** by human-created agents. In both cases, some factor actively causes the mutation to occur. The exact cause of any specific mutation usually cannot be determined, although in experimental situations various agents can be shown to increase the frequency of the occurrence of mutations.

Geneticists believe, however, that many point mutations result from mistakes in the replication of the DNA molecule. Thus, if in the replication of the codon ATA (tyrosine) the incorrect complementary base is incorporated into the DNA molecule, the new codon might read AAA (phenylalanine), resulting in an amino acid substitution. Once the alteration occurs, it becomes the basis for replication of additional DNA with the same error. All but two amino acids are coded by more than one codon, and so some mutations can be genetically neutral. For example, if the codon ATA mutated to ATG, there would be no change in the amino acid since both codons code for the same amino acid, in this case tyrosine.

The factors that initiate spontaneous mutations are for the most part unknown. It was once thought that background radiation from the general environment accounted for the majority of the observed spontaneous mutations, but most geneticists now believe that this is not true. Naturally occurring chemicals and fluctuations in temperature may account for many spontaneous mutations.

The story is different for induced mutations. In 1927 H. J. Muller demonstrated that mutations could be induced in fruit flies by using x-rays. In fact, the increase in the frequency of mutations was directly proportional to the increase in the dosage of radiation (Figure 5–2). This discovery increased awareness of the dangers of artificial radiation from medical or occupational exposure and from nuclear fallout. Although the U.S. Atomic Energy Commission had set what are considered to be safe levels of radiation, it can generally be said that any induced radiation increases the rate of mutation beyond the spontaneous rate.

Certain chemicals added to foods, compounded in medicines, or poured into the atmosphere or waters are known to cause mutations in bacteria, but the effects of many of these agents on multicellular animals are not yet known. Some of these substances, although they may enter the animal, may be kept from the chromosomes by plasma and nuclear membranes. Since many commonly used substances are suspect, it is important that they be fully investigated. In addition, certain viruses are known to cause mutations.

When mutations do occur, they may have no effect on the phenotype of the organism, as is the case, for example, when the mutant allele is a recessive. On the other hand, mutations can pro-

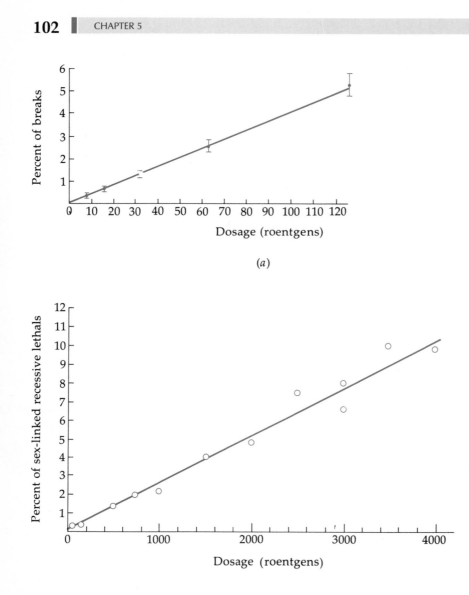

(a)

FIGURE 5–2 *Effects of radiation on the genetic material. (a)* X-ray dosage and frequency of induced chromosomal breaks in the cells of a grasshopper. *(b)* X-ray dosage and frequency of sex-linked recessive lethals induced in fruit fly spermatozoa.

duce phenotypic alterations that range from extremely subtle to drastic. If mutations occur in somatic cells, cell death and abnormal development, including cancer, could result. A single chance mutation taking place in a skin cell, for example, may have virtually no effect on the phenotype, yet the same isolated mutation taking place in a sex cell may have a significant effect on the individual conceived from that sex cell. Such a mutation may result in potentially valuable characteristics, abnormal conditions, or even inviable gametes.

How frequent are mutations? Although mutation rates vary from trait to trait, most estimates for mutations that occur in sex cells are about 1 in every 100,000 gametes per generation per gene (Table 5–4). When the large number of genes per gamete is considered, the probability of a particular gamete's carrying at least one new mutation is about ½. Since many of these new mutations are recessive, they probably will not cause any problems in the immediate offspring.

Effects of Small Population Size

The model of genetic equilibrium is mathematical and assumes an infinitely large population, but natural populations are not infinitely large.

TABLE 5–4

SOME ESTIMATED SPONTANEOUS MUTATION RATES IN HUMAN POPULATIONS

ABNORMALITY	INHERITANCE*	ESTIMATED MUTATION RATE (PER MILLION GAMETES PER GENERATION)	POPULATION	SOURCE†
Retinoblastoma	AD, v	6–7	German	1
Tay-Sachs disease	AR	11	Japanese	2
		4	European	2
Congenital total color blindness	AR	28	Japanese	2
		15	European	2
Albinism	AR	28	Japanese	2
		15	European	2
		33–70	Northern Irish	3
Hemophilia A	XR	13	North American	4
Hemophilia B	XR	0.5	North American	4

*AD = autosomal dominant; AR = autosomal recessive; XR = X-linked recessive, v = incomplete penetrance and/or variable expressivity.
†1 = F. Vogel, "Neue Untersuchen zür Genetik des Retinoblastoms," *Zeitschrift für menschliche Vererbungs und Konstitutionslehre,* 34 (1957), 230, 234; 2 = J. V. Neel et al., "The Incidence of Consanguineous Matings in Japan with Remarks on the Estimation of Comparative Gene Frequencies and the Expected Rate of Appearance of Induced Recessive Mutations," *American Journal of Human Genetics,* 1 (1949), 175–176; 3 = P. Froggart, "Albinism in Northern Ireland," *Annals of Human Genetics,* 24 (1960), 226–227, 231; 4 = I. Barrai et al. "The Effects of Parental Age on Rates of Mutation for Hemophilia and Evidence of Differing Mutation Rates for Hemophilia A and B," *American Journal of Human Genetics,* 20 (1968), 195.

When we deal with small populations, we often see changes in gene frequencies that are due to chance error.

SAMPLING ERROR   Political polls that predict the winners of elections can serve as examples of **sampling error.** Imagine it is election time and you have been hired by a candidate to predict the winner. Because of time and money limitations, you cannot possibly reach all 100,000 eligible voters, and so you decide to take a sample.

The first question is, How large must the sample be to represent the population adequately? If you take only 10 people, they might all be voting for the same person by pure chance. Maybe they are relatives and the only ones voting for this candidate! If you take a sample of 100 individuals, the predictive value of the poll might be increased. Here, too, you must protect against bias by not polling people who might be inclined toward one candidate because of their ethnic background, financial situation, party affiliation, and so forth. One way of achieving an unbiased sample is by randomly polling an adequate-sized sample. The actual size of a representative sample depends on the variation within the population. Statistical formulas can be used to determine what sample size is needed to ensure that predictions will be within a desired level of accuracy.

Consider another example: suppose you wish to take a representative sample of the colors of marking pens in a "population" of such pens. If the entire population is red, a sample of one will be sufficient. However, if there are 10 colors in various frequencies, the sample must be large enough to include all the colors *and* reflect their relative numbers. Any deviation from this would be a sampling error.

One more, slightly different example can be used: flipping coins. Since the odds of landing heads are ½, we would expect that one-half of the flips will always be heads. So, if you flip a coin 10 times, you would expect 5 heads; 100 times, 50 heads; and 1000 times, 500 heads. Yet if the coin is flipped the suggested number of times, the results might deviate from the predicted situation. If, for example, you flip the coin 10 times, you *might* end up with 5 heads; but any number from 0 to 10 is possible. Furthermore, if you flip the coin 10 times repeatedly, the number of heads will fluctuate from series to series

(Table 5–5). If a large number of flips, say, 1000, are performed, not only will you come closer to the ideal probability of ½ heads, but the fluctuations from one series to another will not be as dramatic (Table 5–6).

GENETIC DRIFT   As the genes in a gene pool are being passed from one generation to the next by gametes, we are, in effect, taking a sample. Just as in a sample of voters, colored pens, or coins, all the possibilities may not be represented. If the gene pool is large, and hence the number of matings great, the odds are high that the new gene pool will be fairly representative of the old one. If the gene pool is small, however, the new pool may deviate appreciably from the old. Such chance deviation in the frequency of alleles in a population is known as **genetic drift.**

Figure 5–3 plots the change of allele frequency through time as the result of genetic drift. Note that the fluctuations appear to be random and that, when the allele frequency is high, there is a strong possibility that it will reach 100 percent, with the alternate allele disappearing from the population.

TABLE 5–5

SAMPLING ERROR IN A SET OF ACTUAL TRIALS

POSSIBLE COMBINATIONS FOR TEN THROWS		TIMES COMBINATION THROWN	
HEADS	TAILS	NUMBER	PERCENT
10	0	0	0
9	1	0	0
8	2	3	3
7	3	7	8
6	4	23	26
5	5	23	26
4	6	13	15
3	7	12	14
2	8	5	7
1	9	1	1
0	10	0	0
		87	100

TABLE 5–6

POPULATION SIZE IN A SET OF ACTUAL TRIALS

NUMBER OF THROWS	NUMBER OF HEADS EXPECTED	NUMBER OF HEADS OBSERVED	DEVIATION FROM EXPECTED (%)
250	125	118	5.6
500	250	258	3.2
1000	500	497	0.6

Another form of genetic drift occurs as the result of **population bottlenecking.** This happens when a population is reduced for some reason, such as a natural disaster, to a small size. The initial reduction in the size of the population causes a reduction in variation because of the probability that some variants will be lost by chance as individuals are lost from the population. As the reduced population reproduces, the variability of ensuing populations is less than the variation that existed before the bottlenecking took place.

Recently Naoyuki Takahata and several other population geneticists proposed that a population bottleneck occurred sometime around 400,000 years ago that would explain why there is less genetic variation among humans worldwide than the genetic variation found among geographically close individuals of other species such as gorillas living in the same forest.[3] The proposed bottleneck might have reduced the number of reproducing humans from about 100,000 to about 10,000 individuals. Much of the diversity of the original population could have been lost by chance. The new population of 10,000 individuals would then have given rise to new generations of descendants with reduced variability. Not everyone agrees with this explanation for the relative lack of genetic diversity in modern populations. For example, some statisticians believe that a population of 10,000 is still too large to be a valid bottleneck.

---

[3]A. Gibbons, "The Mystery of Humanity's Missing Mutations," *Science,* 267 (1995), 35–36.

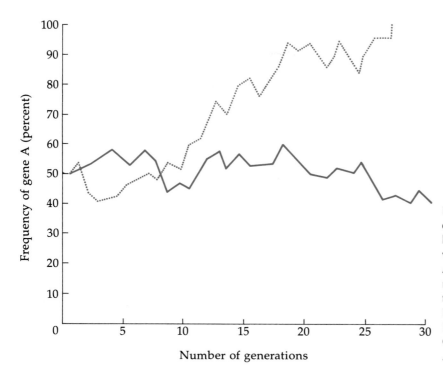

FIGURE 5–3 *Genetic drift.* This diagram traces genetic drift in two hypothetical populations, beginning with an allele frequency of 50 percent. After thirty generations, one allele has reached a frequency of 100 percent and the other has dropped to 40 percent. From "Genetic Drift in an Italian Population" by L. L. Cavalli-Sforza. Copyright © 1969 by Scientific American, Inc. All rights reserved.

FOUNDER PRINCIPLE Another form of drift involves the **founder principle,** which occurs if there is movement of a segment of a population to another area. The migrating group represents a sample of the original, larger population, but this sample is probably not a random representation of the original group. For instance, it may be made up of members from certain family groups whose gene frequencies vary considerably from the average of the original population. If the migrant population settles down in an uninhabited area or restricts mating to itself, it may become the founder population for the larger population that will develop from it (Figure 5–4), it may ultimately merge with other populations, or it may become extinct.

The founder principle is significant in many situations. For example, in a natural disaster, such as a flood or an epidemic, the surviving population may not be representative of the original population. Also, a colonizing group may differ markedly from the general population from which it comes. English descendants in the United States, Australia, and South Africa, for example, differ from each other as well as from the "mother" population.

The Xavante of the Amazon Basin provide an example of the founder principle. The Xavante live in villages with average populations of several hundred individuals. When a village becomes too large, it divides into two villages, each with 100 to 200 people. Consequently, the breeding size of each new village is smaller than that of the original village. The split into two villages

FIGURE 5–4 *Founder principle.* The founders of the new population represent a nonrandom sample of the original population.

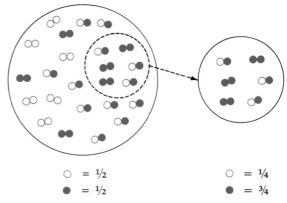

is largely along family lines. Since family members stay together, and many do not mate because of the incest taboo, the effective breeding size of the population is even smaller; that is, the number of potential mates is reduced even further from what we may assume from the size of the population alone. Therefore, the fission of the original village leads to the establishment of new populations that may by chance statistically differ from each other in terms of gene frequencies.

Gene Flow

Movement to an area that is already occupied brings about gene flow. Travelers may bring a previously absent allele to a population. This new allele is analogous in effect to a mutation. If the new allele gives its possessor an adaptive advantage, then it will tend to spread through the population in subsequent generations. Gene flow may alter the effects of genetic drift, since alleles lost or reduced in frequency by chance may be reintroduced into a population by newcomers. Also, gene flow usually has a homogenizing effect. The process generally makes two or more populations more similar to each other than would be the case if gene flow did not occur between them.

Note that the terms *gene flow* and *migration* are not synonymous. Gene flow refers to the transfer of alleles into different gene pools, whereas migration connotes a permanent or long-term move to another area. Thus one person could migrate but contribute no alleles to his or her new population, but a male could go on even a short trip and disperse his gametes. Soldiers, traveling businesspersons, and others have produced gene flow without actually migrating.

Nonrandom Mating

The statistical model of genetic equilibrium calls for random mating. If matings were truly random, the probability of mating with any one member of the opposite sex would be the same as the probability of mating with any other member. In reality, mating is not truly random. When you choose a mate, very definite biases

contribute to the choice—factors such as physical appearance, education, socioeconomic status, religion, and geographical location.

Two basic types of nonrandom matings will be discussed here. The first is **consanguineous mating,** which refers to mating between relatives; the second is **assortative mating,** which involves preference for or avoidance of certain people for physical and/or social reasons.

CONSANGUINEOUS MATING   For most of American society, mating between relatives is now rare. Yet, in some other societies, consanguineous mating is not only common but preferred.

Many societies have cultural patterns of preferential marriage with a particular relative. **Cross-cousin preferential marriage** is one common type. In this system, an example of your preferred marriage partner is your mother's brother's child or your father's sister's child, who in each case is your first cousin. Yet marriage may be prohibited between you and your mother's sister's child or father's brother's child. Cousin marriage is quite common in many parts of the world. Table 5–7 shows the incidence of first-cousin marriage in several societies.

Marriages also occur between second and third cousins, as well as between other types of relatives, such as uncle and niece. In fact, a preferential marriage that is considered repulsive to most Western societies, brother-sister marriage, was once common among the royalty of several societies, including Hawaiians and ancient Egyptians. Some scholars believe that Cleopatra was the offspring of a brother-sister marriage and was at one time married to her brother.

What are the effects of consanguineous matings on a gene pool? Let us look at an example that has been used by L. C. Dunn.[4] Research in Sweden has determined that the frequency of the recessive allele for Tay-Sachs disease is 0.005. This means that the number of individuals who are heterozygous for the trait is 1 percent of the total population. Therefore, the probability of

[4]L. C. Dunn, *Heredity and Evolution in Human Populations,* rev. ed. (New York: Atheneum, 1965), 125–126.

TABLE 5–7

FREQUENCIES OF COUSIN MARRIAGES

POPULATION	PERIOD	NUMBER OF MARRIAGES IN SAMPLE	FIRST-COUSIN MARRIAGES (%)
United States, urban	1935–1950	8,000	0.05
Brazil, urban	1946–1956	1,172	0.42
Spain			
Urban	1920–1957	12,570	0.59
Rural	1951–1958	814	4.67
Japan			
Urban	1953	16,681	5.03
Rural	1950	414	16.40
India, rural	1957–1958	6,945	33.30

Source: From *Principles of Human Genetics,* Third Edition, by Curt Stern. Copyright © 1973 by Curt Stern. Reprinted by permission of W. H. Freeman and Company.

two carriers' mating is 0.01 × 0.01, or 0.0001. Since one-fourth of their offspring would have the trait, we conclude that the probability of two carriers' mating at random and having a child with this abnormality is 0.000025, or $\frac{1}{40,000}$, the observed frequency of the trait.

Now instead of considering two persons who mate at random, suppose two first cousins mate whose common grandfather is a carrier. If the grandfather married a homozygous normal person, the probability of their offsprings being a carrier would be $\frac{1}{2}$. The probability of getting carriers in the third generation, assuming that all people marrying into the family are homozygous normal, would be $\frac{1}{2} \times \frac{1}{2}$, or $\frac{1}{4}$. This is because matings between *AA* and *Aa* individuals would have a probability of $\frac{1}{2}$ for the production of *Aa* offspring and, since we know that the probability of the second-generation parents' being *Aa* is $\frac{1}{2}$, we must multiply $\frac{1}{2}$ by $\frac{1}{2}$, the individual probabilities of the two separate events. In the third generation each cousin has a $\frac{1}{4}$ probability of being a carrier. The probability of the cousins mating and both being carriers is $\frac{1}{4} \times \frac{1}{4}$, or $\frac{1}{16}$. The probability of these cousins' having a child with Tay-Sachs disease is $\frac{1}{16}$ (the probability of the cousins' both being carriers) × $\frac{1}{4}$ (the probability of two carriers' producing a homozygous recessive child), which equals $\frac{1}{64}$ (see Figure 5–5).

In the above problem the cousins' grandfather was a carrier. Of course, it is seldom known

whether a particular ancestor was a carrier or not, but the probability of a common ancestor can be calculated from gene-frequency data for the population in question. In this case the probability of two first cousins having a defective child is $\frac{1}{3200}$, compared with $\frac{1}{40,000}$ if the mating were random.

Consanguineous matings increase the probability of homozygous recessive genotypes. In the example above, the probability of producing a homozygous recessive individual is 12$\frac{1}{2}$ times

FIGURE 5–5 *Cousin mating.* See explanation in the text.

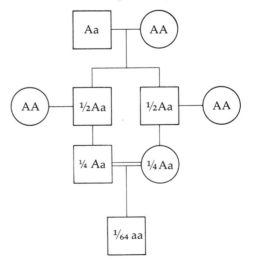

greater if first cousins mate than it is if random mating occurs. In fact, some recessive alleles are so rare that the probability of a carrier's mating with another carrier at random is just about zero. Some recessive abnormalities are sometimes known only from inbred family groups.

The result of consanguineous matings in a population is a reduction in the number of heterozygous individuals and an increase in the number of homozygous individuals. If the homozygous recessive genotype is deleterious, the frequency of the abnormality will increase. Since natural selection can then act upon the abnormal homozygous recessive individuals, a net decrease in the frequency of the allele in the population may result.

Not all inbreeding is the result of preferential marriage. In a small society it may be impossible to find a mate who is not a relative. Because of this, the effects of consanguineous marriages and genetic drift often operate together in the same population, as will be seen in the following example.

THE AMISH   The Amish are a series of small populations that have remained socially isolated for religious and cultural reasons. There are Amish settlements in twenty-three states, in Ontario, Canada, and in Central America, but the most studied group consists of the 20,000 or so Amish of Lancaster County, Pennsylvania. The Amish are one of several religious isolates that are ideal for population studies. They are a strictly defined, closed group with good genealogical records, high nutritional and health standards, and good medical care. Almost all the Amish are at the same socioeconomic level, and they tend to have large families.

Most of the Amish of Lancaster County are the descendants of a founder population of about 200 pre-Revolutionary War ancestors who migrated to Pennsylvania from Europe between 1720 and 1770. Because of the small population size, most available mates are related to some degree, although first-cousin marriages are prohibited.

The Amish represent the results of the founder effect, genetic drift, and consanguineous mating. They have a fairly high frequency of some rather rare alleles, such as the one responsible for Ellis–van Creveld syndrome.

The **Ellis–van Creveld syndrome** is characterized by dwarfism, extra fingers on the hand, and, often, congenital malformations of the heart. The syndrome is quite rare, with fewer than fifty cases being known outside the Amish. Yet among the small Amish population alone, over eighty definite cases are known. A great number of these individuals can trace their descent back to three common ancestors, one of whom was probably a carrier.

Many such isolates, like the Amish, have been studied by students of human evolution. Besides showing a higher incidence of several rare recessive traits, these populations also show allele frequencies for such traits as blood type that differ from the frequencies of the surrounding population. For example, among the Dunkers, a group of 3500 individuals in Pennsylvania descended from German ancestors who migrated to America beginning in 1719, more than 44 percent are of blood-type M. This compares with a frequency of 29 percent for blood-type M found in the present-day populations of the United States and West Germany. Since there is no evidence that these blood-type frequencies are due to natural selection, they are most likely due to the founder principle and/or genetic drift.

ASSORTATIVE MATING   In the United States consanguineous matings are not common. Nevertheless, mating is far from random. Deviation from random mating stems from the fact that Americans choose spouses based on certain cultural conventions they learn from parents, friends, and the mass media. Therefore, out of all potential mates only some are "available." *Assortative* means that people with certain phenotypes tend to mate more or less often than would be expected if matings were random.

Stature provides an interesting example of assortative mating. In American society it is quite common for the husband to be taller than the wife. The reverse is uncommon and is often the source of jokes when it occurs. What effect does this have on the gene pool?

Take two men, one 173 centimeters (5 feet 8 inches) and the other 188 centimeters (6 feet 2 inches). If stature is a convention in mate selection, then the first man will consider women 173 centimeters (5 feet 8 inches) or less, while the second man will consider women 188 centimeters (6 feet 2 inches) or less. The second man has a greater population of women to choose from and might find it easier to find a wife than the first man. Similarly, a woman 183 centimeters (6 feet) tall may have some difficulty finding a mate, since she is "restricted" to men more than 183 centimeters (6 feet) tall. As a result, she may mate later and therefore have a shorter reproductive life and potentially fewer children.

Other important factors that determine mate selection include education and geography. Education is easy to document, and it appears that college-educated people generally prefer to marry other college-educated people. They tend to marry later and produce fewer offspring. Geography is also important. Before you can marry someone, you must meet that person. People tend to meet and marry in the community in which they live. Race and religion also play a significant role in mate selection, as Box 5–2 explains.

Besides showing preferences in choice of a mate, individuals also show avoidances. For example, mentally deficient people are not selected as mates as frequently as mentally normal individuals.

Assortative mating influences gene combination in the F_1 generation. The failure of particular individuals to mate because they are not selected as mating partners prevents certain alleles (such as those causing mental retardation) from being passed on to the next generation's gene pool. Preferences for particular phenotypes might increase the probability that certain gene combinations will be represented in the gene pool of the next generation. For instance, if a tall individual selects another tall individual as a mate, extremely tall offspring might then appear in the next generation, thus bringing about new variation in the population.

Differential Fertility Rates

The model of genetic equilibrium assumes that all matings are equally fertile, but this is obviously not the case. Some couples have three children, others one, and still others no children at all. This means that the contribution to the gene pool of the succeeding generation varies from couple to couple.

V. A. McKusick presents some interesting figures.[5] He estimates that more than half of all zygotes never reproduce: 15 percent are lost before birth, 3 percent are stillborn, 2 percent are lost in the neonatal period, 3 percent die before maturity, 20 percent never marry, and 10 percent marry but remain childless.

Except for identical twins, each zygote is a unique genotype, representing a unique assortment of alleles in a particular combination that will never occur again. Why do more than half of these individuals fail to reproduce at all? Because of some inherited abnormality, many are lost either before or after birth. Others never mate because they are placed in mental institutions. Some die in wars or accidents. Many mate but never have children because of medical problems. And some do not mate or marry, or they marry but choose to have no children.

Of the 47 percent of the original combinations that do reproduce, reproductive rates vary. Some have only one child, others a dozen. What factors determine the differences in fertility? Some are medical, such as blood-type incompatibility, but many are cultural. For instance, many couples today restrict their families to one or two children because of ecological or economic concerns; others believe, on religious grounds, that salvation lies in high fertility. The point is that the next generation is the result of the reproductive activities of the parental generation. Among those who are reproductively active, fertility varies.

What we have been talking about is natural selection, the heart of the theory of evolution. Natural selection is not simply "survival of the fittest." It is the fact that certain individuals tend to have more offspring than other individuals do and therefore make a greater contribution to the gene pool of the next generation. Factors that result in greater fertility, *if genetically determined,*

---

[5]V. A. McKusick, *Human Genetics*, 2d ed. (Englewood Cliffs, N.J.: Prentice-Hall, 1969), 167.

BOX 5–2

ASSORTATIVE MATING IN THE UNITED STATES: RACE AND RELIGION

In Chapter 8, we analyze the concept of race. Yet for the purposes of this box, we will use the term *race* as it is used by the U.S. Bureau of the Census, that is, as a matter of people's self-classification. These self-classifications are based on physical characteristics such as skin color and the perception of one's geographical origin, and so categories used on Census Bureau questionnaires include "black," "white," "Oriental," and "American Indian."

Using these categories, the data clearly show that most Americans marry within their own category. Yet up to 30 percent of the alleles of black Americans were contributed by white ancestors.[1] Most of this admixture occurred not through marriage but through the common practice in which white slave owners used black women as concubines. With the end of slavery, the amount of black-white admixture diminished. However, along with other interracial admixtures, it is again on the rise because of the increased acceptance of interracial marriage. In 1970 all interracial marriages accounted for a scant 0.695 percent of the total marriages for that year; by 1993 that percent had increased to 2.2 percent. Although this is still a relatively small percent of the total, the increase from 1970 to 1993 was about 317 percent. Black-white marriages increased from 0.15 percent of the total marriages in 1970 to 0.45 percent in 1993.[2]

What does admixture mean in evolutionary terms? For one thing, admixture creates a greater variety of gene combinations. Greater genetic variation is evolutionarily advantageous because it provides in-

sulation against extinction. The more varieties of individuals within a population, the less chance that environmental changes will wipe out the population. This concept is explained in the next chapter.

Admixture also can lead to a reduction of homozygous recessive diseases. As a group, the offspring of black-white matings are in some ways statistically better fit than the offspring of either blacks or whites. For instance, blacks have a high carrier rate for sickle-cell anemia (Chapter 4), and whites have a higher carrier rate for cystic fibrosis than blacks. Since both of these diseases are homozygous recessive, both parents would have to be carriers in order for an offspring to have either disease.

The probability of offspring having a recessive abnormality is dependent on the carrier rate in the parents' population. Matings within groups of like people lead to an increase in the number of homozygous allele combinations, a situation referred to as homozygosity. Close relatives show the greatest amount of homozygosity (see the example of Queen Victoria's family in Chapter 4). Matings between people whose common ancestors lived in the remote past give rise to a tendency for more heterozygous allele combination which is called **heterozygosity.**

Because of the tendency toward heterozygosity, admixture between blacks and whites means that the chance of transmitting either sickle-cell anemia or cystic fibrosis to offspring of black-white matings is lower than the chance of transmitting sickle-cell anemia in black-black matings or cystic fi-

brosis in white-white matings. So at least for these two diseases interracial matings would result in a lower incidence of the diseases.

In addition to interracial marriages, marriages between people of different religions have been occurring in greater numbers than in the past. For instance, in the early 1960s, only 6 percent of American Jews married non-Jews; by 1985, that number had increased by about 400 percent to nearly 25 percent.[3] This increase in interreligious mating may bring about a decrease in the frequency of genetic diseases such as Tay-Sachs disease. Tay-Sachs has a high frequency among American Jews, many of whom have ancestors from Eastern Europe, where the gene is thought to have originated. As a consequence, Jewish–non-Jewish matings have a greater chance of producing offspring who are homozygous recessive for Tay-Sachs, and thus have a higher rate of Tay-Sachs disease, than do non-Jewish–non-Jewish matings. However, since the non-Jewish population is so much larger, increased intermarriage would cause the Tay-Sachs allele to become progressively "diluted" (distributed widely within the larger population). This dilution factor, along with an overall lower probability of homozygosity, would lead to an overall reduction in cases of Tay-Sachs disease.

---

[1] T. E. Reed, "Caucasian Genes in American Negroes," *Science* 165 (1969), 762–768.
[2] Bureau of the Census, *Statistical Abstracts of the U.S.:* 1994, 114th ed. (Washington, D.C.: GPO, 1994), 56.
[3] L. Grunson, "Groups Play Matchmaker to Preserve Judaism," *New York Times,* Apr. 1, 1985.

will be passed on to the next generation with greater frequency. Factors that result in lowered fertility or higher mortality, such as genetic abnormalities, will tend to be eliminated.

Summary

Natural populations are not in genetic equilibrium because five mechanisms bring about changes in allele frequency. Mutations, the ultimate source of genetic variability, provide one way in which the predicted frequencies deviate from observed frequencies. Since mutations are usually deleterious to the individual, they rarely "catch on." Their importance lies in providing a potential for adapting to new situations.

Random genetic drift is another factor in evolutionary change. With genetic drift, by chance alone, not all alleles in a population will be represented proportionally in the next generation. The smaller the population, the more pronounced this effect. According to the founder principle, a new population based on a small sample of the original population may show distinctive gene frequencies. Again, the smaller the sample, the greater the potential deviation from the original group. Sampling error is in part responsible for much of the physical variation in different human populations.

Gene flow can bring new alleles into a population, where they may be adaptive and increase in frequency. Gene flow also acts to make populations genetically more similar to each other.

The genetic-equilibrium model assumes random mating, but individuals consciously choose mates for myriad reasons. For example, they may prefer to marry a relative in order to keep power and wealth within the family, or they may want to mate with someone with green eyes for personal aesthetic reasons. Nonrandom mating leads to changes in gene frequencies from generation to generation.

Differential fertility, or natural selection, is a powerful force of evolutionary change. This topic will be a major focus of the next chapter.

As a final note, it should be emphasized that the mechanisms of evolution—mutation, drift, gene flow, nonrandom mating, and natural selection—work *together* to create net change. For instance, natural selection would have nothing to "select" for or against if the variability provided by mutation were not present.

STUDY QUESTIONS

1. Why do we define evolutionary change in terms of changes in relative gene frequencies rather than in terms of changes in phenotype?
2. Genetic equilibrium is a state that never actually exists. Why can it not exist in a real population?
3. What is meant by the term *sampling error*? What types of sampling errors can occur in the reproduction of populations?
4. Cousin marriage is illegal in some states. Does mating between cousins produce more abnormal children than mating between nonrelatives? What genetic factors are involved?
5. What role does mutation play in evolutionary change? Could evolution occur without mutation?
6. Insecticide is sprayed on an insect population. A small percent of the insects survive because of a mutation that allows them to "neutralize" the toxin. Did the mutation arise because the insect population needed it to? Explain.
7. Why is the phrase "survival of the fittest" somewhat misleading?
8. Do you believe that the course of human evolution can be predicted? If so, why and how? If not, why not?

SUGGESTED READINGS

Bowler, P. J. *Evolution: The History of an Idea*, rev. ed. Berkeley: University of California Press, 1989. This book outlines the history of evolutionary theories. Its final chapter looks at modern debates about evolutionary theory, including the ideas of creationists.

Futuyma, D. J. *Evolutionary Biology*, 3d ed. Sunderland, Mass: Sinauer Associates, 1996. This book provides one of the best discussions of population genetics available.

Harti, D. L. *A Primer of Population Genetics*, 3d ed. Sunderland, Mass: Sinauer Associates, 1996. This is a short introduction to population genetics that requires no knowledge of mathematics beyond simple algebra.

Suzuki, D., et al. *An Introduction to Genetic Analysis,* 5th ed. New York: Freeman, 1993. This is a general introduction to genetics with excellent chapters on population genetics. There are numerous solved exercises.

Volpe, E. P. *Understanding Evolution,* 6th ed. Dubuque, Iowa: Brown, 1996. This is a short introduction to evolutionary theory with a good overview of population genetics.

A tortoise and iguana from the Galápagos Islands, visited by Charles Darwin on his trip aboard the HMS Beagle.

I have called this principle, by which each slight variation, if useful, is preserved, by the term Natural Selection.
                Charles Darwin (1809–1882)

CHAPTER 6

NATURAL SELECTION AND THE ORIGIN OF SPECIES

We have phrases in English such as "sweet tooth" to show our preference for sweet food as opposed to other foods. We may take this preference as some kind of logical given. The scientist can provide an evolutionary hypothesis for the preference.

That hypothesis would contend that sweet things provide quick energy and are usually nonpoisonous (bitter-tasting foods are often poisonous). Animals that have a sweet tooth would have a higher survival rate than those that prefer bitter foods. With each generation, more individuals would prefer sweet over bitter.

This chapter deals with the processes involved in establishing an advantage of one type of individual over another. Such an advantage is called a selective advantage. In addition, we will see how one population may fragment into more than one population and, therefore, how life proliferates.

NATURAL SELECTION

Evolution is defined as any change in the gene pool of a population. Such changes accumulate over the generations.

Variation within the population is at the base of biological evolution. If all organisms were genetically identical, there could be no change in gene frequencies, only fluctuations in numbers of individuals or extinction. In reality, variation always exists within a population of organisms. In a relatively stable environment, organisms with characteristics that maintain (or increase) their competitive efficiency in exploiting this environment survive and reproduce at a greater frequency than organisms that lack the advantageous characteristics. If the environment changes, other phenotypes may be better able to survive and reproduce at an increased rate. Any difference in net reproductive success is **natural selection.**

Variability of Populations

All populations display genetic variability. Some of this variability is clearly observable: color, size, and shape, for example. Other differences are observable only through dissection or microscopic and biochemical analyses.

HUMANS AS A VARIABLE SPECIES   Humans are polymorphic. **Polymorphism** refers to the presence of several distinct forms with frequencies greater than 1 percent within a population. An example of this is the presence of individuals with A, B, AB, and O blood types within a population.

Variation in phenotypic traits among human populations in different parts of the world is easy to see. Yet even among siblings from a single family, there are differences in physical features, blood types, and even psychological patterns. Some of these differences vary with sex and age; others are influenced by the cultural or natural environment; and many, such as blood type, are totally genetic.

How many genetically different individuals are possible? Ignoring for a moment identical twins and environmental factors, there are about 10^{963} possible combinations of alleles in humans. This number is a 1 followed by 963 zeros—a number trillions of times larger than the total number of people who have ever inhabited the earth. To this can be added the effects of differing environments, which further increase variability. Because of exposure to differences in the environment, even identical twins differ from each other.

MECHANISMS OF VARIATION   As noted in Chapter 5, mutation is the ultimate source of all genetic variability. Mutations, which provide the raw material for increasing genetic variation, have the potential to enter into new combinations with existing alleles.

Mutations produce new alleles, but variation also develops in another way. Because of independent assortment and crossing-over, a new combination of alleles is produced every time a zygote is formed. This new genotype is unique; it has never existed before and will never exist again. Natural selection acts upon new mutations and recombinations of existing alleles.

Environment, Habitat, and Niche

In Chapter 1 we saw that there are many definitions of the word *culture*. The same is true of the word **environment.** The environment, in its most general sense, is anything and everything external to the subject of discussion. The environment of a specific red blood cell includes other red blood cells, white blood cells, and the plasma. A person's environment includes such things as clothing, furniture, air temperature, trees, and flowers, as well as other people.

This concept of environment is broad, often too broad to be useful. Therefore, the concepts of physical environment, biological environment, cultural environment, and microenvironment prove useful. The **physical environment** refers to the inanimate elements of the surroundings. The living elements surrounding the subject of discussion are more specifically referred to as the **biological environment.** The **cultural environment** contains the products of human endeavor, such as tools, shelters, clothing, toxic wastes,

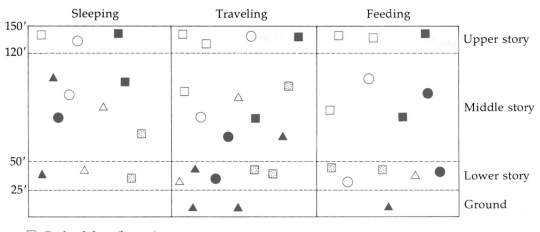

FIGURE 6–1 *Ecological niche.* This chart shows the spatial distribution of seven species of African arboreal monkeys in relationship to diet and three different activities.

and even social institutions. The **microenvironment** is a very specific set of physical, biological, and, for humans, cultural factors immediately surrounding the organism. For example, a particular organism may live in only a certain species of tree and may occupy only the end branches of those trees. There may be a rainfall requirement whereby the animal cannot survive if the environment becomes too wet.

A term related to environment is **habitat,** defined as the place in which an organism lives. Examples of habitats are tropical rain forests, deserts, freshwater marshes, and tundra. Some authors also employ the concept of a **microhabitat,** which is a more specific "address" for an organism, such as the upper story of a tropical rain forest.

The term **niche,** or **ecological niche,** refers, first, to the specific microenvironment in which a particular species lives. The term also includes the anatomical, physiological, and behavioral methods by which the organism exploits physical space and its relationship to other organisms.

Two animals occupying the same physical area, but one consuming leaves and the other consuming fruits, or one being active at night and the other active during the day, are occupying different niches (Figure 6–1). **Ecology** is the study of the relationship of organisms or populations of organisms to their niches.

The Mechanisms of Natural Selection

Differences in mortality and fertility exist within populations. Possessors of some phenotypes live to reproduce and do so to varying degrees; possessors of other phenotypes either die before reproductive age or live but do not reproduce. Numerous factors account for the failure to reproduce in great numbers or the failure to reproduce at all. Some factors are environmental, but many are genetic.

Any factor that brings about a difference in fertility or mortality is a **selective agent.** A selective agent places **selective pressure** upon certain individuals within the population, resulting in a change in the frequency of alleles in the next generation. This is evolution.

An example of selection in a population is smallpox. The selective agent is the smallpox virus. In a population exposed to the virus some individuals will acquire the disease and die, others will develop mild cases and survive, and still others will not contract the disease at all. Factors such as exposure, hygiene, age, diet, and stress play major roles. Research suggests that certain biochemical factors, such as ABO blood types, also play a role in determining who acquires smallpox. Possessors of certain genotypes will have a high death rate, thereby reducing the number of individuals in the population available to transmit their genes to the next generation. Those who survive will live to transmit their genes. Smallpox therefore places selective pressure on the members of the population that results in a subsequent gene pool that is more resistant (better adapted) to the disease environment (Figure 6–2).

Natural selection acts upon the phenotype of an individual. Although the phenotype is influenced by environmental factors, only that part of it that is determined by the genotype can be passed on to the next generation's gene pool.

An environmental factor that may cause death but does not "select" one phenotype over another is not a selective agent. If an atomic bomb were dropped without warning on an area and everyone died, or if only a random sample of people who happened to be in a shelter at the time survived, natural selection would not have taken place. On the other hand, if some people on the periphery of the bomb were biologically more resistant to the radiation than others and hence survived at a greater frequency, this would be an instance of natural selection.

FITNESS   Certain individuals (or populations) may have higher fertility and lower mortality rates than other individuals in a particular niche. These individuals (or populations) are said to display a greater fitness for that niche. **Fitness** is a measure of how well adapted a particular individual or group is to the requirements imposed by the environment. Survival to reproductive age, successful mating, and fertility are not al-

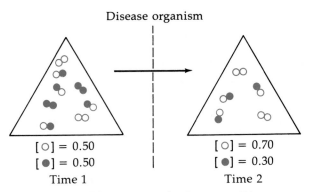

FIGURE 6–2 *Disease as a selective agent.* Disease can bring about different survival rates among the possessors of different genotypes, thereby changing the allele frequencies in the gene pool.

ways related to such factors as size and strength. Fitness also does not necessarily correspond to characteristics that a society values. A highly educated, wealthy, good citizen who has no children has an individual fertility rate of zero.

Fitness varies with the situation. Since environments change and populations may shift into new niches, selective pressures are not always constant. For this reason, a trait that has a high fitness value in one niche may lose this fitness in another. On the other hand, a trait with a low fitness value may gain greater fitness in a new niche.

In general, natural selection affects the frequency of alleles by eliminating alleles and allele combinations that are deleterious to the majority of those who carry them. Natural selection also tends to retain and increase the frequencies of alleles and allele combinations that are adaptive.

An Example of Natural Selection in a Nonhuman Population

Natural selection is not some mystical or hypothetical process that exists only in the mathematical formulations of anthropologists and biologists. It can be seen in action.

A classic example of natural selection is described in a study of the peppered moth (*Biston betulara*) made by the late British biologist H. B. D.

Kettlewell[1]. This example illustrates both how environments can change and how natural selection eliminates disadvantageous alleles while it increases the frequency of beneficial ones.

Before the Industrial Revolution, the English peppered moth rested on light, lichen-covered tree trunks. Its light-colored body with dark peppering effectively camouflaged it from predatory birds. Within the moth population, however, a mutant allele produced individuals with dark gray bodies, and on light-colored trees these mutants were easy prey for birds (Figure 6–3). Consequently, the birds, which represented a selective agent, eliminated the mutant alleles as fast as they arose. In other words, the dark moths had a very low fitness in this particular environment. The dark variant represented less than 1 percent of the total population in 1848.

The Industrial Revolution caused the environment to change. Smoke from coal-burning factories and home stoves killed the lichens on nearby trees and darkened the tree trunks with soot. Now the light-colored moths became more conspicuous, and birds consumed them more frequently than the dark ones. In other words, the fitness of the dark moths increased, while that of the light moths decreased. Selective pressure was reduced on the dark moths and increased against the light ones. By 1898 the dark form made up 99 percent of the total moth population around the city of Manchester!

This is an example of a rapid environmental change caused by human activity. The light moth was no longer adapted to the altered environment, and so its mortality rate increased. At the same time, the dark-colored form became more adapted, its mortality rate decreased, and eventually it made up most of the population. Several other species of animals have adapted to changes in the environment brought about by industrialization in the same way. The change of allelic frequency in industrial areas toward populations with darker coloration is termed **industrial melanism.**

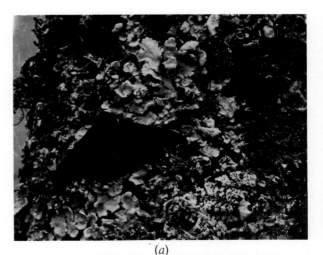

(a)

(b)

FIGURE 6–3 *Natural selection in the peppered moth.* A light and dark form of peppered moth is seen against *(a)* a light-colored and *(b)* a dark-colored tree trunk.

Darkening of the tree trunks did not take place all over England, and so populations of the light-colored moth still exist in some areas. Thus, through natural selection, two different forms of the same species have developed in contrasting environments. In addition, beginning with the passage of the Clean Air Act of 1956 in the United Kingdom, the frequency of the dark

[1]H. B. D. Kettlewell, "A Survey of the Frequencies of *Biston betulara* (L.) (Lep.) and Its Melanistic Forms in Great Britain," *Heredity,* 12 (1958), 51–72.

form of peppered moth is now declining. According to a study began in 1959 near Liverpool, the percentage of dark moths has dropped from a high of 94.2 percent in 1960 to 18.7 percent in 1994.[2]

The rapid changes seen in the peppered moth population resulted from a dramatic environmental change caused by human activity. Before the evolution of humans, and in environments not as greatly altered by human activity, changes also took place, but these changes were generally not as dramatic or as rapid. Consequently, natural selection is usually a much slower and more subtle mechanism.

Natural Selection in Humans

Natural selection is also occurring in human populations. Because of the long time between generations, however, examples of selection in human populations are not easy to document except in cases of lethal traits. Yet several studies have dealt with what might be real, but subtle, examples.

SELECTION AGAINST CERTAIN SIMPLE DOMINANT AND RECESSIVE ALLELES The least complicated cases of natural selection in humans are those involving total selection against a simple dominant abnormality that is completely penetrant and lethal. An example is **retinoblastoma,** a cancer of the retina of the eye in children. This abnormality is fatal unless the entire eye is removed. Since the trait is clear-cut, affects all individuals with the allele equally, and results in death before reproductive age, selection eliminates the allele in the next generation. Because none of the individuals with the abnormality can reproduce (assuming surgery is not performed), the appearance of the trait in any generation is due to new mutations.

Such an allele has a **selective coefficient** (s) of 1.00—selection is complete. The **relative fitness (RF)** of an individual with the allele is given by the formula $RF = 1 - s$. The relative fitness in this case is 0; no offspring are produced by a person with a dominant lethal allele.

If selection is not complete, an abnormal dominant allele will still tend to be eliminated, but more slowly. For example, if the selective coefficient is 0.50, then persons with the trait will leave behind, on the average, only one-half the number of offspring than those without the trait will leave, all other factors being equal. Thus the number of persons with the trait, barring new mutations, will be cut by one-half in each generation.

Natural selection acts much more slowly against a recessive trait. Only homozygous recessive individuals are eliminated. Since heterozygous individuals will carry the allele to the next generation, the allele will tend to be eliminated, but much more slowly than a dominant trait with the same fitness (Figure 6–4).

NATURAL SELECTION AND THE ABO BLOOD TYPES Differences in blood-type frequencies exist in different populations. For example, in a population in India 35.38 percent of the members were of blood type B; 33.21 percent were type O; 24.55 percent were type A; and 6.86 percent were type AB. This contrasts strongly with a Kwakiutl Indian population from British Columbia, Canada, in which 67.74 percent of the members were of type O and 32.27 percent type A. Types B and AB were totally absent.[3]

Why should these differences exist within and between populations? Likely explanations are random genetic drift and natural selection.

Until relatively recent times all people lived in small groups. Group differences developed from group to group because of genetic drift. Likewise, when a small group migrated from one group to establish a new population, differences

---

[2]B. Grant, D. F. Owen, and C. A. Clarke, "Decline of Melanic Moths," *Nature,* 373 (1995), 565; C. A. Clarke, B. Grant, F. M. M. Clarke, and T. Asami, "A Long Term Assessment of *Biston betularia* (L.) in One UK Locality (Caldy Common near West Kirby, Wirral), 1959–1993, and Glimpses Elsewhere," *The Linnean,* 10 (1994), 18–26.

[3]A. E. Mourant et al., *The Distribution of the Human Blood Groups and Other Polymorphisms,* 2d ed. (London: Oxford University Press, 1976).

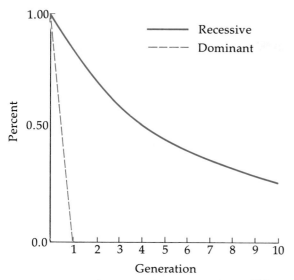

FIGURE 6–4 *Selection against rare genotypes.* This graph shows the rate at which frequencies of rare genotypes are reduced by natural selection. One line shows a dominant abnormality and the other a recessive one. In both cases, the frequencies begin at 1 percent and selection is complete. Assume no new mutations.

developed because of the founder principle. Current evidence suggests that natural selection also played a role in the development of the ABO blood-type system. Here the selective pressures are small, and the changes they caused have developed over hundreds and thousands of years.

In Chapter 4, we discussed hemolytic disease involving the Rh blood-type system. It now appears that in some respects ABO incompatibilities may have a greater selective effect than Rh incompatibilities. Several investigators have noted that in situations in which the mother is blood-type O and the fetus is type A or B, hemolytic disease may develop in the fetus and newborn infant.

Surveys show that when the mother is type O and the father type A, fewer type A children are produced than when the mother is type A and the father type O. The type O mother carries anti-A and anti-B in her blood. These antibodies often, but not always, cross over into the fetal blood system, where, if the fetus is of type A,

damage may occur. In one study 12 percent of all newborns of type O mothers were of type A and B. Of these newborns, 0.5 percent showed clinical symptoms of blood destruction.[4]

It is important to realize that fertility rates differ for different types of matings. We have seen, for example, that a mating between an O mother and an A father produces fewer offspring than a mating between an A mother and an O father. Fewer of the former's children will be of blood-type A. These differences in fertility can bring about subtle, but real, changes in allele frequencies over many generations.

Several diseases also appear to act as selective agents against certain blood types. For example, persons with blood-type A have an elevated incidence of cancer of the stomach, cancer of the pancreas, and pernicious anemia. Blood-type O has been linked to duodenal and stomach ulcers. In populations of European descent, the risk of developing a duodenal ulcer is 35 percent higher among persons of type O than among persons of the other three ABO blood types (Figure 6–5).[5]

Natural Selection and Sickle-Cell Anemia

You have already been introduced to sickle-cell anemia. The genotype Hb^AHb^A results in the manufacture of hemoglobin A. The genotype Hb^SHb^S produces hemoglobin S and the disease sickle-cell anemia. The heterozygote Hb^AHb^S produces both hemoglobins.

The fitness of an individual with sickle-cell anemia is effectively zero. Therefore, as we would expect, natural selection operates to eliminate the allele Hb^S in many areas such as the United States. Nevertheless, populations in many parts of Africa, southern Europe, and the Middle East have very high Hb^S allele frequencies, as high as approximately 0.20. This means

[4]H. Levene and R. E. Rosefield, "ABO Incompatibility," in A. G. Steinberg (ed.), *Progress in Medical Genetics*, vol. 1 (New York: Grune & Stratton, 1961), 120–157.
[5]J. Buettner-Janusch, "The Study of Natural Selection and the ABO(H) Blood Group System in Man," in G. E. Dole and R. L. Carniero (eds.), *Essays in the Science of Culture* (New York: Crowell, 1969), 79–110.

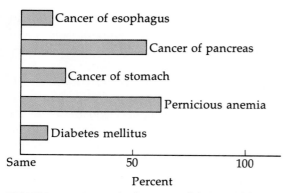

FIGURE 6–5 *Natural selection and the ABO blood types.* This graph shows the relatively greater risk, in percent, of type A individuals developing the diseases listed compared with that of type O individuals. Other blood types also show relatively greater risks for specific diseases.

that as many as 36 percent of the individuals in these populations have the sickle-cell trait or sickle-cell anemia. The high frequency for *Hb*S is startling, especially when we remember that the frequency of the allele for PKU, also a deleterious recessive, is only 0.01 or less in all populations for which data are available. What factors are responsible for the high frequency of *Hb*S?

The British geneticist Anthony Allison was one of the first to realize that the high frequencies of *Hb*S are found in areas characterized by high incidences of falciparum malaria.[6] The distribution of hemoglobin S (seen in Figure 6–6) correlates highly with that of malaria. This suggests that the heterozygote, with both hemoglobin A and hemoglobin S, is relatively resistant to malaria and has a higher fitness than either homozygous type. This increased resistance has been confirmed.

Malaria involves parasites that reproduce in the red blood cell at one stage of their complex reproductive cycle. The malaria parasite cannot infect cells that contain hemoglobin S. The fitness of the anemic individual is low because of the effects of sickle-cell anemia. The fitness of the individual homozygous for hemoglobin A in

malarial areas is depressed because malaria has such a high mortality rate and because malaria often leaves the victim sterile.

The fitness of the heterozygote, however, is relatively high because of lower mortality from malaria. Thus the heterozygote has the greatest probability of surviving, reproducing, and contributing the most genetic material to the next generation. Yet because the heterozygote produces a certain proportion of children with the disease, the death rate from sickle-cell anemia may be high in areas where the allele is plentiful.

People adapt to their environment, and disease organisms are important environmental factors. Some anthropologists believe that malaria as it is known today did not exist in Africa before the development of farming some 13,000 years ago. This cultural change caused an opening of the forest and the creation of stagnant pools of water in which mosquitoes, which are the carriers of the malarial parasites, reproduced. As the rate of malaria increased, so did mortality. A population in a malarial environment has several possible fates. It may die off when the mortality rate is so great that the population is no longer large enough to maintain itself; on the other hand, a chance mechanism for survival might save the population.

Most likely, sickle-cell anemia already existed, but before the rise of malaria, the frequency of the allele *Hb*S was low because of the low fitness of the anemic individual. With the increase and spread of malaria, the fitness of the heterozygote became greater than the fitness of the homozygous *Hb*A*Hb*A individual, and the frequency of the allele *Hb*S increased. Today, population fitness in malarial areas is balanced between mortality due to malaria and mortality due to sickle-cell anemia. The combined death rate is lower than the rate would be for mortality due to malaria alone if the sickle-cell allele did not exist. This situation, in which the heterozygous individual is best fit, is one form of **balanced polymorphism** (Figure 6–7).

A balanced polymorphism is a condition in which two or more alleles are maintained in a population by natural selection. Selection produces an equilibrium so that allele frequencies

[6]A. C. Allison, "Protection Afforded by Sickle-Cell Trait against Subtertian Malarial Infection," *British Medical Journal*, 1 (1954), 290–294.

remain the same from generation to generation. Heterozygote advantage, as seen in the case of sickle-cell anemia, is the simplest type of balanced polymorphism. In such cases, if the frequency of the sickle-cell allele decreases, more people who are homozygous for Hb^A are born and there is increased selection against the Hb^A allele. If the frequency of the Hb^S allele increases, more individuals homozygous for that allele are born and there is increased selection against the Hb^S allele. If the heterozygote is more fit than either homozygous condition, this produces a balance-counterbalance system that keeps the frequencies of alleles stable.

OTHER DISEASES AND MALARIA   Several other genetic conditions are associated with the distribution of malaria. Some of them have been shown to reduce the impact of malaria upon human populations, and others are suspected of performing this function. The picture is complicated by the fact that more than one type of malaria exists and differing genetic traits may protect the individual against different forms of the malarial parasite.

In northwestern sections of Africa an abnormal hemoglobin, **hemoglobin C,** overlaps the distribution of hemoglobin S. Perhaps these two hemoglobins protect against different types of malaria. A series of abnormalities referred to as **thalassemias** differ from the abnormal hemoglobins in that the polypeptide chains are normal. However, some chains, such as the alpha and beta chains, may not be produced, while other hemoglobin types, such as fetal hemoglobin, are produced into adulthood. Thalassemia major, which occurs in the homozygous individual, can be severe and is often fatal. Thalassemia minor, which occurs in the heterozygous individual, is not severe and is believed to be associated with malarial resistance. **Glucose-6-phosphate dehydrogenase deficiency** has also been linked to malaria resistance. Figure 6–6 shows the distribution of some of these traits and of malaria.

Natural Selection and Social Behavior

In the previous sections of this chapter we discussed natural selection in terms of physical characteristics. Over the years most anthropologists have maintained that human behavior and social characteristics are learned. Not having a genetic basis, these characteristics are not subject to the same type of selective forces that physical characteristics are.

On the other hand, sociobiologists maintain that many behaviors that social scientists see as predominantly or strictly learned are indeed influenced by genes. These behaviors include aggression, violence, territoriality, sex-role differences, nepotism, fear of strangers, and homosexuality. Sociobiologists attempt to show that evolutionary processes, such as natural selection, apply to these behaviors. The general idea suggests that, like variations in physical characteristics, variations in social behavior have fitness. Behaviors that are fit for an environment are favored at the expense of nonadaptive behaviors.

ALTRUISM   An example often used in arguments between sociobiologists and anthropologists involves **altruistic acts,** such as saving another at the expense of one's own life. Since altruistic acts are commonplace, the hypothesized gene for an altruistic predisposition must have reached high frequencies by having selective advantage. Stephen Jay Gould relates how a colleague, using an Eskimo example, explained to him the possibility of selection for an altruistic gene.

Among some Eskimos, grandparents sacrifice themselves for the good of their social unit. If food resources become scarce and the group has to move to a new area, older people who might hamper the group's movement stay behind to die. We may assume that this behavior is adaptive for the group as a whole and that the group's members survive at a higher rate than do groups not characterized by this altruistic behavior. In this case the altruistic gene is preserved in the population and rises in frequency relative to a "selfish" gene.

If there is a genetic predisposition to an altruistic act, such as the one in the Eskimo example, it would be an example of inclusive fitness. **Inclusive fitness** consists of an individual's own fitness plus his or her effect on the fitness of any relative. Because inclusive fitness involves al-

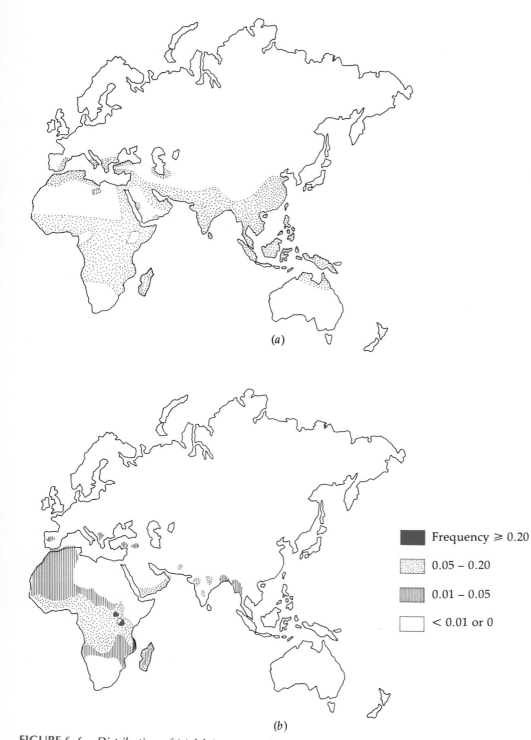

(a)

(b)

Frequency ≥ 0.20

0.05 – 0.20

0.01 – 0.05

< 0.01 or 0

FIGURE 6–6 *Distribution of (a) falciparum malaria, (b) hemoglobin S, (c) hemoglobin C and E, and (d) thalassemia in the Old World.*

HbE

HbC

(c)

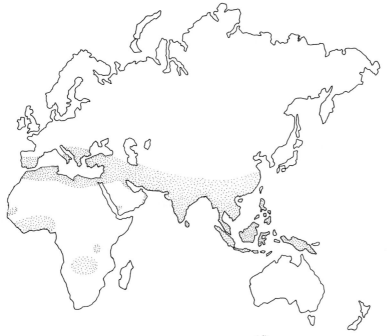

(d)

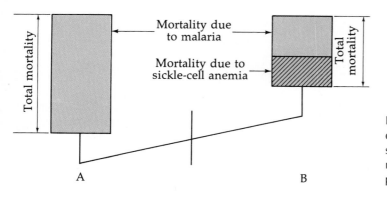

FIGURE 6–7 *Balanced polymorphism.* The total death rate from malaria in a population lacking the sickle-cell allele (A) is greater than the total death rate from malaria and sickle-cell anemia in a population with the sickle-cell allele (B).

truistic acts that benefit relatives, it is referred to as **kin selection.** Kin selection is explained graphically in Box 6–1.

No one suggests that kin selection among the Eskimos is a conscious process. The simple fact is that in the course of evolution, groups who do not practice kin selection are gradually eliminated in favor of those who do practice it. Similar arguments may be made for other behaviors, from panhandling to homosexuality.

GENETIC VERSUS CULTURAL DETERMINISM   The above discussion presents an example of **genetic determinism,** the idea that specific behaviors are influenced by specific genes. On the other side of the coin is the idea of **cultural determinism,** which states that human behavior is almost entirely learned. Each type of determinism in its pure sense attributes complete causality to either learned behavior or genetic influence. What would cultural determinists say about the Eskimo example?

Cultural determinists would say that some groups of Eskimos have a learned tradition of sacrifice. In these families "sacrifice is celebrated in song and story; aged grandparents who stay behind become the greatest heros of the clan. Children are socialized from their earliest memories to the glory and honor of such sacrifices."[7] Again, if such sacrifice is adaptive, then those

groups who *learn* it will survive better than those who do not. No specific gene need be involved.

NATURE AND NURTURE WORK TOGETHER
Except for reflexes, the brain controls human behavior. For instance, only the profoundly retarded, psychotic, injured, or abused fail to acquire or maintain language abilities. This is a human universal. On the other hand, a lizard has no genetic potential for learning a language. Language is one form of communication. Lizards can communicate, but not linguistically (Chapter 12).

Humans not only learn a language but also acquire language skills in the same general order of events: cooing (using vowel sounds only), babbling (combining vowels and consonants), and the one-word stage (when sound and meaning are linked for the first time). Each of these stages begins at the same average age (12 weeks, 5 to 6 months, and 11 to 12 months, respectively) in all societies. These facts strongly suggest that the brain is "prewired" for linguistic abilities. This prewiring, like the evolution of physical traits, is the result of the adaptive value of language and the selective pressures that established it.

The brain and the genes that influence its morphology and function appear to allow for a wide range of *potential* behaviors rather than determining extremely specific behaviors. This flexibility of behavior is one of the things that defines people as human. While the range of potential behaviors has limits, dictated in part by biology, the cultural dimension of human be-

---

[7]S. J. Gould, *Ever Since Darwin: Reflections in Natural History* (New York: Norton, 1977), 256.

BOX 6–1

KIN SELECTION

Presented here is a diagram that illustrates a hypothetical case of kin selection involving altruism. A person whose house is on fire is faced with a dilemma: he must choose between two possible actions. The individual could save himself, but in so doing his siblings would perish in the fire. On the other hand, he could warn his siblings of the danger by running back into the burning house, but then he would die as a result of his act. If his action resulted from the inheritance of an altruistic gene, then his choice would be predestined.

The man warns his siblings and dies in the fire. Let us assume that each sibling ultimately produces the same number of children that the altruist would have if he had lived. By saving the lives of his siblings, the altruist indirectly contributed more genes to the next generation than he would have if he had lived and his siblings had died. His altruistic act increased his inclusive fitness.

The altruist shared 50 percent of his genes with each of his siblings. Therefore, his three surviving siblings contribute 150 percent (3 times 50 percent) of his genes to the next generation (see arrows) compared with what he would have contributed if he had lived and had two children (and three dead siblings).

Good examples of kin selection are provided by ants, bees, and wasps. Genetically controlled or influenced altruism in humans remains a debatable issue.

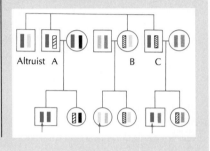

havior allows much greater variation among individuals than does the innately controlled behavior of termites, lizards, or any other animal. Although the human brain evolved with the potential for language abilities, the specific language (such as English, Spanish, Chinese, or Navaho) that one speaks is completely a result of social learning. Any human can learn any language.

Over no issue is the debate about the nature and degree to which human behavior is genetically or environmentally influenced more intense than the issue of human aggression and violence. Partly in response to the sociobiological contention that human aggression and violence are under genetic influence, a 1986 United Nations conference drafted a statement on this matter. This statement, called the Seville Statement on Violence, concludes that there is no scientific evidence to support the proposition that humans are biologically conditioned to practice warfare. Most sociobiologists do not agree with this conclusion, and the search for answers to the questions involving the nature of human violence and other human behaviors continues (Chapter 12).

Summary

Variability is inherent in all populations. The human species is polymorphic, and natural selection operates upon this variability. Natural selection can be seen as differences in reproductive rates among the variants within the population. Possessors of some genotypes reproduce to varying degrees, while others leave behind no offspring. Since the possessors of different genotypes produce differing numbers of offspring, their contribution to the next generation differs, and this brings about changes in the gene pool. Individuals or populations with higher survival or fertility rates are said to be better fitted to the environment in which they live. Still, a genotype that is fit in one environment may lose some or all of its fitness in a new one; the converse is also true.

THE ORIGIN OF SPECIES

Microevolution is the process of establishing and eliminating alleles from a population through

BOX 6–2

THE IMPLICATIONS OF SOCIOBIOLOGY

In reality, the complex social behavior pattern of the human species is the outcome of the complementary interaction of biological evolution and cultural evolution. The key question is not whether there is a genetic foundation of social behavior in humans, but rather how firm and constraining is the foundation. The greater our knowledge and understanding of the degree of genetic determinism, the greater our capacity to modify behavior by cultural changes.[1]

As E. Peter Volpe implies in the above quotation, the degree to which a specific type of behavior is genetically determined or learned has enormous implications for humans. If a behavior has a strong genetic basis, then attempts to alter that behavior by changing sociological processes may be of limited value. If, for example, human aggression derives primarily from the genes, the idea of a peaceful world would be hopeless without universal eugenic alteration of the human genome. If, on the other hand, behavior is completely learned, then any "bad" behavior could be eliminated through behavioral modification programs. We could learn not to be aggressive and violent.

In response to the debate over the causes of human aggression, a committee of scientists meeting in 1986 in Seville, Spain, drafted a statement on human aggression and violence. This statement has been endorsed by many organizations, including the American Anthropological Association. A resolution presented to the American Anthropological Association is as follows.

RESOLUTION ON ENDORSEMENT OF THE SEVILLE STATEMENT ON VIOLENCE

Whereas the levels of interpersonal violence have been increasing in recent years in the United States and elsewhere, and warfare is still prepared for and periodically engaged in by many nations of the world;

Whereas the continued existence of nuclear weapons endangers all life on this planet;

Whereas scientific findings have at times been misused or misinterpreted to justify violence, war, and/or the preparation for war, and the misinterpretation of scientific findings has contributed to widespread pessimism regarding the possibilities of reducing violence and abolishing war;

Whereas such pessimism contributes to passive acceptance of aggression and is not conducive to open-minded exploration of possible alternative means for resolving interpersonal and international conflict;

Whereas anthropology offers considerable scientific insights into human nature, and many anthropologists have studied human violence and warfare; therefore,

Be it resolved that the American Anthropological Association endorses the Seville Statement on Violence, drafted by a committee of scientists from various nations and academic disciplines, including anthropology, in Seville, Spain on May 16, 1986, at a meeting sponsored by the Spanish National UNESCO Commission.[2]

Douglas P. Fry explains the Seville Statement on Violence in the following way:

The Statement on Violence is presented in the form of five major propositions, each one being elaborated upon in the original document. The propositions are: (1) It is scientifically incorrect to say that we have inherited a tendency to make war from our animal ancestors. (2) It is scientifically incorrect to say that war or any other violent behavior is genetically programmed into our human nature. (3) It is scientifically incorrect to say that in the course of human evolution there has been a selection for aggressive behavior more than for other kinds of behavior. (4) It is scientifically incorrect to say that humans have a "violent brain." (5) It is scientifically incorrect to say that war is caused by "instinct" or any other single motivation. The Statement on Violence concludes that humanity is not condemned to war by biology, but to the contrary, humanity is capable of inventing peace, as well as war.

Because of widespread pessimism about the possibilities of reducing interpersonal violence and/or implementing nonviolent alternatives to war, the Statement on Violence merits wide circulation and discussion. Anthropologists and others are requested to reflect upon how they might use, or expand upon, the Statement on Violence in their various roles as teachers, researchers, consultants, and citizens.[3]

The above use of the term *scientifically incorrect* should be taken to mean that no currently valid data exist to support the views being negated in the five statements. It should not be taken to mean that such valid data will never develop. One of the purposes of the Seville Statement on Violence is, according to David Adams of Wesleyan University, to encourage debate and research on human nature as it relates to violence and aggression.[4]

---

[1]E. Peter Volpe, *Understanding Evolution*, 5th ed. (Dubuque, Iowa: Wm C. Brown, 1985), 255.
[2]D. P. Fry, "Resolution on Endorsement of the Seville Statement on Violence," *Anthropology Newsletter*, 28 (January 1987), 24. Reprinted with the permission of the American Anthropological Association from *Anthropology Newsletter* 28, January 1987. Not for further reproduction.
[3]Ibid.
[4]"Seville Statement on Violence Endorsed," *Anthropology Newsletter*, 28 (December 1987), 1.

natural selection and genetic drift. Microevolution is small-scale evolution which can be seen occurring in living populations, as in the case of industrial melanism. Thus far we have been discussing microevolution. **Macroevolution** addresses the evolution of new species and higher taxa such as genera and families. It is evolution that takes place over many generations and can be observed through fossil evidence.

Many think of macroevolution as the accumulation of minute changes in the gene pool over very long periods of time. Recently, however, some researchers have proposed that macroevolution might also operate partly on some principles specific to it. We will explore this possibility shortly.

The Evolution of Subspecies

All natural populations of plants and animals have variation within them, as well as within or between segments of a population. For instance, within your community, your classroom, and your family there are obvious differences in physical appearance in addition to less easily observed differences in such traits as blood type and resistance to disease.

Population variation varies with spatial distribution. The local population itself is a **deme,** a group of organisms that live together, exploit the same habitat, and mate most frequently with one another. Individuals within the deme tend to resemble one another more closely than they do individuals of adjacent demes. A group of neighboring demes occupying similar habitats also share many similar characteristics.

Differences between groups of demes evolve because of many factors, including genetic drift and the founder principle. A particular mutation may occur in one deme and not in another. Mating is nonrandom, and patterns of mating may vary from one group to another. Most importantly, different populations occupy slightly different niches. Populations that occupy slightly different niches are subject to subtle differences in selective pressures. When these populations interbreed with low frequency, distinct characteristics may develop in each. When significant differences occur between groups within a larger

population, we say that **subspecies,** or **races,** have evolved.

What constitutes a significant difference between populations? This question has no clear answer. Determining whether a species is made up of one more-or-less homogeneous group, or whether it has two, twelve, or twenty subspecies, depends on the criteria being used. Different scientists employ different criteria and do not always agree with one another. For example, if two groups of demes within the same population differ greatly with respect to individual size and coloration, most might agree that they are different subspecies. However, if the groups differ only slightly in size and display few other differences, are they one or two subspecies?

Continuous variation is an additional problem. For instance, in California the yarrow plant varies in height according to the altitude at which it grows. It does not vary in distinct jumps but gradually decreases in height with increased altitude. This type of gradient is called a **cline.**

Clines also exist in human populations. For instance, blood-type O reaches a frequency of about 75 percent in western Europe, but it gradually decreases in more eastern populations until it reaches about 50 percent in Russia. Can one draw a line anywhere along the cline and say that on one side one subspecies exists and on the other side a different subspecies? This problem will be considered in detail in Chapter 8.

SPECIATION   Subspecies are populations in the larger population, the species. These subspecific units can differ from one another in many ways, yet they are at the same time interfertile; that is, they can reproduce successfully with one another. Occasional matings between members of adjacent demes counteract, to a degree, the differences that develop between them.

When a member of one subspecies mates with a member of another subspecies, alleles are transferred from one group to the other. For example, if an advantageous mutation develops in subspecies A and occasional matings take place between subspecies A and B, the mutation may be introduced into subspecies B. We speak of **gene flow** as the movement of alleles from one population to another (Figure 6–8). Gene flow acts to keep the gene pool more-or-less uniform

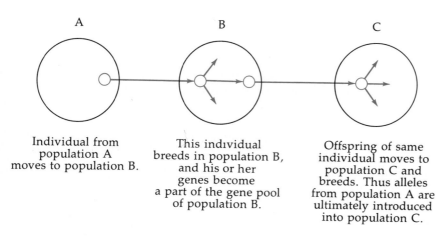

A	B	C
Individual from population A moves to population B.	This individual breeds in population B, and his or her genes become a part of the gene pool of population B.	Offspring of same individual moves to population C and breeds. Thus alleles from population A are ultimately introduced into population C.

FIGURE 6–8   *Gene flow.*

throughout a species range and hence prevents one subspecies from becoming highly differentiated from another. Gene flow also ensures the spread of beneficial mutations throughout a population, while deleterious alleles are eliminated at their points of origin.

If intergroup matings cease, each subspecies will subsequently evolve separately. As an example, Figure 6–9 shows the distribution of demes over a region. When a river changes its course, separating the population into two parts, the inability to swim prevents matings between the two groups of demes, and so gene flow effectively stops.

Once gene flow has ceased, the two subpopulations begin to change as genetic drift and patterns of nonrandom mating operate differently in each group. Selective pressures may differ in the two areas because of subtle differences in the microenvironments on opposite sides of the river. Also, different mutations may occur in each of the separated groups. These factors lead to changes in allelic frequencies between the two groups and to the evolution of new alleles. If the differences in gene frequencies between the two groups become great enough, the groups will no longer be capable of successful reproduction with each other even if the barrier is later removed. Thus, the two groups may begin as two distinct subspecies and eventually evolve into two distinct species.

THE ROLE OF GEOGRAPHICAL ISOLATION

Geographical isolation is a primary initiator of

speciation in animals. It is the process by which members of a population become separated by barriers that prevent the interchange of genes. Such barriers include large bodies of water, mountain ranges, and deserts. **Speciation** occurs when the separated populations have evolved characteristics that prevent reproductive success between them even if the geographical barriers are later lifted. Species that occupy mutually exclusive geographical areas are called **allopatric species.**

Speciation may result from spatial isolation more subtle than major geographical barriers. Organisms may adapt to narrowly defined ecological niches. Within a tropical forest, for example, the tops of trees present microhabitats that may be quite different from those on the tree trunks or near the ground, in which case speciation may result from spatial isolation within the same small area.

THE ROLE OF TEMPORAL ISOLATION

Populations evolve. Genetic changes build up over the generations, and thus a population may be genetically quite dissimilar from its ancestral population. One species becomes two if what was two subspecies are no longer capable of successful reproduction.

Population A evolves over a thousand generations into population B. They may look different, and these differences may be measurable, but we know from work with contemporary species that variation within a species can be great. Since it is impossible to gather reproductive data on an ancient population, the definition of a species known only from the fossil record becomes very difficult and highly problematical.

Paleontologists, who study the record of the past, break up a continuous progression, as seen in the fossil record, into species; species established in this way are called **paleospecies.** This concept will be discussed further in Chapter 14.

REPRODUCTIVE ISOLATING MECHANISMS

Spatial or temporal isolation initiates speciation, but once speciation has taken place, the species may come to reside within the same region. Such species are called **sympatric species** (Figure 6–10). Eight reproductive isolating mechanisms serve to separate closely related species living side by side.

Ecological isolation is the circumstance in which two closely related populations are separated by what is often a slight difference in the niches they occupy. Some species are adapted to such extremely narrow niches that minor differences, such as variations in soil conditions, can

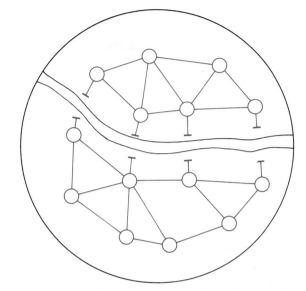

FIGURE 6–9 *First step in speciation.* Geographical isolation of two groups of demes prevents gene flow between them. Small circles represent demes and the connecting lines between them represent gene flow.

FIGURE 6–10 *Allopatric and sympatric species. (a)* Allopatric species occupy mutually exclusive geographical areas. *(b)* Sympatric species live in the same area, but they are prevented from successful reproduction by a reproductive isolating mechanism.

(a) (b)

effectively separate them even when they are living next to each other.

Seasonal isolation occurs when the breeding seasons of two closely related populations do not correspond. For example, a male from one species whose breeding season is in April cannot mate with a female from another species whose breeding season is in June.

Sexual isolation is the condition in which an incompatibility in behavior prevents mating between individuals of closely related populations. For instance, one or both sexes of a species may initiate mating by a pattern of behavior that acts as a stimulus to the other sex of its own species but does not act as a stimulus to the opposite sex in a closely related species. The stimuli might take the form of specific visual signals, such as the mating rituals of certain birds or the light signals sent out by male fireflies. The member of the opposite sex responds only to the signal characteristic of its group. Incompatibility in auditory stimuli, such as calls, and chemical stimuli, such as the release of odoriferous substances, can also act as behavioral isolating mechanisms.

Mechanical isolation occurs because of an incompatibility in the structure of the male and female sex organs. In some cases copulation is attempted, but no sperm is transferred.

Ecological, seasonal, sexual, and mechanical reproductive isolating mechanisms are **premating mechanisms** that prevent species from exchanging gametes. In **postmating mechanisms** gametes are exchanged but either no offspring result or the offspring that do result are inviable, are sterile, or have reduced fertility. Premating mechanisms are less wasteful than postmating mechanisms since in the former gametes are not consumed but in the latter they are.

Gametic mortality is the process by which sperm are immobilized and destroyed before fertilization can take place. This occurs if antibodies in the genital tract of the female kill the sperm or if the sperm cannot penetrate the membrane of the egg. The term **zygotic mortality** describes the situation in which fertilization occurs but development ceases soon after.

Hybrid inviability occurs when a mating between two species gives rise to a fertile hybrid that does not leave any offspring. This process is not well understood, but the lack of success of the hybrid may depend on its inability to compete effectively with nonhybrid individuals. In other words, the hybrid may not be as well adapted as the nonhybrid parents, or it may not display appropriate mating behavior. These adaptive and behavioral limitations may prevent the production of progeny.

Hybrid sterility occurs when the hybrid of two species is sterile. The classic example is the hybrid of the horse and the donkey, the mule, which, with few exceptions, is incapable of reproduction.

SPECIATION IN GENETIC TERMS   Why is isolation necessary for speciation to occur? The answer can be phrased in genetic terms as follows: isolation allows descended populations to develop in an undisturbed manner without the infusion of genes from another closely related population. In this way, the genetic material in the isolated population can be reconstituted, resulting in the development of one of the reproductive isolating mechanisms previously discussed. As long as there is significant gene flow between populations, these mechanisms cannot develop. Mutation, drift, nonrandom mating, and selection operate to bring about speciation in isolated populations. The probability that the *same* mutation will occur, or that mutations will occur in the same sequence, in two different isolated populations is effectively zero. Different mutations create different potential genotypes.

Also, alleles can recombine in an almost infinite number of ways, which is important since a particular allele can have differing selective advantages in the context of variable genotypes. Since each isolated population contains unique gene combinations, new combinations may arise by chance, providing some selective advantage to the population.

In addition, no two habitats are identical. Therefore, separate populations are subject to different selective pressures. The genetic systems of separated populations tend to adapt to the changing environments. In fact, they must, or else they will become extinct. The new populations also represent different sectors of the parental population because of the founder principle, and so they are somewhat different from each other from the very beginning.

Ecology and Speciation

Animal populations are able to expand into new geographical regions and occupy some of the ecological niches that exist in these regions. However, the ability to adapt to new niches varies from an extremely limited potential in some populations to an almost unlimited expansive ability in others. The major factors influencing this capability include the nature of the geographical barriers, the amount of change a group of organisms can tolerate, and the mode or modes of dispersal, that is, the ability of the organism to "get around."

When a population enters a new region, it occupies niches similar to those it occupied in the original area. The niches are not identical either because minor environmental differences may exist or because other niches may already be occupied by another species.

COMPETITION   When two populations occupy the same or parts of the same niche, they are said to be competing with one another. **Competition** does not necessarily mean that individuals belonging to the two populations physically fight one another. It simply means that they eat the same food, seek out the same sleeping places, or are active at the same time of day.

When two populations are competing in the same niche, differences in anatomy, physiology, or behavior may give one population the edge. For example, a population that is able to gain access to food at the expense of the other population will be able to maintain itself in the niche. The other population will either die out, move, or—an important factor in speciation—adapt to another or a more restricted niche. Thus, if one population's diet includes fruits, leaves, and occasionally insects and another population's diet consists of fruits and leaves only, the first might increase its intake of insects. This population may ultimately become primarily insectivorous in its habits.

PREADAPTATION   Populations entering new geographical regions often occupy niches not found in their original area. These populations do not become totally adapted to the new niches since the selective pressures characteristic of these new niches have not been operating on them. Nevertheless, many populations, or individuals within a population, may already have developed characteristics that prove to be adaptive in the new situation. The term **preadaptation** refers to the potential to adapt to a new niche. Organisms do not adapt because they need to but because by chance they have the potential to adapt.

A classic example of preadaptation is the evolution of flight. *Archaeopteryx*, until recently thought to be the earliest known bird, is very similar to small, flightless reptiles of its time (Figure 14–2b). The one distinguishing feature of *Archaeopteryx* is the presence of feathers. Through mutation and selective pressure, reptilian scales evolved into feathers within the *Archaeopteryx* or ancestral population. The evolution of feathers was not in response to any anticipated need for flight. Perhaps feathers had selective advantage over scales in their ability to retain body heat. However, once evolved, lightweight feathers also allowed their possessors to glide through the air. Subsequent mutations and natural selection led to the evolution of modern birds.

A population's niche may change not only because of movement into new regions but also because of changes in the environment within an area. Therefore, preadaptation is important even to species that remain in one locality. Because preadaptation is a chance event, extinction instead of survival often occurs.

ECOLOGICALLY SPECIALIZED SPECIES   A species is **specialized** when it can tolerate little change in its particular niche. A specialized species may not be able to move into new niches, even when the environmental conditions are similar, and may not be able to compete successfully with other populations. An example of an extremely specialized animal in terms of diet is the Australian koala, which eats almost exclusively the leaves of eucalyptus trees. The distribution and proliferation of these trees therefore determine the distribution of the animal. Any change in tree population, resulting from a change in climate or in human use, affects the koala population.

Because a specialized species can tolerate little change in its ecological niche, its ability to disperse is limited. However, as long as the habitat remains stable, a specialized species will be highly competitive toward less specialized species in its habitat and will experience a high degree of reproductive success.

If a small population becomes geographically isolated from the parental population and develops a specialized relationship with the new environment, this ecological specialization will act as an isolating mechanism, preventing gene flow. Hence, speciation will occur.

ECOLOGICALLY GENERALIZED SPECIES   A **generalized species** can survive in a variety of ecological niches. Humans are perhaps the most generalized of all species. Through their cultural ingenuity human populations can adjust to environments such as the extreme cold of the Arctic and the heat and humidity of the tropics by making tools and building appropriate shelters. Now, with the development of life-support systems, people can live for extended periods of time under the sea and in outer space. This ability to move into a variety of habitats has been responsible for the great dispersal of humans over the earth. Perhaps in the future it will be responsible for their dispersal throughout the solar system.

Because of people's lack of precise environmental requirements and because of their ability to adjust culturally, geographical barriers have had little chance to isolate human populations effectively. Since gene flow has been continuous, speciation has not occurred among humans. People are, of course, not the only generalized animals. In fact, *generalized* and *specialized* are relative terms. At one end is the extremely specialized koala, and at the other the very generalized *Homo sapiens*. Within these limits are varying degrees of generalization and specialization.

SPECIALIZED AND GENERALIZED TRAITS
We have been using the concepts of generalization and specialization to refer to the relationship between a population and its niche, but we can also use these terms to label specific characteristics displayed by the members of populations. For instance, the human hand is generalized in that it can be used for many purposes, such as carrying objects and manufacturing tools. The foot, on the other hand, is specialized in that it is used for basically one thing, locomotion. What is important here is that the relative specialization or generalization of a specific trait may make that trait more important for survival than another trait. Generally, the more specialized anatomical, physiological, or behavioral features an animal has, the more specialized the total phenotype is.

Specialization can lead not only to speciation but also to evolutionary dead ends. The more specialized an animal becomes, the less likely it will be to move into new niches; hence the animal has less chance of encountering the isolation necessary for further speciation to occur. When a species becomes so specialized in a particular niche that it cannot tolerate change, it is in greater danger of extinction than a more generalized species. If eucalyptus trees die out, so will koalas. On the other hand, if one of the environments that a particular group of humans occupies becomes unlivable, other environments will support this group.

Rates of Speciation

The rates at which speciation occurs are difficult to determine, and the fossil record is of little help. First, it is difficult or impossible to know when reproductive isolating mechanisms came into being. How can one tell from bones if differences in mating behavior existed between two morphologically similar populations?

Second, even if isolating mechanisms could be observed in the fossil record, they develop in too short a time for the points at which differentiation takes place to be noticed. Reproductive isolating mechanisms might develop quickly, but a fossil sequence most likely consists of forms that lived thousands of years apart.

Although rates of speciation cannot be measured effectively, we can infer that they are dependent on internal and external factors. Internal factors include such things as point mutations, chromosome changes, and other genetic factors that may lead to the development of reproductive isolating mechanisms. External factors include the types of barriers to gene flow, the types of new ecological niches available, and so forth.

We may assume that related populations that have low mutation rates, live in homogeneous environments without physical barriers, and are not under great selective pressure may remain basically stable and not develop sufficient differences for speciation. It follows that high mutation rates, strong selective pressures, differing ecological niches, and separation by geographical barriers may provide the necessary conditions for rapid speciation.

THE TEMPO OF EVOLUTIONARY CHANGE

There are two general views on the tempo of evolutionary change. Charles Darwin called the first "descent with modification." Known today as **phyletic gradualism,** it sees evolution as a slow process characterized by gradual transformation of one population into others. In 1972 paleontologists Niles Eldridge and Stephen Jay Gould proposed a different scheme, called **punctuated equilibrium.**

The phyletic gradualism model of evolution assumes that the rate of evolutionary change is relatively slow and constant through time. The fossil record, however, reveals what appear to be shifts in the pace of evolutionary change within specific lineages. An evolutionary line that has been very "conservative" for millions of years may seem to suddenly undergo a rapid burst of evolutionary change. Evolution may proceed quickly when a population enters a new habitat, but as the population adapts to its new niche, the rate of evolution slows. These shifts in the tempo of evolution are seen as an illusion by phyletic gradualists. Such shifts in tempo are explained as reflections of imperfections in the fossil record caused by such things as changing conditions for fossilization.

The punctuated equilibrium model is consistent with the data from the fossil record. Eldridge and Gould propose that a large population may become fragmented into several new populations by geographical isolation or migration. New populations, now peripheral to the main population, would initially differ from the main population because of the founder effect. In addition, these peripheral populations would be small and therefore subject to the effects of genetic drift. Some researchers believe that in small peripheral populations genetic drift is a much stronger evolutionary force than has previously been proposed in most microevolutionary models. Thus, natural selection and genetic drift may differ in their importance in microevolution and macroevolution in different populations (Figure 6–11).

Other genetic events could be responsible for relatively rapid evolutionary shifts. Among these are chromosomal mutations such as translocations and inversions. Another possibility involves regulatory genes.

In the early 1960s, two French scientists, François Jacob and Jacques Monod, proposed a model of genetic events that seems to account for evolutionary occurrences not explainable by other models.[8] They proposed the existence of two major classes of genes. The first type, called **structural genes,** codes for specific polypeptide chains that make up protein molecules such as hemoglobin and melanin. The second class contains **regulatory genes,** which do not code for any structural or enzymatic features of the phenotype but do control the activity of structural genes. Regulatory genes turn structural genes "on" and "off" and so control the time of production and quantity of polypeptide chains. Mutations in regulatory genes may play an important role in speciation. Such mutations would not affect the coding for a polypeptide chain, but they might change the timing of the production of that structural unit or block its production altogether.

Differences between closely related species may be due more to mutations in the regulation of structural genes than to changes in the structural genes themselves. For example, researchers have found that, on the average, forty-four human and chimpanzee proteins are 99 percent identical, yet these organisms are anatomically quite dissimilar (see Table 13–10). Mary-Claire King and Allan C. Wilson believe that the differences are due mainly to changes in regulatory,

---

[8]F. Jacob and J. Monod, "Genetic Regulating Mechanisms in the Synthesis of Protein," *Journal of Molecular Biology,* 3 (1961), 316–356.

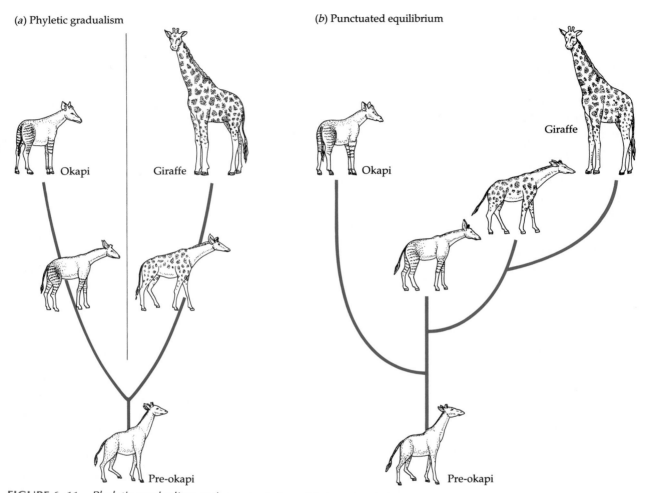

(a) Phyletic gradualism

(b) Punctuated equilibrium

Okapi

Giraffe

Giraffe

Okapi

Pre-okapi

Pre-okapi

FIGURE 6–11 *Phyletic gradualism and punctuated equilibrium.* (a) Phyletic gradualism sees okapi and giraffe evolution as two evolutionary lines slowly diverging from a common ancestor. (b) Punctuated equilibrium sees a small population coming off of the pre-okapi group leading to modern okapis, while several more giraffelike species evolved and became extinct through time.

not structural, genes.[9] Since one regulatory gene may affect many morphological and behavioral traits, a mutation to a single or a few regulatory genes may lead to rapid evolution. This idea will be discussed further in Chapter 13.

Adaptive Radiation

Movement into new ecological niches depends upon many factors. First, there has to be physi-

cal access to the new niche; physical barriers may limit an organism's chance for dispersal. Second, the habitats in which the individuals live must provide a variety of niches. A lowland animal living in a valley surrounded by high mountains has immediate access to a diversity of adjacent altitudinal niches. In contrast, a flatland animal population, while perhaps finding it easier to move more extensively, may encounter only a limited number of flatland niches. Third, the individuals entering the new niche must be preadapted to some degree. Fourth, either the new niche must be unoccupied or the entering individuals must be able to compete successfully

[9]M.-C. King and A. C. Wilson, "Evolution at Two Levels in Humans and Chimpanzees," *Science*, 188 (1975), 107–116.

with other populations already existing in the niche.

A generalized species is usually able to survive in a variety of habitats. Its members may spread into new ecological niches to which they are preadapted and form new populations. Over time, these populations will take on distinctive characteristics as they become more closely adapted to their new niches. Subspecies will form, and in many cases new species will emerge. The evolution of new species is most likely to occur in certain situations: when a species enters an uninhabited environment or one in which competition does not exist (as in the example below), or when a species develops new anatomical or physiological adaptations that allow it to compete successfully in a variety of niches. Such a proliferation of new species is called an **adaptive radiation.**

A classic example of adaptive radiation is the case of the finches of the Galápagos Islands, 965 kilometers (600 miles) off the coast of Ecuador. Darwin observed the many varieties of finches on the islands and later proposed that natural selection was the force behind this variation.

A single species of seed-eating ground finch is found on the mainland of South America. This population is believed to be similar to the ancestral form of at least fourteen distinct species of finches on the Galápagos Islands. When the an-

cestral finches arrived on the islands, they were able to adapt and survive in the varied habitats available to them. There was no competition from other birds for living space and food resources, and the finches were preadapted for survival in the new niches.

The present finch species display differences in diet and in beak size and shape. Some are seed eaters like the ancestral population, but beak size varies among these species. The large-beaked ground finches eat both large, hard seeds and smaller food, while the smaller-beaked birds must rely on the smaller, softer foods only. At the present time, the competition for food is not great, for the large-beaked birds usually ignore the smaller seeds. If these birds were to compete with the smaller-beaked species, the more specialized small-beaked birds would very likely be reduced in number or become extinct.

Finches with other beak forms also evolved. One with a straight beak feeds on the prickly pear cactus, exploiting the nectar and soft pulp. The vegetarian tree finch, with a parrotlike beak, eats leaves, fruits, and buds, and several finches are insectivorous (Figure 6–12). Perhaps the most interesting of the Galápagos finches is the woodpecker finch, which uses a cactus spine or twig to remove insects from cracks or holes in the bark of trees. This bird habitually uses tools in order to obtain its food supply and has even been

FIGURE 6–12 *Darwin's finches.* The diverse bill forms represent adaptations to different niches, an example of an adaptive radiation.

Large seed-eating ground finch

Cactus ground finch

Insectivorous tree finch

Small seed-eating ground finch

Vegetarian tree finch

Woodpecker finch

FIGURE 6–13 *The woodpecker finch.* The woodpecker finch uses and sometimes makes a tool in order to exploit an ecological niche.

observed altering twigs to the most efficient size or shape (Figure 6–13).

Each differing niche presented different selective pressures. In addition, the islands were far enough apart to minimize contact between the populations. As time went on, new subspecies and, ultimately, new species emerged. From the single ancestral population many distinct species evolved.

Extinction

While evolution is constantly bringing about the development of new species, other species are disappearing. When pressures develop in an environment, natural selection does not always bring about new adaptations. In many cases, the organisms involved simply do not have the potential to adapt. Because they are too specialized and are not preadapted to the new situation, they become **extinct.**

Extinction is not an unusual event. Extinctions of the past far outnumber the total number of species that are living today. Humans, through their technology, have increased the rate of extinction. They use guns to kill animals and bulldozers to destroy their habitats. Although there is usually competition between organisms for particular niches, in which some of the competitors are displaced, no large animals can compete

successfully with *Homo sapiens* for any environment. (Interestingly, those organisms that do compete successfully with humans are small forms, such as mice, flies, and disease organisms.) Therefore, the give and take, the periods of change and reestablishment of new balances, and the derivation of new types do not generally occur when people take over an environment.

Humans, in an attempt to improve their genetic heritage through eugenics, might also be lowering the species' ability to adapt and adjust to new environmental situations. This is the subject of Box 6–3.

Summary

Macroevolution includes those processes responsible for the evolution of species and higher taxa. The local reproductive population is the deme, and the forces of evolution operate to bring about changes in gene frequencies within the gene pools of demes. Since different demes of the same species occupy slightly different habitats, selective pressures may differ from deme to deme.

When demes or groups of demes become reproductively isolated, subspecies may develop. The elimination of gene flow between demes, which is usually the result of some type of geographical barrier, allows for the accumulation of different mutations within each deme. These accumulations and gene-frequency changes, generated within and restricted to each deme, ultimately make successful reproduction between the demes impossible. Over time, these populations may become distinct species, called allopatric species.

Sympatric species are closely related species that have come to reside in the same general geographical area. Yet gene flow is effectively prevented by one of several reproductive isolating mechanisms: ecological isolation, seasonal isolation, sexual isolation, mechanical isolation, gametic mortality, zygotic mortality, hybrid inviability, and hybrid sterility.

Populations within a species tend to disperse into new regions where they occupy similar ecological niches, but these new niches can never be identical to the original ones. Certain individuals

BOX 6–3

EUGENICS AND THE REDUCTION OF VARIABILITY

Humans are one of the most ecologically generalized species, primarily because of human culture which allows for flexible responses to diversity and environmental change. Humans also show considerable biological diversity (Chapters 7 and 8) which allows for the exploitation of numerous environments.

Eugenics is the study of various methods that can improve the inherited qualities of a species (Chapter 4). Nevertheless, in some instances eugenic programs could have a very negative effect on the human population by reducing genetic variability.

A major question is, What traits should be eliminated? Genetic abnormalities that lead to an early death, extremely low intelligence, and severe skeletal abnormalities will probably never have any advantages in future generations.

However, what about certain mild metabolic defects or blood disorders which could conceivably have beneficial effects if the environment should change? Also, alleles that are deleterious in the homozygous state may confer adaptive advantage in the heterozygote.

A classic example of this situation is the relationship between sickle-cell anemia and malaria. Sickle-cell anemia is often a lethal trait, bringing about disability and early death, yet the presence of this deleterious allele in the heterozygous individual brings about a resistance to malaria. There are many other examples of alleles which, although disadvantageous in the homozygous recessive state, bring about a greater adaptation in the heterozygous than in the homozygous normal individual. In 1987 the carrier rate for cystic fibrosis, a fatal lung disease, was

found to be higher than expected; one explanatory proposal is that the heterozygous individual has some selective advantage that has yet to be identified.

Imagine a situation whereby, by using eugenic means, we could eliminate the allele for sickle-cell anemia through detection of heterozygotes. This is a fine goal. What would happen, though, if the techniques for controlling malaria become ineffective? Because of the disappearance of the sickle-cell allele, the population would lack the protection from malaria conferred by this allele. This is not farfetched, since the major means of controlling malaria is to destroy the disease-carrying mosquito with an insecticide such as DDT. Already, large populations of mosquitos have evolved that have a resistance to DDT. If malaria became a threat again and the sickle-cell allele no longer existed, the population would be less fit in the new malarial environment than it was in the old one (see figure).

As the situation changes, what was at one time advantageous (the sickle-cell trait) might become disadvantageous, but conceivably it could become advantageous again. Also, new diseases can evolve; if certain types of people are deleted from the population through eugenics, it might later turn out that they were the people who carried the immunity to the new disease.

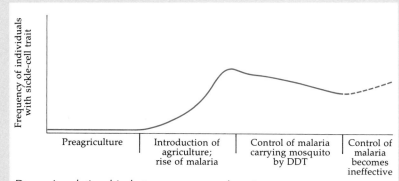

Dynamic relationship between genes and environment.

within the population may possess preadapted variations that increase their adaptation in the new niche. When a population enters an area in which it has no competition, or when a population evolves new anatomical or physiological adaptations, speciation may be quite rapid. This rapid proliferation of species is an adaptive radiation. However, if populations unable to compete in their original niche do not adapt to new or changing niches, extinction may result.

STUDY QUESTIONS

1. What is meant by the statement that evolution is based upon variation within the population and within the niche?
2. Compare the operation of natural selection on a homozygous dominant, homozygous recessive, and heterozygous trait.
3. Often the fitness of a particular trait and the nature of the selective pressures within a population are not obvious. What selective pressures operate upon hemoglobin S in a malarial environment?
4. Speciation follows geographical isolation. What occurs genetically after a population becomes geographically isolated? What factors other than geography serve to isolate populations?
5. Why is necessity not the "mother of invention" in evolutionary terms?
6. Contrast the phyletic gradualism model of evolution with the punctuated equilibrium model.
7. What differentiates a generalized species from a specialized species?
8. Why is extinction less probable in a generalized species than in a specialized one?

SUGGESTED READINGS

Bowler, P. J. *Evolution: The History of an Idea*, rev. ed. Berkeley: University of California Press, 1989. This book outlines the history of evolutionary theories. Its final chapter looks at modern debates about evolutionary theory, including the ideas of creationists.

Edelstein, S. J. *The Sickled Cell: From Myths to Molecules.* Cambridge, Mass.: Harvard University Press, 1986. This book details the history and nature of sickle-cell anemia.

Maitland, A. E., and D. C. Johanson. *Blueprints: Solving the Mystery of Evolution.* New York: Penguin, 1989. Written by a journalist and a well-known paleoanthropologist, this book is an extremely readable introduction to evolutionary theory. It tells the story of how evolutionary and genetic ideas developed through time.

Mayr, E. *Toward a New Philosophy of Biology: Observations of an Evolutionist.* Cambridge, Mass.: Harvard University Press, 1989. One of the best known modern evolutionary theorists discusses his ideas about evolution and the origin of species.

Volpe, E. P. *Understanding Evolution*, 6th ed. Dubuque, Iowa: Wm. C. Brown, 1996. This is a short introduction to the theory of evolution and population genetics.

Three stages in the life of actor George Burns.

The genetic basis of man's capacity to acquire, develop or modify, and transmit culture emerged because of the adaptive advantages which this capacity conferred on its possessors.[1]
Theodosius Dobzhansky (1900–1975)

[1]T. Dobzhansky, *Mankind Evolution* (New Haven, Conn.: Yale University Press, 1962), 20.

CHAPTER
7

HUMAN ADJUSTMENTS AND GROWTH AND DEVELOPMENT

A common dream, which has served as the plot of more than one novel, involves viewing or meeting an exact duplicate of oneself who lives in another place or time. This "second self" can be no more than illusory. Except for identical twins and the possibility of clones, genetic variables alone reduce the probability that two people can be exactly the same to all but zero. Even identical twins show variation due to differences in their environments.

There are three principal mechanisms that bring about variation among individuals and populations. The first is nongenetic adaptations called adjustments: behavioral adjustments are cultural responses to environmental stress, and acclimatory adjustments are reversible physiological responses to such stress. The second mechanism that brings about variation involves the processes of growth and development. Finally, there is microevolutionary change or adaptation. The first two of these mechanisms of variation are the subjects of this chapter. Adaptation will be discussed in Chapter 8.

HUMAN ADAPTABILITY: ADJUSTMENTS

Physiologically, humans are animals who evolved under conditions of the tropical savanna. R. P. Clark and O. G. Edholm write:

> A distinguished biologist, Peter Scholander, coined the phrase—"man is a tropical animal"—many years ago. He was emphasizing that man almost certainly originated in East Africa, in a hot, possibly rather dry, savannah environment, conditions for which man is well adapted. He is extremely well-endowed with sweat glands and has more than any other mammal; because of the ability to sweat at a high rate man can maintain body temperature in hot climates without difficulty. . . . Man is also almost hairless; this is not necessarily a great advantage in any climate but it is less of a disadvantage in hot climates than it is in cool or cold regions. Certainly for a highly sweating animal, a thick fur coat would be incompatible. . . . For all of these and many other reasons, man has the characteristics of a tropical animal.[2]

Today, human populations occupy a wide range of habitats, from the equatorial deserts of north Africa to the icy wastelands of the Arctic. While most animal species have become adapted to relatively narrow niches, humans exist in far-ranging, highly diverse niches.

The human species can survive in a wide diversity of habitats without undergoing microevolutionary change; this is possible because of nongenetic changes termed **adjustments.** However, the genetic potentials that allow for nongenetic adjustments are themselves products of the evolutionary process. A major problem facing researchers in this area is determination of the relative importance of genetic and nongenetic forms of adaptability, which we have termed here *adaptation* and *adjustment*, respectively. In fact, in most situations, both processes probably work together.

Behavioral Adjustments

Behavioral adjustments are cultural responses to environmental stresses. Culture provides human populations with a very important means of adjusting to such stresses. Because these adjustments are nongenetic, they can be continuously altered to meet new environmental situations.

HUMAN HOUSING   An example of how culture allows people to survive in stressful habitats is housing. The type of housing that is used in an area is influenced by such factors as temperature, humidity, wind, rain, and light. A classic example of the use of housing in a stressful habitat is the igloo of the Eskimo. The igloo consists of a dome-shaped structure (Romans and Etruscans were not the only people to develop the arch) connected to the outside by a tunnel (Figure 7–1). The construction material is snow, which is an excellent insulator because air is trapped within the snow itself. Heat within the structure is produced by a small seal-oil lamp. The heat of this lamp causes the snow to melt slightly during the day and refreeze at night, forming an icy reflective layer on the inside. This reflective layer plus the dome shape serve to reflect the heat throughout the igloo. Relatively little heat is lost to the outside since the dome shape minimizes the surface area from which heat can radiate. A long entry way gradually helps warm the air as one enters the structure, and it also serves to block the entry of wind into the habitation area.

Habitation structures are only one aspect of a people's technology. It is through all aspects of technology that people can survive under difficult environmental conditions. In fact, through behavioral adjustments humans have been able to spend limited periods of time deep under the ocean and in outer space.

SOCIAL RESPONSES TO HARSH ENVIRONMENTS   In addition to varying their house types and utilizing other technological adjustments such as clothing, weapons, and other tools, humans adjust their social organization to their environment. For instance, Eskimos who live in extremely harsh habitats may use several strategies to reduce environmental stress. The

---

[2]R. P. Clark and O. G. Edholm, *Man and His Thermal Environment* (London: Edward Arnold, 1985), 134.

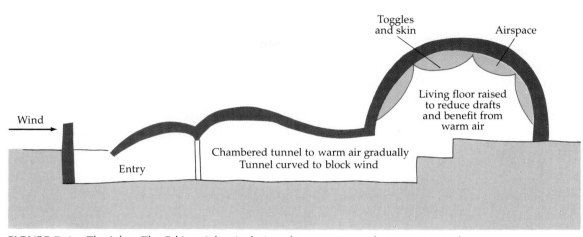

FIGURE 7–1 *The igloo.* The Eskimo igloo is designed to permit people to survive in the extremely hostile arctic environment.

anthropologist Knud Rasmussen discovered during a trip to King William Island that in a sample of eighteen marriages, thirty-eight out of ninety-six female infants born had been put to death.[3] This practice of female infanticide is a strategy used by the Nestilingmuit Eskimos to increase the ratio of males to females. They do this because males are hunters; in the harsh northern environments, such populations believe that females contribute less to survival than males do. Peoples in these harsh habitats may also practice suicide, invalidicide, and senilicide in crisis situations. By all these means, unproductive members are eliminated from the population, thus reducing the stress on those who remain and increasing the chances of survival of the group as a whole.

Infanticide is usually an extreme response to extreme conditions, although it has been found in many human societies. All human societies in some way adjust economic, political, social, religious, and other aspects of their social systems to environmental conditions. This sociocultural flexibility is, in part, what allows humans to exist in so many habitats.

Some sociobiologists propose that there are genetic factors involved in the behaviors of infanticide, suicide, invalidicide, and senilicide. Since, under specific circumstances, these practices improve the probability of the survival of a group, natural selection may tend to select for these practices in certain environments. Many anthropologists today maintain that sociobiological models may be valuable in understanding human behavior. However, other anthropologists remain cautious in accepting any ideas involving biological control of specific behaviors.

Acclimatory Adjustments to Arctic Habitats

Acclimatory adjustments are reversible physiological responses to environmental stress. Examples of acclimatization may be seen in three particularly stressful environments: the Arctic, the desert, and high altitudes.

Perhaps one of the more stressful habitats occupied by humans is the Arctic. Not surprisingly, people occupied the arctic regions late in human prehistory, and humans can become acclimatized to the climate to only a very limited degree.

The primary environmental stress in the Arctic is very low temperatures. Cold stress can lead to frostbite, an actual freezing of the tissues, which usually occurs in exposed, high-surface-area parts of the body such as fingers, toes, and

[3]K. Rasmussen, "The Netsilik Eskimos: Social Life and Spiritual Culture," in *Report of the Fifth Thule Expedition, 1921–1924* (Copenhagen: Cyldendalske Boghandel, 1931), 141.

earlobes. Another result of cold stress is **hypothermia,** or lowered body temperature. Normal body temperature, as measured in the mouth, averages 37°C (98.6°F). When the body temperature falls below 34.4°C (94°F), the ability of the hypothalamus of the brain to control body temperature is impaired. Temperature-regulating ability is lost at 29.4°C (85°F), and death may result.

Unlike other animals that occupy the Arctic, humans are not well adapted to cold stress; this fact is probably a reflection of people's tropical origins. Humans do not possess thick layers of subcutaneous fat or thick fur; in fact, the human body has remarkably little in the way of insulation. The most important factor for survival in the hostile arctic climate is responding with behavioral adjustments such as specialized housing, clothing, and other technologies.

While clothing and shelter provide insulation for humans in the Arctic, it is interesting to see what happens when a human is exposed to cold without the necessary behavioral and even acclimatory adjustments. The nude human body at rest must begin to combat a lowering of body temperature when the air temperature stands at approximately 31°C (87.8°F). This temperature is known as the **critical temperature.**

The subject of this experiment must both increase the heat produced by the body and reduce the loss of heat to the air. Two short-term methods of producing additional body heat are exercise and shivering. As any jogger knows, a high degree of muscle activity yields heat, but such exercise can be maintained only for limited periods of time. More important is shivering. Low body temperature causes the hypothalamus of the brain to stimulate increased muscle tone, which, when it reaches a certain level, results in shivering. At the height of shivering, the increase in muscle metabolism can raise body heat production to five times normal; but, like exercise, shivering cannot continue indefinitely. A major mechanism for conserving heat is peripheral **vasoconstriction.** Constriction of the capillaries in the skin prevents much of the warm blood from reaching the surface of the skin where much of the body's heat would be lost to the air.

People living under arctic conditions for long periods of time are less affected by the cold as time passes. Perhaps the most important accli-

matory adjustment is in the **basal metabolic rate.** The basal metabolic rate, which represents the total energy used by the body in maintaining those body processes necessary for life, is a measure of the minimum level of heat produced by the body at rest. Under cold stress, individuals are able to acclimatize by increasing their basal metabolic rate; this increase can be as much as 25 percent in adults and 170 percent in infants. The increased basal metabolic rate results in the production of additional body heat, but the production of this heat requires that individuals consume a great quantity of high-energy food sources. The native diet in arctic regions, which consists largely of protein and fat, provides the necessary types of food.

Acclimatory Adjustments to Desert Habitats

In some ways humans are better able to survive in the hot and arid climates of the world than in the arctic regions. This ability is due to the general lack of body hair, which, if present, would act as insulating material.

In desert habitats the human body must get rid of excess heat that is being absorbed by the body. In general, a nude human body loses heat in any one of four ways (Figure 7–2). The first is **conduction,** which occurs when heat appears to move from a warmer object to a cooler object by direct contact. Thus, if you touch an object cooler than yourself, heat will move from your body to the cooler object. The second is **convection,** in which the warm object is surrounded by a cooler fluid, either liquid or air. A person who is hot from absorbing solar radiation will lose heat as the heat from the body is transferred to the cooler air. As the air next to the body warms up, it expands, and expanding air rises. As the warm air rises from the skin, cooler air flows down to replace it. Thus currents set up in the air carry away heat.

The third way in which an object can rid itself of heat is by **radiation.** Radiation represents electromagnetic energy that is given off by an object as electromagnetic waves of a characteristic wavelength. Other forms of electromagnetic waves include visible light, ultraviolet radiation, and radio waves.

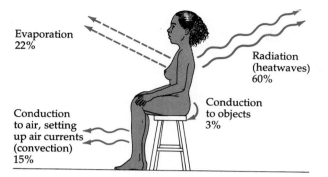

FIGURE 7–2 *Heat loss in a nude human figure.* This figure illustrates the various mechanisms by which heat is lost from a nude human body at rest. The percentages refer to the contribution of each mechanism to the total heat loss.

The fourth way in which an object can lose heat is through **evaporation.** When water is turned from a liquid to a gas, in this case water vapor, a certain amount of energy in the form of heat is required. Therefore, when you get out of a swimming pool on a warm day, you feel cool because some of your body heat is being used in the process of transforming the pool water left on your skin into water vapor.

While conduction, convection, radiation, and evaporation are used by the human body to rid itself of excess heat in warm climates, in air temperatures above 35°C (95°F) body heat is lost primarily through evaporation. Therefore, **sweating** is the most important method of controlling body temperature in warm climates. Humans have a greater capacity to sweat than any other mammal. G. A. Harrison writes: "Human sweating is a highly efficient cooling mechanism making us one of the few species well adapted to high energy expenditure during the day in hot and dry environments."[4]

Humans have a high density of sweat glands over their bodies, although the number per square centimeter differs in different parts of the body. Interestingly, people who go to live in desert environments do not develop additional sweat glands; the number of sweat glands does not differ significantly between desert- and non-desert-dwelling populations.

Acclimatizing to desert life is not well understood, but within a few weeks people living in hot, arid climates seem to reach some type of acclimatory adjustment. In time, the sweat glands become more sensitive and produce more sweat. Of course, sweat is not all water; it also contains salts, and much sodium is lost through sweating. With time, the concentration of salt in sweat is reduced, and the relatively high salt concentrations found in desert water usually compensate for salt loss. Urine volume is also reduced, thus helping the body conserve the water so badly needed for sweating. This same acclimatization ability has been found in peoples from all parts of the world. It appears to represent a basic ability of the human species instead of an adaptation of certain populations.

In addition, there are other short-term responses to increased heat loads. A physiological response is **vasodilation** of the capillaries of the skin. In vasodilation, the bloodstream brings more heat to the body surface as the capillaries of the skin dilate; then the heat is removed by sweating. People can also make a number of behavioral adjustments to hot climates. In desert regions people reduce physical activity during the heat of the day, thereby reducing heat production by the body. Also, desert-dwelling people adopt a relaxed body posture that increases the surface area of the body from which sweat may evaporate.

Adjustment to hot climates is aided by cultural factors such as clothing and shelter. Desert dwellers cover their bodies to protect their skin from sunlight and to reduce the amount of heat from the sun that directly heats the body. Their clothing is designed to permit the free flow of air between the clothing and the body. This airflow is necessary to carry off the water vapor formed by the evaporation of sweat.

It is interesting to note that the color of clothing does not seem to make much difference in hot climates. An experiment involving black and white Bedouin robes showed that the black robes gained about 2½ times as much heat as the white robes. Yet the temperature of the skin under black robes was the same as that under white robes. Most likely, the greater convection cur-

[4]G. A. Harrison, J. M. Tanner, D. R. Pilbeam, and P. T. Baker, *Human Biology*, 3d ed. (Oxford: Oxford University Press, 1988), 451.

rents between the black robe and the skin are responsible for this phenomenon.

Acclimatory Adjustments to High-Altitude Habitats

Joseph de Acosta, describing his travels across the Andes of South America, wrote in 1590:

> There is in Peru a high mountaine which they call Pariacaca. . . . When I came to mount the degrees, as they call them, which is the top of this mountaine, I was suddenly surprised with so mortall and strange a pang, that I was ready to fall from the top to the ground and although we were many in company, yet everyone made haste (without any tarrying for his companion) to free himself speedily from this ill passage. . . . I was surprised with such pangs of straining and casting as I thought to cast up my heart too: for having cast up meate, fleugme and choller both yellow and greene, in the end I cast up blood with the strining of my stomach. To conclude, if this had continued I should undoubtedly have died.[5]

Joseph de Acosta was describing **high-altitude, or mountain, sickness.** The symptoms of high-altitude sickness may include "shortness of breath, respiratory distress, physical and mental fatigue, rapid pulse rate, interrupted sleep, and headaches intensified by activity. There may also occur some slight digestive disorders and in some cases a marked loss of weight. In other cases the individual may feel dyspnea, nausea, and vomiting."[6] Although most people eventually become acclimatized to high altitudes, many do not. They will continue to suffer from chronic mountain sickness as long as they remain at a high altitude.

Less than 1 percent of the world's population lives at high altitudes, yet these people are of great interest to anthropologists. High-altitude environments place many stresses on human populations including low oxygen levels, high levels of solar radiation, cold, high winds, and, often, lack of moisture, rough terrain, and limited plant and animal life.

HIGH-ALTITUDE HYPOXIA   Our previous discussions of arctic and desert environments stressed the great importance of culture as a means of adjustment to stressful environments. Culture plays a major role at high altitudes as well, and it helps people adjust to many of the environmental problems that they face. However, a major situation in which culture plays virtually no role is **high-altitude hypoxia.**

Hypoxia refers to low oxygen pressure, which occurs when low levels of oxygen are supplied to the tissues of the body. High-altitude hypoxia is one of the few environmental stresses that cannot be adjusted to by some cultural means. Although the use of oxygen tanks provides limited adjustment, this solution is available only in high-technology cultures and is practical for only short periods of time (see Box 7–1).

The earth's atmosphere exerts an average of 1.04 kilograms of pressure on every square centimeter (14.7 pounds per square inch) of surface area at sea level. At sea level, this pressure raises a column of mercury in a closed tube to an average height of 760 millimeters (29.92 inches). Therefore, we say that the average air pressure at sea level is 760 millimeters (29.92 inches) of mercury.

The atmosphere is composed of many gases. Approximately 21 percent of air is oxygen; that portion of the total atmospheric pressure that is due to the pressure of oxygen is the **partial pressure** of oxygen. At sea level, the partial pressure of oxygen is 159 millimeters (6.26 inches) of mercury. As one gains altitude, the total air pressure and the partial pressure of oxygen decrease (Figure 7–3). At 4500 meters (14,765 feet) the partial pressure of oxygen decreases by as much as 40 percent, thus substantially reducing the amount of oxygen that can reach the tissues of the body.

The actual entry of oxygen into the bloodstream takes place in the approximately 300 million **alveoli** of the lungs. The alveoli are small air sacs which are richly endowed with blood capillaries. Although the partial pressure of oxygen at

[5]J. de Acosta, *The Naturall and Morall Historie of the East and West Indies* (Seville: 1604), quoted in M. P. Ward et al., *High Altitude Medicine and Physiology* (Philadelphia: University of Pennsylvania Press, 1989), 6.
[6]A. R. Frisancho, "Functional Adaptation to High Altitude Hypoxia," *Science*, 187 (1975), 313. The term **dyspnea** refers to difficult or painful breathing.

BOX 7-1

HOW HIGH CAN PEOPLE LIVE WITHOUT BOTTLED OXYGEN?

The highest human settlement in the world is Aconquija located at an elevation of 5000 meters (16,400 feet) in the Andes. It is possible for some individuals to perform at higher altitudes for short periods of time. "While the well-adapted climber can survive and function adequately for months at 19,000 feet, at 26,000 feet this is possible only for days, if no artificial oxygen is used."[1]

The highest place on earth is the summit of Mount Everest, which lies 8848 meters (29,028 feet) above sea level. The first humans to stand atop Mount Everest were Edmund Hillary and Tenzing Norgay on May 29, 1953. Since then several expeditions have reached the summit with the aid of bottled oxygen. In fact, it was believed that it was impossible for humans to climb that high without the use of bottled oxygen.

On May 9, 1978, two members of an Austrian expedition, Peter Habeler and Reinhold Messner, were the first humans to reach the top of Mount Everest without the use of bottled oxygen.[2] In 1981 the American Medical Research Expedition moved into the Himalayas to conduct research on human physiology at extreme altitudes. Research stations were established at several altitudes, and two members of the team reached the summit of Mount Everest without bottled oxygen and were able to take a limited number of physiological measurements.[3]

The symptoms of high-altitude sickness become exaggerated at extremely high altitudes, even in those who have become acclimatized to some degree. Reinhold Messner describes his feelings enroute to Mount Everest:

My rucksack weighed between 12 and 16 kilos [26 and 35 pounds], and to carry it was such an effort for me that it took all my strength and all the oxygen in my muscles, simply to thrust out my chest to take in air, and then to let it out again. . . . I could only manage 30 or 40 steps without oxygen, and they cost me so much strength, that the possibility of my climbing Everest without oxygen didn't even enter into the question.[4]

At high altitudes mental functions begin to become impaired, as described by Peter Habeler:

Our altitude was now 28,500 feet, and we had obviously reached a point at which normal brain functions had broken down, or at least were severely limited. Our attentiveness and concentration declined; our instinct no longer reacted as reliably as before; the capacity for clear logical thinking had also apparently been lost.[5]

[1]O. Ölz, "Everest without Oxygen: The Medical Fundamentals," in P. Habeler, *The Lonely Victory* (New York: Simon & Schuster, 1979), 220.
[2]P. Habeler, ibid.; R. Messner, *Everest: Expedition to the Ultimate* (New York: Oxford University Press, 1979).
[3]J. B. West, "Human Physiology at Extreme Altitudes on Mount Everest," *Science*, 223 (1984), 784–788.
[4]R. Messner, op. cit., 156.
[5]P. Habeler, op. cit. 183.

sea level is 159 millimeters (6.26 inches) of mercury, the partial pressure of oxygen in the alveoli at sea level is 104 millimeters (4.16 inches) of mercury. This is because not all the air in the lungs is replaced with each breath. The partial pressure of oxygen in the arteries and capillaries of the circulatory system is 95 millimeters (3.80 inches) of mercury, while the partial pressure of oxygen in the tissues is 40 millimeters (1.60 inches) of mercury.

Oxygen diffuses from the higher to the lower partial pressure; therefore, it moves from the blood into the tissues. At high altitudes, however, where the partial pressure of oxygen in the atmosphere is low, the partial pressure of oxygen in the blood is too low to allow diffusion of oxygen from the blood to the tissues unless special physiological adjustments take place. These are the adjustments that make possible human habitation of high-altitude environments.

MOVING INTO HIGH ALTITUDES   When a person who normally lives near sea level first travels into high mountains, he or she will probably notice an increase in the breathing rate, which may reach twice that at sea level. The increased breathing rate brings more oxygen into the alveoli, and it helps increase the partial pressure of oxygen in the blood. This **hyperventilation,** or increased breathing rate, eventually is re-

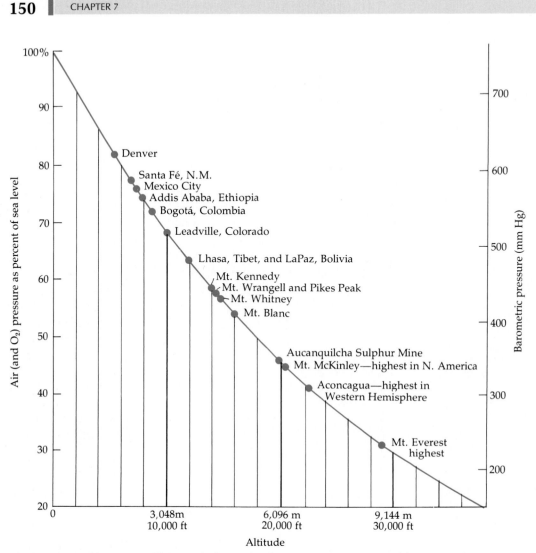

FIGURE 7–3 *Air pressure.* This graph shows the decrease in air pressure with increase in altitude.

duced, and it levels off as the person becomes acclimatized to the high altitude.

About 97 percent of the oxygen in the blood is carried in chemical combinations with hemoglobin in the red blood cells; the other 3 percent is dissolved in the plasma and may be ignored. The chemical association of oxygen and hemoglobin is loose and reversible. When the partial pressure of oxygen is high, as in the alveoli of the lungs, oxygen combines with hemoglobin. When the hemoglobin reaches the capillaries, where the partial pressure of oxygen is low, it is released from the hemoglobin molecule and is free to diffuse into the cells.

When the blood leaves the lungs, the hemoglobin is about 97 percent saturated; that is, oxygen has combined with about 97 percent of the hemoglobin molecules. Some of the oxygen is then given up in the capillaries of the tissues. As a result, the hemoglobin in the veins returning to the heart and lungs is only about 70 percent saturated. At high altitudes, several factors operate to alter these percentages, thereby permitting the hemoglobin molecules to carry more oxygen to the tissues. For example, because of hyperventilation, the concentration of carbon dioxide in the blood decreases, thus altering the blood chemistry in such a way as to increase the amount of oxygen carried in the blood.

Many other acclimatory adjustments take place. In time, the number of capillaries in the body increases, thereby shortening the distance that the oxygen must be carried by the blood to the tissues. In addition, the number of red blood cells increases, and hence the amount of hemoglobin being carried by the blood also increases. Therefore, although the partial pressure of oxygen as it enters the lungs differs at sea level and at high altitudes, the partial pressure of oxygen in the blood is not very different by the time it reaches the capillaries (Figure 7–4). Many changes also occur at the cellular level that enable cells to carry out their metabolic functions at lower oxygen levels.

While the factors discussed above permit people to live at high altitudes, they cannot overcome all the negative biological effects from high-altitude living. For example, high altitude affects reproduction; birth weights are lower, and infant mortality is greater. In addition, the growth and development of children are slower.

Summary

Although *Homo sapiens* is physiologically a tropical species, human populations today occupy a great variety of habitats and are able to survive under stressful environmental conditions. Adjustments are nongenetic physiological mechanisms by which animals can survive in specific habitats.

Behavioral adjustments are cultural responses to environmental stress. The utilization of technology, such as specialized clothing, housing, and tools, and the development of particular forms of social behavior are cultural ways in which humans are able to adjust to hostile conditions.

Humans can also adjust in physical ways by means of reversible physiological responses to environmental stress; these are termed acclimatory adjustments. For example, under conditions of extreme arctic cold, the basal metabolic rate of the body increases, resulting in an increased production of body heat. Under desert conditions the sweat glands become more sensitive and produce more sweat; urine volume is reduced. Changes in blood chemistry permit humans to survive the dangers of hypoxia at high altitudes. Through such mechanisms, human populations have been able to spread over the earth and have

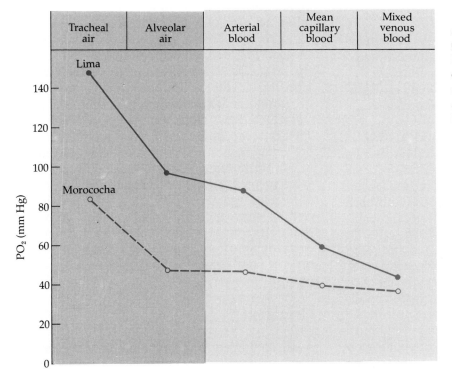

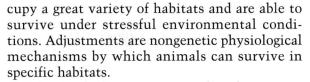

FIGURE 7–4 *Average partial pressure of oxygen.* This chart shows the partial pressure of oxygen in the lungs and in various parts of the circulatory system, comparing individuals living at sea level (Lima, Peru) and at high altitude [Morococha, Peru, at 4540 meters (14,891 feet)].

come to terms with some of the earth's most difficult habitats.

THE NATURE OF HUMAN GROWTH AND DEVELOPMENT

Much of the variation found within populations is due to differences in age and sex. Patterns of growth vary between human populations and form an important area of anthropological research.

Ontology is the study of the growth and development of an organism. **Growth** can be simply defined as an increase in the size or mass of an organism. For example, growth may be observed by measuring the increase in a child's height and weight over time. On the other hand, **development** may be seen as a change over time from an immature to a mature or specialized state. The appearance of the specialized tissues that make up the various organs of the body from the undifferentiated cells of the early embryo, and the changes in the sex organs and other features that occur as an individual passes through puberty, are both examples of development.

The Growth Process

All the body's tissues consist of cells surrounded by intercellular material. Each of the estimated 100 trillion cells of the adult human is ultimately derived from the zygote (single fertilized ovum). The process of growth from this single cell occurs in three ways.

Perhaps the major mechanism for growth is **hyperplasia,** an increase in the number of cells, which is accomplished by the process of mitosis (described in Chapter 4). Mitotic division is very rapid in the early embryo, but once the cells have become differentiated into several types, the different cell types divide at very different rates. In adults some cells undergo continual and rapid mitotic division. This is the case with skin cells. Since large numbers of dead skin cells are shed from the surface of the body daily, rapid cell division is required to keep the total number of skin cells constant. At the other end of the spectrum are nerve cells, which cease to divide soon after birth.

Growth may also occur when individual cells grow larger. Although nerve cells do not divide in the growing child, the long processes that make up the nerve fibers become longer as the body grows and the distances between parts increase. A general increase in cell size, or **hypertrophy,** is limited. Although the expanding volume of a spherical cell increases with the cube of the radius, the surface of the cell increases only with the square of the radius. Thus, the surface area of a growing cell would soon become too small to allow adequate nutrients and chemicals to enter through the cell membrane into the cytoplasm of the cell.

In addition to having cells, the body contains an intercellular matrix. In some cases this matrix, a product of the cells it surrounds, becomes involved in the development of specialized connective tissue such as cartilage. Growth can occur through the process of **accretion,** or increase in the amount of intercellular material.

GROWTH RATES OF TISSUES   Since different types of cells divide at different rates, it follows that different types of tissues and different parts of the body also grow at different rates. This is largely responsible for the differences in body proportions that develop with age, as well as for differences in body composition.

Figure 7–5 shows the growth of different body tissues. The vertical scale indicates the size of the tissue as a percentage of the total growth after birth. The tonsils, the thymus gland, and the lymph nodes are composed of lymphoid tissue which grows very rapidly in early childhood. This type of tissue traps foreign particles in the body and plays a major role in the development of immunity to diseases. By the end of 5 or 6 years the nervous system has reached 90 percent of its adult size; after this, the growth rate is extremely slow. In contrast, the elements of the reproductive system grow very slowly until puberty, when their growth accelerates. Growth rates of fatty tissues will be discussed when we examine puberty.

Osteology

Anthropologists have studied the process of human growth most extensively in the skeleton.

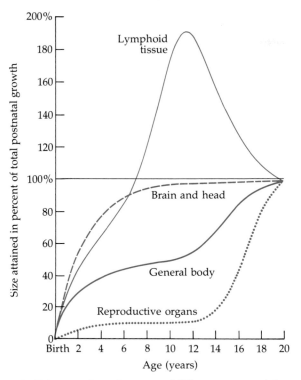

FIGURE 7–5 *Growth curves of different parts and tissues of the body.* This graph illustrates the differences in growth of different tissues and parts of the body, expressed in terms of percent of total growth attained after birth.

Osteology, the study of bones, is a major interest of many anthropologists. Part of this interest stems from archaeological and paleoanthropological fieldwork, which involves careful study of skeletal remains. Information about the population, including sex ratios, age at death, and human variation, provides insights into the biology of prehistoric populations. Methods of burial and artificial deformation of the skeleton tell us much about the cultural practices surrounding life and death. (The names of the various bones and their features may be found in the Appendix.)

THE GROWTH OF BONES   Initially, a fetal limb bone is formed of cartilage. The actual bone first appears at the center of this cartilage, an area called the **primary center of ossification;** in many bones this center appears before birth. The process of **ossification** soon turns most of the cartilage into bone.

The formation of **secondary centers of ossification** occurs most frequently near the ends of long bones such as the humerus and femur. Although considerable variation exists, primary and secondary centers of ossification generally appear in a characteristic order at particular ages. Figure 7–6 shows examples of ages at which centers of ossification appear, from birth to 5 years, in females.

The primary and secondary centers will not merge for some time. In a long bone, the shaft, or primary center, is the **diaphysis,** while the secondary centers near either end are the **epiphyses.** As ossification continues, bone replaces the remaining cartilage, and ultimately the epiphyses and the diaphysis unite to form a single bone.

Growth of mammalian long bones does not occur at the ends, but in very narrow areas between the diaphysis and epiphyses. As the individual increases in size, these areas, called **growth plates,** become increasingly thinner and eventually disappear as the epiphyses fuse with the diaphysis. Once fusion occurs, growth stops. Like the appearance of centers of ossification, fusions of growth plates generally occur in a characteristic order and at certain average ages, although individuals vary. Figure 7–7 shows the average ages of epiphyseal union for selected growth plates in males.

BONE AGE   Certain biological events, such as the appearance of a center of ossification or the fusion of a growth plate, may be used to define a standard **bone age.** In reality, these events occur across a wide range of variation in age in human children. Also, because boys and girls mature at different rates, the definitions of the standard bone ages for the two sexes are different. The standard bone age represents the average chronological age at which these events take place. In contrast, **chronological age** is the time since birth.

The wrist and hand are the parts of the skeleton most often used in determining bone age in children, and x-rays of these parts are particularly useful. First, since the wrist and hand consist of many individual bones, x-rays provide considerable information. Second, because the wrist and hand are thin, extremely low x-ray dosages may be used. Finally, the events of ossi-

BOX 7–2
AGING

Someday genetic-engineering techniques may be used to arrest the aging process, although today the idea is a fantasy of science fiction. All people age. **Aging** is the uninterrupted process of normal development that leads to a progressive decline in physiological function and ultimately to death.

It has been suggested for decades that certain groups of people age at a much slower rate and live considerably longer lives than other groups. Russians from the Caucasus Mountains, Hunzas from the Karakoram Mountains in Pakistan, and Ecuadorans have been represented in the popular literature as including within their populations a very high percentage of people who are well over 100 years old. However, when these cases are carefully examined, these individuals usually turn out to be in their seventies and eighties.[1] In fact, these populations do not show average life expectancies any greater than the general U.S. population.

So, then, why do people exaggerate age? One reason may be that the society is attempting to show that its culture is better than others, or even to display a biological superiority. In some groups, a man of draftable age customarily takes the identity of his father in order to avoid military service. In many societies, great age brings with it increased prestige or fame.

The rates of aging and the time of death are influenced by both genetic and cultural factors. **Life expectancy** is how long a person can, on the average, expect to live. Although average life expectancies differ considerably from population to population, the oldest ages that people attain in different cultures are very similar. For humans, as for each of the other animal species, there seems to be a theoretical maximum age determined by genetic predestiny. This is called the **life span.** Even if heart disease and cancer were eliminated, the present human life span would increase by only about 14 years to about 100 years.[2]

Many investigators of the aging process believe that the maximum life span of a species is due to a developmental "clock." The timing of this clock is controlled, in part, by regulatory genes. These genes determine the appearance and disappearance of biochemical products that control the aging process. Recent studies indicate that another aspect of the genetic developmental clock might involve mitochondrial DNA. As mutations accumulate in mtDNA, the body might age. These models of aging, as well as others that have been proposed, are hypothetical. As of yet, aging is inadequately understood.

Many developmental events contribute to old age. The following may occur as one gets older: loss of bone density, gain of fat but loss of muscle tissue, loss of teeth, dry skin, menopause, decline in sperm count, decline in near and far vision, diminished senses of hearing and taste, rise in cholesterol levels, and increase in susceptibility to many diseases including heart disease, cancer, cerebrovascular disease, chronic pulmonary disease, diabetes, and chronic liver disease. The occurrence and degree of these events are highly variable among individuals within a population as well as variable among populations.

[1] A. Leaf, "Long-lived Populations: Extreme Old Age," *Journal of American Geriatrics,* 30 (1982), 485–487.
[2] L. Hayflick, "The Biology of Human Aging," *Plastic Reconstructive Surgery,* 67 (1981), 536–550.
References: T. Overfield, *Biologic Variation in Health and Illness: Race, Age, and Sex Differences* (Menlo Park, Calif.: Addison-Wesley, 1985); and J. S. Olshansky, B. A. Carnes, and C. Cassel, "In Search of Methuselah: Estimating the Upper Limits to Human Longevity," *Science,* 250 (November 2, 1990), 634–640.

fication in the hand and wrist are well defined and usually accurate.

Figure 7–8 shows the x-rays of two boys, each with a chronological age of 15 years. These x-rays may be compared with x-rays of hands and wrists of standard bone ages. The x-ray on the left shows more unfused epiphyses than the x-ray on the right. The boy on the left has a bone age of 12½ years, whereas the boy on the right has a bone age of 15½ years.

DENTAL AGE   Like other mammals, humans develop two sets of teeth. The first is a set of **deciduous,** or baby, teeth; the second is a set of **permanent teeth.** Humans have twenty deciduous teeth and thirty-two permanent teeth.

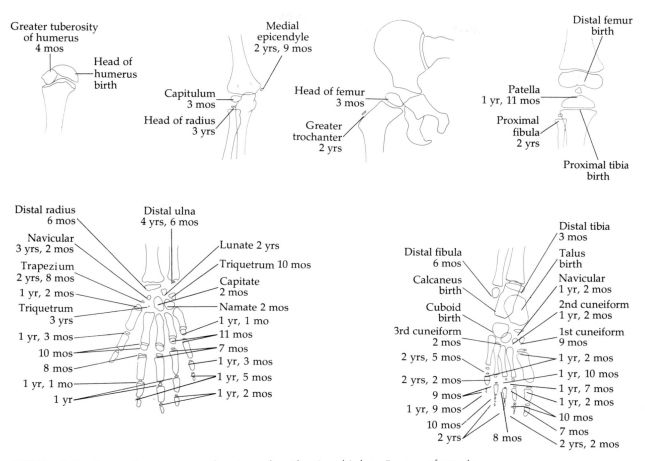

FIGURE 7–6 *Dates of appearance of centers of ossification, birth to 5 years of age, in "white" females.*

In humans, teeth begin to develop in the 5-month-old fetus, and the first deciduous tooth erupts (appears through the gum) about 6 months after birth. By the average age of 3 years, all twenty deciduous teeth have fully erupted and the permanent teeth are developing in the jaws. At 6 or 7 years of age, the deciduous teeth begin to fall out and are replaced by the permanent teeth (Figure 7–9).

Although variation does occur, most of the deciduous and permanent teeth erupt in a fairly consistent order at particular ages. For example, the second permanent molar erupts at an average age of 12 years. (In England the eruption of the second molar was formerly used to decide when a child was old enough to go to work.) Other teeth are not so regular: third molars, the "wisdom teeth," may erupt between the ages of 17 and 80 years and in some individuals may never erupt at all.

Figure 7–10, developed by the American Dental Association, shows the status of the different teeth at various ages. This chart depicts the "typical" sequence and average age of tooth eruption; there is considerable variation in both.

The Adult Skeleton

By the early twenties, most of the epiphyses are fused and all the teeth, with perhaps the exception of the highly variable third molars, are fully erupted. Age-related changes in the adult skeleton are generally degenerative changes such as the closure and obliteration of sutures in the skull, loss of teeth, and degeneration of bone in the skull and other parts of the anatomy.

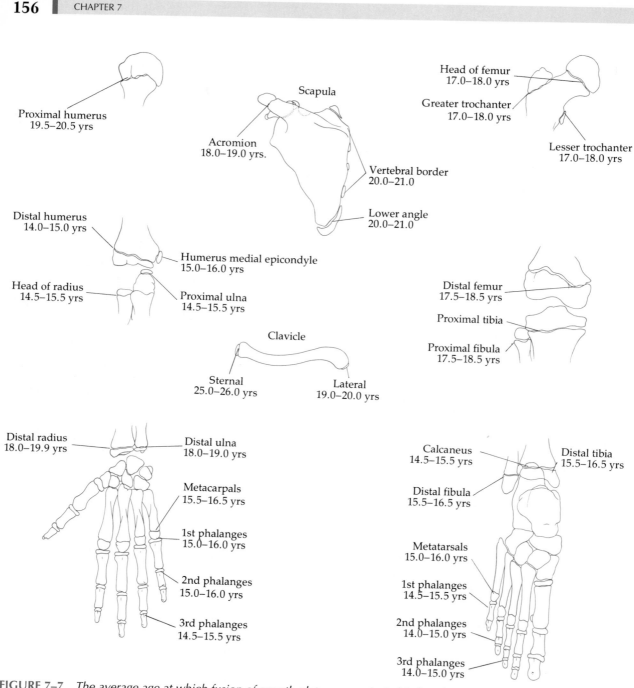

FIGURE 7–7 *The average age at which fusion of growth plates occurs in "white" males.*

An example of age-related changes in the postcranial skeleton may be seen in an analysis of the **pubic symphysis,** which is the part of the pelvis where the two innominates join. (The pelvis consists of two halves, the innominates, which in turn are divided into sections. The front section is the pubis.) Age can be estimated by separating the two innominates and carefully examining the **symphyseal face,** or the surface where one pubis joins the other. Many of these changes can be seen in Figure 7–11. Using analysis of the skull and the postcranial bones in the

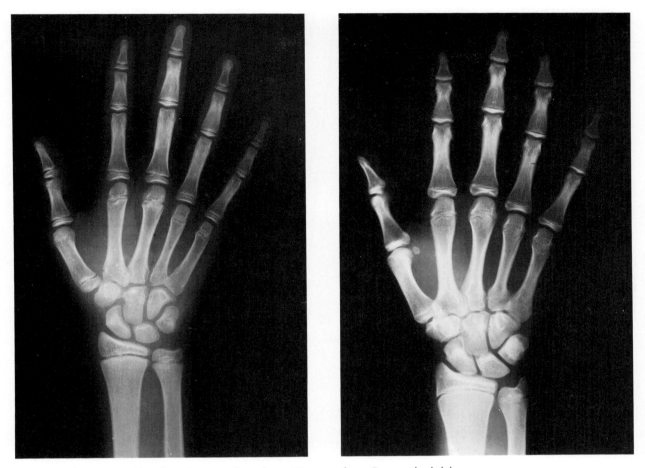

FIGURE 7–8 *X-rays of hands and wrists of two boys 15 years of age.* Boy on the left has a skeletal age of 12½ years, whereas boy on the right has a skeletal age of 15½ years.

adult, a reasonable estimate of age at death can be made.

THE MALE AND FEMALE SKELETONS The adults of many mammalian and primate species show marked differences in size and structure between males and females, a feature referred to as **sexual dimorphism.** Sexual dimorphism is relatively slight in humans, yet various parts of the male and female skeleton do show noticeable differences.

In Figure 7–12, which compares the male pelvis with the female pelvis, adaptations for childbearing can be seen in the female pelvis. Note, for example, that the female pelvis is characterized by a U-shaped and broader subpubic angle, a smaller acetabulum, a larger, wider, and shallower sciatic notch, a circular or elliptical pelvic inlet, and many other features.

Many sexual differences in the human skeleton reflect the male's greater size and heavier musculature. Areas where muscles attach to bone are seen as roughened areas and projections, and the size of these areas and projections is a reflection of the size of the attached muscle.

Growth Curves

On a child's birthday it is customary in many American households to record the child's height on a wall or door, so that over the years the progressive growth of the child can be seen. In the eighteenth century, Count Philibert Guéneau de Montbeillard published the record of his son's

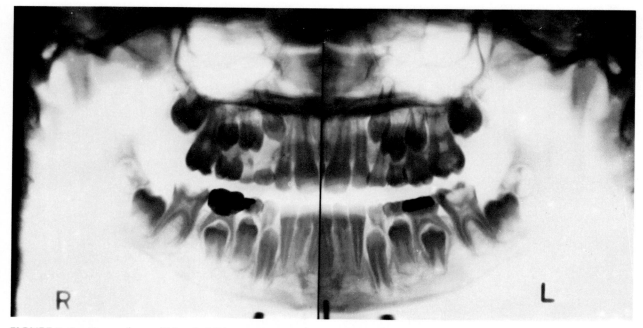

FIGURE 7–9 *X-ray of mandible of child, age 9 years, showing the development of permanent teeth within the jaw.*

growth between the years 1759 and 1777. The data were published by his friend Comte de Buffon, introduced in Chapter 2.[7]

Figure 7–13 plots the height of de Montbeillard's son at various intervals from birth to 18 years of age. This type of curve, called a **distance curve,** shows the total height of the child on a series of dates. Figure 7–14 plots the height gained by de Montbeillard's son in a series of 1-year periods. This type of curve is a **velocity curve.** Looking at this particular curve, we can see that the velocity, or rate of growth, decreased from birth until about 11½ years of age. Then we see a great increase in the growth rate, which peaks at about 14½ years of age. This increase is the **adolescent growth spurt.**

When the growth curves of boys and girls are compared, differences are obvious. In general, girls grow faster than boys. The stages of growth and maturation are the same, and they occur in the same order, but the rates of maturation differ. At birth females are 4 to 6 weeks more mature than males, and females reach puberty

about 2 years earlier. Although males on the average grow taller, girls reach 50 percent of their adult height at 1.75 years of age, while boys reach this landmark at 2.0 years of age.

Puberty

Of all the events in an individual's life cycle, one of the most significant both biologically and socially is **puberty.** In most human societies the onset of puberty occasions a ritual that marks a major transition in the social life of the individual.

One of the major physical changes that occurs in puberty is a rapid increase in stature. In Figures 7–13 and 7–14 we saw an example of the adolescent growth spurt in a male. As noted above, females experience a similar growth spurt, but it occurs earlier than in males. Also, the increase in stature and the speed of growth are less in girls than in boys.

The later onset of puberty in males may account for their greater stature as adults. The hormones involved in the sexual changes at puberty also bring about the end of bone growth in the

---

[7]G. A. Harrison et al., op. cit., 339.

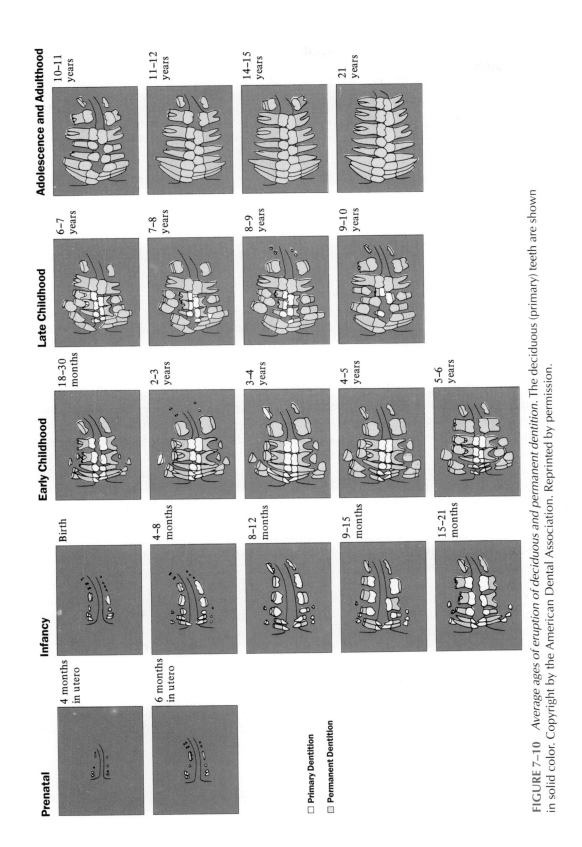

FIGURE 7–10 *Average ages of eruption of deciduous and permanent dentition.* The deciduous (primary) teeth are shown in solid color. Copyright by the American Dental Association. Reprinted by permission.

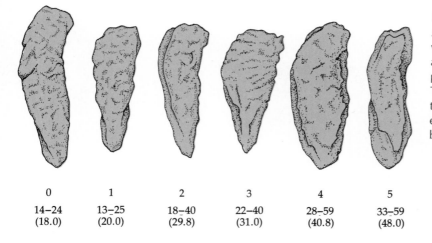

0	1	2	3	4	5
14–24	13–25	18–40	22–40	28–59	33–59
(18.0)	(20.0)	(29.8)	(31.0)	(40.8)	(48.0)

FIGURE 7–11 *Changes in the symphyseal face.* To determine the age at death, various aspects of the symphyseal face are analyzed. This figure shows an example of some of the changes that occur. The age range, with the mean in parentheses, is given for each stage. The final estimate of age is based upon the combined analysis of several factors.

long bones. Thus the later onset of puberty gives males a longer time to grow.

The earliest signs of puberty in males are the enlargement of the testes and changes in the texture and color of the scrotum; these are soon followed by the enlargement of the penis and the growth of pubic hair. Individuals vary in the age at which these events occur. Growth of the penis begins at 12½ years on the average, but it may begin as early as 10½ or as late as 14½. A problem of social adjustment at this time is that some boys may be just beginning puberty after their peers have completed it. Spontaneous ejaculations occur about a year after the onset of penis growth, usually during sleep. Initially, the semen contains fewer sperm than during adulthood, and so boys may be relatively infertile during early adolescence.

The earliest sign of puberty in the female is the development of the **breast bud,** which is an elevation of the breast as a small mound. Also, there is a slight enlargement of the **areolar area,** the dark area surrounding the nipple. In the female there is a sudden and visible event known as **menarche** (rhymes with "monarchy"), the first menstrual flow. Menarche actually appears late in puberty; it represents a mature stage of development of the uterus. It does not, however, mark the development of full reproductive functions. This occurs a year or so later.

Within a given population the age at menarche is quite variable. In addition, when *averages*

from different populations are compared, great variation is apparent as well. In some populations the average age at menarche may be under 13, whereas in other populations the average age may exceed 18 (Table 7–1).

In addition to changes in the reproductive organs, other changes that differentiate males and females occur at puberty. These are the **secondary sexual characteristics.** An example found in males is the development of facial hair and of a deeper voice. The voice change is due to lengthening of the vocal cords, which, in turn, results from the growth of the larynx. A voice change also occurs in the female. Perhaps more important for both sexes, however, are changes in body proportions and body composition.

ANTHROPOMETRIC DATA   One of the oldest studies within the general field of physical anthropology is **anthropometry,** the "systematized art of measuring and taking observations on man, his skeleton, his brain, or other organs, by the most reliable means and methods for scientific purposes."[8]

Anthropometric measurements can be plotted as growth curves. Different parts of the body grow at different rates, and many differences that

[8]A. Hrdlička, *Practical Anthropology* (Philadelphia: Wistar Institute of Anatomy and Biology, 1939), 3.

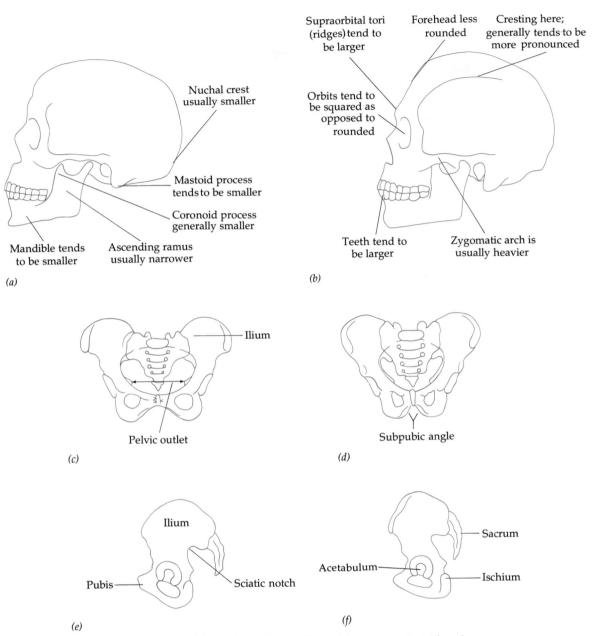

FIGURE 7–12 *Sex determination of the skeleton.* Comparison of the stereotypic *(a)* female skull and *(b)* male skull, and *(c)* female pelvis and *(d)* male pelvis; side view of *(e)* female pelvis and *(f)* male pelvis.

characterize the sexes after puberty simply represent differences in relative growth rates. For example, Figure 7–15 plots two anthropometric measurements against age in the form of velocity curves. The first plots **biacromial width,** a measurement of the width of the shoulders. At puberty males develop relatively broad shoulders. The second graph plots **bitrochanteric width,** a measurement of hip width. Here the greatest growth at puberty is in the female.

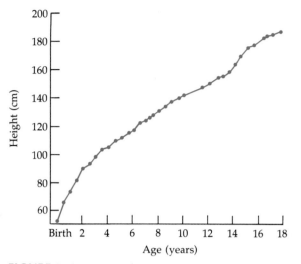

FIGURE 7–13 *Growth in height of de Montbeillard's son from birth to 18 years, 1759–1777.* This example of a distance curve shows total height on each of several dates.

DEVELOPMENTAL ADJUSTMENTS

Some variations in the pattern of growth and development provide a means of adjustment to environmental stress. Such adjustments are called **developmental adjustments.** A good example of developmental adjustment can be seen in differ-

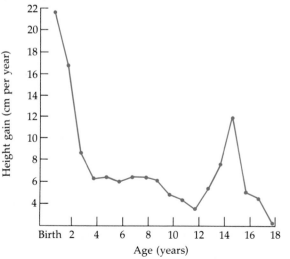

FIGURE 7–14 *Growth in height of de Montbeillard's son from birth to 18 years, 1759–1777.* This example of a velocity curve shows increments in height gained from year to year.

TABLE 7–1
MEDIAN AGE AT MENARCHE (FIRST MENSTRUATION) IN SEVERAL POPULATIONS

POPULATION OR LOCATION	MEDIAN AGE (YEARS)
Wealthy Chinese (Hong Kong)	12.5*
Wroclaw (Poland)	12.6*
California (United States)	12.8*
Moscow (U.S.S.R.)	13.0*
Tel Aviv (Israel)	13.0†
Burma (urban)	13.2*
Oslo (Norway)	13.5*
Wealthy Ibo (Nigeria)	14.1*
Transkei Bantu (South Africa)	15.0*
Tutsi (Rwanda)	16.5‡
Hutu (Rwanda)	17.1‡
Bundi (New Guinea)	18.8*

*J. M. Tanner, "The Secular Trend towards Earlier Physical Maturation," *Trans. Soc. Geneesk.,* 44 (1966), 524–538.
†A. Ber and C. Brociner, "Age of Puberty in Israeli Girls," *Fertility and Sterility,* 15 (1964), 640–647.
‡J. Hiernaux, *La Croissance des écoliers Rwandais* (Brussels: Outre-Mer, Royal Academy of Science, 1965).

ences in growth rates involving chest circumference.

It has been known for some time that individuals growing up at high altitudes develop greater chest circumferences than those growing up at lower elevations (Figure 7–16). This is related to greater lung volume, primarily in what is termed the **residual volume,** the amount of air still remaining in the lungs after the most forceful expiration. Greater residual volume in children growing up at high altitudes appears to develop as a result of rapid and accelerated development of the lungs in childhood.

CHANGES IN BODY COMPOSITION Along with the adolescent growth spurt is a change in the composition of the body. The amount of muscle tissue increases, especially in males. Apart from the large muscles, males develop larger lungs, larger hearts, and a greater capacity for carrying oxygen in the blood in comparison with females. These differences are associated with greater speed, strength, and physical endurance (Figure 7–17).

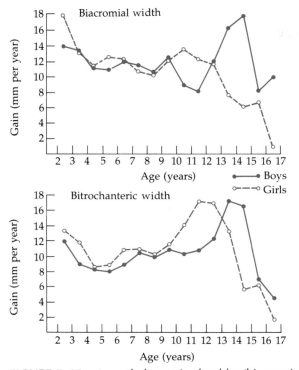

FIGURE 7–15 *Annual change in shoulder (biacromial) width and hip (bitrochanteric) width in boys and girls.*

FIGURE 7–16 *Chest circumferences.* This graph compares the growth of chest circumference of three Peruvian populations found at *(a)* sea level, *(b)* moderate altitude of 2300 meters (7544 feet), and *(c)* high altitudes between 4000 and 5000 meters (13,120 and 18,040 feet). A growth curve from the United States is included for comparison *(d)*.

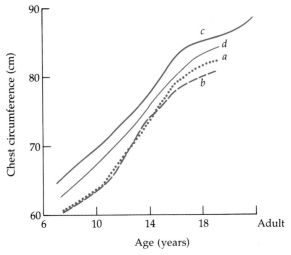

Changes also occur in the amount of **subcutaneous fat,** the fat deposited under the skin. With the onset of the growth spurt, the relative proportion of subcutaneous fat decreases. Because this decrease is greatest in males, females enter adulthood with relatively more subcutaneous fat, especially over the pelvis and on the breasts, the upper back, and the upper arms.

Control of Growth and Development

The nature and rates of growth and development are controlled by the complex interaction of many factors. Among these are the endocrine glands, nutrition, and heredity.

HORMONAL CONTROL OF GROWTH AND DEVELOPMENT   The **endocrine glands** are organs that produce a special group of chemicals called **hormones,** which are secreted directly into the bloodstream and are carried throughout the body.

A number of hormones have an effect on growth and development. For example, **growth hormone,** produced by the pituitary gland, is essential for normal growth, particularly the growth of bone. Children deficient in this hormone reach an average adult height of only 130 centimeters (51 inches) although they have normal body proportions.

Sex hormones play major roles in growth and development, especially at puberty. **Testosterone** is manufactured by cells of the testes. At puberty testosterone stimulates the growth of the testes and the male sex organs, such as the penis and the prostate, and also stimulates the development of secondary sexual characteristics such as facial hair. In the female, **estrogens** are produced by the ovaries. Estrogens stimulate the growth of the female sex organs, such as the vagina and the uterus, and cause secondary changes such as breast development. Other hormones, produced by other glands, also influence the pattern of growth and development in the individual.

NUTRITION AND GROWTH AND DEVELOPMENT   The processes of growth utilize the raw materials taken into the body (ingested) as food. Nutrients help sustain growth and development,

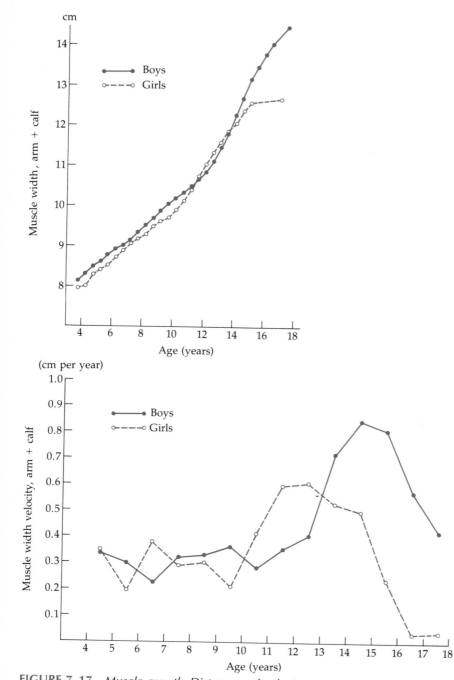

FIGURE 7–17 *Muscle growth.* Distance and velocity curves showing the sum of widths of upper arm and calf muscles as seen in x-rays.

repair damage, and maintain vital processes, and they provide energy for bodily activities. The lack of proper nutrition can seriously retard normal growth and development.

Protein-caloric malnutrition is a broad term covering many nutritional problems. Malnutrition is especially prevalent among developing nations, primarily those undergoing the transition

FIGURE 7–18 *Kwashiorkor and marasmus. (a)* Child with kwashiorkor in Agra, India. *(b)* Child with marasmus, from Diamond Harbor, near Calcutta, India.

to urbanized societies. Severe malnutrition is also frequent during war.

One form of protein-caloric malnutrition is **kwashiorkor,** a Ghanaian word meaning "second-child disease" (Figure 7–18*a*). Kwashiorkor is usually associated with the period immediately following weaning, which often takes place when a second child is born. In many parts of the world, especially in the tropics, the child moves from its mother's milk to a diet of carbohydrates and little protein. The main food is usually a starchy gruel made from yams, taro, corn, rice, or millet; animal protein is scarce and, when available, expensive. Thus the child may receive enough food to satisfy hunger but does not receive the proteins vital to normal health, growth, and development.

Several symptoms characterize kwashiorkor. **Edema,** or water retention, occurs in the feet and lower legs and may occur in other parts of the body. Growth is retarded. Muscle wasting occurs, as seen in the thinness of the upper arms and by the child's difficulty in holding up its head when pulled from a lying to a sitting position. Because the diet is high in carbohydrates, a relatively thick layer of subcutaneous fat and a distended belly are often seen. Many psychomotor changes occur, including retarded motor development. The child is apathetic, miserable, withdrawn, and indifferent to its environment.

Marasmus results from a diet low in both protein and calories (Figure 7–18*b*). It occurs at all ages, but usually in children soon after weaning. Symptoms of marasmus include extreme growth retardation, wasting of muscles and subcutaneous fat, diarrhea, and severe anemia. Since vital nutrients are absent during a critical time for brain growth, mental retardation often occurs. Early death is the rule.

Kwashiorkor and marasmus represent extreme examples of malnutrition and growth retardation. In addition to these conditions, less severe forms of malnutrition and a lack of specific nutrients in the diet can also lead to problems.

Excessive amounts of many nutrients can also lead to health problems. For example, excessive amounts of vitamin D can lead to **hypercalcemia,** which is characterized by high levels of calcium in the bloodstream, sluggish nerve reflexes, sluggish and weak muscles, and unnatural calcification of soft tissue.

In some parts of the world one encounters overnutrition, which produces **obesity.** A person is considered obese when his or her weight is 20 percent greater than a sex- and age-specific weight-for-height standard. Obese children tend to be taller for their age than the average child, and they also mature earlier.

EFFECTS OF DISEASE ON GROWTH AND DEVELOPMENT

Growth and development are affected by many diseases. Many genetic abnormalities, such as PKU (Chapter 3), and chromosomal abnormalities, such as Down's syndrome (Chapter 4), clearly affect growth. Likewise, nongenetic diseases, such as those caused by bacteria, viruses, fungi, and parasites, can influence ontology.

Many childhood diseases may retard normal growth and development. Although measles and chicken pox may have no lasting effect on well-nourished children, severe and prolonged nongenetic diseases inevitably impair growth, especially in malnourished populations.

HEREDITY AND GROWTH AND DEVELOPMENT

Growth is a complex process involving the interaction of cultural, environmental, and genetic factors. The exact role of heredity is not precisely known. Tall parents tend to have, on the average, tall children, but genetic factors are complex and difficult to analyze.

One method of estimating the relative influence of heredity and environment is through twin studies, which were discussed in Chapter 3. Identical, or monozygotic, twins have the same genotype. Thus, monozygotic twins may be compared with fraternal, or dizygotic, twins of the same sex whose genotypes differ to the same extent that genotypes differ among pairs of brothers or sisters who are not twins. In addition, twins raised in the same household may be compared with twins who were separated at birth and grew up in different environments.

Tables 7–2 and 7–3 present data on growth from such twin studies. The similarities between monozygotic twins in stature, weight, and age at menarche, together with the differences between dizygotic twins and pairs of nontwin siblings, suggest a strong genetic influence on these traits. Yet the differences between monozygotic twins, especially when twins are reared apart, show that environmental influences are also present.

Twin studies suggest that genes strongly influence growth, primarily by establishing optimal limits for growth. Thus, an individual may have the genetic potential for a particular stature, yet that stature may not be reached because of malnutrition or childhood disease. The nature of the genetic mechanism, however, is unknown.

TABLE 7–2

AVERAGE DIFFERENCES BETWEEN MONOZYGOTIC AND DIZYGOTIC TWINS AND PAIRS OF SIBLINGS

DIFFERENCE IN	MONOZYGOTIC TWINS	MONOZYGOTIC TWINS REARED APART	DIZYGOTIC TWINS	SAME-SEX SIBLINGS (NOT TWINS)
Stature (centimeters)	1.7	1.8	4.4	4.5
Weight (kilograms)	1.9	4.5	4.5	4.7

Source: H. H. Newman et al., *Twins: A Study of Heredity and Environment* (Chicago: University of Chicago Press, 1937), 72.

TABLE 7–3

AVERAGE DIFFERENCE IN MENARCHE

RELATIONSHIP	DIFFERENCE (MONTHS)
Monozygotic twins	2.8
Dizygotic twins	12.0
Pairs of sisters	12.9
Pairs of unrelated women	18.6

Source: E. Petr, "Untersuchungen zur Erbbedingtheit der Menarche," *Zeitschrift für Morphologie und Anthropologie,* 33 (1935), 43–48.

The Secular Trend in Growth and Development

Occasionally we read a newspaper or magazine article reporting that people are getting larger each generation. Scientists have long been aware of this phenomenon, which is called the **secular trend.** The secular trend is the tendency over the last 100 or so years for each succeeding generation to mature earlier and grow larger (Figure 7–19). This trend has occurred worldwide. In the twentieth century, the change in mean body height per decade has been about 0.6 centimeter (0.25 inch) in early childhood, about 1.3 centimeters (0.5 inch) in late childhood (8 years old for girls and 10 years old for boys), and about 1.9 centimeters (0.74 inch) at midadolescence (age 12 for girls and age 14 for boys).[9]

What causes secular trends? No one knows for sure. Some researchers believe that a general improvement in nutrition, better sanitation, better health services, and less tedious lifestyles are responsible. These factors have permitted individuals to more closely approach their genetically determined potential weight and stature. Today a leveling off of the secular trend appears to be occurring in higher socioeconomic, urban populations.

Summary

Ontology is the study of growth and development. Growth is an increase in the size of an or-

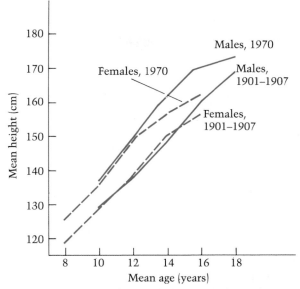

FIGURE 7–19 *Secular trend.* This graph shows the mean height of "white" Australian males and females measured in 1901–1907 and in 1970.

ganism; development is a change from an undifferentiated to a highly organized, specialized state. There are three ways in which growth occurs: hyperplasia is an increase in the number of cells; hypertrophy is a general increase in cell size; and accretion is an increase in the amount of intercellular material.

Osteology is the study of bones; it includes the investigation of patterns of growth and development in teeth and bones. Bone growth begins with the appearance of primary and secondary areas of ossification, areas where bone is replacing cartilage. In long bones, the primary center is referred to as the diaphysis, while the secondary centers near either end are the epiphyses. The diaphysis and epiphyses first appear in a fairly regular order at characteristic ages. When the growth of the long bones ceases, the diaphysis and epiphyses fuse; this occurs in different bones at characteristic ages. The specific pattern of bone appearance and closure of the growth plates between the epiphyses and diaphysis provide a bone age, the average chronological age at which these events occur. The pattern of tooth formation and eruption serves a similar purpose. Anthropologists are able to use these

---

[9]H. V. Meredith, "Findings from Asia, Australia, Europe, and North America on Secular Change in Mean Height of Children, Youths, and Young Adults," *American Journal of Physical Anthropology,* 44 (1976), 321–322.

growth patterns to ascertain the age at death of skeletal material. Differences between males and females, sexual dimorphism, can be used to determine the sex of skeletal material.

Growth can be charted in distance and velocity curves that plot the increase in stature, or some other variable, over time. When examining a growth curve, we notice a period known as the adolescent growth spurt. This is an aspect of puberty which also includes changes in the reproductive organs and the secondary sexual characteristics. Specific anthropometric measurements can also be plotted against age and illustrate aspects of sexual dimorphism. Differences in patterns of ontology may be seen in children growing up in stressful environments; these are known as developmental adjustments.

The nature and rates of growth and development are controlled by the complex interaction of internal and external factors. These factors include the hormones, which are particularly involved in the control of puberty; environmental factors, including the availability and usage patterns of food; diseases, both those that are genetic and those caused by disease organisms; and heredity, which plays a major role by setting the potential limits to growth measurements such as stature. Improvement in nutrition, better sanitation, and better health services may be responsible for an increase in average stature and weight over the years, a tendency referred to as the secular trend.

STUDY QUESTIONS

1. In human populations, behavioral adjustments are the most significant means of responding to the environment. What is meant by this statement?
2. A human wearing little clothing sets out into the arctic winter. Another, similarly dressed, sets out into the Sahara Desert. Describe the physiological events that will take place in each situation.
3. Very high altitudes present what is perhaps the most difficult habitat for human habitation. Describe the various stresses found at

high altitude and the human responses to these stresses.
4. What is the major difference between *growth* and *development*?
5. An archaeologist excavates a prehistoric burial site. Using the information from osteology, what can we find out about the skeletons?
6. Biologically, how do the events associated with puberty differ in males and females?
7. What factors are responsible for differences in the patterns of growth and development among individuals or groups of individuals?
8. What is the secular trend?

SUGGESTED READINGS

Bogin, B. *Patterns of Human Growth.* Cambridge, England: Cambridge University Press, 1988. This book provides a basic introduction to the topic of human growth and development.

Frisancho, A. R. *Human Adaptation: A Functional Interpretation,* rev. ed. Ann Arbor: University of Michigan Press, 1993. This book discusses human adaptations to stressful environments, including heat and cold stress, high-altitude hypoxia, and malnutrition.

Harrison, G. A., J. M. Tanner, D. R. Pilbeam, and P. T. Baker. *Human Biology,* 3d ed. Oxford: Oxford University Press, 1988. The section on human growth, written by J. M. Tanner, provides a concise introduction to the study of growth and related topics.

Joyce, C., and E. Stover. *Witness from the Grave: The Stories Bones Tell.* Boston: Little, Brown, 1991. This book discusses the methods used to decipher the information from skeletal material. It highlights the work of Clyde Snow, a leading forensic anthropologist.

Overfield, T. *Biological Variation in Health and Illness: Race, Age, and Sex Differences.* Menlo Park, Calif.: Addison-Wesley, 1985. In addition to covering the subjects mentioned in the title, this book gives a general overview of human variation.

Polednak, A. P. *Racial and Ethnic Differences in Disease.* New York: Oxford University Press, 1989. This volume addresses the distribution of genetic and nongenetic diseases and other characteristics in human populations.

Sinclair, D. *Human Growth after Birth,* 5th ed. Oxford: Oxford University Press, 1990. This book is a basic text on human growth and development.

Suzanne, C. *Genetic and Environmental Factors during the Growth Period.* New York: Plenum, 1984. As the title indicates, this book looks at the factors that influence human growth and development.

Tanner, J. M. *Foetus into Man: Physical Growth from Conception to Maturity,* 2d ed. Cambridge, Mass.: Harvard University Press, 1990. This is a general introduction to the study of human growth and development.

The whole human species, of course, is tremendously variable. Even within one nation, no matter how isolated, even within one family, we find innumerable differences between individuals. In ways that we do not fully understand, these differences have become partially sorted out according to geographic area (or, as we must say in the modern world, area of ancestry). . . . Some of the differences correlated with area of ancestry probably arose many thousand years ago, when small bands, perhaps a few families, left a group and went out to found new tribes. Their individual and family characteristics became the heritage of what later became large populations. Thus population and racial differences are, in a sense, the lengthened shadow of individual differences.[1]

Alice Brues

[1]A. Brues, "Foreword," in T. Overfield, *Biologic Variation in Health and Illness: Race, Age, and Sex Differences* (Menlo Park, Calif: Addison-Wesley, 1985), x. Reproduced by permission of Theresa Overfield and Alice Brues.

CHAPTER

8

THE ANALYSIS OF HUMAN VARIATION

In the previous chapter we examined the nature of two sources of human variation. First, we discussed adjustments—nongenetic responses to environmental stress. These are behavioral, acclimatory, and development adjustments. Second, we considered the differences that result from the patterns of growth and development.

A third source of variation is microevolutionary changes called adaptations, the subject of the first part of this chapter. The discussion of adaptation will be followed by an examination of the distribution of human variation and the classification of this variation.

ADAPTATION

Adaptation is an important factor bringing about variation within and among populations. Here we will discuss two examples of adaptation in human populations, skin color and body build.

The Nature of Skin Color

People are commonly classified as red, white, black, yellow, or brown. Yet in spite of this apparent rainbow of humanity, only one pigment, **melanin,** is responsible for human coloring. Skin color is also affected by hemoglobin: the small blood vessels underlying the skin give lighter-skinned persons a pinkish cast. The larger the number of blood vessels, the greater the influence of hemoglobin on skin color. In addition, skin color is affected by the thickness of the outermost stratum of the skin. This layer contains keratin which, when present in large quantity in a thick outer layer, is slightly yellow. Keratin also blocks the red color of the hemoglobin from showing through the skin.

Melanin is produced in the outermost layer of the skin, the **epidermis** (Figure 8–1). The pigment is produced in specialized cells called **melanocytes.** Like nerve cells, to which they are related, the melanocytes have several branchlike projections called **dendrites.** While nerve cells send messages along their branches, the dendrites of melanocytes transport the melanin to higher layers of the epidermis. People with dark skin and people with light skin have, on the average, the same number of melanocytes in the same areas of the body. Skin color is determined by the amount of melanin produced, the size of the melanin particles, the rate of melanin production, and the location of the melanin in the skin.

SKIN COLOR AS AN ADAPTATION   People with dark skin are often found in more equatorial regions, while persons with light skin are found farther from the equator. Why is darker skin color adaptive in equatorial regions?

FIGURE 8–1   *Human skin.* A photograph of the outermost layer of the skin (epidermis) as seen through the microscope. In this cross section of dark skin, the concentration of melanin can be seen in the stratum granulosum.

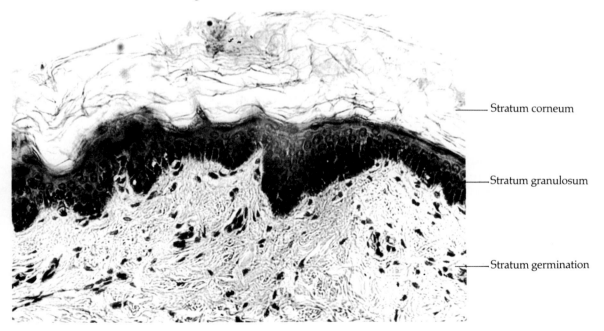

Stratum corneum

Stratum granulosum

Stratum germination

One hypothesis holds that dark skin provides protection against the harmful effects of ultraviolet radiation from the sun. This radiation can cause sunburn and sunstroke and can stimulate the development of skin cancers. Since melanin absorbs ultraviolet radiation, dark skin cuts down the amount of this radiation that passes through the outer layers of the skin.

In many parts of the world the amount of ultraviolet radiation reaching the surface of the earth varies with the seasons. Since ultraviolet radiation stimulates melanin production, the increased amount of radiation during the summer in the middle latitudes causes people to tan. All people are capable of some degree of tanning.

Another hypothesis links skin color with production of vitamin D, which is vital for calcium absorption in the intestines. Calcium is necessary for normal bone development, and the lack of this mineral leads to bone diseases such as **rickets.** Excessive calcium leads to **hypercalcemia,** a condition characterized by malfunctions of the nervous system.

Although some vitamin D comes from digested foods, most is manufactured within the skin. This biochemical reaction requires ultraviolet radiation. The amount of ultraviolet radiation that reaches those layers of the skin where vitamin D synthesis takes place is influenced by the concentration of melanin in the skin.

The geographical areas of most intense ultraviolet radiation are the grasslands of the equatorial regions. People in these areas often have extremely dark skin that always remains dark, as we can see in the Nilotic peoples of the grasslands of east Africa and the aboriginal populations of the Australian desert. Even with very dark skin, the intense ultraviolet radiation characteristic of equatorial regions guarantees that more than enough vitamin D is produced.

Extremely dark skin is not characteristic of indigenous tropical-forest dwellers, since the heavy vegetation filters out much of the solar radiation. The pygmies of the Congo Basin of Africa, for example, are lighter than the people who entered the forest some 2000 years ago from the Cameroons, which lies northwest of the Congo. On the other hand, peoples living in the Arctic are darker than one might expect. Snow reflects ultraviolet radiation, thereby increasing the amount of such radiation that ultimately reaches their skin.

DETERMINATION OF SKIN COLOR   As we have just seen, ultraviolet radiation can act as a selective agent on a population's gene pool, bringing about differences in skin color in different parts of the world. We know that the inheritance of skin color is polygenic. A small number of genes are involved, but the exact genetic mechanisms are not known.

Cultural factors may also affect skin color. For instance, light-skinned people who wear little clothing or make a practice of sunbathing appear darker in the summer than genetically similar people who protect themselves from tanning. Suntan lotions also alter the color of the skin. Of course, darkened skin produced by exposure to ultraviolet radiation or tanning lotions will not be passed on to the next generation. However, if there is an advantage or disadvantage in the ability to tan, natural selection will increase or decrease the frequency of this trait.

Adaptation and Body Build

Natural selection plays a major role in determining the size and shape of the human body. The effects of natural selection are greatest under the most stressful conditions. Thus, if people live in a generally mild climate that is frigid for 3 months of the year, they must be adapted to the harsh conditions as well as to the mild ones. Each time the stressful conditions arise, the genes of those individuals who do not survive are eliminated. Their nonadaptive genes will not be transmitted to the next generation. Over time, the population will become increasingly adapted to its local circumstances.

RADIATION OF HEAT AND BODY BUILD We have already discussed some aspects of the problem of heat loss in desert habitats. Radiation is the most significant mechanism for heat loss from the nude human body at rest, accounting for 67 percent of heat loss at an air temperature of 24°C (75.2°F). The efficiency of radiation as a heat-reducing process depends largely on body build.

The amount of heat that can be lost from an object by radiation depends on the ratio of surface area to body mass. Suppose two brass objects of identical weight, a sphere and a cube, are heated to the same temperature and then left to cool. Which object cools faster? The cube cools faster. Although both objects have the same weight, the cube has more surface area from which the heat can radiate. On the other hand, the sphere has the smallest surface per unit weight of any three-dimensional shape.

While weight increases by the cube, surface area increases only by the square. This is generally true of human beings as well. As seen in Table 8–1, the ratio of body weight to surface area of skin is higher in cooler northern regions and decreases toward the equator. Just as a sphere has the smallest surface area per unit weight, a short, stocky human body also has a low surface area per unit weight. Thus, we would expect that people in arctic regions, in order to reduce heat loss, would be short and stocky and have short limbs. When the Eskimo's body is examined, this expectation is confirmed (Figure 8–2a). In contrast, the Nilotes live in the hot equatorial regions of east Africa and have long, linear trunks with long arms and legs (Figure 8–2b). Such linearity provides a large surface area for the radiation of heat.

Variability extends to other parts of the anatomy. Anthropologists have studied the variation of many features, including the nose, hair texture, and hair color, but the reasons for variability in these features are poorly known. Variation also occurs in various physiological traits, in molecular traits such as blood types, and in the frequencies of genetic disease. Some of these will be discussed in the next section.

Summary

This section has examined two examples of adaptation in human populations: skin color and body build. Human skin color is due primarily to the pigment melanin. In general, people living in equatorial regions tend to have darker skin than those living at higher latitudes. In this case melanin may be acting to protect the body from the harmful ultraviolet rays of the sun and from the possibility of overproduction of vitamin D. People living in equatorial regions also tend to be tall and linear, a body build that maximizes the amount of surface area per unit of body weight.

THE DISTRIBUTION OF VARIABILITY

Adjustments and adaptations are responses to particular environmental conditions. Many of these environmental conditions are associated with particular habitats. For example, dark skin color and linear body build are associated with hot, open, tropical climates. Since such climates are found near the equator, it follows that there will be a characteristic distribution of these traits when they are plotted on a map. This section will examine the distribution of variable features of human populations.

TABLE 8–1

RATIO OF BODY WEIGHT TO BODY SURFACE AREA IN MALES*

POPULATION	MEDIAL LATITUDE	RATIO (KILOGRAMS PER SQUARE METER)
China		
North		36.02
Central		34.30
South		30.90
North Europe to north Africa†		
Finland	65°N	38.23
Ireland	53°N	38.00
France	47°N	37.78
Italy	42½°N	37.15
Egypt (Siwah)	26°N	36.11
Arabs (Yemen)	15°N	36.10

*Women show ratios different from men's. This may be due to differences in the mechanisms of heat regulation between men and women. For example, the ratio for France (women) is 38.4, compared with 37.78 for men, as seen above.
†There is some discontinuous variation in the north Europe to north Africa range. For example, the ratio for Germany is 39.14, even though it is south of Finland.
Source: Eugene Schneider, "Variations morphologiques et différences climatiques," *Biométrie Humaine,* 6 (1971), 46–49. Used with permission of Dr. Schneider.

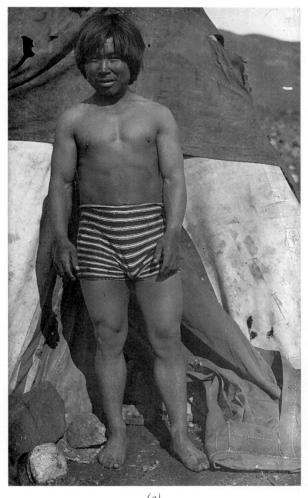

(a)

FIGURE 8–2 *(a) Eskimo and (b) Nilotes (Masai).*

(b)

Some Generalizations about Mammalian Variation

Scientists have made several generalizations based on data on the physical nature of the bodies of various "warm-blooded" animals. One such generalization is **Gloger's rule.** This rule states that within the same species there is a tendency for more heavily pigmented populations to be located toward the equator and for lighter populations to be farther from it.

Bergmann's rule refers to the relationship between surface area and mass or volume of the body. It states that within the same species the average weight of the members of a population

increases and the surface area of the body decreases as the average environmental temperature decreases. **Allen's rule** states that within the same species the relative size of protruding parts of the body, such as the nose and ears, and the relative length of the arms and legs increase as the average environmental temperature increases.

From our discussion of skin color and body build we see that these generalizations hold true for humans in many situations. However, there are also many exceptions. For example, body size is affected by diet, and dietary differences in different parts of the world may account for some of the observed variations in weight. Other facts include the migration of many human groups into new areas to which they bring a body characteristic adapted to their region of origin. If they arrive and cultural factors shield them from the environment, they may retain the original feature. Conversely, cultural factors and selective factors may interact to bring about change.

Clinal Distributions

The frequency of a particular trait may vary from place to place because it may have different selective values in different areas or because it may have spread in a particular pattern throughout its history. When such frequencies are plotted on a map, they may vary systematically. This is seen in Figure 8–3, which plots the frequencies of blood-type B in Europe. Note that the frequencies of blood-type B decrease systematically along a line from the upper right-hand corner of the map to the French-Spanish border.

A distribution of frequencies that show a systematic gradation over space is known as a **clinal distribution.** Clinal distributions may develop in at least two ways. A cline might be determined by a gradual change in some selective pressure. For instance, an increase in the prevalence of the malaria-carrying mosquito as one moves from temperate into more tropical areas may be related to an increase in the frequency of the sickle-cell allele. As the selective pressure changes, so might the distribution of the trait.

A cline may also develop when a particular trait originates in a specific area and spreads outward by means of gene flow. The farther away one is from the center of origin, the lower the frequency tends to be. The distribution of blood-type B may be the result of this process: blood-type B has its highest frequencies in central Asia and may have originated there.

Discontinuous variation occurs when a particular trait appears in high or low frequencies in various areas with little or no gradation between those areas. An example is the frequency of red hair in the United Kingdom (Figure 8–4).

Skin color and body build are generally clinal in nature. Since human populations are mobile, discontinuous variation in skin color and body build occur as peoples with different skin colors and body builds migrate into new areas. Also, the interbreeding of these migratory peoples has

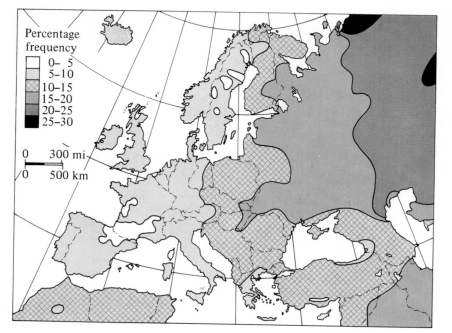

FIGURE 8–3 *Distribution of blood-type B in Europe.* This is an example of a basically clinal distribution.

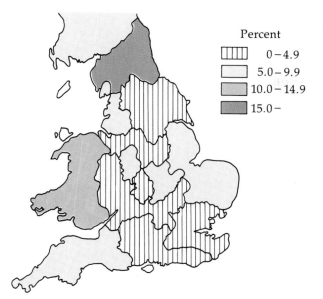

FIGURE 8–4 *Distribution of red hair in the United Kingdom.* This is an example of discontinuous variation.

produced multiple skin-color variants and a variety of body builds. In the following sections we will examine the distribution of other factors.

DISTRIBUTION OF BLOOD TYPES   In Figure 8–3 we examined the clinal distribution of blood-type B in Europe. The clinal distribution of many blood-type antigens, coupled with the nonclinal distribution of still other antigens, suggests that considerable variation occurs in the frequencies of particular blood types from population to population.

Some specific blood antigens are characteristic of specific populations. For example, high frequencies of blood-type A are found in Scandinavia and among the Eskimos; high frequencies of blood-type B are found in central Asia, north India, and west Africa (Figure 8–5); and high frequencies of blood-type O are found throughout most of North and South America and in Australia. The distribution of blood types and their use in the classification of human variation will be discussed more thoroughly in the next section.

As discussed in Chapter 6, selective pressures operate on the ABO blood-type system. For example, researchers have hypothesized that small-pox is more severe and mortality rates are higher among peoples of blood-types A and AB than among peoples of types O and B. If this hypothesis is correct, smallpox, in areas where it is common, would act as a selective agent tending to eliminate A and AB individuals. O and B individuals would be left to produce most of the next generation. Maybe this is why in countries such as India, where smallpox was once common, B is the most common blood type today.

An interesting distributional study focuses on the Diego blood antigen. Table 8–2 shows that this antigen is found only in Asiatics often referred to as "Mongoloids" and to the aboriginal populations of the New World who are derived from the "Mongoloid" peoples of Asia. According to one hypothesis, the "Mongoloids" are of fairly recent origin and the Diego antigen is a characteristic of this population. Presumably, the antigen was carried to the New World when the ancestors of the American Indians migrated across the Bering Strait (Chapter 19). This hypothesis proposes that Diego-positive persons are not found in other adjacent populations because the antigen is relatively new and has not become established. Of course, selective factors cannot be ruled out.

Variability in Frequency of Genetic Disease

Specific genetic diseases, or high frequencies of genetic diseases, characterize all populations. For example, cystic fibrosis is a recessive genetic abnormality. While the abnormal allele is relatively frequent in European populations, it is rare in Asiatic and African populations. Another example is the allele associated with Tay-Sachs disease among Ashkenazi Jews. Generally all populations are associated with high and low incidences of certain genetic abnormalities. Table 8–3 lists some genetic abnormalities associated with particular groups of people.

Why are certain genetic diseases associated with particular populations? Major factors in establishing high frequencies of certain alleles in specific populations include inbreeding in small populations, the preference for consanguineous

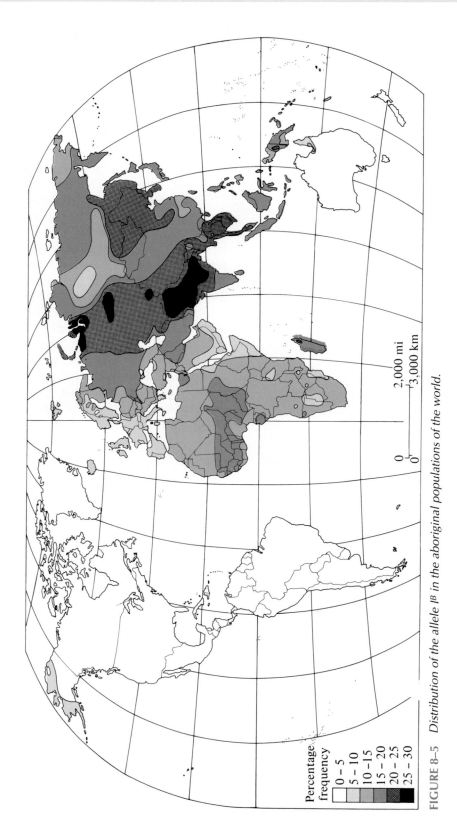

FIGURE 8–5   *Distribution of the allele I^B in the aboriginal populations of the world.*

Percentage
frequency

0 – 5
5 – 10
10 – 15
15 – 20
20 – 25
25 – 30

2,000 mi
3,000 km

0
0

TABLE 8–2

FREQUENCIES (PERCENT) OF DIEGO-POSITIVE PHENOTYPE IN VARIOUS POPULATIONS

POPULATION	FREQUENCY OF DIEGO-POSITIVE
Caingangs (Brazil)	45.8
Carajas (Brazil)	36.1
Caribs (Venezuela)	35.5
Maya Indians (Mexico)	17.6
Guahibos (Venezuela)	14.5
Japanese	12.3
Chippewas (Canada)	10.8
Koreans	6.1
Guajiros (Venezuela)	5.3
Apaches (United States)	4.1
Eskimos (Alaska)	0.8
Lapps (Norway)	0.0
Polynesians	0.0
Aborigines (Australia)	0.0
Whites (United States)	0.0
Asiatic Indians	0.0
Africans (Liberia, Ivory Coast)	0.0
Bushmen (South Africa)	0.0

Source: G. A. Harrison et al., *Human Biology* (New York: Oxford University Press, 1964), 275.

matings in many societies, and the founder principle operating in small migrant populations.

Balanced polymorphism, or heterozygous advantage, has been identified as the mechanism responsible for the relatively high frequency of sickle-cell anemia in many populations in Africa and elsewhere. This mechanism may also be involved in the elevated frequencies of cystic fibrosis, phenylketonuria, schizophrenia, Tay-Sachs disease, and other conditions. Modern technology has alleviated the selective advantage of many balanced polymorphisms, and so it may be impossible to discover the nature of the former advantage that a heterozygous genotype bestows on individuals of a population.

Cultural Variation

Different populations have different technologies, marriage patterns, religions, and economies. They possess different ideas of nature, justice, and law. Even body movements and thought patterns are culturally tempered. Within a group, all these factors are integrated into a functional system, with each element related in some way to the others. The cultural system, in turn, is intimately related to the noncultural environment and to human biology.

Different peoples have different ideas of beauty based on their cultural traditions. To achieve effects that they consider aesthetically pleasing, many groups permanently alter the shape and the structure of the body by artificial means. This alteration often serves to distinguish individuals of high status in cultures in which little clothing is worn. Various societies provide medical and religious justifications for body alterations. Examples of body alterations include circumcision, clitoridectomy (surgical removal of the external portion of the clitoris), scarification, and tattooing.

The face and the head are frequently subject to modification. The Kwakiutl Indians of British Columbia place a board on the soft foreheads of their infants to flatten the front of the skull (Figure 8–6a). Punan women of Borneo slit their earlobes and insert brass rings, eventually drawing each lobe down to the shoulder.

Societies throughout the world alter the body to enhance their beauty, attain status, or become initiated. Several groups pierce the nasal septum, others slit the lips, and, in the United States, many pierce the ear and other parts of the body. Each method allows ornaments to be attached (Figure 8–6b). Foot-binding, plastic surgery, hair and skin transplants, and many other methods of surgically or cosmetically altering the body are practiced in various parts of the world.

Summary

Several generalizations have been proposed to describe the distribution of features in "warm-blooded" animals. Gloger's rule states that within the same species there is a tendency for more heavily pigmented populations to be located toward the equator and for lighter populations to be farther from it. Bergmann's rule states that within the same species the average body weight

TABLE 8–3

THE ETHNIC DISTRIBUTION OF GENETIC DISEASE*

POPULATION	DISEASE	INHERITANCE PATTERN†
Europeans in general	Alkapoturnia	AR
	Anencephaly	PG
	Cystic fibrosis	AR
	Oculocutaneous albinism	AR
	Porphyria variegata	AD
	Spina bifida	PG
Ashkenazi Jews	Guacher's disease	AR
	Hyperuricemia (gout)	AD
	Tay-Sachs disease	AR
Greeks, Italians, and Armenians	G-6-PD deficiency	XLR
	Thalassemia major (Cooley's anemia)	AR
Northern Europeans	Lactase deficiency	AD
	Pernicious anemia	PG
Irish	Phenylketonuria (PKU)	AR
Amish and Icelanders	Ellis–van Creveld syndrome	AR
Africans	G-6-PD deficiency	XLR
	Hemoglobinopathies (hemoglobin S, hemoglobin C)	CD
	Polydactyly	PG
Chinese	Alpha thalassemia	AR
	G-6-PD deficiency, Chinese type	XLR
Japanese	Acatalasia	AR
	Cleft palate	PG
	Wilson's disease	AR

*This table indicates some of the genetic diseases found in high frequencies in particular populations.
†AR, Autosomal recessive; AD, autosomal dominant; PG, polygenic; XLR, X-linked recessive; CD, codominant.
Source: V. McKusick, *Mendelian Inheritance in Man: Catalogs of Autosomal Dominant, Autosomal Recessive, and X-Linked Phenotypes,* 5th ed. (Baltimore: Johns Hopkins, 1978).

of the individuals of a population increases and the surface area of the body decreases as the average environmental temperature decreases. Allen's rule states that within the same species the relative size of protruding parts of the body, such as the nose and ears, and the relative length of the arms and legs increase as the average environmental temperature increases. However, especially among human populations, there is considerable deviation from these generalizations.

Human variation is often clinal in nature, that is, expressed as gradations. Yet some traits appear almost exclusively within one or a few populations. These traits are said to show a distribution that is discontinuous.

Humans differ in their anatomy, physiology, ontogeny, and culture. Except for culture, which is by definition learned, all these factors can have a genetic component. In many instances, the environment also plays a powerful role in creating variation. In fact, it would be more accurate to say that human morphology (form) and behavior are products of the dynamic interaction between cultural, biological, and environmental variables. Because the relationship between these variables is dynamic, the differences between human groups are in a constant state of flux. For any particular trait, two groups may become more or less similar to each other at different times, depending on the particular situations.

BOX 8–1

SKELETAL EVIDENCE OF CULTURAL PRACTICES

While many alterations of the human body are deliberate, many other changes in anatomy are nondeliberate side effects of cultural practices. For example, humans in all cultures habitually assume particular resting postures. In adulthood, the postures learned in childhood have become normal and comfortable. Postures encountered in other cultures may prove difficult and often painful to assume and may permanently affect the anatomy.

D. H. Ubelaker excavated a large number of skeletons at Hacienda Ayalan on the southern coast of Ecuador. On analysis, he found that many of the bones of the foot, specifically the metatarsals and the phalanges (see the Appendix) showed several unusual features such as small bony extensions.

Analysis of the Ecuadoran skeletons suggests that the unique features in the foot skeleton developed from the stresses produced from frequent and extreme hyperdorsiflexion of the metatarsophalangeal joints. The figure illustrates this extreme backward movement of the joints between the meta-

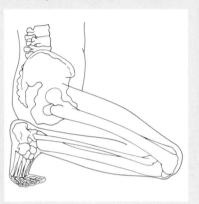

tarsal bones of the ankle and the phalanges of the toes. This movement resulted from the individual's assuming a kneeling position with the weight of the body pressing down on the joints within the foot. Since these features are found most frequently in female skeletons, Ubelaker suggests that this body position was assumed by women as they ground maize on stone metates. Thus, whether describing skeletal material or a living human body, anthropologists must know whether they are dealing with genetic traits, environmentally produced features, or cultural modifications of some genetically determined trait.

Reference: D. H. Ubelaker, "Skeletal Evidence for Kneeling in Prehistoric Ecuador," *American Journal of Physical Anthropology,* 51 (1979), 679–686.

FIGURE 8–6 *Deformation of the head. (a)* An example of head flattening: woman from the Koskimo (Kwakiutl) tribe, Vancouver Island; *(b)* an example of body piercing: American.

(a)   (b)

THE CLASSIFICATION OF HUMAN GROUPS

People are natural classifiers. They see nature as being composed of types of things rather than individual entities. If every rock, tree, or animal had a unique label attached to it, effective communication would be impossible. So people speak in categories; they talk of igneous rocks, pine trees, and mammals.

Each group of people classifies the world around it. Any human group has an answer to the question What kinds of rocks, trees, or animals are there? But the categories expressed by people do not necessarily describe the world as seen by objective science. These categories reflect specific cultural traditions and differ from society to society. Anthropologists refer to such classifications as **folk taxonomies.**

Categorization or classification is necessary in everyday communication as well as in science. Without the ability to generalize, conversation would be difficult and laws and theories could not exist. Nevertheless, folk taxonomies do not always correspond to reality. When the inaccuracies apply to categorizations of people, they often mirror hatred and mistrust.

Folk Taxonomies of Race

In coping with the world, people visualize human variation in terms of categories. The simplest type of classification is one in which a particular people classify themselves as "human" and everyone else as "less than human." For instance, the Navahos call themselves *diné*, which, roughly translated, means "the people." This label implies "a strong sense of difference and isolation from the rest of humanity."[2] This type of conceptualization also existed among the ancient Greeks, who divided humankind into two categories, Greeks and barbarians. Some Greeks believed that the barbarians just made noises or babbled. Today we play a reversal on the Greeks with the saying, "It's all Greek to me."

Especially in urban centers, a person encounters daily a variety of people of different statures, skin colors, and facial features. If people at an American suburban shopping center were asked to list the different types of people in the world, the most frequent answers would probably be Caucasoids, Mongoloids, and Negroids; or whites, African Americans, Indians, Hispanics, and Asians; or some other combination of terms (Figure 8–7).

Such classifications are examples of folk taxonomies that reflect how many Americans perceive human differences. Do they also reflect reality? The answer is both yes and no. Folk taxonomies do have a social reality in that many forms of behavior are determined by them. In a situation requiring interaction with another person, a particular American may behave differently if the other individual is perceived as "white," "black," or "Asian." On the other hand, physical anthropologists deal with biological reality, and here folk taxonomies just do not reflect what we know about human variation.

Few Americans have seen aboriginal peoples from remote regions of the world, such as the Ainu, the Australian aborigine, the San, or the Lapp (see color insert: "The Faces of Human Variation"). Most Americans have contact primarily with peoples whose origins are in Europe, the Middle East, West Africa, Latin America, and parts of Asia, particularly Japan, China, and southeast Asia. A person who looks somewhat different from the people normally encountered is forced into an existing category. Thus, American soldiers during World War II often illogically classified the Melanesians of the western Pacific as "Negro."

Anthropological Classifications of Human Variation

"Races do not exist; classifications of mankind do."[3] Scientific classifications of people, like folk taxonomies of people, are attempts to divide

---

2C. Kluckhohn and D. Leighton, *The Navaho*, rev. ed. (New York: Doubleday, 1962), 23.

3G. A. Dorsey, "Race and Civilization," in C. A. Beard (ed.), *Whither Mankind: A Panorama of Modern Civilization* (New York: Longmans, Green, 1928), 254.

(a)

(b)

(c)

FIGURE 8–7 *Four American racial stereotypes.* (a) Jay Silverheels as Tonto in *The Lone Ranger,* (b) Warner Oland as "Charlie Chan," and (c) Hattie McDaniel and Vivian Leigh in *Gone with the Wind.*

human beings into specific groups, but this is where the similarity ends.

A scientific classification is not an end in itself. It is a means of discovering the processes that create the phenomenon being classified, in this case, human variation. A scientific classification of human variation would be a model serving a function similar to that of other scientific models, such as the Hardy-Weinberg formula. This formula is a way of discovering whether forces of evolution are working on a population. Similarly, a classification of human variation should be a way of discovering the processes involved in creating human genotypic and phenotypic variation.

Folk taxonomies are usually based on ethnocentric ideas about the inherent differences in physical appearance and behavior between groups. Although some of these beliefs may be partly based on observation, most are based on mythology. In contrast, the criteria used in scientific classification must be derived from empirical studies. In other words, the attributing of different characteristics to different populations must be validated through procedures of the scientific method.

The History of Scientific Classification

Carolus Linnaeus (1707–1778), introduced in Chapter 2, was perhaps the first person to apply systematic criteria in a uniform way in classifying humans. His contribution, the first scientific taxonomy of the living world, included people. This taxonomy will be described in Chapter 9.

Linnaeus labeled all humans *Homo sapiens,* from *Homo,* meaning "man," and *sapiens,* meaning "wise." He then divided the human species into four groups based on the criteria of skin color, geographical location, and personality traits. These four categories are *H. sapiens Africanus negreus* (black), *H. sapiens Americanus rubescens* (red), *H. sapiens Asiaticus fucus* (darkish), and *H. sapiens Europeus albescens* (white).

Among scientists this classification did not stand the test of time. For one thing, it excluded many peoples. Where were the peoples of Oceania, India, and other areas to be placed? Could it legitimately be said that all peoples of Africa had the same skin color? North Africans are light-skinned; the San of south Africa are brownish-yellow; and the Bantu are dark. While Linnaeus's general system of classification of plants and animals was readily adopted by the scientific community, his classification of people was not. Nevertheless, his notion of four races is still used by many Europeans and Americans.

NINETEENTH-CENTURY CLASSIFICATION

Johann Friedrich Blumenbach (1752–1840) was a German physician and student of comparative human anatomy. He divided the human species into five "races": *Caucasian, Mongolian, Ethiopian, Malayan,* and *American.* The term *Ethiopian* was later changed to *Negro.*

Anders Retzius (1796–1860) noted many variations within the five types proposed by Blumenbach. Deciding that the shape of the head was an important criterion for classifying people, Retzius developed the cephalic index as a means of comparing populations. The **cephalic index** is the breadth of the head relative to the length, as given by the formula

$$\frac{\text{Head breadth}}{\text{Head length}} \times 100$$

These early attempts set up two criteria for the classification of human variation: outward physical characteristics and geographical origin. The measurements made and the indices calculated led to classifications that were wholly descriptive in nature. They did not explain the process that created the observed variations. Often the classifications arrived at did not appear to fit the real world, as when members of the same family were placed in different "races" on the basis of the criteria used.

USE OF BLOOD TYPES IN CLASSIFICATION

With the development of genetic theory, anthropologists began to question the use of the traditional criteria of classification. Skin color, they argued, was a poor standard, since its mechanism of inheritance is unknown and it is affected by environment and culture. Therefore, some anthropologists turned to the blood-type systems

as a basis for classification. Blood type is easy to determine; in most cases blood-typing can be done in the field. A given blood type is either present or absent, and it is not affected by environmental factors. Finally, the mechanisms of inheritance of blood types are, for the most part, known (Chapter 4).

In 1950 William Boyd published the following classification based on an analysis of the frequencies of specific blood types: (1) *Early European* (hypothetical category, represented today only by the Basques of Spain), (2) *European* (Caucasoid), (3) *African* (Negroid), (4) *Asiatic* (Mongoloid), (5) *American Indian,* and (6) *Australoid.*[4]

Boyd defined these categories on the basis of blood-type frequencies. For example, he defined the European group in terms of a high frequency of Rh-negative and A_2, one of the two major varieties of blood-type A. The Asiatic group, however, was characterized by a low frequency of Rh-negative and A_2 but a high frequency of A_1 and a variety of Rh-positive, Rh_2.[5]

The basic problem with this method is that clearly defined categories do not always emerge. Although it is possible to generalize for a large geographical area, specific groups often deviate from this generalization. For instance, most North American Indians show a high frequency of blood-type O; the Cherokee are 96 percent O, and the Chippewa are 88 percent. However, the Blackfeet show an O frequency of only about 25 percent.[6]

On the other hand, specific populations from different parts of the world can show similar blood-type frequencies. For example, the frequencies of blood-types O, A, B, and AB for the Atayal of Taiwan are 45.2, 32.6, 17.1, and 5.1 percent, respectively. The same frequencies for a population from Macedonia, Greece, are 45.2, 32.3, 19.3, and 3.2 percent.[7] Although their

---

[4]W. C. Boyd, *Genetics and the Races of Man* (Boston: Little, Brown, 1956).
[5]Ibid., 268.
[6]A. E. Mourant, A. C. Kopeč, and K. Domaniewska-Sobczak, *The Distribution of the Human Blood Groups and Other Polymorphisms,* 2d ed. (London: Oxford University Press, 1976). Figures for North American Indians are for groups with no known, or minimal, gene flow from Europeans.
[7]Ibid.

blood-type frequencies are very similar, these two populations clearly belong to different categories on the basis of geography and physical appearance. Are we therefore to say that the Blackfeet are not North American Indians because the frequencies of their blood types deviate from those of most other North American Indians? Are we to place the Atayal and Macedonians in the same group purely on the basis of similarity of blood types?

A major problem with the use of blood-type frequencies as the sole criterion for categorizing human populations is that most of these frequencies show a clinal distribution. Although major differences may exist in two populations from either end of the cline, this distinctiveness is blurred by subtle differences in frequencies in intermediate populations.

CLASSIFICATION AND THE FOSSIL RECORD

To some people, there is a fixed number of categories of people that correspond to basic divisions from the remote past. A classification based on the fossil record is that of Carlton S. Coon, who, in his 1962 book *The Origin of Races,* divided the human species into five categories: *Australoids, Mongoloids, Caucasoids, Congoids* (dark-skinned Africans), and *Capoids* (Bushmen and Hottentots).[8]

Coon postulated that humankind separated into these five divisions before the evolution of our species, *Homo sapiens.* To him human fossils represented early stages in this pre-*sapiens* development. An early fossil found in Java would be an early Australoid, while a fossil from China would be an early Mongoloid, and so on.

Coon's ideas have been rejected by most anthropologists. Clear-cut evolutionary ties between specific fossils and specific modern populations simply do not exist. Yet since the late 1980s the subject of the origins of anatomically modern humans has held a center stage in physical anthropology. The question of possible relationships between fossils and modern forms has once again become an important topic of study. This will be explored in detail in Chapter 19.

GEOGRAPHICAL RACES   Another approach to the classification of human variation is the 1961 scheme of Stanley Garn.[9] He observed that people living in the same large geographical area tend to resemble one another more closely than they resemble people in different geographical areas. Of course, this is a generalization with many exceptions. Garn divided the human species into nine large **geographical races.** Geography alone is the major criterion for classification, not some arbitrarily chosen trait such as skin color, blood type, or cephalic index. Since gene flow takes place more frequently within a major geographical zone than between adjacent zones, populations in the same major geographical areas generally show some similar gene frequencies.

Garn's nine geographical human races are (1) *Amerindian* (the aboriginal inhabitants of North and South America), (2) *Asiatic,* (3) *Australian,* (4) *Melanesian* (peoples of New Guinea and neighboring islands), (5) *Micronesian* (peoples of the islands of the northwest Pacific), (6) *Polynesian,* (7) *Indian* (peoples of the subcontinent of India), (8) *African,* and (9) *European.*

Garn divided these large geographical races into a series of **local races,** which are of two basic types. The first type consists of distinctive, partly isolated groups, usually remnants of once-larger units. Examples used by Garn include the Ainu of Japan and the San of southern Africa. Much larger local races make up the second basic type. Large local races are not as isolated as small ones, and a greater degree of gene flow occurs between them. An example of a large local race is the northwestern European.

Considerable variation exists within larger local races. If allele frequencies within the northwestern European local race are mapped, for example, constant changes in frequencies often are found as we travel in a particular direction—a clinal distribution exists. Garn arbitrarily divided the large local races into several small units called **microraces.** Precise boundaries cannot be drawn, and specific individuals within one microrace may look more like members of

---

[8]C. S. Coon, *The Origin of Races* (New York: Knopf, 1962).

[9]S. M. Garn, *Human Races* (Springfield, Ill.: Charles C. Thomas, 1961).

another microrace than like each other. Still, one fact remains: people living in the same community tend to mate more frequently with one another than with individuals of other communities.

THE CHANGING NATURE OF HUMAN VARIATION   Human variation is dynamic, and the shape of clines is constantly changing. Old microraces are broken down, and new ones are established. Between 1845 and 1854, 3 million people migrated to the United States. Between 1881 and 1920, 23½ million people entered the United States from such countries as Great Britain, Italy, Germany, Spain, Russia, Portugal, and Sweden. Some of these people formed partial isolates, such as Germans in Pennsylvania, Welsh in upper New York, and Scandinavians in Wisconsin and Minnesota. More recently the U.S. Immigration and Naturalization Service reports that from the 1950s through the 1980s about 2 million persons entered the United States from Mexico, 700,000 from Cuba, 900,000 from the Dominican Republic, Haiti, and Jamaica, and 500,000 from Vietnam. With each migration the gene pool is reconstituted, and hence a description of the people in a geographical area at one specific time may not hold at another time (Figure 8–8).

The Genetic Relationship between Human Races

We discussed earlier the work of William Boyd, who used blood-type frequencies in developing a classification of human races. His was an early attempt to employ the study of human variation on the molecular level. Since the 1950s great progress has been made in the analysis of molecular variation. Now, both nuclear and mitochondrial DNA can be studied directly. The methodologies that have been developed for such studies have provided scientists with a wealth of data for studying the genetic relationships among populations.

Two important conclusions can be drawn from the molecular data. First, the average genetic differences between geographically separated human populations are fewer than the genetic differences within a single population. Second, because of the relatively small number of genetic differences among geographically separated populations, these populations should not be assigned to separate subspecies. The differences in human populations are fewer than those that zoologists consider significant enough to separate nonhuman species into subspecies. The relatively small degree of genetic variation in contemporary human populations could be due to a population bottleneck that occurred about 400,000 years ago in a population that was ancestral to modern humans (Chapter 5).

In 1988 Luigi Luca Cavalli-Sforza and his colleagues collected published data on gene frequencies from forty-two aboriginal populations of Africa, North and South America, Oceania, Europe, and Asia.[10] They then constructed a genetic tree that diagrammed these genetic relationships. A tree showing the relationships among thirty-eight populations is shown in Figure 8–9.

According to this study, the forty-two human populations may be separated into two large divisions. The first contains the Africans; the second may be broken down into two major groupings: the north Eurasians and the southeast Asians.

The north Eurasian "supercluster" includes the Caucasoids, a group comprising the peoples of Europe, north Africa, southwest Asia, and India. A major subdivision includes two further groupings. The first consists of the peoples of northeast Asia, such as the Mongols, Tibetans, Japanese, arctic peoples of Asia, and Eskimos. The second grouping is made up of the aboriginal peoples of North and South America.

The second major "supercluster" is that of the southeast Asians. This group includes the peoples of mainland and insular southeast Asia, such as those of Thailand, Indonesia, Malaya, and the Philippines; the peoples of the Pacific islands, including those of Polynesia, Micronesia, and Melanesia; and the peoples of Australia.

This study does not attempt to develop a clas-

---

[10]L. L. Cavalli-Sforza et al., "Reconstruction of Human Evolution: Bringing Together Genetic, Archaeological, and Linguistic Data," *Proceedings of the National Academy of Sciences*, 85 (1988), 6002–6006.

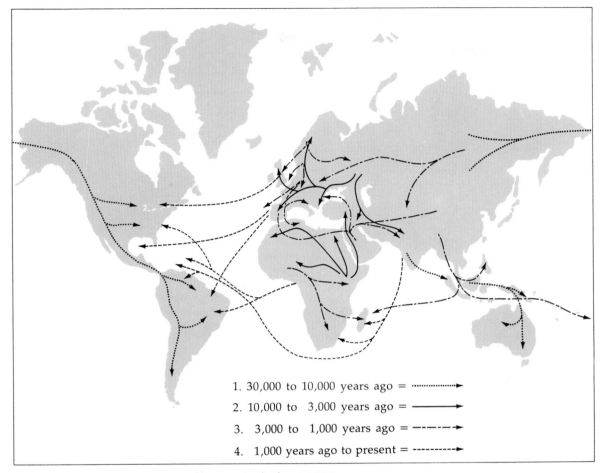

1. 30,000 to 10,000 years ago = ········▶
2. 10,000 to 3,000 years ago = ───────▶
3. 3,000 to 1,000 years ago = ──·──·──▶
4. 1,000 years ago to present = ─ ─ ─ ─ ─▶

FIGURE 8–8 *Major movements of humans in the last 30,000 years.*

sification of human populations per se; rather, it tries to determine the genetic relationships among these populations. Linguistic models of the distance between groups generally correspond to the genetic data. Two linguistic super-families show very close correspondence with the two major divisions based on genetic data markers. We will return to this general topic in Chapter 19 when we look at the molecular, paleontological, and archaeological evidence for the emergence of modern human populations.

The Nature of Human Variation and Its Classification

In traditional systems of classification, arbitrary traits are often used to divide humankind into a finite number of groups. When one, two, or twenty traits are used in such classifications, the underlying assumption is that groups so classified will be different from each other in traits not used in the classification. This is not necessarily true. If another set of traits is used, the classification might be different. The species *H. sapiens* is a collection of tens of thousands of characteristics. Isolating the variation between groups for a few of these characteristics does not explain all similarities and differences or even a small portion of them. Also, when a trait shows continuous gradation, the point at which the cline is broken into two groups becomes arbitrary.

Many populations that resemble each other in one way differ in other respects. This is illustrated in Table 8–4. Here we see the frequencies

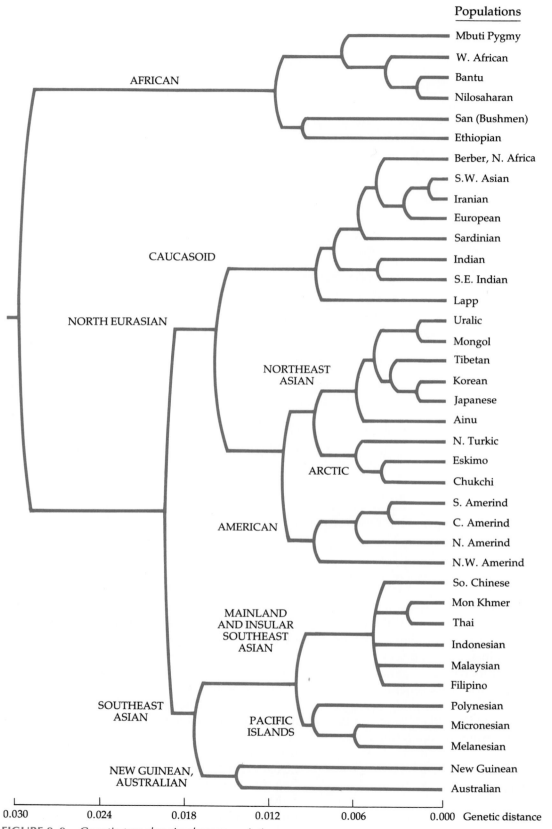

Populations

Mbuti Pygmy
W. African
Bantu
Nilosaharan
San (Bushmen)
Ethiopian
Berber, N. Africa
S.W. Asian
Iranian
European
Sardinian
Indian
S.E. Indian
Lapp
Uralic
Mongol
Tibetan
Korean
Japanese
Ainu
N. Turkic
Eskimo
Chukchi
S. Amerind
C. Amerind
N. Amerind
N.W. Amerind
So. Chinese
Mon Khmer
Thai
Indonesian
Malaysian
Filipino
Polynesian
Micronesian
Melanesian
New Guinean
Australian

AFRICAN

CAUCASOID

NORTH EURASIAN

NORTHEAST ASIAN

ARCTIC

AMERICAN

MAINLAND AND INSULAR SOUTHEAST ASIAN

PACIFIC ISLANDS

SOUTHEAST ASIAN

NEW GUINEAN, AUSTRALIAN

0.030   0.024   0.018   0.012   0.006   0.000   Genetic distance

FIGURE 8–9   *Genetic tree showing human variation.*

TABLE 8–4

COMPARISON OF TRAITS IN FIVE POPULATIONS*

	POPULATION				
TRAIT	SOUTH AMERICAN INDIAN	WEST AFRICAN	ENGLISH	JAPANESE	GREEK
PTC nontasting[†]	1.2	2.7	31.5	7.1	
Blood-type B[‡]	0–5	15–20	5–10	20–25	10–15
Lactase deficiency[§]	Up to 100	Up to 100	32	90	88
Sickle-cell trait and anemia[¶]	Up to 16	Up to 34	0	0	Up to 32

*Data are expressed in average percentages.
[†]G. A. Harrison et al., *Human Biology* (New York: Oxford University Press, 1964), 274.
[‡]A. E. Mourant, A. C. Kopeč and K. Domaniewska-Sobczak, *The Distribution of the Human Blood Groups and Other Polymorphlsms,* 2d ed. (London: Oxford University Press, 1976).
[§]See Robert D. McCracken, "Lactase Deficiency: An Example of Dietary Evolution," *Current Anthropology,* 12 (1971), 479–517; and Norman Kretchner, "Lactose and Lactase," *Scientific American,* 277 (October 1972), 76.
[¶]Frank B. Livingstone, *Abnormal Hemoglobins in Human Populations* (Chicago: Aldine, 1967), 162–470.

of phenylthiocarbamide (PTC) nontasting (Chapter 3), blood-type B, lactase deficiency (lactase is an enzyme required to break down lactose, or milk sugar), and sickle-cell trait and anemia. With respect to PTC nontasting and lactase deficiency, west Africans are closest to South American Indians; yet, in relation to sickle-cell anemia, west Africans are closest to Greeks.

DO HUMAN RACES EXIST?   The answer to this question depends on what is meant by *race* and by *exist*. People certainly act toward other people in specific ways that depend on perceptions of how those other people fit into stereotyped groups called "races." However, this only means that "races" exist in a social sense.

Do races exist in a biological sense? One problem is that the biological concepts of race and subspecies are not precisely defined. No one debates the existence of human variation—that certainly does exist. What is debated is how this variation should be described. Those who believe that the race concept can be applied divide the human species into a finite number of groups, each having a label attached to it and representing a bounded gene pool. Those who see variation in humans but no finite number of categories prefer to describe human variation in terms of distribution and the adaptive significance of specific traits.

Because human variation is so complex and dynamic, it may not be subject to categorization.

Not all phenomena are amenable to empirical study, and perhaps not all things can be organized into neat categories that have explanatory potentials. An approach that looks at each trait individually might be more logical and explanatory in light of what we do know about human variation. It would facilitate the description of the distribution, clinal or discontinuous, of each trait and the generation of hypotheses regarding the reasons for the distribution that is observed. Are natural selective forces at work? To what degree is sampling error responsible for the distribution? What contributions do nonrandom mating patterns make to the establishment of the distribution in question?

THE POLITICS OF "RACE"   The exploration of differences between human groups is a valid scientific pursuit. However, history is filled with examples of genocide, slavery, and discrimination based, in part, on false notions of biological differences between peoples. Any examination of the relationship of human biological variation and differences in behavior is sure to cause controversy. A proposed 1992 Conference on Genetic Factors in Crime was canceled because of fears that certain populations might be labeled as biologically more prone toward crime than others (Box 8–2). At the annual meeting of the American Association of Physical Anthropologists in 1995, a session on human variation turned emotional as participants argued over

BOX 8–2

VIOLENCE AND RACE

Is there a gene for violent behavior? In 1993 Hans G. Brunner and his colleagues in the Netherlands published information on an X-linked mutation. They suggested that this allele correlated with aggressive behavior. Various men in a Dutch family apparently possessed this allele through five generations; the affected men committed acts of aggression including attempted rape and various acts of assault. A defective gene in one family that appears to affect brain function does not mean that there is a gene or genes that predispose people in general to violent acts. However, it does not mean that such genes do not exist.

Individuals with characteristics beneficial to their survival and reproductive potential are selected over those who do not possess such features. Aggression may be an important aspect of human nature. Early hominids were hunters and/or scavengers, and successful hunting may be related to aggressive behavior. For example, we can image the behavior of an early hominid male chasing large scavengers away from a kill. Not only would success in procuring meat

aid in the survival of the individual and the group by providing an important food source, but a successful food provider might also have elevated status in society, marry earlier, and produce a large number of children.

There is a link between a neurotransmitter called serotonin and aggressive behavior. (A neurotransmitter is a chemical messenger used by nerve cells to communicate with each other or with other tissues that help to control the body's activities.) In studies on both humans and nonhuman primates, more impulsive and aggressive individuals often have low levels of serotonin.

In 1992 a Conference on Genetic Factors in Crime was canceled because of the fear that some investigators might make claims that certain populations are more genetically inclined toward violence than other groups. For instance, if average serotonin levels are found to differ in different populations, would this mean that some groups are more predisposed toward aggressive behavior than other groups? In the years since the cancelation of the conference,

some tentative conclusions about violent behavior have been suggested, although not all agree.

- Violent behavior is not controlled by a single gene.
- Biological factors that appear to relate to violence are extremely complex.
- Biological factors that affect violent behavior need not be genetic. Certain elements of the social environment may affect a person's biology. For example, serotonin level may rise or drop depending on one's status within the society and one's level of prestige and self-worth.
- There is no established link between genetic differences that characterize populations and differences in levels of aggressive behavior.

References: V. Morell, "Evidence Found of a Possible 'Aggressive Gene'", *Science,* 260 (1993), 1722–1723; J. E. Stevens, "The Biology of Violence," *BioScience,* 44 (1994), 291–294; J. van Williams, "Violence, Genes, and Prejudice," *Discover,* 15 (November 1994), 93–102; and R. Wright, "The Biology of Violence," *The New Yorker* (March 13, 1995), 69–77.

whether or not the Human Genome Diversity Project (Chapter 4) would reinforce the false idea that some populations are "purer" than others. These and other concerns make it difficult to make any conclusions about human variation without being accused of having a political motive.

As controversial as delving into the nature of human biological diversity is, there is general consensus that the idea of a fixed number of groups has so far not been fruitful and that it may be the wrong way to approach the subject.

Not only has this approach failed to explain most human variation, but it has also allowed people to conclude, erroneously, that a group differing in a few traits must differ in a large number of traits. Such conclusions have been implied in several popular books including *The Bell Curve,* published in 1994.[11] These conclusions, in turn, have led to judgments concerning the su-

[11]R. Herrnstein and C. Murray, *The Bell Curve: Intelligence and Class Structure in American Life* (New York: Free Press, 1994).

periority or inferiority of particular populations. Such judgments are not based on empirical data, as scientific conclusions must be. The following sections deal with this error and with the idea mentioned at the beginning of this discussion—the social "reality" of race.

RACE AND INTELLIGENCE   There have been great debates over the relationship between race or ethnic affiliation and intelligence. In the early part of this century, the focus of this question was on the relative intelligence of members of ethnic groups, such as the Poles, Greeks, Italians, and Jews, who were entering the United States in great numbers. Immigrant populations were extensively tested during World War I, and they were consistently found to average about 20 points lower than the national average on IQ tests. By the 1970s the descendants of these immigrants were scoring at the national level or higher. It has become obvious to researchers that the early low scores were due primarily to environmental and cultural factors such as malnutrition, language difficulties, and lack of experience with tests and the types of questions being asked.

RACE AND INTELLIGENCE TESTING   Intelligence testing in the United States is big business. Yet IQ testing has been under attack for a variety of reasons. During most of the twentieth century, intelligence has been equated with IQ score, but results of IQ tests show that different ethnic groups have different average scores. For instance, people socially classified as "blacks" score about 15 points lower on the average than do "whites." Is this difference due to environmental causes or differences in innate potentials?

IQ tests use symbols that are common within the particular culture that administers the test. The test is said to be **culture-bound.** This means that if the test has relevance at all, it will have relevance only for members of the culture that uses the symbols (language and general concepts) employed in the test.

As an example, American middle-class individuals may think that the question illustrated in Figure 8–10 is a perfectly logical one to ask. Yet, on closer examination, it becomes clear that making the correct choice in the time given depends on previous experience. If this question were given to Australian aborigine trackers, for example, who had little or no contact with the concepts of two-dimensional geometry, they would probably answer it incorrectly because of their lack of experience with the items pictured. On the other hand, if a city-dwelling American were asked to identify which of several close friends had made a set of footprints, he or she would probably fail where the Australian tracker would succeed.

Verbal exams are equally biased. In one of these, a battery of questions is asked, such as the name of the person who wrote *Faust*. The answer to this, Goethe (Gounod wrote the opera), might be familiar to children who emigrated from Germany or who have German parents. Or it might be known by a college student who enrolled in world literature as opposed to one who enrolled in English literature. Going one step further, the upper-middle-class teenager who does not have to work after school to help support his or her family may spend leisure time reading. A person from a poor family who must work may have no time or motivation to read books. Also, a poor family may simply maintain a household without books.

On the same test, by the way, is the question: What is ethnology? Ethnology is a branch of anthropology, but the answer given as correct for

FIGURE 8–10   *Intelligence testing.* This is an example of a test for the measurement of spatial ability. The subject is asked to mark the drawing that will make a complete square with the first figure. Speed is important. This type of test would be extremely difficult for members of a society in which geometric shapes are not utilized to the same degree as in U.S. society.

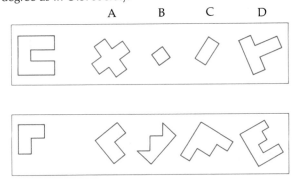

this question conforms to none of the modern anthropological definitions of this term.[12] In other words, an incorrect response might be marked "correct"! The point is that these tests are biased toward white middle-class experiences, and in some cases the answers expected by the testers are imprecise.

In the light of the preceding observations, one can easily see why various ethnic groups in the United States tend to score, on the average, lower than "whites" on standard IQ tests. These tests embody questions that are considered important to the "white" middle-class population. In fact, such commonly used tests as the Stanford-Binet were standardized by using "white" subjects only, "with no explanation about this on the part of the authors."[13]

IQ tests emphasize mathematical manipulation, a subject that middle-class children usually are exposed to early in life. Their parents may have been to college, and many of these children have had early preschool experience as well. In lower socioeconomic communities the parents often had to go to work early in life; few have gone to college. Thus mathematical logic is both less important and less attainable to them. Such parents often do not value the existing educational systems because they do not see the schools as helpful in preparing their children for jobs or in providing social mobility. As a result, children from lower socioeconomic groups often do not attend preschool. In addition, vocabulary and other dialect differences exist between social classes, ethnic groups, and regions of the country. Lower IQ scores often reflect a lack of understanding of the question because of the way in which it is worded.

Another important point is that even when comparisons are made between ethnic groups in the United States with differing lifestyles and experiences, the differences in IQ scores within each group greatly exceed the differences between groups. Whereas the scores of people from the same ethnic group might differ by 50 points or more, the averages of two different groups might vary by only about a dozen or so points. This means that many members of one population individually score either higher or lower than the average score of another population.

Little evidence exists to suggest that the average differences in IQ scores that are observed between groups are due to innate differences. Richard Herrnstein and Charles Murray in *The Bell Curve* imply that such innate differences do exist. They point out that African Americans who have attained middle-class or higher economic status on the average score higher than lower socioeconomic class African Americans and whites. Yet these middle-class African Americans still on the average score lower than middle-class whites.[14] People matched for economic status, however, are not necessarily matched for other social dimensions. African Americans as a social group have had very different social experiences in the United States than have whites who have not suffered prejudice and discrimination. The behaviors and values most inducive to creating children with high IQ scores might be less frequently found in African American and other minority groups even if they have attained middle or higher economic status. Cross-culturally, it can be shown that economic status is only one factor correlated with IQ scores. Japanese children on the average score higher than American children, as is discussed in Box 8–3.

In addition, IQ scores tell us little or nothing about a person's creative, social, musical, or artistic talents. Intelligence as tested by an IQ test leaves us with an imprecise, culture-bound definition of intelligence. The culture boundedness of IQ tests has led one state to enact a controversial law. In California, African Americans referred to remedial classes cannot be administered IQ tests.[15]

In response to the controversy over IQ testing, the 1980s and 1990s have seen new theories on what intelligence is and how it should be tested. Howard Gardner believes that there are several relatively separate types of intelligence, includ-

---

[12]M. L. Moerman, "Ethnology, the Dictionary, and IQ," *Anthropology Newsletter*, 16 (May 1975), 24.
[13]J. Ryan, "IQ, the Illusion of Objectivity," in K. Richardson and D. Spears (eds.), *Race and Intelligence* (Baltimore: Pelican, 1972), 53.

[14]R. Herrnstein and C. Murray, op. cit., 286–289.
[15]B. Bower, "I.Q.'s Generation Gap," *Science News*, 132 (1987), 108–109.

BOX 8–3

ARE THE JAPANESE, ON THE AVERAGE, SMARTER THAN AMERICANS?

In October 1986, Yasuhiro Naka-sone, Prime Minister of Japan, of-fered an explanation of why Japan competes so well against the United States: the Japanese people score higher on IQ tests than Americans. Indeed, the mean na-tional IQ score in Japan is about 111 as compared to 100 in the United States. Nakasone's remark seems to suggest a belief in a con-nection between race and intelli-gence. More specifically, he be-lieves that racial and ethnic minorities in the United States im-pair American performance in world trade.

It is a fact that ethnic and racial minorities in the United States score lower than the white major-ity. Nakasone, however, seems to be blaming the differences in scores on innate factors. In exam-ining Japanese culture, no innate factors need be postulated to ex-plain the 11-point IQ-score advan-tage that the Japanese appear to display.

Here are some reasons that could explain the differences in average scores between Japanese and Americans.

1. Japanese children attend school for an average of 240 days a year; American children attend school for less than 180 days a year.
2. The quality of education is uni-formly high in Japan. Most Japanese are of the same social class, and about 99 percent are of the same ethnic group.
3. Discipline and expectations of students in Japan are much greater than in the United States.
4. Japanese students are assigned heavier course loads and more homework than their American counterparts.
5. Economic success in Japan is absolutely dependent on acade-mic achievement. Although aca-demic achievement increases the chances of economic suc-cess in the United States, it is not absolutely essential.
6. Almost all Japanese value edu-cation. The consequences of dropping out of school are ex-tremely negative. Only 2 percent of Japanese high school seniors drop out of school as compared to 27 percent of high school se-niors in the United States.

It is therefore no wonder that mean IQ scores are higher in Japan than in the United States. The Japanese place a greater value on education. As a result, Japanese children take educational goals more seriously and spend more time in school and on homework than American children. The dif-ferences in average IQ scores be-tween groups labeled as different races or ethnic groups in the United States are most likely also due to a mix of sociocultural fac-tors rather than innate differences.

Even though the American mean IQ is not as high as that of the Japanese, Americans are re-sponsible for innovating more of this century's new technologies than any other nationality, and they have won more Nobel Prizes than the members of any other culture. IQ scores do not test such things as creativity. American soci-ety emphasizes creativity.

References: E. Brown, "Nakasone's World-Class Blunder," *Time,* Oct. 6, 1986, 66–67; "A Racial Slur Stirs Up a Storm," *Newsweek,* Oct. 6, 1986, 35; and T. Watanabe, "Cookie-Cutter Education," *Los Angeles Times* (June 24, 1990), D10–D11.

ing linguistic, musical, logical-mathematical, spatial (the perception and re-creation of the vi-sual world), bodily-kinesthetic (skill in handling objects), and personal (skill, for instance, that gives "access of one's own feelings").[16]

Robert Sternberg believes that intelligence is exercised in three areas. Contextual intelligence guides a person in selecting the appropriate en-vironments to be in and in adapting to environ-ments. Experiential intelligence is the ability to confront new situations on the basis of previous experiences. And internal intelligence is the abil-ity to plan, monitor, and change an approach to solving a problem.[17] Both Gardner and Sternberg agree that intelligence is more than a single score on a single type of test.

[16]H. Gardner, *Frames of Mind: The Theory of Multiple Intel-ligence* (New York: Basic Books, 1983); and W. Winn, "New Views of Human Intelligence," *New York Times Magazine,* Apr. 29, 1990, 16.

[17]R. Sternberg, *Beyond IQ: A Triachic Theory of Human In-telligence* (New York: Cambridge University Press, 1985).

RACE AND CULTURAL CAPABILITIES   It's believed by some that "nonwhite" peoples are incapable of developing **civilizations.** The term *civilization* is like the term *culture*: everyone has a different idea of what it is. It is beyond the scope of this text to discuss the various schools of thought on the subject although it is discussed further in Chapter 19. Instead, let us define it in terms of the common elements in most definitions. Civilization usually implies technological complexities such as a large number and variety of artifacts, often including monumental architecture, metallurgy, and a body of "scientific" knowledge. Most importantly, it implies complex social arrangements such as occupational specialization, centralized governments, religious and political hierarchies, social classes, and codes of law and conduct. In civilizations the individual becomes subject to regulations of a "state," whereas in noncivilizations the family (including extensions of the family, such as clans) is the single most important regulating agent.

Civilization arose in areas characterized by a maximum of trade and movement of people, which provided for the diffusion of artifacts and ideas. Because innovation is basically a recombination of things existing in a society into new forms, as the number of elements increases in a society, the rate of innovation increases. The cart could not have been invented if the wheel had not come first.

Civilizations did not arise in central Africa because the terrain was not suitable for quick movement of people or goods. The rivers of this area are not navigable because of great fault systems that create rapids along their courses. Restricted travel, a hot, humid climate, dense vegetation, and endemic disease, not innate inferiority, hampered the early development of civilization in the Congo Basin. Yet in areas of Africa where these conditions did not exist, early civilizations did arise and spread into the forest areas. The empires of Ghana, Kanem-Bornu, Mali, and Songhai rose to greatness when their goods were traded throughout the world. The people involved were not members of the "white race."

ARE THERE "PURE RACES"?   The assertion that some races are "purer" than others, which Hitler used to justify the killing of millions of people, is not validated by any factual data. People are spread over an extremely large area, and physical variation exists in all directions without extensive discontinuities. Through gene flow and migration or invasion, all areas of the world are constantly interchanging genes. This may be an extremely slow process, as in the case of the Australian aborigines, or a very dynamic process, as in Europe.

The "racial" picture is a changing one. Since no two people are alike through time and space, the same is true of human populations. If we were to move back in time 50,000 years, the people inhabiting the earth would not fall into the groupings or clinal patterns of today. Even today, certain groups, such as the Ainu and the San, are changing, primarily through intermarriage with other groups. New groups are emerging. Those Americans labeled "African American" are in many ways dissimilar to the African populations from which some of their ancestors came. During the days of slavery, interracial matings were common, and some famous "white" American men had children by "black" women. In fact, some historians believe that Thomas Jefferson had several such children.

Estimates indicate that today's African-American gene pool contains between 20 and 30 percent European and American Indian alleles. This is seen in the statistics for such traits as lactase deficiency. The Africans who were brought to America came from such groups as the Yoruba and the Ibo of west Africa, groups that display close to 100 percent lactase deficiency. African Americans, on the other hand, are only 70 percent lactase-deficient. This is partly due to the flow of northern European genes into this population's gene pool. In addition, a limited number of American Indian genes have entered gene pools that are derived predominantly from Africa and Europe. On the other side of the coin, the groups in the United States generally classified as "white" have a certain frequency of genes within their gene pools that are derived from African, American Indian, Asiatic, and other non-European sources. As we have emphasized throughout this chapter, human gene pools are always being reconstituted; there are no stable divisions of *Homo sapiens.*

Summary

People are socially classified into "races" that do not correspond to biological facts. Folk taxonomies of race are frequently linked to ideas of superiority and inferiority, and they serve as justification for the socioeconomic stratification that benefits the ruling group. It is easier to subject a group to harsh and unjust treatment if the people in it are relegated to a completely different ancestry and if they are portrayed as being inferior.

While anthropologists have become more realistic about the nature of human variability, people in general still use the simplistic division of humankind into a small number of stereotyped "races." This section has discussed the problems that concern race as a social category. Race has often been correlated with differences in intelligence and cultural capabilities. Upon examination, these differences either are not supported by factual data or, where they do exist, are not traceable to genetic components.

In the case of intelligence, an additional problem exists. There is no consensus on just what intelligence is—so how can it be measured? In the 1980s, new ideas about the nature of intelligence were proposed by investigators who were generally critical of IQ-type intelligence tests. We conclude that behavioral differences between peoples are almost always the result of cultural influences. Nevertheless, a genetic component may be involved in such things as the linearity of the Nilotes, which facilitates spear throwing. Researching the heritability of human traits is a legitimate activity of scientists, but as in any research, the variables must be carefully defined and controlled.

STUDY QUESTIONS

1. How does *adaptation* differ from *adjustment*?
2. Why would one expect peoples living in hot equatorial grasslands to be very tall and linear and to have dark skin?
3. What environmental factors can be correlated with the distribution of differences in skin color?
4. How are skin color and general body build related to one another?
5. What factors are responsible for the clinal nature of the distribution of some traits? Why are the distributions of many traits discontinuous?
6. In what ways are folk taxonomies different from scientific classifications?
7. Many people classify "races" on the basis of a single criterion, such as skin color. What are the inherent dangers of using only one or a few criteria to classify human populations?
8. A legitimate scientific pursuit is the exploration of possible intellectual differences between groups. Explain why IQ and other standardized tests are not good measures of the comparative intelligence of different populations.

SUGGESTED READINGS

Two general texts in the field of human biological variation are

Brues, A. *People and Races,* 2d ed. Prospect Heights, Ill.: Waveland, 1990.
Molnar, S. *Human Variation: Race, Type, and Ethnic Groups,* 3d ed. Englewood Cliffs, N.J.: Prentice-Hall, 1991.

The following books deal with intelligence and intelligence testing:

Gould, S. J. *The Mismeasure of Man.* New York: Norton, 1981.
Sternberg, R. *Beyond IQ: A Triachic Theory of Human Intelligence.* New York: Cambridge University Press, 1985.

Additional books that deal with human variation are

Cavalli-Sforza, L. L., P. Menozzi, and A. Piazza. *The History and Geography of Human Genes.* Princeton, N. J.: Princeton University Press, 1994. Using genetic, geographic, archaeological, ecological, anthropological, and linguistic data, the authors attempt to reconstruct the origin and evolution of human populations. This 1032-page book is a detailed analysis of human variation—and it is not without its critics.

Harding, S. (ed.) *The "Racial" Economy of Science: Toward a Democratic Future.* Bloomington, Ind.: Indiana University, 1993. The book is a group of essays that deal with a number of issues on race including how Western science has contributed to racist ideas.

Jenkins, J. B. *Human Genetics,* 2d ed. New York: Harper & Row, 1990. Chapter 14 of this book offers an excellent discussion of the relative contribution of genetic and sociocultural factors to intelligence (as measured by IQ tests).

Mascie-Taylor, C. G. N., and G. W. Lasker (eds.). *Biological Aspects of Human Migration.* Cambridge: Cambridge University Press, 1988. The editors have included eight essays on the evolutionary significance of migration.

The issue of human variation has been covered by articles in several popular magazines. A series of articles appeared in the November 1994 issue of *Discover* and the October 24, 1994, issue of *Newsweek.* The latter concentrates on the book *The Bell Curve.*

THE FACES OF HUMAN VARIATION

Homo sapiens is a polytypic species (Chapter 6). People live in local populations, and populations and groups of populations take on particular physical characteristics. Many of these characteristics are those that evolve through natural selection as an adaptive response to environmental circumstances. For example, an adaptive relationship exists between ultraviolet radiation, melanin production in the skin, and vitamin D production.

These pictures show a very few faces of human variation. As you examine them, keep the following facts in mind. First, there are no typical individuals; every population is greatly varied. Second, physical differences are relatively minor, and in the final analysis, the major differences among people are learned cultural ones.

AFRICA

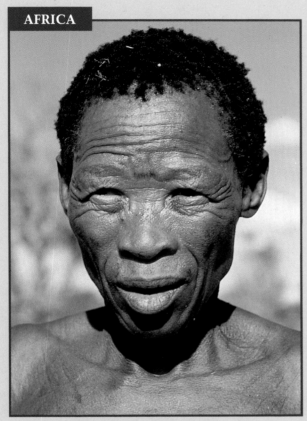

FIGURE 8-A   San, Kalahari Desert, Botswana

FIGURE 8-B   Efe, Ituri Forest, Zaire

FIGURE 8-C   Somba, Dahomey

FIGURE 8-D Ainu, Hokkaido, Japan

FIGURE 8-F Bangalore, India

FIGURE 8-E Bagish, China

FIGURE 8-G Hmong, Laos

FIGURE 8-H   Aborigine, Arnhem Land, Australia

FIGURE 8-J   Tonga, Polynesia

FIGURE 8-I   Mendi, South Highlands, New Guinea

FIGURE 8-K   Hamadan, Iran

FIGURE 8-N   Yanomama, Brazil

FIGURE 8-L   Kauto Keino Lapp, Norway

FIGURE 8-O   Taos Pueblo, New Mexico

FIGURE 8-M   Tbilisi, Georgia

CAROLI · LINNÆI, SVECI,

DOCTORIS MEDICINÆ,

SYSTEMA NATURÆ,

SIVE

REGNA TRIA NATURÆ

SYSTEMATICE PROPOSITA

PER

CLASSES, ORDINES,

GENERA, & SPECIES.

O JEHOVA! Quam ampla sunt opera Tua !
Quam ea omnia sapienter fecisti !
Quam plena est terra possessione tua !
Psalm. civ. 24.

LUGDUNI BATAVORUM,

Apud THEODORUM HAÀK, MDCCXXXV.

Ex TYPOGRAPHIA
JOANNIS WILHELMI DE GROOT.

Cover page of *Systema Naturae*, 1735, by Carolus Linnaeus, which set forth the form of the classification of animals still in use today.

It was to reveal the divine design that a young Swedish naturalist called Carl von Linné (generally known by his pen-name of Linnaeus) began the first great catalogue of animals and plants which culminated in the publication in 1752 of Philosophia Botanica, *written in Latin, in which he classified all plants according to class, genus, and species. . . . In his view the universe was static and atemporal, unchanged since it had first been created by God. He was interested only in the number, figure, proportion and situation of the organisms he classified, because these data were essential if the full complexity of God's design were to be revealed. Linnaeus conceived of a perfectly balanced nature, advocating zoos with cages each containing one pair of each type of animal, separated from other types, without interaction between them. According to him such a zoo would reproduce conditions as they had been on earth immediately after Creation.*[1]

James Burke

[1]From James Burke, *The Day the Universe Changed* (Boston: Little, Brown, 1985). Copyright ©1985 by London Writers Limited. By permission of Little, Brown and Company and BBC Enterprises Ltd.

9

CHAPTER

PEOPLE'S PLACE
IN NATURE

Humans are animals. They are part of a great diversity of living things, all of which share certain basic traits. Within the depths of the cell, biochemical mechanisms are remarkably similar wherever they are found. Yet, upon this base, life has evolved into an amazing variety of forms.

Early naturalists, including Carolus Linnaeus, viewed the complexity of life as a manifestation of the divine design that revealed itself at the creation. Although Linnaeus's view was a far cry from the vision of evolutionary change published by Charles Darwin over 100 years later, the classification of the living world was an important step in the development of such a theory. Classification provided biologists with a system for discussing, comparing, and contrasting living forms. This chapter discusses biological classification and looks at how humankind is related to the rest of the animal kingdom.

TAXONOMY

All human societies attempt to put order into their world. To understand the nature of living things and their diversity, people sort this diversity into a manageable number of categories. These categories can then be related to one another.

All peoples have systems of classification. Folk taxonomies of human variation were examined in Chapter 8. Since ordering is the first step in science, the scientist, too, is involved in the development of classification schemes. If we are to consider variability scientifically, we must precisely define the units of study and how they are related to one another. A system of organizing data is a **classification.** The science of classifying organisms into different categories is known as **taxonomy.**

Linnaeus's Classification

The most significant attempt to order the living world was that of the Swedish naturalist Carolus Linnaeus (1707–1778) (Figure 9–1). Although fundamental differences exist in theory, the system developed by Linnaeus is the basis of the system of classification used in modern biology.

The basic unit of classification in Linnaeus's scheme is the species, which Linnaeus considered to be a unit of creation, unchanging and distinct through time. His task was to define all the species known to him and to classify them. In his tenth edition of *Systema Naturae*, published

FIGURE 9–1 *Carolus Linnaeus (1707–1778).*

in 1758, he listed 4235 animal species. Today, according to biologist Edward O. Wilson, there are approximately 1,032,000 known animal species (Box 9–1).[2]

---

[2]E. O. Wilson, *The Diversity of Life* (Cambridge, Mass.: Belknap Press, 1992).

BOX 9–1

THE DIVERSITY OF LIFE

The typical urban American student is probably aware of only a very small number of animal species. The first that come to mind are those we keep as pets, including the familiar dogs and cats and the less familiar tropical fish, turtles, and iguanas. Perhaps more significant are those urban species we would rather not think about: rats, spiders, flies, and cockroaches. William Jordan describes several animal species that have made notable adaptations to an urban lifestyle in the suburbs of Los Angeles: the opossum, coyote, skunk, crow, parrot, alligator lizard, argentine ant, cellar spider, and feral cat.[1] Yet the totality of urban fauna is rather limited.

Moving to a larger venue, we may ask: How many animals worldwide have been identified and named by biologists? Not surprisingly, this list is a great deal longer. Yet most of the animals on this list are known only from a few specimens in a dusty museum drawer or a drawing in a technical scientific journal. This state of affairs makes it extremely difficult to arrive at an accurate estimate of the number of animal species that do exist on earth. Estimates vary tremendously, and many biologists agree that the number of animal species described and named may be only a fraction of the species that actually exist.

Biologist Edward O. Wilson ponders this question.[2] As a result of his search he estimates that 1,032,000 animals are presently described and named. If we examine the number of animals in each of the animal phyla as seen in the figure we observe that the vast number of known animal species are the arthropods, the phylum that includes the beetles, spiders, ants, and butterflies. And of the animal species yet to be discovered, the vast majority will probably turn out to be the arthropods living in the world's tropical rain forests. Biologists are very concerned about the rapid destruction of the rain forest that is annihilating tens of thousands, if not millions of unknown animal species. The loss of some of these species could have a major impact on human survival and the quality of human life.

And what of the mammals, the group of animals to which we belong? Only about 4000 mammals

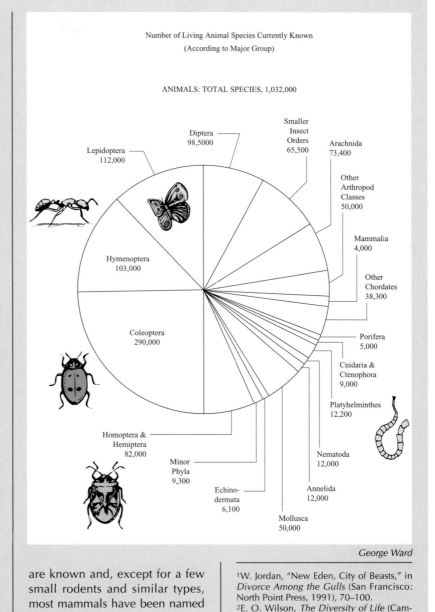

Number of Living Animal Species Currently Known
(According to Major Group)

ANIMALS: TOTAL SPECIES, 1,032,000

- Lepidoptera 112,000
- Diptera 98,5000
- Smaller Insect Orders 65,500
- Arachnida 73,400
- Other Arthropod Classes 50,000
- Mammalia 4,000
- Hymenoptera 103,000
- Other Chordates 38,300
- Coleoptera 290,000
- Porifera 5,000
- Cnidaria & Ctenophora 9,000
- Platyhelminthes 12,200
- Homoptera & Hemiptera 82,000
- Nematoda 12,000
- Minor Phyla 9,300
- Annelida 12,000
- Echinodermata 6,100
- Mollusca 50,000

George Ward

are known and, except for a few small rodents and similar types, most mammals have been named and described.

[1]W. Jordan, "New Eden, City of Beasts," in *Divorce Among the Gulls* (San Francisco: North Point Press, 1991), 70–100.
[2]E. O. Wilson, *The Diversity of Life* (Cambridge, Mass.: Belknap Press, 1992).

BINOMIAL NOMENCLATURE Linnaeus realized that a given animal is often known by different names in different parts of the world. Indeed, the same kind of animal often has several names in the same language. For these reasons, he decided to give species new Latin names. He chose Latin not only because it was the language of science but also because it was unchanging and politically neutral.

The system developed by Linnaeus is called a **binomial nomenclature** because each species is known by a **binomen,** or a two-part name. For example, Linnaeus gave the human species the name *Homo sapiens. Homo* is the generic name, or the name of the **genus** to which people belong. A genus is a group of similar species. This name is always capitalized, and no two genera (plural of *genus*) in the animal kingdom can have the same name. The second name is the specific name. The specific name is never capitalized, and it must always appear in association with the generic name. The generic and specific names are always in italics or underlined. Thus, humans belong to the genus *Homo* and the species *Homo sapiens.*

CLASSIFICATION OF SPECIES   According to Linnaeus, the characteristics of each animal species were the result of creation and a reflection of the divine plan. Variations within a species did exist, but these variations were considered irrelevant. The basic unit of study was actually the divine blueprint, or **archetype,** of a particular species.

Linnaeus noted that some animals are more alike than others. No one can doubt that monkeys resemble humans quite closely and that humans resemble dogs more than they do fish. Scientists of the eighteenth century believed that these similarities in structure were due to similarities in archetype. To study the similarities between animal forms, and to classify them on this basis, was to reveal the divine plan.

Archetypes were found on different levels. Each species had an archetype. Because humans, monkeys, and apes shared a great many features, Linnaeus placed them in a common group on the basis of these similarities. The archetype for the primates was simply a less specific blueprint than the archetype for the individual species. Going one step further, Linnaeus placed humans, monkeys, dogs, horses, and others in an even larger group, Mammalia. Here again, an archetype existed, but with even more generalized specifications.

The Basis of Modern Taxonomy

Biologists no longer think of species as fixed units of creation. As defined in Chapter 5, the species is a population whose members are able to reproduce successfully among themselves but are unable to reproduce with members of other species. The species is a dynamic unit, constantly changing through time and space; a species living at one point in time may be quite different from its descendants living millions of years later. Segments of a species may evolve into subspecies and, finally, may form a separate species. Species are not defined by physical similarities per se but rather on the criterion of their reproductive success. Species are placed into higher taxonomic levels on the basis of their evolutionary relationships.

THE TAXONOMIC HIERARCHY   The species is the basic unit of the modern system of classification. Closely related species are placed in a common genus. A genus represents a group of species with a fairly recent common ancestry; these species are populations that in the recent past were merely subspecies of some larger population. A genus is an example of a **taxon** (plural, taxa), which is a group of organisms at any level of the taxonomic hierarchy.

Taxa above the level of genus are often referred to as **higher taxa.** The existing system of classification contains five higher taxa: **family, order, class, phylum,** and **kingdom.** A family is a group of closely related genera; an order is a group of closely related families; and so forth. As we go higher in the hierarchy, each succeeding level is defined by more generalized characteristics. Because the higher taxa encompass so much variation, the included species have fewer characteristics in common.

Humans belong to the species *Homo sapiens* and the genus *Homo.* Although the genus *Homo* contains only one living species, it includes the extinct species *Homo habilis* and *Homo erectus.* The genus *Homo* is part of the family Hominidae, which also includes the extinct genus *Australopithecus.* The family Hominidae belongs to the order Primates, as do the monkeys, apes, tarsiers, and prosimians. The order Primates, in turn, is part of the next higher taxon, the class Mammalia. Other examples of mammals are dogs, cattle, whales, elephants, and bats. The class Mammalia is included in the phylum Chordata, which also encompasses birds, reptiles, amphibians, and fish. Finally, the chordates belong to the kingdom Animalia, which includes all animal forms.

The seven taxonomic levels, however, are not enough for a complete and satisfactory classification. The prefixes *super-, sub-,* and *infra-* are used to create additional levels. Thus, there can be a superfamily, a suborder, an infraclass, and so

TABLE 9–1

THE CLASSIFICATION OF *HOMO SAPIENS*

KINGDOM: Animalia
  PHYLUM: Chordata
    SUBPHYLUM: Vertebrata
      CLASS: Mammalia
        SUBCLASS: Theria
          INFRACLASS: Eutheria
            ORDER: Primates
              SUBORDER: Anthropoidea
                SUPERFAMILY: Hominoidea
                  FAMILY: Hominidae
                    GENUS: *Homo*
                      SPECIES: *Homo sapiens*

on. Table 9–1 presents a detailed classification of the species *Homo sapiens.*

Determining Evolutionary Relationships

Phylogeny refers to the evolutionary history of species. Since the development of classifications depends on the knowledge of evolutionary relationships among taxa, this section will discuss some of the problems in determining these evolutionary relationships.

HOMOLOGOUS FEATURES   A comparison of two different animals may reveal many anatomical similarities. In the reconstruction of a phylogeny, the taxonomist looks for structural similarities that are the result of inheritance from a common ancestor. Such similarities are known as **homologies.**

To convey the significance of homologous structures, we must point out a fundamental fact: once a new structure has evolved, the probability that it will evolve back into the exact thing from which it came is highly unlikely. It can, however, disappear or evolve further into something else. Furthermore, new structures do not simply appear from nowhere; they evolve from preexisting structures.

Figure 9–2 shows the forelimbs of a series of vertebrates. Externally, these forelimbs are quite different and serve different functions: manipulating objects, running, flying, and swimming. Yet all are derived from the same basic structure found in a common ancestral form. While the whale flipper reminds one of a fish fin, upon dissection the derivation of the flipper becomes obvious. It is an elaboration of the basic structure of the forelimb of a four-footed land vertebrate (see Box 9–2).

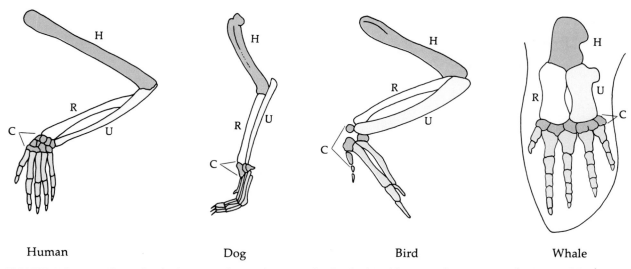

Human   Dog   Bird   Whale

FIGURE 9–2   *Vertebrate forelimbs.* Homologous bones in the forelimbs of four vertebrates are (H) humerus, (U) ulna, (R) radius, and (C) carpals. Homologies are similarities resulting from inheritance from a common ancestor.

BOX 9–2

THE FEET OF WHALES

Transitional forms are very rarely recovered from the fossil record. A very small percentage of the creatures that once lived are found as fossils. It is rather improbable that we will ever recover a representative of a rapidly evolving transitional form. This makes it difficult for some people to accept evolutionary history as fact.

From comparative anatomical and molecular studies of living forms, investigators hypothesize that modern cetaceans, the order that includes modern whales and porpoises, evolved from the mesonychids, a group of prehis-

Reconstruction of *Ambulocetus* (A) standing on land and (B) at the end of the power stroke during swimming.

toric even-toed hoofed animals related to modern deer, camels, and pigs. Yet until recently fossils of early whales had not been recovered. In December 1989, the husband-and-wife paleontology team of Philip Gingerich and Holly Smith discovered a whale with hind limbs in the Zeuglodon Valley in what is now the Egyptian desert.

The 40-million-year-old Egyptian fossils represent several bones of the pelvis and hindlimbs of *Basilosaurus.* The 20-inch-long leg articulates with a 10-inch-long pelvis which in turn articulates with the spine of an animal some 50 feet long when adult. Although the hindlimbs are extremely tiny when compared with the body, they are fully functional. Philip Gingerich suggests that they may

have been used to align the animal during copulation.

In 1994 fossil evidence of the earliest fully marine ancestor of the whale, *Rodhocetus,* was published. This form dates from about 47 to 46 million years ago and was found in Pakistan. An even older species is *Ambulacetus,* also from Pakistan. Unlike the younger *Rodhocetus, Ambulacetus,* having functioning legs, could move on land as well as in the water. Weighing about 300 kilograms (660 pounds), this early cetacean lived in shallow seas. Its skeleton shows a large, elongated hand, toes ending in hooves, and a long tail. It moved around on land very much like a modern sea lion and swam by means of undulations of the spine and paddling with its hindlimbs (see the figure). Other fossil cetaceans are known, the oldest dating from 52 million years ago and also found in Pakistan.

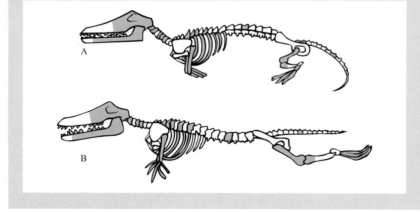

References: P. D. Gingerich, "The Whales of Tethys," *Natural History* (April 1994), 86–88; P. D. Gingerich et al., "New Whale from the Eocene of Pakistan and the Origin of Cetacean Swimming," *Nature,* 368 (1994), 844–847; P. D. Gingerich, B. H. Smith, and E. L. Simons, "Hind Limbs of Eocene Basilosaurus: Evidence of Feet in Whales," *Science,* 249 (1990), 154–157; and J. G. M. Thewissen et al., "Fossil Evidence for the Origin of Aquatic Locomotion in Archaeocete Whales," *Science,* 263 (1994), 210–212.

HOMOPLASTIC FEATURES   It is, of course, possible for structures in two different species to be similar without being homologous. Such similarities are said to be **homoplastic.** Homoplasy can come about in three different ways: parallelism, convergence, and chance.

Homoplastic features may be found in related species that independently evolved similarities

World (Africa, Europe, and Asia) evolved in Africa, the evolution of monkeys in the New World and Old World occurred independently of one another. Many similarities between these two major groups of monkeys arose independently in the two hemispheres but from a common premonkey ancestor (Figure 9–3).

Convergence refers to similar developments in less closely related evolutionary lines. Figure 9–4 shows a North American wolf, a Tasmanian wolf, and a whale. If a biologist had to classify these animals based on their evolutionary relationships, what criteria would be used?

A comparison of North American and Tasmanian wolves shows similarity in body size and shape, type of dentition, and diet—but it also shows great differences as well. The North American wolf and the whale are both placental mammals. In these species the fetus is nourished through a placenta until birth. The placenta is an example of an ancestral structure found in many descendant species. In contrast, the Tasmanian wolf, which is thought to be extinct today, is a marsupial, or pouched mammal, like the kangaroo. The marsupials evolved before the evolution of the placenta.

The complex method of fetal nourishment characterized by the placenta is more indicative of a close evolutionary relationship than are size and shape. Yet the similarities seen in the North American wolf and the Tasmanian wolf are striking. They are due to the fact that similar selective pressures can bring about similar adaptations in divergent evolutionary lines; this is convergence. (For another example of convergence see Figure 9–12.)

Another important concept is that of **analogy.** As seen in Figure 9–5, the wings of a bat, a bird, and a butterfly apear to be similar and serve the same function—flying. Structures that serve the same function are said to be analogous. Analogous structures may be homologous or homoplastic depending on whether or not the structure existed in the common ancestor. The three wings in the figure are homoplastic. For example, the common ancestor of the two flying vertebrates, the bat and the bird, did not possess

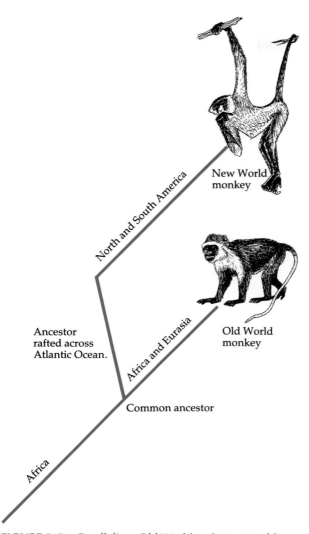

FIGURE 9–3 *Parallelism.* Old World and New World monkeys had a common origin in Africa. After rafting to South America, the New World monkeys evolved along lines similar to those of the Old World monkeys because of the common origin and similarities in ecological niches.

that did not exist in the common ancestor. However, the common ancestry did provide initial commonalities that gave direction to a parallel evolution in the two lines. This is called **parallelism.** For example, while the common ancestor of the monkeys of the New World (Central and South America) and the monkeys of the Old

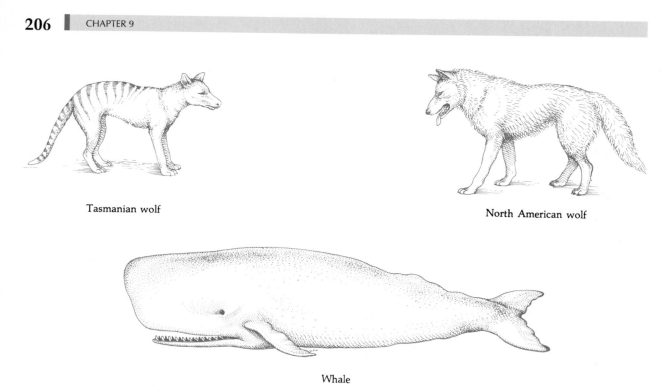

Tasmanian wolf

North American wolf

Whale

FIGURE 9–4 *Convergence.* The similarities between the Tasmanian wolf and the North American wolf result from convergent evolution. Actually, the North American wolf is more closely related to the whale.

FIGURE 9–5 *Analogy.* The wings of the butterfly, the bird, and the bat are analogous structures. They serve the same function, flying, but were independently evolved in different evolutionary lines.

Butterfly

Bat

Bird

wings. Wings arose independently among birds and mammals. While appearing to be similar, their skeletal structures are different.

Cladistics

An important approach to the theory of classification is **cladistics.** This term comes from the word **clade,** which refers to a set of species descended from a particular ancestral species. The practitioner of cladistics looks for homologous features. A major concern in this search is how far back in time it was that the homologies first appeared.

In cladistics, homologies that appeared recently and are therefore shared by a relatively small group of closely related taxa are called **shared derived (synapomorphic) features.** Homologies that first appeared a longer time ago and are shared by a larger group of species are called **shared ancestral (symplesiomorphic) features.** The task of the taxonomist is to identify which features are shared derived and which are

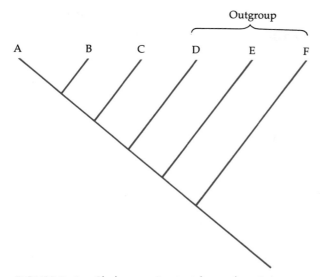

FIGURE 9–6 *Cladogram.* See text for explanation.

shared ancestral, and to separate both these types from features that are unique (**autapomorphic**) to a particular species or group of species.

Conducting a cladistic analysis is relatively straightforward. Let us say that we wish to determine evolutionary relationships among three species (or three genera, families, and so forth). These are species A, B, and C in Figure 9–6. We include in our analysis several other species that are closely related to the three in question; these additional species are called an **outgroup.** Features that appear in all or most of the species including the outgroup (A through F in Figure 9–6) are assumed to be shared ancestral features. (It is possible for a particular shared ancestral feature to be absent from a particular species because the feature has disappeared in that species.) Features that are found in the original set of species (A, B, and C) but not in the outgroup are assumed to be shared derived features.

From a cladistic analysis a **cladogram** can be drawn that graphically presents the evolutionary relationships among the species (or other taxa) being studied (Figure 9–7). While such a diagram appears to convey an evolutionary history, the time element is not present. Thus the cladogram, while depicting relationships among taxa, does not depict temporal relationships.

Summary

Central to the scientific study of the diversity of life is a system of ordering data, which is known as classification; the science of classifying organisms into different categories is known as taxonomy. In 1758 Linnaeus published the tenth edition of his classification of the living world; the form of this classification is still used today. Linnaeus gave all living species a binomial name, or binomen, and placed species in genera, genera in families, and so forth up the taxonomic hierarchy. Species were seen as unchanging, divinely created units, each of which had an archetype, or divine blueprint. Similar-looking animals were placed in categories based upon increasingly generalized archetypes.

Modern taxonomists think of the species as a dynamic unit defined in terms of reproductive success. Evolutionary relationships between species can be deduced on the basis of structural similarities that are the result of inheritance from a common ancestor; such similarities are known as homologies.

On the other hand, structures in two different animals can be similar without being homologous; such similarities are said to be homoplastic. Homoplasy can come about in several different ways. Independent evolution of similarities in related species is referred to as parallelism. Convergence refers to developments that arise in divergent evolutionary lines when similar selective pressures cause similar adaptations. Similarities can also come about by chance. In cladistics, a distinction is made between homologies that have appeared recently and are shared by a relatively small group of species or taxa (shared derived features) and homologies that first appeared a much longer time ago and are shared by a relatively large group of species or taxa (shared ancestral features).

PEOPLE AND THE ANIMAL WORLD

The Animal Kingdom

An important step in the classification of species is to divide them into large, basic units known

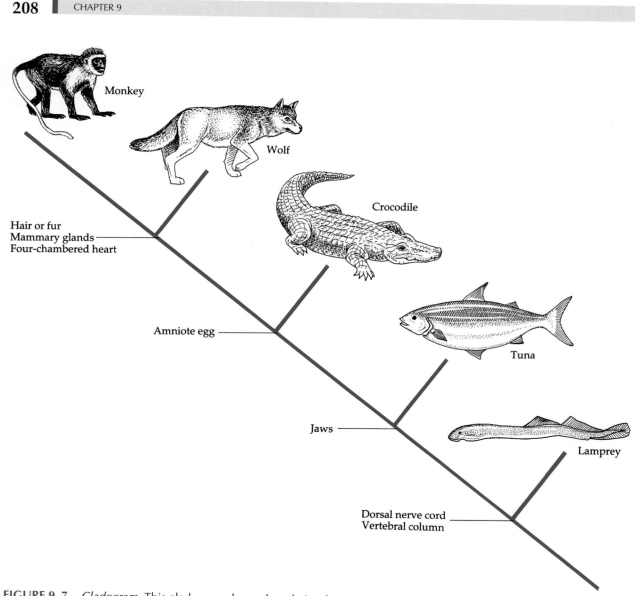

FIGURE 9–7 *Cladogram.* This cladogram shows the relationships among representatives of five vertebrates. Each branch point is defined by one or more newly evolved shared derived features.

as *kingdoms.* It was once thought that all organisms could be placed in either the plant kingdom or the animal kingdom. Today, however, taxonomists realize that many forms, such as acellular organisms, bacteria, and fungi, do not fit neatly into either of these two groups; they are placed in other kingdoms, bringing the total number of kingdoms to five (Table 9–2).

Members of the animal kingdom differ from plants in a number of ways. Animals are incapable of synthesizing food from inorganic materials; they must obtain their nutrients by consuming other organisms. Most animals are

highly mobile and have contracting fibers such as muscles. In addition, animals are composed of

TABLE 9–2

THE FIVE KINGDOMS OF LIFE*

KINGDOM:	Animalia (sponges, earthworms, grasshoppers, shellfish, starfish, reptiles, mammals)
KINGDOM:	Planti (pine trees, flowering plants)
KINGDOM:	Fungi (mushrooms)
KINGDOM:	Protista (unicellular organisms)
KINGDOM	Monera (bacteria, blue-green algae)

*With examples.

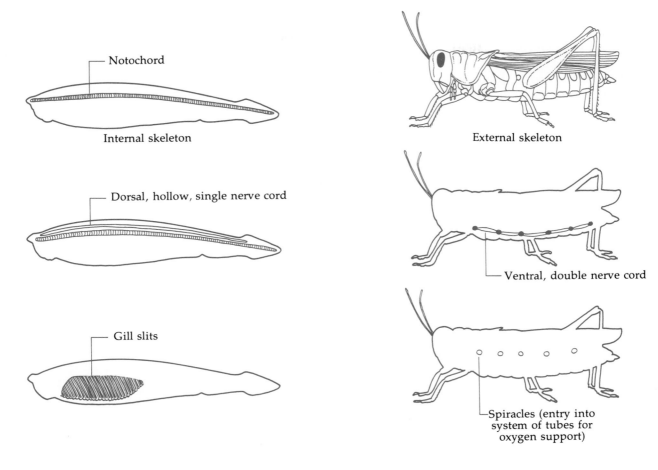

Amphioxus (Chordata)   Grasshopper (Arthropoda)

FIGURE 9–8   *The phyla Chordata and Arthropoda.* The major characteristics of the phylum Chordata are contrasted with those of the phylum Arthropoda.

specialized kinds of cells. Most animals can respond quickly to changes in their environment because they have nerves, muscles, and special sensing organs.

The animal kingdom is divided into several units known as *phyla*, with each phylum representing a basic body plan. The number of recognized phyla varies from author to author, but the total number is usually more than eighteen. Most familiar animals belong to the following nine phyla (examples of animals in each are given in parentheses): Porifera (sponges), Coelenterata (jellyfish, sea anemones), Platyhelminthes (planaria, tapeworms), Aschelminthes (nematode worms), Mollusca (snails, scallops, octopuses), Annelida (earthworms), Echinodermata (star-

fish), Arthropoda (spiders, butterflies, crayfish), and Chordata (fish, reptiles, birds, mammals).

The Phylum Chordata

Humans belong to the phylum Chordata. **Chordates** include such forms as the tunicates, fish, amphibians, reptiles, birds, and mammals.

It is instructive to compare the phylum Chordata with another, such as, for example, members of the phylum Arthropoda. Figure 9–8 compares a grasshopper, an arthropod, with an *Amphioxus*, a small, ocean-dwelling chordate. Some points of similarity can be noted. Each is **bilaterally symmetrical**; that is, each can be cut down the middle to form two halves that are generally mirror images of each other. Each animal has a head and a tail and a digestive system with openings at both ends.

A major feature of the chordates is the presence of an internal skeleton. Part of this skeleton is a cartilaginous rod, called the **notochord,** that runs along the back of the animal. In all chordates the notochord is present in the embryonic stage, but in most chordates it is replaced by the spine in the adult. In the grasshopper (arthropod) the skeleton is external; the animal has no notochord.

In chordates, a single hollow nerve cord lies on top of the notochord (**dorsal** to the notochord). In the arthropods, the nerve cord is double and solid, and it is located on the **ventral,** or bottom, side of the animal.

In addition, all chordates have **gill slits** at some time in their life history. Although gills do not actually develop in people, structures that appear in the human embryo are thought by embryologists to be **gill pouches.** Arthropods such as grasshoppers supply air to their tissues through a series of tubes that open to the outside through their outer covering. Others such as crayfish have feathery gills but no gill slits.

The Vertebrates

The phylum Chordata includes the subphylum Vertebrata, which includes most of the animals within the phylum. There are seven living classes of vertebrates: the jawless vertebrates, the sharks and rays, the bony fish, the amphibians, the reptiles, the birds, and the mammals (Table 9–3).

The early **vertebrates** were similar in many ways to *Amphioxus,* but in place of a notochord, a true vertebral column, or spine, developed. Like the early chordates, the early vertebrates were filter feeders. Because they lacked jaws, they swam with open mouths; forcing water into their mouths and out through their gills, they filtered out food particles. Vertebrates ultimately developed bone in place of cartilage, and many early forms were covered by bony plates. Today, the jawless vertebrates are represented by the highly specialized lamprey and hagfish.

TABLE 9–3
THE CLASSIFICATION OF THE CHORDATES*

PHYLUM: Chordata
  SUBPHYLUM: Tunicata (tunicates)
  SUBPHYLUM: Cephalochordata (*Amphioxus*)
  SUBPHYLUM: Vertebrata
  CLASS: Agnatha (lampreys, hagfish)
  CLASS: Chondrichthyes (sharks, rays)
  CLASS: Osteichthyes (perch, herring, salmon)
  CLASS: Amphibia (frogs, salamanders)
  CLASS: Reptilia (turtles, lizards, snakes)
  CLASS: Aves (robins, vultures, ostriches, penguins)
  CLASS: Mammalia (dogs, elephants, whales, gorillas)

*With examples.

THE ORIGIN OF JAWS   A major event in vertebrate evolution was the evolution of jaws. New structures do not simply arise from nothing; they develop as modifications of preexisting structures. The jawless vertebrates have skeletal elements, **gill bars,** that support the gill slits. In the early fish, the first gill bars enlarged to become a primitive jaw (Figure 9–9).

While filter feeding restricted the jawless vertebrates to very small food particles, the evolution of jaws enabled them to prey on one another and to proliferate. Today these jawed vertebrates are represented by the sharks and rays and the bony fish. Land vertebrates eventually evolved from a population of freshwater bony fish.

THE ORIGIN OF LAND VERTEBRATES   The ancestors of the land vertebrates were freshwater bony fish adapted to drought conditions, which were common at the time. Periodically, lakes and streams dried up or became small ponds of stagnant water. These vertebrates had lungs for supplementing their oxygen supply in oxygen-deficient water.

The origin of land vertebrates also depended on the evolution of legs. Unlike the fish of today, these early fish had bony elements in their fins. The constant drying up of lakes and streams gave a local selective advantage to these fish, which could move overland from one pond to the next.

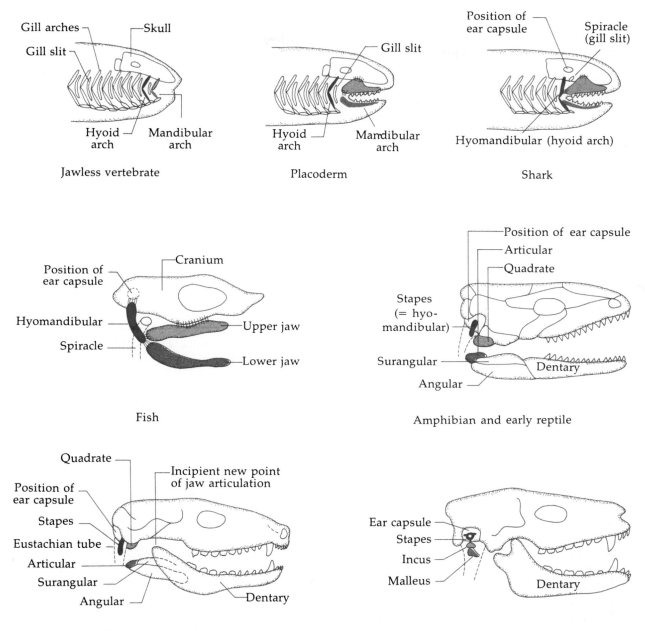

FIGURE 9–9 *Evolution of the jaws and middle-ear bones.* Note the many examples of homologies. For instance, the malleus (a bone of the middle ear) of the mammal is homologous to the articular bone of the lower jaw in the amphibian and early reptile.

As was pointed out by the vertebrate paleontologist Alfred S. Romer, land vertebrates did not arise because there was opportunity on land.[3] Organisms do not evolve structures to meet the requirements of new potential habitats. No fish ever lifted its head out of the water, surveyed the land, and decided that since the land was devoid of competition and food was plentiful, it would then evolve lungs and limbs. The structures that make life on land possible evolved as adaptations to aid the fish in *water* under drought conditions. In retrospect it appears as if the population evolved new adaptations in order to enter new niches on land. In reality the evolution of new adaptations for life in water merely allowed the animal to adapt to new terrestrial habitats, an example of preadaptation.

AMPHIBIANS AND REPTILES   The earliest land vertebrates were the amphibians. Amphibians, however, were tied to the water. Most needed to keep their skin moist, especially to aid in breathing through the skin, and all had to lay their eggs in water. This prevented an extensive exploitation of terrestrial habitats.

A life spent totally on land was made possible by changes in the breathing apparatus, which increased the efficiency of the lungs; a waterproof skin; and the **amniote egg.** The amniote egg may have evolved as a method of protecting eggs in water; but once it had developed, reproduction on land became possible.

The embryo in an amniote egg develops within a shell (Figure 9–10). Fertilization must take place inside the body of the female before the shell is formed. Within the shell, several membranes develop from embryonic tissue. The embryo itself is contained inside a fluid-filled **amnion,** which forms from the embryo's side. A second membrane, the **chorion,** is derived from the amnion; the chorion lies just beneath the shell and acts as a surface for oxygen absorption. Growing out of the embryo's digestive tract is the **yolk sac,** which is filled with yolk in reptiles

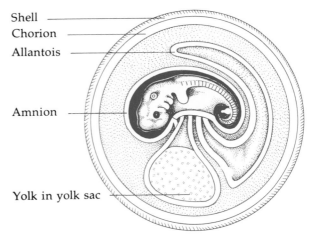

Shell
Chorion
Allantois

Amnion

Yolk in yolk sac

FIGURE 9–10   *Amniote egg.* This type of egg could be laid on land.

and birds, and the **allantois,** where waste material is deposited.

With the development of the amniote egg, vertebrates were no longer tied to the water. The earliest true land vertebrates were the reptiles, which began to spread over the land some 300 million years ago. From this radiation evolved the dinosaurs and modern reptiles, as well as the birds and mammals.

The Mammals

The reptilian group from which the mammals ultimately emerged appeared very early in the reptilian radiation. These early mammal-like reptiles did not resemble modern reptiles; from the beginning they showed marked mammalian features and soon evolved into true mammals. The mammals coexisted with the dinosaurs throughout most of their history. With the demise of the dinosaurs, mammals became the dominant form of large terrestrial animal.

THE REGULATION OF BODY TEMPERATURE
A lizard sleeps through the cold desert night in an underground shelter. When it senses the warmth of the sun, it emerges into the daylight and suns itself. At last it is ready to perform the activities of the day. Yet when the desert sun is

[3]A. S. Romer, "Major Steps in Vertebrate Evolution," *Science,* 158 (1967), 1629–1637.

BOX 9–3

WERE DINOSAURS "WARM-BLOODED"?

Humans try to understand extinct forms by analogy, thinking of them in terms of modern species. Since dinosaurs are placed in the class Reptilia, modern reptiles have been used as models for reconstructing how dinosaurs actually lived. Yet prehistoric species may have been quite different from similar-appearing modern ones.

Throughout the museums of the world dinosaurs were once shown essentially as large lizards, lumbering, quadrupedal beasts. Because of the discoveries and new interpretations of the past few decades, our picture of the life of dinosaurs is rapidly changing. One major conclusion of some paleontologists is that some dinosaurs were "warm-blooded." John Ostrom describes the small, predatory dinosaur *Deinonychus:* "It must have been a fleet-footed, highly predacious, extremely agile and very active animal, sensitive to many stimuli and quick in its responses. These in turn indicate an unusual level of activity for a reptile and suggest an unusually high metabolic rate."[1]

Deinonychus, a predatory dinosaur from Montana.

Some evidence suggests endothermy, although the picture is far from clear and controversy reigns. For example, skeletons and preserved footprints show that most dinosaurs were erect bipeds, a posture and gait that occur today only in the endotherms, mammals and birds. The relatively large vertical distance between the heart and the brain requires that there be sufficient blood pressure to get the blood to the brain, which suggests a fully developed four-chambered heart. Many conclude that these animals were capable of high activity levels and running speeds.

Other bits of evidence include specialized dentition among the plant-eating dinosaurs that is associated with the processing of large amounts of food that would be required for endothermy. In some, the anatomical structure of the mouth separates the nasal from the mouth cavity, permitting simultaneous eating and breathing. Microscopic examination of the structure of the bone of some species shows similarities to that of endothermic mammals and birds and differences from that of modern reptiles. Analysis of the skeletons of young dinosaurs shows a rapid rate of growth that is characteristic of modern mammals and birds but quite different from the slow growth rate of modern reptiles.

Other evidence comes from an analysis of a mixture of the isotopes of oxygen in some fossil bones. In modern reptiles there is a significant temperature difference between the internal body core and the extremities; such a marked difference is not found in endothermic mammals. Body temperature is reflected in the ratio of isotopes of oxygen. Analysis of such data reveals a mammalian, hence a "warm-blooded," pattern in some dinosaurs. Although not universally accepted, this latest evidence adds another piece to this fascinating puzzle.

---

[1]John Ostrom, quoted in J. N. Wilford, *The Riddle of the Dinosaurs* (New York: Knopf, 1985), 172.
References: R. T. Bakker, *The Dinosaur Heresies* (New York: William Morrow, 1986); R. E. Barrick and W. J. Showers, "Thermophysiology of *Tyrannosaurus rex:* Evidence from Oxygen Isotopes," *Science,* (1994), 222– 224; J. N. Wilford, op. cit.; J. H. Ostrom, "The Evidence for Endothermy in Dinosaurs," in R. D. K. Thomas and E. C. Olsen (eds), *A Cold Look at the Warm-Blooded Dinosaurs* (Washington, D.C.: American Association for the Advancement of Science,

high, the lizard must seek shelter, for it cannot function in the desert's fierce heat.

A cold wind is blowing down the mountainside, yet the mouse wakes up before dawn. In the dark, safe from its enemies, it forages for food. Unlike the lizard, the mouse can function in the cold of night or in the fierce heat of day.

Contemporary reptiles are said to be "cold-blooded," while mammals are described as "warm-blooded," but these terms are far from descriptive since the body temperature of a lizard may be as high as that of a mammal. The primary distinction between the body temperatures of reptiles and mammals lies in the source of the body heat. Reptiles are **ectotherms;** that is, they derive most of their body heat from outside their bodies. Reptiles can and do maintain a high and constant body temperature, but they accomplish this primarily through behavior. During the cold of the night the lizard seeks a relatively warm underground burrow; in the early morning the animal suns itself on a rock; and during the heat of the day it finds the shade of a plant or rock. This method of maintaining relatively constant temperature is termed **behavioral thermoregulation.** To maintain a constant temperature, the reptile must vary its activity with changes in the environment.

Like the lizard, the mouse also maintains a relatively high, constant body temperature. Unlike the lizard, however, mammals are **homeothermic;** that is, mammals can control their body temperature through physiological means and can maintain a high body temperature largely independent of the environmental temperature. This is accomplished by the ability to generate body heat internally (**endothermy**) and by special mechanisms for regulating the body temperature. This means that mammals can maintain a relatively constant, high level of activity with a fair degree of independence from the constraints of environmental temperature.

Homeothermy requires a complex of interrelated features such as the evolution of regulating mechanisms in the brain, the growth of fur or hair to provide a layer of insulation, and the development of sweat glands to allow cooling of the body if necessary. In addition, it requires a reliable and fairly large intake of food. A snake may eat once every other week. It simply swallows an entire animal, which then dissolves slowly in the digestive juices in its stomach; the bones and fur are excreted. Mammals do not swallow animals whole. Instead, meat-eating mammals tear their prey into small pieces, and plant eaters bite off small amounts which they then chew into small pieces.

SOME OTHER CHARACTERISTICS OF THE MAMMALS   Mammals are characterized by **heterodont** dentition, the regional differentiation of teeth (Figure 9–11). Unlike reptiles, whose teeth are all simple, pointed structures (**homodont**), mammals evolved different types of teeth—incisor, canine, premolar, and molar—that serve the different functions of tearing, piercing, and chewing. Mammals have two sets of teeth (**diphyodonty**), the deciduous teeth and the permanent teeth; reptilian teeth are continuously replaced (**polyphyodonty**).

The growth and development of teeth parallels the pattern of growth and development of the skeleton. Reptiles continue to grow throughout their lives. Their teeth are continuously being replaced, and their long bones are capped with cartilage where bone growth likewise continues to take place. On the other hand, mammalian deciduous teeth are replaced in childhood by permanent teeth that serve the mammal throughout adult life. Also, as was discussed in Chapter 7 with respect to human growth, mammalian bone growth occurs in growth plates between the diaphysis and epiphyses of the bone. At characteristic ages bone growth ceases, and the growth plates disappear as adult size is reached.

The lower teeth of the mammals are embedded in one bone on either side of the lower jaw, or mandible, which is a solid structure able to take the stresses of chewing. The reptilian lower jaw is composed of six bones, while the mammalian lower jaw or **mandible** is composed of two bones that are often fused into a single struc-

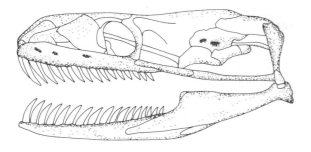

Snake

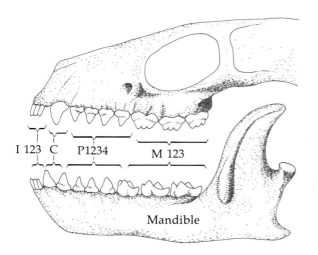

Mammal

FIGURE 9–11 *Mammalian jaws and teeth.* The jaws and teeth of a mammal are compared with those of a reptile (a snake). The mammal pictured is a hypothetical generalized placental mammal. The teeth are (I) incisors, (C) canines, (P) premolars, and (M) molars.

ture. Two of the reptilian jawbones have been transformed into middle-ear bones, giving mammals three bones in the middle ear in contrast to the single bone in reptiles. While the eardrum, or **tympanic membrane,** is found near the surface of the body in reptiles, the mammalian tympanic membrane and middle ear are encased in bone.

Many other anatomical features in mammals aid in adapting to terrestrial habitats. These include the **diaphragm,** which is a muscle lying beneath the lungs that functions in breathing; the **hard palate,** which separates the nasal from the oral cavity and permits the animal to breathe and chew at the same time; and the **four-chambered heart,** which allows efficient separation of oxygenated and deoxygenated blood.

MAMMALIAN REPRODUCTION AND BE-HAVIOR   The amniote egg, which is laid on land, evolved with the reptiles. In order to maintain their populations, most reptiles lay eggs in great numbers; however, the eggs of most reptiles are given minimal care.

One of the most important aspects of mammalian reproduction is that the offspring develop inside the mother. The embryo and fetus are not exposed to the outside environment. This ensures a higher chance of survival for the fetus, which means that fewer young are required to maintain the population.

Behavioral changes are as important as anatomical and physiological changes. Newborn mammals cannot obtain their own food; they are nourished by taking milk from their mothers' **mammary glands.** The ability of the mother to produce a high-quality, dependable food also increases the mammalian infant's chances of survival. The care given the young by the mother and often by the father is equally important. Among some mammals, adults other than the parents care for infants. Unlike many reptilian young, who often never see their parents, mammalian young develop close bonds with their mothers and sometimes their fathers and siblings.

Bonding and protection of offspring not only function to protect the offspring but also make the transmission of learned behavioral patterns possible. To a large extent, mammals also adjust to their niches through behavior. In contrast to insect behavior, which is basically innate, much of mammalian behavior is learned. Behavioral adjustments can thereby change rapidly, even within a single generation, in response to changing environmental pressures. Anatomical adaptations, such as improvements in the nervous system, including the elaboration of the brain,

FIGURE 9–12 *The echidna* (Tachyglossus aculeatus). This is an example of a prototherian mammal. The spines on the body resemble those of the porcupine, a placental mammal, yet they have a different internal structure. This is an example of convergent evolution.

are important in creating the potential for behavioral adjustments.

CLASSIFICATION OF THE MAMMALS   The mammals belong to the class Mammalia, which is divided into two subclasses containing three groups that correspond to the three major kinds of mammals. The subclass Prototheria consists of the egg-laying mammals; the pouched mammals and the placental mammals belong to the subclass Theria.

Prototherian mammals, also known as the **monotremes,** include only two living forms, the platypus and the echidna (Figure 9–12). These animals lay eggs but also produce milk. In most ways they possess both reptilian and mammalian characteristics, and for this reason some taxonomists consider them to be mammal-like reptiles. Modern mammals did not evolve from prototherian-like ancestors. They represent a branch of the mammalian class that evolved a number of distinctive traits after the monotremes had branched off the main mammalian evolutionary line.

The **therian** mammals, which produce live young, can be divided into two infraclasses. The infraclass Metatheria contains the **marsupials,** or pouched mammals (Figure 9–13). Most of them live in Australia, although the opossums are a well-known North American group. They differ from other mammals in many ways but most importantly in method of reproduction. Metatherian offspring are born while they are still fetuses. The fetus then crawls into the mother's pouch or fold, where it continues to develop and mature.

The remainder of the mammals, and by far the larger number of species, belong to the infraclass Eutheria. These are the **placental mammals.** Their young remain inside the mother, nourished by the **placenta,** until they reach an advanced state of development. The placenta is an organ that develops from fetal membranes. It

FIGURE 9–13   *Matchie's tree kangaroo* (Dendrolagus matchiei). This is an example of a metatherian mammal, or marsupial.

penetrates the lining of the uterus where the placental blood vessels come into close contact with the mother's blood. Oxygen, nutrients, and other substances pass from the mother's bloodstream into that of the fetus. Waste material passes in the opposite direction.

THE RELATIONSHIP OF PRIMATES TO OTHER MAMMALS   Today there are eighteen (some count more) living orders of placental mammals, which are listed in the classification in Table 9–4. Since the major subject of physical anthropology is people, we are most interested in the order Primates, which is the subject of the next several chapters.

The traditional classification of taxa is based upon the analysis of anatomy and paleontology. More recently, molecular and chromosome data have been considered (Chapter 13), which has led to many discussions about the relationships

TABLE 9–4

THE CLASSIFICATION OF THE MAMMALS*

CLASS: Mammalia
　SUBCLASS: Prototheria
　　ORDER: Monotremata (platypuses, echidnas)
　SUBCLASS: Theria
　　INFRACLASS: Metatheria
　　　ORDER: Marsupialia (kangaroos, koalas, opossums)
　　INFRACLASS: Eutheria
　　　ORDER: Insectivora (shrews, hedgehogs, moles)
　　　ORDER: Macroscelida (elephant shrews)
　　　ORDER: Scandentia (tree shrews)
　　　ORDER: Chiroptera (bats)
　　　ORDER: Dermoptera (flying "lemurs")
　　　ORDER: Edentata (armadillos, anteaters, tree sloths)
　　　ORDER: Pholidota (pangolins)
　　　ORDER: Primates (lemurs, tarsiers, monkeys, apes, humans)
　　　ORDER: Rodentia (squirrels, beavers, mice, porcupines)
　　　ORDER: Lagomorpha (rabbits, hares)
　　　ORDER: Cetacea (whales, porpoises, dolphins)
　　　ORDER: Carnivora (dogs, bears, cats, hyenas, seals)
　　　ORDER: Tubulidentata (aardvarks)
　　　ORDER: Perissodactyla (horses, rhinoceroses, tapirs)
　　　ORDER: Artiodactyla (pigs, camels, deer, cattle, hippopotamuses)
　　　ORDER: Proboscidea (elephants)
　　　ORDER: Sirenia (sea cows, dugongs)
　　　ORDER: Hyracoidea (hyraxes, conies)

*With examples.
This classification is based upon that of E. H. Colbert and M. Morales, *Evolution of the Vertebrates,* 4th ed. (New York: Wiley-Liss, 1991), 434–437. The classification of other authors may differ. For example, many zoologists place the seals and walruses into their own order, the Pinnipedia. The Cetacea and Chiroptera each are often divided into two orders instead of one.

among various groups of animals, such as the orders of placental mammals. Although there is no consensus on this issue, Figure 9–14 shows one attempt, based upon molecular data, to picture the relationship among the mammalian orders.[4]

As can be seen in Figure 9–14, some biologists place the order Primates in a superorder named

Archonta. The Archonta includes the primates along with the Scandentia (tree shrews), the Dermoptera (flying lemurs), and the Chiroptera (bats). More will be said about the tree shrews in Chapter 10 and about the flying lemurs in Chapter 15.

Summary

People belong to the animal kingdom. This large group of organisms is divided into several phyla that represent basic body plans. The phylum Chordata, which encompasses all vertebrates, is characterized by a notochord, dorsal hollow nerve cord, and gill slits. In the vertebrates, the notochord is replaced by a vertebral column. One group of early vertebrates gave rise, through the refinement of lungs and limbs, to the first land vertebrates, the amphibians. With the evolution of the amniote egg, reproduction was no longer tied to water. This evolutionary development resulted in the great reptilian radiation, which included a line of reptiles that were mammal-like. Through a long evolutionary history, these reptiles ultimately gave rise to the mammals.

The mammals are a class of vertebrates. They are characterized by homeothermy and endothermy, heterodont dentition, mammary glands, and complex patterns of learned behavior. The mammals have radiated into eighteen living orders. Included in one of these orders, the order Primates, are people.

STUDY QUESTIONS

1. Although the form of Linnaeus's system of biological classification is still in use, the concept of classification has changed considerably. In what ways does the theory of taxonomy of the eighteenth century differ from that of the twentieth century?

[4]M. J. Novacek, "Mammalian Phylogeny: Shaking the Tree," *Nature,* 356 (1992), 121–125.

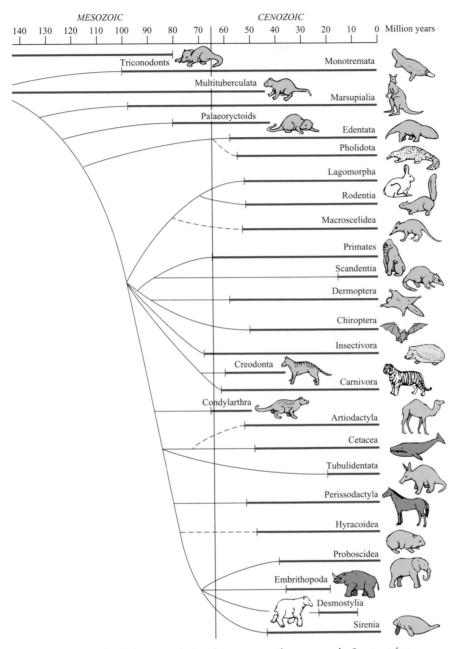

FIGURE 9–14 *Evolutionary relationships among the mammals.* See text for explanation.

2. One line of evidence for evolutionary relationships is homologous structures. How does the taxonomist distinguish between two similar structures that are truly homologous and those that are the result of convergent evolution?

3. What is the theoretical basis of the cladistic approach?

4. Each animal phylum represents a basic body plan. What features characterize the phylum Chordata? Can these features be identified in humans?

5. What selective pressures operating on the water-dwelling bony fish resulted in a preadaptation for life on land?

6. What major adaptations have been largely responsible for the success of the mammals at the expense of the reptiles?

7. Think about what humans are like today. Why is it unlikely that a humanlike creature would evolve in the class Reptilia?

SUGGESTED READINGS

Anderson, S., and J. K. Jones Jr. (eds.). *Orders and Families of Recent Mammals of the World.* New York: Wiley, 1984. This book contains several very detailed discussions of modern mammals, including their characteristics and classification.

Colbert, E. H., and M. Morales. *Evolution of the Vertebrates,* 4th ed. New York: Wiley-Liss, 1991. This book presents the history of the vertebrates, including the fossil record and a survey of living forms.

Mayr, E. *Principles of Systematic Zoology.* New York: McGraw-Hill, 1969; Simpson, G. G. *Principles of Animal Taxonomy.* New York: Columbia University Press, 1961. Although somewhat dated, these are the two classic texts on modern animal taxonomy.

Nielsen, C. *Animal Evolution: Interrelationships of the Living Phyla.* New York: Oxford University Press, 1995. This book provides a detailed cladistic analysis of animal species, including the primates.

Radinsky, L. B. *The Evolution of Vertebrate Design.* Chicago: University of Chicago Press, 1987. A well-written and easily understood book on the evolution of vertebrate anatomy.

The white-handed gibbon, *Hylobates lar lar.*

I confess freely to you, I could never look long upon a monkey without very mortifying reflections.

William Congreve, *Letters to Dennis*, 1695

CHAPTER

10

THE LIVING PRIMATES

In 1758 Linnaeus classified humans together with the monkeys and apes into the same category. Since then, many people have attempted, as Richard Passingham says, to "put animals back in their proper place."[1] Different rationales have been posited to put distance between humans and the other primates—for that matter, all animals—but today biologists no longer debate the issue.

Humans *are* primates; they share with other primates many basic primate characteristics. This perhaps explains the tremendous fascination that people have for monkeys and apes in zoos. Anthropologists, too, are fascinated by primates. Studies of their natural history, behavior, and anatomy provide important clues for the reconstruction and understanding of the human evolutionary history.

This is the first of several chapters that examine the relationship of humans to their nonhuman primate relatives. This chapter defines what a primate is and then surveys the animals that make up this order.

---

[1]R. Passingham, *The Human Primate* (Oxford: Freeman, 1982), 1.

THE PRIMATE ORDER

The order Primates is one of the eighteen orders of placental mammals recognized by biologists today. We can define most of these mammalian orders on the basis of some distinctive adaptation. Members of the order Chiroptera, the bats, have wings; members of the order Carnivora, which includes the bears, lions, and dogs, have sharp teeth for slicing and tearing meat; and so on.

Unlike animals in other mammalian orders, members of the order Primates are not characterized by one or more conspicuous traits, such as the wings of bats or the specialized teeth of carnivores. This fact has led to considerable difficulties concerning the definition of the order. In this section we will examine the features that are usually associated with the living primates.

The Nature of the Primate Order

This problem of defining the primates was noted by the British anatomist Wilfred LeGros Clark, who pointed out that primates are best defined in terms of their adaptability. This adaptability may be thought of as a response to the **arboreal** habitat. Almost all primates live in trees; even the more terrestrial forms, such as the baboons, readily take to the trees. Humans also have the potential to climb. In fact, children from many cultures enjoy playing in trees, and many athletes and performers achieve great proficiency in arboreal maneuvers.

The arboreal habitat differs significantly from the terrestrial one. An arboreal animal must constantly be aware of the three-dimensional nature of its habitat. In moving through the trees, the animal is moving not only forward and backward, left and right, but also up and down. The arboreal habitat is not a solid one, and any miscalculation can send an animal falling to the ground from great heights. Sometimes branches sway in the wind or shift as an animal leaps from one branch to the next. This habitat is also unpredictable, as can be seen when a primate leaps to a branch that then breaks. The difficulties of living in such a situation should be kept in mind as we review the characteristics of the order.

Another basic theme in primate evolution is related to the ecological niche thought to have been filled by the earliest primates—arboreal insect predation. Although only some primates living today eat insects, many features of the living primates can be seen as specializations for moving along the thin branches of low-lying bushes and trees hunting for insects. As we examine specific features of the primates, we shall attempt to relate them to the requirements of arboreal habitats and arboreal insect predation.

THE *SCALA NATURAE*   A major difficulty in discussing primate characteristics is the variability of the group. Early biologists saw humans as the "ideal" primate and placed the primates in a rank order according to how closely they conform to the ideal. Their rank-order sequence might list, in ascending order, the tree shrew (not a primate), lemur, tarsier, monkey, chimpanzee, and, at the top, human. This conception, known as the *Scala naturae,* suggests an evolutionary sequence consisting of modern forms, one in which modern living forms are our direct ancestors.

Of course, a species cannot be a descendant of its contemporary. Some modern forms may have specific characteristics that were present in populations ancestral to ourselves, and so these forms may share a common ancestry with humans. Still, we must remember that modern nonhuman primates are products of long evolutionary sequences, just as people are; thus they cannot be the ancestors of humans.

A Definition of the Order Primates

Today we realize that we must take great care when isolating the specific characteristics that form the basis of the definition of a taxon. While members of a taxon, such as an order, share many homologous features, as we discussed in Chapter 9, we must be careful to distinguish between different kinds of homologies.

Some similarities found among the primates are shared ancestral traits that are found in many mammalian orders, having been inherited from the same ancestral placental mammal. For example, all primates are characterized by the presence of the clavicle, a pair of bones commonly called the "collarbone." Yet the clavicle is present in other mammalian orders and in fossil placental mammals. This is an example of a trait retained in the primates although it has been lost in some other orders. Of course, we must also recognize that a trait that is present in the primates and other mammalian orders may have arisen through parallelism or convergence.

Other traits that are found among the primates are shared derived features that are unique to the order and therefore may be used to distinguish the primates from other groups of mammals. Examples include the replacement of the claw by nails (although some primates have retained claws on some digits) and the details of the structure of the skull that houses the middle ear (to be discussed in Chapter 13).

MOVEMENT IN THE TREES   As has been mentioned, primates are generally arboreal animals, and many shared derived features of their anatomy are related to movement in arboreal habitats. Primates have evolved a degree of prehension of the hand and foot whereby they are able to grasp; a monkey walking along a branch grasps that branch.

The evolution of a grasping big toe is perhaps one of the most important diagnostic features of the primates. Except for humans, all primates can grasp objects with the big toe. The grasping big toe plays an important role in arboreal insect predation by allowing the animal to anchor itself on a branch by its feet as it leaps up and catches an insect with its hands. The adaptation for this niche served to differentiate the early primates from other early mammalian stocks.

Many, but not all, primates have a grasping thumb. In many cases the thumb has become truly **opposable;** that is, the thumb can rotate so that the terminal pad of the thumb comes into contact with the terminal pad of one or more of the other digits. This grasping ability is another important factor in the primates' ability to manipulate objects in their habitats.

A squirrel scampers up a tree by digging its claws into the bark. As a primate moves up a tree, it grasps the trunk. In most primates claws have evolved into nails (Figure 10–1). The fingers of primates end in **tactile pads;** these pads not only act as friction pads in grasping but also con-

Claw   Nail

FIGURE 10–1   *Nail versus claw.* The nail is homologous to the outer layer of the claw.

fer a refined sense of touch that helps convey information about the environment.

Besides having these shared derived features, the primates have also retained many shared ancestral features. The forelimb structure of the primate corresponds well to the generalized limb structure of early placental ancestors. For example, all primates have retained the clavicle (collarbone), the two separate bones in the lower arm (the ulna and radius), and five fingers (**pentadactylism).** (See the Appendix for a discussion and diagrams of the bones of the skeleton.) This arrangement permits a great degree of flexibility in the shoulder, forearm, and hand, which facilitates movement through the trees.

In many modern placental mammals one or more of these features have disappeared. We can look at the horse as an example. The horse is suited to high-speed running over hard ground. This means of locomotion results in a great amount of jarring, but it does not require any real degree of flexibility in the forelimb. Such flexibility has been lost in the horse, and as a result, many elements of the skeleton have been lost. The clavicle has disappeared, the shoulder has lost its flexibility, the two bones of the lower arm have fused, and the five fingers have been reduced to one, the hoof (Figure 13–5). The anatomical structures that play major roles in movement and locomotion will be described in more detail in Chapter 13.

THE SENSE OF SMELL   Among terrestrial mammals, the **olfactory** sense, or sense of smell, plays a crucial role. Hunters realize that when they approach an animal like a gazelle, the animal is not apt to see them, especially if they freeze when it is looking up; but they had better stalk the animal from downwind to avoid being detected by their smell.

Smells are relatively unimportant in the trees. Most odors hug the ground, and the wind, as it blows through the trees, eliminates their usefulness. Also, the sense of smell does not give an arboreal animal the type of information it needs, such as the exact direction and distance of one branch from another. Thus, in the primates, the sense of smell has diminished; over time it has proved to have little selective advantage.

In the primates, the nasal structures of the skull are reduced in size, and the muzzle or snout is relatively small (Figure 10–2). While a few primates have retained a **rhinarium,** the moist, naked area surrounding the nostrils, most primates lack this feature. Also, the olfactory regions of the brain are reduced.

VISION   Most mammals see only a two-dimensional black-and-white field; they depend more on the olfactory sense. Most primates see both in three dimensions and in color, although the degree of development of color vision does vary among different groups of primates. Color vision helps them distinguish detail, since similar colors, such as various shades of green in a tropical forest, may blend if seen only in black and white. In addition, stationary objects stand out in a three-dimensional field.

Primate vision developed in response to the selective pressures of the arboreal environment, where precise information on direction and distance is crucial. Once developed, vision provided the primates with more detailed information about their habitats than was available to any other mammalian form. Also, excellence in vision combined with fine motor coordination and manipulative ability allowed the development of superb hand-eye coordination.

The primate eye is large, and its **retina** contains two types of cells, **rods** and **cones,** that are sensitive to light. Rods respond to very low intensities of light and are responsible for black-and-white vision. Cones, while not as sensitive to low light intensities, sense color and have high acuity. In the central area of the retina is the **macula,** an area consisting of only cones. Within the macula is a depression, called the **fovea,** that contains a single layer of cones with no overlapping blood vessels. This is the area of greatest visual acuity; it permits the fine visual discrimination characteristic of the primate eye (Figure 10–3).

FIGURE 10–2   *The primate face.* The facial skeleton of a monkey is compared with that of a tree shrew. Note the reduction of the olfactory apparatus and the relatively flat facial skeleton of the monkey.

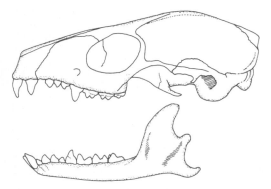

Tree shrew

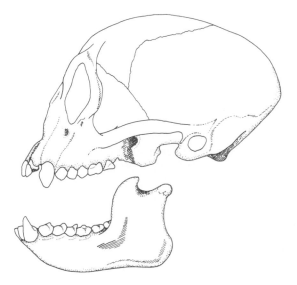

Monkey (*Cebus*)

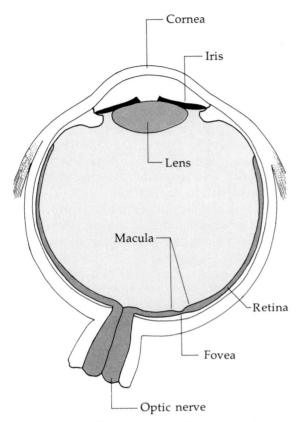

FIGURE 10–3 *The primate eye.* A diagrammatic cross section of the human eye.

The primate eyes have come to lie on the front of the face. As a result, the visual fields seen by each eye overlap extensively, producing a broad **binocular field.** Thus the brain receives images of the same objects simultaneously from both eyes. This fact is a prerequisite for three-dimensional or **stereoscopic vision.** The evolution of stereoscopic vision is not only dependent upon binocular vision but also upon significant changes in the optic nerves and the brain.

Stereoscopic vision enables the arboreal primate to determine distance with a high degree of precision, which aids the animal in moving rapidly through the trees. The origins of stereoscopic vision, however, like those of the grasping big toe, may lie in arboreal insect predation in the early primates. Three-dimensional vision improves the accuracy of the final strike when the primate is pursuing fast-moving insect prey.

In the primates, the eye is supported on the side by a **postorbital bar** (Figure 10–4*b*). This skeletal feature is found in all living primates and in some other mammalian groups. However, the morphological details of the postorbital bar differ among the different mammalian taxa, and the evolution of the postorbital bar in different orders most likely represents a case of convergent evolution.

In some primates, and in other mammal orders, the orbit, the space that contains the eye, is

FIGURE 10–4 *The eye socket.* (a) An eye socket is absent in the cat. (b) While an eye socket is absent in the slender loris, the eye is surrounded by a complete bony ring. (c) The monkey skull displays a complete eye socket.

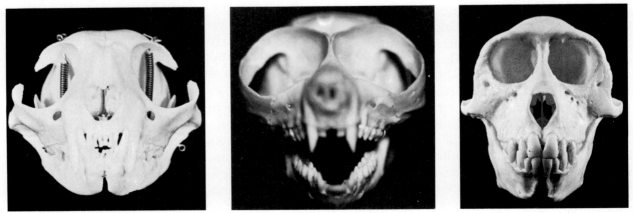

(a)   *(b)*   *(c)*

not separated from the muscles behind it. In most primates a bony **postorbital septum** is found behind the eye that isolates it from these muscles and forms a bony socket in which the eye lies (Figure 10–4c).

Primates are highly social animals, and vision plays a key role in primate communication. Unlike dogs, who smell one another on meeting, primates communicate largely through visual stimuli, although vocalizations also play important roles. Primates frequently use body postures and facial expressions as means of communication. Facial expression is made possible in many primates by differentiation of the muscles of the face. The facial musculature in other mammals is relatively undifferentiated. Also, unlike other mammals, many primates have an upper lip that is not attached to the upper gum. This allows a wide range of gestures, including the kiss.

The Growth and Development of Primates

The life of an individual can be divided into several phases or periods: **prenatal,** from conception to birth; **infantile,** from birth to the eruption of the first permanent teeth; and **juvenile,** which encompasses the time from the eruption of the first teeth to the eruption of the last permanent teeth. This is followed by the **adult** period. Figure 10–5 shows the relative length of these subdivisions of growth and development in several primate forms.

THE PRENATAL PERIOD The primate placenta differs from that of other placental mammals. In most mammals, the blood vessels of the fetus and those of the mother come into close contact, and nutrients and other substances pass through two vessel walls from the maternal to the fetal bloodstream. In the **hemochorial placenta,** which is found in most primates, the fetal blood vessels penetrate the lining of the uterus. The uterus undergoes cellular changes, and the fine blood vessels of the mother break down to form a spongy, blood-filled mass. The result is that maternal blood surrounds the fetal blood vessels, and so materials pass through only a single vessel wall in moving from one blood system to the other (Figure 10–6).

The period of time between conception and birth is known as **gestation.** The primates are characterized by the prolongation of gestation. To illustrate this point, we can compare three mammals of similar size: the chimpanzee (a primate), the impala (a hoofed mammal), and the coyote (a carnivore). Gestation is 224 days in the chimpanzee, 191 days in the impala, and 63 days in the coyote. The length of gestation in several primates is listed in Table 10–1.

There is a famous and somewhat formidable saying, at least in biological circles: "Ontogeny recapitulates phylogeny." This means that **ontogeny,** the development of the individual, resembles **phylogeny,** the evolutionary history of the species. Early biologists saw in the developing embryo a history of the evolutionary stages of the species. For example, the human embryo develops a tail and even structures considered gill pouches. In fact, the early embryo of a human is practically indistinguishable from that of other vertebrates (Figure 10–7).

The embryo, of course, does not literally pass through the evolutionary stages of the species; the early stages of development are simply conservative and have changed little over time. Most specializations occur later in embryonic and fetal development, and many are the result of alterations in growth pattern.

Besides the lengthened prenatal period, a rapid rate of growth characterizes the human fetus. For example, the orangutan fetus grows at an average rate of 5.7 grams (0.2 ounce) per day, while the rate for the human fetus is about 12.5 grams (0.44 ounce) per day. Because the placenta develops earlier in humans, rapid growth begins soon after conception and remains rapid throughout the gestation process.

LIFE AFTER BIRTH Along with a lengthened childhood period is a lengthened life span in general. Primates are relatively long-lived animals. Among mammals longevity is related to body size, with the larger mammals, in general, living longer than the smaller ones. Yet when other mammals of similar size are compared with pri-

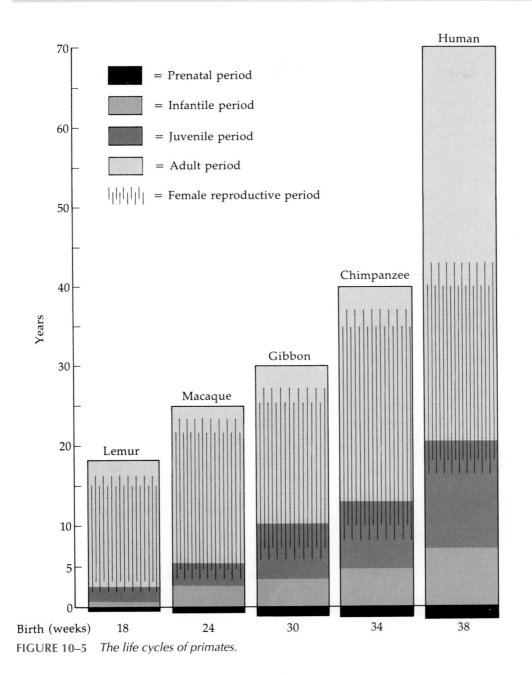

FIGURE 10–5 *The life cycles of primates.*

mates, the latter tend to exhibit a longer life span. Other life-cycle events also take longer in primates. The age at which the female gives birth to her first offspring is 14 years in the chimpanzee, 2 years in the impala, and 3 years in the coyote. Finally, the life span is approximately 41 years in the chimpanzee, 12½ years in the impala, and 16 years in the coyote.

Other Features of the Primates

Dentition is discussed in detail in Chapter 13, but it should be mentioned here that primate dentition is characterized by fewer teeth than the number found in the ancestral placental mammal. This ancestral form had forty-four teeth, whereas many primates, including humans,

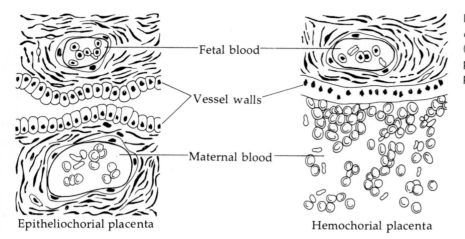

FIGURE 10–6 *Hemochorial placenta*. The hemochorial placenta (right), found in humans, is compared with the epitheliochorial placenta (left), found in lemurs.

Epitheliochorial placenta

Hemochorial placenta

have only thirty-two. Primate teeth are relatively simple in structure, especially when they are compared with those of grazing animals or carnivores.

Primates are known for their great intelligence. The primate brain is large in relation to the size of the body, and the areas that control complex behavioral patterns are well developed. This permits a great degree of behavioral flexibility. The anatomy of the primate brain is discussed in Chapter 13.

TABLE 10–1

LENGTH OF GESTATION IN PRIMATES

PRIMATE	GESTATION PERIOD (DAYS)
Lemur	120–135
Slender loris	160–174
Marmoset	142–150
Spider monkey	139
Squirrel monkey	165–170
Guenon	150–210
Macaque	162–186
Langur	196
Baboon	164–186
Orangutan	240–270
Gorilla	270
Chimpanzee	216–260
Human	266

Source: A. G. Hendrick and M. L. Houston, "Gestation," in E. S. E. Hafez (ed.), *Comparative Reproduction of Nonhuman Primates* (Springfield, Ill.: Charles C. Thomas, 1971). Used with permission of Charles C. Thomas, Publisher.

Much primate adaptability is the result of learned behavioral adaptations. Most primates live in large social units, usually produce single births, and have a long childhood period; these factors facilitate learning. The social behavior of primates is the topic of Chapter 11.

Summary

Unlike animals in other mammalian orders, primates are not characterized by one or more conspicuous traits. Instead, primates are best defined in terms of their adaptability, which may be thought of as a response to the arboreal habitat and arboreal insect predation.

Among the most significant diagnostic features of the order are a grasping big toe, a grasping thumb that is opposable in many groups, digits ending in nails and tactile pads, pentadactylism, and retention of the clavicle. Among primates the olfactory sense has been reduced along with the skeletal apparatus for smell and the olfactory areas of the brain. The sense of vision has become predominant; primates see in color and possess stereoscopic vision. The eye is supported by a postorbital bar, and in most primates a postorbital septum forms a bony socket that lies on the front of the face.

During the prenatal period the primate fetus is nourished through a hemochorial placenta in which the fetal blood vessels are bathed in the

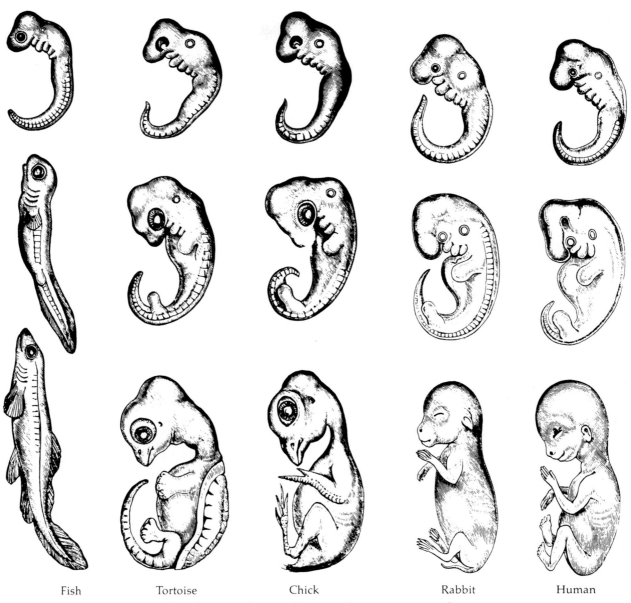

Fish	Tortoise	Chick	Rabbit	Human

FIGURE 10–7 *Comparative embryology.* Vertebrate embryos are shown at corresponding stages of development.

maternal blood. The primates are characterized by the prolongation of gestation, during which the fetus grows rapidly, as well as by a long childhood period and a prolonged life span. Other characteristics of the order include the retention of a relatively unspecialized dentition, increased brain size, adjustment through learned patterns of behavior, and life in social groups.

THE LIVING PRIMATES

Approximately 185 species of primates have been described. The classification of primates, however, like taxonomy in general, is open to some debate. The purpose here is not to enter into these controversies but simply to recognize their existence.

This section will follow the classification shown in Table 10–2. When looking at the classification of the living primates, we see that the order Primates is divided into three suborders and eleven families. In this section we will discuss representative species in each family in terms of their classification and natural history. More detailed information on behavior, anatomy, and other subjects will be presented in subsequent chapters.

The Prosimians

The first suborder within the Primates is the Prosimii. These animals often lack some of the features described as characteristic of the order. Most, but not all, prosimians are **nocturnal** (active at night), with eyes adapted for nocturnal vision. Their sense of smell is well developed, facilitated by a long snout ending in a rhinarium. Many also have specialized scent glands, and olfaction plays an important role in their social behavior. Unlike their other fingers and toes, which end in nails, their second toes end in claws. These **toilet claws** are used by the animal in scratching and cleaning its fur. Finally, the lower front teeth, the incisors and canines, are thin and narrow, and they project forward horizontally to form a **dental comb.**

Because the prosimians lack many of the features of the monkeys, apes, and humans, it is easy to think of them as primitive ancestral forms. Although they retain many ancestral features, they are modern, highly specialized animals. Figure 10–8 shows the distribution of the prosimian families.

THE PROSIMIANS OF MADAGASCAR   Three closely related families of the primates—the Lemuridae, Indriidae, and Daubentoniidae—live on the island of Madagascar (Malagasy Republic), which is located about 400 kilometers (250 miles) off the southeast coast of Africa. Primatologists believe that the early ancestors of these animals found their way to the island by rafting across the channel, which was once narrower

---

TABLE 10–2

CLASSIFICATION OF THE LIVING PRIMATES

ORDER: Primates
  SUBORDER: Prosimii
    INFRAORDER: Lemuriformes
      SUPERFAMILY: Lemuroidea
        FAMILY: Lemuridae (lemurs)
        FAMILY: Indriidae (indris, avahis, sifakas)
      SUPERFAMILY: Daubentonioidea
        FAMILY: Daubentoniidae (aye-ayes)
    INFRAORDER: Lorisiformes
      SUPERFAMILY: Lorisoidea
        FAMILY: Lorisidae (lorises, galagos)
  SUBORDER: Tarsioidea
      FAMILY: Tarsiidae (tarsiers)
  SUBORDER: Anthropoidea
    INFRAORDER: Platyrrhini
      SUPERFAMILY: Ceboidea
        FAMILY: Callitrichidae (marmosets, tamarins)
        FAMILY: Cebidae (squirrel, spider, howler, and capuchin monkeys)
    INFRAORDER: Catarrhini
      SUPERFAMILY: Cercopithecoidea
        FAMILY: Cercopithecidae (guenons, mangabeys, baboons, macaques, langurs)
      SUPERFAMILY: Hominoidea
        FAMILY: Hylobatidae (gibbons, siamangs)
        FAMILY: Pongidae (orangutans)
        FAMILY: Panidae (chimpanzees, gorillas)
        FAMILY: Hominidae (humans)

Source: J. R. Napier and P. H. Napier, *The Natural History of the Primates* (Cambridge, Mass.: M.I.T., 1985), 14. The classification of the Hominoidea has been modified.

---

than it is today, on masses of vegetation. Once on the island they were isolated from the mainland, and thus they were protected from the later-evolving monkeys and apes. In isolation and because of the lack of competition from other mammals, the Madagascar prosimians were able to move into many diverse niches; this is reflected in their numbers and diversity. However, today their natural habitats are being rapidly destroyed, and many species observed by early explorers are known only from their skeletal remains.

The family Lemuridae includes the lemurs (Figure 10–A in the color insert). In general, the small lemurs are nocturnal, solitary, and **omnivorous** and eat a variety of foods. The larger lemurs, including the well-known ring-tailed

BOX 10–1

TREE SHREWS: A PROBLEM OF TAXONOMY

The tree shrews are most unprimate in appearance, as suggested by their family name, Tupaiidae, which is derived from a Malayan word meaning "squirrel." Some early primatologists, such as W. E. LeGros Clark, included the tree shrews in the Primate order. They based this classification on the relatively well-developed eye and visual areas of the brain and the many similarities between the tree shrews and members of the family Lemuridae, for example, the presence of dental combs. However, these similarities actually represent shared primitive features or parallelisms; they are not indicative of an evolutionary relationship between the tree shrews and the primates. Detailed studies of the anatomy, physiology, and behavior of this animal place it more clearly in the order Insectivora.

Nevertheless, discussion of the tree shrew is important to anthropology. First, it serves to remind us that neat taxonomic categories do not exist in nature. Classification schemes are simply attempts to impose order on an extremely complex and dynamic system. Second, the tree shrew serves to give us some general idea of what the earliest primate may have been like. This should not suggest, however, that the primates evolved from tree shrews. Modern tree shrews are highly evolved contemporary forms.

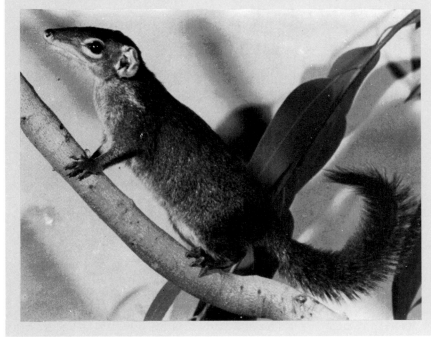

Reference: W. P. Luckett (ed.), *Comparative Biology and Evolutionary Relationships of Tree Shrews* (New York: Plenum, 1980).

---

lemur, are more **diurnal** (active during the day), live in large social units, and include plant food as a major part of their diet (Figure 10–9). The smallest are the mouse lemurs and dwarf lemurs (Figure 10–B in the color insert); one species averages only 60 grams (2 ounces) in weight. The largest lemurs weigh almost 4 kilograms (9 pounds).

Although the eyes of the lemur are located on the front of its head, stereoscopic vision is not as well developed as in the monkeys and apes. On the other hand, the ring-tailed lemur's sense of smell is well developed. When it is disturbed, it often rubs its anal region against a tree, a behavior termed **scent marking.** The male ring-tailed lemur has a specialized gland on his forearm that is also used in scent marking. Like all prosimians, the lemurs possess a dental comb and a toilet claw on the second toe.

Also living on the island of Madagascar, the family Indriidae consists of the indri, avahi, and sifaka (Figure 10–10). The indri, which is totally diurnal, is the largest of the Madagascar prosimians, weighing about 6.3 kilograms (14 pounds). Their diet consists primarily of plant material, especially leaves. When they are resting, they

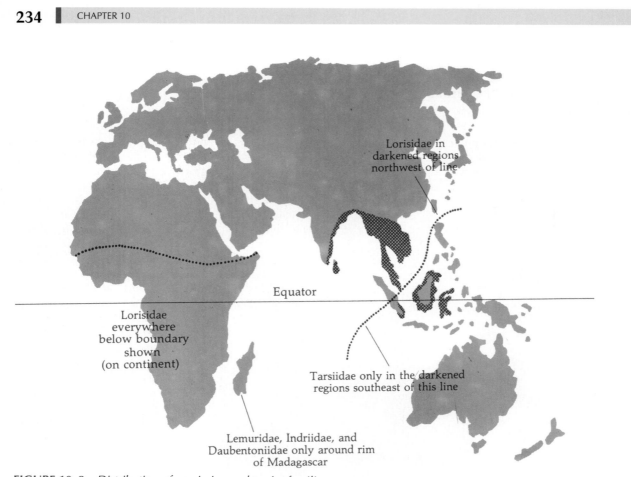

Lorisidae in
darkened regions
northwest of line

Equator

Lorisidae
everywhere
below boundary
shown
(on continent)

Tarsiidae only in the darkened
regions southeast of this line

Lemuridae, Indriidae, and
Daubentoniidae only around rim
of Madagascar

FIGURE 10–8   *Distribution of prosimian and tarsier families.*

cling upright on a vertical branch; when moving, they use their very long legs to leap from branch to branch, maintaining an upright posture. The indri is the only Madagascar prosimian that lacks a tail.

The family Daubentoniidae contains only one species, the aye-aye, now on the verge of extinction (Figure 10-C in the color insert). The aye-aye was once thought to be a rodent since it has large, continuously growing front teeth which are separated from the rest of the teeth by a large gap. The hand is characterized by a long, thin, middle finger, and all the digits except the big toes end in claws. During the night the aye-aye uses its front teeth to tear open the outer layers of bamboo or the bark of trees to get at the insects inside; the insect is then extracted with the elongated finger.

The aye-aye provides us with an interesting example of convergence of function or analogy. Three animals that feed on insects directly beneath the bark are the aye-aye, the woodpecker (a bird), and *Dactylopsila*, an Australian marsupial. Like the aye-aye, *Dactylopsila* has a thin, elongated finger on each hand and large incisors.

THE FAMILY LORISIDAE   The lorises probably have survived competition with the monkeys and apes in Asia and Africa because of their nocturnal habits. The family is divided into two subfamilies. The subfamily Lorisinae contains species that walk along branches very slowly and deliberately, hand over hand. These animals have very powerful grips, enhanced by the reduction of their index fingers to mere bumps. Like the

FIGURE 10–9 *Prosimian*. Ring-tailed lemur, *Lemur catta*.

FIGURE 10–10 *Prosimian*. Sifaka, *Propithecus verraeux*.

lemurs, they have dental combs as well as grooming claws on their second toes. The lorises live alone or in pairs. Their diet is varied, consisting of fruits, leaves, seeds, birds and birds' eggs, lizards, and insects. The Asiatic members of the subfamily are the slender loris and slow loris (Figure 10–11); the African members are the potto and angwantibo.

The African subfamily Galaginae includes the galagos, also known as bush babies (Figure 10–12). These are small animals weighing between 65 grams (2.3 ounces) and 1.3 kilograms (3 pounds). Although they show a variety of locomotor patterns, these nocturnal primates are noted for their leaping ability, which is made possible by their elongated legs. In one study, the small *Galago senegalensis*, with a center of gravity perhaps 3.75 centimeters (1.5 inches) off

the ground, leaped vertically in the air 2.25 meters (7 feet 4.75 inches).[2] This leaping ability enables the animal to move quickly through the branches searching for and catching insects.

The Tarsiers

The suborder Tarsioidea includes only one family, the Tarsiidae. The five species of tarsier are found on islands in southeast Asia, including Borneo, Sumatra, and the Philippines (Figure 10–8).

The tarsiers are very small primates, weighing between 60 and 200 grams (2 and 7 ounces) (Figure 10–13). Their name is derived from their

---

[2]E. C. B. Hall-Craggs, "An Analysis of the Jump of the Lesser Galago *(Galago senegalensis)" Journal of Zoology*, 147 (1965), 20–29.

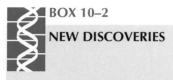

BOX 10–2

NEW DISCOVERIES

A modern tragedy is the destruction of the tropical rain forest and the loss of its lush vegetation and the extinction of its diverse animal life. In contrast to the daily stories of destruction and extinction comes the periodic discovery of new species.

In 1984 a new species of guenon was found in an undis-turbed primary forest in central Gabon, in west Africa. The primate was named the sun-tailed guenon (*Cercopithecus solatus*). The guenons are the most common African arboreal monkey with over twenty described species.

In 1985 and 1986, a new species of lemur was seen in the southeastern rain forest of Mada-gascar. This animal was named *Hapalemur aureus,* the golden bamboo lemur, and is the third species within the genus *Hapale-mur,* the bamboo lemurs.

In 1989 another lemur was "re-discovered." Although a few individuals had been seen earlier and five specimens exist in museum collections, the hairy-eared dwarf lemur, *Allocebus trichotis,* has never been studied. This species of dwarf lemur is very small, weighing only 80 grams (2.8 ounces), and was re-discovered in the rain forest on the northeastern coast of Madagascar.

In 1988 a population of tarsiers was observed on the Indonesian island of Sulawesi that appeared to differ from the four known tarsier species in their anatomy, behavior, and chromosomes. The species was named *Tarsius dianae,* in honor of the late primatologist Dian Fossey, known for her work among the mountain gorillas.

In another part of the world, Brazil, coastal rain forests are being rapidly destroyed. In 1990, on a small island south of São Paulo, primatologists discovered a new species of New World monkey, the black-faced lion tamarin, *Leontopithecus caissara* (see the accompanying Figure). All five of these newly found primates, the sun-tailed guenon, the golden bamboo lemur, the hairy-eared dwarf lemur, the Sulawesi tarsier, and the black-faced lion tamarin, are rare and highly endangered.

References: M. J. S. Harrison, "A New Species of Geunon (Genus *Cercopithecus*) from Gabon," *Journal of Zoology, London,* 215 (1988), 561–575; B. Meier et al., "A New Species of *Hapalemur* (Primates) from South East Madagascar," *Folia Primatolog-ica,* 48 (1987), 211–215; B. Meier and R. Al-bignac, "Rediscovery of *Allocebus trichotis* Günther 1985 (Primates) in Northeast Mada-gascar," *Folia Primatologica,* 56 (1991), 57–63; C. Niemitz et al., "*Tarsius dianae:* A New Primate Species from Central Sulawesi (Indonesia)," *Folia Primatologica,* 56 (1991), 105–116; W. Stolzenburg, "Tamarin Tale: Tracking Down a New Species," *Science News,* 137 (June 30, 1990), 406.

FIGURE 10–11 *Prosimian.* Slow loris, *Nycticebus coucang.*

FIGURE 10–12 *Prosimian.* Galago, *Galago senegalensis.*

elongated tarsal (ankle) bones, which enable them to leap long distances. The tarsiers leap among the thin, vertical saplings near the ground, keeping their bodies in a vertical position. At rest they press the lower part of their long tails against the tree trunk for support (Figure 13–2).

Tarsiers are strictly nocturnal. Their eyes have become so large that they cannot be moved by the eye muscles, which have become degenerate. Instead, the animal is capable of turning its head almost 180 degrees to look behind itself. Tarsiers feed on insects and lizards; they do not eat plant food.

The tarsiers share several characteristics with the prosimians, such as the toilet claw on the second toe. (The tarsiers actually have additional toilet claws on the third toes as well.) Unlike the prosimians, they lack dental combs. Their eye socket is partially closed; in this they resemble more closely the monkeys and apes than the prosimians. They also show a number of specialized features that are unique among primates, such as the fusion of the tibia and fibula (the two bones of the lower leg). This feature is also found in the rabbits and hares.

FIGURE 10–13 *Tarsier.* Mindanao tarsier, *Tarsius syrichta carbonarious.*

At one time, early tarsiers were thought to be ancestral to the monkeys and apes. Today, paleontologists believe that tarsiers represent an ancient, specialized primate group, perhaps best placed in its own suborder, the Tarsioidea.

The Monkeys

The third major division of the order Primates is the suborder Anthropoidea. This suborder includes the primates that are familiar to most people: the New World monkeys, Old World monkeys, lesser and great apes, and humans.

The term *monkey* embraces a large number of species found throughout the tropics of the Old World (Africa, Europe, and Asia) and the New World (North, Central, and South America). Although most people see the monkeys as a single group, in reality the monkeys of the Old World and those of the New World are fairly distinct. Many anthropologists theorize that the ancestral monkeys first evolved in Africa. Later some populations rafted across the Atlantic Ocean to populate the New World (Chapter 15). Isolated in their own hemisphere for over 30 million years, each group evolved many unique features. Yet the Old World and New World monkeys, build-

ing upon the same basic anatomy, retained and evolved many similarities as well. This is an example of parallelism. These two groups of monkeys are usually divided into two superfamilies: the Cercopithecoidea of the Old World and the Ceboidea of the New World. Figure 10–14 shows the distribution of the two monkey superfamilies.

THE NEW WORLD MONKEYS   The monkeys of the New World belong to the superfamily Ceboidea. These monkeys are easily identified by the **platyrrhine nose,** in which the nostrils are usually separated by a broad nasal partition, or septum, and open facing forward or to the side (Figure 10–15). This nose form contrasts with the noses of the Old World monkeys, apes, and humans. Consequently the New World monkeys are often referred to as the platyrrhine monkeys and are sometimes placed in the infraorder Platyrrhini.

The New World monkeys share several features that contrast with those of the Old World monkeys. The New World monkeys tend to be smaller than those of the Old World, and they are strictly arboreal. The New World monkeys have three premolars in each quarter of the mouth; some, but not all, have **prehensile tails** that can be used to hang onto branches and even

FIGURE 10–14   *Distribution of the monkeys.*

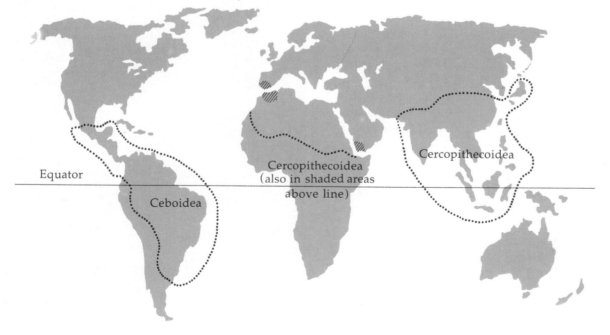

FIGURE 10–15 *New World monkey.* Hairy saki, *Pithecia monachus.*

to pick up objects (Figure 13–1); the thumb is nonopposable, in some forms it has disappeared.

The New World monkeys are divided into two families. The first family, the Callitrichidae, includes the marmosets and tamarins (Figure 10-H in color insert). These are small animals weighing between 70 and 550 grams (2.5 and 19.5 ounces). The thirty-four species of marmosets and tamarins are found throughout the forests of Central and South America. The marmosets and tamarins live in small family units, and the females usually produce twins at birth. The father carries the infants and transfers them to the mother for feeding (Figure 11–1).

Unlike most primates, the marmosets and tamarins possess modified claws on all their digits except their big toes, which have true nails. Like all ceboid monkeys, they have three premolars in each quadrant of the mouth, but this family is distinguished from other New World monkeys in having only two molars per quadrant; all other monkeys have three. They are generally omnivorous and include insects in their diet. Unlike the tamarins, the marmosets rely heavily on sap and gums. This dietary specialization is reflected in their dentition. In contrast to the teeth of the tamarins, the lower incisors

of the marmosets are relatively long and the lower canines project only a little above the level of the incisors. The animals use their specialized lower teeth to make holes in the bark of trees to tap the sap and gums.

Most of the New World monkeys belong to the second family, the Cebidae. In contrast to the

FIGURE 10–16 *New World monkey.* Representative of the Cebidae: squirrel monkeys, *Saimiri sciureus.*

Callitrichidae, the cebids are larger, weighing between 750 grams and 15 kilograms (1.5 and 33 pounds). They have nails on all digits, three premolars and three molars per quadrant of the mouth, and are characterized by single births. The larger cebids habitually move and feed while suspended under branches, and many have evolved a prehensile tail as an aid in suspension.

The cebids are divided into five subfamilies. The subfamily Cebinae includes the small squirrel monkeys (Figure 10–16) and the well-known capuchins, the common organ-grinder monkeys. Capuchins have a moderately developed prehensile tail. The subfamily Aotinae includes the titi monkey and the owl monkey, or douroucolis; the owl monkey is the only completely nocturnal monkey (Figure 10–17). The subfamily Pithecinae includes the sakis (Figure 10–15) and uakaris (Figure 10–I in the color insert). Uakaris are bald-headed primates with very short tails whose naked faces are often bright pink.

The next two subfamilies are characterized by the presence of a prehensile tail. The subfamily Alouatinae contains the howler monkeys (Figure 10–18). This genus possesses a highly specialized larynx and a modified hyoid bone that forms a chamber which acts as an amplifier and is responsible for the monkey's loud and distinctive call. The spider monkeys, the woolly monkeys, and the rare muriquis are in the subfamily Atelinae. Spider monkeys are noted for their dexterous prehensile tail, which serves as a third "hand." The underside of the lower part of the tail lacks hair and appears to be sensitive to touch. This monkey's hand lacks a thumb, and the remaining four fingers form a hook that the animal uses as it suspends itself underneath a branch (Figure 13–1).

FIGURE 10–17 *New World monkey.* Representative of the Cebidae: owl monkey, *Aotus trivirgatus.*

FIGURE 10–18 *New World monkey.* Representative of the Cebidae: red howler monkey, *Alouatta seniculus.*

Because of the fairly remote relationship of the ceboids to humans, they have not been studied as extensively as the Old World monkeys. Interest is mounting, however, and data on these species, especially on their social behavior, are becoming increasingly available.

THE OLD WORLD MONKEYS Old World monkeys, apes, and humans make up the infraorder Catarrhini. This infraorder can be divided into two superfamilies. The superfamily Cercopithecoidea are the Old World monkeys which consists of the single family Cercopithecidae.

Old World monkeys comprise a large number of species that are spread over Africa and Asia, and they include one small population in Europe.

Members of this family are characterized by the **catarrhine nose** where the nostrils are separated by a narrow nasal septum and open downward (Figure 10–19). The catarrhine nose is also characteristic of apes and humans. Old World monkeys, as well as people and apes, have only two premolars per quadrant of the mouth. In contrast to the New World monkeys, the Old World monkeys tend to be fairly large. Although many are arboreal, some genera are semiterrestrial. None has a prehensile tail, and the thumb is well developed in most forms and is opposable.

The Cercopithecidae are divided into two subfamilies. Except for the macaques, members of the subfamily Cercopithecinae live in sub-Saharan Africa. Macaques are found in north Africa, on the Rock of Gibraltar in Europe, and in southern and southeast Asia and southern Japan. Members of this subfamily weigh between 1.2 and 15 kilograms (2.7 and 33 pounds), and many species exhibit a marked **sexual dimorphism,** that is, a major difference in size and nonsexual features between sexes. A distinguishing feature of these monkeys is the presence of **ischial callosities** in the anal region of the animal; these callouses are in contact with the branch or ground when the animal sits. The female usually

FIGURE 10–19 *Old World monkey.* Representative of the subfamily Cercopithecinae: Hamlyn's guenon, *Cercopithecus hamlyni.*

FIGURE 10–20 *Old World monkey.* Representative of the subfamily Cercopithecinae: Chacma baboon, *Papio cynocephalus ursinus.* A female chacma baboon shows a swelling of the sexual skin. Underneath the swelling on the left can be seen part of the ischial callosity.

has a **sexual skin** that often turns bright pink or red and sometimes swells when the female is in **estrus,** the period of sexual receptivity (Figure 10–20). The Cercopithecinae are omnivorous, and they have **cheek pouches** that open into the mouth and are used for temporary food storage.

Many arboreal and all of the semiterrestrial monkeys of Africa belong to the Cercopithecinae. The many species of guenons and mangabeys (Figure 10–19) are spread throughout the African rain forest, woodland, and savanna habitats. The ground-dwelling monkeys of the savanna are the baboons. One species, the hama-

dryas baboon, lives in the semidesert regions of southern Ethiopia where the baboons sleep at night on cliffs rather than in trees. Baboons are often referred to as the "dog-faced monkeys" because of their well-pronounced muzzles. Associated with the muzzle are large, formidable canine teeth, especially in the adult males (Figure 11–8). Other African cercopithecoids include the patas monkey, vervet monkey, drill, mandrill (Figure 10–D in the color insert), and gelada (Figure 10–21).

The Asiatic representatives of the Cercopithecinae are the macaques. The dozen

FIGURE 10–21 *Old World monkey.* Representative of the subfamily Cercopithecinae: gelada, *Theropithecus gelada.*

macaque species live in a great diversity of habitats, including tropical rain forests and semi-deserts; in contrast, the Japanese macaques endure winter snow. The only European monkey is a macaque living on the Rock of Gibraltar (Figure 10–22). The diet of the macaques is quite varied, including fruits, roots, and other vegetable material, as well as insects and shellfish.

The other subfamily, the Colobinae, or leaf-eating monkeys, also inhabits both Africa and Asia. The members of this subfamily lack cheek

pouches. They are able to digest mature leaves because of the presence of a complex sacculated stomach in which bacterial action is able to break down the cellulose found in leaves.

A major group of leaf-eating monkeys is the langurs of south and southeast Asia (Figure 10–23). One population lives in the Himalayas at elevations up to 3650 meters (12,000 feet). Others are found in very dry habitats, where they can survive because of their ability to digest dry, mature leaves and bark. Other Asiatic forms include the snub-nosed langurs (Figure 10–F in the color insert) and the proboscis monkey. The African representatives of this subfamily are the colobus monkeys, or guerezas (Figure 10–24).

The Apes

The last four primate families belong to the superfamily Hominoidea. Figure 10–25 shows their distribution. The first three families are referred to as the apes; these are the Hylobatidae, Pongidae, and Panidae.

THE FAMILY HYLOBATIDAE   The family Hylobatidae includes the smallest of the apes, the gibbons and siamangs, which are sometimes called the **lesser apes.** Gibbons range over a larger area than any of the other apes. They are found in much of southeast Asia including Indonesia, Malaysia, Thailand, Burma, and the east Indian state of Assam. The gibbons are the smaller of the lesser apes, weighing about 6 kilograms (13 pounds) and standing about 90 centimeters (3 feet) tall (Figure 10–26). They exhibit virtually no sexual dimorphism. They have short, com-

FIGURE 10–22   *Old World monkey.* Representative of the subfamily Cercopithecinae: Barbary "ape" macaque, *Macaca sylvanus.*

FIGURE 10–23   *Old World monkey.* Representative of the subfamily Colobinae: common langur, Nepal, *Presbytis entellus.*

FIGURE 10–24   *Old World monkey.* Representative of the subfamily Colobinae: red colobus monkey, *Colobus badius.*

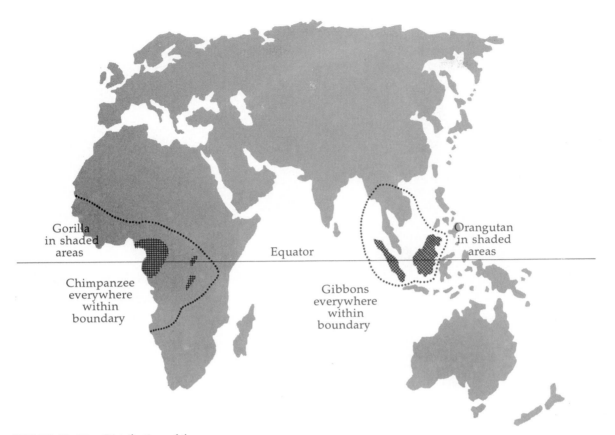

FIGURE 10–25 *Distribution of the apes.*

pact bodies with exceedingly long arms—a body build suited for **brachiation,** which is hand-over-hand locomotion under a branch (Figure 13–3). The gibbons are the classic brachiators in the primate order.

While gibbons are primarily arboreal, they do walk bipedally on the ground. Their diet consists of fruit, leaves, and buds, supplemented with birds' eggs, young birds, and insects. Gibbons live in small family groups consisting of a mature pair with several young. Each group occupies a distinct territory that is defended by loud vocal displays by the male.

The siamangs are found in Sumatra and on the Malay Peninsula (Figure 10–27). They are similar to the gibbons, but they are larger (10.7 kilograms or 23.5 pounds) and have longer arms in proportion to their bodies. A distinctive feature is an air sac under the chin which inflates when the animal vocalizes, producing a very loud call.

THE FAMILY PONGIDAE Until comparatively recent times, the family Pongidae was considered synonymous with the **great apes,** which included the two African great apes, the chimpanzee and gorilla, and the Asiatic great ape, the orangutan. However, studies of molecular biology and cytogenetics (Chapter 13) have demonstrated the very close evolutionary relationship of the African great apes to humans. Therefore, many anthropologists today have moved the chimpanzee and gorilla out of the Pongidae, leaving the orangutan as the sole member of this family.

The orangutan is found today only on the islands of Sumatra and Borneo (Figure 10–G in the color insert). Orangutans are quiet, slow-moving, arboreal vegetarians. Young orangutans stay close to their mothers; adult orangutans, however, are solitary. They sleep in nests that can be as high as 24 meters (80 feet) above the ground.

FIGURE 10–26 *Lesser ape.* Representative of the family Hylobatidae: white-handed gibbon, *Hylobates lar lar.*

FIGURE 10–27 *Lesser ape.* Representative of the family Hylobatidae: island siamang, *Symphalangus syndactylus.*

Their locomotor behavior can be described as **quadrumanous;** that is, they use their upper arms to hold onto branches above their heads, but they do not actually suspend themselves from these branches. They exhibit great sexual dimorphism; the males are large, weighing more than 70 kilograms (154 pounds) at maturity, while the females average about 37 kilograms (81.5 pounds). Males average 1.37 meters (4½ feet) in height, and females average about 1.15 meters (3 feet 10 inches) in height. Some males develop large pouches under the chin and flanges of flesh on the cheeks. These physical features are not found in the females.

THE FAMILY PANIDAE   The increase in the number of comparative studies of the African great apes, in addition to new theoretical approaches to the study of taxonomy, has led many anthropologists to reconsider traditional classifications. This has led to several new schemes that attempt to show more accurately the relationship between the apes and humans. Table 10–3 shows some examples of recently proposed classifications. In this text we will adopt the classification that places the African great apes in the family Panidae, and humans in the family Hominidae.

The family Panidae includes the gorilla and the chimpanzee. The largest living primates are the gorillas of Africa; an adult male gorilla weighs about 150 kilograms (331 pounds) and is about 1.83 meters (6 feet) tall. Females weigh about 92 kilograms (203 pounds). Gorillas are divided into three subspecies: the lowland gorilla of west Africa (Figure 10–28), the lowland gorilla of east Africa, and the highland gorilla of east Africa (Figure 10–E in the color insert). Recent

TABLE 10–3

THREE DIFFERENT CLASSIFICATIONS OF HUMANS AND APES

SIMPSON (1945)[*]	ANDREWS AND CRONIN (1982)[†]	ANDREWS (1990)[‡]
Superfamily: Hominoidea	Superfamily: Hominoidea	Superfamily: Hominoidea
Family: Pongidae	Family: Hylobatidae	Family: Hylobatidae
Subfamily: Hylobatinae	Genus: *Hylobates*	Genus: *Hylobates*
Genus: *Hylobates*	Genus: *Symphalangus*	Genus: *Symphalangus*
Genus: *Symphalangus*	Family: Pongidae	Family: Hominidae
Subfamily: Ponginae	Genus: *Pongo*	Subfamily: Ponginae
Genus: *Pongo*	Family: Hominidae	Genus: *Pongo*
Genus: *Pan*	Subfamily: Gorillinae	Subfamily: Homininae
Genus: *Gorilla*	Genus: *Pan*	Tribe: Gorillini
Family: Hominidae	Genus: *Gorilla*	Genus: *Pan*
Genus: *Homo*	Subfamily: Homininae	Genus: *Gorilla*
	Genus: *Homo*	Tribe: Hominini
		Genus: *Homo*

[*]Simpson, G. G., "The Principles of Classification and a Classification of Mammals," *Bulletin of the American Museum of Natural History*, 85 (1945), 1–350.
[†]Andrews, P., and J. E. Cronin, "The Relationships of *Sivapithecus* and *Ramapithecus* and the Evolution of the Orang Utan," *Nature*, 297 (1982), 541–546.
[‡]Andrews, P. cited in L. Aiello and C. Dean, *Human Evolutionary Anatomy* (London: Academic Press, 1990) p. 9.

studies of gorilla DNA suggest that the west African and east African subspecies may actually be separate species.[3] Lowland gorillas are the ones that are usually seen in zoos. The highland gorillas have been the subject of several studies in the wild.

Gorillas are basically terrestrial vegetarians. They walk on all four limbs, but instead of placing the palms of their hands flat on the ground, they walk on their knuckles. Although their size prevents them from moving easily through the trees, gorillas sometimes choose to build their sleeping nests there.

Perhaps the best known ape is the chimpanzee. This genus includes three subspecies of the common chimpanzee, found north of the Zaire (Congo) River (Figure 10–29). However, recent analysis of the DNA found in hair samples shed in the wild suggests that the western subspecies may actually be a separate species.[4] The other known species is the rare bonobo, or pygmy chimpanzee, found south of the river (Figure 10–30). Common chimpanzee males average about 45 kilograms (100 pounds) in weight, with females averaging about 37 kilograms (82 pounds). Chimpanzees range in height from 1 to 1.7 meters (3¼ to 5½ feet). Although the word "pygmy" implies small size, the bonobo is only slightly smaller than the common chimpanzee.

Sociable and curious, chimpanzees are much more active than gorillas. They live in flexible social groups, which is not generally true of other nonhuman primates. Like the gorillas, chimpanzees build nests in trees and are also knuckle walkers.

The Hominids

The family Hominidae contains only one living species—*Homo sapiens*. Humans display moderate sexual dimorphism, with the average height of women generally between 5 and 10 percent less than the average height for men. The average height in different populations, however, can differ significantly. The world's shortest people are the Efe of Zaire, Africa. Efe males average about 1.42 meters (4 feet 8 inches) in height. On

[3]M. Ruvolo et al., "Gene Trees and Hominoid Phylogeny," *Proceedings of the National Academy of Sciences*, 91 (1994), 8900–8904.

[4]P. A. Morin et al., "Kin Selection, Social Structure, Gene Flow, and the Evolution of Chimpanzees," *Science*, 265 (1994), 1193–1201.

FIGURE 10–28 *Great ape.* Representative of the family Panidae: lowland gorilla, *Gorilla gorilla gorilla.*

FIGURE 10–29 *Great ape.* Representative of the family Panidae: common chimpanzee, *Pan troglodytes.*

the other hand, the Dinka of the Sudan, also in Africa, display the greatest average height, with males averaging 1.85 meters (6 feet 1 inch) in height.

Unlike the other primates, humans have lost much of their locomotor flexibility. While they are still capable of climbing trees, and some individuals do become skillful aerialists, humans are essentially habitually erect, terrestrial bipeds. This pattern of posture and locomotion is not unique to *H. sapiens*, but only this species among all primates has become anatomically specialized for it. While the human skeleton is similar to the ape skeleton in the upper torso, from the pelvis down the human skeleton has become highly specialized for bipedal walking and running (Chapter 13).

FIGURE 10–30 *Great ape.* Representative of the family Panidae: bonobo or pygmy chimpanzee, *Pan paniscus.*

BOX 10–3

VANISHING PRIMATES

Today, over half of the living primate species are in some danger of becoming extinct. Leading the list of endangered species are the muriqui and lion tamarin of the Atlantic forests of eastern Brazil, the mountain gorilla of Africa, the twenty-eight species of primates on the island of Madagascar, and the lion-tailed macaque and the snub-nosed monkeys from Asia.

The major threat to primates in the wild is destruction of their habitats, which is occurring primarily in the tropical forests where the vast majority of modern primates live. Because the rapidly increasing human populations in these parts of the world cannot be supported on the traditional agricultural land or in the large cities, vast areas of tropical forest are being converted into farmland and ranchland. Other factors responsible for much of the destruction of the tropical forest are the need for firewood, poor management of industrial logging, and the construction of hydroelectric projects.

In many parts of the world primates are hunted for food or to procure skins and other body parts. The skins of the black-and-white colobus monkey (see the accompanying Figure) have been used for rugs, coats, and native headdresses.

Finally, primates are used extensively for scientific research. Although today the importation of primates from the wild has markedly decreased, only a few decades ago thousands of animals were imported for research and the pet trade.

Today, major efforts to preserve the primate fauna have been initiated in many countries. Yet while laws have been passed to promote the conservation of primates, they are often impossible to enforce. The major problem is the exploding population characteristic of many tropical countries. The need to feed and house this expanding population has made it difficult to preserve endangered primate species.

Reference: R. A. Mittermeier and D. L. Cheney, "Conservation of Primates and Their Habitats," in B. B. Smuts et al. (eds.), *Primate Societies* (Chicago: University of Chicago Press, 1986), 477–490.

Humans are omnivorous, with meat eating playing a significant role in almost all human societies. The only other primates known to kill and eat other mammals are baboons and chimpanzees. While chimpanzees have been observed to manufacture a limited number of tools, the manufacture of large numbers of complex tools by humans has led to the development of elaborate and complex technologies.

Humans have one of the longest gestation periods of any primate, although they produce the most helpless infants. The period of infant de-

A PORTFOLIO OF ENDANGERED PRIMATES

The tropical forests of the world are home to the greatest diversity of plant and animal species on the planet, yet many of these unique life forms are rapidly disappearing, primarily because of deforestation brought about by human activity. On these pages are just a few primate species that are classified as endangered or vulnerable by the International Union for Conservation of Nature and Natural Resources. Species classified as *endangered* are those that are in great danger of extinction, especially if conditions do not change. Some endangered species may already be extinct. Species classified as *vulnerable* are those that are very likely to be reclassified as endangered in the near future.

FIGURE 10-B Hairy-eared dwarf lemur, *Allocebus trichotis,* from Madagascar, was thought to be extinct but recently has been rediscovered. It is considered endangered.

MADAGASCAR

FIGURE 10-A Golden bamboo lemur, *Hapalemur aureus,* from Madagascar, is newly discovered and has not yet been classified.

FIGURE 10-C Aye-aye, *Daubentonia madagascariensis,* from Madagascar, is classified as endangered.

FIGURE 10-D   Mandrill, *Mandrillus sphinx*, from Cameroon, Congo, Equatorial Guinea, and Gabon, is considered to be vulnerable and is likely to be classified as endangered in the near future.

FIGURE 10-E   Mountain gorilla, *Gorilla gorilla beringei*, from Rwanda, Uganda, and Zaire, is endangered.

FIGURE 10-G Orangutan, *Pongo pygmaeus*, from Sumatra and Borneo, is endangered.

FIGURE 10-F Golden snub-nosed monkey, *Rhinopithecus roxella-nae*, from China, is considered to be vulnerable and is likely to be classified as endangered in the near future.

FIGURE 10-H Golden lion tamarin, *Leontopithecus rosalia,* from Brazil, is endangered. This primate has been successfully bred in several zoos in the United States and is currently being introduced back into its native habitat in Brazil.

FIGURE 10-I Red uakari, *Cacajao calvus,* from Brazil, Colombia, and Peru, is considered to be vulnerable and is likely to be classified as endangered in the near future.

pendency is very long, with adult status often not reached until the second decade of life. This long childhood provides an opportunity for the development of complex patterns of learned behavior. Indeed, this is *H. sapiens'* most significant distinction: the dependence upon culture for adjusting to the environment.

Summary

This section has introduced the various primate groups in anticipation of the chapters to follow. The order Primates is divided into three suborders. The first, Prosimii, includes the lemurs, sifaka, aye-aye, lorises, and galagos. The second, Tarsioidea, contains the tarsiers. The final suborder, Anthropoidea, includes the New World and Old World monkeys, apes, and humans.

STUDY QUESTIONS

1. What is meant by the idea that adaptability is the primate's way of coping with its habitat? How is this related to the arboreal environment?

2. In what ways can the primate be said to possess a generalized anatomy? In what ways is a generalized anatomy more advantageous than a more specialized one?

3. An animal's awareness of its environment depends upon data received through the sense organs. What senses have been refined in the primates? How do the refinements of these senses provide adaptations to arboreal habitats?

4. What are some of the characteristics of the primates that can be considered shared derived (synapomorphic)? What characteristics can be considered shared ancestral (symplesiomorphic)?

5. How does the suborder Prosimii as a group contrast with the suborder Anthropoidea?

6. In what ways have the evolution of New World monkeys and Old World monkeys paralleled each other? What features can be used to distinguish between the two groups?

SUGGESTED READINGS

Coimbra-Filho, A. F., and R. A. Mittermeier (eds.). *Ecology and Behavior of Neotropical Primates.* Rio de Janeiro: Academia Brasileira de Ciencias, 1981. This book discusses the taxonomy and fossil history of the New World monkeys and the ecology and behavior of sixteen representative species.

Fleagle, J. G. *Primate Adaptation and Evolution.* San Diego: Academic, 1988. The first half of this book is a discussion of the primate order and the various primate taxa.

Jolly, A. *The Evolution of Primate Behavior*, 2d ed. New York: Macmillan, 1985. Although this book is primarily concerned with behavior, it has excellent introductory chapters on the primates in general.

Jolly, A. *A World of Their Own: Man and Nature in Madagascar.* New Haven: Yale University Press, 1980. This book is an introduction to the flora, fauna, and people of the island of Madagascar; it is written by a foremost expert on the Madagascar primates.

Kavanagh, M. *A Complete Guide to Monkeys, Apes and Other Primates.* New York: Viking, 1983. Well illustrated, with many color photographs, this relatively nontechnical book introduces each primate genus.

Martin, R. D. *Primate Origins and Evolution.* Princeton, N.J.: Princeton University Press, 1990. This large volume presents a wealth of detailed information about many aspects of the primate order.

Napier, J. R., and P. H. Napier. *The Natural History of the Primates.* Cambridge, Mass.: M.I.T., 1985. The first five chapters of this book deal with characteristics of the primates, primate origins, anatomy, and behavior. This is followed by profiles of each primate genus, illustrated with black-and-white and color photographs.

Richard, A. F. *Primates in Nature.* New York: Freeman, 1985. This book focuses on primate ecology, with excellent discussions of distribution, diet, demography, and social organization.

Tylinek, E., and G. Berger. *Monkeys and Apes.* New York: Arco, 1985. After a general introduction, this book proceeds to present a paragraph or so on each primate species. The book is abundantly illustrated with line drawings as well as black-and-white and color photographs.

Wolfheim, J. H. *Primates of the World: Distribution, Abundance, and Conservation.* Seattle: University of Washington Press, 1983. This listing of all living primate species includes a distribution map with data on abundance and diversity, habitat, factors affecting populations, and conservation activities. An extensive bibliography is provided for each species.

Primatologist Sarah Blaffer Hrdy observes langurs on Mt. Abu, India.

Studies of nonhuman primates form an important part of a scientific enterprise that is giving us increased understanding of the world about us, of the evolutionary processes that gave rise to it, and of our place within it. Beyond that, however, nonhuman species, and especially nonhuman primates, provide an important source of data for understanding many aspects of human behavior and physiology in terms of causation, developmental processes, function, and evolution.[1]

Robert A. Hinde

[1]R. A. Hinde, "Can Nonhuman Primates Help Us Understand Human Behavior?" in B. B. Smuts et al. (eds.), *Primate Societies* (Chicago: University of Chicago Press, 1987), 413. Copyright © 1986 by the University of Chicago. All rights reserved.

11

CHAPTER
PRIMATE BEHAVIOR

From casual observers at a zoo to scientists engaged in research, people are fascinated with animal behavior. The physical anthropologist is most interested in the nonhuman primates since all primates, including humans, are united by a common ancestry.

Millions of years have passed since all primates had a common ancestor, or even since humans and apes did. Yet studies of nonhuman primate behavior throw light on current human behaviors—such as the need for physical contact. By studying contemporary nonhuman primate behavior, we can develop ideas on what some of the selective pressures operating on early hominid populations might have been.

Although there are many similarities between human and nonhuman primate behavior, humans have taken a different evolutionary path from any other primate. This chapter considers the behavior of the nonhuman primates, while the next chapter discusses human behavior in comparison to the nonhuman primates.

PRIMATE BEHAVIOR

Discussions of adaptation usually involve analyses of anatomical structures, yet animals also cope with the requirements of their ecological niches by means of behavior. This is illustrated by the social insects, whose complex behavioral patterns are imperative to their survival. These innate patterns, as well as aspects of the insects' anatomy and physiology, are determined by the genetic code.

Primates also rely on behavior to contend with the requirements of their niches, but unlike insect behavior, a large proportion of primate behavior is learned and hence variable. Because of this, problems arise about the validity of generalizations drawn from a limited number of studies. Behavioral patterns differ not only from species to species but also from group to group within the same species. Nevertheless, the study of primate behavior is essential to a complete understanding of the primate complex. Today, studies of primate behavior are a major division of the field of **primatology.**

Methods in the Study of Primate Behavior

Early studies of primate behavior were conducted primarily with zoo populations, and data from these studies led to many erroneous conclusions. Today we realize that these data reflect the unnatural and overcrowded conditions in the cage. When a zoo population is given adequate space and a good food supply and is maintained in a natural social grouping, its behavior is very similar to that of wild populations.

Several studies have compared wild populations with caged populations of the same species. In a report on one such study, T. Rowell writes of baboons: "The same units of social behavior were observed in both wild and caged populations, and no behavior patterns were seen in one and not the other."[2] She notes, however, that the intensity of social interaction is much greater in the caged population.

Perhaps the most valid study is one in which the observer spends enough time with a natural population to recognize individuals. Since animals become familiar with the observer as well, close observation becomes possible. The disadvantages of such studies are that it takes long periods of time to make contact with the animals and the yield of data is relatively low.

Many of these problems are solved, to a great extent, through studies of **provisionized colonies,** which are natural populations in which feeding stations are established. Because the primate group travels to the feeding stations daily, the researcher can observe individuals closely and can collect census data, such as information on births and deaths. Studies conducted away from the feeding stations are made easier by the primate group's increased tolerance of the observer. The yield of data is greater than that achieved with the standard field study of a nonprovisionized group, and new observers can be introduced into the research situation quite readily. Well-known provisionized colonies include those of the Japanese macaque at Takasakiyama, Japan, and the rhesus macaque colony on Cayo Santiago, Puerto Rico (see Box 11–1).

While natural and provisionized populations are the most frequently studied, many universities and research stations maintain artificial colonies. In addition, laboratory studies, conducted primarily by psychologists, involve manipulation of the animals in a laboratory situation.

Primate Social Behavior

Primates are, for the most part, social animals; most live in social groups of varying sizes. A social group is "made up of animals that interact regularly and know one another individually. Its members spend most of their time nearer to one another than to nonmembers and are often hostile toward nonmembers."[3]

---

[2]T. Rowell, "A Quantitative Comparison of the Behaviour of a Wild and a Caged Baboon Group," *Animal Behavior,* 15 (1967), 499, 501.

[3]A. F. Richard, *Primates in Nature* (New York: Freeman, 1985), 291.

BOX 11–1

THE RHESUS MONKEYS OF CAYO SANTIAGO

Cayo Santiago is a 15.2-hectare (37.6-acre) island located 1 kilometer (0.6 miles) from the southeast coast of Puerto Rico. In 1938 a population of rhesus monkeys *(Macaca mulatta)* from India was established on this uninhabited island. The colony has been continuously maintained since 1938.

The idea of developing a colony of free-ranging monkeys in the New World was developed by Clarence Ray Carpenter. In 1938 there was much interest in the project because of the possibility that the political situation in Europe might result in the cutting off of the importation of monkeys from Asia, especially the rhesus monkey, commonly used in laboratory studies. In 1939 Carpenter traveled to

A rhesus mother and her infant rest in the branches of a tree on Cayo Santiago.

India to trap 500 rhesus monkeys, including 100 females with infants. All were tested for tuberculosis, a major cause of illness and death among monkeys, and those showing a positive reaction were not shipped. It took 47 days to transport the animals from India to New York. The animals arrived on Cayo Santiago on November 14, 1938, and beginning in December 409 rhesus monkeys were set free.

Before the arrival of the monkeys, Cayo Santiago was covered primarily with grass and was used as pasture for goats. A variety of trees and shrubs were planted in anticipation of the monkeys. Little was known about the naturalistic behavior of rhesus monkeys. For example, some people thought that rhesus monkeys were cave dwellers and they constructed many small artificial caves; none were ever used.

By 1941 the colony was firmly established, and many primatologists were using the animals in their research. However, the financial support of the colony was becoming precarious and large numbers of monkeys were removed from the island and transported to laboratories in the United States. In 1956 the Laboratory of Perinatal Physiology of the National Institute of Neurological Disease and Blindness (NINDB) and the University of Puerto Rico took over administration of the island colony.

Under new management, improvements in the care of the animals were made and major research was initiated on the island. It was at this time that animals were marked so that individuals could be identified. Annual censuses were conducted, and longitudinal studies of specific animals following their development from birth to death were begun. These long-term studies are extremely difficult in natural populations. Although many animals were removed for laboratory studies, the population increased in size annually. In the 1960s the Cayo Santiago monkeys were used to found new monkey colonies on other islands in the area. In 1970 the island became part of what is now the Caribbean Primate Research Center of the University of Puerto Rico School of Medicine.

References: R. G. Rawlins and Matt J. Kessler, "The History of Cayo Santiago Colony," in R. G. Rawlins and M. J. Kessler (eds.), *The Cayo Santiago Macaques: History, Behavior and Biology* (Albany, N.Y.: State Univ. of New York Press, 1986), 13–45.

TABLE 11–1

PRIMATE SOCIAL GROUPS

GROUP	DESCRIPTION	EXAMPLE
Female and her offspring	Range overlaps ranges of other female-offspring groups and those of the males	Mouse lemur
Monogamous family	Male-female pair and preadult offspring	Marmosets; gibbons
One-male group (harem)	Male and several females; called a harem when the group is a subunit of a larger unit	Hamadryas baboon
Multimale group	Several males with several females and young	Savanna baboon; rhesus macaque
Fission-fusion society	Several groups varying in size and composition	Common chimpanzee

There are many advantages to living in social units. The social group provides both males and females with access to individuals of the opposite sex as mating partners; once offspring are produced, the group provides protection for the helpless young. The group also serves as a pool of information, which is vital for animals whose primary means of adaptation involves learned behavior.

Much of the activity of primates is based upon the availability and distribution of food. Larger social units often can take precedence over smaller units with regard to food, and the collective memory of the social group creates a vast store of knowledge about the location of food supplies. Also, although mammals usually flee from danger, a large group of primates may act as an effective deterrent against predators, important in populations that feed on the ground during the day.

PRIMATE SOCIAL ORGANIZATION   In part because primate social behavior is largely learned, we find great variety in the form and composition of primate social groups and in the patterns of social interactions of individuals within groups. Primate social units range from loosely organized associations of relatively solitary animals to large, highly integrated troops of well over 100 individuals. While it is not possible to discuss all the forms of primate social organization, we can examine some of the more common social groupings (Table 11–1).

A relatively simple form of social grouping is found in many small nocturnal prosimians, such as the galagos, mouse lemurs, and dwarf lemurs. The basic social unit is the female and her immature offspring. Each female-offspring unit occupies a specific space termed a **home range.** The ranges of females may overlap extensively, and females with their young often share the same nest. Males occupy larger ranges that overlap several ranges occupied by females. Males and females do not interact with each other on a regular basis; for example, they do not feed together. They do have periodic contact, and when the female is sexually receptive, mating occurs. The social unit of the mouse lemur is described in Box 11–2.

The **monogamous family** is a relatively simple unit that consists of an adult male-female pair, usually mated for life, and their offspring. The young normally leave the group when they reach puberty. This type of social unit is characteristic of the marmosets and tamarins and the lesser apes.

Attempts to breed highly endangered marmosets and tamarins in captivity gave rise to the realization that the social behavior of these New World primates is distinct from that of other taxa. The marmoset and tamarin males play major roles in the rearing of offspring. Twins are usually born, and the father carries the infants, transferring the young to the female only for feeding (Figure 11–1). The group often contains three sets of twins of successive ages. This social unit, however, is not as simple as it might first

BOX 11–2

THE BEHAVIOR OF THE MOUSE LEMUR

While primates are usually thought of as highly social animals, some of the small nocturnal prosimians lead a relatively solitary existence. Among the smallest of the primates are the mouse lemurs of Madagascar. The head and body of the lesser mouse lemur are only 13.3 centimeters (5 inches) long; the tail adds another 14 centimeters (5.5 inches). Mouse lemurs spend the daylight hours in leaf nests built in the dense foliage or in holes in trees. During the night hours they forage for a variety of plant and animal food including fruits, insects, spiders, and frogs. A very important part of their diet are gums and insect secretions which they scrape off the bark and leaves with their dental comb. Here we will look briefly at the social behavior of the slightly larger Coquerel's mouse lemur, *Microcebus coquereli.*

Adult mouse lemurs occupy relatively small core areas that average 1.5 hectares (3.7 acres) for males and 2.5 to 3 hectares (6.2 to 7.4 acres) for females. The core area is surrounded by a larger peripheral area of over 4 hectares (10 acres). There is some overlapping of the home range, especially in the case of a female and her young or a male and a female. Peripheral areas overlap more extensively, allowing adults of the same sex to come into social contact. However, although the core area makes up only 30 percent of the home range, 80 percent of their activity occurs here. Like most lemurs, the mouse lemur marks its core area with urine, feces, and secretions from specialized glands.

While occupying the core area, the mouse lemur engages in solitary activities such as autogrooming, feeding, and resting; these activities typically occur during the earlier part of the night. After midnight the animal may move out into the peripheral area where it may contact another mouse lemur. These include encounters between the sexes and territorial activities between males.

Reference: E. Pages, "Ethoecology of *Microcebus coquereli* during the Dry Season," in P. Charles-Dominique et al., *Nocturnal Malagasy Primates* (New York: Academic Press, 1980), 97–116.

FIGURE 11–1 *Golden lion tamarin.* Marmosets and tamarins usually produce twins, which are carried by the father and transferred to the mother for nursing.

appear. Young animals may transfer from one family group to another, and in some groups a second adult male may be present. Understanding the social behavior of these tamarins has led to a highly successful breeding program. Monkeys born in captivity are now being released into the Brazilian forest.

A more common form of group organization consists of a single male associated with several females. This type of group may exist as a small, independent **one-male group,** or it may be a subunit, sometimes called a **harem,** of a larger unit. The social organization of the hamadryas baboon consists of harems and all-male groups bound together in a hierarchy of larger social groupings.

Perhaps the most familiar form of primate society is the **multimale group,** which consists of a fairly large number of animals, including many adult males and adult females. The distinction between one-male and multimale groups, how-

ever, is not always clear. The social organization of the savanna baboon is an example of a multimale group society.

Finally, there are many primates that exhibit a variety of social groupings. The size and organization of the various types of groups often depend on the activity of the group and the season of the year. This is typical of the common chimpanzees, whose social organization may be referred to as a **fission-fusion society** because large groups break into smaller units and smaller groups coalesce into larger ones.

Summary

Generalizations about primate behavior are difficult to make. Since much primate behavior is learned, great differences exist not only among different species but also among different populations of the same species.

Primates are social animals that live in social groups of varying sizes. Within the groups we find differences in age and sex categories, as well as complex behavioral patterns among the various individuals. Although primate groups vary in size and structure, certain general patterns can be identified.

The social unit of many small nocturnal prosimians is the female and her offspring; several units occupy overlapping ranges. Males occupy larger ranges that overlap those occupied by the females. The marmosets and tamarins live in monogamous family units in which the male often plays a major role in the rearing of offspring.

Many primate groups consist of a single male associated with several females. This type of group may be a small, independent one-male group or a subunit, called a harem, of a larger unit. A common form of primate society is the multimale group, which consists of a fairly large number of animals, including many adult males and adult females. Finally, many primates, such as the common chimpanzee, exhibit a fission-fusion society in which a variety of social groupings exist. The size and organization of the various groups depend on the activity of the group and the season of the year.

CASE STUDIES OF PRIMATE BEHAVIOR

This section deals with the social organization and social behavior of the monkeys and apes. We will examine a small series of anthropoids—the gibbon, gelada, baboon, and chimpanzee—by outlining their basic social organizations and discussing selected aspects of their social behaviors. This is not an exhaustive study, but it is one that will provide some understanding of the basic patterns and general nature of primate behavior.

Social Behavior of the Gibbon

The monkeys and apes are generally characterized by relatively large, complex social units, although small social groups do exist. Since many basic concepts are easier to understand in the context of small groups, we will begin our discussion with a description of the monogamous family group.

The monogamous family group is a relatively small social unit consisting of a single mated pair and their young offspring. It is found among the lesser apes (Hylobatidae)—the gibbons and the siamang (Figure 11–2). In this section, we will examine some aspects of the social behavior of the

FIGURE 11–2 *The monogamous social unit of the gibbon.* Adult male (black) and female (blond) with offspring.

white-handed gibbon, *Hylobates lar,* which was studied by J. O. Ellefson in the lowland rain forests of the Malay Peninsula.[4]

THE GIBBON SOCIAL GROUP   In the monogamous family group, the adult male and female mate for life. The close relationship between the adult pair is seen in both grooming and sexual activity.

Grooming is a behavioral pattern common to most primates. In grooming, the animal uses its hands to search and comb through the fur, although prosimians use the dental comb instead. Grooming involves the search for dirt, dry pieces of skin, and parasites in the fur. The removal of this material keeps the fur relatively clean and groomed. An animal may spend time grooming itself as a part of this cleaning process; this is called **autogrooming.** The animals also spend a great deal of time grooming one another; this is referred to as **allogrooming.**

Allogrooming in primates is an important form of social behavior, as it aids in the development and maintenance of close social bonds. It is especially common between closely related individuals and is characteristic of close social ties such as those between mother and child. Among gibbons, grooming is important in the maintenance of the adult male-female bond. The adult gibbon pair groom one another several times a day, primarily in the afternoon. This grooming is reciprocal; the male grooms the female for about as long as the female grooms the male.

Sexual behavior is another important aspect of social behavior. An analysis of the spacing of births suggests that sexual behavior in the white-handed gibbon takes place during short periods every 2 years or so. No courtship behavior has been observed.

THE GIBBON LIFE CYCLE   The infant stage of gibbon development lasts from birth to approximately 2 to 2½ years of age. Within a few months after birth the infant begins to eat solid food. At the end of this stage it is weaned and also stops sleeping with its mother. Even the very young infant can cling tightly to its mother's fur as she rapidly moves through the high branches of the trees. The mother and other members of the group do not pay a great deal of attention to the infant. As the infant grows older, it moves farther away from its mother for longer periods of time and interacts with older siblings if it has any.

The juvenile period begins between 2 and 2½ years and ends between 4 and 4½ years. Important during this stage of gibbon development is **play** behavior. Play is difficult to define, yet play behavior appears to be important among primates and it occupies a great deal of the waking hours of juveniles. Play often involves intense, repetitive physical activity that results in the development and refinement of physical skills. Ellefson describes the play of the white-handed gibbon as including "chasing, grappling, hitting, kicking, jerking, holding, biting, stretching, pushing and dropping."[5] It is through play that young primates learn rules of objects, that is, the relationship between the body and objects. For example, what objects the juvenile can move and how trees respond to jumping on a branch. Play also provides a setting for the development of social skills and the formation of social bonds between specific individuals.

There is a major difference, however, between the play activities of gibbons and those of many other primates. In larger primate groups, several **play groups** many form, each including many animals of similar age. In the small gibbon family, the sole playmate of an older juvenile is its younger sibling. Thus the older juvenile is always larger and stronger than the younger, and the physical activity of the older must be controlled to avoid injuring the younger. Also, gibbons spend less time playing than do most other primates.

During the juvenile period, the adults become less and less tolerant of the juvenile's feeding close by. When the juvenile is about 4 years of age, the adults actively threaten it away from

---

[4]J. O. Ellefson, "A Natural History of White-Handed Gibbons in the Malayan Peninsula," in D. M. Rumbaugh (ed.), *Gibbon and Siamang,* vol. 3 (Basel: Karger, 1974), 1–136.

[5]Ibid., 84.

many food sources. Their **threat gestures** include staring, shaking a branch, and lunging toward the young animal.

The adolescent gibbon is between 4 and 6 years of age. At about 6 years of age the animal attains full adult size and full sexual maturity. This is the period of **peripheralization.** At this time, the adults (more often the adult male) become aggressive toward the adolescent and actively keep it away from the area in which they are eating. Also, the adolescent gibbon begins to move away from the group to forage and feed on its own.

The subadult phase of gibbon development lasts from the age of 6 until the animal mates, but the age of first mating is variable. As the animal becomes more and more separated from its group of birth, possibilities arise for the formation of a new social unit. Although the exact mechanisms are not known, peripheral subadult males do attract subadult females, and new male-female pairs are established.

TERRITORIALITY   All animals occupy space. The area in which a group feeds, drinks, grooms, sleeps, plays, and so forth, is its home range. The home ranges of gibbon groups measure about 40 hectares (100 acres) in size. We must always keep in mind, however, that primates utilize three-dimensional space and that the actual space occupied in a tropical forest, with its tall trees, is considerably larger than that suggested by the ground measurement. The area that a group defends against other members of its own species is its **territory.** The territory, which is usually smaller than the home range, represents the boundaries at which the animal actively begins to defend an area against another group.

Gibbons are highly territorial animals, and most of the home range is defended territory. Among the white-handed gibbons studied by Ellefson, territories overlap about 20 percent, and so the neighboring group may be found within the overlapping area. Actual conflict between neighboring males takes place, on the average, about every other day. Conflicts always occur in the area of the overlapping territories, which is usually about 23 to 69 meters (25 to 75 yards) wide.

FIGURE 11–3   *Gibbon vocalization.*

Territorial conflict is expressed primarily in terms of vocalization and display. Early in the morning the southeast Asian forest rings with the sound of the great call of the gibbon (Figure 11–3). These morning calls broadcast the location of the various gibbon groups. Upon hearing the morning call of a nearby group, a male may lead his group over to the vicinity of that neighboring group. A typical conflict period lasts about an hour, the first half of which is spent in vocalizations and displays by adult males. These are usually followed by chases, but the chases rarely penetrate deep into any group's territory. Actual contact between adult males is rare.

Territorial behavior serves several functions. It spreads individual members of a population over a large area, thereby preventing a concentration of animals and overutilization of resources in a relatively small area. A map of gibbon territories shows a mosaic of small territories throughout a relatively large area. Territoriality also serves to control population size since an animal cannot begin to produce offspring until it has found a mate and established its own territory. The number of territories available is stable.

Social Behavior of the Gelada

Geladas, *Theropithecus gelada*, are large, primarily terrestrial monkeys. They once ranged over large areas of east Africa, and they are even represented in the fossil record. Today, the geladas are found only in a dry, desolate, mountainous region of Ethiopia. Although the geladas are not true baboons (baboons belong to the genus *Papio*), they are similar to baboons in many ways.

The social organization found in this hot, dry habitat may be an adaptation to the environment. Primates that spend a great deal of time on the ground searching for food tend to form large groups, primarily for protection against predators. Primates that are more arboreal are relatively secure in the trees, and so they tend to form smaller and more loosely organized groups. Although trees are few and far between in the barren wastes where the geladas live, large social units are not always able to locate adequate food supplies in the hot, dry habitat. Thus, when food is scarce, the larger gelada group breaks up into its constituent groups. These smaller units are a better size for foraging for food under the harsh conditions. The following description of gelada social organization is based on the field studies of Robin and Patsy Dunbar.[6]

AGE-SEX CATEGORIES   Different animals behave in different ways within a social group. The most important differences in social behavior are determined by the sex and age of the individual.

Therefore, we need to divide the members of the gelada groups into a series of age-sex categories, as we previously did with the white-handed gibbon.

The early infant phase lasts from birth to 6 months of age. The infant is black or dark brown in color, a marked contrast to the reddish coat color of the adult. This distinctive difference in color between infant and adult, which is characteristic of many primate species, makes the infant easily recognizable. The black gelada infant is a focal point of the group, and all members will protect the infant if it is in danger. During infancy the young gelada stays very close to its mother. Toward the end of infancy, when the coat color begins to change to the adult color, the adults relax their vigilance and the infant is freer to move around and explore its environment.

The 6- to 18-month-old infant is adult in color, yet it still spends considerable time near its mother. At about 1 to 1½ years of age, the infant is weaned. Then the animal is classified as a juvenile, a phase lasting from 1½ to 3½ years of age. During this period the juvenile becomes increasingly independent of its mother, and most of its social interactions take place in play groups.

The subadult female, aged 3½ to 4½ years, is sexually mature but has not quite reached adult size. As the female completes growth, she associates primarily with other adult females and their offspring and is soon bearing offspring of her own.

The male is considered a subadult for a much longer time than the female—from 3½ to 6 years of age. In part, this is because the male continues to grow for a longer period of time than the female. While the canine teeth erupt early in the subadult period, full growth of the large canines characteristic of males does not take place until the end of the subadult period. Only at this time do the males take their place in adult life. Because of this longer growth period, the adult male is larger than the female. This larger size, plus other distinctive features such as the cape of fur around the shoulders, makes it easy to distinguish the adult male from the adult female. Such a difference in the physical appearance between the male and female is an example of sexual dimorphism (Figure 10–21).

---

[6]R. Dunbar and P. Dunbar, *Social Dynamics of Gelada Baboons* (Basel: Karger, 1975).

FIGURE 11–4 *The gelada.* A female gelada sits behind and grooms an older male.

Sexual dimorphism is common among the more terrestrial monkeys. Because monkeys are vulnerable to predation on the ground, the larger size of the males provides the group with a mechanism for defense against predators. In addition, there appears to be a correlation between the degree of development of sexual dimorphism and the size and complexity of the monkey social unit. Instant recognition of individuals is relatively easy in small units such as the gibbon family, but recognition becomes a problem in larger social groups. In case of danger, a gelada female needs to identify an adult male, and the distinctive physical appearance of the male makes this easy.

SOCIAL ORGANIZATION OF THE HAREM UNITS   The basic social unit of the gelada is the one-male–several-females unit, or harem. Besides harems, small all-male groups also exist.

A typical harem consists of about eleven members: one adult male, five adult females, and five juveniles and infants. The most cohesive bonds in the unit appear to exist between females, who express their closeness in terms of grooming (Figure 11–4). In many ways the male is peripheral to the group. The females form a stable unit that maintains itself with little herding by the male. If a female from a neighboring harem comes too close, the females will chase her off. The males appear to respect each other's females, and they threaten females from other groups who come too close.

One form of behavior that is often seen in social interactions within the harem or between harems is **agonistic behavior.** This is behavior involving "fighting, threats, fleeing and other related displays."[7] Much agonistic behavior takes the form of display and gesture instead of actual fighting. Agonistic gestures and facial expressions include staring, raising the eyebrows, and lunging in space (Figure 11–5).

SOCIAL DEVELOPMENT   The juvenile male spends most of his time in play groups with other young animals within his harem, although juveniles from adjacent harems play with one another. As he grows older, he pays less attention to the members of the harem of his birth and begins to associate with an all-male group consisting of older juveniles, young subadult and adult males without females. The older subadult male begins to show interest in the harem groups, and he attaches himself to one as a follower. These follower males are peripheral to the unit; they interact primarily with the juveniles and a few females of the group and generally avoid the adult male.

The juvenile female also participates in play groups until the time of puberty. She then begins to show interest in the adult males, mothers, and young infants and spends her time following the infants around and attempting to play with them. As she reaches sexual maturity, she becomes interested in the group leader. Since the

---

[7]N. Chalmers, *Social Behavior in Primates* (Baltimore: University Park Press, 1980), 63.

FIGURE 11–5   *The gelada.* Two males are fighting on the right. Note threat gesture at left.

adult male usually has little interest in the young female, the possibility arises that the female will become attached to a young male.

New harem units may arise in a variety of ways. Typically a follower male forms an attachment with a young female. Once this bond becomes established, the young male and female slowly move away from the larger unit to form a new unit. A less frequent possibility is that a young male will attack an older harem male and take over the harem.

LARGER GELADA UNITS   While the basic social units of the gelada are the harem and the all-male group, these groups do not wander independently of one another. Instead, they gather into **bands** consisting of harems and male groups that share a home range. During certain seasons, the band comes together in areas where food is plentiful. During times when food is less plentiful, the band breaks up and forages as individual harems and all-male groups.

Under very good grazing conditions, many bands come together to form a **herd.** Herds form in areas where band ranges overlap. In the Dunbars' study at Sankaber, Ethiopia, the herd contained 762 animals divided into 6 bands; in all there were 68 harems and 9 all-male groups.

Social Behavior of the Savanna Baboon

Perhaps one of the best-studied primates other than humans is the savanna baboon. In large part this is because savanna baboons live on the open grassland where humans can easily observe them. This contrasts with the very difficult observing conditions in forest areas. Also, many anthropologists have been intrigued by the fact that both baboons and early hominids are primates that left the forest and became adapted to life on the savanna.

Baboons range throughout large areas of Africa where they are the most commonly seen monkeys; in some places they are considered agricultural pests. The savanna baboons are divided into four kinds: olive (or anubis), yellow, chacma, and Guinea baboons. Many primatologists believe that the four groups represent four subspecies of the species *Papio cynocephalus*.

Many populations of savanna baboon have been studied in many parts of Africa. Baboon social organization is quite flexible and varies from one group to another. For example, the baboon troops at Amboseli, Kenya, exhibit intergroup aggression when in close proximity, yet baboons studied in Uganda show frequent movement of individuals from one group to another. In contrast, the baboons of Nairobi Park, Kenya, show much stability.

The conclusion we must draw from the wealth of field observations of baboons and other primates is that primate societies are variable in their adjustments to the environment. Differences in physical habitat, for example, are reflected in differences in the size of the home range, the troop size, and the general nature of intergroup interactions. This variability is a reflection of the fact that, in general, primate social behavior is not innate—determined by the genetic code. Through the formation of learned behavioral patterns, each primate population has developed its particular guide for survival.

The following discussion is based on studies of two populations of savanna baboons living in Kenya, the baboons of Nairobi Park, studied by Irvin DeVore and his colleagues, and the baboons of Amboseli, studied by Stuart and Jane Altmann and their associates.[8]

THE BABOON TROOP   Baboons live in a social unit called a **troop.** In both Nairobi Park and Amboseli, troops average about forty animals. The baboon troop remains within a home range with distinct boundaries, a fact illustrated by the

[8]I. DeVore and K. R. L. Hall, "Baboon Ecology," and K. R. L. Hall and I. DeVore, "Baboon Social Behavior," in I. DeVore (ed.), *Primate Behavior: Field Studies of Monkeys and Apes* (New York: Holt, 1965), 20–52, 53–110; S. A. Altmann and J. A. Altmann, *Baboon Ecology: African Field Research* (Chicago: University of Chicago Press, 1970); J. Altmann, *Baboon Mothers and Infants* (Cambridge, Mass.: Harvard University Press, 1980).

inability of an observer to drive a troop across these boundaries. Boundaries are never defended; hence, territories do not exist. The home ranges of neighboring troops usually overlap extensively (Figure 11–6). In contrast to the territorial behavior of the gibbon, when more than one baboon troop occupies sections of an overlapping area, the troops tend to ignore one another and to avoid contact. When contact between baboon troops is unavoidable, such as around a water hole during the dry season, several troops often drink side by side. They ignore one another, or the smaller troop simply gives way to the larger.

The baboons of Kenya occupy ranges of about 23 to 24 square kilometers (8.9 to 9.3 square miles). The size appears to depend upon the size of the troop and the concentration of food. Within the home range are certain **core areas,** which may contain a concentration of food, a water hole, a good resting area, or sleeping trees. The core areas are used exclusively by a single troop, which spends more than 90 percent of its time within the two or three core areas that are found in its home range.

Baboons inhabit the savanna, which is essentially a dry grassland with scattered groups of trees. The primary food of the baboon is grass, which makes up about 90 percent of its diet during the dry season. This is supplemented by other vegetable matter such as seeds, flowers, and fruits. The baboon also consumes insects and some small reptiles and occasionally eats mammalian flesh.

Although food is easily found, the baboon must obtain much of this food on the ground, where danger from predators poses a real threat. The location of sleeping trees is extremely important for safety during sleeping hours, and the troop must reach the safety of these trees by nightfall. During the day, the troop depends upon the collective protection of the large males, and it relies to an extent on the alarm calls of other animals to warn it of the proximity of predators.

STRUCTURE OF THE BABOON TROOP
Within the baboon troop, several distinct classes of individuals can be identified. The age-sex categories, similar to those of the gelada, include infants, juveniles, subadult males, adult females, and adult males.

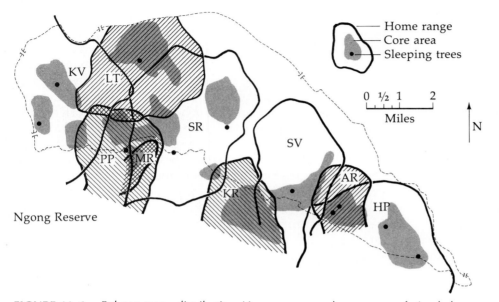

Boundary of Nairobi Park

Home range
Core area
Sleeping trees

0   ½   1   2
Miles

N

Ngong Reserve

FIGURE 11–6 *Baboon troop distribution.* Home ranges and core areas of nine baboon troops in Nairobi Park, Kenya. The troops vary in size from twelve to eighty-seven individuals, with home ranges varying from slightly over 5 to 40 square kilometers (2 to 15.5 square miles).

The adult males play an especially important role in baboon social life, for the troop is dependent upon them for protection when foraging in the open. The baboons show a greater degree of sexual dimorphism than do most other monkey species. The very long canine teeth of the male are deadly weapons even against the most powerful carnivores.

Figure 11–7 is a diagram of a typical baboon troop moving through the savanna. The largest, most dominant males are in the center of the troop, where they protect the juveniles and females, especially the females with young infants. Surrounding the troop are the less dominant males and the subadult males, who act as the first line of defense in the presence of a predator. In such situations, the adult males form a line of defense between the source of danger and the troop, thus allowing the troop to gain the safety of the trees. Few carnivores will bother to approach a line of alerted adult males.

The adult males are arranged in a **dominance hierarchy.** While this hierarchy is usually thought of as strictly linear, the relative ranks of the lower-ranking males are not always sharply defined. Also, a pair of males may form an alliance that permits the pair to occupy a position in the system at a higher level than either could occupy alone. The existence of a hierarchy makes it possible for several aggressive adult males to coexist within the same troop.

The most dominant males are usually in good physical condition. They appear to be confident and aggressive, and they are able to attract the support of other males. The most dominant males also seem to be the offspring of the highest-ranking females. The presence of a high-ranking mother enables a male offspring to intimidate other animals higher in rank than himself but lower in rank than the mother, who is quick to back up her young in a conflict situation. Also, the offspring of high-ranking mothers associate more closely with the dominant males than do other offspring.

Once formed, the hierarchy is stable although changes do occur, especially as members grow

FIGURE 11–7 *A baboon troop moving through a savanna.* When a troop is moving through the savanna, the dominant adult males are in the center of the troop, along with females and small infants and older infants. A group of young juveniles is seen below the center and older juveniles above. Other adult males and females lead and bring up the rear. Two estrus females (dark hindquarters) are in consort with adult males.

old and die. Young males entering the system simply cannot challenge the most dominant male for his position, for the dominant male is likely to be supported by other dominant males. Some high-ranking males are able to maintain their high rank even after they have become old and weak, with their canine teeth worn down to the gums.

Physical aggression is rare, and most aggression is expressed by gesturing rather than by actual fighting. Such agonistic behavior includes staring, raising the eyebrow to expose the distinctively colored eyelid, slapping the ground, or jerking the head back and forth. When you next visit the zoo and observe a baboon male "yawning," do not feel that he is bored or tired. He is probably displaying his canine teeth as a threat gesture directed toward you, the observer (Figure 11–8).

The dominance system operates in a variety of situations. A dominant male receives his preference of choice food and can monopolize sexually receptive females. A subordinate gives up his sitting place to a more dominant male, a behavior that is termed **displacement.** A subordinate male approaching a more dominant male will **present** his anal region to him and often will be **mounted** by him. The observer uses data on such behaviors as displacement, presenting, and mounting to gain a picture of the dominance system within the troop.

Adult females also form dominance hierarchies, although dominance interactions are not observed as often among females as they are among males. The rank of a female is determined largely by the rank of her mother, and she usually ranks just below her mother. The relative rank of a female baboon with respect to her mother, sisters, and daughters is more significant among females than among males since a female spends most of her time in the company of family members.

In contrast to females, subadult males leave the troop of their birth and migrate to other troops. These migrations often cover long distances and expose the young males to much danger. This is a major reason why males have a higher death rate than females. As a result, adult males in a given troop have all migrated in from other troops and do not form close kinship bonds as do females.

The relative position of a female varies somewhat depending on whether she is sexually receptive to the male or is associated with a young infant. These changes are related, in part, to the interest of the adult male in receptive females and the concern of the male about the safety of the young. Females in either situation find them-

FIGURE 11–8 *Threat gesture.* The canine display.

selves close to the dominant males, thus elevating their social rank in the troop. Also, other females show great interest in infants, and they present to or groom the mother in an attempt to come into close association with the infant.

SEXUAL RELATIONSHIPS The reproductive cycle in the baboon female is about 35 days long. At approximately the midpoint of the cycle, a mature ovum moves from the ovary to the fallopian tube; this event is called **ovulation.** If sperm are present in the female reproductive tract around the time of ovulation, conception may occur.

Sexual activity in most primates occurs only around the time of ovulation. This period of sexual receptivity is termed **estrus.** Since sexual behavior functions to ensure the presence of sperm in the female reproductive tract at the time when an ovum is available for fertilization, sexual activity is normally restricted to the estrus period.

During most of her life, the female baboon is not sexually receptive to the male. She is recep-

tive only during estrus, but estrus does not occur during pregnancy or **lactation** (nursing). In addition, sexual activity among many monkey species is restricted to a definite mating season, in which case no sexual activity may take place within a troop for many months of the year. It is therefore apparent that sexual activity is limited among baboons and may be absent for long periods of time.

Estrus in the savanna baboon is marked by certain physical and behavioral changes, and prominent among them is the swelling of the sexual skin (Figure 10–20). As the swelling enlarges, the female becomes receptive to the advances of the males. The swelling, in turn, serves as a signal to the males that the female is indeed in estrus. In most mammals, olfactory cues signal sexual receptivity. While this is true to a degree in primates, the prominence of a visual cue underscores the importance of vision to primates.

Early in a female's ovulation period, the more subordinate males make sexual advances; they are short in duration. As the female approaches the time of ovulation, she actively solicits sexual interest from the dominant males. The dominant male and female form a **consort pair,** and they remain together for several hours to several days. Since the dominant males are copulating around the time of ovulation, they probably will father most of the young.

GROUP COHESION Unlike many mammalian societies, most monkey troops are not held together by herding on the part of the males. The members of the troop appear to prefer to remain with the group of their birth, among familiar individuals with whom they have formed social bonds. Consequently, it is difficult to force a member to leave a troop or to introduce a new member into a troop.

Group cohesion appears to be based on the attraction of troop members to three categories of individuals: dominant males, infants, and old females. At rest, the dominant males are surrounded by females and young, who are attracted to their presence. This is especially true of very young animals and mothers of newborns. Infants also become focal points of troop interest. When a newborn appears in a troop, the female mem-

FIGURE 11–9 *Baboon friends.* Zena, an adult female, seen on the right, sleeps next to her best friend, Hector. These baboons are members of the Eburru Cliffs troop who live near the town of Gilgil, Kenya.

bers attempt to look at it and handle it and they pay a great deal of attention to the mother.

Lengthy studies of some monkey species have demonstrated a bond that exists between mothers and their adult daughters. A basic subunit of the troop is an old female with her grown daughters and their respective offspring. When the troop is at rest, the females settle down in **grooming clusters** that are composed of several closely related females. As we have seen in other species, grooming symbolizes a closeness between individual primates.

Other close relationships exist among baboons. Barbara Smuts has recognized friendships that occur between adult males and females among the olive baboons in Kenya.[9] Female baboons are wary around the larger adult males, yet females form friendships with specific males in which the relationship is quite different. An adult female is relaxed around her male friend and often grooms him (Figure 11–9). A male friend appears to protect both the female and her offspring from aggression from other animals. The male may carry the infant as a way of in-

hibiting aggression against himself on the part of other males. When in estrus, the female is more likely to form a consort pair with her friend, which means that the infant being protected is very likely to be his offspring.

Social Behavior of the Chimpanzee

Perhaps one of the most extensive studies of a primate population in its natural habitat is that of the chimpanzee, *Pan troglodytes*, in the Gombe Stream National Park in Uganda. Begun in 1960 by Jane Goodall, this study continues today.[10] Although chimpanzees normally inhabit dense forests, the more open forest of the park has made observation easier.

The chimpanzee is primarily arboreal. Its food is found principally in trees, and about 50 to 70 percent of the day is spent feeding and resting in trees. The animals sleep in trees, building new nests each evening. Yet most traveling between

---

[9]B. B. Smuts, *Sex and Friendship in Baboons* (New York: Aldine, 1985).

[10]J. van Lawick-Goodall, *In the Shadow of Man* (Boston: Houghton Mifflin, 1971); and J. Goodall, *The Chimpanzees of Gombe: Patterns of Behavior* (Cambridge, Mass.: Belknap Press, 1986); G. Goodall, "Gombe: Highlights and Current Research," in *Understanding Chimpanzees*, P. G. Heltne and L. A. Marquardt (eds.), (Cambridge, Mass: Harvard University Press, 1989), 2–21.

TABLE 11–2

STAGES IN THE LIFE OF CHIMPANZEES

STAGE	MALE	FEMALE
Infancy	0–5 years	0–5 years
Childhood	5–7 years	5–7 years
Adolescence	8–15 years	8–14 years
Maturity	16–33 years	14–33 years
Old age	33 years to death	33 years to

trees is done on the ground. Chimpanzees travel many miles each day, with the availability of food determining the length and direction of travel.

The diet of the chimpanzee is primarily vegetarian, including fruits, leaves, seeds, and bark. In addition, the animal occasionally eats insects, such as ants and termites, and sometimes hunts and eats meat. Six to seven hours each day are spent actively feeding.

FIGURE 11–10 *Chimpanzee social unit.* Fifi (left) a chimpanzee in Africa's Gombe Stream National Park, nuzzles her brother, Flint, while their mother, Flo, holds the baby.

CHIMPANZEE SOCIAL ORGANIZATION

Like that of the gibbon, gelada, and baboon, the life cycle of the chimpanzee can be divided into stages. The most notable difference between the life-cycle stages of chimpanzees and those of monkeys is that chimpanzees have a longer life span and mature more slowly. The stages in the life of chimpanzees are summarized in Table 11–2. Chimpanzees probably live into their fifties.

The chimpanzee social unit is an ever-changing association of individuals that is perhaps best described as a fission-fusion type of society. In contrast to the savanna baboon troop, with its relative day-to-day stability and constancy, the chimpanzee **community** consists of a series of small units whose membership is constantly changing. A community consists of individuals who occupy a particular range and who, in the course of a year, have some contact with one another. The size of the community varies depending on births, deaths, and migrations. In 1980 the Gombe Stream community consisted of forty-two individuals.

An individual chimpanzee may display a great deal of independence as he or she establishes new associations, sometimes on a day-by-day basis; or, on occasion, he or she may travel alone. The typical chimpanzee group usually contains five or fewer adults and adolescents in addition to juveniles and infants, but a number of different kinds of groups can form (Figure 11–10). The eight different kinds of groups are summarized in Table 11–3. Many variables are responsible for the changes in group composition, including the availability of food, the presence of infants, the number of estrus females, and the invasion of a home territory by neighbors.

SOCIAL RELATIONSHIPS AMONG THE CHIMPANZEES As with monkeys, social interactions between chimpanzee males can be described by the terms *dominance* and *submission*. Many instances of dominance interactions between two males have been described. For example, if two males go after the same fruit, the subordinate male holds back. Likewise, if a dominant male shows signs of aggression, the subordinate male responds with gestures of submis-

TABLE 11–3

COMPOSITION OF CHIMPANZEE
SOCIAL GROUPS

TYPES OF SOCIAL GROUPINGS	DESCRIPTION
All-male party	Two or more adult and/or subadult males
Family unit	Mother and her offspring
Nursery unit	Two or more family units; may include unrelated childless females
Mixed party	One or more adult or adolescent males with one or more adult or adolescent females, with or without offspring
Sexual party	Mixed party in which one or more females is in estrus
Consortship	One adult male with one adult female with or without offspring
Gathering	Group including at least half of the members of the community and at least half of the adult males
Lone individual	A single animal

sion, such as reaching out to touch the dominant animal and crouching. Although clear-cut dominance interactions do take place, a rigid dominance hierarchy, such as that found among baboons, does not exist.

Much of chimpanzee aggression takes the form of gesture and display, and one animal can achieve dominance over the others by the fierceness of his display activity. One such male, Mike, rose from the bottom of the ladder to the top by incorporating into his display some of Goodall's kerosene cans. He would hurl the cans in front of him as he charged the other males, and they would quickly get out of his way and respond with a submissive gesture. Goodall sees Mike's behavior as evidence of his superior intelligence relative to that of the other chimpanzees in his community.

Goodall and other researchers have discovered that adult male chimpanzees are usually more sociable (interactive) than adult females. In contrast to the baboons, it is the female chimpanzee that usually migrates from one community to another. Thus closely related males, often broth-

ers, form a close bond within the community in contrast to the females who often spend time alone with their offspring. Closely related males are more likely to travel and cooperate with one another.

Most male interactions are with other males. Goodall found that males groom each other about twice as long as males and females groom each other. Males also display their affinity for each other by holding and embracing one another much more than they hold and embrace females. Unlike human groups and some nonhuman primate groups, "male chimpanzees do not have long-lasting close relationships with particular females; their closest relationships are with other adult males."[11]

The female reproductive cycle is evidenced in the chimpanzee by the periodic swelling of the sexual skin. The female may initiate sexual contact, but generally sexual behavior is a consequence of male courtship displays. The male leaps into a tree and for about a minute swings from branch to branch with the hair of his head, shoulders, and arms erect. As the male approaches the female, she crouches down in front of him. Consort pairs are not always formed, and mating can be quite promiscuous.

The mother-infant bond is extremely close. At first, the infant is totally dependent upon its mother and is constantly held and carried by her. Later, the infant sits upright on her back and begins to move away from her. Mothers frequently play with their babies, and the babies' playmates also include other young and adult animals. After the infant stops riding on its mother's back, it associates more frequently with a play group (Figure 11–11). Play becomes less important when puberty is reached and the animal begins to enter adult life.

THE TERMITE STICK   The chimpanzee's practice of feeding upon termites is of special interest to students of human evolution, for the chim-

---

[11]R. C. Baily and R. Avunger, "Humans as Primates: The Social Relationships of Efe Pygmy Men in Comparative Perspective," *International Journal of Primatology*, 11 (1990), 141.

FIGURE 11–11
Chimpanzee young at play.

panzee manufactures and uses a tool for this purpose. At one time, anthropologists defined humans as *the* toolmaking animal. This definition has now been revised since chimpanzees and other animals have been observed deliberately manufacturing tools (see Box 11–3).

Termite feeding becomes an important activity at the beginning of the rainy season. For as many as nine weeks, chimpanzees spend one or two hours each day feeding on termites. This is the time when sexually mature termites grow wings in order to leave the termite mound to found new colonies. Passages within the mound are extended to its surface, but the openings to the outside are sealed over while the termites await ideal flying conditions.

The chimpanzee, upon locating a mound in this condition, scrapes away the thin seal over one of the passages. It then takes a **termite stick** and pokes it down the hole. After a moment, the tool is withdrawn with the termites hanging on it, ready to be licked off by the chimpanzee (Figure 11–12).

In manufacturing a termite stick, the chimpanzee pays attention to the choice of material

FIGURE 11–12 *The termite stick.* A 5-year-old chimpanzee uses a tool she made herself, by stripping down a blade of grass, to fish for insects in a termite mound.

BOX 11–3

THE DISCOVERY OF TOOLMAKING IN CHIMPANZEES

Jane Goodall describes the first observation of tool manufacture among the chimpanzees of the Gombe Stream National Park:

It was October and the short rains had begun. The blackened slopes were softened by feathery new grass shoots and in some places the ground was carpeted by a variety of flowers. The Chimpanzees' Spring, I called it. I had had a frustrating morning, tramping up and down three valleys with never a sign or sound of a chimpanzee. Hauling myself up the steep slope of Mlinda Valley I headed for the Peak, not only weary but soaking wet from crawling through dense undergrowth. Suddenly I stopped, for I saw a slight movement in the long grass about sixty yards away. Quickly focusing my binoculars I saw that it was a single chimpanzee, and just then he turned in my direction. I recognized David Greybeard.

Cautiously I moved around so that I could see what he was doing. He was squatting beside the red earth mound of a termite nest, and as I watched I saw him carefully push a long grass stem down into a hole in the mound. After a moment he withdrew it and picked something from the end with his mouth. I was too far away to make out what he was eating, but it was obvious that he was actually using a grass stem as a tool.

For an hour David feasted at the termite mound and then he wandered slowly away. When I was sure he had gone I went over to examine the mound. I found a few crushed insects strewn about, and a swarm of worker termites sealing the entrances of the nest passages into which David had obviously been poking his stems. I picked up one of his discarded tools and carefully pushed it into the hole myself. Immediately I felt the pull of several termites as they seized the grass, and when I pulled it out there were a number of worker termites and a few soldiers, with big red heads, clinging on with their mandibles. There they remained, sticking out at right angles to the stem with their legs waving in the air.

On the eighth day of my watch David Greybeard arrived again, to-

gether with Goliath, and the pair worked there for two hours. I could see much better: I observed how they scratched open the sealed-over passage entrances with a thumb or forefinger. I watched how they bit the ends off their tools when they became bent, or used the other end, or discarded them in favor of new ones. Goliath once moved at least fifteen yards from the heap to select a firm-looking piece of vine, and both males often picked three or four stems while they were collecting tools, and put the spares beside them on the ground until they wanted them.

Most exciting of all, on several occasions they picked small leafy twigs and prepared them for use by stripping off the leaves. This was the first recorded example of a wild animal not merely *using* an object as a tool, but actually modifying an object and thus showing the crude beginnings of tool*making*.[1]

[1]Excerpt from *In the Shadow of Man* by Jane van Lawick-Goodall. Copyright © 1971 by Hugo and Jane van Lawick-Goodall. Reprinted by permission of Houghton Mifflin Company. All rights reserved.

and the nature of the tool. The termite stick is fashioned from a grass stalk, twig, or vine, and it is usually less than 30.5 centimeters (12 inches) long. If a twig is too long to use, the chimpanzee breaks it to the right length. If a twig or vine is leafy, the animal strips it of its leaves before using it.

Young chimpanzees do not appear to have an interest in collecting termites. Goodall reports that while a mother chimpanzee spends hours termiting, the young become impatient and attempt to get her to leave. The art of termiting and termite-stick making is learned. When young chimpanzees begin to show an interest, their first termite sticks are poorly made. They

have difficulty inserting the stick into the hole and withdrawing it without losing the termites hanging on to it. Through watching their mothers, the young chimpanzees learn, although some are better students than others and are able to make better tools.

Goodall and others describe other examples of tool manufacture. For example, a chimpanzee will make a sponge by chewing a leaf and then use it to take up water. One chimpanzee was observed making a series of different tools to extract honey from a dead stump.

Many natural objects are used as tools: sticks as clubs, rocks as missiles, and leaves as towels. Nevertheless, although chimpanzees, like people, do

FIGURE 11–13 *Chimpanzee eating meat.* Adult male chimpanzee (hair wet from rainstorm) dismantles and eats a juvenile baboon carcass.

make tools in the wild, their inventory of tools does not even begin to approach the complexity of human technology or the degree of human dependence upon tools for survival.

CHIMPANZEES AS HUNTERS   Unlike most primates, chimpanzees eat meat. Chimpanzees have been observed killing and eating a variety of animals, including bushbucks, bushpigs, rodents, and young and adult monkeys, such as the baboon and the red colobus monkey (Figure 11–13). Cannibalism and the attacking of human infants have also been reported. While chimpanzees may simply surprise an animal in the

undergrowth and then kill and eat it, they also appear to hunt animals deliberately for food.

The decision to hunt is often triggered by the distress call of a young baboon, and a spontaneous kill frequently leads to more purposeful activity. Hunting is most often a male activity in which several males cooperate in trapping the animal. The prey is killed by slamming it against a tree or the ground, by crushing its skull between their teeth, or simply by tearing it apart.

After the kill, other chimpanzees arrive to share the meat. They form temporary groupings called **sharing clusters,** and most members of a cluster eat some of the prey. Observations show

BOX 11–4

THE SEXUAL BEHAVIOR OF THE BONOBO

The bonobo *(Pan paniscus)* lives in a small dense tropical forest in Zaire south of the Congo River. As early as 1929, the bonobo population had been reduced by the hunting practices of local peoples. Today, few natural groups exist, and even fewer captive populations are available for study. Beginning in the 1970s, considerable research has been carried out on the remaining wild populations.

The social behavior of this ape differs in many ways from that of the common chimpanzee and bears some interesting resemblances to human behavior. They

Two adult female bonobos in a typical genitogenital rubbing position.

live in communities of about fifty animals, but they spend most of their time in smaller groups of two to ten individuals. Compared with chimpanzees, the bonobos are more social, more peaceful, and spend more of their time in groups.

Bonobo sexual behavior shows some features that are not found in other apes. Bonobos mate face to face (ventroventral) about a quarter of the time. This copulatory position is not found among chimpanzees and is rare among mammals in general; it is found primarily among whales, porpoises, and humans. Female bonobos exhibit a prolonged period of sexual receptivity, with copulations occurring during early phases of the estrus cycle.

Among chimpanzees males usually initiate sexual behavior; among the bonobos males and females initiate sexual behavior in an egalitarian manner. Finally, investigators have observed behavior, primarily among females, that has been labeled "homosexual" behavior. The behavior observed is described as genitogenital rubbing and is usually seen during feeding sessions or before or after heterosexual mating by one or both of the females.

References: B. G. Blout, "Issues in Bonobo *(Pan paniscus)* Sexual Behavior, " *American Anthropologist,* 92 (1990), 702–714; T. Kano, "The Bonobo's Peaceable Kingdom," *Natural History* (November 1990), 62–70; and R. L. Susman (ed.), *The Pygmy Chimpanzee* (New York: Plenum, 1984).

that the time spent in eating the meat varies from 1 hour and 40 minutes to more than 9 hours.

Some individuals, especially subadults and adult females, simply pick up pieces of meat that have been dropped by other individuals. Other animals tear off a section of a larger piece being consumed by another animal, usually a female. Often a particular animal requests meat by the characteristic gesture of holding a hand, open and palm up, under the possessor's chin while making characteristic vocalizations. Any chimpanzee may make such a request, but it is more often ignored than rewarded.

The head seems to be the choicest part of the kill by chimpanzee standards. The animals enlarge the foramen magnum (the large hole in the base of the skull) with their teeth and fingers to get at the brain. They eat the soft tissue together with leaves.

Summary

We have just examined some aspects of the social behavior of four primate species: the gibbon, the gelada, the savanna baboon, and the chimpanzee. None of these species is typical, for each represents its own set of adaptations and adjustments to the environments in which it lives. Yet certain themes of behavior emerge from our studies. For example, agonistic behavior appears to be characteristic of each of our groups. In multimale groups, male dominance hierarchies tend to form, yet most dominance behavior is expressed by gesturing rather than actual fighting. Grooming behavior occurs frequently among primates as an expression of close social ties. The protection and care of the infant by the mother and other adults of the social unit also appears to be a universal theme of primate social behavior.

STUDY QUESTIONS

1. Describe some of the different kinds of social groups found among primates.
2. What is grooming behavior? How does grooming affect the social relationships of the members of a primate group?
3. Gelada society is organized into a hierarchy of groups. Describe this organization and explain how it relates to changes in the environment.
4. Compare the use of space by the savanna baboon troop with that by the gibbon group. What differences in their habitats would help explain differences in their use of space?
5. Baboon troops are relatively stable and peaceful. Ingroup fighting is rare. How does the existence of the dominance hierarchy promote the stability of the group?
6. Periods of sexual activity in primates are usually limited. Describe the sexual cycle of a female monkey and discuss how the period of receptivity in the female affects the social unit.
7. What is meant by a fission-fusion type of social organization? Describe the various types of social groups found among chimpanzees.
8. In the context of hunting, chimpanzees exhibit several behavioral traits that are usually not encountered in other social activities. What are some of these traits?

SUGGESTED READINGS

Erwin, J., T. L. Marple, and G. Mitchell (eds.). *Captivity and Behavior: Primates in Breeding Colonies, Laboratories, and Zoos.* New York: Van Nostrand Reinhold, 1979. This book is a compilation of several studies of primates in nonnatural situations.

Goodall, J. *The Chimpanzees of Gombe: Patterns of Behavior.* Cambridge, Mass.: Belknap Press, 1986. This book brings together the data gathered from over two decades of research on the chimpanzees of the Gombe.

Hamburg, D. A., and E. R. McCown (eds.). *The Great Apes.* Menlo Park, Calif.: Benjamin/Cummings, 1979. This book contains thirty-one papers on field studies of the great apes.

Heltne, P. G., and L. A. Marquardt (eds.). *Understanding Chimpanzees.* Cambridge, Mass.: Harvard University Press, 1989. This volume includes thirty-three papers on chimpanzees.

Jolly, A. *The Evolution of Primate Behavior,* 2d ed. New York: Macmillan, 1985. This is an excellent introduction to the general topic of primate behavior.

Peterson, D., and J. Goodall. *Visions of Caliban.* Boston: Houghton Mifflin, 1993. Written for a general audience, this volume discusses chimpanzee behavior and the relationship between humans and chimpanzees.

Richard, A. F. *Primates in Nature.* New York: Freeman, 1985. This is an excellent introduction to the general topic of primate behavior. The author also discusses primate distribution, diet, and communication.

Smuts, B. B., D. L. Cheney, R. M. Seyfarth, R. W. Wrangham, and T. T. Struhsaker. *Primate Societies.* Chicago: University of Chicago Press, 1987. This is a collection of papers covering a variety of topics including primate socioecology, communication, and intelligence.

van Lawick-Goodall, J. *In the Shadow of Man.* Boston: Houghton Mifflin, 1971. This is a nontechnical discussion of the behavior of chimpanzees and the early experiences of Jane Goodall in the field.

Anthropological field work in the South Pacific.

The human condition has led to an open adaptive system based on culture. Culture may have its own set of biological restraints. Mental patterns may be partially shaped by genes, but these can only set the outer limit on the range of possible human behavior. Actual behavior, in specific conditions, can never be understood without an understanding of the cultural and historical process that shapes it. The nature of human nature is essentially cultural.[1]

Alexander Alland, Jr.

[1]A. Alland, Jr., *To Be Human* (New York: Wiley, 1980), 621–622.

CHAPTER 12

HUMAN BEHAVIOR IN PERSPECTIVE

Many anthropologists have studied the structure of nonhuman primate society for clues to the origins of human society. They have assumed that human societies were derived from social systems similar to those of the living monkeys and apes. Yet the social systems of modern nonhuman primates also have been developing through the millennia, and so they do not necessarily represent ancestral patterns. Comparative studies of all behavioral systems can provide us with new insights as to the limits and possibilities of human behavior.

THE HUMAN BAND

Most humans today live in farming and industrial societies. Yet farming is a recent human development, probably no older than 13,000 years, and industrialism is a product of the eighteenth century. Anthropologists turn to contemporary societies that practice a foraging (hunting-gathering) strategy when they are comparing humans with other animal societies.

All contemporary foraging societies have been affected by technologically more advanced peoples. In recent centuries foragers have lived essentially in marginal areas, where farming is not practical. Today these societies are rapidly changing as they come increasingly under the influence of neighboring agricultural or industrial peoples. Most of the data for our comparisons come from the many anthropological studies of hunter-gatherers conducted during the first half of the present century.

The Structure of the Human Band

The basic social unit of foraging peoples is the **band,** which typically contains about thirty-five to fifty members. Bands can be much larger, however, and band membership is often quite variable. Small bands may join into larger, multiband units when food is plentiful.

Like the monkey troop and the chimpanzee community, the human band consists of many males and females—adults, subadults, juveniles, and infants. In contrast to the nonhuman primate societies we have surveyed, the adult members of the human band are, for the most part, involved in exclusive male-female relationships. The gibbon social unit consists of a single male and female with their immature offspring, but a third adult normally is not tolerated; within the human band, several male-female partnerships coexist.

Among the many factors related to permanent male-female bonding is the fact that human sexuality does not appear to be cyclic, as it is in most mammals. Human females do not exhibit any conspicuous physical indication of estrus, such as the swelling of the sexual skin in baboons and chimpanzees. Human females also are potentially receptive to the male at all phases of their reproductive cycle.

The lack of a clearly defined estrus in humans may be related to the development of bonds of cooperation among the males of the band and the lessening of male-male competition over estrus females. Since all females are potentially receptive throughout the year, males do not need to compete for the few females in the band who are near the time of ovulation. Specific factors regulating receptivity and male interest are usually cultural.

Monkey troops and chimpanzee communities are, to a large degree, closed units. Relationships with adjacent groups are often hostile. Chimpanzee males from one community have been observed attacking and killing members of a neighboring community. Animals of one sex born into a particular troop often remain with that troop for their entire lives and form close bonds with siblings of the same sex. Adolescent animals, male baboons and female chimpanzees, for example, leave the society of their birth and migrate to other units. Once the animal has left the unit of its birth, it no longer has any social relationships with its parents or siblings.

Human bands are similar to baboon troops and chimpanzee communities in that members of one sex, usually females in foraging societies, leave the group of their birth and join—in the case of humans marry into—a neighboring group (Figure 12–1). What is different with humans is that although individuals leave the band of their birth, they maintain close ties throughout their lives with relatives in their natal band as well as other bands. Thus an adult woman, for example, lives in a band with her husband and children and maintains close relationships with the band of her parents and brothers, the band of her sister and her sister's husband, the band of her daughter and her husband, and so on. She visits these other bands and even lives in another band for a period of time. As a result, important social and economic relationships are formed between these bands. Kinship is the basic means of social organization, with the relationships of the family extended throughout the society.

The extent of territoriality among hunter-gatherers varies. In many parts of the world, these people do not look upon an area of land as

FIGURE 12–1 *San family.*

something owned by a particular group, although locations such as particular water holes and sacred areas are often traditionally regarded as being within the realm of a group. In the case of a water hole, other groups show their courtesy by asking permission to use it, and this permission is seldom refused. Warfare as we know it in agricultural and industrial societies does not occur among hunter-gatherers, but formalized skirmishes or feuds do occur. The motivation for these is usually a belief that a death in one group was caused by the sorcery of a member of another. The victim's group may engage the suspected sorcerer's group and kill or injure one or a few people for revenge.

Hominids as Hunters

Humans are primarily omnivores. Although different societies emphasize different foods, humans eat a variety of animal and vegetable material. What a society considers edible or inedible is defined by its culture.

The significance of meat eating varies from society to society, and some societies do not include mammalian flesh on their menu. Yet foraging societies appear to emphasize meat as an important source of sustenance and hunting as an important social activity. Some anthropologists view "man the hunter" as the key to understanding human evolution. The hunting activities of contemporary foragers are projected back to prehistoric times. Hunting becomes the main explanation for the evolution of manual dexterity, erect bipedalism, the human brain, and culture.

Predatory activity is rare in primates. Many primates consume insects, birds, small reptiles, and small mammals, but only three primates— baboons, chimpanzees, and humans—have been observed eating the flesh of medium to large mammals. Although baboons and chimpanzees deliberately hunt, hunting is a minor activity in terms of the total diet and social behavior. For example, a group of chimpanzees living in Tanzania consumed 3 kilograms (6.6 pounds) of meat per offspring, 8 kilograms (17.6 pounds) of meat per female, and 25 kilograms (55 pounds) of meat per male in an average year.[2]

THE SOCIAL CARNIVORES   In 1969 George Schaller and Gordon Lowther proposed that social systems are determined to a large extent by ecological conditions.[3] Schaller and Lowther note that in many respects human society bears a closer resemblance to that of the social carnivores, such as lions, tigers, and wild dogs, than to that of the apes. As an example, we can explore the social behavior of wild dogs in east Africa.[4]

Wild dogs live in packs containing an average of five to seven adults, with more adult males than adult females. These packs range over large areas following the migratory herds that are their prey.

The pack usually hunts at dusk and dawn, stalking a herd of animals such as gazelles, their most frequent prey. When the herd becomes aware of the pack and begins to flee, the pack begins the chase. The leader chooses the prey, usually the slowest animal, and the rest of the pack follows its lead. Even if another potential victim crosses the path of a pack member, it continues to chase the victim chosen by the leader. Members of the pack intercept the prey when it changes its course, and in this way the pack acts as a cooperative unit.

The chase usually lasts from 3 to 5 minutes, covering 1.6 to 3.2 kilometers (1 to 2 miles). The prey, when overtaken, is exhausted and often stunned, and it is immediately killed. Pack members literally tear the body apart, and they swallow the meat in large pieces within a very short time. Over 85 percent of the chases are successful.

The dog pack stalks a herd and then chases down the prey. The lion patiently waits, hiding in the grass near a water hole, for a prey animal to come to drink. Human hunting techniques are quite different. While humans can run down small animals, such as young gazelles, their basic method of hunting is to get close to an animal and to wound it. Only rarely do humans kill an animal outright; they may spend several hours or even several days catching up with the fleeing and wounded prey. Unlike the carnivores, humans can maintain a steady pace, walking for most of the day and covering many miles as they follow the wounded animal. Of course, people also can construct a variety of traps so that they need not even be present when an animal is caught. Wounding, butchering, and sometimes transporting meat all involve the use of tools.

HUNTING AND SOCIAL BEHAVIOR   In many ways the social behavior of humans more closely resembles that of wild dogs than that of chimpanzees. For example, chimpanzees construct new nests each night in different sleeping trees. Wild dogs establish **home bases,** at least during the 3 months before the pups are old enough to follow the migratory herds. When the pack goes hunting, a guard, which may be either a male or a female, is left behind. When the pack members return from the hunt with pieces of unchewed meat in their stomachs, the hunters disgorge some meat in response to a begging gesture. Thus the guard and the pups can share in the kill (Figure 12–2).

As we have seen, human hunter-gatherers also establish home bases. Human groups move their home bases periodically, but normally a specific camp serves as a home base for several months. Unlike a pack of wild dogs, a human group is likely to have infants present at all times of the year.

Among humans hunting is almost always a male activity. The female, who is primarily responsible for the care of infants, gathers wild vegetable food and may also fish or aid in the hunt.

[2]R. W. Wrangham and E. van Z. B. Riss, "Rates of Predation on Mammals by Gombe Chimpanzees, 1972–1975" *Primates*, 31 (1990), 167.

[3]G. B. Schaller and G. R. Lowther, "The Relevance of Carnivore Behavior to the Study of Early Hominids," *Southwestern Journal of Anthropology*, 25 (1969), 307–341.

[4]R. D. Estes and J. Goddard, "Prey Selection and Hunting Behavior of the African Wild Dog," *Journal of Wildlife Management*, 31 (1967), 52–70; W. Kühme, "Communal Food Distribution and Division of Labor in African Wild Dogs," *Nature*, 205 (1965), 443–444; and D. G. Kleiman and J. F. Eisenberg, "Comparisons of Canid and Felid Social Systems from an Evolutionary Perspective," *Animal Behavior*, 21 (1973), 637–659.

FIGURE 12–2   *Wild dogs, Tanzania.* Female (not the mother) regurgitates meat to pups.

Among most hunter-gatherers the female contributes the bulk of the food by weight, but the male provides the more culturally valued food, meat. A general **sexual division of labor** appears to characterize all human societies, although the distinction between male and female activities may be vague in some (Figure 12–3). In modern industrial societies, this distinction has lessened considerably.

Just as the hunting dog brings meat to the home base and shares it with the guards and pups, **food sharing** is an important aspect of human social behavior. A factor related to food sharing is the highly portable nature of meat, although humans also transport vegetable food. (Perhaps tools for the transport of food, such as baskets, were among the earliest tools manufac-

tured by hominids.) It would be difficult for a herbivore to transport a quantity of grass or for a chimpanzee to transport a large amount of leaves or fruit; but meat, which is pound for pound higher in nutritional value than vegetable food, can be transported with little difficulty. A chimpanzee can carry a dead animal in its hand or drag a carcass along the ground; a wild dog can transport meat in its stomach; a human can simply fling a carcass over his or her back or cut it into several large pieces, or transport the meat in a container.

Once back at the home base, humans can share with one another the results of their hunting and gathering activities. Food sharing is a significant feature of the human band, but males and females do not contribute in the same way

FIGURE 12–3   *San hunters and gatherers.* Two San men carry home palm hearts.

to the food supply. The males and females complement each other with their varied contributions to the food supply.

Children and elders can make up as much as half of the population of the band. Sharing acts as an effective method of ensuring "social security" that goes beyond the immediate family to include all the members of the band. The hunter who is having bad luck can obtain meat from a successful hunter, who will be repaid when the situation is reversed. Those too old to hunt not only are supported by the younger band members but also are valued for their experience and knowledge.

In human groups, sharing goes well beyond food and often includes tools, weapons, and labor. Most important, though, is the sharing of knowledge. If a hunter discovers a new method of trapping prey or a better way of making a tool, he does not keep it secret, for the greater the sum of knowledge in the society, the greater the po-

tential for that society's survival. The sharing of knowledge is the basis for all technological advancement.

The monkey troop is characterized by a general absence of food sharing. Except for the nursing of infants, each animal obtains its own food supply. Males and females are essentially equal in their abilities to obtain food, but the males monopolize choice foods that are scarce. Chimpanzees occasionally share food; interestingly, meat is the food they most often share.

SOCIAL BEHAVIOR IN HUNTING BANDS
Dominance is a recurrent feature of male-male and female-female social relationships among nonhuman primates. In the human band the typical nature of male-male and female-female relationships is generally egalitarian. Although individuals, usually males, may be considered leaders because of their skills and leadership abilities, hunting and gathering societies are charac-

terized by cooperation and the absence of strict hierarchical systems. This cooperation is essential for successful hunting-gathering. Power hierarchies and class systems are not inherent in human society.

Among wild dogs the females form a linear hierarchy during the breeding season. Although one male usually dominates, males are generally not ranked. Normally, only the dominant male and dominant female mate. The dominant female prevents other females from mating through aggressive behavior, and if another female should give birth, her pups are killed. Therefore, usually only a single litter of six or seven pups is produced. Some biologists suggest that producing only one litter per pack minimizes the time that must be spent near a den.

Cooperation on the hunt and the lack of a dominance hierarchy characterize human hunting-gathering societies. Efficient hunting demands cooperation, and a dominance system is not consistent with food sharing. Among the baboons, meat is monopolized by the dominant males, whereas chimpanzees not only cooperate in hunting but often share the kill. Wild dogs, too, cooperate in hunting and share food, although they show a dominance hierarchy with respect to mating. Usually, dominance systems do not develop within human hunting-gathering groups, although leadership patterns do appear. Leadership is based primarily upon skill, and the leader usually has no coercive power, simply the influence that comes from respect.

Other Hypotheses on the Origins and Nature of Human Societies

WOMAN THE GATHERER   Not all anthropologists agree that hunting was the primary factor in the development of hominid society. They note that when the sources of the diet are accurately noted and weighed, women often provide the bulk of the calories. For example, in one study over a 28-day period, Richard Lee notes that among the !Kung San of South Africa women provide 57 percent of the calories and men provide another 13 percent *through gather-*

FIGURE 12–4   *San hunters and gatherers.* San women gathering.

ing; only 30 percent of the calories came from the hunt (Figure 12–4).[5]

Unlike gathering, hunting is not predictable. Dean Falk comments:

> In modern hunting and gathering societies that live in habitats similar to those of early hominids, the men may go hunting, but, on a day-to-day basis, it is the women who end up providing most of the nourishment for the entire group. While *he* is out trying his luck at hunting, *she* (often accompanied by children) collects the more widely available plant food, insects, and small animals. She ensures that neither her children nor her hunter will go hungry tonight![6]

[5]R. B. Lee, *The !Kung San* (Cambridge, Mass.: Cambridge, University Press, 1979), 262.
[6]From *Braindance* by Dean Falk. Copyright ©1992 by Dean Falk. Reprinted by permission of Henry Holt and Co., Inc.

Another criticism of the carnivore model is that careful analyses of the bone remains suggest that early hominids were not necessarily hunters but were very likely scavengers instead.

REPRODUCTIVE STRATEGIES AND THE ORIGINS OF HUMAN SOCIETY   Owen Lovejoy believes that the key to understanding the development of early hominid society lies in an understanding of reproductive strategies.[7] In nonvertebrate forms a female produces an enormous quantity of ova, but she gives the ova little or no care. Only a few offspring survive to adulthood from millions of ova.

In the mammals, and especially in the primates, far fewer offspring are produced, but with increasing parental care the probability of survival of each individual offspring becomes very great. Thus, instead of spending reproductive energy to produce numerous progeny, primates devote much of their reproductive energy to caring for a small number of offspring. This increases the odds of surviving to adulthood. This is seen in single rather than multiple births and the long interval between successive births. The child is helpless at birth and requires a fairly long childhood to learn the behaviors required for survival in adulthood.

This reproductive strategy, however, can lead to a situation in which the population declines in size and becomes in danger of extinction because of an inadequate birthrate. There has been a steady decline in the ape populations over the centuries. The average female chimpanzee produces one offspring every 5.6 years. She does not reach sexual maturity until 10 years of age. This means that she must live until 21 years of age if she is to produce two offspring to replace her and her mate. However, there are many biological and environmental factors which may prevent this from happening.

A chimpanzee mother must forage for food in trees. Movement in the trees creates dangerous situations during which an infant may fall; this is a major cause of infant mortality. Since the chid must be carried, the mother is not able to carry two young offspring at the same time; this is related to the long interval between successive births.

Lovejoy postulates that a solution to these problems developed among the earliest hominids through a partial separation of the feeding ranges of the males and females. The males exploited a much larger range, being unrestricted by the presence of a young infant. With less competition from the male, the female confined her foraging to a much smaller area. Less mobility resulted in a lowered accident rate and permitted an increase in parenting behavior.

Besides the necessity of obtaining an adequate food supply, male access to the female is necessary for reproductive purposes. A system by which the male was associated exclusively with a single female provided a system where the male was guaranteed access to a female. This decreased competition with other males, while at the same time the male did not compete with the female and offspring for food supplies.

According to Lovejoy's hypothesis, the next step was the collection of distant food by the male who transported the food to the female and her offspring. The mother spent more time caring for the offspring and could take care of more than one immature offspring at a time (Figure 12–5). This reduced the time between successive births. The total birth and survival rates increased. All of this benefited the male, who increased the probability of his genes being represented in the next generation. Habitual erect bipedalism allowed the male to carry food more efficiently with his hands. Lovejoy believes that the earliest tools made were devices for carrying food.

Once this stage had been reached, other features that characterize human social organization emerged. For example, the loss of the outward signs of estrus and continual sexual receptivity on the part of the female increased the intensity of the male-female bond. Increased participation of the male in parenting led to development of the nuclear family.

This model, however, has not found universal acceptance. Direct evidence of early hominid be-

[7]C. O. Lovejoy, "The Origin of Man," *Science*, 211 (1981), 341–350; C. O. Lovejoy, "Modeling Human Origins: Are We Sexy Because We're Smart, or Smart Because We're Sexy?" in D. T. Rasmussen (ed.), *The Origin and Evolution of Humans and Humanness* (Boston: Jones and Bartlett, 1993), 1–28.

FIGURE 12–5 *San mother and children.*

havior is practically nonexistent. While anthropologists may develop hypotheses using data from a variety of sources, our knowledge of what really occurred is strictly limited.

Summary

For a significant part of human evolution, people lived as foragers. The present human condition was shaped, in part, by evolutionary forces acting on hunting-gathering groups. The basic social unit of foragers is the nomadic band, which consists of adult males and females, subadults, juveniles, and infants. Bands, as well as other human social arrangements such as tribes and states, are characterized by exclusive long-term male-female relationships and a sexual division of labor. Human societies are most often outbreeding, which functions to establish or maintain social and economic relationships between bands. Kinship links within and between bands are the primary means of social organization in band society. The degree of territoriality and intragroup

fighting varies in different hunting-gathering societies. However, the concept of private ownership of land or warfare over territory is foreign to foragers. The motivation for feuds is often one group's accusations of sorcery leveled against another group.

Humans are omnivorous; however, meat is usually considered to be a more culturally valued food than plant material. Humans use a variety of methods to hunt, including wounding an animal and then "running down" the injured prey. The meat, as well as gathered vegetable materials, is brought back to a home base where the food is shared. Although food sharing occurs in a variety of nonhuman species in the animal kingdom, sharing is rare in primates.

The social structure of humans includes many features of nonhuman primate social groups, but in many other ways human societies resemble those of the social carnivores. Social carnivores share food, cooperate in hunting, and show other similarities to human hunters. Various models of the origin of human society have been proposed. Some see human society evolving along parallel lines with carnivore society, some see great significance in the gathering activities of women, while others see human reproductive biology and behavior as the prime factor.

COMMUNICATION

In his book *Language, Thought and Reality*, the linguist Benjamin Lee Whorf claims, "Speech is the best show man puts on."[8] Indeed, anthropologists consider language to be such an important aspect of our nature that an entire branch of anthropology, **linguistics,** is devoted to its description and analysis. The understanding of linguistic behavior is important to the anthropologist's understanding of human adaptations and adaptability.

Language is but one means of communication. **Communication** is a very general term that, in its broadest application, simply means that some

---

[8]B. L. Whorf, in J. B. Carroll (ed.), *Language, Thought and Reality: Selected Writings of Benjamin Lee Whorf* (Cambridge, Mass., and New York: Technology Press and Wiley, 1956), 249.

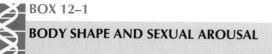

BOX 12–1

BODY SHAPE AND SEXUAL AROUSAL

For years investigators who study nonverbal communication have pointed out that differences in male and female anatomy act as signals that initiate sexual arousal in the opposite sex. Anthropologists Frederick S. Szalay and Robert K. Costello have an idea about how this dimorphism evolved and how it is related to sexual signals in contemporary nonhuman primates.

Sexual dimorphism in modern hominids is not restricted to size differences. For instance, the dissimilarity in fat distribution in human males and females is very

great compared to other animals. Szalay and Costello argue that the human female's hairless fatty buttocks and breasts act as a signal that sexually arouses males in a way that is similar to the hairless and swollen sexual skin in many nonhuman primate females, such as chimpanzees and baboons. The temporary swelling of the sexual skin in nonhuman primates is related to the estrus cycle and attracts the male only when the female is in estrus. The permanently large buttocks and breasts of human females allow for sexual arousal of the human male at any time.

Szalay and Costello suggest that this human female characteristic, which they call a **permanent estrus display,** evolved along with and as a consequence of bipedalism. They hypothesize that the periodic perineal swelling of quadrupeds would not be effective as a sexual signal in bipedal animals. (The perineal area includes the anus and vulva.) Instead, as quadrupeds, seen in the figure (bottom right), evolved through intermediates (center left and top) into fully bipedal hominids (top right), labial swelling during estrus was replaced by anatomical mimicry. This mimicry involves fat deposits in the hips, thighs, and breasts.

Reference: F. S. Szalay and R. K. Costello, "Evolution of Permanent Estrus Displays in Hominids." *Journal of Human Evolution,* 20 (1991), 439–464.

stimulus or message is transmitted and received. On more specific levels, communication means different things to the physicist, mathematician, engineer, and behavioral scientist. We are concerned with its usage in relation to animals; in this context, communication means that one animal transmits information to another animal. This information can simply convey the presence of the animal, or it can indicate such things as dominance, fear, hunger, or sexual receptiveness. Communication does not necessarily imply thought, but as neurological complexity evolves, so do the methods, mechanisms, and potential of communication.

Methods of Primate Communication

Social animals are constantly communicating with one another; even the spatial positions they assume in relation to one another can be forms of communication. Primates communicate through olfactory, tactile, visual, and auditory signals.

Compared with other mammals, the primates, in general, have a reduced olfactory sense. The sense of smell is much more important to prosimians and New World monkeys than to Old World monkeys and apes. Some prosimians, such as the ring-tailed lemur, have specialized scent glands that excrete odoriferous substances. The animal uses this material, along with urine and feces, to mark off territory. Many of the New World monkeys use the olfactory sense also and, like prosimians, have permanent scent glands.

Although the sense of smell is less important in Old World monkeys and apes, it still serves as a means of communication. Male rhesus monkeys, for example, recognize an estrus female by specific odors originating in the vagina. The great emphasis on deodorants and perfumes indicates the role played by olfactory signals in human communication.

The tactile sense is likewise important in primates, and they spend long periods of time touching one another. Grooming, for example, functions not only to remove dirt and parasites from the fur but to communicate affection. Grooming is found among all categories of individuals: between adult males, between a male and an estrus female, and between a female and

her infant. The close physical contact between a mother and her infant appears to be essential for the normal development of the individual.

Visual communication is of great importance to primates. The positioning of animals in relationship to one another convey information about dominance, feeding, sexual behavior, and attitude, and general body posture can signal tension or relaxation. Motivational researchers have concluded that a political candidate, newscaster, or other person talking to a large group should stand slightly sideways rather than face directly ahead. The latter position, supposedly taken as a dominance display, is said to make an audience nervous.

In addition to the positioning of the body, facial gestures are used extensively among primates to convey information. Various examples of gestures were given in the discussion of the social behavior of the baboon in Chapter 11.

VOCAL COMMUNICATION One thing is certain: primates, including people, do not have to open their mouths to communicate a wide range of information. Many primate sounds are nonvocal. For instance, the gorilla beats its chest, shakes branches, or strikes the ground to communicate frustration. Likewise, a bit of silence is often as meaningful as noise itself and often indicates danger. Anyone who has been to a zoo, however, and heard the vocalizations of the siamangs, or, for that matter, anyone who has visited a schoolyard knows that primates not only vocalize but do so with a great deal of noise. Some arboreal monkeys and apes are among the loudest and most vocal of mammals.

Nonhuman primates produce a number of vocalized sounds. In prosimians and some monkeys, these sounds tend to be **discrete.** A discrete signal is one that does not blend with other signals; it is individually distinct. Anthropoids also produce some discrete calls, but other calls grade into one another, forming a **call system.** This blending makes it difficult to estimate the number of calls, or specific messages, produced, but the number of calls for most species seems to average between ten and twenty.

Although the meaning of different sounds varies a great deal from one species to another, some generalizations can be made. Barking sounds serve as alarm signals among gorillas, chimpanzees, baboons, rhesus monkeys, and langurs. Screeching and screaming sounds often signal distress; growling indicates annoyance. Animals produce different types of grunts while moving around, seemingly to maintain contact between the animals in a group.

One animal can produce sounds that direct the attention of another toward specific objects. Other sounds convey quantitative information, specify a particular type of behavior that should be used, or initiate a whole sequence of related behaviors. Primates also have a great ability to inform one another about their moods at particular moments through subtle changes in their vocalizations.

LANGUAGE   Nonhuman animals, especially other primates, share many of the features of human language. Nevertheless, several characteristics of language are, as far as we know, unique. Other features are developed to a higher degree in human language than in any other communication system.

Human language is both **open** and discrete. Openness refers to the expansionary nature of language, which enables people to coin new labels for new concepts and objects. The hunter-gatherer who sees an airplane for the first time can attach a designation to it; in the same manner, a biologist who discovers a new species can give it a name.

Most nonhuman primate signals are not discrete. The gibbon who is content one moment and frightened the next simply grades one call into the next. Recently, research has shown that a limited number of nonhuman anthropoid signals do seem to be discrete, such as the two very acoustically different alarm calls of vervet monkeys, one that signals the initial approach of a neighboring group and another that signals a more aggressive approach (Figure 12–6). However, all the messages of language are discrete. Through language, the human can say, "I am content" or "I am frightened," delivering a distinct message that never blends with any other message.

The discrete units of language are **arbitrary.** A word, for example, has no real connection to the thing it refers to. There is nothing about a pen that is suggested by the sound "pen." If we all agreed, a pen could be called a "table." Even though the potential for sound formation is innate, the meanings of the arbitrary elements of a language must be learned.

One of the most important and useful things about human language is **displacement,** which is the ability to communicate about events at times and places distant from those of their occurrence. Displacement enables a person to talk and think about things not directly in front of him or her. This is the characteristic of language that makes learning from the past, as well as planning for the future, possible. Displacement is to a large degree responsible for creativity, imagination, and illusion.

For a communication system to be called *language*, it must have a lexicon and a grammar. A

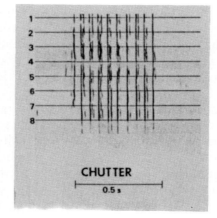

(a)   *(b)*

FIGURE 12–6 *Discreteness in vervet monkey alarm calls.* The *wrr* and chutter are both calls that are given in the presence of another group. *(a)* The *wrr* is given when a neighboring group has first been spotted. *(b)* The acoustically different chutter is produced under more aggressive conditions of contact. Pictured are spectograms, which are visualizations of sound.

lexicon is a vocabulary, a set of meaningful units such as words (or hand positions in sign language). A **grammar** is a set of rules used to make up these words and then to combine them into larger utterances such as phrases and sentences. Most rules of a grammar are unconsciously known. If a system has a lexicon and a grammar, it need not be oral to be considered language. Thus, a system such as American Sign Language (ASL) is considered a language, since specific rules govern the combination of the nonvocal signs used.

Symbolic Behavior in Chimpanzees

As research on primates continues, the uniqueness of humankind diminishes. Several apes, including the chimpanzee Washoe, the bonobo Kanzi, and the gorilla Koko, have cast doubt on the claim that language is exclusively a human characteristic.

For almost half a century, researchers have been attempting to teach chimpanzees language. In the 1940s a chimpanzee named Vicki, after years of training, was with difficulty and lack of clarity able to say three words: *mama, papa,* and *cup.*

The chimpanzee's larynx (voice box) is higher in the throat than is the human larynx. This and other anatomical features of the chimpanzee prevent the animal from producing sounds with the qualities of human speech sounds. Also, chimpanzees do not show development of **Broca's area** of the brain, the area that in humans controls the production of speech (Figure 18–14). Since chimpanzees and other apes are not equipped to produce human speech sounds, systems of nonvocal communication, which have a lexicon and a grammar as well as the design features of language not related to speech, have been tried in experimental situations. Washoe and Koko have been taught to use the American Sign Language for the deaf, and Kanzi has been taught to use a computer that employs arbitrary symbols to represent words or concepts.

WASHOE   In the American Sign Language for the deaf, different positions of the hand correspond to different concepts. The language is arbitrary; that is, the hand positions are not produced automatically but must be learned. The positions can be combined to form sentences, and different signs can appear at different places in different sentences. ASL is also an open system in that the potential exists for inventing new "words" by new hand configurations.

At the age of 7 years, Washoe could use 175 signs. She had learned her first sign at about 15 months and had acquired a vocabulary of some 50 signs at the age of about 3 years (Figure 12–7). The fact that she could learn individual signs and use them in the proper context is interesting in itself, but what is more significant is that she could apparently invent both sentences and signs. For example, when Washoe saw a swan for the first time, she signed "water bird." This represents both the invention of a term and the use of a sequence of meaningful units to create a phrase. She often made such combinations.

In 1970 Washoe was moved to the Institute for Primate Studies, in Norman, Oklahoma, where Roger Fouts had trained other chimpanzees in the use of ASL. An especially interesting question was whether Washoe would transmit her knowledge of ASL to her offspring. Other studies provide evidence that chimpanzees communicate with one another using sign language (Figure 12–8).

Washoe had a baby in 1979, but unfortunately, the baby died at 8 weeks of age. In what was a controversial move, Fouts took another chim-

FIGURE 12–7 *Washoe.* Washoe uses the ASL sign for "hat."

(a)

(b)

(c)

(d)

FIGURE 12–8   *Chimp-to-chimp communication.* In this sequence two young males, Booee (right) and Bruno (left), communicate using ASL. Booee is requesting some fruit slices from Bruno: *(a)* "you"; *(b)* "feed"; *(c)* "Boosee" (his name sign); *(d)* Bruno gives Booee the fruit.

panzee infant from its natural mother and gave the 10-month-old baby to Washoe. After a rocky start, Washoe and the baby, named Loulis, accepted each other.

At 3 years of age, Loulis was placed in contact with three other chimpanzees, and by 1987, Loulis was using about fifty signs. Fouts claims that Loulis learned the signs exclusively from other chimpanzees, not from his human keepers. Some were learned from Washoe, others from the other chimpanzees in the colony. Although even Fouts believes that some of Loulis's signs were learned strictly by imitation, he also maintains that others were deliberately

taught. He cites as an example the way in which Loulis acquired the sign for "food" from Washoe: taking Loulis's hand, Washoe pushed his fingertips together and tapped them on his mouth.

By 1991 Washoe had a signing vocabulary of 240 signs. In 1992 she was moved to a new research facility at Central Washington University. Here she joined other signing chimpanzees and is participating in many projects, including the study of chimp-to-chimp signing.

KANZI   In the late 1980s, reports of a young bonobo named Kanzi began to appear. Although raised around chimpanzees who were being taught to use a computer, Kanzi had no training in this skill. The computer had 250 symbols on a keyboard (Figure 12–9). Each symbol, called a **lexigram,** represented a word. Investigators at the Yerkes Regional Primate Center in Georgia were amazed when Kanzi spontaneously began to use the computer and "asked" to be chased. Kanzi also seems to understand spoken language and responds correctly to certain oral commands.

Some of those who work with Kanzi maintain that he has a simple understanding of grammar. For instance, if a chimpanzee named Matata initiated an action, Kanzi would describe the incident by putting the verbal aspect second—"Matata bite." However, if Matata was acted upon, the verb would go first, as in "grabbed Matata," meaning someone grabbed Matata. By 1991 Kanzi's custodians said the 6-year-old bonobo knew 90 lexigrams and understood 200 spoken words and 650 sentences (see Box 12–2).

KOKO   Gorillas were once thought to be less intelligent than chimpanzees, but this is being disproved by the gorilla Koko (Figure 12–10). By the age of 7 years, Koko had an active vocabulary of 375 ASL signs, many more than Washoe or other chimpanzees had acquired at any age. According to her handlers, Koko scores between 85 and 95 on the Stanford-Binet IQ test, identifies herself in the mirror and in photographs, and invents words and phrases. These and other behaviors indicate an intelligence far beyond what was expected before the study began.

SKEPTICISM ABOUT APE-LANGUAGE STUDIES   The above information has been presented from the point of view of the researchers involved in the studies. With few exceptions, the general scientific community of the 1960s and 1970s accepted these reports at face value, but in 1979 and the early 1980s, the first extensive criticisms began to appear.

One of the most vocal critics of the ape-language studies is H. S. Terrace.[9] Terrace is not

FIGURE 12–9   *Kanzi.* Kanzi is a bonobo who, in some ways, seems more adept at learning language than common chimpanzees. Kanzi communicates by pointing to symbols on keyboards.

BOX 12–2

THE QUESTION OF THE INNATENESS AND UNIQUENESS OF LANGUAGE

Anyone concerned with the study of human nature and human capacities must somehow come to grips with the fact that all normal humans acquire language, whereas acquisition of even its barest rudiments is quite beyond the capacities of an otherwise intelligent ape.[1]

Noam Chomsky, one of the best known linguists of the twentieth century, expressed the above sentiment in 1972. It mirrored the traditional view about people: humans are distinct from all other animals in possessing language. In an attempt to explain this uniqueness, Chomsky and others proposed that there is a yet-to-be-found language acquisition area of the brain that allows children to unconsciously, and without being directly taught, learn language. If this language acquisition area exists, it would be an innate feature of humans that is prewired for what Chomsky calls a Universal

Grammar. The Universal Grammar is a set of proposed rules that underlies the specific grammars of all languages. All that is needed for a child to learn any language is a sample of utterances provided by the linguistic environment.

There is no doubt that a human brain evolved specially equipped for language acquisition. Although linguists debate the existence of a Universal Grammar, it is an established fact that all human children go through the same stages of language development at about the same age, regardless of the language of their culture.

Also, there is no doubt that the ability to acquire language is much more developed in humans than in any other species. However, Chomsky's contention that "acquisition of even its barest rudiments is quite beyond the capacities of an otherwise intelligent ape," may not be correct.

Research on bonobos, such as Kanzi, indicates that they can "use symbol combinations as a means of specifying more than a single symbol can express."[2] Some of Kanzi's two-element combinations are *bite-chase, slap-grab, tickle-hide, chase-ball, grab-head, grab-Matata,* and *food-orange*. The use of these two-element combinations may reflect the chimpanzee's ability to reach, very rudimentarily, what is called the two-word stage of language development. So, as with many other characteristics once thought to be the exclusive province of humankind, very simple and partial language-type abilities may be found in nonhuman primates.

[1]N. Chomsky, *Language and Mind* (New York: Harcourt Brace Jovanovich, 1972).
[2]E. S. Savage-Rumbaugh, "Language Acquisition in a Nonhuman Species: Implications for the Innateness Debate," *Developmental Psychobiology*, 23 (1990), 615.

---

convinced that the apes display an understanding or use of grammar. He points out that in word sequences, the ape might simply be using two or more behaviors that individually get the same reward. For example, Terrace believes that Washoe's use of the sequence "more drink" does not display the animal's knowledge of *more* as a modifier of *drink*. Instead, he believes that the ape has learned through conditioning that either the word *more* or the word *drink* will be rewarded with food, a hug, a pat, or other positive reinforcement; the combination of signs maximizes the chance of reward and need not imply any knowledge of grammar.

The contention that Kanzi understands word order may also be premature. Not enough data have been presented to make a strong argument for his understanding of grammar. If the apes

have no real understanding of grammar, then this might mean that ASL or a computer readout does not have the same meaning for the ape as it does for the human. If this is so, then the ape's lack of a true lexicon and grammar indicates a lack of language abilities, at least as reflected in the ape-language studies done so far.

Terrace also offers another type of criticism. He believes that the ape researchers were giving their subjects subtle subconscious clues as to the correct response. He noted this in his own research with Neam Chimpsky ("Nim" for short), the chimpanzee named for the famous linguist Noam Chomsky (see Box 12–2). When Terrace studied videotapes of his own assistants communicating with Nim, he discovered subtle nonverbal prompting. He saw the same type of prompting in films of other subjects.

FIGURE 12–10 *Koko.* Koko was the first gorilla to be taught a form of American Sign Language. Here she is shown making the sign "smoke" for her cat Smoky.

Terrace also found that Nim's utterances did not increase in length over time and that Nim's responses were not usually spontaneous but followed the researcher's utterances 88 percent of the time. In addition, many of Nim's responses were imitations of the human utterances; the ape rarely added information to a "conversation" and had no concept of turn talking. In other words, to Terrace, what Nim and other apes were doing did not look like human language.

There is much debate over Terrace's observations. Researchers A. Allen Gardner and Beatrice Gardner, who worked with Washoe, have labeled Terrace's Nim project "poor" and a "gross oversimplification."[10] Others have said that Terrace is making distinctions between human language and ways in which apes produce utterances that have no basis in fact.

If Terrace is correct, then language may indeed be a uniquely human potential. On the other hand, if Washoe, Kanzi, and Koko are really using language, then language can no longer be qualitatively considered the exclusive domain of our species. In the long run, both schools of thought may be missing the point. Duane Rumbaugh points out that language may not be simply an all-or-none phenomenon.[11] If apes are evolutionarily as close to humans as all areas of study indicate, then perhaps ape and human linguistic abilities evolved from a common ability of an ancient ancestor. The two abilities may have simply evolved differently, maintaining some similarities because of a common source. Whatever the answers are, this decade's ape-language studies are guaranteed to be exciting and controversial.

Summary

The terms *communication* and *language* are not synonymous. All organisms communicate in

[10]J. Greenberg, "Ape Talk: More Than 'Pigeon' English?" *Science News*, 117 (1980), 298.

[11]Ibid., 298–300.

that they transmit and receive messages. These messages need not be symbolic or involve any form of thought; they simply give information. Language has been regarded as a uniquely human form of communication that involves symbolic representations that are arbitrary and discrete. These characteristics, along with openness and displacement, as well as other features not discussed in this text, when taken as a whole differentiate language from the call systems of nonhuman primates and the communication systems of all other organisms.

Nevertheless, experimental work on apes has raised questions regarding the linguistic abilities of nonhuman primates. Can apes be taught human language and then transmit this knowledge to their offspring or other untrained apes? Some investigators believe that the research done with Washoe, Kanzi, Koko, and other apes shows that they have at least rudimentary linguistic ability. Other researchers see the supposed linguistic behavior of apes as nothing more than stimulus-response learning. Still others take a position somewhere between these two conclusions. As new research methods are developed, the 1990s may be a time when more concrete answers are provided to the question of the ape's linguistic abilities.

ARE HUMANS UNIQUE?

Throughout history many philosophers have attempted to distance humans from other living organisms. Social scientists have searched for characteristics that mark humanity as unique. On the other hand, modern evolutionary biologists and sociobiologists see continuity in the living world. They see differences, especially differences in closely related species, as quantitative rather than qualitative. In this section we will explore the uniqueness of the human species and the question of human universals.

Intelligence in Nonhuman Primates

The concept of intelligence is an elusive one. Social scientists cannot even form a consensus on the nature of intelligence in humans (Chapter 8).

The concept is even more problematic in nonhumans. The fact that apes may use arbitrary and discrete symbols in an open way to convey displaced information suggests a continuity with human thought processes. Recent research on monkeys also displays this continuity.

WHAT DO MONKEYS KNOW?   Dorothy L. Cheney and Robert M. Seyfarth provide insight into the question of monkey intelligence.[12] They designed experiments to see whether African vervet monkeys understand the concept of rank within their dominance hierarchy.

To form powerful alliances, individual vervet monkeys attempt to groom other monkeys that are higher in rank. If a monkey approaches a grooming pair, the invader will displace the monkey it outranks. If the intruder outranks both grooming monkeys, which one will the intruder displace? In 29 out of 30 cases the more dominant intruder displaced the lower-ranking monkey of the pair (Figure 12–11). Cheney and Seyfarth conclude that the monkey who stays put knows its own rank relative to the invading monkey and knows its rank relative to the monkey who is displaced. The monkey who stays also knows the other two monkeys' relationship to each other. "In other words, she [the monkey who stays] must recognize a rank hierarchy."[13]

Cheney and Seyfarth also explore the extent to which vervets understand their own calls. Vervet monkeys are territorial; when a monkey from one group first sights a neighboring group approaching, they produce a *wrr wrr* warning (Figure 12–6a). If the neighboring group approaches aggressively, the members of the invaded group produce a chuttering sound (Figure 12–6b).

The researchers conducted an experiment in which they played a recording of one vervet's *wrr*s to its group when no neighboring group was in sight. The other animals soon learned to ignore the false alarm and also ignored the chutters of the recorded monkey. However, the animals reacted normally to all other calls of the

[12]D. L. Cheney and R. M. Seyfarth, *How Monkeys See the World* (Chicago: University of Chicago Press, 1990).
[13]Ibid., 82.

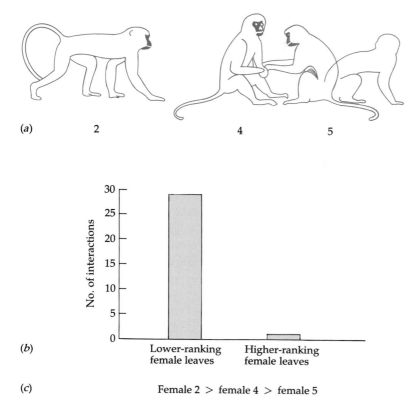

(a) 2 4 5

(b)

(c) Female 2 > female 4 > female 5

FIGURE 12–11 *Competition over access to a grooming partner in vervet monkeys. (a)* A high-ranking female (2) approaches two lower-ranking females (4 and 5). *(b)* The lower-ranking female (5) is almost always supplanted. *(c)* This suggests that the monkeys recognize a rank hierarchy.

monkey who had "cried wolf." Cheney and Seyfarth concluded that since the *wrr*s and chutters are acoustically dissimilar, the vervets can perceive that *wrr*s and chutters carry similar meaning. Since the recorded monkey was unreliable with one alarm call *(wrr)*, the vervets also ignored its other alarm call (chutter).

Cheney and Seyfarth's work, and the work of several other primatologists, suggests that monkeys generalize about relationships between individuals and represent meaning in their calls. Unlike the case with humans, the monkeys' potential in these areas is very limited. Even if every primate call had meaning, a primate species usually has fewer than twenty calls; the English language contains about 500,000 words. This represents an enormous quantitative difference. Cheney and Seyfarth point out that there are also qualitative differences between monkeys and humans. For instance, monkeys do not know what they know; that is, they do not seem to be aware that they know things. Also, monkeys seem unable to "attribute mental states to oth-

ers or to recognize that others' behavior is . . . caused by motives, beliefs, and desires."[14]

WHAT DISTINGUISHES PRIMATES? The work with vervet monkeys suggests that intelligence is not an all-or-none characteristic. The developing body of evidence from monkey and ape research projects has led Susan Essock-Vitale and Robert M. Seyfarth to summarize some of the things that set primates apart, at least quantitatively, from most other animals. These behaviors include the facts that primates

recognize each other as individuals, distinguish kin from nonkin, and behave differently toward those of different dominance ranks. Experiments suggest that these social skills are learned and that they develop with experience. Moreover, primates can remember past interactions, seem able to predict the behavior of others based on prior observations, and

[14]Ibid., 312.

discriminate among their own and other individuals' close associations. . . . Finally, although primates are not qualitatively different from other animals in this respect, they do seem outstanding in their ability to maintain simultaneously many different kinds of relationships, each finely tuned to the individual characteristics of the participants.[15]

These qualities point to the nonhuman primates' great mental abilities as compared with those of other animals. Yet we can only speculate as to the evolutionary meaning of this complex behavior. As with humans, behavior based on learning allows for more behavioral flexibility than that determined strictly by heredity. This behavioral flexibility allows the animal to choose a variety of strategies, which is especially important when unusual events occur and biologically stereotyped behavior may prove disastrous. In the complexity of the nonhuman primates' social behavior, and in their ability to manufacture tools, we see reflections of what may have been the roots of human culture.

Protoculture

Humans have been described as cultural animals who cope with the conditions of their niches largely by means of cultural adjustments. Culture represents a body of behavioral patterns and knowledge that is learned and passed down from generation to generation. (See Chapter 1 for a discussion of *culture.*) Primatologists are becoming increasingly aware of the fact that not only can nonhuman primates adjust to new situations by means of learned behavior but also that many behavioral patterns are passed down from generation to generation as a type of social heredity. Those who feel that the transmission of learned behavior is common among these forms believe that primates do have a **protoculture;** that is, they are characterized by the simplest, most basic aspects of culture.

PROTOCULTURE IN MONKEYS   Many behavioral patterns in the monkey are certainly genetically determined. Laboratory studies, in which animals have been reared away from the social unit or reared by a human substitute mother, have shown that certain vocalizations and dominance gestures occur in the isolated monkey. Since the animal had no contact with its natural mother or troop, such similarities between isolated and troop-reared behavior must be interpreted as being genetically determined.

On the other hand, many behavioral patterns are apparently learned. One infant raised with its natural mother never learned to use its cheek pouches for food; its mother never used hers. Later the animal was placed in a cage with another monkey. The second monkey would rush to the food and place much of it in his cheek pouches, leaving little for the first. Very quickly, however, the original animal learned the proper use of the pouches.

Some of the best data on the degree to which learned behavior is developed in nonhuman primates come from studies of the Japanese macaque. Primatologists have attempted to introduce new foods in provisionized populations. The Japanese macaque does not eat everything available in its natural habitat and does not always accept the introduction of new foods. Candy was accepted readily by the infants, who generally show a greater amount of exploratory activity than do adults, but even after several years, candy was not accepted by the entire troop. On the other hand, the dominant males accepted the introduction of wheat immediately, and this behavior spread throughout the troop in only 4 hours.

Some of the best examples of behavioral changes occurred on Koshima Island, Japan, where primatologists introduced sweet potatoes as a food. Normally, macaques rub dirt off food with their hands, but one day a young female took her sweet potato to a stream and washed it. Apparently providing greater efficiency in dirt removal, the pattern of sweet-potato washing soon spread to the other members of her play group and then to the mothers of these young monkeys. Four years later, 80 to 90 percent of the

---

[15]S. Essock-Vitale and R. M. Seyfarth, "Intelligence and Social Cognition," in B. B. Smuts et al. (eds.), *Primate Societies* (Chicago: University of Chicago Press, 1987), 452. ©1986 by the University of Chicago. All rights reserved.

monkeys in the troop were washing sweet potatoes (Figure 12–12). Later some monkeys began to wash their sweet potatoes in salt water, the salt probably improving the flavor. Often they carried the sweet potatoes a short distance to the shore, and in carrying sweet potatoes, the animals moved bipedally. Therefore, erect bipedalism has become a more frequent locomotor pattern of this troop on land (Figure 12–13).

This later development is of interest to students of human evolution. The earliest hominids developed erect bipedalism as a dominant form of locomotion. The shift to erect bipedalism was not necessarily sudden; rather, a slow increase in the frequency of this mode of locomotion could have occurred in response to some environmental factor. Anthropologists are not quite sure what this environmental change was, although the replacement of tropical forest by grassland has been suggested.

On Koshima Island the investigators saw the increased use of this locomotor pattern in response to a new learned behavioral pattern, washing sweet potatoes in salt water. Conceivably, if a behavioral pattern like this had some selective advantage, animals biologically more

FIGURE 12–13 *The Japanese macaque.* Bipedal transport of sweet potato to the ocean for washing.

capable of bipedalism might contribute more genes to the gene pool of the next generation. At any rate, the behavioral changes in the Japanese macaque at least suggest how changes in the frequency of an anatomical trait might result from a change in a behavioral pattern.

PROTOCULTURE IN CHIMPANZEES   Protocultural behavior is also present in the chimpanzee. Some of this learned behavior was discussed in Chapter 11 in relation to the use of termite sticks by young chimpanzees and the use of human-made objects to obtain status. In addition, young chimpanzees learn a great deal about chimpanzee society in their play groups. For instance, they learn who the dominant adult females are by the actions taken against them if they get into a fight with another youngster. Chimpanzee females also appear to learn how to be effective mothers from watching their own mothers and taking care of their siblings. Jane Goodall reports that a young female who took care of her orphaned brother seemed to be a more experienced mother when she had her first offspring than other first-time mothers.

FIGURE 12–12 *The Japanese macaque.* Sweet-potato washing.

The point of this discussion is that the beginning of cultural behavior can be seen in monkey and ape societies. Continuing investigations into these phenomena can aid the physical anthropologist in understanding the possible ways in which culture developed in humans.

Human Universals

Many anthropologists, probably most of them, are skeptical of statements that generalize about what all peoples do. But are there not generalizations of that sort that really do hold for the wide array of human populations? There are—and not enough has been said about them. This skepticism and neglect of human universals is the entrenched legacy of an era of particularism in which the observation that something *doesn't* occur among the Bongo Bongo counted as a major contribution of anthropology. The truth of the matter is, however, that anthropologists probably always take for granted an indefinite collection of traits that add up to a very complex view of human nature.[16]

Just as all baboons share many behavioral characteristics, all humans share certain behavioral potentials. For instance, except for individuals profoundly affected by disease or injury, all humans can learn a language—baboons cannot. The potential for learning language, and other characteristics of human nature, evolved as a result of evolutionary and cultural forces acting on these behaviors. Just as there is a "prewired" genetic potential for learning language, it is equally true that a specific language, such as English, Chinese, or Navaho, is learned by exposure to an environment in which that language is spoken (or signed). There is no biological propensity to learn one specific language over another. These facts are relatively noncontroversial.

THE SEXUAL DIVISION OF LABOR   The general relationship between nature (biological destiny) and nurture (learning) concerning language abilities may be relatively clear. However, what about other behaviors, say, the division of labor between males and females? Is this behavior a result of nature or nurture or some combination of both factors?

One way that this issue has been approached is by asking questions such as this: Are women as a category universally subordinate to men as a category? However, this question is perhaps too loaded with emotion to deal with objectively. Also, a scientific explanation depends on precisely defined concepts, but it is hard to define *subordinate.*

So who is right? Are women subordinate to men in all societies or not? Certainly, ethnographers have been biased—but does this bias explain their consistent reports of female subordination? Certainly, the Iroquois and other peoples demonstrate that women in some societies have achieved considerable control over their own lives and even over public decision making—but do such cases represent full equality of males and females? Indeed, would we know "full general equality" if we saw it in a society? What would it look like? Would men and women have to carry out the same kinds of economic tasks before we could say they are equal? Is monogamy necessary, or can a society be polygynous and still qualify? Shall we require that women occupy 50 percent of all leadership roles before we say they have equal rights? How should domestic life be organized before we can say that husbands in general do not dominate their wives?[17]

So perhaps the question about the relationship between the sexes should be phrased something like this: Are there biological differences between the sexes that universally affect behavior in a consistent manner? Besides the most apparent primary sexual differences between men and women, other biologically controlled differences exist. The average man is stronger (more muscular) than the average woman. Many women seem to experience a decrease in fertility if they engage in very heavy exercise; men are not affected in this way. Women not only give birth, but in all

---

[16]D. E. Brown, *Human Universals* (New York: McGraw-Hill, 1991), 1.

[17]Reprinted by permission from *Humanity: An Introduction to Cultural Anthropology* by J. Peoples and G. Bailey. Copyright ©1994 by West Publishing Company. All rights reserved.

societies they care for infants and young children more than men do.

The character of each culture determines the precise way that the above biological facts are interpreted. For instance, in modern industrial societies, in which machines often substitute for human muscle power and in which the birth rate is low, biological differences between men and women have fewer social consequences than in nonindustrial societies. Yet these biological factors are at least partially responsible for the male-female division-of-labor specializations found in societies throughout the world. Hunting, trapping, mining, lumbering, butchering, building boats, and working with stone, bone, shell, and metal seem to be overwhelmingly male activities in all societies studied. Gathering wild plant foods, shellfish, and mollusks, collecting resources for use as fuel, fetching water, making clothing, weaving, and taking care of small animals are predominantly female tasks.

OTHER HUMAN UNIVERSALS   We have been discussing sexual differences in task specialization as an example of a human universal. Donald E. Brown lists hundreds of other possible human universals.[18] There are different degrees of consensus on the universality of the items he lists, but various anthropologists, psychologists, sociologists, sociobiologists, and others have suggested each item as a candidate for universal status.

Some researchers believe that all human societies change through time, have some concept of privacy, have some form of art, practice body ornamentation, distinguish between good and bad behavior (have a moral system), make jokes, have languages that conform to a universal set of grammatical rules, display universal stages of language acquisition, distinguish between general and particular, display ethnocentrism, solve some problems by trial and error, use tools, have kinship terms, have rules about sexual behavior, are aware of the individual self as distinct from others, have a social structure influenced by accumulated information, show collective decision

making, have leadership, have some form of play and games, have a world view, and have children that show a fear of strangers. Some people also believe that individuals within all societies have the potential for aggression, hope, anxiety, lying, feeling loss and grief in respect to the death of close kin, have a sense of duty, and feel boredom.

Humans share some of the above characteristics with other animals. Chimpanzees make a limited number of tools, and some researchers suggest that they might feel grief when certain other chimpanzees, such as a mother, die. Yet the list of human universals taken as a whole describes only one animal—*Homo sapiens*.

Summary

Perhaps most anthropologists would agree that members of our species are the only living organisms with the capability of asking the questions: What am I? and Why am I? In the search for the answers to these questions, anthropologists are carefully studying the behavior of closely related species. Some nonhuman primates display mental characteristics that were once thought to be distinctly human. These include the ability to categorize experiences and convey distinct and discrete meaning in their calls.

Research into primate behavior reveals that many nonhuman primates, especially monkeys and apes, show protocultural behavior. The study of the ways in which behavior is learned and transmitted in nonhuman primates will, we hope, aid in the understanding of the development and nature of human culture.

Finally, although there is a general evolutionary continuity between closely related taxa, humans are distinguished by a complex of characteristics that, when taken as a whole, differentiate them from other primates. These universal characteristics result in a human nature that evolved as a result of biological and evolutionary factors such as mutation and natural selection.

STUDY QUESTIONS

1. What is the nature of the human band? What are some points of comparison between the

---

[18] Brown, op cit., 157–201.

human band and other primate social arrangements?

2. What characterizes male-female relationships in human societies? In what ways do these relationships differ from those of other primates? From those of the social carnivores?

3. Compare hunting behavior among the wild dog, chimpanzee (consult Chapter 11), and human. What features do humans share with wild dogs and chimpanzees?

4. Are the words *language* and *communication* synonymous? Explain.

5. In what ways is language different from other animal communication systems?

6. Why is there controversy over the contention made by some researchers that apes can learn human language?

7. Research on vervet monkeys has shown these animals to be capable of behaviors once thought to be unique to humans. What are these behaviors, and in what ways did investigators discover that monkeys were capable of them?

8. What is meant by the term *protoculture?* How do monkeys show protocultural behavior?

9. Describe some human universals.

SUGGESTED READINGS

Brown, D. E. *Human Universals.* New York: McGraw-Hill, 1991. This brief book discusses the nature-nurture debate in terms of the concept of human universals. The extensive bibliography lists sources, both recent and historical, that deal with this topic. The book is a must for people interested in exploring the concept of a universal human nature.

Cheney, D., and R. Seyfarth. *How Monkeys See the World.* Chicago: University of Chicago Press, 1990. This book explores such questions as, What do monkeys know about the world? Are they aware of what they know? It presents the results of research into these and other questions dealing with the issues of primate intelligence and cognition.

Goodall, J. *The Chimpanzees of Gombe: Patterns of Behavior.* Cambridge, Mass.: Belknap Press, 1986. This book brings together the data gathered from over two decades of research on the chimpanzees of the Gombe.

Heltne, P. G., and L. A. Marquardt (eds.) *Understanding Chimpanzees.* Cambridge, Mass.: Harvard University Press, 1989. This volume includes thirty-three papers on chimpanzees, seven of which deal with ape-language studies and chimpanzee intelligence.

Michel, A. *The Story of Nim: The Chimp Who Learned Language.* New York: Knopf, 1980. This is a short book with marvelous photographs explaining how H. S. Terrace attempted to teach language to a chimpanzee.

Parker, S. T., R. W. Mitchell, and M. L. Boccia. *Self-Awareness in Animals and Humans: Developmental Perspectives.* New York: Cambridge University Press, 1994. This collection of original articles explores the meaning of self-awareness, how to measure self-awareness, and which species are capable of it and why.

Sebeok, T. A., and J. Umiker-Sebeok. *Speaking of Apes: A Critical Anthology of Two-Way Communication with Man.* New York: Plenum, 1980. This book looks at ape language from a skeptical point of view.

Terrace, H. S. *Nim.* New York: Knopf, 1979. This book presents the first systematic and extensive negative criticism of the ape-language studies of the 1960s and 1970s.

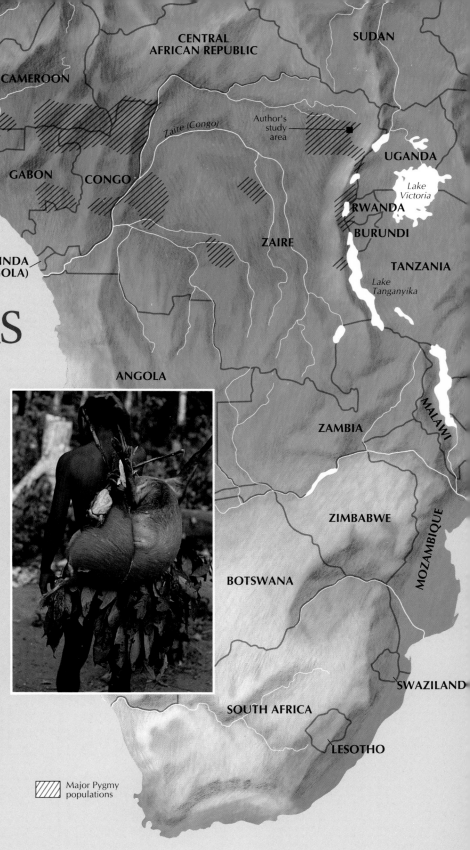

THE EFE: FORAGERS OF THE CONGO BASIN

Between 150,000 and 200,000 short-statured people, known to outsiders as Pygmies, live in the tropical rain forest in seven African countries. Anthropologist Robert C. Bailey has studied a group called the Efe. The semi-nomadic Efe are foragers who provide the Lese, a larger-statured group of farmers, with forest products and field labor in return for the garden food that provides the Efe with two-thirds of their calories.

FIGURE 12-A An Efe man carries an 18-kilogram (40-pound) duiker, a type of antelope, which he killed with a metal-tipped arrow.

Major Pygmy populations

FIGURE 12-B A group of men divide up a kill. The largest portion of meat always goes to the hunter who first wounds the animal. Because the men do many things besides hunt as a group, they spend a lot of time together. However, the one individual a married man spends the most time with is his wife.

FIGURE 12-C An Efe man repairs arrows while his wife sits at the entrance of the hut preparing food. The man's daughter-in-law (far right) is also involved in the food preparation. Efe women do much of the heavy work, as well. They gather and carry large pieces of fire wood to the camp and carry most of the family's belongings when the camp is moved. When Bailey asked an Efe man why the women carry more than the men, the man dismissed the question by replying: "Women are stronger than men. ...I could never carry all that weight. Besides, men have to be free to use their weapons. What if an elephant charges?"*

*R.C. Bailey, "The Efe: Archers of the African Rain Forest," *National Geographic*, 176 (November 1989), 686.

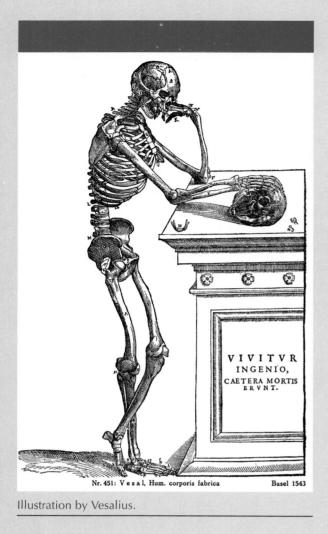

Nr. 451: V e s a l, Hum. corporis fabrica   Basel 1543

Illustration by Vesalius.

*In order to interpret the fossils, to determine
what hominid fossils were like in life, it is
necessary to compare the structure of their fossil
bones and teeth to those of humans, apes and
other primates. This can help us to determine
not only that they were on the human line, but
also details about their function, how they
moved and what they ate. Only by such analogy
with modern humans and non-human primates
can we have confidence in our conclusions
about the nature of our evolutionary ancestors.[1]*
        Leslie Aiello and Christopher Dean

[1]L. Aiello and C. Dean, *An Introduction to Human Evolutionary Anatomy* (London: Academic, 1990), 1.

13

CHAPTER
COMPARATIVE STUDIES: ANATOMY AND GENETICS

New anatomical structures usually evolve gradually as modifications of preexisting structures. Thus, closely related forms exhibit homologous anatomical features. These homologies are established through careful comparative studies.

Most of the evidence of primate evolution is found in the study of skeletons, both the skeletons from living primates and those found in the fossil record. Skeletal material is easier to study than other parts of the anatomy and, with rare exceptions, skeletal material is all that is available in the fossil records. For these reasons, physical anthropologists have become specialists in skeletal anatomy.

Anatomical structures should be discussed within the context of their functions, which in turn can be related to the behavior of the animal. It is important to realize from the beginning that anatomical changes evolve within the context of behavioral changes. New behavioral patterns often provide the selective pressures for evolutionary development. For this reason this chapter will examine those aspects of comparative anatomy that relate to the changes thought to be of fundamental importance in the evolution of the hominids: the evolution of erect bipedalism, the evolution of fine manual dexterity, the increase in the size of the brain, and the reduction in the size of the teeth and jaw.

Not all comparisons are made on the anatomical level. Physical anthropologists are increasingly studying similarities and differences on the molecular level which includes the analysis of DNA and protein molecules which are direct reflections of the genetic code. This chapter examines the skeletal, cytogenetic, and molecular evidence of primate evolution.

COMPARATIVE ANATOMY OF LOCOMOTION AND MANIPULATION

Humans are erect bipeds, but they are not the only erect bipeds in the animal kingdom, nor are they the only primates capable of this method of locomotion. Unlike other primates, however, hominids habitually depend upon this mode of locomotion. They have evolved many anatomical features that have made efficient and habitual erect bipedalism possible. As we will see in later chapters, these anatomical features evolved over 4 million years ago.

Likewise, primates in general share a refined manual dexterity. For example, most Old World monkeys and the apes share with humans an opposable thumb. Humans, however, have evolved a high degree of manual dexterity that permits the creation of a complex technology. This section will explore the anatomy of locomotion and manual dexterity.

Locomotor Patterns among Primates

Locomotor specializations characterize most mammalian orders; some obvious examples are the bats, the whales, and the hoofed mammals. On the other hand, primates retain a rather large repertoire of locomotor behaviors. This is consistent with the theme of primate adaptability. The primates, as a group, display a variety of locomotor patterns, and a wide range of locomotor patterns may characterize a single species. Table 13–1 lists several general types of locomotion behavior.

LOCOMOTOR PATTERNS OF PROSIMIANS, TARSIERS, AND MONKEYS **Quadrupedalism** is the basic locomotor pattern of terrestrial vertebrates. The quadruped moves on all four limbs. The body is held parallel to the ground, a position known as **pronograde** posture. We can recognize several categories of quadrupedalism, with a major division being made between arboreal and terrestrial quadrupedalism.

In **arboreal quadrupedalism,** or **branch running and walking,** the primates walk, climb, jump, and leap on and among the branches. The

TABLE 13–1 PRIMATE LOCOMOTOR PATTERNS	
TYPE OF LOCOMOTION	REPRESENTATIVE PRIMATES
QUADRUPEDALISM	
Slow climbing	Loris
	Potto
Branch running and walking	Lemur
	Tamarin
	Capuchin monkey
	Guenon
Ground running and walking	Macaque
	Gelada
	Baboon
	Mandrill
New World semibrachiation	Spider monkey
	Howler monkey
Old World semibrachiation	Colobus monkey
	Langur
VERTICAL CLINGING AND LEAPING	
Vertical clinging and leaping	Tarsier
	Galago
	Sifaka
APE LOCOMOTION	
True brachiation	Gibbon
	Siamang
Quadrumanous	Orangutan
Knuckle walking	Chimpanzee
	Gorilla
ERECT BIPEDALISM	
Erect bipedalism (heel-toe stride)	Human

branches may be quite small and uneven, and they are frequently unstable as they move in the wind or in response to the motion of another animal. Arboreal quadrupeds use their hands and feet to grasp a branch as they move along the top of the branch. Their arms and legs are of roughly equal length, although all their limbs tend to be shorter than those of other primates; shorter limbs bring the body closer to the branch, thus aiding stability. Arboreal quadrupeds also have long tails that aid in balancing on top of the branches. Their fingers and toes are relatively long to facilitate grasping the branches, but they are not as long as those of primates that suspend themselves under branches.

We can recognize several subtypes of arboreal quadrupedalism. Many quadrupeds, for example,

FIGURE 13–1 *New World semibrachiation.* A spider monkey (*Ateles geoffroyi*) is seen suspending itself by an arm and prehensile tail.

suspend themselves and move beneath branches. In **New World semibrachiation,** the animal, such as the spider monkey and the howler monkey, uses its prehensile tail and arms to suspend its body (Figure 13–1). In **Old World semibrachiation,** leaping is common, with the arms extended to grasp a branch. The colobus monkeys and langurs frequently use this form of locomotion. Both types of semibrachiation are forms of **suspensory behavior.** Suspensory behavior is not only a method of locomotion but is also a major means of feeding.

Some monkeys are more terrestrial in their habits. In **terrestrial quadrupedalism,** or **ground running and walking,** the animal spends much of its time on the ground, feeding. Movement on

the ground does not involve grasping with their hands. Also, these animals do not leap or climb as they move along a relatively flat, continuous surface. Compared with arboreal quadrupeds, terrestrial quadrupeds have shorter fingers and toes, longer arms and legs of nearly equal length, and often a short or externally absent tail. Terrestrial quadrupeds include such monkeys as the baboons and gelada.

Vertical clinging and leaping is the dominant locomotor pattern of the tarsier and many prosimians such as the galagos and sifakas (Figure 13–2). As the term suggests, the animal rests on a tree trunk in a clinging position; it keeps its body in a vertical, or **orthograde,** posture. In moving from one tree to another, it leaps, landing vertically with its hindlimbs on the new trunk. On the ground, the animal either hops or moves bipedally. These animals have long, powerful hindlimbs.

HOMINOID LOCOMOTION   A highly specialized form of suspensory behavior is **true brachiation,** which is found in the lesser apes, the gibbons and siamang. In true brachiation the body, suspended from above, is propelled by arm swinging (Figure 13–3). The animal rapidly moves hand over hand along a branch, maintaining an orthograde posture.

When feeding, a gibbon can suspend itself under a branch by one arm for up to 20 minutes at a time. In this position the gibbon, because of its very long arms, can collect various fruits, berries, buds, and flowers growing on branches beneath it with its free hand. A quadruped would be unable to reach many of these items since they often grow on the ends of branches that would not support the animal's weight. The true brachiators are bipedal on the tops of large branches and on the ground, where they also maintain an orthograde posture.

Orangutans are much larger and more cautious animals than lesser apes. While they often suspend themselves under branches, their movements are slow and they use their forelimbs and hindlimbs to a great extent, a locomotor pattern described as **quadrumanous.** Quadrupedal on the ground, the orangutan usually does not walk on the palm of the hand as monkeys do, but often walks on the side of the hand or fist.

The locomotor behavior of the African great apes is best described as **knuckle walking** (Figure 13–4). Unlike orangutans, which frequently move from tree to tree without descending to the ground, the chimpanzees and gorillas usually move on the ground. Here they are essentially semierect quadrupeds. They support the upper part of their bodies on the knuckles of their hands, unlike the monkeys, which use their palms. In knuckle walking, the fingers are flexed and the animal places its weight on special knuckle pads that lie on the backs of the fingers.

Many primates exhibit **erect bipedalism** over short distances, but only in humans is erect bipedalism the habitual means of locomotion.

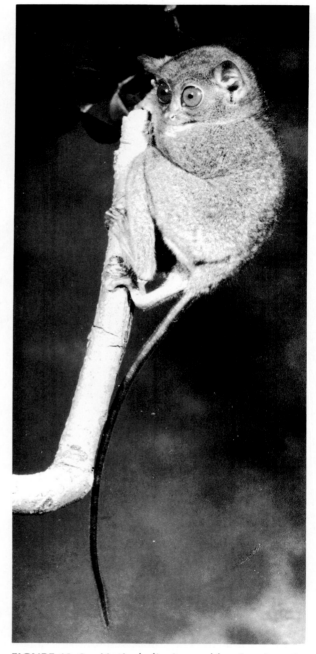

FIGURE 13–2   *Vertical clinging and leaping.* A tarsier (*Tarsius syrichta*) is shown clinging to a vertical branch.

Humans maintain an orthograde posture while standing and walking. As a human walks, the heel of the foot strikes the ground first; the cycle ends when the individual pushes off with the big toe. This is called the **heel-toe stride.**

FIGURE 13–3 *Brachiation.* A siamang (*Symphalangus syndactylus*) is caught in the act of brachiating.

Comparative Anatomy of Primate Locomotion

A major focus of hypotheses on early hominid evolution is the origin of erect bipedalism. If hominid and ape locomotor patterns share a common ancestry, evidence should be found by comparing those parts of the anatomy that relate to locomotion. From such an analysis a hypothetical common ancestor can be reconstructed. In comparing modern forms and the reconstructed ancestor, the evolutionary history of habitual erect bipedalism reveals itself.

This section is not intended as a complete survey of comparative anatomy. Rather, it discusses the method of comparative anatomy and some of the major conclusions of this method. This section focuses upon the parts of the skeleton that function in locomotor activities. An introduction to the skeleton, including the identification of the various bones, is presented in the Appendix.

VARIATIONS OF THE BASIC MAMMALIAN SKELETON The basic mammalian skeleton is greatly modified in many mammalian orders. For example, the horse skeleton is adapted for high-speed running (Figure 13–5). This type of locomotion involves constant jarring of the body and transmits great forces through the limbs to the body. As the horse skeleton has no clavicle, the scapula attaches directly to the rib cage by muscles that absorb the forces generated by running. Of course, flexibility in the shoulder has been lost, but a grass-eating animal running across the plains has little need to lift its forelimb above its head. The radius and ulna in the horse skeleton have fused; four of the five digits on each limb have been lost, and the remaining digit has evolved into a hoof.

In contrast to the horse and most other mammals, the primates, for the most part, have retained a basically generalized skeleton. All primates have retained the clavicle, and most are able to rotate their forearms. With a few excep-

FIGURE 13–4 *Knuckle walking.* A chimpanzee (*Pan troglodytes*) is seen in a knuckle-walking stance.

tions, primates have five fingers or toes at the end of each limb.

The Hominoid Skeleton

In contrast with the hominoids, monkeys carry their bodies parallel to the ground. The spine forms an arch supported by the limbs; the trunk is relatively long and narrow. The hominoid (ape and human) trunk is relatively short and broad; for example, the spine of the gorilla contains three to four lumbar vertebrae compared with seven in the rhesus monkey. Unlike the monkey's back, the hominoid back does not play any important role in locomotion. The ape body is semivertical to the ground, whereas the human body is completely erect. The back muscles of the hominoids are fairly small, and the spine is relatively inflexible.

Figure 13–6 shows the relative positions of the bones of the shoulder girdle. In a monkey, the scapula lies on the side of the trunk, with the head of the humerus pointing backward. In a

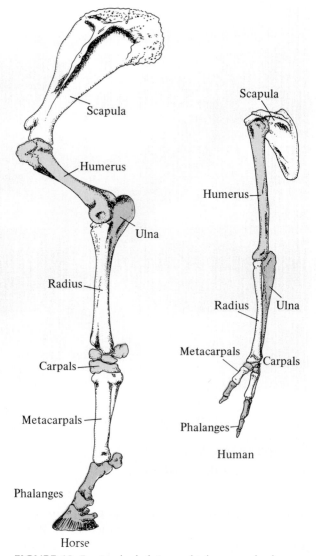

FIGURE 13–5 *Limb skeletons of a horse and a human.* While the forelimb of the horse has been highly specialized for running on hard ground, the primate forelimb has remained relatively generalized. Note the fusion of the radius and ulna and the loss of four of the five digits in the horse.

hominoid, the long clavicles place the arms well to the side of the body. The clavicles extend backward so that the scapula lies on the back and the head of the humerus points inward.

The socket of the scapula is relatively shallow in humans and apes, permitting a greater degree of rotation of the humerus than occurs in mon-

BOX 13–1

HUMANS AS ERECT BIPEDS

Erect bipedalism as a habitual means of locomotion is relatively rare in the animal kingdom. Many anthropologists have stated that humans as bipeds are physically unstable, slow, and weak. The physical disadvantages of human bipedalism are compensated for by superior intelligence and the ability to make and use tools. This concept, however, poses a major dilemma in the evolution of erect bipedalism. How could an early bipedal animal with limited intelligence and poor toolmaking abilities survive?

John Devine has reviewed the many recent studies of erect bipedalism.[1] He has concluded that, contrary to traditional beliefs, bipedal humans are rather formidable animals. The problem seems to be that we tend to visualize humans as they exist in industrial societies. People in these societies do not engage in the same types of physical activities that are common among hunters and gatherers and non-Western horticulturalists.

Preindustrial humans walk and run long distances on a regular basis. In some countries where people normally do not own cars and where public transportation is not available, it is not unusual for people to walk many miles to their tasks in the fields. Hunters frequently walk 40 miles a day; families with young children may move 30 miles or more. Many cultural groups regularly engage in running either for communication or as a sport. For example, the Tarahumara of Mexico hunt deer by chasing down the animal over a 2-day period until the deer falls from exhaustion. A Tarahumara can easily run 283 kilometers (176 miles) without stopping. (By the way, the longest distance run by a human in a 24-hour period is 169 kilometers or 105 miles!)

Recent studies have shown that humans are not all that slow. They can run various distances with speeds from 11 to 37 kilometers per hour (7 to 23 miles per hour). In comparison, hoofed animals such as antelope have been clocked between 25 and 50 kilometers per hour (16 and 31 miles per hour). Thus a human can outrun many potential food sources. Under many circumstances, an early bipedal hominid could have outdistanced a predator.

[1] J. Devine, "The Versatility of Human Locomotion," *American Anthropologist*, 87 (1985), 550–570.

---

keys. Thus, a hominoid can easily hold its arm directly overhead, as when an ape suspends itself from an overhead branch. In addition, hominoids can rotate their forearms to a much greater extent than can monkeys. Humans can rotate their forearms about 160 degrees, allowing them to do pull-ups with palms either toward the body or away from it.

These are some of the many characteristics common to apes and humans in the shoulder and arm. These features are adaptations to suspensory behavior and suggest that hominids evolved from an ancestor adapted to arboreal locomotion. This does not mean that the ancestor was a specialized brachiator like the modern gibbon, with elongated forearms and fingers; the ancestor may have simply been an animal that engaged in some degree of suspensory behavior and emphasized the arms in locomotion.

The length of the leg in quadrupedal monkeys is nearly the same length or somewhat longer than the arm. The ratio of arms to legs is seen by comparing the **intermembral index.** Table 13–2 lists this index for several primates.

More precisely, the index compares the length of two bones in the arm (the humerus and the radius) with the length of two bones in the leg (the femur and the tibia). The equation for calculating the intermembral index is

$$\frac{\text{Length of humerus} + \text{length of radius} \times 100}{\text{Length of femur} + \text{length of tibia}}$$

The number that results from this formula provides an indication of the relative proportion of the forelimb and the hindlimb. An index of 100 means that the arms and legs (excluding the hand and foot) are of equal length. An index over

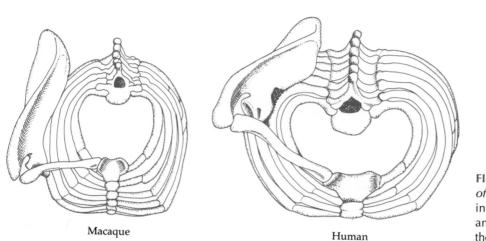

Macaque   Human

FIGURE 13–6 *Cross section of trunk.* Note the differences in the shape of the rib cage and the relative positions of the clavicle and scapula.

TABLE 13–2

PRIMATE INTERMEMBRAL INDICES

TYPE OF LOCOMOTION	REPRESENTATIVE PRIMATES	INTERMEMBRAL INDEX*
QUADRUPEDALISM		
Slow climbing	Loris	92
	Potto	88
Branch running and walking	Lemur	70
	Tamarin	82
	Capuchin monkey	81
	Guenon	84
Ground running and walking	Macaque	89
	Gelada	94
	Baboon	95
	Mandrill	94
New World semibrachiation	Spider monkey	105
	Howler monkey	98
Old World semibrachiation	Colobus monkey	79
	Langur	78
VERTICAL CLINGING AND LEAPING		
Vertical clinging and leaping	Tarsier	55
	Galago	62
	Sifaka	64
APE LOCOMOTION		
True brachiation	Gibbon	129
	Siamang	148
Quadrumanous	Orangutan	144
Knuckle walking	Chimpanzee	107
	Gorilla	117
ERECT BIPEDALISM		
Erect bipedalism (heel-toe stride)	Human	70

*Average for sample.
Source: Data taken from J. R. Napier and P. H. Napier, *A Handbook of Living Primates* (London: Academic, 1967), 393–395. Used with permission of Academic Press and J. R. Napier. Human index taken from A. H. Schultz, "Proportions of Long Bones in Man and Apes," *Human Biology,* 9 (1937), 281–328.

100 indicates longer arms than legs, while an index under 100 means that the legs are longer. Note that this index in the quadrupedal monkeys is nearly or somewhat below 100. On the other hand, apes, with their characteristically elongated arms, typically have intermembral indices above 100.

Adaptations for Erect Bipedalism

In general, the skeleton of the human trunk, shoulders, and upper limbs shows adaptations to suspensory behavior similar to those found in apes. However, other parts of the human anatomy, particularly the pelvis, leg, and foot, show specializations for erect bipedalism.

A chimpanzee occasionally assumes an upright stance. For the bipedal ape, the major problem is maintaining a balance of the trunk since in an upright position the center of gravity shifts to the front of the pelvis and legs. The chimpanzee must therefore bend the leg at the knee, resulting in an awkward and inefficient form of bipedalism.

In humans, the position of the skull on top of the spine and the development of curvatures of the spine, especially the **lumbar curve,** have resulted in a trunk balanced over the pelvis. The ilium of the pelvis has become short and broad, which provides the surfaces necessary for the attachment of muscles involved in erect bipedalism. With changes in the shape and position of the ilium, the human sacrum has come to lie in a new position, closer to the point of articulation between the femur and the pelvis than it is in the ape. Consequently, the weight of the trunk is transmitted more directly to the legs (Figure 13–7).

Three muscles having an important role in hominoid stance and movement are the **gluteus maximus, gluteus medius,** and **gluteus minimus.** In the ape, all three act as **extensors,** extending the leg at the hip. In the chimpanzee, the gluteus medius is the largest of the three.

The modification of the pelvis in human evolution has brought about reorganization of the muscles involved in movements of the leg. In hominids, changes in the structure and orientation of the ilium have resulted in repositioning of the

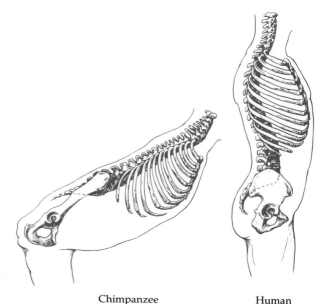

Chimpanzee   Human

FIGURE 13–7   *The pelvis and trunk.* A comparison of the pelvis and trunk in the chimpanzee and the human.

gluteus medius and gluteus minimus. These muscles now act as **abductors,** moving the thigh away from the midline of the body and rotating it laterally as well. Both muscles are responsible for keeping the trunk in a stable, upright position during walking. The gluteus maximus has become a very large muscle and acts as a major extensor of the leg in running and climbing (Figure 13–8).

The leg and foot have also been modified for erect bipedalism. The leg is long and powerful (see Table 13–2 for the human intermembral index). Instead of extending straight down from the pelvis, the thigh extends down at an angle bringing the knees close together for better balance (Figure 16–21).

The foot shows great evolutionary changes and is among the most specialized of human features. In other primates, the big toe is well developed and is capable of movements to the side of the foot; this capability allows these primates to grasp with their feet. In walking, their body weight is borne between the first and second toes. In contrast, the human foot is fairly inflexible, and an arch has developed. The toes are short, including the big toe, and they are inca-

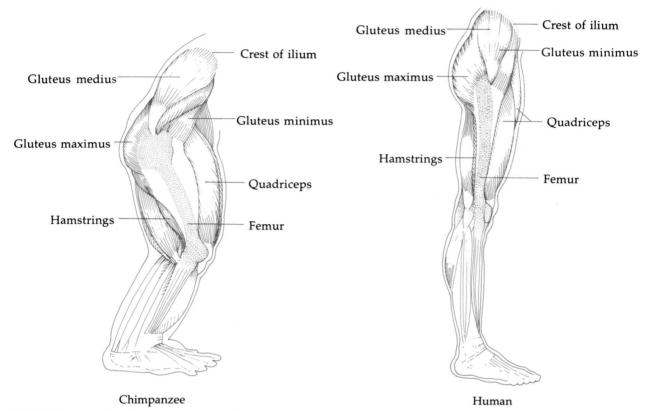

FIGURE 13–8   *Gluteal musculature in a chimpanzee and a human.*

pable of extensive sideways movement. Thus, humans have only a limited grasping ability; they are not capable of manipulating objects with their feet to the degree found in other primates (Figure 13–9). In walking, the heel hits the ground first and the push of the step-off is on the big toe itself.

Comparative Anatomy of the Hand

A major feature of the hominids is their ability to manufacture tools. Evidence for toolmaking comes from two sources. The first is the discovery of stone tools; the earliest archaeological material dates to about 2.6 million years ago. It is also very likely that tools made of perishable materials such as wood and vines date back much earlier in time. The second line of evidence is the anatomy of the hand whose structure permits the fine coordination required for tool manufacture.

The hand serves a number of functions. It is an organ of locomotion, manipulation, and sensation. In most primate species, the locomotor function dominates the manipulative function. In humans, who normally use only their lower limbs in getting from one place to another, the hands are freed for exclusive manipulative activity. This activity is enhanced by a refined sense of touch.

As we have already seen, the primates are characterized by pentadactylism; they have retained the five fingers characteristic of the early placental mammals (Figure 13–10). (In a few species—the spider monkey and the colobus monkey, both semibrachiators—the thumb has been lost.) The palm and fingertips of the primate hand are devoid of hair and are covered with fine **epidermal ridges** that are richly endowed with nerve endings and are responsible for the highly developed sense of touch. The claws characteristic of many mammals have been replaced with nails.

Most prosimians, tarsiers, and New World monkeys, can draw their fingers back against the palm of the hand, facilitating the grasping of branches and other objects. In these primates, movement of the thumb is restricted to the joint between the metacarpal and first phalanges, and to the joint between phalanges.

In the Old World monkeys, apes, and humans, the development of a saddle configuration in the joint between the carpal and metacarpal allows the thumb to be directly opposed to the other fingers (Figure 13–11). Humans differ primarily in the degree of movement possible at this joint. The human thumb is able to oppose the other fingers, and so the fleshy tip of the thumb comes into direct contact with the fleshy tips of all the fingers. In the apes the fingers are elongated, and the metacarpals and phalanges are curved; in humans these bones are straight.

The hand is capable of several types of prehensile functions. In the **power grip,** the animal grabs an object between the palm and the fingers (Figure 13–12); in this position, much force can be applied. All primates are capable of the power grip. More important for fine manipulation of objects is the **precision grip,** where the animal holds an object between the thumb and the fingers. This is made possible by the presence of an opposable thumb. Humans have developed pre-

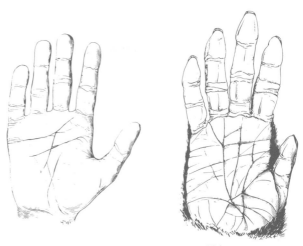

Human   Chimpanzee
FIGURE 13–10   *Hands of a chimpanzee and a human.*

cision handling to a degree not found in other primates.

Summary

Primates display a variety of locomotor patterns, not only among the various species within the order but also within a given species itself. Many fundamental locomotor patterns can be identified within the primate order. These include vertical clinging and leaping, arboreal and terrestrial quadrupedalism, New World semibrachiation, true brachiation, knuckle walking, and erect bipedalism.

While the skeleton of most mammals, such as the horse, is highly specialized for locomotion, the primate skeleton is relatively generalized. It has retained many traits of the generalized mammal, such as five fingers on all limbs and the clavicle, but some degree of skeletal specialization does exist.

The skeletons of living apes and humans are adapted to suspensory behavior. Some of the skeletal features needed for suspension include a short, broad trunk; fewer lumbar vertebrae in the spine; clavicles that extend backward; a scapula that lies on the back of the trunk, with the head of the humerus pointed inward; a shallow socket on the scapula; and the ability to rotate the lower

FIGURE 13–9   *Foot skeletons of a gorilla and a human.*

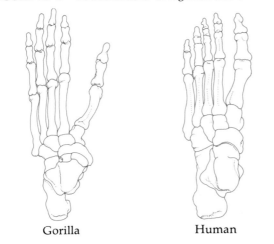

Gorilla   Human

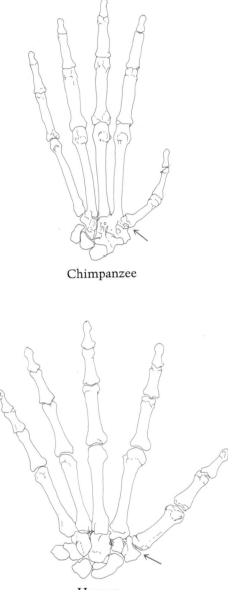

Chimpanzee

Human

FIGURE 13–11 *Hand skeletons of a chimpanzee and a human.* Arrows point to the joint between the carpal and metacarpal of the thumb. In Old World monkeys, apes and humans this joint has a saddle configuration that permits the thumb to be directly opposed to the other fingers.

arm 160 degrees. From studies of the anatomy of the hominoids, many anthropologists have concluded that the common ancestor of humans and apes was an arboreal primate adapted to some degree of suspensory behavior.

Unlike the skeletons of most primates, the human skeleton has become specialized for erect bipedalism. Some modifications that made this possible include the development of the lumbar curve, changes in the shape and orientation of the pelvis, changes in the function of the gluteal musculature, elongation of the leg relative to the arm, and the evolution of a short, stout big toe and an arch of the foot.

One of the most significant characteristics of the hominids is the development of the hand as a fine instrument of manipulation. The primate hand possesses five fingers and fingernails and is covered with fine epidermal ridges. The thumbs of the Old World monkeys, apes, and humans are opposable and thus capable of a fine precision grip.

COMPARATIVE ANATOMY OF THE SKULL AND THE BRAIN

The skull is a very complex part of the skeleton, composed of twenty-eight separate bones plus thirty-two teeth in the adult. A description of the skull and an identification of the individual bones are included in the Appendix.

The skull contains the brain and the sense organs for seeing, hearing, tasting, and smelling, as well as the jaws and teeth, the organs of mastication. The structure of the skull reflects its position on the spine and the nature of the animal's diet. This section discusses many of these points, as well as the structure of the brain itself.

Some Features of the Skull

The skull articulates with the spine by the **occipital condyles,** two rounded projections on the cranial base. The occipital condyles are located on the sides of a large hole, the **foramen magnum,** in the cranial base; the spinal cord passes through the foramen magnum to merge with the brain.

Figure 13–13D shows a bottom view of the skulls of a cat and several primates. The occipital condyles on the cat skull are located far to the rear of the skull. This animal is pronograde; the

(a)

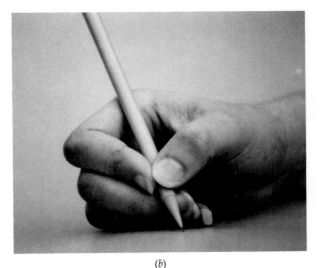

(b)

FIGURE 13–12 *Human hand showing (a) power grip and (b) precision grip.*

skull attaches directly to the front of the spine, where the powerful **nuchal muscles** keep the head up. These muscles in animals such as the cat are relatively large. In the cat, a flange, known as the **nuchal crest,** has formed on the back section of the brain case, where it provides additional surface area for attachment of the nuchal musculature.

Apes are characterized by a degree of orthograde posturing. Consequently, the occipital condyles have moved forward on the cranial base to articulate better with the top of the spine in a

vertical position. In the gorilla, the massive facial skeleton weights the head so that powerful nuchal muscles are needed, hence the presence of a prominent nuchal crest. In humans, the condyles lie in a position almost directly in the center of the underside of the skull. With the reduction of the facial skeleton and the enlargement of the brain case, the skull has achieved a good balance on top of the spine. Note the absence of a prominent nuchal crest.

THE SENSE ORGANS   Seeing, smelling, and hearing are characterized by special sense organs: the eye, nose, and ear. These organs are, in part, housed within the skull. Therefore, the structure of the skull reflects the nature of these organs.

The eyes of most primates are located on the front of the head instead of on the sides of the head as in most other animals. This allows for binocular vision. The lower part of the eye in most mammals is supported on the side by the **zygomatic arch,** or cheekbone; the eye itself is separated from the musculature behind it by a membrane. In living primates, the eye is further supported by the **postorbital bar,** created by the fusion of a process coming down from the top of the orbit and a process coming up from the zygomatic arch. In the anthropoids, and to a large degree in the tarsiers, a bony **postorbital septum** is found behind the eye. It connects the postorbital bar to the brain case, creating a complete eye socket in the anthropoid skull. While a postorbital bar is found in some other mammals, the postorbital septum is a primate specialization (Figure 10–4).

In primates, because of the general reduction in the sense of smell, the nasal region of the skull is relatively small. This results in a general flattening of the face. Associated with the reduction in olfaction is a reduction in the surface area of the nasal membranes and the bony plates that support these membranes. For example, the lemurs possess four pairs of bony plates, called the **ethmoturbinals,** while anthropoids have only two pairs.

The organ of hearing, the ear, consists of the external ear, a tube leading to the eardrum, the eardrum itself, the three middle-ear bones, a coiled tube containing the nerve endings that

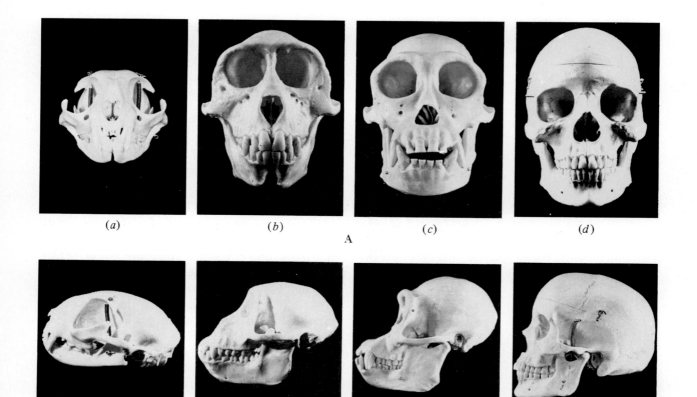

FIGURE 13–13 *Comparative anatomy of the skull.* (*A*) Front view, (*B*) side view, (*C*) back view, and (*D*) bottom view of the skulls of a (*a*) cat, (*b*) rhesus monkey, (*c*) chimpanzee, (*d*) human. (Note: Not to scale.)

sense the vibrations created by sound, and fluid-filled chambers associated with movement and orientation. Most of the ear is housed within the skull.

The middle ear, containing the three middle-ear bones, lies within the **auditory bulla,** a flat or inflated structure that forms in the floor of the skull. Primates are unique among mammals in that the bulla is formed from a small bone of the skull called the petrosal. The tympanic membrane, or eardrum, is supported by a bony element called the **ectotympanic.** The relationship of the ectotympanic to the auditory bulla varies among living primates (Figure 13–14).

The architecture of the skull is a reflection of the organization of the brain, teeth, and sense organs. In the primates the facial skeleton has be-

come relatively small, primarily because of the reduction of the sense of smell. This contrasts with the enlargement of the cranium. In prosimians, the facial skeleton is located to the front of the brain case, but in anthropoids, and especially in humans, the relatively small facial skeleton has moved below the large brain case. Although the nasal apparatus is reduced in size, the massiveness of the teeth and jaw in some species, such as the baboon and gorilla, results in a **prognathism,** which is a jutting forward, of the jaw.

The Evolution of the Primate Brain

The human brain, which allows for the complexity of behavior and culture, is a remarkable organ and is one of the most distinctive features of

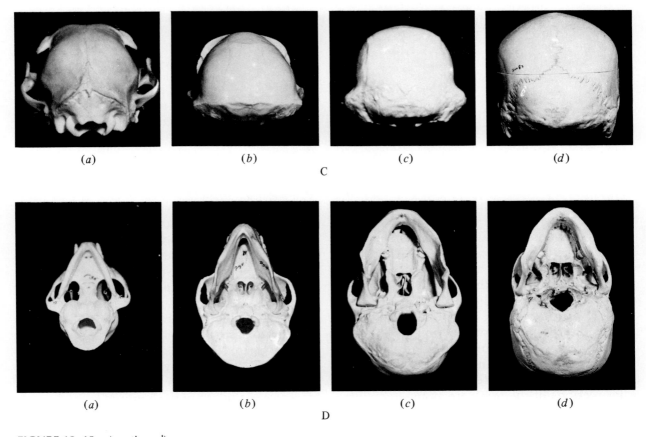

C

(a)   (b)   (c)   (d)

D

(a)   (b)   (c)   (d)

FIGURE 13–13   (continued)

Homo sapiens. The anatomy of the brain is discussed in the Appendix.

The major element of the nervous system in the primitive vertebrate is the single, hollow nerve cord. At the front end of the cord, the primitive brain developed. Here are the sense organs; information gathered by these structures is fed into the brain, which then produces some type of response. The primitive vertebrate brain consists of three swellings in the hollow nerve cord associated with a thickening of walls: the **forebrain, midbrain,** and **hindbrain.** These swellings established the basic structure of all vertebrate brains, including those of the primates (Figure 13–15). In early vertebrates, differentiation of each of the three divisions of the brain already had taken place. Three sections make up the forebrain: the

thalamus, the cerebral hemispheres, and the olfactory bulbs. The midbrain also developed special structures, including the optic lobes. The cerebellum developed as a large swelling on the hindbrain, with the thick lower portion becoming the medulla oblongata. These are only the major features of the early vertebrate brain, for many other structures were also developing. In the early vertebrates, the paired cerebral hemispheres of the forebrain were smooth swellings; they were associated primarily with the sense of smell.

In the early reptiles, the cerebrum enlarged. Although it is still associated with smell, a new area appeared, the **neocortex,** a gray covering on the cerebrum. This cortex is involved with the association and coordination of various impulses

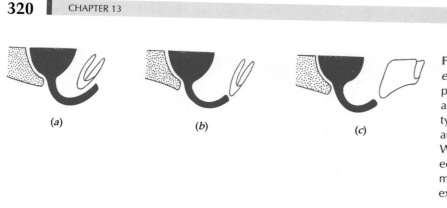

FIGURE 13–14 *Primate middle ears.* (*a*) In the lemurs, the ectotympanic is a simple ring. (*b*) In the lorises and New World monkeys, the ectotympanic is fused to the rim of the auditory bulla. (*c*) In the tarsiers, Old World monkeys, and hominoids, the ectotympanic is fused to the outer margin of the auditory bulla and is extended into a tube.

coming from the sense organs and other areas of the brain.

In early mammals, the area of the cerebrum associated with smell was important, but the neocortex begins to show an expansion. The neocortex is separated from the rest of the cortex by a groove. This new area is the major part of the covering, or cortex, of the brain. This part of the mammalian brain expanded in size, and convolutions are seen on the surface in many species. In this expanded cortex many of the functions that were controlled in the early mammals by other sections of the brain are associated with the cerebral cortex. For example, in mammals visual stimuli are received by the cerebral cortex rather than by the optic lobes of the midbrain. Several vertebrate brains are compared in Figure 13–16.

THE PRIMATE BRAIN   The evolution of the primate brain is characterized by a general increase in brain size relative to body size. As the size of the body increases, so does the size of various parts of the body. Not all body parts increase at the same rate; some parts of the body, such as the brain, increase at a faster rate. This is the concept of **allometric growth.** In many large animals, the brain is relatively larger than it is in closely related smaller species.

Since humans are large primates, we expect to see a large brain due to allometric growth. The increase in the size of the hominid brain through time, however, is greater than can be explained by allometric growth alone. The increase in brain size over and beyond that which can be explained by an increase in body size is termed the **encephalization quotient (EQ).** Table 13–3 gives

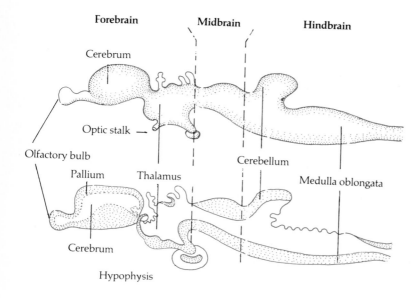

FIGURE 13–15 *The vertebrate brain.* A generalized and schematized representation of the vertebrate brain. The lower figure is a longitudinal section showing differences in the thickness of the brain wall.

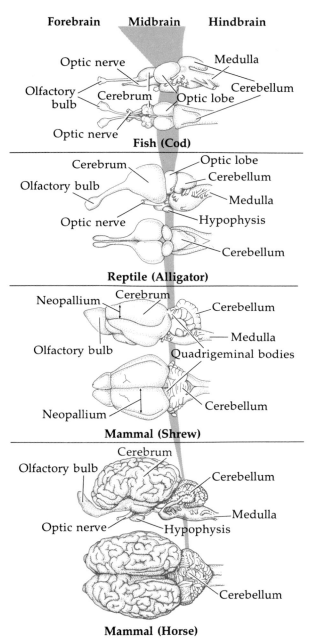

Forebrain   Midbrain   Hindbrain

Fish (Cod)

Reptile (Alligator)

Mammal (Shrew)

Mammal (Horse)

FIGURE 13–16   *Comparison of vertebrate brains.* Side and top views of four vertebrate brains. Note expansion of the forebrain in the mammals.

TABLE 13–3	
ENCEPHALIZATION QUOTIENT IN SOME PRIMATES	
PRIMATE	EQ
Tarsier	1.29
Spider monkey	2.33
Rhesus monkey	2.09
Hamadryas baboon	2.35
Gibbon	2.74
Orangutan (male)	1.63
Gorilla (male)	1.53
Chimpanzee (male)	2.48
Human (male)	7.79

Source: H. J. Jerison, *Evolution of the Brain and Intelligence* (New York: Academic, 1973).

Many convolutions greatly increase its surface area, and the cerebral cortex in humans completely covers the olfactory lobes and the midbrain. In the course of primate evolution, the different areas that are associated with specific functions have become more clearly defined (Figure 13–17). Areas of the brain concerned with the sense of smell have undergone reduction, while areas associated with vision and the sense of touch have become elaborated.

The evolution of toolmaking abilities, language, and other human characteristics has affected the evolution of the brain. The cortical areas associated with hand coordination are about three times as extensive in the human brain as they are in the ape brain, and the expansion of the areas concerned with language is even greater.

The cerebral cortex makes possible a level of complex behavior that we call intelligence, which is most highly developed in humans. The cortex also allows for **social intelligence,** through which the knowledge and images that originate in an individual's brain can be transferred by speech (and in the last 5000 years, writing) to the brains of others. The knowledge of an entire society, which is always greater than the knowledge of any one individual, can be drawn on to meet crises. This is one major factor that differentiates humans from other species.

several examples of this measure. Note the tremendous difference between humans and other primates.

THE CEREBRAL CORTEX   The neocortex covers the entire cerebrum in the Anthropoidea.

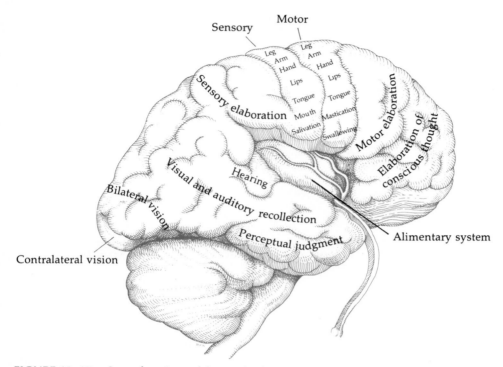

Sensory

Motor

Leg
Arm
Hand
Lips
Tongue
Mouth
Salivation

Leg
Arm
Hand
Lips
Tongue
Mastication
Swallowing

Sensory elaboration

Motor elaboration

Elaboration of conscious thought

Hearing

Visual and auditory recollection

Bilateral vision

Perceptual judgment

Contralateral vision

Alimentary system

FIGURE 13–17 *Some functions of the cerebral cortex.*

Erect Bipedalism and the Human Brain

In the evolution of the human pelvis, discussed earlier, a repositioning of the sacrum in hominids has created a complete bony ring through which the birth canal passes. In the chimpanzee, the articulations of the sacrum to the innominate bones and the pelvis to the femur are farther apart than in humans, which means that the birth canal has a bony roof at one point and a bony floor at another. In humans, the bony roof has moved over the bony floor, creating a complete bony ring through which the head of the child must pass at birth (Figure 13–18). The flexibility of the human infant's skull, however, allows for a certain degree of compression as the child passes through the birth canal, and for a great deal of growth after birth.

Other animals' brains are almost completely developed at birth. For instance, the rhesus monkey at birth has a brain that is approximately 75 percent of its adult size, and the brain of a chim-

panzee newborn is 45 to 50 percent of its adult size. In contrast, the human newborn has a brain less than 30 percent of its adult size, attaining over 90 percent of its adult size by the fifth year of life. Consequently, the child is dependent upon others for a long time, and it is during this extended period that learning and mental abilities develop.

The Brain Case

As the brain enlarges, so does the neurocranium in which the brain is housed. In most mammals, as in the cat, the facial skeleton is relatively large in relation to the brain case, and it is located in front of the brain case. In primates, the brain case is larger than the facial skeleton, and the facial skeleton is located underneath the brain case rather than in front of it (Figure 13–13).

The volume of the interior of the brain case is the **cranial capacity.** Note that cranial capacity is the volume of the brain case, *not* the size of the

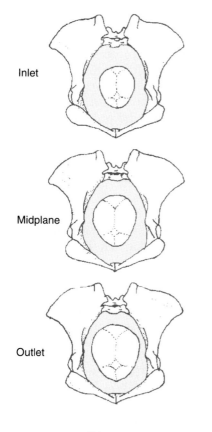

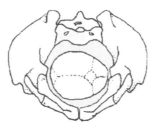

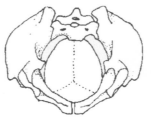

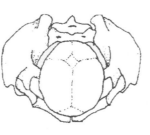

Inlet

Midplane

Outlet

Chimpanzee

Human

FIGURE 13–18 *Pelvis and fetal head.* A female pelvis of a chimpanzee and a human from below. Note the size of the head of the fetus in childbirth at the level of the pelvic inlet, midplane, and pelvic outlet.

brain (Table 13–4). Although the two are close, the brain itself is covered by tissue, nerves, and blood vessels, and so its volume is always less than that of the cranium.

Wide variation of cranial capacity is usually seen within a given species. While we note that the average cranial capacity of modern humans is 1350 cubic centimeters, the nonpathological range runs from about 900 to more than 2000 cubic centimeters. Within this range, there appears to be no correlation between brain size and intelligence. Even between species, the structure and physiology of the brain are more important than its size.

Since the inside of the brain case does conform roughly to the outside surface of the brain, it can convey some information about the brain itself. Often a cast is made of the inside of a cra-

TABLE 13–4

CRANIAL CAPACITIES OF THE LIVING HOMINOIDEA

PRIMATE	AVERAGE CRANIAL CAPACITY (CUBIC CENTIMETERS)
Gibbon	102
Chimpanzee	399
Orangutan	434
Gorilla	535
Human	1350

Source: P. V. Tobias, "The Distribution of Cranial Capacity Values among Living Hominoids," *Proceedings of the Third International Congress of Primatology, Zurich, 1970,* vol. 1 (Basel: Karger, 1971), 18–35.

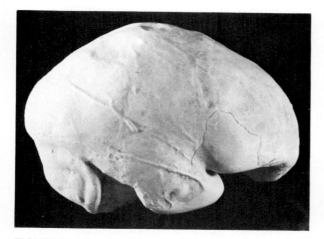

FIGURE 13–19 *An endocranial cast.* An endocranial cast of *Homo erectus,* a fossil hominid from China.

nium of a fossil find; the result is an **endocranial cast** like the one in Figure 13–19. From such a cast the relative proportion of the lobes of the brain and other information can be inferred. Remember, however, that this is not a fossil brain but simply a cast of the inside of the brain case.

Primate Dentition

The ingestion of food is a major prerequisite for life in animals and involves several parts of the anatomy. In vertebrates, the teeth, jaw, and muscles used for chewing are used in preparing food for intake into the digestive system of the body. We have already seen that mammals are characterized by heterodonty, the regional differentiation of teeth into different kinds of teeth that serve different functions, and diphyodonty, the development of two sets of teeth, the deciduous dentition (milk teeth) followed by the adult dentition. In general, the primates have retained a fairly unspecialized tooth structure; the reduction in the number of teeth has not progressed to the degree that it has in many other mammalian orders.

PRIMATE TEETH   Among mammals we recognize four different kinds of teeth: incisors, ca-

nines, premolars, and molars (Figure 13–20). Among primates in general, the incisor tends to be a broad, cutting type of tooth with a rather simple structure; it is often described as "spatulate." The incisors are used to grasp food. Primates that eat fruit use their incisors to tear off small pieces that can then be properly masticated (chewed) by the premolars and molars. Smaller food objects, such as seeds and grasses, are usually passed directly back to the chewing teeth. Primates that specialize in this type of diet often have smaller incisors than do the fruit eaters.

As we saw in Chapter 10, prosimians are characterized by the development of a dental comb, which is formed by lower incisors and canines that project forward horizontally (Figure 13–21). The lower canine often takes on the appearance of an incisor and is included in the comb. In this situation, the functions of the canine are taken over by the first premolar, which then becomes caninelike in appearance. The upper incisors are frequently reduced in size. The animal uses the comb for grooming the fur and for scraping gum and resins off the bark of trees.

The canine is a simple, pointed, curved tooth, usually larger than the other teeth. This tooth serves many functions, such as grasping, stabbing, ripping, and tearing food, and plays a role in defense and agonistic display. Canines of the

FIGURE 13–20 *Four types of primate teeth.* Human dentition from half of the upper jaw and half of the lower jaw.

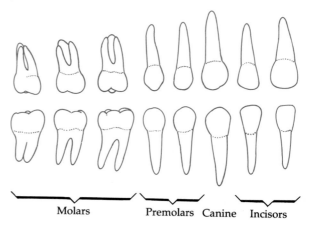

Molars   Premolars Canine Incisors

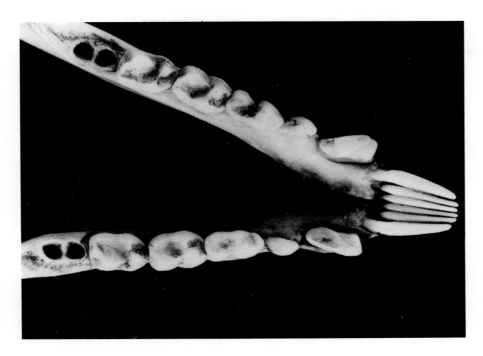

FIGURE 13–21 *The dental comb.* The lower jaw of a lemur. The dental comb is made up of the lower two canines and four incisors.

Anthropoidea tend to be much larger in males than in females, another example of sexual dimorphism. Canines, highly developed in the terrestrial male baboon, act as a weapon in troop defense.

The premolars and molars are often called the **cheek teeth;** these are the teeth used in chewing. The premolars, or bicuspids in dental terminology, are simple teeth that usually have two **cusps,** or points. In many mammals, including some primates, the premolar either has developed additional cusps to become more molarlike or possesses only a single cusp; for this reason anthropologists do not call the premolars bicuspids.

The molars are the most complex teeth in structure because of the formation of several cusps and minor cusps, ridges, and valleys. The molars chew and prepare the food for passage to the stomach for digestion. This process is especially critical for processing leaves and insects, which are composed, in part, of cellulose and chitin, respectively. Food is sheared between the crests on the surface of the molars and is crushed and ground between the various cusps, thus reducing the size of the food particles. The smaller the food particles, the greater the surface area per unit of volume upon which the digestive enzymes can act.

DENTAL FORMULAS   The types and numbers of teeth are designated in **dental formulas,** some of which are listed in Table 13–5. Since dentition is bilaterally symmetrical, we need only note the numbers and kinds of teeth on one side of the jaw. The teeth of the upper jaw are shown above the line, and those of the lower jaw, below the line. While the notations for the upper and lower jaws are generally the same, there are exceptions. In the formula, the four numbers, separated by dots, are the number of incisors, canines, premolars, and molars, respectively, per quadrant. Paleontologists have reconstructed the dental formula of the common ancestor of living placental mammals as

$$\frac{3.1.4.3}{3.1.4.3}$$

Primate evolution is characterized by a loss of teeth in the dental formula, although the total reduction in tooth number in primates is not as great as that found in some other mammalian orders.

TABLE 13–5

ADULT DENTAL FORMULAS OF LIVING PRIMATES

PRIMATE	DENTAL FORMULA	TOTAL NUMBER OF TEETH
Lemurs	$\frac{2.1.3.3}{2.1.3.3}$	36
Indris	$\frac{2.1.2.3}{1.1.2.3}$	30
Aye-ayes	$\frac{1.0.1.3}{1.0.0.3}$	18
Marmosets	$\frac{2.1.3.2}{2.1.3.2}$	32
New World monkeys	$\frac{2.1.3.3}{2.1.3.3}$	36
Old World monkeys, apes, and humans	$\frac{2.1.2.3}{2.1.2.3}$	32

The dental formulas for the prosimians show much variation. All the Ceboidea are characterized by three premolars per quadrant; among the ceboids, the cebids have retained three molars while the marmosets and tamarins have two. All the Old World anthropoids have thirty-two teeth and the dental formula

$$\frac{2.1.2.3}{2.1.2.3}$$

In apes and humans a further reduction in the dental formula is possible since one or more of the third molars (wisdom teeth) do not develop at all in some individuals. Also, when the third molars erupt, the human jaw is often too small to accommodate them, and the resulting impacted molars require surgical removal.

APE DENTITION   Because of a common ancestry, the dentition of the panids and that of the hominids have many traits in common. Even so, each evolutionary line has evolved several distinctive features (Figure 13–22). The incisors of the great apes are quite broad and spatula-like, and the upper incisors of these animals are implanted in the jaw at an angle.

The ape canine is large and projecting. When the animal closes its mouth, the canines interlock, each fitting into a space, or **diastema,** in the opposite jaw. In the upper jaw the diastema is in front of the canine, while in the lower jaw it is behind the canine. Thus, in chewing, the chimpanzee cannot use the more rotary motion characteristic of hominids. The canines of gorillas and orangutans show marked sexual dimorphism.

When the mandible of a prosimian is looked at from above, the row of teeth, or **dental arcade,** presents the outline of the letter V. With the evolution of large, projecting canines in the ape, the front of the mandible has broadened so that the ape dental arcade is in the shape of the letter U.

The first lower premolar in the ape is also specialized because the canine in the upper jaw shears directly in front of it. This premolar is larger than the other and has an enlarged cusp. This tooth, known as a **sectorial premolar,** presents a sharpening edge for the canine. The cheek teeth, the premolars and molars, are arranged in two straight rows that parallel each other, although they often converge toward the back of the jaw.

The basic structure of the molars in humans is the same as that in chimpanzees. The upper molar contains four cusps, and the lower molar has five. The arrangement of the five cusps and the grooves between them suggests a letter Y and therefore is called the **Y-5 pattern** (Figure 13–23). This contrasts with the **bilophodont** molar struc-

FIGURE 13–22   *Dentition of a chimpanzee.*

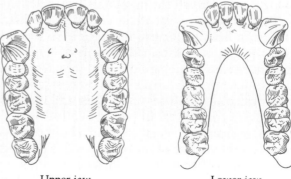

Upper jaw   Lower jaw

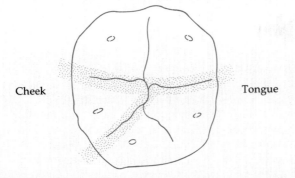

FIGURE 13–23 *The Y-5 molar pattern.* Note the arrangement of the valleys and five cusps in the lower hominoid molar.

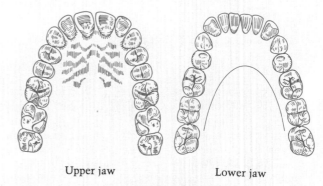

Upper jaw   Lower jaw

FIGURE 13–24 *Human dentition.*

ture in the monkey, whose lower molar consists of four cusps with a small constriction separating them into two pairs.

MODERN HOMINID DENTITION

In the evolution of hominid dentition, the size of the teeth has decreased and the length of that portion of the jaw that holds the cheek teeth has decreased relative to the length of the skull. When viewed from the side, all the teeth are at the same level; the canine is not projecting, and the first lower premolar is not sectorial. As shown in Figure 13–24, the teeth are arranged in a curved, or parabolic, dental arcade with no diastema.

The human incisors, in contrast to those of the ape, are narrower and are implanted vertically in the jaw. Human canines are small, with a spatulate cutting edge; they do not project or interlock, nor do they show much sexual dimorphism. This contrasts markedly with the ape canines, which are pointed, projecting, and interlocking and show great sexual dimorphism. Diastemas associated with the ape canines are absent in humans.

Like the ape molars, the human upper molars have four cusps (although the upper third molar tends to have only three), while the lower molars exhibit the Y-5 pattern. In contrast to ape molars, human molars show more rounded and compacted cusps. These features are due to the fact that hominid teeth have relatively thick enamel,

the outer covering of the teeth. Thick enamel, characteristic of both living and fossil hominids, is suited to the increased crushing and grinding required in the processing of hard, tough food materials. Most of the apes possess relatively thin enamel; the thickness of enamel in the orangutan is intermediate between that of humans and the other apes. Box 13–2 discusses the importance of tooth enamel in comparative anatomy.

As we saw earlier, the permanent teeth normally erupt in a predictable pattern. Monkeys and apes are similar in that the canine tends to be the tooth that erupts last or next to last. This may be related to the fact that the large, projecting canine can be an effective and dangerous weapon. The monkey and ape canine erupts after the animal has attained full adult size and social status. The human canine erupts before the second and third molars and, in some individuals, may even erupt before one or more of the premolars.

Besides differences in the order of eruption, the time over which the teeth erupt is extended in humans as a consequence of the extended childhood period. Thus, by the time the second molar erupts, the first molar has had the opportunity to be partially ground down by abrasion from some types of food particles. When the third molar erupts, it shows a high relief with its patterns of cusps and valleys, compared with the second molar, which is somewhat ground down, and the first molar, which is ground down even further. This steplike wear pattern in a fossil jaw

BOX 13–2

THE ULTRASTRUCTURE OF TOOTH ENAMEL

The development of the scanning electron microscope has made possible the development of comparative studies on a microscopic level. This technology has been used to study tooth enamel, the hard outer layer of the tooth. These studies are exciting because enamel changes very little during the process of fossilization and teeth are very common in the fossil record. In fact, many extinct species are known by their teeth alone.

Tooth enamel is 96 percent mineral—crystals of apatitic calcium phosphate. These crystals form into rods or prisms which are then assembled into even larger units. Electron microscope studies have shown that the structure of tooth enamel is very regular, yet variations exist among species.

There are three major patterns in the arrangement of prisms. Distinct differences in pattern exist between living hominids and living and fossil anthropoids. Pattern 1 prisms are found in insectivores and many bats. Pattern 2 prisms are found in most hoofed mammals, rodents, and marsupials. Prisms with pattern 3, often called the "keyhole" pattern, are commonly found in humans. Many subtypes also exist. All three enamel types can be found in the primate order. While pattern 3 is found in human enamel, pattern 2 is frequently found in the enamel of the rhesus monkey, and pattern 1 in the lemurs.

Differences are also found among the various species of hominoids. In general, pattern 3 enamel characterizes the great apes and humans. However, the relative abundance of some of the subtypes differs. A specialist in the microstructure of tooth enamel can distinguish human enamel from chimpanzee and gorilla enamel when viewed with a scanning electron microscope.

Because of variation in structure, pattern differences become a valuable diagnostic tool. Remember that teeth are the most common parts of the skeleton to be preserved in the fossil record. Since teeth are largely composed of minerals, few changes are found in teeth that have been buried in the ground. Analysis of the microstructure of tooth enamel can therefore provide valuable clues as to the evolutionary relationship of a particular fossil tooth and living primate forms.

References: A. Boyde and L. Martin, "The Microstructure of Dental Enamel," in D. J. Chivers, B. A. Wood, and A. Bilsborough (eds.), *Food Acquisition and Processing in Primates* (New York: Plenum, 1984), 341–367; T. G. Bromage and M. C. Dean, "Re-evaluation of the Age at Death of Immature Fossil Hominids," *Nature,* 317 (1985), 525–527; and D. B. Gantt, "Enamel Thickness and Ultrastructure in Hominoids: With Reference to Form, Function, and Phylogeny," in D. R. Swindler and J. Erwin (eds.), *Systematics, Evolution, and Anatomy* (New York: Liss, 1986), 453–475.

may be indicative of an extended childhood period.

The reduction in the size of the teeth may be related to the development of tool use and a more meat-oriented diet. The apes, for example, use their large front teeth to break open hard fruits; humans might use a chopping tool held in the hand in the same situation. Another suggestion is that a major function of the large, projecting canine is its role in agonistic display. With the development of cooperative hunting in human societies, such displays probably no longer occurred. Also, for defense, humans use weapons instead of canines.

Remember, however, that use and disuse of a structure during a lifetime does not directly af- fect the evolution of that structure. The reduction of the canine represents a shift in frequencies from the alleles that produce larger canines to those that produce smaller ones; that is, mutations were originally responsible for creating a range of variation in canine size. When the large canines lost their selective advantage, the smaller canines may have gained some selective advantage; through time, the frequency of large canines gradually decreased.

The Jaw

The human jaw is smaller and is shorter relative to the skull than is the ape jaw. Since human food is usually cut up or in some way processed into smaller pieces so that it is easier to chew, humans do not need to exert as much pressure when chewing as the apes do. In time, of course, fire was used to cook meat, thus tenderizing it.

In the anthropoids, the mandible, or lower jaw, consists of two fused symmetrical halves. In the ape, the forces generated by the jaw in eating are great, and the curved front section of the mandible, where the two halves of the mandible have fused, is reinforced internally by a buttress, the **simian shelf.** This shelf rarely occurs in the hominids. In modern humans, the evolution of a small jaw has resulted in a **chin,** a product of changes in the growth and development pattern of the jaw (Figure 13–25).

The muscles that operate the jaw have also changed in the course of human evolution, becoming, for the most part, smaller. The **temporalis** muscle arises on the side of the skull and inserts on the jaw (Figure 13–26). In the gorilla this muscle is very large, while the brain case is relatively small, and so a large flange, the **sagittal crest,** develops across the top of the skull, providing the surface area necessary for muscle attachment. The **masseter,** another muscle that functions in chewing, arises on the zygomatic arch of the skull and inserts on the mandible. An animal with large teeth and jaw and, consequently, a large masseter, has a robust zygomatic. Since the temporalis passes through the opening formed by the zygomatic and the side of the skull, a large temporalis is associated with a

flaring zygomatic arch. In modern humans the zygomatic arch is slender and not flaring.

Also related to the size of the mandible is the development of **brow ridges.** The brow ridge acts to reinforce the skull and absorb the forces generated by the process of chewing. Thus, animals with large jaws have large brow ridges, and those with small jaws have small brow ridges or none at all.

Summary

The human skull, composed of twenty-eight separate bones plus thirty-two teeth in the adult, is a very complex part of the skeleton. The skull articulates with the spine by means of the occipital condyles on the base of the skull. In most mammals the condyles are located toward the rear of the skull, while in primates they are located underneath the skull. In humans they are positioned almost directly in the center of the skull; this achieves a good balance of the skull atop the spine. The general trend in primate evolution has been a reduction in the facial skeleton. The nasal apparatus is reduced in size, and the eyes are encased in bony eye sockets located on the front of the skull.

Within the primate order we see the progressive enlargement of brain volume and development of the cerebral cortex. The human neocortex makes possible higher mental activities. In association with other features, such as bipedal-

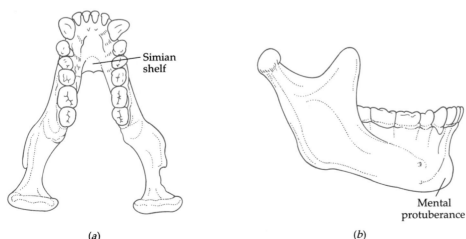

Simian shelf

(a)

Mental protuberance

(b)

FIGURE 13–25 *Simian shelf and chin.* Note the simian shelf in the ape mandible and the chin or mental protuberance on the human mandible.

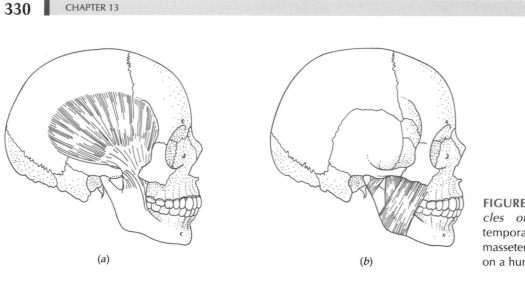

FIGURE 13–26 *The muscles of the jaws.* The temporalis muscle (*a*) and masseter muscle (*b*) as seen on a human skull.

(*a*)

(*b*)

ism and manual dexterity, the cerebral cortex allows for social as well as individual intelligence. It is this social intelligence that enables humans as a species to interact with the environment. This interaction can be advantageous, as seen in the general increase in comfort and living standards that technology can bring, or devastating, as evidenced by pollution, war, and depletion of resources.

The increase in the size of the human brain is reflected in the increased volume of the cranium, or brain case. While the average cranial capacity is 1350 cubic centimeters, the range of variation is large. Within normal limits, no correlation between brain size and intelligence exists.

The primates have retained a fairly unspecialized tooth structure. The New World monkeys have three premolars per quadrant of the mouth, and most have a total of thirty-six teeth. All the Old World anthropoids have only two premolars, for a total of thirty-two permanent teeth. General characteristics of modern hominid dentition are a reduction in tooth size, lack of a sectorial premolar, a parabolic dental arcade, lack of a diastema and projecting canine, vertical implantation of the incisors, early eruption of the canine, a differential wear pattern of the molars, and thick tooth enamel.

The human jaw is smaller and shorter, relative to the skull, than is the ape jaw; a chin is present. The muscles that operate the jaw are smaller. The temporalis muscle in the ape is very large, while the brain case is relatively small. A large flange, the sagittal crest, develops across the top of the skull, providing the surface area necessary for muscle attachment. The large masseter muscle is associated with a robust, flaring zygomatic arch. The large brow ridge acts to reinforce the skull and absorb the forces generated by the process of chewing. The modern human skull lacks a sagittal crest and is characterized by small or absent brow ridges and a slender, nonflaring zygomatic arch.

MOLECULAR BIOLOGY AND CYTOGENETICS

Evolution has been defined on the genetic level as changes in the gene pool of a population. Ultimately, this refers to changes in the genes themselves. This section examines **comparative cytogenetics,** the comparative study of chromosomes, and **molecular biology,** the comparative study of the molecules of living organisms.

Comparative Cytogenetics

The genetic material within the cell is found in small bodies called chromosomes (Chapter 4). Comparative cytogenetics is the comparative study of chromosomes from the cells of different species of plants and animals. Such studies shed

TABLE 13–6

SOME CHROMOSOME NUMBERS OF PRIMATES

PRIMATE	FAMILY	NUMBER OF CHROMOSOMES
Owl monkey	Cebidae	54
Spider monkey	Cebidae	34
Capuchin monkey	Cebidae	54
Woolly monkey	Cebidae	62
Squirrel monkey	Cebidae	44
Common marmoset	Callitrichidae	46
Red-crowned mangabey	Cercopithecidae	42
Vervet monkey	Cercopithecidae	60
Patas monkey	Cercopithecidae	54
Rhesus monkey	Cercopithecidae	42
Baboon	Cercopithecidae	42
Indian langur	Cercopithecidae	44
White-handed gibbon	Hylobatidae	44
Crested gibbon	Hylobatidae	52
Siamang	Hylobatidae	50
Orangutan	Pongidae	48
Gorilla	Panidae	48
Chimpanzee	Panidae	48
Human	Hominidae	46

Source: T. C. Hsu and K. Benirschke, *Atlas of Mammalian Chromosomes,* vol. 10 (Berlin: Springer-Verlag, 1977), pt. 4.

light on the evolutionary relationships and histories of these species.

CHROMOSOME NUMBER   A species is associated with a characteristic number of chromosomes. In *Homo sapiens* nondividing body cells contain forty-six chromosomes. Table 13–6 lists the chromosome numbers of a variety of primate species, varying from thirty-four in the spider monkey to sixty-two in the woolly monkey.

Chromosome number is not necessarily consistent within any given taxonomic group such as a family; closely related species may have differing chromosome numbers. For example, the white-handed gibbon has forty-four chromosomes, while the crested gibbon has fifty-two, yet both species belong to the same genus. On the other hand, widely differing species may share the same number of chromosomes. The Old World patas monkey and the New World owl monkey both have the same chromosome

number, fifty-four. It therefore follows that chromosome number is not evidence of evolutionary relationships. All the great apes, however, share the same chromosome number of forty-eight.

CHROMOSOME MORPHOLOGY   As we saw in Chapter 4, chromosomes differ in size and position of the centromere. On the basis of these characteristics, chromosomes may be classified and arranged in a standard way; this standardized arrangement of chromosomes is a **karyotype.** Human karyotypes are shown in Figure 4–1.

Chromosomes may be placed in one of four classes, depending on the relative position of the centromere (Figure 13–27). A chromosome is **metacentric** when the centromere appears approximately in the center of the chromosome; the two arms of the chromosome are of roughly the same length.

A **submetacentric** chromosome has a centromere lying to one side of the chromosome's center; this produces arms of unequal length, the short and long arms. An **acrocentric** chromosome has a centromere near one end; this produces arms of very unequal length, and the short arm is often extremely small. A **telocentric** chromosome is characterized by a centromere located at the very end of the chromosome. The human karyotype includes no telocentric chromosomes.

Figure 13–28 shows a composite karyotype comparing chimpanzee and human chromosomes. Although the chromosome numbers differ, the chromosomes exhibit a high degree of similarity in their appearance. Hypothetically, their similarity is the result of a common inheritance; in other words, these chromosomes are

FIGURE 13–27 *Types of chromosomes.* Chromosomes, as seen in metaphase, can be classed into four types based on the position of the centromere: (*a*) telocentric, (*b*) acrocentric, (*c*) submetacentric, (*d*) metacentric.

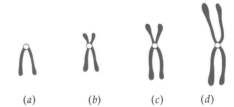

(*a*)   (*b*)   (*c*)   (*d*)

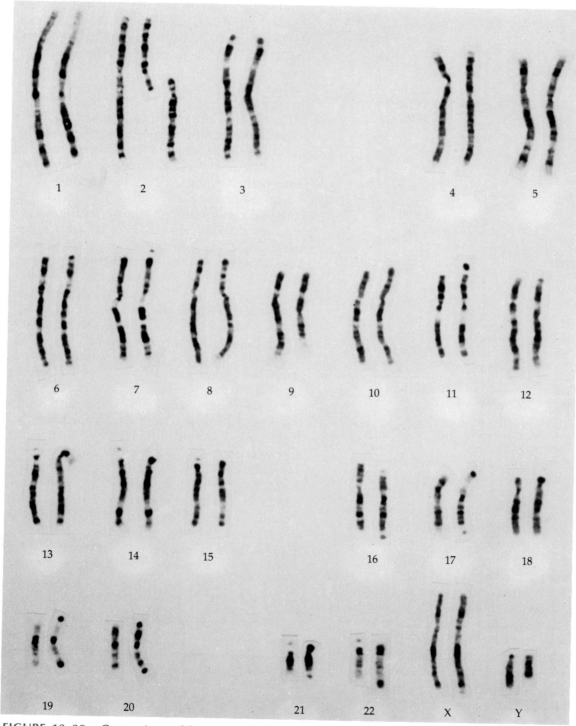

FIGURE 13–28 *Comparison of human and chimpanzee chromosomes.* The great similarity of human and chimpanzee chromosomes is shown in this composite karyotype. For each pair, the human chromosome is shown on the left and the chimpanzee chromosome on the right.

homologous. Through gene mapping, homologous genes are being found in the same position on human and chimpanzee chromosomes.

In Chapter 4 we saw how abnormal numbers of chromosomes result in particular abnormalities. A chimpanzee with forty-nine chromosomes has been reported, and the animal exhibits physical features very similar to those of Down's syndrome in humans. Human patients with this abnormality have three number 21 chromosomes; the chimpanzee with the similar group of symptoms has three number 22 chromosomes. In both humans and chimpanzees these are very small acrocentric chromosomes, and strong evidence indicates that human chromosome 21 is homologous to chimpanzee chromosome 22.

The Nature of Chromosome Evolution

Human and chimpanzee chromosomes are very similar, but they are not identical. Beginning with a common ancestor, several small evolutionary changes have occurred independently in the human and chimpanzee evolutionary lines. What are the mechanisms of this chromosomal evolution?

In Chapter 4 we listed four mechanisms of chromosome alteration: deletion, duplication, translocation, and inversion (Figure 4–5). The first two, deletion and duplication, usually result in a visible abnormality since genetic material is either missing or present in excess. Individuals with such abnormal chromosomes are not likely to survive and reproduce.

The other alterations, translocation and inversion, may lead to a viable chromosome since the genetic material is only being rearranged. In addition, a chromosome can break into two smaller chromosomes, or two small chromosomes can fuse together to form one larger chromosome. All these mechanisms would result in the evolution of new chromosome numbers and/or morphology.

COMPARATIVE STUDY OF BANDED CHROMOSOMES Because the members of a particular chromosome group in a karyotype are often so similar, they can be paired only by using special techniques. Specific chromosomes can be differentiated by several methods that reveal a pattern of bands. The banding pattern is specific for each chromosome. In addition, the use of banding techniques makes it possible to observe extremely detailed structures of chromosomes.

The chromosomes seen in Figure 13–28 are giemsa-banded. Detailed analysis of the banding patterns leads to the conclusion that "essentially every band and subband observed in man has a direct counterpart in the chimpanzee chromosome complements."[2] Since the banding pattern is largely a reflection of the genetic content of the chromosomes, this supports the theory of close genetic similarity between chimpanzees and humans.

Comparisons of human and chimpanzee banded chromosomes reveal many interesting differences. Figure 13–29b illustrates a **pericentric inversion** in which two breaks occur, one on either side of the centromere. The centerpiece turns around and rejoins the two outside pieces. Thus, human chromosome 4 and its chimpanzee counterpart both contain the same bands, but their relative positions are different. Nine human chromosomes differ from their chimpanzee counterparts in such a manner.

Ten other chromosomes, including the X chromosome, differ from their chimpanzee counterparts because they contain extra chromosome material called **constitutive heterochromatin.** Geneticists believe that this material does not contain any actual genes (Figure 13–29c).

We have already noted that the human karyotype contains one less chromosome pair than the chimpanzee karyotype does. When we carefully pair up each human chromosome with a chimpanzee chromosome that appears to be similar, we find that human chromosome 2 does not have a homologous chromosome from the chimpanzee set. Also, two small acrocentric chimpanzee chromosomes are left unmatched.

One hypothesis proposes that human chromosome 2 evolved from a fusion of two acrocentric ancestral chromosomes. Such an event is il-

---

[2]J. J. Yunis, J. R. Sawyer, and K. Dunham, "The Striking Resemblance of High-Resolution G-Banded Chromosomes of Man and Chimpanzee," *Science,* 208 (1980), 1145.

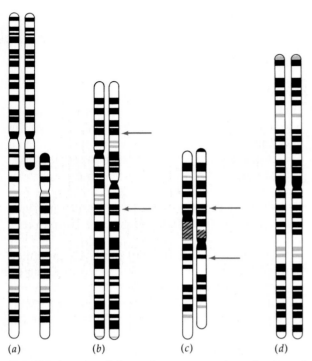

FIGURE 13–29 *Schematic representation of selected human and chimpanzee chromosomes.* Human chromosomes are on the left. (*a*) Human chromosome 2 shows similarities with two chimpanzee chromosomes. (*b*) Chromosome 4 shows an inversion; breaks (shown by arrows) occur on either side of the centromere, and the centerpiece becomes turned around. (*c*) Chromosome 9 shows an inversion plus chromosomal material, indicated by hatched lines, that is not thought to contain any actual genes. (*d*) Chromosome 3 shows virtually no variation between the human and the chimpanzee.

FIGURE 13–30 *The evolution of human chromosome 2.* It is hypothesized that human chromosome 2 evolved from a fusion of two small ancestral chromosomes: (*a*) ancestral chromosomes; (*b*) short arms broken off; (*c*) centromeres fused together.

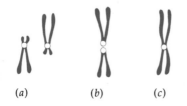

lustrated in Figure 13–30. The two short arms of the two acrocentric chromosomes break off. If these small, short arms carry no important genes, their loss would not adversely affect the organism. Then the two centromeres fuse, forming a new, larger chromosome. Once this becomes fixed in the population, the number of chromosomes is reduced from forty-eight to forty-six. We can conclude that the common ancestor of humans and chimpanzees possessed forty-eight chromosomes, which is the chromosome number of the other great apes as well. Figure 13–29*a* compares human chromosome 2 with two acrocentric chimpanzee chromosomes. The matching bands support the hypothesis that this human chromosome arose through a fusion of the two smaller ancestral chromosomes.

The Study of Molecular Structure

In the previous sections we saw how evolutionary relationships can be established upon analysis of the genetic material on the cellular level. In the following sections we will examine similarities on the molecular level, looking first at protein molecules and then at the DNA molecule itself.

In sickle-cell anemia, the abnormal hemoglobin S differs from the normal hemoglobin A by a single amino acid substitution. This substitution is a reflection of a single base change in the DNA molecule controlling beta-chain synthesis (Chapter 4). However, not all substitutions produce abnormalities. In the course of evolution, occasional substitutions occur that either produce no undesirable changes or, less commonly, produce an improvement. Thus, in the divergence of two evolutionary lines which begins with common protein structures, successive substitutions will occur. In time, the two divergent populations will possess proteins with similar yet differing structures. The amino acid sequences of the same types of protein or, more accurately, homologous proteins, may be compared. Those with the more recent common ancestor should show the greatest similarities in the amino acid sequence; that is, they should show the least number of amino acid substitutions.

IMMUNOLOGICAL STUDIES   The determination of the exact sequence of amino acids in a protein can be time-consuming. Other methods of comparing proteins can be used, such as **immunological comparison.** As an example, we will summarize the studies of the serum albumins conducted by Vincent Sarich.[3]

The serum albumins are single chains of about 570 amino acids found in all land vertebrates. Sarich took samples of purified serum albumin from human and nonhuman primate blood and injected them into rabbits. The rabbits responded by manufacturing antibodies against the injected proteins. These antibodies were used as the test reagent since they reflect the structure of the injected protein.

The antisera that developed from the injection of human serum albumin reacted strongly to human serum albumin. The reaction of antihuman serum albumin to chimpanzee serum albumin, however, was less strong, and to rhesus monkey serum albumin it was even weaker. The strong reaction between the antisera and the sera from which the antisera were derived is said to indicate an **immunological distance (ID)** of zero; therefore, the ID between one human and another is zero. The weakest measurable ID is about 200. Antisera were developed to serum albumin samples from humans, chimpanzees, rhesus monkeys, and spider monkeys and were then tested against the serum albumins from these four species. The results are listed in Table 13–7. The smaller the ID, the closer the evolutionary relationship.

STUDIES OF AMINO ACID SEQUENCES
Since each amino acid is specified by one or a few codes in the DNA molecule itself, the determination of amino acid sequences provides us with a reconstruction of the genetic code. Since some amino acids are determined by more than one code, some changes in the code itself will not result in an amino acid substitution. Therefore, the amino acid sequence provides us with

---

[3]V. Sarich, "A Molecular Approach to the Question of Human Origins," in P. Dolhinow and V. Sarich (eds.), *Background for Man* (Boston: Little, Brown, 1971), 60–81.

TABLE 13–7	
IMMUNOLOGICAL DISTANCE SEPARATING PRIMATE PAIRS	
PAIR	ID
Human–chimpanzee	7
Human–rhesus monkey	32
Human–spider monkey	58
Chimpanzee–rhesus monkey	30
Chimpanzee–spider monkey	56
Rhesus monkey–spider monkey	56

Source: Adapted from Vincent Sarich, "A Molecular Approach to the Question of Human Origins," in P. Dolhinow and V. Sarich (eds.), *Background for Man* (Boston: Little, Brown, 1971), 66.

the minimum number of changes or substitutions in the nucleotide sequence of the DNA molecule.

As an example, we can look again at the hemoglobin molecule. The alpha chain of a hemoglobin molecule consists of 141 amino acids. In a group of primates studied all but 17 of these 141 were identical. Table 13–8 lists the variable positions in the polypeptide chain and identifies the variant amino acid in each position for several representative primates. Molecular biologists have determined amino acid sequences for several proteins in over 100 primate species.

DIRECT STUDIES OF DNA   A direct study of the DNA molecule itself provides the most detailed information about the genetic code, and one method of study is **DNA hybridization.** Segments of normal double-stranded DNA are processed to produce single-stranded DNA. Single-stranded DNA segments from two different species are mixed, and these single strands come together to form double-stranded hybrid DNA. Since the strands are derived from different populations, the nucleotides on the two strands are not always complementary. Therefore, these hybrids are less stable than normal double-stranded DNA.

The DNA strands can be separated through the use of heat. Hybrid DNA dissociates at a lower temperature then natural DNA, and a lowering of this critical temperature by 1.1° C (2° F)

TABLE 13–8

VARIABLE AMINO ACIDS IN PRIMATE ALPHA-GLOBIN CHAINS

	AMINO ACID NUMBER																
	8	12	15	19	21	23	53	57	67	68	71	73	78	111	113	118	129
Primate ancestor	Thr	Ala	Gly	Gly	Ala	Asp	Ala	Ala	Thr	Asn	Ala	Val	Ser	Ser	His	Asp	Leu
Anthropoid ancestor	—	—	—	—	—	—	—	Gly	—	—	—	—	Asn	Ala	—	—	—
Tarsier	—	—	Asp	—	—	—	Ser	Gly	—	Thr	Gly	Ile	Asn	Cys	—	—	Val
Capuchin monkey	—	Thr	—	—	—	—	—	Gly	Ser	—	—	—	Asn	Ala	—	—	—
Rhesus macaque	Ser	—	—	—	—	Glu	—	Leu	Gly	Leu	Gly	—	Asn	Ala	Leu	Glu	—
Human	—	—	—	Ala	—	Glu	—	Gly	—	—	—	—	Asn	Ala	Leu	Glu	—

Source: Adapted from J. M. Beard and M. Goodman, "The Hemoglobins of *Tarsius bancanus,*" in M. Goodman, R. E. Tashian, and J. H. Tashian (eds.), *Molecular Antrhopology* (New York: Plenum, 1976), 243.

means that about 1 percent of the nucleotides in the molecule are mismatched. Thus the change in temperature becomes a measure of the dissimilarity of the DNA between two species, and this can be interpreted as a measure of evolutionary divergence. Other methods of comparing DNA exist, including the direct determination of the genetic code itself and comparisons of mitochondrial DNA from different species.

Phylogenetic Trees

The quantitative data derived from the comparisons of homologous proteins or DNA may be used to develop **phylogenetic trees.** These are graphic representations of the evolutionary relationships among animal species.

A phylogenetic tree appears as a series of points connected by lines to form a branching pattern. The single most ancestral point is the root of the tree, and each ancestral point produces two, and only two, descendants. Earlier we noted that changes in amino acids can be accounted for by more than one pattern of change in the genetic code; therefore, alternate branching patterns can be constructed. An important principle in the construction of phylogenetic trees is the **maximum parsimony principle.** Simply stated, the most probable phylogenetic tree is the one based on the fewest changes in the genetic code.

Figure 13–31 is an example of a phylogenetic tree. It is based upon the combined amino acid sequence of six proteins: alpha- and beta-hemoglobin, myoglobin, fibrinopeptides A and B, cytochrome *c,* and alpha lens crystallin. Let us read this tree from the top down.

All the primates listed in Figure 13–31 exhibit a common ancestry distinct from the other eutherian orders shown. The order Primates appears to be most closely related to the orders Lagomorpha and Insectivora. The first group of primates to branch off the line leading to humans is the prosimians; shown in the diagram are the slender loris, the slow loris, and the Lemuroidea (lemurs). The next primates to branch off are the tarsiers, followed by the New World monkeys, represented by *Saimiri* (the squirrel monkey), *Cebus* (the capuchin), Atelinae (spider monkeys), and the marmosets.

Following the New World monkeys, the Old World monkeys branched off, forming a distinct group consisting of the langur, vervet monkeys, the patas monkey, the rhesus and Japanese macaques, mangabeys, and baboons. Finally, the phylogenetic tree shows the close relationships among the members of the Hominoidea and the especially close relationship of humans to chimpanzees.

HUMAN-APE RELATIONSHIPS The construction of hominoid phylogenetic trees has ultimately led to a restructuring of hominoid

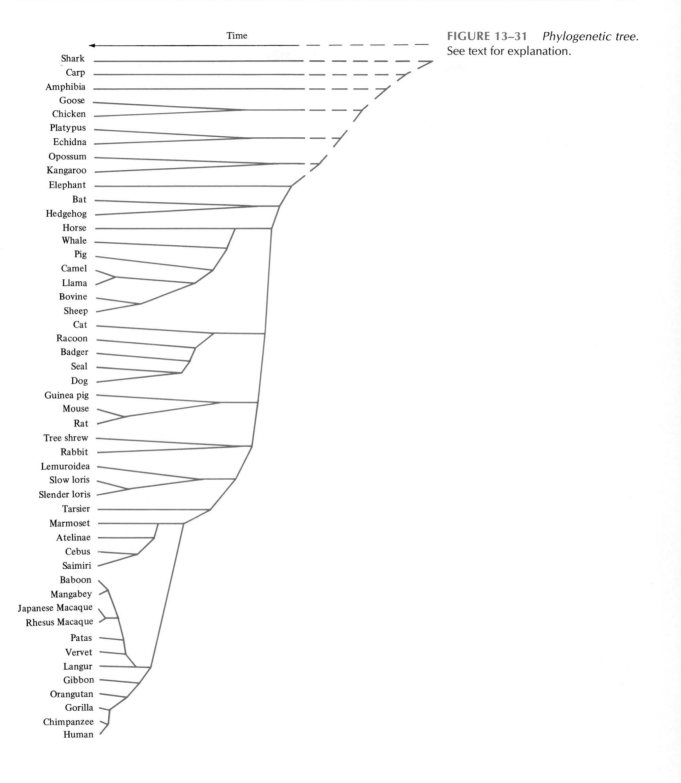

FIGURE 13–31 *Phylogenetic tree.* See text for explanation.

taxonomy. Traditionally, the superfamily Hominoidea was divided into three families: Hylobatidae (gibbons and siamang), Pongidae (orangutan,
gorilla, and chimpanzees), and Hominidae (humans). Molecular data, however, have clearly
shown the closeness of the human-chimpanzee
evolutionary tie and, to a slightly lesser degree,
the human-gorilla tie. Orangutans appear to be
more distantly related to humans than are the
African great apes, which has led many primate
taxonomists to keep *Pongo*, the orangutan, in the
family Pongidae and to move the chimpanzees
and gorillas into the family Panidae. We have followed this practice in this text (Chapter 10).

Table 13–9 illustrates the differences between
humans and several primate species by measuring the percentage of differing amino acids in a
series of proteins. The close relationship between *Homo sapiens* and the African great apes
is apparent. Table 13–10 summarizes the differences in the amino acid sequences of twelve proteins in humans and chimpanzees. From these
data we see that 99.3 percent of the human and
chimpanzee polypeptides studied are identical.

We may conclude, then, that the differences
in structural genes between *Homo sapiens* and
the living chimpanzees are very small. They are
of the same order of magnitude as differences existing between similar-appearing, very closely related species such as the horse and the zebra or
the grizzly and the polar bear. On the other hand,
the anatomical differences between humans and
chimpanzees are substantial. It has been suggested that most of the changes that have taken
place in hominid evolution are based on changes
in regulatory or modifier genes and on the relative positions of the genes on the chromosomes,
rather than on mutations of structural genes.

FETALIZATION   Another interesting aspect of
recent studies on regulatory genes is the new life
this research has given to an old concept: the **fetalization hypothesis.** This idea was proposed in
the 1920s by the Dutch anatomist Louis Bolk,
who hypothesized that humans are characterized
by infantilization. According to Bolk, humans
have carried fetal or infant characteristics of the
apes into adulthood; he said that a human adult
is a primate fetus that has become sexually ma-

TABLE 13–9

AMINO ACID DISTANCES BETWEEN HUMANS
AND SELECTED PRIMATES

PRIMATE	AMINO ACID DISTANCES BETWEEN HUMAN AND NONHUMAN PRIMATES*
Chimpanzee	0.27
Gorilla	0.65
Orangutan	2.78
Gibbon	2.38
Macaque†	3.89
Ceropithecus†	3.65
Squirrel monkey‡	8.78
Spider monkey‡	6.31
Capuchin monkey‡	7.56
Slow loris§	11.36

*Percent of differing amino acids.
†Old World monkey.
‡New World monkey.
§Prosimian.
Source: Adapted from M. Goodman, "Protein Sequence and Immunological Specificity," in W. P. Luckett and F. S. Szalay (eds.), *Phylogeny of the Primates* (New York: Plenum, 1975), 224.

ture. Bolk presented twenty features that humans share with fetal apes and monkeys, such as
a rounded bulbous cranium, small jaw, and a
nonrotated, nonopposable big toe.

The recent work on regulatory genes has convinced some scientists that Bolk was essentially
correct. Changes in regulatory genes may have
slowed down certain developmental characteristics in humans. This may account for the fact
that humans and apes evolved from a common
ancestor without much change in structural
genes. The adaptive advantage of fetalization
may be that it permits a prolongation of the time
in which learned behavior is accumulated.

THE MOLECULAR CLOCK   The construction
of phylogenetic trees enables anthropologists and
biologists to establish the relative evolutionary
distances and relationships between different
taxonomic groups. Early investigators of the
structure of hemoglobin and cytochrome *c* went
one step further and proposed the existence of a
"molecular clock." They felt that by using this
clock, the molecular distance between groups
could be translated into a known period of time.

TABLE 13–10

DIFFERENCES IN THE AMINO ACID SEQUENCES OF HUMAN AND CHIMPANZEE PROTEINS

PROTEIN	NUMBER OF AMINO ACID DIFFERENCES	NUMBER OF AMINO ACIDS IN PROTEIN
Fibrinopeptides A and B	0	30
Cytochrome *c*	0	104
Lysozome	0*	130
Hemoglobin α	0	141
Hemoglobin β	0	146
Hemoglobin ^γ	0	146
Hemoglobin Gγ	0	146
Hemoglobin δ	1	146
Myoglobin	1	153
Carbonic anhydrase	3*	264
Serum albumin	6*	580
Transferrin	8*	647
Total	19	2633

*Approximation based on methods other than analysis of known amino acid sequences.
Source: Reprinted from M.C. King and A. C. Wilson, "Evolution at Two Levels in Humans and Chimpanzees," *Science,* 188 (1975), 108. Copyright 1975 American Association for the Advancement of Science.

The existence of a molecular clock is based upon the assumption that the rate of amino acid replacement for any given protein is relatively constant. If this assumption is correct, then the clock can be calibrated by correlating a particular evolutionary distance between two groups with the actual time of divergence as known through the dating of the fossil record. Thus the molecular clock is only as good as the calibration date. (The problems of dating the fossil record will be discussed in Chapter 14.) Once this calibration has been accomplished, investigators can use the clock to establish the divergence time for pairs of taxa for which fossil records do not exist.

If the concept of a molecular clock is to be valid, several assumptions must be shown to be true. First, the rate of amino acid substitutions in protein molecules, or nucleotide substitutions in DNA, must be constant over time. This may not be the case, however; research suggests that different proteins exhibit different substitution rates. Also, substitution rates may differ in different evolutionary lines. In comparisons with other mammalian groups, the molecular clock may actually run slower in the Hominoidea and slower still in the Hominidae. The critical factor in this difference in clock rate may be the length of the generation. Second, for the concept of the molecular clock to be valid, the majority of mutations or substitutions must be neutral so that these substitutions can accumulate without being acted upon by natural selection. Anthropologists do not agree on the validity of these assumptions.

Summary

Since the genes are located within the chromosomes, comparative analysis of human and nonhuman chromosomes has provided information for determining evolutionary relationships. When we examine human and chimpanzee karyotypes, we can easily pair up each human chromosome with a chimpanzee counterpart. The only exception is human chromosome 2, which appears to have evolved from the fusion of two smaller chromosomes.

In recent years, detailed biochemical studies of protein molecules have added a valuable perspective to evolutionary studies. By a comparison of protein and DNA molecules from various living species, the evolutionary closeness of these species can be estimated. From these data phylogenetic trees can be drawn to illustrate the most probable evolutionary relationships among species.

STUDY QUESTIONS

1. How does the anthropologist use data from comparative anatomy to determine evolutionary relationships?
2. In what ways can the primate skeleton be said to be generalized?
3. What is meant by the term *suspensory behavior?* Discuss the evidence for the hypothesis that hominids evolved from a generalized suspensory ancestry.
4. Some hominid fossils show the presence of crests, ridges, and pronounced brow ridges on

the skull. How can these features be interpreted?

5. Compare the dentition of modern humans with that of modern apes.

6. What are the major features of the evolution of the primate brain?

7. Describe the evolution of the human karyotype from an ancestral panid karyotype.

8. As animals evolve, so do protein molecules. Discuss the use of comparative biochemical studies in the determination of evolutionary relationships.

9. While humans and chimpanzees show a 99 percent similarity in their structural genes, they still display many phenotypic differences. Discuss the factors that have brought about these differences.

SUGGESTED READINGS

Aiello, L., and C. Dean. *An Introduction to Human Evolutionary Anatomy.* London: Academic, 1990. A detailed description of human anatomy, this book emphasizes the anatomical evidence for human evolution.

Ankel-Simons, F. *A Survey of Living Primates and Their Anatomy.* New York: Macmillan, 1983. This is a rather complete introduction to the primate order, emphasizing various aspects of their anatomy, including the skeleton.

Cook, N. D. *The Brain Code.* London: Methuen, 1986. This is a fascinating book on how information is stored and transmitted within the brain.

Martin, R. D. *Primate Origins and Evolution: A Phylogenetic Reconstruction.* Princeton: Princeton University Press, 1990. This book contains several detailed chapters summarizing comparative primate anatomy.

Napier, J., revised by R. H. Tuttle. *Hands.* Princeton, N.J.: Princeton University Press, 1993. This book includes discussions of the anatomy, evolution, and social and cultural aspects of the hand.

Ornstein, R., and R. F. Thompson. *The Amazing Brain.* Boston: Houghton Mifflin, 1986. This is a well-illustrated and well-written introduction to the anatomy and functioning of the human brain.

Swindler, D., and C. D. Wood. *An Atlas of Primate Gross Anatomy.* Melbourne, Fla.: Krieger, 1982. This book contains a series of detailed line drawings illustrating the comparative anatomy of the baboon, chimpanzee, and human.

A. L. Zihlman, *The Human Evolution Coloring Book.* New York: Barnes & Noble, 1982. This "coloring book" is not a children's book but a very complete workbook written by a noted physical anthropologist. It includes important "lessons" on human evolution including anatomy and molecular genetics.

Paleontological fieldwork at Dinosaur National Monument.

Most fossil animals no longer possess soft tissues like muscles, flesh, and brain; their bones are no longer articulated, and some of their bones are broken or destroyed. Their bones and teeth have been mineralized. Fossil animals do not live in social groups; they have no home range or preferred habitat; and they do not move, feed, play, learn, reproduce, fight, or engage in any other behaviors. Their bones are not associated with those of the animals they interacted with in life. In short, through death most evidence of the interesting information about animals—what they look like, what they eat, how they move, where they live, and so on—is lost. Only through indirect evidence and painstaking study can any information about their habits and lifestyle be reconstructed.[1]

Pat Shipman

[1]P. Shipman, *Life History of a Fossil: An Introduction to Taphonomy and Paleoecology* (Cambridge, Mass.: Harvard University Press, 1981), 3. Reprinted by permission of Harvard University Press.

CHAPTER 14

THE RECORD OF THE PAST

Confucius wrote, "Study the past, if you would divine the future." Through the ages, people have pondered their history. The anthropologist is interested in the past for what it will reveal about the nature and development of humans as biological, social, and cultural beings. The anthropologist believes, as Confucius did, that a knowledge of the events leading to the present human condition is an important tool for coping with the problems that confront us.

The past reflects a type of biological immortality. Life begets life, and through the processes of reproduction, the present becomes a slightly modified reconstruction of the immediate past. There is, however, still another type of immortality—that of the fossilized remains of an organism. It is through the preservation of body parts that the anthropologist can see into the past and attempt to reconstruct the history of life.

FOSSILS AND THEIR INTERPRETATION

A **fossil** is the remains or traces of an ancient organism. Fossils have interested people for thousands of years; in fact, prehistoric societies may have attached magical or religious significance to fossils. The Greeks and Romans not only knew of fossils but also made some assumptions about their meaning. About 500 B.C., some believed that fossil fish represented the ancestors of all life. During the Middle Ages, knowledge and theories about fossils changed. Fossils were considered remnants of attempts at special creation, objects that had fallen from the heavens, and even devices of the devil.

In the fifteenth century Leonardo da Vinci wrote: "The mountains where there are shells were formerly shores beaten by waves, and since then they have been elevated to the heights we see today." From that time on, debate has raged over the true meaning of geological formations and the fossils found in them. Only in the past few hundred years have scholars agreed that fossils are the remains of ancient organisms and that they can tell us much about the history of life.

The Nature of Fossils

The "immortality" of the body is limited; most organisms have left no traces of their existence upon our planet. Their dead bodies were consumed by other organisms and eventually, through the process of decay, were absorbed into the soil.

Taphonomy is the study of the processes that affect an organism after death, leading in some cases to fossilization. Fossilization is actually a rare event, since several conditions must be met in order for an organism to be preserved.

First, the remains of the organism must be suitable for fossilization. Different parts of the body decay at different rates. It is therefore not surprising that the vast majority of fossils uncovered are those with hard tissues such as teeth, bones, and shell. These decay more slowly than soft tissues such as skin, brain, and muscles.

Vast numbers of ancient organisms that lacked hard material probably will never be known.

Second, the carcass of the animal must be buried very quickly after death, before it is consumed by scavengers or destroyed by natural elements. The probability of fossilization is greatly increased when the body settles in stagnant water. The lack of oxygen discourages bacterial decay, and the lack of currents in the water minimizes movements of the body. More unusual are volcanic eruptions or violent storms that quickly cover the body with layers of volcanic ash or mud.

Finally, the material in which the remains are buried must be favorable for fossilization. Some soils, such as the acidic soils of the tropics, actually destroy bone. Also, minerals must be present that will infiltrate the bone, teeth, or shell and replace the organic matter. This is the process of fossilization.

Only on rare occasions are entire organisms found that include soft tissue. In 1991 a partially freeze-dried body of a man was found at an elevation of 3200 meters (10,500 feet) in the Italian Alps near the Austrian border. The corpse was not the victim of a recent skiing accident; it was the victim of a misfortune that took place about 5300 years ago. Even the man's internal organs, clothing, and tools had been preserved (Figure 14–1). Entire bodies of mammoths and woolly rhinoceroses have also been recovered in the permanently frozen ground of Siberia.

Insects and spiders are found embedded in amber, which is fossilized tree resin. Mummified remains are known from the hot, dry regions of Egypt, the American Southwest, and the western coastal deserts of South America. Preserved bodies are also known from the peat bogs of northern Europe. These finds, though rare, are extremely valuable since they provide direct evidence of skin, hair, stomach contents (for diet analysis), and much more.

The vast majority of fossils exist in the form of mineralized bone (Figure 14–2a). As the bone lies buried in the ground, minerals replace the organic matter in the bone. Traces of ancient life forms also may be found as molds and casts. A **mold** is a cavity left in firm sediments by the decayed body of an organism; nothing of the organ-

FIGURE 14–1 *The "Ice Man."* The partially freeze-dried body of a man who died about 5300 years ago.

ism itself is left. This mold, if filled with some substance, becomes a **cast** that reflects the shape of the fossil (Figure 14–2*b*). Tracks and burrows of animals have been preserved this way (Figure 14–2*c*). Materials that were ingested and excreted by animals also can be preserved; they tell us much about the diet of the animals. These forms of preservation, however, are rarely found in the primate fossil record; ancient primates are best known by their fossilized bones and teeth.

Biases in the Fossil Record

The fossil record is not a complete record of the history of living organisms upon the face of the earth. It is but a sample of the plants and animals that once lived. Charles Darwin wrote:

> I look at the natural geological record, as a history of the world imperfectly kept, and written in a changing dialect; of this history we possess the last volume alone, relating only to two or three countries. Of this volume, only here and there a short

chapter has been preserved; and of each page, only here and there a few lines.[2]

SAMPLING ERROR IN THE FOSSIL RECORD
Because the probability of preservation varies from region to region, some organisms are better represented in the fossil record than others—while still others are totally unknown. Species living under conditions in which the odds of fossilization are good, such as freshwater lakes and ponds, will be common as fossils. Terrestrial animals, especially those living in tropical areas, are fossilized much less often.

Because of differential preservation, the frequency of fossil specimens does not necessarily reflect the size of the living populations represented by the fossils. Birds, for example, are not preserved as frequently as mammals, and so the fossil record shows a scarcity of bird species. In

---

[2]C. Darwin, *On the Origin of Species by Means of Natural Selection* (London: J. Murrary, 1859), 310–311.

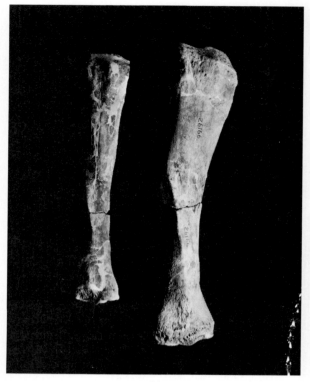

(a)

(b)

(c)

FIGURE 14–2 *Fossils.* The remains of prehistoric life may take the form of *(a)* fossilized bone (limb bones of *Baluchterium), (b)* cast *(Archeopteryx),* and *(c)* tracks (dinosaur).

reality, birds may have been a predominant life form in a particular area at a particular time.

Another factor in sampling is the accessibility of sites. In some areas important fossil beds may have formed, but they are not exposed at the surface. Some areas, such as southwestern France and Kenya, have been extensively explored, while other areas, such as southeast Asia, remain virtually untouched. A major reason for this geographical sampling error is politics. Some governments have been hostile to anthropological research, and military activity has made visits to other areas impossible. On the other hand, many governments and governmental institutions, such as the National Museums of Kenya, have been extremely active in this type of research. The result has been an uneven sampling of sites in various regions of the world.

An important factor determining the locations excavated is the individual interests of paleoanthropologists. Most excavations occur in deposits representing geographical areas and geological periods that are considered important at the time the research is planned. As time goes on and our knowledge of human paleontology grows, new areas and new periods are considered critical.

Another factor that affects geographical sampling is money. Fieldwork can be very expensive, and the research interests of a scientist must be mirrored by the agencies financing the project. Several factors affect the cost of paleoanthropological research. A low-paid graduate student working in his or her own country may be able to conduct a short-term project for relatively little money. On the other hand, a full-scale overseas multidisciplinary operation may cost several hundred thousand dollars.

GAPS IN FOSSIL SEQUENCES   It is sometimes possible to follow the evolution of successive populations for millions of years, only to encounter a period characterized by an absence of fossils. This, in turn, may be followed by reemergence of the population or a somewhat more evolved form. Such gaps are common, and we will see many examples in subsequent chapters.

Several factors can cause gaps to appear in the fossil record. For one thing, organisms do not necessarily stay in the same habitat or niche. If a species moves into a new habitat, the probability of fossilization may change. Although the population seems to have disappeared, in reality it simply may not have been preserved during the time it resides in that habitat.

Another factor bringing about gaps in the fossil record is a change in **sedimentation,** which is the deposition of materials carried in water, wind, or glaciers. Most fossils are found in sedimentary deposits. If sedimentation ceases in a particular area, preservation may also cease and a gap in the fossil record will result. In addition, erosion may destroy sedimentary beds that have already been laid down.

SAMPLING OF POPULATIONS   Within a given species, the collection of actual specimens re-

covered represents a sample of the individual organisms that once lived. Anna K. Behrensmeyer estimates that only 0.004 percent of the hominids once living at Omo, Ethiopia, are represented in the fossil record.[3]

Fossilization is a chance phenomenon; it represents a sample of individuals of a given population. This forces us to question if a specific individual is an average member of the population, especially if a species is known only from fragmentary remains or from a single individual. Since the probabilities for fossilization are so low, it is very difficult to know the range of variation of a species and we must often define a species on the basis of a single specimen.

In situations in which a species is defined on the basis of a reasonable sample of individuals, some unrepresentative fossils are known. For example, the first relatively complete Neandertal skeleton to be discovered is the one from La Chapelle-aux-Saints, France. This skeleton became the prototype of the Neandertals. The Neandertals were pictured as creatures with unusual posture, hunched over and bowlegged, with massive brow ridges and bestial features (see Box 18–2).

The specimen from La Chapelle-aux-Saints is not an average Neandertal, however, but is the skeleton of an old man suffering from an advanced case of arthritis of the spine. If a number of Neandertals are compared, this particular individual is one of the least modern in appearance. Today we know that the term *Neandertal* is a general designation for a group of hominids that show a great deal of intraspecific variation (Chapter 18).

Differential Preservation

As we have seen, whether a particular organism or parts of an organism are preserved or not depends on a number of factors. The probability of a bone's being preserved after death is known as that bone's **preservation potential.** By observing

---

[3]A. K. Behrensmeyer, "Taphonomy and Paleoecology in the Hominid Fossil Record," *Yearbook of Physical Anthropology 1975* (Washington, D.C.: American Association of Physical Anthropologists, 1976), 36–50.

the fate of dead bodies in the field and by conducting many laboratory experiments, taphonomists have gathered data showing that the preservation potential of a particular bone depends upon its size, shape, and composition and its behavior in water.

Bone size can be thought of in terms of volume. Very large bones, such as skulls and mandibles, are preserved more frequently than small bones. Bone composition is also a factor. Because carnivores prefer spongy bone, compact bones are more frequently left to be incorporated into the fossil record. Also important is the shape of the bone. Relatively thin, flat bones, such as the innominate and scapula, tend to break easily. These bones are infrequently found as fossils and, when recovered, are often broken and fragmented.

The **hydraulic behavior** of a bone refers to its transport and dispersal in water. Most fossils are derived from bodies that have been deposited in water environments; the fossils are found in sedimentary beds that are formed in water. A bone's composition, its size, and its shape are all important factors in determining what will happen to the bone in water. Ribs and vertebrae are easily transported by water, and so they are frequently moved by water considerable distances from the rest of the skeleton. As they move, they are often abraded by the gravel beds of the stream or river. On the other hand, skulls and mandibles are transported only by rapidly moving streams. Table 14–1 and Figure 14–3 summarize the forces that act to destroy bones after the death of an organism.

What Can Fossils Tell Us?

The fossil record is like a puzzle with many pieces missing and still others distorted. Yet a picture, although incomplete, does emerge. Often the image is only an outline of the past; sometimes it is a well-documented history.

With a few exceptions, the fossil record consists solely of skeletal remains, but much can be inferred about the body from the skeleton. For example, areas of muscle attachment can be seen on the surface of bone, often as ridges or roughened areas. From this information, the shape, size, and function of various muscles can be re-

TABLE 14–1	
DESTRUCTIVE FORCES ACTING ON BONE	
DESTRUCTIVE FORCE	EFFECTS
Predators and scavengers (including hominids)	Consumption, gnawing, breakage
Use of bones as tools	Breakage, wear
Hydraulic transport	Winnowing of assemblage, abrasion
Subaerial transport (rolling, sliding along streambed)	Abrasion, breakage
Aeolian (wind) transport	Pitting, winnowing of assemblage
Weathering	Cracking, crumbling, exfoliation
Decay by chemicals, roots, insects, soil, water	Disintegration, breakdown of structure

Source: Adapted from P. Shipman, *Life History of a Fossil: An Introduction to Taphonomy and Paleoecology* (Cambridge, Mass.: Harvard University Press, 1981), 41. Reprinted by permission of the Harvard University Press.

constructed. This is important in the reconstruction of locomotor patterns.

Once the musculature has been reconstructed, we can get some idea of what the organism might have looked like by placing a skin over the musculature (Figure 14–4). The fossil record, however, gives no indication of the color of the skin or of the amount of hair on the body.

The relative size of the eye socket, nasal cavities, and hearing apparatus can tell us a great deal about which senses were most important when the animal was alive. The evolution of vision in the primates can be seen in the formation of the eye socket and the frontal position of the eyes on the skull.

Brains are never fossilized, although brain matter has been found from fairly recent times in bodies preserved in wet sites such as bogs. However, some inferences about brain size can be made from the brain case. An examination of the inside surface of the brain case, which conforms to the general size and shape of the brain, gives some idea of the gross structure of the brain itself. In addition, grooves in the brain case, which are clearly seen in an endocranial cast, are indications of arteries, veins, and nerves (Figure 13–19). While such data have led to inferences re-

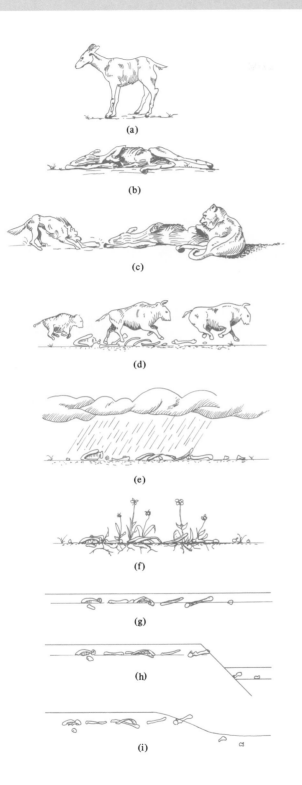

garding intelligence, the development of culture, and the presence or absence of speech, one must view these conclusions with a great deal of caution.

Patterns of growth and development are mirrored in the fossil record when one discovers a sequence of specimens representing individuals of different ages. **Computerized tomography** and other medical technologies are being used by paleoanthropologists to discover features such as nonerupted teeth that are embedded within the fossil jaw. These findings provide evidence for reconstructing age at death and patterns of dental development and maturation, as well as for reconstructing life expectancies and population structure. **Paleopathology** deals with investigations of injuries and disease in prehistoric populations, such as arthritis and dental caries (cavities in teeth) in Neandertal skeletons.

In addition to information about the individual and the species, the presence of fossil remains of animals in association with human remains, the remains of human activity, and the geological context all tell us much about the living patterns and ecological relations of the early hominids. Figure 14–5 shows the interrelationships of various types of data and interpretations that can be used to build a picture of the early hominids.

Hominid fossils and **artifacts,** the material remains of human behavior, are the primary data used in the reconstruction of technology, subsistence activities and diet, land-use patterns, and even, to a limited extent, group social structure. **Paleoanthropology,** the interdisciplinary study of prehistoric hominids and related forms, combines data from many disciplines, such as geology, **paleontology** (the study of fossils), **palynol-**

FIGURE 14–3 *The process of fossilization. (a)* A living animal. *(b)* The carcass of the recently dead animal. *(c)* Predators feed on the carcass, destroying and disarticulating many bones. *(d)* Trampling by other animals further breaks up the bones. *(e)* Weathering by rain, sun, and other elements cracks and splits many of the bones. *(f)* The roots of plants invade many bones. *(g)* The bones are fossilized. *(h)* Faulting displaces and further breaks bones. *(i)* Fossils are exposed on the surface by erosion.

ogy (the study of fossil pollen), **paleoecology,** and taphonomy, to reconstruct the environment in which the hominids functioned. Of course, the most important information anthropologists derive from the fossil record is evidence of evolutionary processes. For it is in the fossil record that the actual remains of early forms are found.

Taxonomy and the Fossil Record

In 1963 George Gaylord Simpson wrote:

> Men and all recent fossil organisms pertinent to their affinities are animals, and the appropriate language for discussing their classification and relationships is that of animal taxonomy. . . . It is notorious that hominid nomenclature, particularly, has become chaotic.[4]

Prerequisite to any discussion of the fossil record is an understanding of the problems of taxonomy and fossils.

THE SPECIES CONCEPT IN THE FOSSIL RECORD Fossil taxonomy is one of the most provocative areas in paleoanthropology. With each new find, a new debate begins over the fossil's placement in the evolutionary scheme, and a major problem is the definition of species when applied to fossils. Since the definition of species for living populations is based upon the criterion of reproductive success, the difficulties of applying this concept to the fossil record are obvious.

There are two schools of thought concerning the definition of species in the fossil record, and they are diametrically opposed to each other in philosophical outlook. The **typological** viewpoint embodies the ancient philosophy developed by Plato, which holds that basic variation of a type is illusory and that only fixed ideal types are real. According to this concept of the archetype, which was introduced in the discussion of taxonomy in Chapter 9, two fossils that

FIGURE 14-4 *Flesh reconstruction.* A flesh reconstruction of *Homo erectus* from China.

differ from each other in certain respects represent two types and, hence, are two different species.

The typological viewpoint has dominated human paleontology for what are probably psychological reasons more than anything else. The discovery of a new fossil is a highly emotional experience, and a new find becomes more significant if it can be said to represent a new species rather than simply being another specimen of an already known species.

The **populationist** viewpoint, on the other hand, maintains that only individuals have reality and that the type is illusory. More precisely, the populationists argue that since no two individuals are exactly alike, variation underlies all existence.

Let us consider an example of the populationist viewpoint. The heights of four individuals are 155 centimeters (5 feet 1 inch), 160 centimeters (5 feet 3 inches), 170 centimeters (5 feet 7 inches),

---

[4]G. G. Simpson, "The Meaning of Taxonomic Statements," in S. C. Washburn (ed.), *Classification and Human Evolution,* Viking Fund Publications in Anthropology, No. 37 (New York: Wenner-Gren Foundation for Anthropological Research: 1963), 4–5.

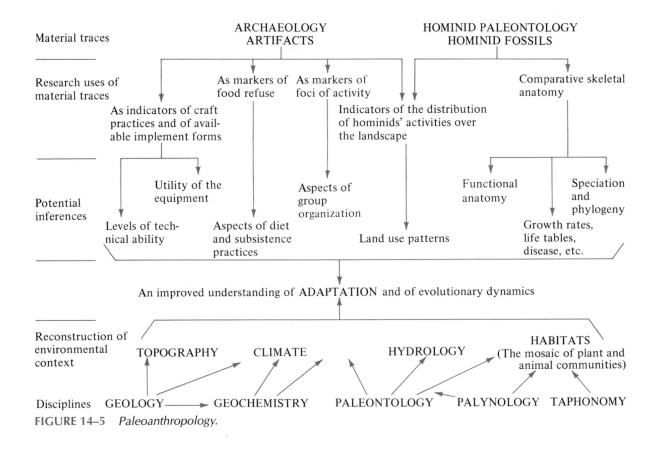

FIGURE 14–5 *Paleoanthropology.*

and 178 centimeters (5 feet 10 inches). Their average height is 166 centimeters (5 feet 5 inches). First, note that the individuals in the sample vary by 23 centimeters (9 inches), and second, note that no one individual in the sample is average. According to this reasoning, variation in fossil finds can be explained as divergence from a statistical average. If this variation is no greater than that which might be found within a related living species, the populationist sees no reason to separate the finds into different taxonomic categories.

To illustrate this point, Figure 14–6 shows a series of skulls that display a fair degree of variation in appearance. How many species are represented here? In this case they are all modern gorillas, members of the species *Gorilla gorilla.* Yet a series of hominoid fossils that show this degree of variation would be broken up by many paleoanthropologists into a number of distinct species.

THE PALEOSPECIES   Among living organisms, the species is defined in the objective terms of reproductive isolation, yet neither reproductive isolating mechanisms nor gene frequencies can be seen in the fossil record. At best, geographical isolation can be inferred in some situations. In dealing with the fossil record, the taxonomist is restricted to an analysis of morphological variation, and, as has already been noted, variation within a species can be great.

Many anthropologists have concluded that since reproductive criteria cannot be applied to the fossil record, the species concept cannot be legitimately applied to fossil forms. Instead, we must speak of the **paleospecies,** which resembles the species but is defined in terms of morphological variation rather than in terms of genetic isolation and reproductive success. (Some paleoanthropologists speak of **chronospecies,** which are arbitrarily defined divisions of an evolutionary line.) A paleospecies is a group of similar fossils

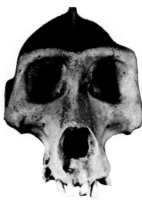

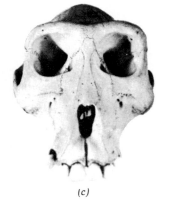

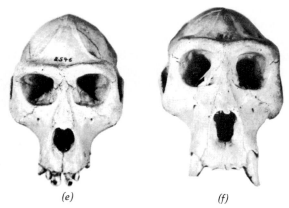

FIGURE 14–6 *Intraspecific variation.* A series of six skulls, all members of the same species, *Gorilla gorilla.* Note the degree of variation: *(b)* and *(f)* are males, *(a)* and *(c)* are probably males, and *(d)* and *(e)* are probably females.

whose range of morphological variation does not exceed the range of variation within a closely related living species. Determination of a paleospecies requires detailed statistical analysis of both the fossil series and the living species being used for comparison.

Yet some paleontologists suggest that the range of variation may have been greater in some earlier populations than among related contemporary species. For example, over 1000 apelike fossils have been recovered from Lufeng, China. Some paleoanthropologists see clear evidence of two distinct species, *Ramapithecus lufengensis* and *Sivapithecus yunnanensis.* Charles E. Oxnard writes: "The marked differences between *Ramapithecus* which is always smaller and *Sivapithecus* is clear. These differences are far greater than those generally found between the sexes of extant forms, even between the sexes of such markedly dimorphic species as gorillas and orang-utans."[5] On the other hand, an analysis by Jay Kelley and Xu Qinghua leads them to the conclusion that these specimens represent a single species that exhibits a degree of sexual dimorphism in dimensions of the teeth that exceeds the degree of sexual dimorphism found among living orangutans and gorillas.[6]

It may be difficult to resolve this difference of opinion. The evidence consists primarily of teeth, although other parts of the skeletal anatomy are known; determination of sex on the basis of dental evidence is difficult. It is also very possible that a group of fossils includes the remains of individuals that originally lived at different times.

REASONS FOR VARIABILITY IN THE FOSSIL RECORD   Many differences among fossil specimens represent the emergence of new species and higher taxonomic groups. Nevertheless, much of the variation that often is interpreted as interspecific actually is intraspecific.

One form of intraspecific variation is that of age. Figure 14–7 shows the skulls of an infant

---

[5]C. E. Oxnard, *Fossils, Teeth and Sex* (Seattle: University of Washington Press, 1987), 93.
[6]J. Kelley and Xu Qinghua, "Extreme Sexual Dimorphism in Miocene Hominoids," *Nature,* 352 (1991), 151–153.

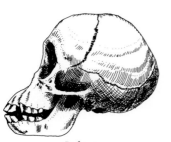

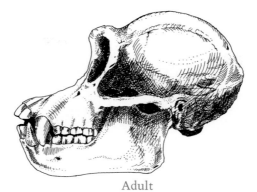

Infant   Adult

FIGURE 14–7   *Age differences in chimpanzee skulls.* The skulls of an infant and an adult chimpanzee.

and an adult chimpanzee; note the absence of a prominent brow ridge and the generally more "human" appearance of the infant's skull. One must be extremely careful when using anything other than adult material in interpreting the fossil record.

Sexual dimorphism was discussed in Chapter 11. We saw that the male adult baboon is larger than the female, has longer canines, and has a mantle of fur over his shoulder. Thus, the sex of an adult baboon is easy to determine even from a skull alone. On the other hand, the gibbon shows little sexual dimorphism; unless the female is nursing a child, male and female gibbons cannot be distinguished at a distance. Evidence suggests that the early hominids showed a greater degree of sexual dimorphism than *Homo sapiens* does today.

Finally, variation within a species can be due to the simple fact that, as we saw in the discussion of genetics, no two individuals are phenotypically identical. One cannot expect any two fossil specimens to be exactly alike. Consider, for example, the tremendous variation within the species *Homo sapiens* with respect to stature, body build, and cranial capacity.

Summary

The remains and traces of ancient organisms make up the fossil record, yet this record is far from being a complete history of life on earth. The process of fossilization is the subject matter of taphonomy. Fossilization is a rare event because it depends on an organism's having hard parts, such as bones, teeth, or shells, and being buried immediately after death. The work of predators and scavengers, and the weathering effects of rain, heat, cold, and wind, often serve to destroy most or all of an organism before final burial takes place.

Because of the nature of fossilization, the fossil record is a biased sample of the totality of life that once existed. Fossilization is more apt to occur in some areas, such as at the bottom of lakes, than others, such as in tropical rain forests. Aquatic animals are preserved more frequently than those living in terrestrial habitats. Some parts of the world and some geological time spans have been more thoroughly explored for fossils than have others. A major problem of sampling is the realization that a fossil is a single individual. Is that individual typical of the species, or does it represent a deviation from the norm?

Fossils provide a great deal of information if they are studied carefully. From skeletal remains, the musculature can be reconstructed; from the musculature, one can get a good picture of the physical appearance of the animal when it was alive. The brain case provides some information about the brain itself. In addition, fossils provide data on growth and development patterns and injury and disease. The associated remains of animals, artifacts, and the geological context tell us much about ecological relationships and even, to some extent, the behavior of prehistoric populations.

BOX 14-1

WHAT IS A MILLION?

As we saw earlier, paleontologists today hypothesize that the first life arose on earth about 3.8 billion years ago. The Cenozoic, or the Age of Mammals, began about 65 million years ago. In the chapters to come are many dates more than 1 million years before the present.

Part of the task of the student is learning these dates, as they are approximations of when the major events of primate evolution took place. It is one thing to memorize a date; it is quite another to comprehend that date that is so many times greater than the human life span.

Yet failure to comprehend this vastness of time is a failure to understand a major aspect of evolutionary history. Evolutionary changes are slow changes that take place over vast durations of time. Even relatively fast changes, such as those postulated by the concept of punctuated equilibrium, occur over enormous stretches of time.

A million is 1000 thousand, and a billion is 1000 million. Thus, saying that life began 3500 million years ago is the same as saying it began 3½ billion years ago. A trillion is 1000 billion. These are huge numbers. Astronomer Carl Sagan tells us how long it would take to count to these numbers if we were to count one number per second, night and day, starting with 1. It would take seventeen minutes to count to a thousand, twelve days to count to a million, and thirty-two years to count to a billion![1]

To get a better feel for the depth of time, we can equate time with distance. Let us say that the history of the earth is represented by a highway stretching from New York to Los Angeles and that New York represents 4½ billion years ago, the age of the earth, and Los Angeles represents today. As we travel along this highway from east to west, the first forms of life appear in Indianapolis, the first animal life in Phoenix, and the first primates around Disneyland. The hominids are evolving on the shores of the Pacific Ocean.

[1]C. Sagan, "Billions and Billions," *Parade Magazine* (May 31, 1987), 9.

A major problem in paleoanthropology is the application of taxonomic principles to the fossil record. The species concept as defined in terms of reproductive success cannot be applied to the fossil record. Instead, we must speak of paleospecies, which are defined in terms of morphological similarities and differences.

GEOLOGICAL TIME

It is somewhat paradoxical that in order to learn more about the earth, scientists have investigated the nature of the moon. Yet both bodies, along with the sun and the other planets, are thought to have been formed at about the same time. Because the crust of the moon has not undergone as much alteration as that of the earth, the examination of moon rocks may give a better estimate of the age of the earth than an examination of the earth itself. This estimate now stands at about 4.6 billion years.

When people believed that the earth was only about 6000 years old, it was impossible to conceive of evolutionary theory in both the biological and the geological senses. Evolution requires an extremely long time span. Because the concept of deep time is so central to paleoanthropology, we must attempt to gain a feeling for long periods of time (see Box 14–1). This section looks at methods for determining the age of fossils and the way in which geologists and paleontologists organize geological time.

Stratigraphy

If a glass of river water sits for a period of time, a thin layer of material soon appears on the bottom of the glass; this layer consists of dirt and other debris that were suspended in the moving water of the river. The atmosphere, through wind and corrosive activities, and bodies of water, through their movements, erode away the land. When the water stops moving, the eroded material, called **sediment,** settles to the bottom under the influence of gravity, and a thin layer forms. In lakes, this process occurs on a much greater scale. Dead animals wash into lakes, where many settle into the bottom mud and become a part of the sedimentary deposit.

Over time, many layers develop, one on top of another. These layers, called **sedimentary beds,** or **strata,** are said to be stratified. Eventually, a lake will dry up, leaving a series of strata that, at some later point in time, may give up their fossils to the paleontologist. The investigation of the composition of the layers of the earth and their relationship to one another is the study of **stratigraphy.**

The basis of stratigraphic studies is the principle of **superposition.** Simply stated, this principle says that under stable conditions the strata on the bottom of a deposit are older than the ones on top. The reasoning behind the principle of superposition is relatively straightforward: the materials from a given point in time are deposited on top of materials deposited earlier. Since the compositions of these materials differ at different times, the various layers can often be visually identified. Areas such as the Grand Canyon in Arizona graphically illustrate stratigraphic succession (Figure 2–3).

In excavating a paleontological or archaeological site, one encounters progressively older remains at increasingly deeper levels. In general, an object that is found deeper in the ground is older than one located closer to the surface. Fossil and cultural remains can be relatively dated based on their position in a deposit (Figure 14–8).

In practice, stratigraphic sequences are not easy to interpret. Neat layers are not always present, and intrusions, such as burials, can place more recent fossils at the same level as much older material (Figure 14–9). Careful analysis of the soil can often reveal such intrusions. Earthquakes, volcanic eruptions, and other cataclysmic events can also alter stratigraphic sequences.

In addition, if long periods of time elapsed during which deposits did not form or deposited sediments were eroded away, long gaps in time will occur between a particular stratum and the layer just above and/or below it. The surfaces of layers that represent such breaks in the geological record are called **unconformities.** For a particular strati-

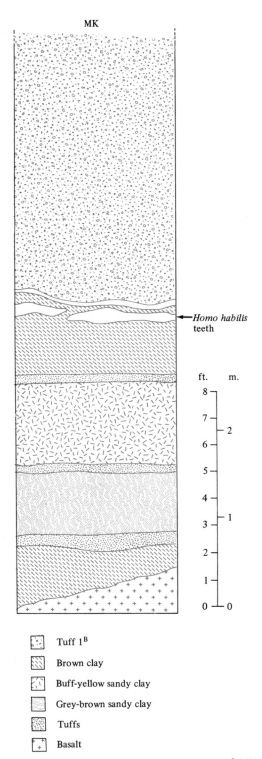

FIGURE 14–8 *Stratigraphic cross section of MK site, Olduvai Gorge, Tanzania.* Note the location of teeth belonging to the extinct hominid species *Homo habilis,* to be discussed in Chapter 17.

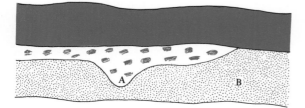

FIGURE 14–9 *Stratigraphic cross section.* In this hypothetical cross section of an archaeological site, a hole has been dug into a lower layer. An object lying at the bottom of the hole *(A)* is therefore found at the same level as much older material *(B)*.

graphic sequence, unconformities may represent more unrecorded time than the time represented by the strata that are present.

INDEX FOSSILS   In the late eighteenth century, an English geologist, William Smith (1769–1839), noted that particular combinations of fossil animals and plants occurred together in certain sedimentary formations. He realized that if these combinations of fossil species were found in areas other than the original, the periods in which the sedimentary layers were laid down in the two areas must be approximately the same. Therefore, strata from one area could be correlated with strata from another.

In this way, certain fossils or combinations of fossils become markers for particular periods of time; certain key fossils are known as **index fossils.** An index fossil is a species that had a very wide geographical distribution but existed for a short period of time. The appearance of an index fossil in a particular stratum immediately provides the investigator with a relative date for that stratum. If a date is established for the index fossil, any other fossil found in association with it is given the same date.

FLUORINE DATING   Paleontologists have developed several ways to test whether or not objects in a site are contemporary. As bones and teeth lie in the ground, they absorb fluorine and other minerals dissolved in the groundwater. On the other hand, the nitrogen content of the bones decreases as the material ages. The amount of minerals absorbed and the amount of nitrogen

lost can be used to calculate the relative chronology of the material in a site. Since the rates of absorption and loss depend on the specific nature of the groundwater, however, these methods can be used only for fossils found in the same area.

The most frequent application of these methods is in determining whether bones found in association are indeed of equal age. If one could show that a human skull and a mammoth rib lying next to it contain the same amount of fluorine, then it follows that both creatures were alive at the same time. On the other hand, if the mineral contents of the two bones differ, with the skull containing less fluorine, one could conclude that the human skull was placed at the lower level through burial. Box 14–2 describes a famous hoax that was resolved through the use of fluorine dating.

Chronometric Dating Techniques

Chronometric dates refer to specific points in time and are noted in specific calendrical systems. **Calendrical systems** are based on natural recurring units of time, such as the revolutions of the earth around the sun or the appearance of the new moon; they note the number of such units that have preceded or elapsed with reference to a specific point in time. For instance, *On the Origin of Species*, by Charles Darwin, was first published in 1859. This date is based on the Gregorian calendar, and it refers to 1859 revolutions of the earth around the sun since the traditional date of the birth of Christ. The same book was published in 5620 according to the Hebrew calendar and in the year 1276 according to the Muslim calendar. The former date is based on the biblical origin of the world, the latter, on the flight of Mohammed.

A chronometric date is often given as 10,115 years ago or 10,115 B.P., in which B.P. stands for "before the present." The problem with this type of designation is that one must know the year in which the date was determined. For example, if a date was determined to be 780 B.P. in 1950, it would have to be changed to 830 B.P. in the year 2000, and so on. Many anthropologists use 1950 as the reference point for all B.P. dates.

BOX 14–2

THE PILTDOWN SKULL

As Darwin's theory became widely accepted, the search for "missing links" began. In 1912 Charles Dawson found a skull in a site on Piltdown Common, England, which became known as *Piltdown Man*. The find consisted of a brain case, which was very much like that of a relatively modern human, and a lower jaw, which was similar to that of an ape (see accompanying figure). Some additional material was discovered later at a nearby site (Site II). Here was the missing link!

In the years that followed, paleontologists discovered other transitional forms that differed considerably from Piltdown. Piltdown showed a large, developed brain case associated with a modified apelike jaw. More recently discovered forms showed a relatively small brain case associated with essentially modern teeth and jaws.

In 1953 the Piltdown skull was declared a hoax. When paleontologists subjected the fossils to fluorine analysis, they found that many of the different fossils contained different percentages of fluorine. The "hominid" material contained less fluorine than the bones of other extinct animals found with it, indicating that the Piltdown brain case was more recent than the estimates made on the basis of soil analysis.

Fluorine analysis also revealed that the jaw did not belong to the rest of the skull. Although the brain case appeared to be a real fossil of fairly recent date, the jaw was a modified orangutan mandible.

The actual percentages of fluorine found in the various individual fossils are listed in the following table.

FOSSIL	FLUORINE (%)
From the original site:	
Cranial fragments	0.10
Jaw	0.03
Elephant, mastodon, rhinoceros	1.9–3.1
Hippopotamus	0.05
From Site II:	
Cranial fragments	0.10
Molar tooth	0.01

The culprit who had masterminded the hoax had filed down the canine teeth and stained the bones to make them appear to be of the same age as known prehistoric animals. These diverse fragments were then secretly placed in the sites. To this day, the perpetrator is still unknown.

References: C. Blinderman, *The Piltdown Inquest* (Buffalo: Prometheus, 1986); F. Spencer, *Piltdown: A Scientific Forgery* (London: Oxford University Press, 1990); and J. S. Weiner, *The Piltdown Forgery* (London: Oxford University Press, 1955).

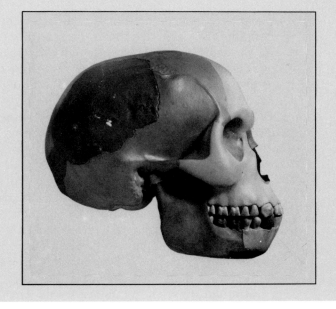

Chronometric dates in paleontology are often given in the following form: 500 B.P. ± 50 years. The "plus or minus 50 years" does *not* represent an error factor. It is a probability statement that is necessary when certain types of determinations are made. This probability is expressed as a **standard deviation.** For example, a standard deviation of 50 years means that the probability of the real date's falling between 550 and 450 B.P. is 67 percent. The probability of the real date's falling between two standard deviations, in our example between 600 and 400 B.P., is 95 percent.

Chronometric dates are sometimes called *absolute dates*, yet some paleontologists and archaeologists believe that this term is misleading. The paleontologist Chris Paul writes:

> There is a natural human tendency to believe that mathematical calculations are somehow more reliable than logic expressed in words. Thus chronometric dates given in years are often thought to be more accurate than relative ages. In fact we *know* with absolute certainty that the Jurassic preceded the Cretaceous, but the current best estimate of fifty-five to sixty million years for the duration of the Jurassic is very much open to question.[7]

Often the paleontologist must use both chronometric and relative dates together. For example, if one fossil is dated at 30,000 ± 250 B.P. and another at 30,150 ± 250 B.P., it is not possible to tell which of the two fossils is the oldest since the ranges of both dates overlap (29,750 to 30,250 B.P. and 29,900 to 30,400 B.P.). Deciding which fossil is older would be impossible with only the chronometric dates, but a relative dating technique might solve the problem.

AMINO ACID RACEMIZATION   An example of chronometric dating is **amino acid racemization.** Many organic molecules, such as the amino acids, occur in two forms that are identical in structure but are mirror images of each other. The amino acids found in proteins in living organisms are, by convention, called *left-handed* or L-amino acids; the L refers to *levo-*, or "left." Mirroring them are the *right-handed* or D-amino acids; the D refers to *dextro-*, or "right." When an organism dies, the L-amino acids slowly turn into D-amino acids, a process known as racemization.

Amino acid racemization is used to date fossil material that contains amino acids; such material includes bone, teeth, **coprolites** (fossilized fecal material), corals, and sea shells. The process can be used to determine the age of material up to 200,000 years old. Its reliability decreases with

age, however, and some types of material can be dated more accurately than others.

Amino acids are found in fossils since only 40 to 70 percent of the amino acids in datable material decomposes. Each amino acid is associated with a characteristic speed of racemization at a given temperature. This is expressed as the racemization rate, which is the time it takes for half of the molecules to change to the D form. For example, the racemization rate of aspartic acid is 15,000 years at 20°C (68°F).

Problems occur with the use of this method, however, since many variables can affect the speed of racemization. The most significant variables are temperature and acidity of the soil. Because of this, calibrated ratios can be used only in a specific geographical area, and the consistency of temperatures over long periods of time needs to be demonstrated.

Radiometric Dating Techniques

A number of dating methods exist that produce chronometric dates. Examples are **tree-ring dating,** or **dendrochronology,** in which the age of a wood sample is determined by counting the number of annual growth rings, and amino acid racemization, which we have just discussed. Nevertheless, the development of **radiometric dating methods,** based upon the decay of radioactive materials, has brought about a major revision of the age of the earth and the fossils it contains.

As we saw in Chapter 4, all matter is composed of one or more elements. The elements carbon, oxygen, nitrogen, and hydrogen are important constituents of all plants and animals, while the elements potassium, silicon, and oxygen are important elements in rocks and minerals.

Although most elements are stable, that is, one element does not change into another, many are unstable, or **radioactive.** Also, an element often occurs in more than one form; the different forms of an element are called **isotopes.** Sometimes some isotopes are radioactive while others are not.

Radioactivity means that the atom is unstable and will decay into another type of atom. Predicting when a given atom will decay is impos-

---

[7]C. Paul, *The Natural History of Fossils* (New York: Holmes & Meier, 1980), 182. Reprinted by permission of Holmes & Meier.

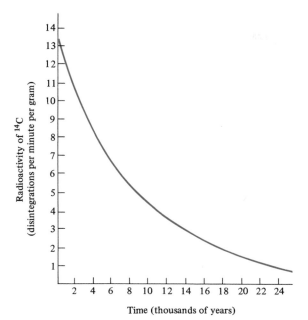

FIGURE 14–10 *Decay curve of ¹⁴C.* At time 0, the ¹⁴C in the animal tissue is in equilibrium with the ¹⁴C in the atmosphere, with the radioactivity of ¹⁴C in the tissue sample measured at 13.56 ± 0.07 disintegrations per minute per gram (dpm/g). When the animal dies, no new ¹⁴C is incorporated into the tissue, and the radioactivity decreases over time.

sible, but we can express the rate of decay as a probability statement. If we have a given number of atoms, we can say that one-half of those atoms will have decayed in a given number of years. This number is known as the **half-life.**

Radioactive decay is uniform throughout time and is unaffected by external conditions such as temperature, pressure, or the presence of other elements. Figure 14–10 plots the rate of decay of radioactive carbon; the number of half-lives is shown on the horizontal axis. In one half-life, exactly one-half of the original atoms have decayed and one-half are left. In two half-lives, three-quarters (one-half plus one-half of one-half) of the original atoms have decayed and one-quarter remain. Notice that this is a geometric curve.

Some radioactive elements have been around from the time the earth was formed. Because their half-lives are so long, they still exist in measurable quantities within the crust of the earth. About twenty such elements have been found, and four exist in enough quantity to be useful for dating: potassium 40, rubidium 87, uranium 235, and uranium 238. Although all four, and some others, have been used as a basis for radiometric dating, potassium 40 has proved to be the most useful.

POTASSIUM-ARGON DATING **Potassium-argon dating** is based upon the radioactive decay of potassium 40, which has a half-life of 1250 million years. One out of 10,000 potassium atoms found in rocks is the radioactive isotope potassium 40 (⁴⁰K). Over time ⁴⁰K decays into calcium 40 (⁴⁰Ca) and argon 40 (⁴⁰Ar); the latter is a gas that accumulates within certain minerals.

In order to make use of this technique, the mineral must meet two criteria. First, although potassium is a common constituent of minerals, the method can be used only on material with a sufficiently high potassium content. Second, the material must arise in association with volcanic activity. Under the very high temperatures that accompany volcanic activity, the argon gas is expelled. When the material cools and solidifies, it contains a certain amount of potassium 40 but no argon 40. As time goes on, the amount of ⁴⁰K decreases while the amount of ⁴⁰Ar increases. These two variables are used in the determination of the chronometric date.

A new form of the potassium-argon technique is **argon 40/argon 39** (⁴⁰Ar/³⁹Ar) dating. The material is radiated so that the nonradioactive ³⁹K is transformed into ³⁹Ar. The argon gas is extracted, and the amounts of ⁴⁰Ar and ³⁹Ar are measured. A variation of this technique involves the use of a laser to melt individual crystals to release the argon. This is termed **single-crystal fusion.** This method reduces the effects of contamination and reduces the size of the sample needed. Recently this dating method was used to date the most ancient hominid finds (Chapter 16).

The potassium-argon technique is limited, with few exceptions, to volcanic ash falls and lava flows. The technique is seldom used to date an actual object, but it is used to date fossilized bones with respect to their placement in relationship to volcanic layers in the surrounding material (Figure 14–11).

(a)   (b)

FIGURE 14–11 *Potassium-argon dating. (a)* Hypothetical live animal. *(b)* After death, the body of the animal becomes incorporated into a sedimentary bed (lake deposit). Periodic volcanic eruptions have created volcanic lenses in this bed, and the volcanic material can be dated by the potassium-argon technique. The age of the fossil is inferred from its context in relationship to the dated volcanic lenses.

Similar techniques can be used with other radioactive isotopes. Table 14–2 lists the radioactive isotopes used in radiometric dating. In practice, several different isotopes are used; if similar dates result from the application of two or more techniques, the determined date is considered reliable.

RADIOCARBON DATING **Radiocarbon dating,** developed by Willard F. Libby in the late 1940s, was the first radiometric dating technique. One isotope of carbon, carbon 14 (^{14}C), is radioactive and will eventually decay into nitrogen 14 (^{14}N). The half-life of ^{14}C is 5730 years.

Carbon 14 forms in the upper atmosphere by the bombardment of nitrogen by cosmic radiation. The amount of ^{14}C formed in the atmosphere is relatively constant over time; although variations in the amount of solar radiation pro-

duce fluctuations in the amount of ^{14}C, it is often possible to correct for these fluctuations.

The ^{14}C in the atmosphere combines with oxygen to form carbon dioxide. Carbon dioxide, in turn, is incorporated into plants by photosyn-

TABLE 14–2

ISOTOPES USED IN RADIOMETRIC DATING

ISOTOPES		HALF-LIFE (YEARS)	USEFUL TIME RANGE (YEARS)
PARENT	DAUGHTER		
^{238}U	^{206}Pb	4.50×10^9	10^7 to origin of earth*
^{235}U	^{207}Pb	0.71×10^9	10^7 to origin of earth
^{87}Rb	^{87}Sr	4.7×10^{10}	10^7 to origin of earth
^{40}K	^{40}Ar	1.3×10^9	10^5 to origin of earth
^{14}C		5730 ± 40	0—50,000

*Currently estimated at 4.55×10^9 years.
Source: C. Paul, *The Natural History of Fossils* (New York: Holmes & Meier Publishers, Inc., 1980), 184. Reprinted by permission of Holmes & Meier.

thesis and into animals by consumption of plants or other animals (Figure 14–12). As long as the organism is alive, the proportion of ^{14}C to nonradioactive ^{12}C in the body remains constant since the amount of new ^{14}C being incorporated into the body balances the amount being lost through decay. When the organism dies, no new ^{14}C atoms are incorporated into the body, and the atoms present at death continue to decay. The age of the organism at death is calculated by comparing the proportion of ^{14}C to ^{12}C in the prehistoric sample with that in a modern sample. Since nitrogen 14 is a gas, it moves from the body into the atmosphere, where it is indistin-guishable from atmospheric nitrogen and hence cannot be measured.

In the conventional method of radiocarbon dating, the ^{14}C is measured by means of a special counter that measures the emissions given off by carbon-14 atoms when they decay. Another method of radiocarbon dating uses accelerator mass spectrometry to measure the ratio of ^{14}C to ^{12}C directly.

Radiocarbon dating can be used to date any organic material, including, but not limited to, wood and charcoal, cloth, seeds and grasses, bones, ivory, and shell. Unlike the case with potassium-argon dating, carbon 14 dates the ac-

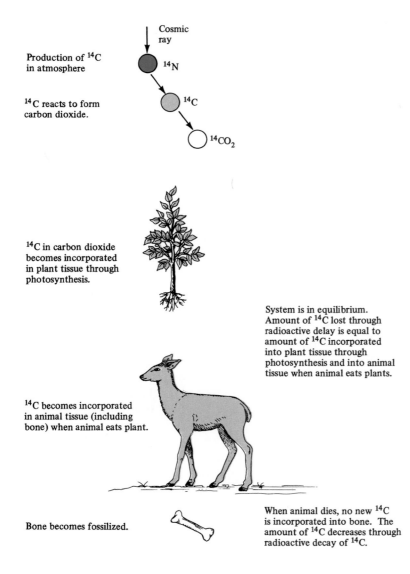

FIGURE 14–12 *Radiocarbon dating.*

Cosmic ray

Production of ^{14}C in atmosphere

^{14}N

^{14}C reacts to form carbon dioxide.

^{14}C

$^{14}CO_2$

^{14}C in carbon dioxide becomes incorporated in plant tissue through photosynthesis.

System is in equilibrium. Amount of ^{14}C lost through radioactive delay is equal to amount of ^{14}C incorporated into plant tissue through photosynthesis and into animal tissue when animal eats plants.

^{14}C becomes incorporated in animal tissue (including bone) when animal eats plant.

Bone becomes fossilized.

When animal dies, no new ^{14}C is incorporated into bone. The amount of ^{14}C decreases through radioactive decay of ^{14}C.

tual material. The material that is being dated is consumed in the process. The maximum age that can be determined by the conventional method at the present time is 40,000 to 50,000 years. The direct method has a theoretical maximum of 100,000 years, but under present conditions the maximum is between 40,000 and 60,000 years. The direct method uses much smaller quantities of the sample being dated.

None of the radiometric dating methods is infallible. The accuracy of the equipment used and the skill of the technician can influence the validity of the date determination. Also, a sample may have been contaminated with radioactive materials in the soil or by substances that contacted the sample after excavation, such as oils from a sweaty hand or smoke from a cigarette. Therefore, samples should be picked up with forceps and placed in a special container, but an inexperienced excavator may forget to do this or may not know that it should be done.

FISSION-TRACK DATING   Another type of radiometric dating technique is **fission-track dating.** Like potassium-argon dating, fission-track dating dates the minerals in a deposit. Minerals are crystalline in nature, which means that their atoms form an orderly three-dimensional structure based on the repetition of modular units. As the nucleus of a heavy isotope such as uranium 238 breaks apart, its decay particles rip holes in the orderly crystal structure of the mineral. In so doing, the particles leave tracks in these crystals.

The tracks can be used to determine a chronometric date. After being chemically treated to make them larger, such tracks can be seen under magnification and counted. The number of atomic disintegrations is directly related to the number of tracks produced. If the concentration of the isotope under study is known, then a count of the tracks left will indicate the age of the mineral being dated. This method can give us dates ranging from twenty years after the specimen formed to as far back as the beginning of the solar system.

THERMOLUMINESCENCE DATING   When some materials, such as crystals, are heated, they give off a flash of light, a phenomenon known as **thermoluminescence.** Minerals in the ground are constantly exposed to radiation from naturally occurring radioactive elements, primarily uranium, thorium, and potassium 40. The radioactivity causes some electrons to separate from the atoms; these electrons then fall into defects in the structure of the crystal where they remain, accumulating through time. When the material is exposed to heat, the trapped electrons are liberated and, in the process, give off characteristic wavelengths of light at particular temperatures.

If the mineral has been exposed to constant radiation through time, then the amount of light will be proportional to the age of the material. In addition, immediately after heating, no more light is seen until the mineral has been exposed to new radiation. Thus, the zero point for determining a date is the last heating of the material or the point at which the mineral was crystallized.

Thermoluminescence can be used to date archaeological finds, such as ceramics, burnt stones (such as those that make up a fire pit), and burnt flint tools, as well as geological material, such as volcanic debris. This technique can be used to date fairly young objects, as well as objects from as far back as 300,000 years ago, depending on the nature of the material being dated.

ELECTRON SPIN RESONANCE DATING   In our discussion of thermoluminescence, we saw that naturally occurring radioactivity causes some electrons to separate from the atoms and then fall into defects in the structure of the crystal. Most of the time these electrons are trapped as pairs, but when an odd number of electrons become trapped, they behave like small magnets. In **electron spin resonance (ESR) dating,** an analysis of this property is used to establish a chronometric date.

Electron spin resonance dating can be used for dates back to the Paleozoic, depending upon the material being dated and other conditions. The method can be used to date many materials, including limestone, coral, shell, and teeth. In Chapter 19 we will see how ESR dating has provided dates that have helped paleontologists understand the evolution of our species.

The Geomagnetic Time Scale

The invention of the compass made possible long-distance ocean voyages of exploration. The needle of a compass points toward the north magnetic pole. Today geologists believe that the earth's magnetism arises from motions within the outer liquid core of the earth caused by the rotation of the earth. The positions of the magnetic north and south poles are not stable, however. They move their position, reverse their polarity, and change in intensity over time.

No one has ever observed the occurrence of reversals in the polarity of the earth. Geologists, however, have found crystals in rock that act as small magnets. In molten rock these crystals orient themselves to the poles before the rock solidifies. Once "frozen" they leave a record of the polarity of the earth at that point in time. The study of the polarity of these materials, both on land and on the sea floor, enables geologists to create a chart showing the sequence of magnetic reversals. When specific reversals are dated by radiometric techniques, a **geomagnetic reversal time scale (GRTS)** can be drawn. If a pattern of normal and reversed polarity is found in a rock formation, the pattern can be matched with the GRTS and dates can be assigned to the formation. Fossils are given approximate dates with respect to their context within the formation.

Figure 14–13 shows a portion of the GRTS. In the figure, intervals of normal polarity, that is, polarity that corresponds to what we find today, are pictured as solid black, while intervals of reversed polarity are seen as white. This scale is constantly being improved as new dates or more detailed profiles are determined. Large divisions of the scale that show primarily a single polarity are called **chrons,** while small subdivisions within a chron are known as **subchrons.** Geomagnetic patterns are known back as far as the Middle Jurassic, but some sections are better known and better dated than others. This method is most useful for 10,000 to 10,000,000 years ago. A major advantage of this technique is

that it can be applied to sedimentary deposits where radiometric techniques cannot be used.

The Geological Time Scale

Large sections of stratigraphic sequences are exposed in many parts of the world. The layers, of various colors and textures, are composed of different types of materials that represent the diverse environmental conditions existing at the time the layers were laid down. In addition, the fossil contents also differ. The study of the stratigraphic sequence of geological features and fossils provides the basis for the geological time scale.

Geologists have divided the history of the earth, as revealed in the stratigraphic record, into a hierarchy of units: the **era, period,** and **epoch.** Each division of geological time is characterized by a distinct fossil flora and fauna and major geological events such as extensive mountain building. In general, the farther back in time we go, the more difficult it is to determine the events that occurred since more recent events often obliterate signs of earlier events. The geological time scale is outlined in Figure 14–14.

Plate Tectonics

The surface of the earth can loosely be compared to a cracked eggshell. Like the fractured shell, the earth's surface is made up of several areas separated by distinct boundaries. These areas, called **tectonic plates,** are segments of the **lithosphere,** the hard outer layer of the earth. Unlike the segments of the eggshell, lithospheric plates move relative to one another as they float at about the rate of 2.5 centimeters (1 inch) a year atop a softer, more fluid layer of the earth. This process of constant plate movement, called **plate tectonics,** is in large part responsible for the formation of mountains and valleys, for earthquakes and volcanoes, for the rise of islands out of the sea, and for many other geological occurrences.

Some plates are completely covered by the sea, while others contain landmasses such as the continents and islands. Since the plates move, it

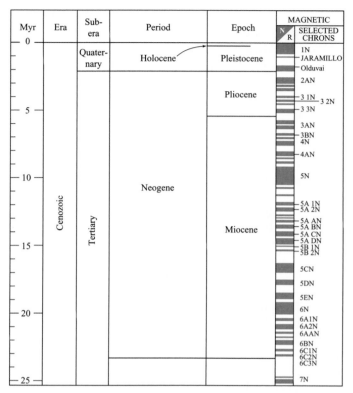

Myr	Era	Sub-era	Period	Epoch	MAGNETIC

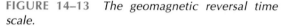

FIGURE 14–13 *The geomagnetic reversal time scale.*

follows that continents move, or "drift." Continents may move into each other; "slide" past each other; or break up, with the parts moving away from each other. Except for earthquakes, this movement occurs so slowly in relationship to a human lifetime that it can be detected only with very sensitive equipment.

Yet continents have been mobile for hundreds of millions of years. Approximately 225 million years ago, plates carrying all the major landmasses that existed at the time came together, forming one large continent called Pangaea (which is Greek for "all the earth"). By about 200 million years ago, this single landmass was breaking up.

Figure 14–14 illustrates the relationship of the continents to each other at various points in time. An important point about continental drift is that it constantly, but slowly, has established and destroyed migration routes. Therefore, understanding the patterns of continental drift is extremely important in explaining why animals and plants are where they are today, that is, their distribu-

tion. The fact that different boundaries existed at different times for a population means that the population was at various times subject to different availability of food, different patterns of predation, different climates, and other changes in environmental pressures.

A Brief History of the Cenozoic

Geological time is divided into three large eras: the Paleozoic, the Mesozoic, and the Cenozoic; the time before the beginning of the Paleozoic is called the Proterozoic. The Cenozoic is called the Age of Mammals because it represents the time of the adaptive radiation of mammals into the numerous and various ecological niches that they occupy today. The Cenozoic began about 65 million years ago. The dividing line between the Mesozoic and the Cenozoic is marked by the relatively rapid extinction of a very large number of organisms, including the dinosaurs which had dominated the earth for so long (see Box 14–3).

The Cenozoic can be divided into two **suberas,**

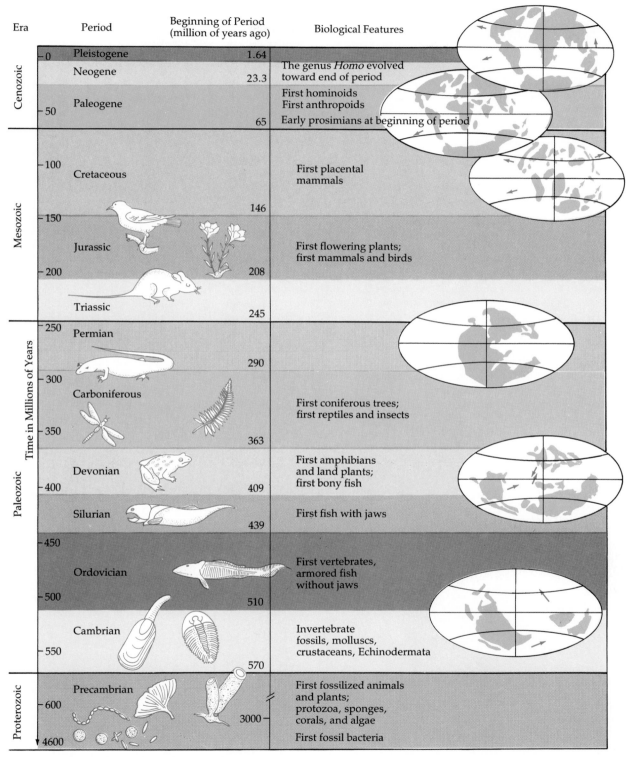

Era	Period	Beginning of Period (million of years ago)	Biological Features
Cenozoic	Pleistogene	0 — 1.64	The genus *Homo* evolved toward end of period
	Neogene	23.3	
	Paleogene	50 —	First hominoids First anthropoids
		65	Early prosimians at beginning of period
Mesozoic	Cretaceous	100 —	First placental mammals
		146	
	Jurassic	150 —	First flowering plants; first mammals and birds
		200 — 208	
	Triassic	245	
Paleozoic	Permian	250 —	
		290	
	Carboniferous	300 —	First coniferous trees; first reptiles and insects
		350 — 363	
	Devonian	400 —	First amphibians and land plants; first bony fish
		409	
	Silurian	439	First fish with jaws
	Ordovician	450 —	First vertebrates, armored fish without jaws
		500 — 510	
	Cambrian	550 —	Invertebrate fossils, molluscs, crustaceans, Echinodermata
		570	
Proterozoic	Precambrian	600 —	First fossilized animals and plants; protozoa, sponges, corals, and algae
		3000 —	
		4600	First fossil bacteria

Time in Millions of Years

FIGURE 14–14   *The geological time scale.*

BOX 14–3

WHERE HAVE ALL THE DINOSAURS GONE?

At 5 A.M. on July 10, 1990, an asteroid (a small rocky interplanetary object) traveling about 35,406 kilometers per hour (22,000 miles per hour), sped across the earth's orbit at a distance of about 4.8 million kilometers (3 million miles) from the earth. Although 4.8 million kilometers may seem very distant, in astronomical terms it represents a near miss. Since 1973 observers at Palomar Observatory in California have spotted thirty-nine asteroids that have passed close to earth. None of these objects hit the earth, but scientists have now identified about 120 "impact structures" left from previous strikes, and about five new ones are identified each year. We may assume that many craters have yet to be found, while others have been obliterated by geological processes such as volcanism, erosion, and sedimentation.

One of the best known impact structures is Meteor Crater in Arizona (see Figure). It was formed when an asteroid hit the earth about 30,000 years ago. The result was a crater that is 1200 meters (4000 feet) in diameter and 200 meters (700 feet) deep. The July 10, 1990, asteroid could have been three times as large as the one that formed Meteor Crater.

Although a dramatic sight, Meteor Crater represents a minor impact compared to that made by an asteroid or comet that may have crashed into the earth 65 million years ago. Some scientists believe that at that time an extraterrestrial object 10 kilometers (6 miles) or more across struck the planet. The object would have hit the earth with a force 10,000 times more powerful than that of all the world's nuclear weapons. A candidate for the crater that resulted from the impact is located on the Yucatan Peninsula of Mexico. Although some scientists believe that other forces such as massive volcanic eruptions caused or contributed to the Cretaceous/Tertiary extinctions, the impact may have been responsible for the extinction of about 75 percent of all animal species living directly before the impact. This mass extinction is one of at least twelve such episodes that have occurred over the last 800 million years.

The discovery that led to the impact-extinction hypothesis dates back to 1978. At that time, a thin layer of iridium-rich clay was discovered in Gubbio, Italy. Since 1978, iridium, a rare element on earth but frequently found in meteorites (the earthly remains of asteroids), has been discovered in 65-million-year-old layers of the earth worldwide. The 65-million-B.P. date corresponds to the boundary between the Cretaceous and Tertiary periods and to the mass extinction.

If an interplanetary object was responsible for the extinctions, the impact may have created an enormous dust cloud of global proportions; as a consequence, sunlight was blocked and plants could not photosynthesize. As plants died out, the animals that were dependent upon them for food also perished. Predators became extinct as their herbivorous prey succumbed. Because solar energy reaching the earth's surface was partially blocked, the planet also cooled. After the initial cooling period, a study of plant life suggests that a heating period occurred (the greenhouse effect). Many organisms that initially survived may have been wiped out by these climatic changes.

Another idea is that hot ejecta (objects thrown upward) were

thrown into the atmosphere on the impact of the asteroid or comet. On returning to earth, these objects could have caused global wildfires that precipitated a variety of cataclysmic effects, including acid rain that killed off sea, lake, and river life, creating a rippling food chain die-off.

It is probable that a large asteroid or comet will again hit the earth. Some scientists are now discussing the possibility of using the Star Wars Defense System, origi-

nally designed to destroy incoming enemy missiles, to divert the course of potentially dangerous interplanetary objects.

We are currently experiencing the thirteenth mass extinction. This time the cause is earth-bound. People, through their destruction of the world's environments and overhunting, are the direct and indirect cause of most of the approximately 100 extinctions of plants and animals that are now occurring every day.

For further information see the following: L. W. Alvarez, "Experimental Evidence That an Asteroid Impact Led to the Extinction of Many Species 65 Million Years Ago," *Proceedings of the National Academy of Sciences,* 80 (1983), 627–642; H. J. Melosh et al., "Ignition of Global Wildfires at the Cretaceous/Tertiary Boundary," *Nature,* 343 (1990), 251–254; V. E. Courtillot, "A Volcanic Eruption," *Scientific American,* 263 (October 1990), 82–92; G. S. Paul, "Giant Meteor Impacts and Great Eruptions: Dinosaur Killers?" *BioScience,* 39 (1989), 162–172; and J. A. Wolfe, "Palaeobotanical Evidence of a Marked Temperature Increase Following the Cretaceous/Tertiary Boundary," *Nature,* 343 (1990), 153–156.

the Tertiary and the Quaternary, concepts first defined in the eighteenth century. Today, many geologists and paleontologists divide the Cenozoic into three periods: the first two, the Paleogene and the Neogene, are divisions of the Tertiary; the Pleistogene is the only period within the Quaternary subera. As can be seen in Table 14–3, these periods are further divided into epochs: the Paleocene, Eocene, Oligocene, Miocene, Pliocene, Pleistocene, and Holocene (or Recent). In paleoanthropology, the Cenozoic era and its periods and epochs are of major concern since during this time the primates, including *Homo sapiens,* evolved.

THE PALEOGENE   The most ancient period of the Cenozoic, the Paleogene, contains three epochs: Paleocene, Eocene, and Oligocene. The first mammals evolved in the Mesozoic era, but it was not until the beginning of the Cenozoic, the Paleocene, that they began their major adaptive radiation. At the beginning of this epoch, the mammals found new opportunities for diversification into the ecological niches left vacant by the dinosaurs, which were by that time extinct. Although no modern mammalian families came into being during this epoch, the ancestors of modern families were present.

During the Paleocene, North America and Europe were connected as a single continent. The western and eastern parts of North America were separated by a large sea, and northwestern North America was connected by land to northeastern Asia. Other waterways covered parts of what is now South America, Africa, and Eurasia.

During the Paleocene, climates were warm and wet and mountains rose to new heights. De-

TABLE 14–3

THE GEOLOGICAL TIME SCALE: THE CENOZOIC ERA

SUBERA	PERIOD	EPOCH	BEGINNING (MILLIONS OF YEARS)
Quaternary	Pleistogene	Holocene	0.01
		Pleistocene	1.64
Tertiary	Neogene	Pliocene	5.2
		Miocene	23.3
	Paleogene	Oligocene	35.4
		Eocene	56.5
		Paleocene	65.0

Source: W. B. Harland et al., *A Geologic Time Scale 1989* (Cambridge: Cambridge University Press, 1990).

ciduous broad-leaved forests extended northward to approximately the latitude of today's Oslo, Norway, and Seward, Alaska, and conifer forests extended farther northward. Much of the present-day western United States was covered with subtropical forests and savanna. The early primates evolved within this setting.

During the Eocene the land bridge between North America and Europe began to separate; the connection was gone by the end of this epoch. Large seas in Eurasia effectively isolated western Europe from the rest of the Old World. South America, Africa, and Australia were all surrounded by water. In the latter part of the Eocene, temperatures began to cool, seasons became more pronounced, glaciers began to form in Antarctica, and climates became dryer and more diverse. Nearly all the modern orders of mammals were present by the Eocene. Primates were widespread, and the earliest anthropoids were present by the end of this epoch.

During the Oligocene climates continued to be characterized by increased cooling, drying, and alternating seasons. Africa and South America were much closer together than they are today. Many paleoanthropologists believe that African anthropoids could have rafted across the then narrow Atlantic Ocean to South America. Some Oligocene primates are known from South American sites. All Old World primate fossils, which include early anthropoids, come from Africa which was separated from Europe and Asia.

THE NEOGENE   The Neogene period consists of the Miocene and Pliocene epochs. In the early Miocene we find the earliest Old World monkeys and apes in east Africa; the first hominids may have appeared during this epoch as well. By the middle Miocene, African primates had begun to migrate over a newly formed land bridge into Asia and Europe. In general, climates in the Miocene were somewhat warmer than those in the Oligocene; by the late Miocene climates were becoming cooler and drier. The continents were pretty much in their present position, but sea levels were higher than they are today and seas still covered large areas of land.

During the Pliocene, climates became cooler and more varied, as the Antarctic ice cap continued to expand. Mountain building continued,

and the mammals reached their high point in variety and size. During this epoch the direct ancestors of *Homo sapiens* evolved.

THE PLEISTOCENE   The epoch comprising all but the last 10,000 years of the Pleistogene period is the Pleistocene, an epoch marked by major fluctuations in the earth's geology and climate. The Pleistocene was the time of many giant mammals, such as the giant ground sloths, mammoths and mastodons, and the saber-toothed cat; it was also the time of their extinction. During the Pleistocene, hominids became efficient hunters, and they were probably responsible for the extinction of many of these mammals.

The Pleistocene is noteworthy because during this time large, long-lasting masses of ice, glaciers, were extensive. Great ice ages had already occurred several times in the history of earth, but the Pleistocene Ice Age is the most recent, and it is certainly the best known. When one speaks of an ice age, the image of a world dominated by freezing temperatures and covered with ice comes to mind; but ice never covered the entire earth. The extent of the continental glaciers is shown in Figure 14–15.

The Pleistocene was not a time of continuous glaciation; rather, it was marked by both **glacial** and **interglacial** periods. During glacials the glacial ice expanded, but during interglacials the climates were as warm as or even warmer than those prevailing today. Actually, each of the major glacials and interglacials was a complex event, comprising cooler and warmer episodes.

During the last glacial, sea levels dropped at least 100 meters (330 feet) below their present level, primarily because large amounts of water were "locked up" in glacial ice. Land connections came into existence wherever shallow water had separated two or more landmasses. For example, during the periods of glaciation, Asia was connected by land to North America; thus animals, including humans, were able to cross between the two at the point of connection. The Pleistocene Ice Age also caused changes in vegetation patterns: as glaciers advanced and retreated, forests turned into grasslands. Great herds of mammals flourished, fed by the grasslands at the foot of glacial ice; but as forests

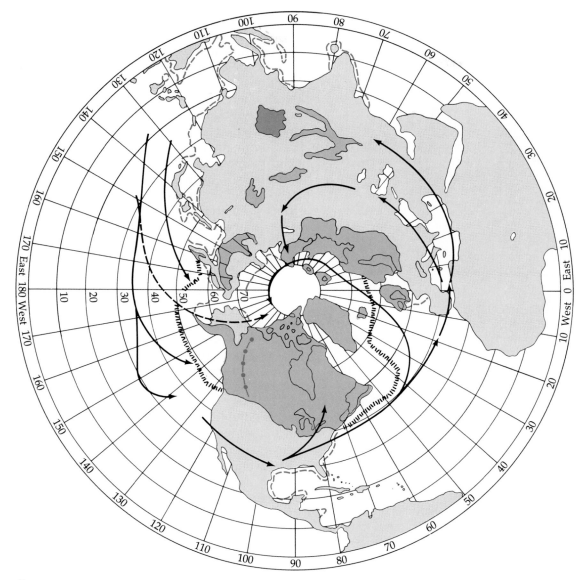

Key:

Principal areas
covered by glacier
ice. *(Very small
areas not shown. In
central and northeastern
Asia, includes areas of more
extensive earlier glaciation.)*

Area not completely glaciated but
in which glaciation was extensive.

∿∿∿∿∿∿∿ Inferred outer limit of pack
ice at annual maximum.

⟶ Inferred major storm tracks *(annual mean)*.

⤍ ⤍ ⤍ Inferred occasional and seasonally
important storm tracks *(annual mean)*.

━●━●━●━ Zones of contact between coalescent major glaciers.

━ ━ ━ ━ 100-meter isobath.

FIGURE 14–15 *Pleistocene glaciations.* Glacial ice did not cover the entire earth during
the Pleistocene but was confined to areas of Europe, North America, and Siberia.

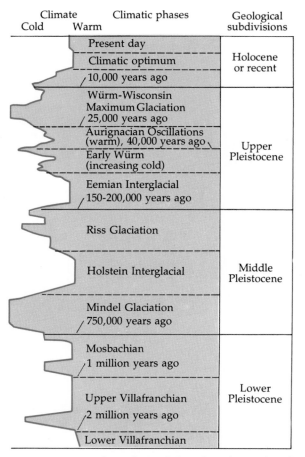

Climate Cold — Warm	Climatic phases	Geological subdivisions
	Present day	Holocene or recent
	Climatic optimum	
	10,000 years ago	
	Würm-Wisconsin Maximum Glaciation 25,000 years ago	Upper Pleistocene
	Aurignacian Oscillations (warm), 40,000 years ago	
	Early Würm (increasing cold)	
	Eemian Interglacial 150-200,000 years ago	
	Riss Glaciation	Middle Pleistocene
	Holstein Interglacial	
	Mindel Glaciation 750,000 years ago	
	Mosbachian 1 million years ago	Lower Pleistocene
	Upper Villafranchian 2 million years ago	
	Lower Villafranchian	

FIGURE 14–16 *Chronology of glacials and interglacials.* This chart presents one of several ways of dividing up the Pleistocene. Also, different names are applied to glacial and interglacial episodes in different parts of the world. Note the fluctuations in temperature within the glacials and interglacials.

again replaced the grasslands, the herds declined.

Figure 14–16 presents a general timeline of the glacials and interglacials during the Pleistocene. The sequence and duration of glacial episodes differed from area to area, however, and the later glacials destroyed much of the detailed evidence of earlier glacials. Therefore, the chart in Figure 14–16 must be viewed in very general terms.

Summary

The interpretation of the fossil record demands accurate dating of fossils. Relative dating provides information on the sequence of fossils in terms of which are older and which are younger. Stratigraphy is based upon the principle of superposition, which states that the lower strata in a deposit are older than those above. One major difficulty with stratigraphy is the possibility that newer material has intruded into older material via burial or cataclysms. Methods like fluorine analysis can help establish whether two bones are contemporary.

Chronometric dating provides an actual calendrical date. The most important chronometric dating methods are based upon the decay of radioactive elements. Carbon-14 dating was the first radiometric technique developed, but is theoretically limited to the last 100,000 years. Potassium-argon dating is based upon the radioactive decay of potassium 40, which has an extremely long half-life; consequently, this method can be used to date the age of the earth. Other dating techniques are fission-track dating, amino acid racemization, thermoluminescence, electron spin resonance, and geomagnetism.

The history of the earth is divided, in terms of geological and paleontological events, into four eras. Each era is divided into periods, which, in turn, are divided into epochs. Thus, the Cenozoic era, which is the Age of Mammals, can be discussed in terms of its many subdivisions.

The evolution of life has been greatly affected by earth dynamics. Landmasses move in relationship to each other, thus creating new migratory routes and destroying others. In addition, plate tectonics is responsible for many climatic alternations, and it may have been a prime cause of the cooling that led to the Pleistocene Ice Age. This was a time of fluctuating temperatures and environments, and as such, it presented a series of changing selective pressures that helped to shape human evolution.

STUDY QUESTIONS

1. What does the field of taphonomy tell us about the development of the fossil record? Why is fossilization a relatively rare event?
2. Why are some animals better represented in the fossil record than others? What are the various "sampling errors" found in the fossil records?

EXCAVATIONS AT DIK DIK HILL, OLDUVAI GORGE

Paleontological excavation is a difficult and exacting activity. In these photographs, we observe some of the phases in the excavation of a *Homo habilis* skeleton. (The species *H. habilis* is discussed in Chapter 17.)

FIGURE 14-A A group of paleoanthropologists are working at the base of Dik Dik Hill, named for the dik dik, a small east African antelope. This is one of several sites within Olduvai Gorge. The formation known as the Castle is in the foreground.

FIGURE 14-B The first fragment of hominid bone, a piece of right ulna, is found at the site.

FIGURE 14-C The research team sets up to begin excavation.

FIGURE 14-D Paleoanthropologists (right to left) Prosper Endeessokia, Tim White, and Mrisho Ramadhani excavate Dik Dik Hill.

FIGURE 14-F Soil is passed through a screen to recover small fragments.

FIGURE 14-E In this aerial view of the completed excavation, white cards indicate where important fragments of the skeleton were found.

FIGURE 14-G The elbow region is represented by the partial remains of a humerus, an ulna, and a radius.

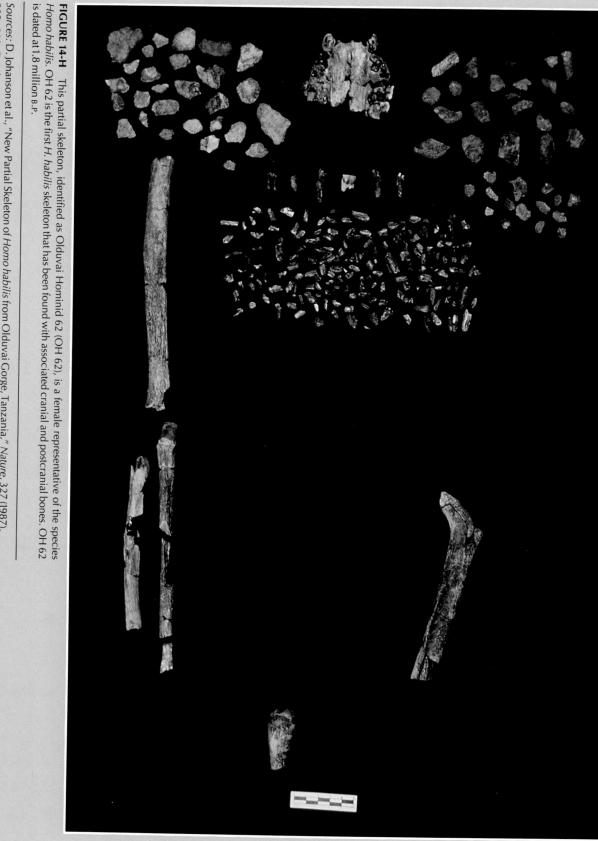

FIGURE 14-H This partial skeleton, identified as Olduvai Hominid 62 (OH 62), is a female representative of the species *Homo habilis*. OH 62 is the first *H. habilis* skeleton that has been found with associated cranial and postcranial bones. OH 62 is dated at 1.8 million B.P.

Sources: D. Johanson et al., "New Partial Skeleton of *Homo habilis* from Olduvai Gorge, Tanzania," *Nature,* 327 (1987), 205–209; D. Johanson and J. Shreeve. *Lucy's Child: The Discovery of a Human Ancestor* (New York: William Morrow, 1989).

3. Although the fossil record is fragmentary, paleontologists are able to reconstruct a great deal about once-living animals. Describe some of the types of information that can be deduced from fossil evidence.

4. Species are defined in terms of reproductive isolation. Since evidence for this cannot be inferred from the fossil record, how does the paleontologist handle the concept of prehistoric species?

5. Individual fossils that were considered representatives of different species have sometimes turned out to belong to a single species. What factors are responsible for variation within species as represented in the fossil record?

6. Distinguish between relative and chronometric dating. What are some examples of each type of dating method?

7. Geological events often have a profound influence on the evolution of living organisms. Briefly describe the impact of continental drift on the evolution of plants and animals.

SUGGESTED READINGS

Behrensmeyer, A. K., and A. P. Hill. *Fossils in the Making: Vertebrate Taphonomy and Paleoecology.* Chicago: University of Chicago Press, 1980. This is a collection of articles on taphonomy.

Binford, L. R. *Bones: Ancient Men and Modern Myths.* Orlando, Fla.: Academic, 1987. This is a provocative book on the science of taphonomy.

Ciochon, R. L., and A. B. Chiarelli. *Evolutionary Biology of New World Monkeys and Continental Drift.* New York: Plenum, 1980. This book presents a collection of essays on the significance of plate tectonics to primate evolution.

Gould, S. J. *Time's Arrow and Time's Cycle: Myth and Metaphor in the Discovery of Geological Time.* Cambridge, Mass.: Harvard University Press, 1987. In this book, Stephen Jay Gould discusses the history of the discovery of deep time, particularly the writings of Thomas Burnet, James Hutton, and Charles Lyell.

McCown, T. D., and A. R. K. Kennedy (eds.). *Climbing Man's Family Tree: A Collection of Major Writings on Human Phylogeny, 1699–1971.* Englewood Cliffs, N.J.: Prentice-Hall, 1972. This collection of essays shows how methods of collecting fossils and interpreting these data have changed over the past three centuries.

Paton, T. R. *Perspectives on a Dynamic Earth.* London: Allen & Unwin, 1986. This relatively short book presents an introduction to earth history and includes sections on radiometric dating and plate tectonics.

Paul, C. *The Natural History of Fossils.* New York: Holmes & Meier, 1980. This is a basic introduction to paleontology with information on the nature of fossils, why fossils form, dating, and more.

Roth, E., and M. Ménager, (eds.). *Nuclear Methods of Dating.* Dordrecht, Netherlands: Kluwer Academics, 1989. This book contains a series of articles that discuss, in technical detail, many of the radiometric dating techniques.

Shipman, P. *Life History of a Fossil: An Introduction to Taphonomy and Paleoecology.* Cambridge, Mass.: Harvard University Press, 1981. This book can serve as an introductory text to taphonomy.

Spindler, K. *The Man in the Ice.* New York: Harmony Books, 1994. The lead archaeologist studying the "Ice Man" describes the 5300-year-old frozen fossil and the artifacts found with him.

Taylor, R. E. *Radiocarbon Dating: An Archaeological Approach.* Orlando, Fla.: Academic, 1987. This volume discusses the history, methodology, and problems of carbon 14 dating.

The Paris Basin in the Late Eocene. The diurnal *Adapis parisiensis* feed on leaves, while at night the tiny *Pseudoloris* hunts an insect and *Necrolemur* (left) and *Microchoerus* (right) cling to branches.

Primate paleontology is an important focus of anthropological research and through its study we can gain a better appreciation of both human evolutionary biology and the circumstances leading to the emergence of our family—the Hominidae. The study of primate paleontology entails not only the investigation of the "hard evidence" of actual fossil remains; consideration is also given to analysis of the nature of past primate diversity, including an assessment of primate adaptive radiations, the divergence times of primate adaptive radiations, the divergence times of major primate lineages, primate distribution and dispersal patterns in time and space, and the ecological adaptations of past primate populations. If we are to place our origins in proper perspective, we must, therefore, be concerned not only with identifying our immediate and processional ancestors, but also with developing an appreciation of the true extent of primate diversity in the past, for it is from amidst this diversity that we emerged.

Russell L. Ciochon and Dennis A. Etler[1]

[1]R. L. Ciochon and D. A. Etler, "Reinterpreting Past Primate Diversity," in R. S. Corruccini and R. L. Ciochon (eds.), *Integrative Paths to the Past: Paleoanthropological Advances in Honor of F. Clark Howell* (Englewood Cliffs, N.J.: Prentice Hall, 1994), 37.

CHAPTER

THE EARLY PRIMATE FOSSIL RECORD

We may think of the story of human evolution as a complex, three-dimensional jigsaw puzzle. The surface of this puzzle represents the present surface of the earth, beneath which lie previous surfaces now covered by sediments. The paleoanthropologist explores the present surface of the earth and excavates down to previous surfaces to discover the fossils and artifacts that provide the clues needed to form hypotheses about human evolution. Yet after decades of search and discovery, only some of the pieces of the puzzle are tentatively in place.

In the previous chapter we discussed many of the reasons for the sketchiness of the fossil record, but these difficulties have not discouraged individuals who are deeply motivated to uncover the roots of humankind. Indeed, the past few decades have been filled with many important paleontological discoveries. Anthropologists, as well as newspaper reporters and the public, have crowded into conference rooms to hear reports of new discoveries that are extending our knowledge of prehistoric populations far back in time.

The problem is that newspaper reporters, students, and even many paleontologists, thirst for a clear, understandable picture of primate evolution. Instead, paleoanthropologists provide hypotheses and tentative sketches. Yet that is how science progresses. As Barnard Campbell put it:

> If our science is to progress at all, new data will prove every hypothesis to be wrong, and will require that every hypothesis be revised. The successive preparation and publication of such hypotheses is part of the necessary means by which science

moves on from one approximation to another, each better and more accurate than the last.[2]

This is the first of several chapters that examine the fossil record. In this chapter we will tell the story of the earliest known primates and the evolution of the nonhominid primates as seen through interpretations of the fossil record.

EVOLUTION OF THE EARLY PRIMATES

A dominant interest in evolutionary studies is that of origins—the origins of humans, of primates, of animals, and of life itself. Yet origins are difficult to identify since the earliest members of a taxonomic group often lack many characteristics of the later and better known members of that group. Furthermore, these earliest members often resemble the population from which they evolved. In our search for the earliest primates, we would hardly expect to find a creature with a fully evolved set of features like those that characterize contemporary animals.

The search for the earliest primate finds us in the north African country of Morocco. There, in 1990, ten tiny teeth were found dating from the Late Paleocene, about 60 million years ago. The fossils were placed in a new genus, *Altiatlasius,* named after the High Atlas Mountains.[3] Primates may have originated earlier, perhaps during the Early Paleocene, or possibly as far back as the Late Cretaceous.

Whether or not *Altiatlasius* was the earliest primate, the existing fossil record and studies of comparative anatomy give us a picture of what the early primates were probably like. Robert Martin looks back in time and sees the earliest primates as small, arboreal, nocturnal mammals living in tropical and subtropical forests. They occupy niches characterized by small, thin branches and saplings. Weighing no more than 500 grams (1.1 pounds), they show anatomical specializations for effective life in trees, such as a grasping foot. The skin of the palm and fingers are covered with epidermal ridges associated with a refined sense of touch. The diets of these earliest primates consist of plant material, such as fruits, and small animals, primarily insects. The animal's precise stereoscopic vision aids in the hunting of small animal prey. The primate carefully stalks its prey. Then, anchoring its body with its grasping feet, it reaches forward and grabs the prey with its hands, bringing the prey to its mouth, where it is killed by biting.[4]

The Early Primate Fossil Record

In the early Cenozoic the surface of the earth looked quite different than it does today. For example, during the Eocene, which began about 56.5 million years ago and lasted about 21 million years, climates were warm and tropical; yet by its end climates began to cool and become drier, and marked seasons developed. North America and Europe began to break apart during the middle of this epoch, and by its end North America and Europe were separated from one another.

Two distinct morphological patterns are found among the early primates; one characterizes the family Omomyidae and the other the family Adapidae. The oldest-known primate, *Altiatlasius,* may be an early omomyid. By the Early Eocene both adapids and omomyids are present in North America and in Europe. These early adapids and omomyids are much more similar to one another than are later forms, suggesting a common ancestry in Paleocene times.

THE ADAPIDS   The family name Adapidae is derived from the generic name *Adapis.* The original specimen was described in 1821 by Georges Cuvier (Chapter 2). Cuvier, however, believed it to be a transitional form between the even-toed

[2]B. Campbell, "A New Taxonomy of Fossil Man," *Yearbook of Physical Anthropology 1973* (Washington, D.C.: American Association of Physical Anthropologists, 1974), 195.
[3]B. Sigé et al., "*Altiatlasius koulchii* n. gn. et sp., Primate Omomyidé du Paléocène Supérieur de Maroc, et les Origines des Euprimates," *Palaeontographica,* 2140 (1990), 31–56.

[4] R. D. Martin, *Primate Origins and Evolution* (Princeton: Princeton University Press, 1990), 656–660.

BOX 15–1

THE CASE OF THE PLESIADAPIFORMES

At one time a major candidate for the honor of being labeled the earliest primate was a group of fossils that make up the suborder Plesiadapiformes. This suborder dates from the Late Cretaceous through the Early Eocene. These fossils are divided into four to six families and are found in both North America and Europe.

The plesiadapiforms were first discovered over 100 years ago. They are known primarily from teeth and jaw fragments and some recently discovered postcranial material. The earliest specimen, known

Plesiadapis, a Paleocene plesiadapiforme. From "The Early Relatives of Man" by E. L. Simons. Copyright ©1964 by Scientific American, Inc. All rights reserved.

exclusively from a single right lower molar, is *Purgatorius* from the Purgatory Hills of Montana.

The plesiadapiforms lack most of the features we associate with the order Primates. They display a relationship with the primates only through similarities of molar morphology; to many paleoanthropologists these similarities are far from convincing. They lack a grasping foot and all digits end in large claws. This suggests a locomotor pattern quite different from those we associate with living primates.

The relatively small orbits, the lack of a forward rotation of the orbits, and the lack of a postorbital bar suggest that plesiadapiform vision was not highly developed. The brain is relatively small. Many of the plesiadapiforms possess rodent-like teeth with large incisors, no canines, and a large diastema

separating the incisors from the premolars. These differences that separate the plesiadapiforms from the more familiar primates have led many primatologists to label the plesiadapiforms "archaic primates," as compared with the "primates of modern aspect" or euprimates ("true" primates).

The interpretation of the plesiadapiforms as early primates has changed during the past several years because of discoveries in the late 1980s of postcranial material. These bones suggest that these animals possessed a gliding membrane anatomically similar to that of the flying lemurs, or colugo *(Cynocephalus),* of the Philippines. (The modern flying lemurs, however, do not fly, nor are they lemurs; indeed they are not even primates but form their own order Dermoptera.) For example, while the phalanges, or finger bone, closest to the palm is the longest in most mammals, the middle bone is the longest in the plesiadapiform *Phenacolemur* and in the modern flying lemur; this is an adaptation for support of a gliding membrane.

References: K. C. Beard, "Gliding Behaviour and Palaeoecology of the Alleged Primate Family Paromomyidae (Mammalia, Dermoptera)," *Nature,* 345 (1990), 340–341; R. F. Kay, R. W. Thorington, Jr., and P. Houde, "Eocene Plesiadapiform Shows Affinities with Flying Lemurs, Not Primates," *Nature,* 345 (1990), 342–344.

hoofed mammals and the primates, hence the name *Adapis*, or "toward the sacred bull Apis."

Members of the Adapidae resemble in some ways the modern lemurs and lorises, and they are often placed within the infraorder Lemuriformes. In other ways they are very dissimilar; for example, the adapids do not possess the dental comb that is so characteristic of modern prosimians. The relationship of the adapids to modern lemurs and lorises is not known.

The adapid skull exhibits an elongated snout. The size of the brain case compared with the size of the facial skeleton is larger than in most mammals, and studies of the brain case show an enlargement of the frontal portion of the brain. A complete bony ring encircles the eye, and the forward position of the eyes results in overlapping fields of vision. The relatively small eye sockets suggest that the animal was diurnal. The **mandibular symphysis,** the area where the two halves of the mandible join, is usually fused, and the two halves of the lower jaw are almost parallel to one another. The dentition of different adapid species suggests different dietary adaptations, including specializations for eating insects, fruits, and leaves.

The adapids weighed over 500 grams (1.1 pounds). Nails are present on fingers and toes. The several relatively complete skeletons exhibit long trunks, legs, tails, and grasping feet with divergent big toes; these are adaptations for leaping and grasping behavior. These and other features are summarized in Table 15–1. A member of this family, *Smilodectes,* is seen in Figure 15–1.

The family Adapidae is divided into two subfamilies: Notharctinae and Adapinae. The two subfamilies represent geographically independent developments reflecting the separation of North America from Europe. The Notharctinae, which includes *Smilodectes,* are primarily found in North America, while the Adapinae are found in Europe and Asia. Most Notharctinae became extinct during the Middle Eocene. Most Adapinae disappeared from the fossil record in the Late Eocene, although a few genera survived into

TABLE 15–1

CHARACTERISTICS OF THE ADAPIDAE AND OMOMYIDAE

CHARACTERISTIC	ADAPIDAE	OMOMYIDAE
Average body size	Above 500 grams	Below 500 grams
Snout	Elongated	Short
Mandibular symphysis	Usually fused	Unfused and mobile
Tooth row	Almost parallel	V-shaped
Incisors	Spatulate and more vertically implanted	Pointed and protruding
Size of central incisor relative to lateral incisor	Smaller	Equal or larger
Canines	Large, with marked sexual dimorphism	Small, with no sexual dimorphism
Lower anterior premolar	Sectorial	Not sectorial
Size of orbit	Small	Large
Number of premolars	Usually four	Usually fewer than four
Activity	Diurnal	Nocturnal
Postorbital closure	Absent	Absent or beginning
Nails	Present	Present
Tibia and fibula	Unfused	Fused
Tarsal bones	Not elongated	Elongated
Probable diet	Insects, fruit, leaves	Insects

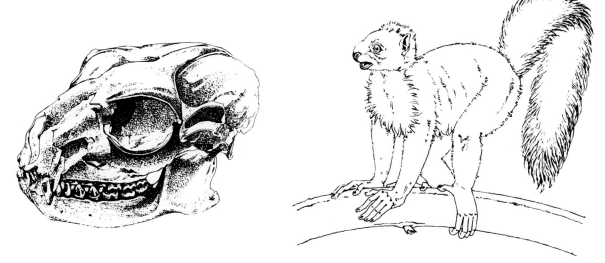

FIGURE 15–1   Smilodectes. An Eocene adapid. From "The Early Relatives of Man" by E. L. Simons. Copyright ©1964 by Scientific American, Inc. All rights reserved.

the Late Miocene in India, Pakistan, and China. A possible adapid has been recovered from the African Eocene.

THE OMOMYIDS   The family Omomyidae consists of a variety of primates that show similarities to the tarsiers; the family is often placed within the suborder Tarsioidea. However, many of the tarsier-like features are superficial, and the relationship between the omomyids and tarsiers is questionable. It is possible that the omomyids evolved from an early adapid. The omomyids first appeared in the Early Eocene and continued through the Early Oligocene. Omomyid fossils are found in North America, Europe, and Asia. A single specimen has been found in Early Oligocene beds in Africa.

The omomyids differ from the adapids in many ways. The skull exhibits a short snout with a V-shaped jaw; the mandible symphysis is unfused and mobile (Figure 15–2). The eye socket is encircled by a complete bony ring, and some species possess the beginning of a postorbital closure. The large size of the orbits compared with the length of the skull suggests that the omomyids were nocturnal. The omomyids are smaller than the adapids, weighing generally

under 500 grams (1.1 pounds). The tibia and fibula are fused, and the tarsal bone elongated, features that resemble those of living tarsiers. These and other features are summarized in Table 15–1.

One of the best known omomyid finds, represented by several skulls in France, is *Necrolemur* (Figure 15–3). The name *Necrolemur* is one of many confusing designations that often are applied to both living and fossil taxa. The name implies that the fossil is similar to the lemurs, whereas it is, in fact, considered by many to be related to the tarsiers. According to the International Rules of Zoological Nomenclature, however, once a name is given to a taxon, it cannot be changed simply because it later becomes inappropriate. The appearance of more than one name for a species in the literature would lead to confusion.

The Evolution of Modern Prosimians and Tarsiers

A single upper molar from Egypt suggests that a loris was present in Africa in the Early Oligocene; other lorises are known from the Early Miocene of Africa and the Late Miocene of Asia.

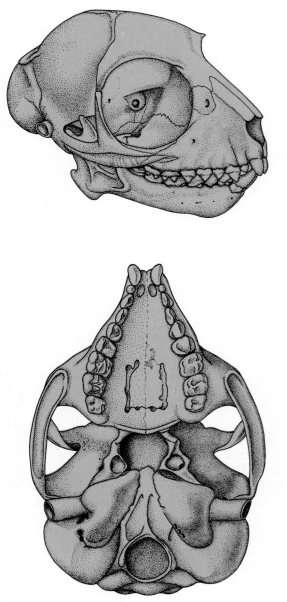

the African mainland by rafting across the Mozambique Channel; even today, natural rafts of tangled vegetation form in the large rivers that flow into the Indian Ocean. Although the island is 400 kilometers (248 miles) from the mainland, the distance was only about 80 kilometers (50 miles) in Early Eocene times.

The omomyids are thought by many paleoanthropologists to be closely related to the tarsiers, but the relationship is far from clear. *Shoshonius*, a fossil genera that was first recovered during the mid-1980s in Wyoming, has been dated to the Early Eocene, about 50.5 million years ago. *Shoshonius* shows many features that link it with the modern tarsiers (Figure 15–4). Its orbits are large relative to skull length, and it possesses a postorbital bar; however, a postorbital plate is not present.

In 1994 paleoanthropologists described excavations that have been taking place since 1992 near the village of Shanghuang in southern Jiangsu Province, China. Many primate fossils have been recovered that date from the Middle Eocene, about 45 million years ago. Both adapid and omomyid fossils have been found. An important discovery is that of teeth belonging to a new species that has been placed in the same genus as the modern tarsier. If this is an appropriate classification, the tarsiers have an evolutionary record that dates from the Middle Eocene to modern times.

FIGURE 15–2 Necrolemur. The skull of the omomyid *Necrolemur.*

FIGURE 15–3 Necrolemur. *Necrolemur's* possible appearance is seen in this drawing by E. L. Simons.

The galagos first appeared in the Early Miocene of Africa.

Although fossil lemurs have not been found in Africa, there are many similarities between the fossil lorises from the African continent and the lemurs of Madagascar. Anthropologists believe that the ancestral lemurs reached the island from

BOX 15–2

DENTITION AND DIET

Living primates show, in general, three basic dietary adaptations; they may be classified as **insectivores** (insect eaters), **frugivores** (fruit eaters), and **folivores** (leaf eaters). In actuality many primates show a combination of these patterns, and some specialized dietary patterns also exist. Since the teeth play major roles in the procurement and processing of food,

we would expect to find special dental adaptations related to the special requirements of various types of diet. Once we understand these adaptations in living primates, we can look for similar adaptations in fossil primates, and we can attempt to gain some understanding of their dietary habits.

The molar teeth are well represented as fossils, and because of

their complex nature, differences in molar morphology can be related to specific diets. The ingestion of leaves and of insects both require that the leaves and the insect skeletons be broken up and chopped into small pieces. This process increases the total surface area of the food, and this increased exposure to the digestive enzymes results in an efficient digestion. The molars of folivores and insectivores are characterized by the development of shearing crests on the molar that function to cut the food into small pieces. Insectivores' molars are further characterized by high, pointed cusps capable of puncturing the outside skeletons of insects.

Frugivores, on the other hand, have molar teeth with low, rounded cusps; their molars have few crests and are characterized by broad, flat basins for crushing and mashing their food. Low, rounded cusps are also seen on molars of primates that consume hard nuts or seeds, but these molars are also characterized by very thick enamel.

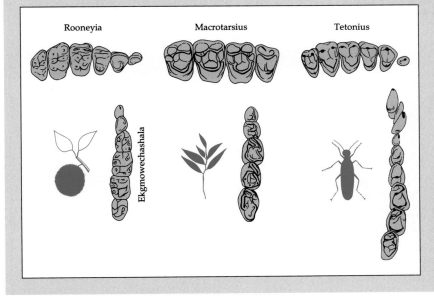

NEW SURPRISES   While most of the early primate fossils belong to the Omomyidae or Adapidae, the fossil record is full of surprises. This is to be expected since many adaptive radiations must have occurred with the majority of new species becoming extinct. In 1994 a new fossil was described from Locality 41 at a site in Egypt known as the Fayum. This site is an important source of early primate fossils and will be discussed in detail shortly. The fossil is dated by geomagnetic dating and faunal correlations to about 36 million years B.P. The new fossil, *Plesiopithecus*, is unlike

any other known fossil. In fact, it belongs in its own new family, Plesiopithecidae, and superfamily, Plesiopithecoidea, within the suborder Prosimii.[5]

Investigators have recovered an almost complete, but badly crushed, skull of *Plesiopithecus*.

[5]E. Simons and D. T. Rasmussen, "A Remarkable Cranium of *Plesiopithecus teras* (Primates, Prosimii) from the Eocene of Egypt," *Proceedings of the National Academy of Science,* 91 (1994), 9946–9950.

FIGURE 15–4 Shoshonius. Reconstruction of the omomyid *Shoshonius cooperi*.

As in other prosimians, the skull possesses a post-orbital bar but lacks a complete eye socket. Elongated lower front teeth resemble a dental comb. The upper canines are sharp and dagger-like. This discovery reminds us that each new excavation has the potential to yield something unique and exciting.

Summary

Altiatlasius, named after the High Atlas Mountains in Morocco, is the earliest known primate in the fossil record dated at 60 million B.P. (Late Paleocene). This find suggests that the primates probably originated during the Early Paleocene or, possibly, the Late Cretaceous. Among the Eocene primates, two distinct morphological patterns are found in North America and in Europe; one characterizes the family Adapidae and the other the family Omomyidae. The adapids resemble in some ways modern lemurs and lorises, although they lack many features of these modern animals, including the dental comb. On the other hand, the omomyids resemble the tarsiers, although many tarsier-like features may be superficial.

The lorises were probably present in the Early Oligocene and Early Miocene of Africa and the Late Miocene of Asia. The galagos date from the Early Miocene of Africa.

The tarsiers may be represented by *Shoshonius,* dated to the Early Eocene of Wyoming. A new find placed in the genus *Tarsius* has been recovered from Shanghuang, China, and is dated at 45 million B. P. (Middle Eocene).

EVOLUTION OF THE ANTHROPOIDEA

The suborder Anthropoidea is the division of the order Primates that includes the living monkeys, apes, and humans. Since the anthropoids were already established by Oligocene times, we must look back into the Eocene to uncover their origins.

The Origins of the Anthropoids

There is much debate in the literature on the origins of the Anthropoidea. Some paleoanthropologists point to the many anatomical similarities between the living tarsiers and anthropoids and suggest that the latter originated from the tarsier-like omomyids. On the other hand, others suggest that the anthropoid origin may be found among the lemurlike adapids. More recently, many paleontologists have suggested that the anthropoids evolved from a yet-undiscovered prosimian group which may have arisen as part of a major mammalian adaptive radiation that took place some 55 million years ago. If this proves to be a viable hypothesis, then the anthropoids may be older than anthropologists have traditionally believed. Another question to be resolved is:

Where did the anthropoids first evolve, Africa or Asia?

There are three major problems in trying to unravel the early history of the anthropoids. First, there are a limited number of early anthropoid fossils, although many new finds have been made since 1988. Second, we can assume that there was a significant branching of early anthropoid forms, with the majority becoming extinct. It is not always clear from the fossil record which early anthropoids gave rise to the later forms. Finally, although anthropoids are distinguished from the prosimians and tarsiers by several diagnostic features, many early anthropoids show a mosaic of features.

Elwyn Simons and Tab Rasmussen delineate the major specialized features that the Late Eocene and Oligocene anthropoids share with living anthropoids which distinguish the early anthropoids from the prosimians and tarsiers.

> These include (1) complete bony "eye sockets" or postorbital closure; (2) a fused metopic suture (i.e., there is a single frontal bone rather than a right and a left); (3) an annular ectotympanic bone attached to the lateral bullar margin (the ear drum is supported by a bone hoop tightly anchored to the bony wall of the ear); (4) lower molars that have reduced trigonids and are bunodont in structure (having rounded puffy cusps for crushing and grinding); and (5) deep mandibles with broadly curved angular regions, steep ascending rami, and fused midline symphyses (indicating a chewing system capable of generating great forces).[6]

The Anthropoids of the Fayum

The richest fossil site from the Late Eocene and Early Oligocene is the Fayum in Egypt. During the Eocene and Oligocene the Fayum was a tropical forest bordering on a large inland sea. The dense forests, swamps, and rivers were the homes of rodents, insectivores, bats, crocodiles, rhinoceros-size herbivores, miniature ancestors of the elephants, water birds such as herons, storks,

---

[6]E. L. Simons and T. Rasmussen, "A Whole New World of Ancestors: Eocene Anthropoidean from Africa," *Evolutionary Anthropology,* 3 (1994), 128–139.

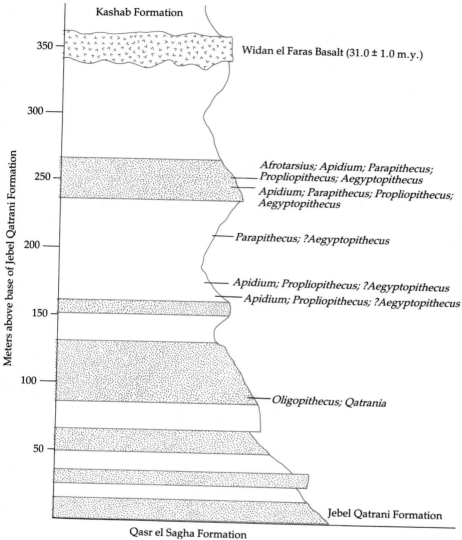

Kashab Formation

350

Widan el Faras Basalt (31.0 ± 1.0 m.y.)

300

Afrotarsius; Apidium; Parapithecus;
Propliopithecus; Aegyptopithecus
Apidium; Parapithecus; Propliopithecus;
Aegyptopithecus

250

Parapithecus; ?Aegyptopithecus

200

Apidium; Propliopithecus; ?Aegyptopithecus
Apidium; Propliopithecus; ?Aegyptopithecus

150

Meters above base of Jebel Qatrani Formation

100

Oligopithecus; Qatrania

50

Jebel Qatrani Formation

Qasr el Sagha Formation

FIGURE 15–5   *The Jebel Qatrani Formation, Fayum.*

and cranes, and many species of primates. Today the once-lush tropical forest is a desert with little plant or animal life.

The rich deposits of fossil primates are a part of a series of sedimentary beds that make up the Jebel Qatrani Formation. This formation, some 350 meters (1400 feet) thick, is capped by a layer of basalt that has been dated by the potassium-argon method at 31 million B.P. Since this formation most likely spans the period from 36 to 31 million B.P., the primate fossils found here date from the Late Eocene and Early Oligocene.

Beneath the Jebel Qatrani Formation lies the beds of Locality 41 which date from the Late Eocene.

The Fayum has been the scene of many expeditions. The greatest number of fossils were collected by a team of Yale University paleontologists under the direction of Elwyn Simons in the 1960s. Excavations by the Geological Survey of Egypt and the Duke University Primate Center in the 1970s and 1980s and later excavations have added greatly to our knowledge of the Late Eocene and Early Oligocene. Figure 15–5 shows a cross section of the Jebel Qatrani Formation and the location of several finds.

The Fayum primates have been assigned to several genera and species. Generally these primates can be placed into two families, the Parapithecidae and the Propliopithecidae. Some species, however, are known by so few fossils that their taxonomic placement cannot be determined at this time. The family Parapithecidae probably split off the anthropoid line at a very early date; it eventually became extinct. The family Propliopithecidae is probably ancestral to the later Old World monkeys, apes, and eventually, the hominids. The primates from the Fayum are listed in Table 15-2.

THE PARAPITHECIDAE   The oldest fossil primates were recovered from the Late Eocene fossil bed of Locality 41, where primate fossils were first recovered in 1988. These include members of the family Parapithecidae. The parapithecids are very small, similar in size to the living marmosets and tamarins. The few postcranial bones recovered suggests that they were probably branch runners-and-walkers and leapers; the structure of the teeth suggests that their diet most likely consisted of fruits rather than insects. This group includes *Qatrania, Serapia,* and *Algeripithecus;* other paleospecies may also be included.

The Early Oligocene parapithecids are small animals; one species, weighing about 300 grams (0.7 pound), is the smallest known living or extinct Old World anthropoid. One genus of this group, *Apidium,* is known from hundreds of individual fossils and is one of the most common mammals in the Fayum beds (Figure 15–6).

The parapithecids display several anthropoid features, yet they resemble the tarsiers in some details of dentition and other features. The mandible is V-shaped, and the canines show a marked sexual dimorphism. The molars show low, rounded cusps characteristic of living fruit eaters, and the thick enamel of the molars suggests the inclusion of hard nuts in the diet as well. Their dental formula is 2.1.3.3/2.1.3.3. This is the dental formula found today among New World monkeys, and it may represent the primitive dental formula of all anthropoids.

THE PROPLIOPITHECIDAE   The propliopithecids are a group of extinct species that lived

---

TABLE 15–2

SOME FOSSILS FROM THE FAYUM, EGYPT

QUARRY*	EPOCH	AGE (MYR)	SPECIES	FAMILY
Quarries I, M	Early Oligocene	33.1–33.4	*Aegyptopithecus zeuxis*	Propliopithecidae
			Propliopithecus chirobates	Propliopithecidae
			Apidium phiomense	Parapithecidae
			Parapithecus grangeri	Parapithecidae
			Qatrania fleaglei	Parapithecidae
			Afrotarsius chatrathi	Tarsiidae
Quarries V, G	Early Oligocene	33.8–34.0	*Propliopithecus haecheli*	Propliopithecidae
			Propliopithecus ankeli	Propliopithecidae
			Apidium moustafai	Parapithecidae
Quarry E	Late Eocene	34.0–35.1	*Oligopithecus savagei*	Propliopithecidae
			Qatrania wingi	Parapithecidae
Quarry L-41	Late Eocene	35.6–35.9	*Catopithecus browni*	Propliopithecidae
			Proteopithecus sylviae	Propliopithecidae
			Serapia eocaena	Parapithecidae

* Quarries refer to specific deposits where fossils have been excavated.
Dates from E. L. Simons and T. Rasmussen, "A Whole New World of Ancestors: Eocene Anthropoidean from Africa," *Evolutionary Anthropology,* 3 (1994), 128–139.

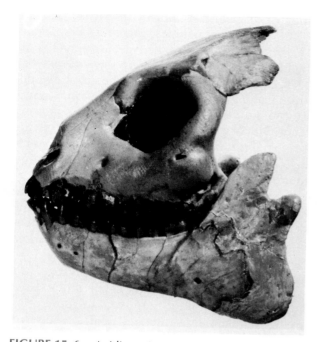

FIGURE 15–6   Apidium. A reconstruction of *Apidium*, a member of the family Parapithecidae from the Fayum.

from Early Oligocene to Late Miocene times. They, or some yet-undiscovered closely related population, probably gave rise to the Old World monkeys and the hominoids.

Several early propliopithecids have been found in Locality 41 in the Fayum. The best known is *Catopithecus*. In 1992 and 1993, several nearly complete skulls were recovered[7]. *Catopithecus* exhibits many anthropoid characteristics such as spatulate incisors, relatively large and long canines, the catarrhine dental formula, marked sexual dimorphism, fusion of the metopic suture forming a single frontal bone, eye socket, and others. Yet the mandible consists of nonfused halves, a distinctive nonanthropoid feature. Many of the dental features of *Catopithecus* suggest that the anthropoids evolved from an adapid ancestor.

These are small animals, about the size of a modern marmoset. The dentition suggests a diet of insects and fruits and the diameter of the eye socket falls within the smaller numbers characteristic of living diurnal primates. Analysis of the few known postcranial bones suggests that *Catopithecus* was a branch runner-and-walker and leaper, moving through its habitat in a way that resembles the smaller living New World monkeys today.

The best known propliopithecid is *Aegyptopithecus*. Although the first sparse fossil remains of *Aegyptopithecus* were discovered in 1906, today we are able to study many skulls and some postcranial material (Figure 15–7). The *Aegyptopithecus* male probably weighed about 6 kilograms (13 pounds) and is the largest of the Fayum primates.

Aegyptopithecus is one of the best transitional forms found in the fossil record, incorporating characteristics of the prosimians, monkeys, and apes. Its long snout and relatively small brain case remind us of the adapids. The size of the eye sockets suggests that the animal was diurnal. The relative expansion of the visual areas of the brain and the relative decrease in the olfactory areas, as seen in the endocranial cast, provide evidence for the importance of vision over smell. The dentition points to an affinity with the hominoid line; details of the teeth and jaw are similar to those of the Miocene and Pliocene hominoids.

FIGURE 15–7   Aegyptopithecus. The reconstructed skull of *Aegyptopithecus zeuxis* from the Oligocene of the Fayum.

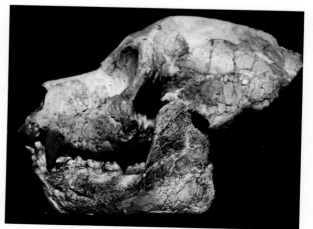

---

[7]E. L. Simons, "Skulls and Anterior Teeth of *Catopithecus* (Primates: Anthropoidea) from the Eocene and Anthropoid Origins," *Science,* 268 (1995), 1885–1888.

The locomotor behavior of *Aegyptopithecus* is known from the analysis of several postcranial bones (Figure 15–8). John G. Fleagle and Elwyn Simons conclude:

> Functionally, both the ulna and humerus indicate that *Aegyptopithecus* was a largely quadrupedal, arboreal animal and that the best models for locomotor behaviour of early hominoids are neither the extant apes nor the extant [Old World] monkeys. Instead, closest resemblances are with the larger arboreal quadrupeds among [New World] monkeys, in particular the howler monkey *Alouatta,* which seems to demonstrate today a forelimb morphology similar to that exhibited by Oligocene apes.[8]

This in no way suggests genetic affinities with the howler monkey, but it does suggest similarities in locomotor adaptations. The howler monkey is adapted for suspensory behavior, but it also possesses a prehensile tail, an organ that is not a part of *Aegyptopithecus* anatomy.

The large number of *Aegyptopithecus* specimens makes it possible to analyze the material for variation within the species. Differences in tooth size suggest a marked sexual dimorphism. Living primates, such as baboons, that live in large social units containing several adults of both sexes exhibit a high degree of sexual dimorphism. In contrast, primates, such as gibbons, that live in small social units show very little difference in size and proportions between the male and female. The fact that *Aegyptopithecus* shows a marked sexual dimorphism suggests that these primates lived in complex social groups consisting of many adult males and females.

The many similarities between *Aegyptopithecus* and modern apes have led some paleoanthropologists to view it as an early member of the Hominoidea. Yet recent studies have emphasized the many features that are more similar to features of the New World and Old World monkeys. It is very likely that the propliopithecids represent a group of primates ancestral to both the cercopithecoids and the hominoids.

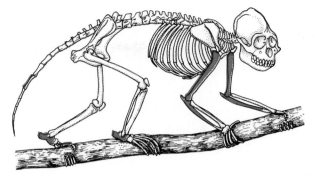

FIGURE 15–8   Aegyptopithecus. The reconstructed postcranial skeleton of *Aegyptopithecus zeuxis*. Bones shown in color have been recovered.

Other Eocene and Oligocene Anthropoids

In 1927 G. E. Pilgrim described a jaw fragment from the Late Eocene of central Burma that he named *Amphipithecus;* another jaw fragment was found in 1938 representing a second species, *Pondaungia.* In 1978 two additional jaw fragments were found in the same geological beds in central Burma. Again, each specimen represented one of the two species discovered earlier (Figure 15–9). These fossils date from the Late Eocene, some 44 to 40 million years ago.

The Burmese fossils are classified by many as anthropoids because of the detailed structure of their dentition. For example, low, rounded cusps are present on the teeth in contrast with the more pointed cusps on prosimian teeth and the mandibles are deep and relatively thick. Nevertheless, they retain many features found in earlier prosimian fossils.

Other early anthropoids have been recently discovered in Oman, Algeria, Tunisia, China, and Thailand, greatly enhancing our knowledge of the early anthropoids. The site near Shanghuang, China, contains several fossils which may be early anthropoids. At least four anthropoid species have been described, the best known belonging to the genus *Eosimias.* If this material is indeed anthropoid, then the anthropoids existed as far back as the Middle Eocene, 45 million years ago. However, not all paleoanthropologists see *Eosimias* as an anthropoid; some do not even think it is a primate.

---

[8]J. G. Fleagle and E. L. Simons, "Humeral Morphology of the Earliest Apes," *Nature,* 276 (1978), 705–707.

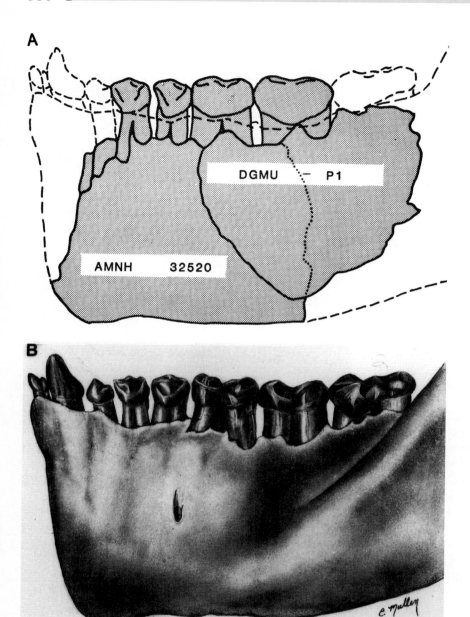

FIGURE 15–9 *Eocene anthropoids.* Reconstruction of the lower jaw of *Amphipithecus mogaungensis* from the Late Eocene of Burma.

The Evolution of the New World Monkeys

A topic of controversy in paleoanthropology revolves around the origins of the superfamily Ceboidea. The consensus is that the New World monkeys evolved from the early African anthropoids. Many Fayum anthropoids, which date from the Early Oligocene, resemble in some ways the later ceboid monkeys; for example, some Fayum anthropoids possess three premolars per quadrant.

Throughout most of the Cenozoic, South America was separated from North America. Although there was never a land connection between South America and Africa during that era, a major lowering of sea levels occurred in the Middle Oligocene. This event would have exposed much of the African continental shelf, and many islands would have surfaced above the South Atlantic waters. Aided by these islands, the ancestral ceboid monkeys could have crossed the Atlantic Ocean on naturally formed rafts. Although the New World monkeys and Old World monkeys evolved independently, the facts that they are descended from a common ancestor and that they occupy similar ecological niches have led to many similarities in their appearance. This is an example of parallelism (Chapter 6). The earliest New World monkeys appear in the Late Oligocene.

FOSSIL CEBOIDS   The oldest fossil member of the superfamily Ceboidea is *Branisella*, which lived 27 million years ago, during the Late Oligocene, in Bolivia. This and another Late Oligocene fossil, *Dolichocebus*, from Patagonia in southern Argentina, show little similarity with any contemporary primate population. Other fossils from Patagonia, dating from the Late Oligocene and Early Miocene, exhibit similarities to the modern subfamily Aotinae, which includes the owl monkeys; in fact, they may represent ancestral populations of this subfamily.

In early 1994 a skull was uncovered in the Abanico Formation near Termas del Flaco in the Chilean Andes.[9] The cranium is very well preserved with very little deformation. The upper dentition is virtually complete. The skull dates from the Early Miocene with an ^{40}Ar/^{39}Ar date of 20.1 million years B.P. The animal, named *Chilecebus*, in life weighed about 1 kilogram (2.2 pounds) and exhibits the same dental formula characteristic of the living New World monkeys.

It appears that the differentiation of New World monkeys into their present subfamilies had occurred by Middle Miocene times. Fossils from La Venta, Colombia, and other sites include possible ancestors of the subfamily Cebinae (the modern squirrel and capuchin monkeys), the subfamily Alouattinae (the modern howler monkeys), and the subfamily Pithecinae (the modern sakis and uakaris). The similarity between the fossil and the modern owl monkey (subfamily Aotinae) is so close that they have been placed in the same genus, *Aotus* (Figure 15–10). Finally, an early representative of the marmosets, family Callitrichidae, may also be present.

The Evolution of the Old World Monkeys

Over 10 million years separates the anthropoids of the Fayum from the fossil hominoids of the Early Miocene. The earliest fossil evidence of the Old World monkeys is *Prohylobates* and *Victoriapithecus*, which make up the family Victoriapithecidae. The former are found in fossil beds from the Early Miocene in north Africa and Kenya; the latter are found in beds from the Early and Middle Miocene of Uganda and Kenya. Both

FIGURE 15–10   Aotus. The mandible of *Aotus dindensis* from the Middle Miocene (below) and of the modern *Aotus trivigatus* (above).

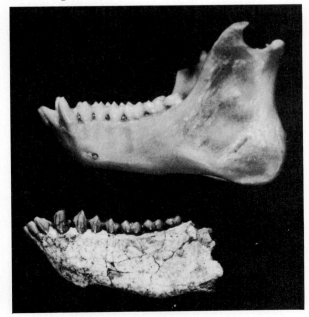

[9]J. J. Flynn et al., "An Early Miocene Anthropoid Skull from the Chilean Andes," *Nature*, 373 (1995), 603–607.

genera are known primarily from dental remains. Although the teeth are essentially cercopithecoid in character, they are more primitive than the teeth of the later monkeys. Recent discoveries of dental, cranial, and postcranial material on Maboko Island in Kenya suggest that *Victoriapithecus* was a small primate, weighing about 3.5 to 4 kilograms (7.7 to 8.8 pounds). It moved quadrupedally in the trees and on the ground.

The origin of the Cercopithecoidea is uncertain. Some paleoanthropologists view the Old World monkeys as a very specialized primate group that evolved as part of an earlier and more generalized anthropoid radiation. Certainly the anthropoids had undergone a major adaptive radiation and had become very diverse and numerous by Early Miocene times. Yet at this time the cercopithecoids, represented by the victoriapithecids, were fairly uncommon. Hominoids occupied many of the ecological niches that would later be occupied by the monkeys. Only later, when the diversity and number of hominoids diminished, did the cercopithecoids assume a dominant role in the mammalian fauna.

Prohylobates and *Victoriapithecus* preceded the divergence of the two subfamilies of the family Cercopithecidae: Cercopithecinae and Colobinae. In fact, they possessed features of both later subfamilies: their dentition resembles that of the cercopithecines, while their facial skeleton resembles that of the colobines.

THE CERCOPITHECINES AND COLOBINES

There is a gap of 10 million years between the last record of the Victoriapithecidae and the next-oldest known fossil evidence of the Old World monkeys. The monkeys become more frequent in the Late Miocene fossil record. By this time the Old World monkeys had divided into the cercopithecines and colobines.

The fossil cercopithecines closely resemble living populations, to which they were undoubtedly ancestral or closely related. The earliest macaques lived in the late Miocene or Early Pliocene of northern Africa. Other members of the genus *Macaca* are found in several localities in Europe, southern Russia, the Near East, northern India, Pakistan, China, and southeast Asia.

Parapapio, from the Lower Miocene of eastern and southern Africa, is probably close to the origin of the baboons *(Papio)* and the mangabeys *(Cercocebus)*. Fossil members of *Papio* are well represented in eastern and southern Africa; although they closely resemble modern baboons, they tend to be larger.

The geladas *(Theropithecus)* are confined today to a small range in the Ethiopian desert. They were once widespread throughout Africa, extending eastward to India. One species, *T. oswaldi*, is the largest known monkey (100 kilograms, or 220 pounds) (Figure 15–11). The guenons *(Cercopithecus)*, today one of the most common monkeys in Africa, are represented by fragmentary dental remains in Pliocene and Pleistocene beds in east Africa.

While the prehistoric cercopithecines are very similar to extant populations, this is not true for the colobines. Fossil members of the subfamily Colobinae are quite different from modern forms and are also found throughout a greater range. They are present in Late Miocene and Pliocene Europe. While they were also present in Asia, the fossils are fragmentary.

Summary

The richest fossil site from the Late Eocene and Early Oligocene is the Fayum in Egypt. The Jebel Qatrani Formation dates from 36 to 31 million B.P. Beneath lies the beds of Locality 41 which dates from the Late Eocene. Most of the Fayum primates can be placed into two families, the Parapithecidae and the Propliopithecidae. The family Parapithecidae includes several species from Locality 41 and *Apidium* from the Jebel Qatrani Formation. This family is probably an early branch of the anthropoids that eventually became extinct. The early propliopithecids, including *Oligopithecus* and *Catopithecus*, have been found in Locality 41. The best known propliopithecid is *Aegyptopithecus* from the Jebel Qatrani Formation. The family Propliopithecidae is probably ancestral to the later Old World monkeys, apes, and eventually, the hominids. Early anthropoids have also been found in Oman, Algeria, Tunisia, Burma, Thailand, and China.

The ceboids, or New World monkeys, were probably derived from early African anthropoids

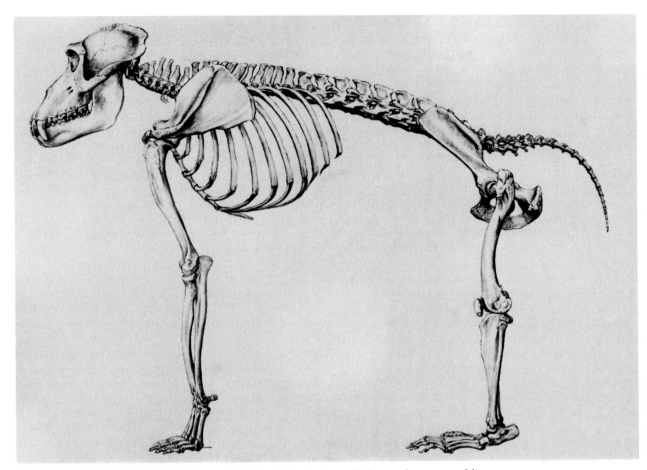

FIGURE 15–11 Theropithecus. A reconstruction of the skeleton of *Theropithecus oswaldi,* an extinct species of gelada from the Pleistocene at Olduvai Gorge.

that traveled across the then-narrower Atlantic Ocean on natural rafts. The earliest known ceboid is *Branisella,* from the Late Oligocene of Bolivia. In general, New World monkey fossils are not well known; those that have been recovered are similar to modern forms, which suggests that the division of the ceboids into their present subfamilies took place by the Middle Miocene.

The cercopithecoids, or Old World monkeys, were relatively scarce in the Miocene; yet by the Pliocene and Pleistocene they became common animals, especially in Africa. The earliest known fossil primates belong to the family Victoriapithecidae, which dates from the Early and Middle Miocene. Beginning in the Late Miocene the monkeys underwent a divergence into the two subfamilies. The subfamily Cercopithecinae includes a wide range of fossil forms that closely resemble living species such as macaques, mangabeys, baboons, geladas, and guenons. Many extinct species, however, were significantly larger. On the other hand, the subfamily Colobinae contains a number of populations that differ considerably from modern colobines.

EVOLUTION OF THE HOMINOIDEA

The superfamily Hominoidea, which contains the living apes and humans, is well represented in the Miocene fossil record in terms of both number of specimens and species. Paleoanthropologists have known of Miocene hominoids for well over a century. The first, discovered in France, was described in 1856, three years before Charles Darwin published *On the Origin of Species.*

Early Miocene Hominoids

The earliest hominoids to appear in the fossil record are from the fossil beds of east Africa. They most likely evolved from Oligocene primates, perhaps the propliopithecids of the Fayum. These early Miocene hominoids date from about 22 to 18 million B.P. and represent an important primate adaptive radiation. They are sometimes called "dental apes" because their dentition resembles the dentition of modern apes, while their postcranial skeleton is monkeylike or perhaps simply primitive.

The African Early Miocene hominoids were first discovered in the 1930s. Among the several genera that have been named and described are *Proconsul, Rangwapithecus, Dendropithecus, Limnopithecus, Micropithecus,* and perhaps others. Most specimens have been found in Kenya, but they are also known from Uganda and Saudi Arabia.

The best known Early Miocene African hominoids belong to the genus *Proconsul.* These species vary in size from that of a small monkey to that of a female gorilla. The largest collection of *Proconsul* fossils is from Rusinga Island in Lake Victoria, Kenya.

The cranial remains show many features that are found in the earlier Old World anthropoids, such as a slender mandible and a robust zygomatic arch. *Proconsul* dentition, compared with modern ape dentition, is characterized by more vertically implanted incisors and canines, slender canines, semisectorial lower anterior premolars, and thin enamel on the molars. The relative width of the jaw between the canines is less than that in modern apes. These features are associated with a V-shaped dental arcade (Figure 15–12). This contrasts with the U-shaped dental arcade of the modern chimpanzee and gorilla. The skull of *Proconsul africanus* is shown in Figure 15–13. Note the prognathous face and the

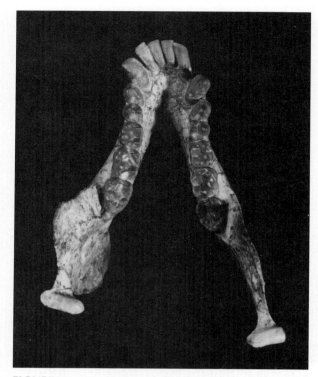

FIGURE 15–12 Proconsul. The lower jaw of *Proconsul africanus* from Rusinga Island, Kenya.

lack of brow ridges. The skull appears more delicate in build than the skulls of contemporary apes (compare with Figure 13–13c).

Some *Proconsul* postcranial material is known, but the fossils are primarily unassociated fragments rather than articulated skeletons. An exception is a small juvenile *P. africanus* skeleton (Figure 15–14). In life this specimen weighed about 15 to 20 kilograms (33 to 44 pounds). The skeleton has an intermembral index of 89, more typical of monkeys than of apes. This animal was probably an arboreal quadruped that lacked specializations for suspensory behavior. However, the discovery of a last sacral vertebra in 1984 shows that *Proconsul,* like all contemporary apes, had no tail.

Charles Darwin theorized that humans originally evolved in Africa because Africa was the home of the chimpanzee and gorilla. From that time on paleoanthropologists have debated this question, with Africa and Asia both being proposed as the hominoid homeland. The Oligocene

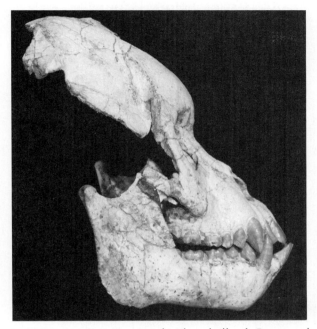

FIGURE 15–13 Proconsul. The skull of *Proconsul africanus* from Kenya.

FIGURE 15–14 Proconsul. A reconstruction of the skeleton of *Proconsul africanus*. Bones shown in color have been recovered.

and Early Miocene evidence strongly supports an African origin for the Hominoidea. Yet many fossils that resemble the African material have been recovered from the early Miocene site of Sihong in eastern China. If the date of 19 to 17 million B.P. is correct, than an Asian origin is a possibility. However, no Oligocene anthropoids have been found in Asia.

The Miocene Hominoid Radiation

At the beginning of the Miocene the continent of Africa was isolated by water from Europe and Asia. The fossil record shows that animals were evolving in Africa that were distinct from those evolving in the rest of the Old World.

About 16 to 14 million years ago, in the Middle Miocene, the Afro-Arabian tectonic plate collided with the Asian plate, and a land connection developed between the two continents. Following this event, the fossil record reveals major migrations of Asiatic species into Africa and migrations of African species into Asia (Figure 15–15). Once the African hominoids reached Eurasia

they spread into a variety of ecological niches. The result is known as the Miocene hominoid radiation.

The geological processes involved in the formation of a land connection between Africa and Eurasia also played a major role in bringing about important geographical and climatic changes. The forces produced by the two large tectonic plates coming together, along with volcanic and earthquake activity, led to the development of mountainous regions. These mountain ranges greatly affected climatic patterns. On the side of the mountains farthest from the sea, the land lay in a rain shadow and received little precipitation. In addition, the average annual temperature gradually decreased during the Miocene and glacial ice expanded in the areas known today as Antarctica and Iceland.

Across wide expanses of Africa, Europe, and Asia, the once low-lying landscape, covered by a continuous tropical forest, turned into a mosaic of discontinuous and contrasting habitats. The tropical forests diminished in size and in many areas were replaced by woodlands (with their lesser density of trees), woodland savannas

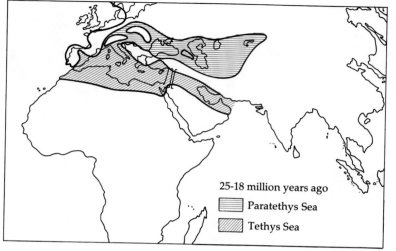

(a)

25-18 million years ago

▤ Paratethys Sea

▨ Tethys Sea

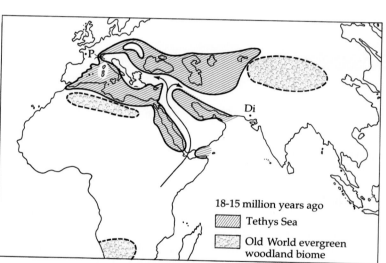

(b)

18-15 million years ago

▨ Tethys Sea

▧ Old World evergreen woodland biome

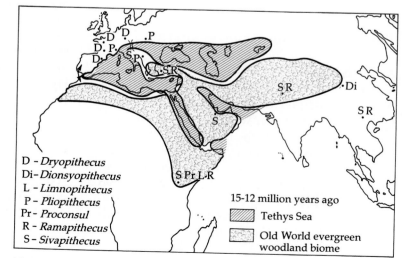

(c)

D - *Dryopithecus*
Di - *Dionsyopithecus*
L - *Limnopithecus*
P - *Pliopithecus*
Pr - *Proconsul*
R - *Ramapithecus*
S - *Sivapithecus*

15-12 million years ago

▨ Tethys Sea

▧ Old World evergreen woodland biome

FIGURE 15–15 *Afro-Arabian/Eurasian land bridge.* *(a)* Between 25 and 18 million years ago the Afro-Arabian Plate came together with the Eurasian Plate. The initial land bridge (‖) permitted the interchange of African and Eurasian mammals. Interference with the currents of the Tethys Epicontinental Seaway brought about major climatic changes. *(b)* Between 18 and 15 million years ago a major land corridor was established, and the first hominoids appeared in Europe. During this time woodland and woodland savanna habitats began to replace the tropical forest. *(c)* Between 15 and 12 million years ago these open country habitats expanded, as did the number of hominoid species. These maps are based on the work of Raymond L. Bernor.

(grasslands dotted with trees), true savanna grasslands, and semiarid regions (Figure 15–16).

Many animals adapted to the forest niches remained in the diminishing forests. As the area occupied by tropical forests decreased, competition for forest niches became more intense. Other populations entered the newly developing habitats. Thus the scene was set for an adaptive radiation into a variety of genera and species occupying Africa, Europe, and Asia.

THE MIOCENE HOMINOIDS The variability and complexity of the Miocene hominoids is bewildering, and paleoanthropologists vary in their interpretations: Are we dealing with a few highly variable species or with many individual species? Stephen Jay Gould addresses this issue by pointing out that the correct image for the visualization of evolution is that of a "copious branching bush," as opposed to that of a tree or ladder. We easily visualize evolutionary history as a ladder, since only a few twigs of the "bush" survive. If the bush model is a more accurate reflection of evolutionary history, early hominoid evolution could have been characterized by a proliferation of species and genera.[10] Only through additional fieldwork and further analysis will be able to sort out the relationships that existed among these creatures and ascertain their relationships to modern forms.

---

[10]S. J. Gould, "Empire of the Apes," *Natural History* (May 1987), 20–25.

FIGURE 15–16 *Miocene habitats.* During the Miocene the once low-lying tropical forest gave way to a mosaic of habitats including the woodland savanna, true savanna, and semiarid regions.

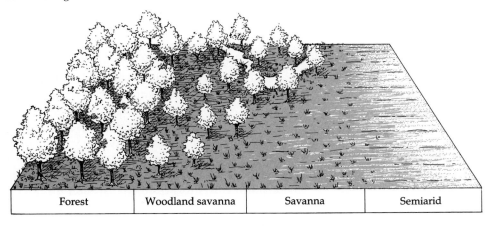

| Forest | Woodland savanna | Savanna | Semiarid |

◀─── Decreasing rainfall ───▶

BOX 15–3

A SOUTHERN HOMINOID

In Chapter 14 we saw that the fossil record is an imperfect chronicle of evolutionary history. Many periods of time and many areas of the world, where prehistoric animals may have existed, have not given up their fossils if fossils actually do exist. For example, practically all of the African Miocene hominoids have been found in east Africa. Did other hominoids roam different parts of the continent?

In 1991 a partial mandible was found at Berg Aukas, in the Otavi Mountains of Namibia, in southwest Africa. Although only one specimen has been found, this 13-million-year old hominoid extends the Miocene hominoid range into the southern part of the continent. Named *Otavipithecus*, its place in the evolutionary scheme is still unclear.

Reference: G. C. Conroy et al., "*Otavipithecus namibiensis*, First Miocene Hominoid from Southern Africa," *Nature*, 356 (1992), 144–148.

The taxonomy of the Miocene hominoids is controversial, and several interpretations exist. Here we will follow the lead of Glenn C. Conroy and simply divide these forms into three major categories.[11] These are not taxonomic terms but are groupings of species that share similar morphological characteristics. The first group of Miocene hominoids includes the **dryomorphs** from the Early and Middle Miocene of east Africa and Eurasia. The second cluster consists of the **ramamorphs** from the Middle Miocene of east Africa and Eurasia. The final group is the **pliomorphs.**

THE DRYOMORPHS   The dryomorphs existed primarily in Africa, although they are also found in Europe and possibly Asia. These were very successful forms and several east African species existed with little evolutionary change from the Early Miocene to the Middle Miocene (about 22 to 14 million B.P.). These are the early Miocene hominoids, including *Proconsul*, that were discussed earlier in this section. The Eurasian dryomorphs occurred later in time, first appearing about 13 to 12 million years ago. They disappear from the fossil record about 10 to 9 million years ago.

The European dryomorphs belong to the genus *Dryopithecus.* The first fossil hominoid to be discovered was *Dryopithecus fontani* which was found in 1856 in France. The genus was named after the oak nymphs, or dryads, of Greek mythology because of evidence of oak trees in the site. Today several specimens are known from various parts of Europe including Spain, Germany, Hungary, and Greece. The European dryomorphs differ from their African counterparts chiefly by differences in the details of their dentition. There is some evidence that dryomorphs may have existed in Asia as well.

THE RAMAMORPHS   The ramamorphs are found in eastern Europe, Turkey, Pakistan, India, and China. A few specimens are also known from east Africa. Through the years many genera and species have been defined. Many paleoanthropologists today believe that all the fossil material can be divided into two genera, *Sivapithecus* and *Gigantopithecus*. The term *ramamorph* is derived from the genus *Ramapithecus*, which most paleoanthropologists no longer consider to be a valid genus; fossils previously classified into the genus *Ramapithecus* are now classified into the genus *Sivapithecus*. These changes reflect the fact that the original taxonomic determinations were based on a few fragmentary fossils; interpretations change as more information becomes available.

Ramamorph morphology, as seen in *Sivapithecus*, contrasts with that of the dryomorphs in many ways. *Sivapithecus* dentition is characterized by thick dental enamel on the molars,

---

[11]G. C. Conroy, *Primate Evolution* (New York: Norton, 1990), 201.

BOX 15–4

THE ITALIAN SWAMP APE

The Late Miocene witnessed a major adaptive radiation of hominoids. Although many species have been identified, it is not surprising that occasionally a fossil appears that does not seem to fit into the established scheme. One example is *Oreopithecus*.

The first fossil to be assigned to the genus *Oreopithecus* was a juvenile mandible first described in 1872. Throughout the years several *Oreopithecus* fossils have been found, primarily in Italy. In 1958 a badly flattened partial skeleton of a young adult male was discovered in an Italian coal mine. The material in which the skeleton was found

is lignite, which is a soft form of coal that originated in a swampy forest habitat. Some fossils that may be related to the European *Oreopithecus* have been found in Africa.

Oreopithecus possesses large canines, a high degree of sexual dimorphism, teeth adapted to processing leafy materials, and a short, wide face (see the Figure). The postcranial skeleton exhibits longer forelimbs than hindlimbs and several features related to flexibility of the shoulder, elbow, and wrist. The ankle was very flexible, and the primate had a powerful grasping foot. Some paleoanthropologists in-

terpret the skeleton as belonging to a primate that could climb vertical tree trunks and moved by means of suspensory behavior. This suite of locomotor patterns would have been adapted to movement in a swampy forest region.

Oreopithecus has been placed in its own family, the Oreopithecidae, but the placement of the Oreopithecidae in the rest of the primate taxonomy has been the subject of some debate. While we are presenting the genus here as part of the Miocene hominoid radiation, some believe that it is more closely related to the cercopithecoids.

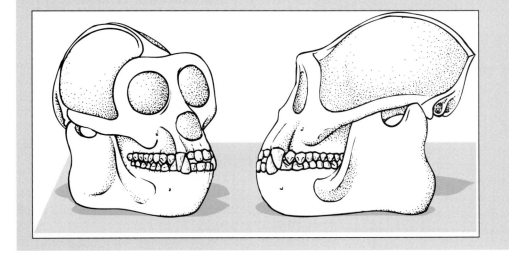

with the relatively low cusps of the large premolars and molars wearing flat, by relatively small canines with pronounced sexual dimorphism, and by broad central incisors. The mandible is relatively deep, the zygomatic arches flaring, and the face **orthognathous** (nonprojecting) (Figure 15–17).

This dental pattern has been associated with the small-object-feeding complex, which is a

dental adaptation to coarse materials, such as grasses and seeds, that are characteristic of drier and more open habitats. Similar dental patterns have been observed in other animals characterized by similar diets and habitats, including the modern gelada and the modern panda. Not all anthropologists share this view, however. Richard F. Kay believes that these dental characteristics indicate a "nut-cracking complex," in

FIGURE 15–17 Sivapithecus. The skull of *Sivapithecus*.

which the animal "ate forest fruits with hard, tough rinds that require tremendous forces to open but, once opened, provided a rich source of nutrients."[12] Such a complex could have evolved in a forest environment.

The difficulty encountered in interpreting diet by means of the dental pattern highlights a critical problem in paleoanthropology. As we discussed in Box 15–2, the relationship of dentition to diet is based primarily on analysis of living forms, in which diet can be directly observed. If the dental pattern of a fossil form matches that of a living form, researchers conclude that the fossil animal shared a common diet with the modern animal. Jay Kelley and David Pilbeam write:

The problem with attempting to interpret, in terms of diet and feeding behavior, the dental-gnathic [jaw] morphology of *Sivapithecus* is that we are at-

tempting to explain a novel morphology. It resembles to a greater or lesser extent certain extant species in selected features of morphology, but as a whole it is quite unique. It may be that its diet was correspondingly novel in terms of the physical properties of food items or in the proportions with which foods of certain properties were utilized. Attempts to slot *Sivapithecus* into existing dietary "categories" based on selected presumed similarities with living species may be misleading.[13]

Similar problems exist in the interpretation of posture and locomotion in *Sivapithecus*. Known limb, hand, and foot bones lack the specializations found in the semibrachiators and knuckle walkers. The ramamorph locomotor pattern has been described as arboreal quadrupedalism with a degree of climbing and suspension.

GIGANTOPITHECUS   A very unusual genus of ramamorph deserves special attention. As its name implies, *Gigantopithecus* was a large "ape"; in fact, it was probably the largest ape that ever lived. It may have been as tall as 2.75 meters (9 feet) and may have weighed as much as 272 kilograms (600 pounds).

In 1935 Ralph von Koenigswald found teeth of *Gigantopithecus* in a Chinese pharmacy in Hong Kong, where fossilized teeth, known as "dragon's teeth," are used as medical ingredients. In the late 1950s and the 1960s three mandibles and over a thousand teeth were discovered in caves in Kwangsi Province in southern China. These remains belonged to *G. blacki*, which inhabited China and Vietnam during the Pleistocene. Of the many apes that evolved in Asia as part of the Miocene hominoid radiation, only two survived to be contemporary with members of the genus *Homo*: *Gigantopithecus* and the orangutan. An early species, *G. giganteus*, is known from the Late Miocene of India and Pakistan.

Figure 15–18 compares the mandible of *Gigantopithecus* with that of *Gorilla*. Dental features of *Gigantopithecus* include relatively

[12]R. F. Kay, "The Nut-Crackers—A New Theory of the Adaptations of the Ramapithecinae," *American Journal of Physical Anthropology*, 55 (1981), 141.

[13]J. Kelley and D. Pilbeam, "The Dryopithecines: Taxonomy, Comparative Anatomy, and Phylogeny of Miocene Large Hominoids," in J. Erwin and E. R. Swindler (eds.), *Comparative Primate Biology*, Vol. 1: *Systematics, Evolution, and Anatomy* (New York: Liss, 1986), 261–411.

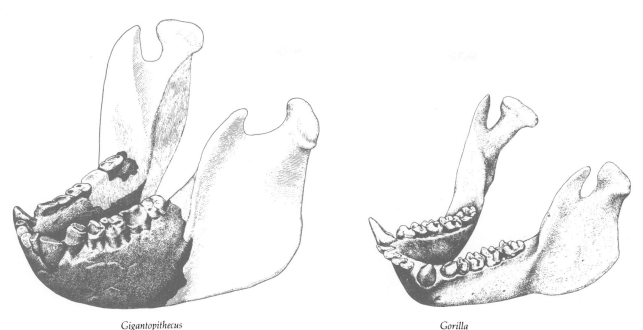

Gigantopithecus   *Gorilla*

FIGURE 15–18   *Mandibles of* Gigantopithecus *and* Gorilla. From "Gigantopithecus" by
E. L. Simons and P. C. Ettel. Copyright ©1970 by Scientific American, Inc. All rights reserved.

small, vertically implanted incisors, reduced canines worn flat by the chewing of coarse vegetation, lack of a diastema, crowding of the molars and premolars, and so forth—all of which contrast markedly with the dentition of the gorilla. Note also the extremely heavy mandible in the region of the molars (see Box 15–5).

THE PLIOMORPHS   The pliomorphs first appeared about 16 million years ago in Europe; they were the earliest Eurasian hominoids. They disappeared from the European fossil record about 12 million B.P., but they survived in China until 8 million B.P. They were small, gibbon-sized primates weighing between 6 and 10 kilograms (13 and 22 pounds).

The pliomorphs include the genus *Pliopithecus* in Europe and *Laccopithecus* in Asia (Figure 15–19). The robust mandible and large temporalis muscle, as indicated by the skull, suggest that the pliomorphs were primarily leaf-eating primates capable of consuming tough vegetation.

An analysis of the postcranial skeleton of the pliomorphs suggests that they were arboreal quadrupeds adapted for suspensory behavior in the manner of the New World semibrachiators such as the spider monkeys. Although it is uncertain whether they possessed tails, they most likely did not suspend themselves with prehensile tails. However, *Pliopithecus* does not show anatomical adaptations for the true-brachiation type of locomotion characteristic of modern gibbons and siamang.

The Origins of the Modern Hominoids

The population that evolved as part of the Miocene hominoid radiation was the common ancestor of modern apes and humans. Russell Ciochon has described the hypothetical Middle Miocene hominoid that became the common ancestor of the lineages leading to the modern apes and humans.

. . .the middle Miocene stem hominoid can be described hypothetically as a medium-sized ape with

BOX 15–5

WHAT DID *GIGANTOPITHECUS* HAVE FOR DINNER?

Most of what we know about fossil populations pertains to their skeletal anatomy. An important challenge in paleoanthropology is the reconstruction of other information about the life of extinct forms, including diet. Important clues about diet are provided by the structure of the teeth, the jaw, and the musculature of chewing, as well as microscopic markings on the teeth.

Another line of evidence for reconstructing diet comes from microscopic particles that are found in plants and that sometimes adhere to the surface of the teeth. Being minerals, these particles, called **phytoliths,** persist through the process of fossilization. Phytoliths are very tiny pieces of silica and are visible only under a scanning electron microscope. Phytoliths form from the silicon dioxide dissolved in the water that enters the plant. Once in the plant, the silicon dioxide solidifies into phytoliths. The phytoliths that form in different plants are often very distinctive in shape. The identification of specific phytoliths in association with archaeological and paleontological material can connect that material with a specific plant or plant group.

Gigantopithecus teeth were subjected to study under a scanning electron microscope. Two kinds of phytoliths were found adhering to the surface of the tooth enamel. One is characteristic of grasses. Unfortunately, the same type of phytolith is found on different kinds of grasses, and so the actual plant from which the phytoliths came could not be ascertained. The presence of these phytoliths, however, supports the hypothesis that bamboo, a member of the grass family, formed a major part of the diet of *Gigantopithecus.* The other type of phytolith is most likely associated with durians, a fruit that is common throughout southeast Asia. Thus the use of modern microscopic technology and the microscopic structure of plants have added important information about the life of these extinct hominoids.

References: R. Ciochon et al., "Opal Phytoliths Found on the Teeth of Extinct Ape, *Gigantopithecus blacki:* Implications for Paleodietary Studies," *Proceedings of the National Academy of Sciences,* 1990; and D. R. Piperno, *Phytolith Analysis: An Archaeological and Geological Perspective* (San Diego: Academic Press, 1988).

a short and broad face, broad interorbital region, smooth forehead lacking pronounced toral development, . . .molar teeth with thin enamel. . ., and a thorax and upper limb skeleton adapted for below-branch suspensory behaviors.[14]

The fossil primate that most closely resembles this hypothetical ancestor is the genus *Dryopithecus.*

It would be nice if we could present a diagram showing the exact relationships of the modern primates to their Miocene and Pliocene ancestors. When the number of fossils was few, many paleoanthropologists did just that; but as more and more specimens are recovered, we are seeing that the Miocene radiation represents a great diversification of primates—many became extinct and some have evolved into modern populations. Russell Ciochon has reviewed the evidence and has suggested some possible relationships.[15]

Many fossils of the lesser apes, the gibbons and siamangs, date from the Middle and Late Pleistocene of China, southeast Asia, and Indonesia. Molecular data suggest that the lesser apes diverged from the rest of the hominoids about 15 million years ago. There are no clearly defined gibbon/siamang fossil ancestors known before the Pleistocene, although some candidates have been suggested.

The orangutan is found today only on the islands of Sumatra and Borneo. Fossil orangutans from Pleistocene sites show a distribution from southern China through southeast Asia and into Indonesia. The orangutan lineage, however, is

---

[14]R. L. Ciochon and D. A. Etler, op cit, 50.

[15]Ibid.

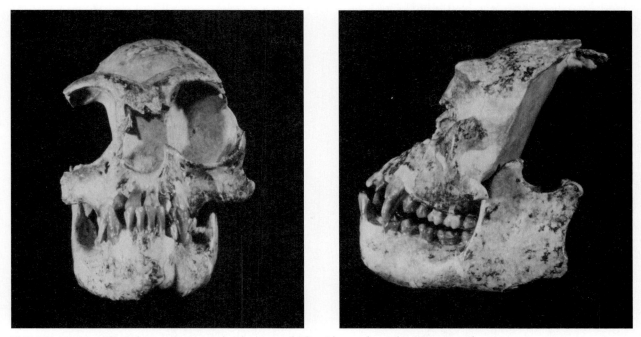

FIGURE 15–19   Pliopithecus. Front and side view of *Pliopithecus* from the Miocene of Europe.

thought to have split off from the rest of the hominoids some 12 million years ago.

There is evidence, however, of an orangutan ancestor to the west. A find from southern Pakistan includes a fairly complete skull of *Sivapithecus indicus* that dates from the Late Miocene, about 8 million years ago. The skull shows a close resemblance to the modern orangutan skull, with a distinctive dish-shaped face, narrow width between the eye sockets, oval-shaped eye sockets, and flaring zygomatic arches (Figure 15–20). This specific constellation of features is not found in the African great apes or the lesser apes.

The common ancestor of the African great apes—the chimpanzee, bonobo, and gorilla—most likely split off the line leading to the hominids between 7.5 and 5 million years ago. However, there is no Pleistocene fossil record of these primates. Although many candidates have been suggested, there is no consensus as to the identification of the ancestral African great ape.

Of course, from our point of view, perhaps the most significant questions are those surrounding

the origins of the family Hominidae. Unfortunately, a gap in the fossil record occurs during the time when the hominids most likely diverged from the apes. By the Pliocene the earliest hominid fossils appear; these are the subjects of the next chapter.

Summary

The earliest hominoids appear in the Early Miocene beds of east Africa. These early hominoids probably evolved from Oligocene primates such as those retrieved from the Fayum, but the exact relationships between the Oligocene and Early Miocene primates have yet to be worked out. Several genera and species have been identified, but the best known belong to the genus *Proconsul*. The skull of *Proconsul* exhibits more vertically implanted incisors and canines, semisectorial lower anterior premolars, thin enamel on the molars, a V-shaped dental arcade, a prognathous face, and a lack of brow ridges. Postcranial material suggests that *Proconsul* was probably an arboreal quadruped that lacked the

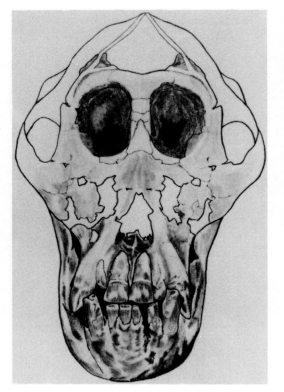

FIGURE 15–20 *Facial skeleton of* Sivapithecus.

The dentition of *Sivapithecus* was characterized by thick dental enamel on the molars, relatively low cusps of the large premolars, molars wearing flat, relatively small canines with little sexual dimorphism, broad central incisors, a relatively deep mandible, flaring zygomatic arches, and an orthognathous (nonprojecting) face. The animal's pattern of locomotion has been described as arboreal quadrupedalism with a degree of climbing and suspension. Some skulls show a close resemblance to the modern orangutan skull, having a narrow snout, a broad zygomatic arch, a narrow nasal aperture, and high orbits. The other ramamorph genus was *Gigantopithecus*, which was probably the largest ape that ever lived.

The pliomorph *Pliopithecus* possesses a robust mandible and a large temporalis muscle, suggesting that it was primarily a leaf-eating primate capable of consuming tough vegetation. The postcranial skeleton is that of an arboreal quadruped adapted for suspensory behavior in the manner of the New World semibrachiators such as the spider monkeys.

specializations for suspensory behavior that are found in modern apes.

Before the Middle Miocene the continent of Africa was isolated from Europe and Asia by water. In the Middle Miocene, the Afro-Arabian tectonic plate came into contact with the Asian plate, and a land connection developed between the two continents. This permitted the migration of the African hominoids into Asia between 16 and 14 million B.P.; in Asia, they underwent a major adaptive radiation. In addition, the forces produced by the coming together of the two large tectonic plates significantly altered the lay of the land, climate, and vegetation.

The taxonomy of the Miocene hominoids is complex and often confusing. However, we can categorize them into three morphological groups. The dryomorphs, which includes the Early Miocene species and *Dryopithecus*, lived during the Early and Middle Miocene. The ramamorphs, including *Sivapithecus*, lived during the Middle Miocene in east Africa and Eurasia.

STUDY QUESTIONS

1. What is the earliest fossil evidence of the primates? What were these early primates like?
2. Two distinct morphological patterns exist in the Eocene, the adapid and omomyid. Describe the general features that distinguish one pattern from the other.
3. Describe the fossil evidence for the origins of the anthropoids.
4. The anthropoids can be divided into three infraorders: Parapithecoidea, Platyrrhini, and Catarrhini. Briefly describe these infraorders and give examples of primates that belong in each one.
5. Contrast the relative diversity and frequency of hominoid and cercopithecoid fossils in the Early Miocene and the Late Miocene. What is the relationship between the early hominoids and the early cercopithecoids?
6. Briefly describe the major features and distribution in both space and time of the dryomorphs, ramamorphs, and pliomorphs.
7. What is the possible relationship of *Sivapithecus* to modern primates?

SUGGESTED READINGS

Ciochon, R., J. Olsen, and J. James. *Other Origins: The Search for the Giant Ape in Human Prehistory.* New York: Bantam, 1990. This nontechnical book describes the search for *Gigantopithecus* fossils in Vietnam and reviews the evidence of hominoid prehistory in Asia.

Conroy, G. C. *Primate Evolution.* New York: Norton, 1990. This volume contains a very detailed and well-illustrated discussion of the fossil primates and includes discussions of the paleoclimates and biogeography of each period of time.

Fleagle, J. G. *Primate Adaptation and Evolution.* New York: Academic, 1988. This book surveys primate evolution from 65 million years ago to the present.

Larsen, C. P., R. M. Matter, and D. L. Gebo. *Human Origins: The Fossil Record,* 2d ed. Prospect Heights, Ill.: Waveland, 1991. This is a handbook that presents a series of drawings and brief discussions of important fossils. Although it focuses on fossil hominids, it does describe a few key early hominoid specimens.

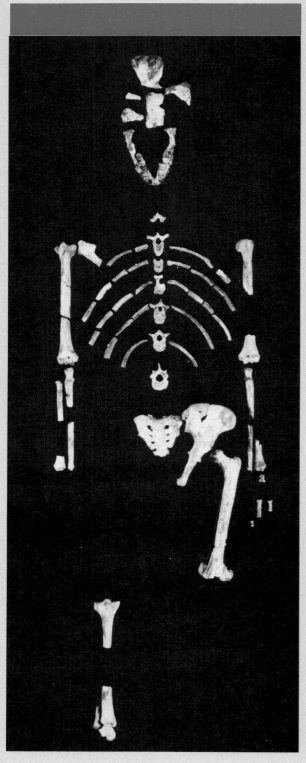

"Lucy" (AL 288-1), a female australopithecine skeleton from Hadar, Ethiopia.

No matter what kind of clothes were put on Lucy, she would not look like a human being. She was too far back, out of the human range entirely. That is what happens going back along an evolutionary line.

Her head, on the evidence of the bits of her skull that had been recovered, was not much larger than a softball. Lucy herself stood only three and one-half feet tall, although she was fully grown. That could be deduced from her wisdom teeth, which were fully erupted and had been exposed to several years of wear. My best guess was that she was between twenty-five and thirty years old when she died. She had already begun to show the onset of arthritis or some other bone ailment, on the evidence of deformation of her vertebrae. If she had lived much longer, it probably would have begun to bother her.[1]

Donald C. Johanson and Maitland A. Edey

[1]D. C. Johanson and M. A. Edey, *Lucy: The Beginnings of Humankind* (New York: Simon and Schuster, 1981), 20–21. Copyright ©1981 by Donald C. Johanson and Maitland A. Edey. Reprinted by permission of Simon and Schuster, Inc.

16

CHAPTER

AUSTRALOPITHECUS

On November 30, 1974, an international interdisciplinary research team, led by Donald Johanson, uncovered an incomplete skeleton of a hominid that lived over 3 million years ago. This find was placed in a new species, *Australopithecus afarensis,* and given the formal acquisition number AL 288-1. She is known to the team, however, as "Lucy," after the Beatles song "Lucy in the Sky with Diamonds."

The earliest well-known genus of the family Hominidae is *Australopithecus,* which lived from about 5 million years ago, or earlier, to about 1 million years ago. The genus *Homo* probably evolved from an australopithecine; during the latter time of its existence *Australopithecus* was contemporary with *Homo.* This chapter examines the genus *Australopithecus:* the history of its discovery, a description of many important finds, its anatomy, and its role in the story of human evolution.

The 1977 television miniseries *Roots* was the most watched series of its time. People seem to be fascinated with tracing their line of descent back through several hundred years of time. Many are drawn to physical anthropology by their curiosity about their even deeper roots. The exploration of the origins of humanity raises many interesting questions: With what other contemporary animals do we have a close common ancestry? Why did the hominid line go off in the direction it did? At what point should we use the word "human" to describe our ancestors? What made these ancestors human? What makes us unique?

This chapter is about the australopithecines, a group of primates considered by anthropologists to be the earliest forms in the direct line leading to modern humans. The genus *Australopithecus* is one of the two known genera of the family Hominidae; the other genus is *Homo*. *Australopithecus* includes several species of hominids that lived in Africa during Pliocene and Pleistocene times; australopithecines have never been found outside Africa. While some fragmentary australopithecine fossils occur in Late Miocene and Early Pliocene deposits, most of the fossils are younger than 4.5 million B.P.

The australopithecine finds exhibit wide variation in morphology because of sexual dimorphism, evolutionary changes throughout their long history, and variation due to reproductive isolation. A major debate in paleoanthropology centers on the identification of australopithecine species and the relationships of these species to one another. Researchers have placed the material in six species: *A. anamensis, A. afarensis, A. africanus, A. aethiopicus, A. robustus,* and *A. boisei*. All paleoanthropologists have not accepted all of these species, and still other species have been proposed. In addition, some place *A. aethiopicus, A. robustus,* and *A. boisei* in a different genus, *Paranthropus*.

Homo most likely evolved from an australopithecine population. The details of this story are not clear, however, for the australopithecines are represented by several species that existed at different points in time; in fact, some australopithecine populations were contemporary with

early *Homo*. The australopithecines became extinct approximately 900,000 years ago.

THE EARLIEST HOMINIDS

In this chapter we discuss the origin of the hominids. That origin seems to lie some time between 7½ and 5 million years ago in Africa. No fossils found before 7½ million years ago show enough of the hominid complex of characteristics to be considered hominid. Starting about 5 million years ago we begin to see this complex evolve in the genus *Australopithecus*. Recently discovered fossils which have been placed into a new genus *Ardipithecus* share some hominid features with the australopithecines. This chapter is primarily about the australopithecines, but we will begin the discussion with what might be a sister genus of *Australopithecus, Ardipithecus*.

In 1992 and 1993 hominid material was recovered from the site of Aramis in the Middle Awash area of Ethiopia by Tim White, Gen Suwa and Berhane Asfaw.[2] Almost 650 vertebrate fossils were collected, including the remains of birds, reptiles, rodents, bats, carnivores, and many herbivore species. A colobine monkey is among the most common vertebrates.

Among the fossils collected the paleontological team also found 17 hominid fossils; 15 of these are cranial remains. The cranial fossils include a fragment of mandible and the remains of a cranial base; the remainder are teeth (Figure 16–1). A few fragmented pieces of limb bones were also found. Early in 1995 a new find was announced which consisted of more than 90 fragments representing about 45 percent of an adult skeleton. These include parts of the skull, arms, vertebral column, pelvis, and legs.[3]

The mammalian bones at Aramis appear to have been fragmented before fossilization, and

---

[2]T. D. White, G. Suwa, and B. Asfaw, "*Australopithecus ramidus*, a New Species of Early Hominid from Aramis, Ethiopia," *Nature*, 371 (1994), 306–312.
[3]H. Gee, "New Hominid Remains Found in Ethiopia," *Nature*, 373 (1995), 272.

FIGURE 16–1 Ardipithecus ramidus. Jaw fragment with teeth found at Aramis, Ethiopia.

tuffs, the Daam Aatu Basaltic Tuff (DABT) and the lower Gàala Tuff Complex (GATC). (*Daam aatu* is "monkey" and *gàala* is "camel" in the Afar language.) These two tuffs lie beneath the VT–1/Moiti horizon which has been dated at about 3.9 million B.P. Because of contamination of the tuffs with older Miocene rocks, it has not been possible to date the DABT, but the GATC, located just beneath the fossil bed, has been dated by the single-crystal laser fusion $^{40}Ar/^{39}Ar$ method to 4.4 million B.P. This date provides the maximum age of the fossils.[4]

The Morphology and Taxonomy of the Aramis Hominids

The teeth found at Aramis are hominid-like in many ways. For example, they exhibit a reduced incisor-like canine. Many other dental features, however, are significantly different from those of later hominids. For example, the canine, although incisor-like in form, is larger than the postcanine teeth. These and other features place this hominid closer to the chimpanzee than to the australopithecines. For example, while the hominids are generally characterized by thick tooth enamel, the Aramis fossils possess tooth enamel of a thickness intermediate between that of the later hominids and chimpanzees.

Analysis of the newly discovered partial adult skeleton is eagerly awaited since it will provide very critical information about the origins of erect bipedalism. The cranial and dental material examined so far suggest that this species, some 4.4 million years old, is very closely related to the chimpanzee and may represent the earliest stage in the evolution of erect bipedalism. Yet because of the fragile nature of the more than 90 skeletal pieces, it will be some time before they can be removed from the site and studied.

The discoverers of these new fossils originally placed them in a new hominid species, *Australopithecus ramidus*. *Ramid* is the word for 'root'

the most common specimens are isolated teeth and fragments of the shafts of limb bones. Carnivore tooth marks are commonly found on the bones. Aramis at that time appears to have been a flat plain on which the carcasses of medium and large mammals were torn apart by carnivores. Many fossilized plants and seeds were also recovered. Analyses of the plant and animal remains suggest Aramis was a wooded habitat at that time.

The geology of this area is characterized by sedimentary beds layered between volcanic **tuffs,** layers of volcanic ash that have been solidified through the pressure of being buried in the earth. Most of the fossils were found on the surface in association with sediments lying between two

---

[4]G. WoldeGabriel, T. D. White, G. Suwa, P. Renne, J. de Heinzelin, W. K. Hart, and G. Helken, "Ecological and Temporal Placement of Early Pliocene Hominids at Aramis, Ethiopia," *Nature,* 371 (1994), 330–333.

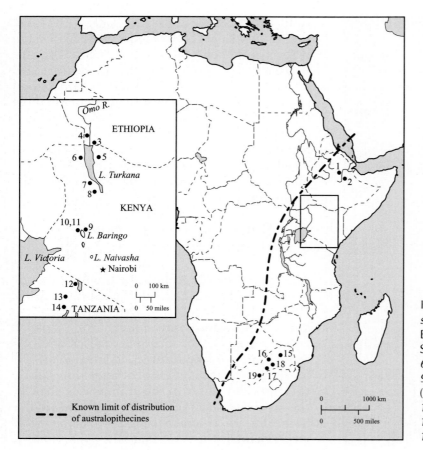

FIGURE 16–2 *Map of early hominid sites. 1* Hadar, *2* Middle Awash (Maka, Belohdelie, Aramis), *3* Fejej, *4* Omo (Usno, Shungura), *5* West Turkana (Koobi Fora), *6* West Turkana, *7* Lothagam, *8* Kanapoi, *9* Chesowanja (Chemoigut), *10* Baringo (Tabarin) *11* Baringo (Chemeron), *12* Peninj, *13* Olduvai Gorge, *14* Laetoli, *15* Makapansgat, *16* Sterkfontein, *17* Swartkrans, *18* Kromdrai, *19* Taung.

in the language of the Afar people who live in the area of the Middle Awash River. The name suggests that this species lies near the point in hominoid evolution when the hominids split off from the line leading to the modern apes.

In 1995 the discoverers decided to place the new species into its own genus, the genus *Ardipithecus*.[5] This move was based on the idea that *Ardipithecus ramidus* is not directly ancestral to *Australopithecus*, but is a sister group sharing an as yet unknown common ancestor.

---

[5]T. D. White, G. Suwa, and B. Asfaw, "Corrigendum to '*Australopithecus ramidus*, a New Species of Early Hominid from Aramis, Ethiopia,'" *Nature*, 375 (1995), 88.

THE DISCOVERIES OF THE AUSTRALOPITHECINES

We will begin the story of the australopithecines by recounting the history of their discovery and reviewing the important sites where their remains have been found. Australopithecine material is known from two regions of Africa, south Africa and the east African countries of Tanzania, Kenya, and Ethiopia (Figure 16–2).

The South African Australopithecines

Much of southern Africa rests on a limestone plateau. Limestone is often riddled with caves, and many have become completely filled in with

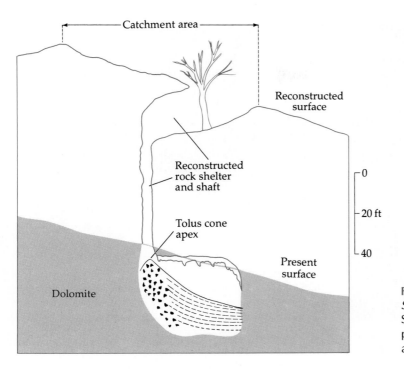

FIGURE 16–3 *Reconstruction of the cave at Swartkrans.* Diagrammatic section through the Swartkrans hillside. The upper reconstructed part has been removed by erosion since the accumulation of the fossil deposit.

debris. The 1920s was a period of tremendous population growth in South Africa, and the need for limestone, a constituent of cement, brought about an increase in quarrying activities. The blasting activities of workers in limestone quarries often expose the ancient cave fills. The material that fills these caves is a **bone breccia.** This is a mass of bone cemented together with calcium carbonate that has dissolved out of the limestone. It is a material that is very difficult to work.

C. K. Brain has reconstructed what one of the caves was like when the fossils were deposited. At this time, the cave was an underground cavern connected to the surface by a vertical shaft (Figure 16–3). Because of a concentration of moisture, trees were found in the region of the shaft in an otherwise relatively treeless region. Leopards often drag their prey into trees, where the carcass is relatively safe from scavengers and other carnivores. Some of the remains of the prey animals fell out of the trees and down the shaft into the cave. This accounts for the relative lack of postcranial remains, which would be destroyed to a large extent by chewing (Figure 16–4). The

hominids would have been among the prey species hunted.[6]

TAUNG   In 1924 fossil material from the quarry at Taung was delivered to Raymond A. Dart of the University of Witwatersrand in Johannesburg, South Africa. A small skull was embedded within the bone breccia. Dart spent 73 days removing the limestone matrix from the skull; he then spent 4 years separating the mandible from the rest of the skull. The fossil that emerged from the limestone matrix consisted of an almost complete mandible, a facial skeleton, and a natural endocranial cast (Figure 16–5). The jaw, containing a set of deciduous teeth along with the first permanent molar, was that of a child. Dart called his find the "Taung baby." A modern human child with the same dental pattern would be about 6 years old. As we will see later in this chapter, however, studies of

---

[6]C. K. Brain, *The Hunters or the Hunted? An Introduction to African Cave Taphonomy* (Chicago: University of Chicago Press, 1981).

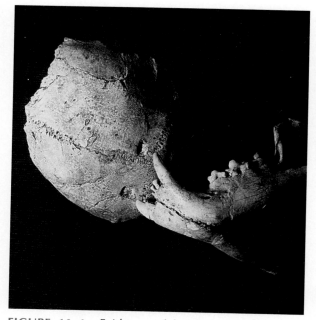

FIGURE 16–4 *Evidence of leopard predation.* This photograph shows part of the skull (parietal) of a juvenile australopithecine from Swartkrans. The two holes in the skull match the lower canines of a leopard. The leopard mandible came from the same deposit.

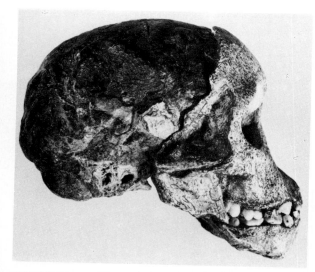

FIGURE 16–5 *"Taung baby."* The mandibular fragment, facial skeleton, and natural endocranial cast of *Australopithecus africanus* found at Taung, South Africa, in 1924.

the growth pattern of the australopithecines suggest that the child may be several years younger.

Dart published his find on February 7, 1925.[7] He named the skull *Australopithecus africanus,* from *australo,* meaning "southern," and *pithecus,* meaning "ape." Dart saw in this skull the characteristics of a primitive hominid, the most primitive of humankind's known ancestors. Dart based his opinion upon the hominid-like structure of the teeth, the nature of the endocranial cast, and the forward position of the foramen magnum which was consistent with erect bipedalism. Other paleoanthropologists, however, were not convinced. They noted the difficulties of making valid comparisons using an incomplete juvenile skull, and some argued that the skull showed close affiliations with the apes. Yet

Dart persisted in his contention that the "Taung baby" was a bipedal hominid, and the years have proved him correct.

The site of Taung has been very difficult to date. First, the actual site where the fossil was found has been destroyed. Second, the geological nature of the area is not suitable for chronometric dating. However, fieldwork conducted in 1988 and 1989 in nearby deposits has yielded many new nonhominid fossils. Analysis of these fossils suggests that the site is about 2.6 to 2.4 million years old, placing it in the same general time range as other *A. africanus* sites from South Africa.[8]

THE STERKFONTEIN VALLEY Most paleoanthropologists rejected Dart's interpretation of *Australopithecus africanus.* An exception was Robert Broom who, after retiring from his Scottish medical practice, went to South Africa in the 1930s and 1940s. Broom investigated three caves in the Sterkfontein Valley, which is located between Johannesburg and Pretoria. Broom excavated the first cave, Sterkfontein, between

[7]R. A. Dart, *"Australopithecus africanus,* the Man-Ape of South Africa," *Nature,* 115 (1925), 195; see also R. A. Dart, "Recollections of a Reluctant Anthropologist," *Journal of Human Evolution,* 2 (1973), 417–427.

[8]J. K. McKee, "Faunal Dating of the Taung Hominid Fossil Deposit," *Journal of Human Evolution,* 25 (1993), 363–376.

BOX 16-1

NAMING FOSSILS

Fossils are given designations that include an abbreviation for the site (and sometimes the museum housing the specimens) and an acquisition number. The latter is usually given to fossils in the order that they are discovered. The site abbreviations used in this book are AL (Afar Locality), ER (East Rudolf, the former name for East Turkana), KNM (Kenya National Museums), KP (Kanapoi), LH (Laetoli Hominid), MLD (Maka-pansgat Lime Deposit), OH (Olduvai Hominid), SK (Swartkrans), Sts (Sterkfontein), and WT (West Turkana).

1936 and 1939; he almost immediately uncovered the first adult specimens of *A. africanus* (Figure 16–6). Further excavations by John T. Robinson, C. K. Brain, Phillip V. Tobias, and A. R. Hughes have brought the inventory of australopithecine fossils to over 300. Correlation of recovered fossil mammals with similar fossils from east Africa dated by radiometric dating techniques suggests a date for Sterkfontein of about 2.5 million B.P.

Another important site in the Sterkfontein Valley is Swartkrans, where Broom, Robinson, and Brain excavated the remains of over 100 individuals. These australopithecines differ from those found at Sterkfontein (Figure 16–7). They belong to the species *Australopithecus robustus* and are often called the "robust" australopithecines. One difference between the robust australopithecines and *A. africanus*, sometimes referred to as the "gracile" form, is that the robust form has larger posterior teeth and larger jaws. Many paleoanthropologists consider the two species to belong to the same genus. Others place the robust australopithecines in the genus *Paranthropus*, the genus created by Broom for the early specimens. The Swartkrans australopithecines are younger than those from Sterkfontein, dating from about 1.7 to 1.1 million B.P.

The third site in the Sterkfontein Valley is Kromdraai, which has been excavated by Broom, Brain, and Elizabeth S. Vrba. The Kromdraai specimens are all robust australopithecines.

FIGURE 16–6   Australopithecus africanus. Specimen Sts 5 from Sterkfontein, South Africa.

FIGURE 16–7   Australopithecus robustus. Specimen SK 48 from Swartkrans, South Africa.

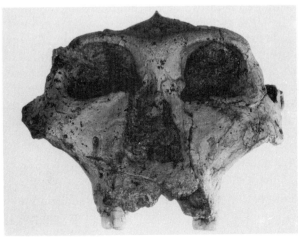

FIGURE 16–8 Australopithecus africanus. (Top) Taung mandible; (middle and bottom) gracile mandibles from Makapansgat, South Africa (MLD 2 and MLD 18).

OTHER SOUTH AFRICAN SITES   Located about 200 miles north of Pretoria is the largest of the South African cave sites, Makapansgat, which was excavated by J. W. Kitching, Dart, and Hughes. The Makapansgat australopithecines belong to the species *A. africanus* and date from about 3 to 2.6 million B.P. (Figure 16–8).

In 1992 two unerupted teeth were found at Gladysvale, located some 13 miles east of Sterkfontein. The teeth, probably belonging to *Australopithecus africanus*, are somewhat more developed than those of the Taung child. Additional fossils from Gladysvale may contribute to our understanding of australopithecine development.

The East African Australopithecines

Many regions of east Africa contain sedimentary deposits hundreds of meters thick that represent former rivers, lakes, and deltas. These extensive deposits are interrupted by layers of basalt and volcanic ash. These layers, which can be dated by several chronometric techniques such as potassium-argon and fission-track dating, act as time markers. Many volcanic eruptions produced ash falls that were swept by the winds and fell over thousands of square miles. Since each ash fall is characterized by a unique chemical composition, it is possible to correlate layers of ash, or tuffs, that formed in different regions from a particular eruption. Figure 16–9 diagrams some important sedimentary beds from which hominid fossils have been recovered.

The Plio-Pleistocene sediments of east Africa are rich in fossils, including those of hominids. Generally, most fossils come from three major regions: Olduvai Gorge and surrounding areas in Tanzania; the Turkana Basin, including Lake Turkana in Kenya and the Omo River region in southern Ethiopia; and Hadar and surrounding areas in northern Ethiopia.

OLDUVAI GORGE   Olduvai Gorge, in Tanzania, is a 25-kilometer-(15½ mile-)long canyon cut into the Serengeti Plain of Tanzania (Figure 16–10). The sedimentary beds, some 100 meters (328 feet) thick, have yielded bones of ancient hominids along with the tools they made and the remains of the animals they may have consumed.

Geologically, the sequence of sedimentary layers at Olduvai is divided into a series of beds. Bed I and the lower part of Bed II show a continuous sequence of sediments deposited when a large lake existed on what is now part of the Serengeti Plain. Hominid sites are located at what were once lake margins or the banks of streams. These areas provided the early hominids with a source of water and a concentration of animal food. In addition, fossilization occurs more frequently in these habitats as opposed to savanna grasslands and tropical forests. The oldest hominid site is located just above a layer of basalt with a potassium-argon date of 1.9 million B.P. Bed I and Lower Bed II span the time from 1.9 to 1.5 million B.P. Hominid material has also been recovered from Middle and Upper Bed II, dated between 1.5 and 1.1 million B.P. During this time

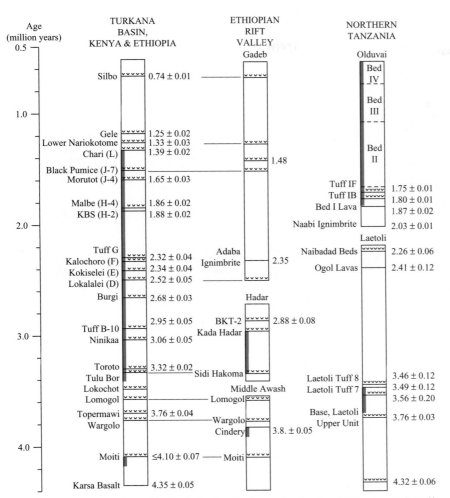

FIGURE 16–9 *Stratigraphic beds in the Turkana Basin, the Ethiopian Rift Valley, and Northern Tanzania.* Dated units are shown in each stratigraphic column. The heavy line on the left edge of each column indicates an interval in which hominid fossils have been found. (Fossils have been lumped into 0.1-million-year intervals.)

the freshwater lake became smaller, and much of the landscape became a dry grassland.

The story of Olduvai Gorge is the story of Louis and Mary Leakey. Louis Leakey was predisposed to think of the australopithecines as a side branch of the hominid line that played no role in the evolution of modern humans. He saw the genus *Homo* as a lineage of great antiquity whose major features were a large brain and the ability to manufacture tools. Although he and Mary later went on the make several important

discoveries of early *Homo*, to be described in the next chapter, their earliest significant find was that of an australopithecine.

Louis Leakey began his work in Olduvai in 1931; Mary arrived on the scene in 1935. Although the discoveries of animal fossils and important archaeological material were made early, the first significant hominid find did not appear until 1959. In that year, Mary Leakey found an almost complete hominid skull (the mandible was missing). The fossil, designated as OH 5,

FIGURE 16–10 *Olduvai Gorge, Tanzania.*

lived at Olduvai Gorge about 1.75 million B.P. (Figure 16–11). This date was the first to be determined by the then-new potassium-argon dating technique. At a time when most anthropologists considered hominid evolution to be confined to the last 1 million years, this new information almost doubled the time span estimated for human evolution. First named "*Zinjanthropus boisei*," this fossil was later placed in the species *Australopithecus boisei.* Since then many other specimens of *A. boisei* have been recovered from several sites. *Australopithecus boisei* resembles *A. robustus* in many ways, but the former possesses larger molars and premolars and has a more powerful jaw. It is often referred to as a "superrobust" australopithecine.

OMO RIVER BASIN   From 1966 to 1974 teams of American, French, and Kenyan paleoanthropologists, including F. Clark Howell, Yves Coppens, and Richard Leakey, explored the Omo River Basin of southern Ethiopia, just north of Lake Turkana. Two major sedimentary formations occur in this area, located some 25 kilometers (15½ miles) apart. The Shungura Formation,

about 760 meters (2493 feet) thick, consists of sediments representing prehistoric rivers, lakes, and deltas. Major tuffs divide the Shungura Formation into a series of members, with Member A

FIGURE 16–11 "*Zinjanthropus boisei.*" A superrobust australopithecine (OH 5) from Olduvai Gorge.

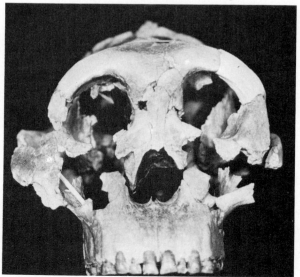

being the oldest. Australopithecine fossils have been recovered from Members B through lower G, dating from 3.3 to 2.1 million B.P. The smaller Usno Formation, approximately 170 meters (558 feet) thick, overlaps the Shungura Formation in time, dating to about 3.3 to 3.0 million years ago. Additional australopithecine fossils are known from these deposits.

The early sediments of the Omo River Basin represent fairly wet conditions. Lake Turkana was larger than it is today, and many fossils are associated with past marsh conditions. The recovered fossils appear to be similar to the early australopithecines from Hadar and Laetoli, to be described shortly.

The remains of *A. boisei* appear in the middle of the Shungura sediments. The earliest appearance of the robust australopithecines is associated with major ecological changes in the Omo Basin. Open habitats, such as grasslands, were slowly replacing the forest and marsh environments. Earlier fossils are fragmentary and more difficult to assign to a species.

KOOBI FORA   A significant series of sites is located in the Koobi Fora region of Kenya. This area of sediments covers approximately 1000 square kilometers (386 square miles) and extends some 25 kilometers (15½ miles) inland along the eastern shore of Lake Turkana. The Koobi Fora Formation is some 560 meters (1837 feet) thick and is divided by tuffs into eight members. The hominid fossils all occur between the Tulu Bor tuff, dated at 3.3 million B.P., and the Chari tuff, dated at 1.4 million B.P. The fossils fall into two groups: those above and those below the KBS tuff, which is dated at 1.88 million B.P.

This region has been studied since 1969 by Richard Leakey, the son of Louis and Mary, and his colleagues, and over 200 fossil hominids have been recovered so far. The australopithecine material appear to include members of the species *A. boisei* and a kind of gracile australopithecine as well (Figure 16–12). In addition, Koobi Fora has revealed an excellent fossil record of pollen, freshwater shellfish, and many mammalian groups including prehistoric members of the pig, cattle, horse, and elephant families. This fossil record has enabled geologists to reconstruct many geological and climatic events in the area.

The record also serves to correlate the area with other regions based on similarities among the fossils recovered.

WEST LAKE TURKANA   Explorations began west of Lake Turkana in 1984 where the Nachukui Formation extends 5 to 10 kilometers (3 to 6 miles) inland along the western shore of the lake. Investigators found a cranium, WT 17000, at the site of Lomekwi. The find was named the "Black Skull" because of its black color, derived from the manganese-rich sediments in which it was found (Figure 16–13). WT 17000 appears to resemble *A. boisei*, yet this specimen is characterized by a small cranium and the retention of some primitive features from earlier australopithecines. WT 17000 is dated at 2.5 million B.P., somewhat earlier than the 2.2 to 1.2 million B.P. range for *A. boisei*. Some investigators place this find in the species *Australopithecus aethiopicus*.

KANAPOI   In August 1995, Meave G. Leakey, the wife of Richard Leakey, and her colleagues published the description of a new australopithecine species.[9] Named *Australopithecus anamensis*, the fossils were found at the site of Kanapoi, located southwest of Lake Turkana in Kenya. Additional material has also been found 30 miles away at Allia Bay on the eastern side of Lake Turkana. The sediments at both sites were once a part of an ancient lake of which Lake Turkana is a remnant. The name *anamensis* comes from *anam* which means *lake* in the language of the Turkana people.

The fossil beds at Kanapoi have been known for some time; a humerus was recovered at Kanapoi in 1965. The new material has been discovered beginning in 1994. The specimens from Kanapoi include a mandible with all its teeth intact but missing the rami (Figure 16–A in the color insert: "Hominid Fossils"), a partial left temporal, additional jaw fragments and isolated teeth, a distal left humerus, and the proximal

---

[9]M. G. Leakey, G. S. Feibel, I. McDougall, and A. Walker, "New Four-Million-Year-Old Hominid Species from Kanapoi and Allia Bay, Kenya," *Nature,* 376 (1995), 565–571. Additional photographs of the Kanapoi fossils and site can be seen in M. Leakey, "The Dawn of Humans: The Earliest Horizon," *National Geographic,* 188 (September 1995), 38–51.

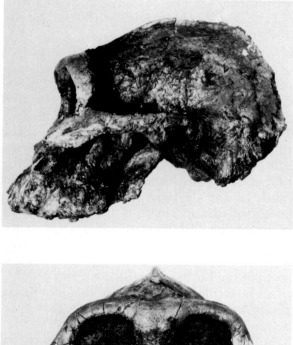

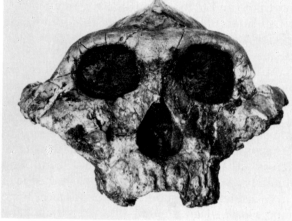

FIGURE 16–12 *Australopithecus boisei.* Side, front, and top views of KNM-ER 406 from Lake Turkana, Kenya.

and distal sections of a right tibia (Figure 16–B in the color insert: "Hominid Fossils"). The material from Allia Bay consists primarily of teeth.

The Kanapoi fossils have been dated by $^{40}Ar/^{39}Ar$ dating and by correlation with dated sediments at other east African sites. The fossils found in the lower horizon, dated by the $^{40}Ar/^{39}Ar$ method, date between 4.17 and 4.12 million years ago. The upper horizon, which contains the postcranial material, is not as precisely dated. Based on correlation with horizons at other sites, it is thought to date from between 4.1 and 3.5 million B.P. The Allia Bay fossils, which consists mainly of teeth, were found within and below the Moiti Tuff which has been dated at 3.9 million B.P. The Kanapoi beds also include fossil fish, aquatic reptiles, and many terrestrial mammals. The habitat may have been one characterized by dry open woods or brush with gallery forest along the rivers.

One of the most striking observations about the new species is that jaws and teeth that in many ways are similar to those of Miocene apes are associated with postcranial material similar in many ways to that of early *Homo*. Since the dental and cranial material is found primarily in the lower horizon and the postcranial material in the upper horizon at Kanapoi, the assertion that they belong to the same species will remain open to question until additional material is found.

HADAR AND THE MIDDLE AWASH   The International Afar Research Expedition, led by Yves Coppens, Maurice Taieb, and Donald Johanson, began working in 1973 at Hadar, which is located in the Afar Basin in central Ethiopia. Because of the unique conditions of burial and fossilization, some fossils are very well preserved. The original work was conducted between 1973 and 1977, during which over 240 hominid fossils were recovered. The stratigraphic beds date between 3.6 and 2.9 million b.p.

The first hominid find, consisting of four leg bones, was made in the fall of 1973. A partial femur and tibia fit together to form a knee joint, providing the oldest skeletal evidence of fully de-

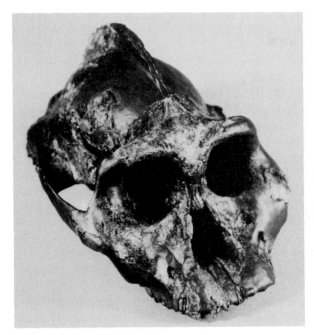

FIGURE 16–13 *The "Black Skull," WT 17000.*

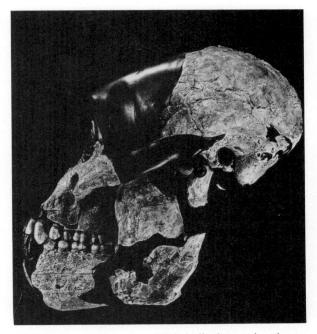

FIGURE 16–14 *Reconstructed skull of* Australopithecus afarensis.

veloped erect bipedalism. Perhaps the best known fossil is "Lucy" (AL 288-1), found in 1974 (see chapter opening). This remarkable find consists of 40 percent of a skeleton. "Lucy" provided the first opportunity for anyone to study cranial and postcranial australopithecine remains from the same individual. In the following year, 1975, the team discovered a collection of 197 bones representing at least thirteen individuals, adults and immatures. Some believe that these individuals, called the "First Family," all died at the same time, possibly killed and buried by a sudden flood or other catastrophe. This material is placed in the species *Australopithecus afarensis* (Figure 16–14).

After a break in time, paleoanthropologists returned to Hadar in 1990, and since then they have recovered fifty-three new specimens attributed to *A. afarensis*.[10] Among these is a cranial fragment dated at 3.9 million B.P., which makes it the oldest known specimen of this species.

Another exciting find is three-quarters of a skull that was pieced together from more than

200 fragments and announced in 1994 (Figure 16–15). This specimen (AL 444-2) is dated at approximately 3.0 million B.P., which is about 200,000 years younger than "Lucy." The skull is

FIGURE 16–15 Australopithecus afarensis. Skull of a male (AL 444-2) from Hadar.

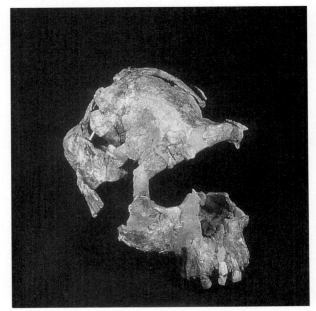

---

[10]W. H. Kimbel, D. C. Johanson, and Y. Rak, "The First Skull and Other New Discoveries of *Australopithecus afarensis* at Hadar, Ethiopia," *Nature*, 368 (1994), 449–451.

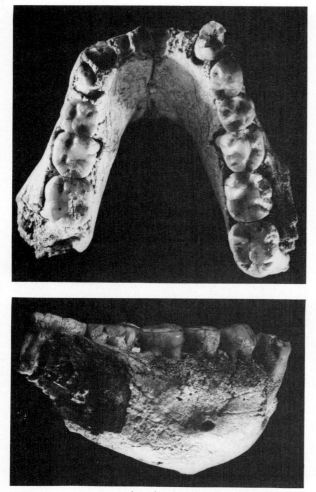

FIGURE 16–16 Australopithecus afarensis. Top and side views of the mandible LH 4 from Laetoli, Tanzania.

of Olduvai Gorge. Mary Leakey and Tim White excavated the remains of several hominids dated between 3.8 and 3.6 million B.P. These fossils have been placed in the species *A. afarensis* (Figure 16–16).

One day at Laetoli about 3.6 million years ago, a light fall of volcanic ash fell over the land and a light drizzle moistened the ash; later, hominids walked across the ash field. A day or so later, another ashfall covered their tracks; the remaining impressions were discovered in 1978 (Figure 16–17). The site consists of two footprint trails over 27.5 meters (90 feet) long. Thirty-eight footprints of a small hominid make up the left trail, and thirty-one footprints of two hominids make up the right trail. The footprints exhibit a well-developed arch and a nondivergent big toe, specializations of the human foot. These footprints provide evidence that "the unique striding bipedal mode of locomotion employed by modern people had been established much earlier than previous evidence had suggested."[12]

Summary

The fossil evidence of the australopithecines has been found in south Africa and the east African countries of Ethiopia, Kenya, and Tanzania. the first fossil to be discovered was at Taung, South Africa, in 1924. Raymond Dart placed the juvenile skull in the species *Australopithecus africanus*. Today we have many fossils from several South African caves. The fossils fall into two major groups: the gracile australopithecines *(A. africanus)* and the robust australopithecines *(A. robustus)*.

The australopithecines are well known from several east African sites associated with extensive sedimentary deposits. Prehistoric volcanic activity associated with these beds provides material for chronometric dating. The most significant sites are those of Olduvai Gorge, the Omo River Basin, Koobi Fora, West Lake Turkana, Kanapoi, Hadar, the Middle Awash, and Laetoli. The fossils have been assigned to several species. The earliest in time are *A. anamensis* and

larger than that of "Lucy"; in fact, it is the largest known australopithecine cranium. Many paleoanthropologists believe that it probably represents a male. Other important finds include an ulna and a partial humerus.

Several sites are located south of Hadar on both sides of the Awash River located within the Afar Basin. Four incomplete mandibles, teeth, and several postcranial bones were discovered in 1990 at Maka by Tim White and his team.[11] These fossils are dated at 3.4 million B.P.

LAETOLI   Laetoli is located in Tanzania near Lake Eyasi, some 50 kilometers (30 miles) south

[11]T. D. White et al., "New Discoveries of *Australopithecus* at Maka in Ethiopia," *Nature*, 366 (1993), 261–265.

[12]T. D. White, "Evolutionary Implications of Pliocene Hominid Footprints," *Science*, 208 (1980), 176.

FIGURE 16–17
Hominid footprints at Laetoli, Tanzania.

A. afarensis; the robust australopithecines belong to the species *A. aethiopicus* and *A. boisei.*

Figure 16–2 is a map of many of the African sites that have yielded australopithecine material. No evidence has been found suggesting that the australopithecines existed outside the African continent. It appears that Charles Darwin was correct when he stated that human ancestors originated in Africa. It was not until after the origin of the genus *Homo* that populations belonging to this genus ventured out of Africa and began the odyssey that ultimately led humans to the far corners of the planet Earth.

Table 16–1 lists most of the australopithecine sites, including some minor sites that have not been discussed. The table also lists for each site the species of *Australopithecus* found; however, there are many controversies surrounding the placement of particular fossils in particular species. The dates for many hominid sites are also tentative.

This section has introduced six species of *Australopithecus.* Not all of these species are considered valid by all paleoanthropologists; other paleoanthropologists have suggested the

existence of still other species. These species are summarized in Table 16–2.

THE AUSTRALOPITHECINES: INTERPRETATIONS OF THE EVIDENCE

The australopithecines are a group of African hominids characterized by a small cranial capacity, a relatively large projecting facial skeleton, large premolars and molars with thick enamel, and postcranial features that suggest that their primary means of locomotion was erect bipedalism. Other than these general features, the genus *Australopithecus* is quite variable. The vast length of time that the genus existed, its considerable geographical variation, and the fragmentary nature of much of the fossil material make it difficult to make broad generalizations about the genus.

What follows are descriptions and interpretations of the evidence. The ideas presented here are hypotheses that will be modified as new evidence is uncovered and new ways of interpreting

TABLE 16–1

SUMMARY OF MAJOR AUSTRALOPITHECINE SITES

SITE*	LOCATION	ESTIMATED AGE (MILLION YEARS B.P.)	SPECIES PRESENT
Taung	South Africa	2.6–2.4	*A. africanus*
Sterkfontein	South Africa	2.5	*A. africanus*
Swartkrans	South Africa	1.7–1.1	*A. robustus*
Kromdraai	South Africa	?	*A. robustus*
Makapansgat	South Africa	3.0–2.6	*A. africanus*
Gladysvale	South Africa	?	*A. africanus*
Olduvai Gorge	Tanzania	1.75	*A. boisei*
Peninj	Tanzania	1.3	*A. boisei*
Laetoli	Tanzania	3.7–3.5	*A. afarensis*
Koobi Fora	Kenya	3.3–1.4	*A. boisei*
Allia Bay	Kenya	3.9	*A. anamensis*
Lomekwi	Kenya	2.5	*A. aethiopicus*
Lothagam	Kenya	5.5–5.0	?
Kanapoi	Kenya	4.2–3.5	*A. anamensis*
Chesowanja	Kenya	1.4	*A. boisei*
Tabarin	Kenya	4.15	*A. afarensis*
Omo	Ethiopia	3.3–2.1	*A. afarensis,* *A. aethiopicus* *A. boisei*
Hadar	Ethiopia	3.6–2.9	*A. afarensis*
Maka	Ethiopia	3.4	*A. afarensis*
Fejej	Ethiopia	4.2	*A. afarensis*

* Sites in boldface are discussed in the text.

the evidence are developed. The transitory nature of interpretations made in paleoanthropology is evident in the variety of interpretations of the evidence and the many debates found in the pages of anthropological journals.

The major landmarks of hominid evolution are the evolution of habitual erect bipedalism, the development of tool use and tool manufac-

TABLE 16–2

SUMMARY OF AUSTRALOPITHECINE SPECIES

SPECIES	TIME PERIOD (MILLION YEARS B.P.*)	GRACILE/ ROBUST
A. anamensis	4.2–3.5	—
A. afarensis	3.9–3.0	Gracile
A. africanus	3.0–2.4	Gracile
A. aethiopicus†	3.5	Robust
A. robustus†	2.0–1.0	Robust
A. boisei†	2.5–1.2	Robust

* Estimates based on presently known dates.
†Robust australopithecines are sometimes placed in the genus *Paranthropus.*

ture, reduction in the size of the dentition, and enlargement of the brain. In a very general sense these landmarks evolved in the order listed. We will discuss the evidence in the same order.

The Australopithecines as Erect Bipeds

The anatomical evidence for erect bipedalism is found in the postcranial skeleton, although, as Raymond Dart observed, the forward position of the foramen magnum in the base of the skull can also be used to infer upright posture. A modest number of australopithecine postcranial bones are known.

The size of the australopithecines can be estimated from the dimensions of the postcranial bones. The australopithecines are relatively small when compared with modern humans and the great apes. The average reconstructed weight for the four best known species (*A. afarensis, A. africanus, A. robustus,* and *A. boisei*) ranges from 40 to 49 kilograms (88 to 108 pounds) for males and from 29 to 34 kilograms (64 to 75

TABLE 16–3

ESTIMATED SIZES OF HOMINID PALEOSPECIES

PALEOSPECIES	BODY WEIGHT (KILOGRAMS)			STATURE (CENTIMETERS)		
	MALE	FEMALE	FEMALE AS % OF MALE	MALE	FEMALE	FEMALE AS % OF MALE
A. afarensis	45	29	64	151	105	70
A. africanus	41	30	73	138	115	83
A. robustus	40	32	80	132	110	83
A. boisei	49	34	69	137	124	91
H. sapiens	65	54	83	175	161	92

Source: Adapted from H. M. McHenry, "How Big Were Early Hominids?" *Evolutionary Anthropology,* 1 (1992), 18.

pounds) for females (Table 16–3). The average reconstructed stature ranges from 132 to 151 centimeters (52 to 59 inches) for males and from 105 to 124 centimeters (41 to 49 inches) for females. The degree of sexual dimorphism is greater than that found in the genus *Homo.*

The australopithecine postcranial skeleton is that of an erect biped. The pelvis, bowl-shaped and shortened from top to bottom, is similar in basic structure to the pelvis of *H. sapiens* (Figure 16–18), and the spine shows a lumbar curve. Erect bipedalism is also deduced from analysis of the footprints discovered at the site of Laetoli in Tanzania.

THE LOCOMOTOR PATTERN OF *AUSTRALOPITHECUS AFARENSIS*   The postcranial skeleton of *A. afarensis* shows several features that suggest its transitional status (Figure 16–19). The skeleton of the arm is relatively long when compared with the relatively short hindlimb.

The ulna, which is curved, is long relative to the humerus. The elbow, however, lacks the specializations found in the ape that allow the ape to support the weight of the upper body on its hands when knuckle walking. One indicator of this feature is the **humerofemoral index** which presents the relative proportions of the humerus and femur (length of humerus × 100/length of femur). The index for "Lucy" is 85, which is between that of a modern human pygmy population (74) and the modern bonobo (98).

Randall Susman and others have interpreted these features as suggesting some arboreal locomotion in association with erect bipedalism.[13] The curved and slender fingers and curved toes intermediate in relative length between those of apes and humans suggest a degree of grasping

[13]R. L. Susman, J. T. Stern, Jr., and W. L. Jungers, "Arboreality and Bipedality in the Hadar Hominids," *Folia Primatologica,* 43 (1984), 113–156.

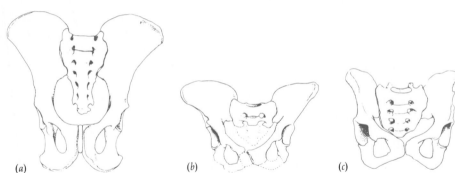

(a)   (b)   (c)

FIGURE 16–18 *Australopithecine pelvis.* The pelvis of *(b) Australopithecus africanus* compared with the pelvis of *(a)* a modern chimpanzee and *(c)* a modern human.

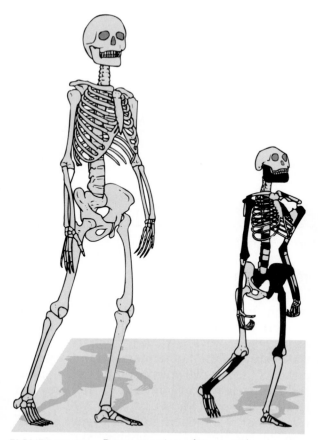

FIGURE 16–19 *Reconstruction of "Lucy."* The drawing on the right represents a reconstruction of AL 288-1 from Hadar. The original fossils are shown in black except in the skull. The remainder of the reconstruction is based upon construction of mirror images of known parts of the skeleton and reconstructions based upon other fossils. Note the long arms and curved fingers. A modern human skeleton is shown for comparison.

foot possesses a humanlike arch, and the big toe is nongrasping. Another important feature is the distinct angle formed at the knee between the bottom portion of the femur and the top portion of the tibia (Figure 16–20). The result is the positioning of the knees close together when the individual is standing. When walking, the weight of the body is centered over one leg while the other leg is moving.

Although *A. afarensis* moved bipedally on the ground, the pattern of this bipedalism was somewhat different from that seen in later australopithecines and *Homo*. The short legs suggest that *A. afarensis* had a significantly shorter stride, which meant that its speed on the ground was likely to have been slower than that seen in humans today.

NEW FOSSIL EVIDENCE   In 1995 paleoanthropologists in South Africa announced that they had recovered four bones of the left foot of an australopithecine from a box of mammalian bones originally found in 1980 at the site of Sterkfontein[14]. These bones (Stw 573) fit together to form an arch extending from the heel of the foot to the beginning of the big toe. The bones show a mixture of human-like and ape-like features, with the ape-like features being more evident in the bones closer to the toe. The investigators conclude that the foot with its grasping big toe was adapted for arboreal climbing as well as bipedal locomotion. Dated between 3.5 and 3.0 million years ago, these bones represent the oldest australopithecines found in south Africa. Not enough evidence is present to determine the species to which this individual belongs.

Finally we can examine the new postcranial bones of *A. anamensis* from Kanapoi, Kenya, which may date between 4.1 and 3.5 million B.P.[15] These postcranial bones are very *Homo*-like in appearance and support the idea that erect bipedalism is very ancient within the family Hominidae.

The proximal and distal sections of a right

that could have functioned as part of an arboreal locomotor pattern. The ability to sleep in trees and to use trees for protection from predators may have been an important factor in the survival of early australopithecine populations. In addition, these populations may have emphasized arboreal food resources. All of this would make a great deal of sense since a transitional form would be expected to show anatomical features for both arboreal locomotion and terrestrial erect bipedalism.

Yet the skeleton of *A. afarensis* makes it clear that this species was also an efficient erect biped. The blade of the ilium is short and broad, the

[14]R. J. Clarke and P. V. Tobias, "Sterkfontein Member 2 Foot Bones of the Oldest South African Hominid," *Science,* 269 (1995), 521–524.
[15]M. G. Leakey, G. S. Feibel, I. McDougall, and A. Walker, op. cit.

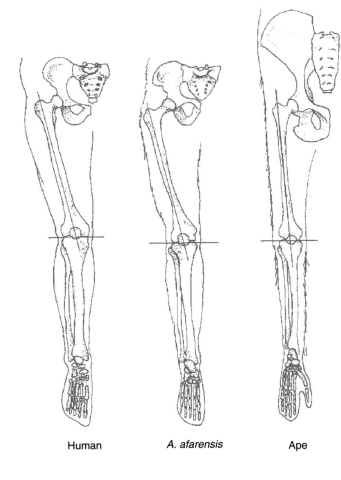

Human   A. afarensis   Ape

FIGURE 16–20 *Australopithecine knee.* In contrast with that of the ape, the human upper leg angles inward, bringing the knees directly under the body. The australopithecines exhibit this human pattern.

tibia have been recovered (Figure 16–B in the color insert: "Hominid Fossils"). At the proximal end, the condyles, which make up part of the knee joint, are at right angles to the shaft. The socket-like condyles are both concave (in an ape one would be convex) and are unequal in size (the lateral condyle is larger than the other). The region where the fibula articulates with the tibia is reduced, which suggests that the fibula and the associated flexors of the big toe are reduced in size. This implies a loss of mobility of the big toe. In general, the bone strongly supports the conclusion that these australopithecines were erect bipeds.

Even though the middle portion of the tibia is missing, an estimate of living weight can be made from measurements of this bone. The individual is thought to have weighed between 47 and 55 kilograms (104 and 121 pounds). *A. ana-*

mensis was somewhat larger than the *A. afarensis* males and 1.7 times than the *A. afarensis* females, based upon estimate weights.

FUNCTIONS OF ERECT BIPEDALISM   Many hypotheses have been put forth to explain the advantages of erect bipedalism. Upright posture positions the animal's eyes high above the ground where it can see a greater distance, and this is important in spotting predators. Erect bipeds can walk a greater distance using less energy than quadrupeds can. In erect bipedalism the hands are freed from locomotor functions and can evolve into organs for fine manipulation. The freeing of hands also enabled the early hominids to carry things such as food, tools, and helpless infants. Perhaps each of these hypotheses contains an element of truth since erect bipedalism allows for a complex interaction of several functions.

THE ART OF STANDING TALL

The anatomy of an animal can be seen as a complex of interrelated parts. The evolution of upright posture and habitual erect bipedalism in the hominids is most clearly seen in the anatomy of the spine, pelvis, legs, and feet. Other parts of the body, however, have had to adjust to this unique locomotor pattern as well. For example, as noted by Raymond Dart in the Taung specimen, the forward position of the foramen magnum is related to upright posture and can be used to infer this unusual stance.

Another part of the anatomy of the head is also correlated with changes in posture. This is the vestibular system that is related to body movements and the perception of one's position in space. The major organ of this system is the bony labyrinth of the inner ear which consists of the three semi-circular canals. Although this part of the anatomy is very difficult to observe in skulls, high-resolution computed tomography can be used to produce cross-sectional images of the middle ear while leaving the fossil skull intact. Paleoanthropologists have used this modern medical technology to study the inner ear of several fossil hominids including the australopithecines.

The three semicircular canals are filled with fluid and are lined with small hairs. Motions of the body create movements within the fluid that are sensed by these hairs. Experiments have demonstrated that the size of the canals is related to locomotor behavior. The investigators took CT scans of thirty-one living primates, including *H. sapiens,* and twelve fossil skulls, including those of *A. africanus* and *A. robustus.* They measured the height and width of the semicircular canals and calculated the radius of the curvature of the arc of each canal.

Modern humans have larger anterior and posterior canals and a smaller lateral canal than the great apes. While fossil specimens classified as *Homo* show proportions similar to those of modern humans, those of the australopithecines show a pattern more like that of the great apes. This can be seen in the table at the top of column 3.

The four great apes possess similar proportions for the three semicircular canals. This likely represents the ancestral condition. The evo-

SPECIES	ASC*	PSC	LSC
H. sapiens	37	36	26
Chimpanzee	34	35	31
Bonobo	35	34	32
Gorilla	32	34	34
Orangutan	35	33	31
A. africanus	34	36	30
A. robustus	34	34	32

* The relative radius of curvatures in percent. The sum of the three columns for each species equals 100. (Sums in this table may not equal 100 because of rounding off.) ASC, PSC, and LSC refers to the anterior, posterior, and lateral semicircular canals, respectively.

lution of the human condition is represented by an increase in size of the anterior and posterior canals and decrease in size of the lateral canal. This may be related to the coordination of upright posture. The more apelike pattern seen in the australopithecines is consistent with the idea that australopithecine locomotor behavior, although including erect bipedalism, also included a significant degree of arboreal locomotion.

Reference: F. Spoor, B. Wood, and F. Zonneveld, "Implications of Early Hominid Labyrinthine Morphology for Evolution of Human Bipedal Locomotion," *Nature,* 369 (1994), 645–648.

Another possible function of erect bipedalism is suggested by biologist Pete Wheeler. He believes that one advantage of erect bipedalism is to lower body temperature, especially in the open grasslands where many of the australopithecines lived.[16] Upright posture raises the body above the ground into faster-moving air currents. It also reduces the surface area of the body that is exposed to the sun, especially when the sun is high in the sky. At noon the sun is shining down on the entire back of a four-legged animal, but only on the head and shoulders of an erect biped. While hairlessness encourages evaporative cooling through sweating, the hair remaining on top of the human head serves as a layer of insulation, further protecting the brain from overheating.

---

[16]P. E. Wheeler, "The Thermoregulatory Advantages of Hominid Bipedalism in Open Equatorial Environments: The Contribution of Increased Convective Heat Loss and Cutaneous Evaporative Cooling," *Journal of Human Evolution,* 21 (1991), 107–115.

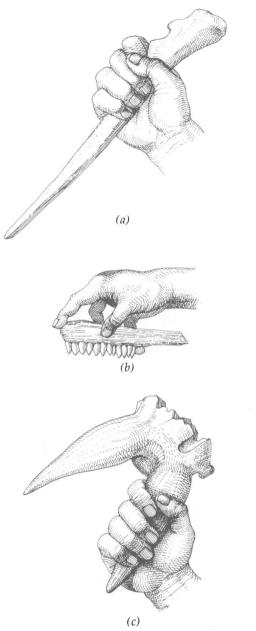

(a)

(b)

(c)

FIGURE 16–21 *Osteodontokeratic tools.* Raymond Dart proposed that broken bones were used by the australopithecines as tools. He proposed that *(a)* an antelope ulna was used as a dagger, *(b)* part of a small antelope mandible was used as a knife blade, and *(c)* horn cores and a portion of the cranium of a fossil reedbuck were used as a piercing instrument. Today, paleoanthropologists believe that these fragmented bones are the result of leopard predation.

Australopithecine Tool Use

Raymond Dart noted the presence of many broken bones in the deposits at Makapansgat. He concluded that they were a result of the deliberate manufacture of bone tools (Figure 16–21). He termed this an **osteodontokeratic culture,** from *osteo,* meaning "bone," *donto,* meaning "tooth," and *keratic,* meaning "horn" (keratin is a main constituent of horn). He saw a femur as a club, a broken long bone as a sharp cutting tool, and a piece of mandible as a tooth scraper. However, later studies by C. K. Brain of the bone material from Swartkrans demonstrated that the features of the bones that suggest deliberate toolmaking are more likely the result of carnivore activity.

In spite of the difficulties in interpreting the bone material in south Africa, paleoanthropologists still believe that tool use and tool manufacture are an important element in early hominid behavior. The fact that chimpanzees manufacture tools (Chapter 12) suggests that such behavior could have characterized the early hominids. Also, the fact that the earliest australopithecines were erect bipeds means that these forms would have had their hands freed from locomotor functions, although the earliest australopithecines may have used their hands for some degree of arboreal locomotion. These facts lead us to expect an early expression of culture in these prehistoric populations.

The earliest hominid tools were most likely made of perishable materials such as wood, bark, leaves, and fibers. The evidence for tool use in the archaeological record, however, consists primarily of stone objects. Early stone tools were probably nothing more than fortuitously shaped natural objects. An example is a small, rounded stone that would fit comfortably in the hand and could be used to crack open a nut to obtain the meat or to break open a bone to obtain the marrow. Such unaltered stones were probably used as tools by early hominids for a long period of time before stones were deliberately altered to achieve a specific shape. It is very difficult to interpret stones found in a site in association with hominid fossils since such stones may have been unaltered stones used as tools or simply stones deposited in a site through geological activity.

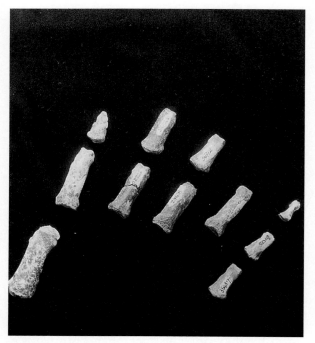

FIGURE 16–22 *Australopithecine hand bones from Swartkrans.*

The first concrete evidence of the manufacture of stone tools comes from a site near the Gona River in Ethiopia, dated between 2.6 and 2.5 million B.P., and the Shungura Formation at Omo, dated between 2.5 and 2.4 million B.P. Stone tools are also known from many sites dated between 2.5 and 1 million B.P.

The australopithecines were contemporary with *Homo* from 2.4 million years ago. The simple presence of a stone tool with an australopithecine bone does not establish that the australopithecine made the tool. However, if stone tools really are 2.6 to 2.5 million years old, this would place them in the australopithecine time range before the emergence of *Homo*. In addition, given the toolmaking ability of chimpanzees, it is very possible that both early *Homo* and late australopithecines could have made stone tools, but perhaps for different purposes.

THE AUSTRALOPITHECINE HAND   Further evidence for australopithecine toolmaking lies in the australopithecine hand. The hand of *A. afarensis* is known from fifty-one bones including carpals, metacarpals, and phalanges. Hand bones of *A. robustus* have been recovered from Swartkrans, South Africa, and are dated from about 1.8 million B.P. (Figure 16–22). They consist of twenty-two carpals, metacarpals, and phalanges.

Randall Susman has studied the hand bones of *A. afarensis* and *A. robustus* along with hand bones from *H. erectus* and fossil *H. sapiens* and contemporary humans, chimpanzees, and bonobos.[17] He notes that the ape hand is most frequently used in a power grip, where an object is held by the fingers against the palm of the hand. Ape hands are characterized by long, curved fingers, narrow fingertips, and relatively small thumbs. The metacarpal of the thumb has a narrow head, a relatively narrow, parallel-sided shaft, and a small base.

Humans, on the other hand, have relatively short, straight fingers. The human thumb is relatively long, resulting in a ratio of thumb to finger length that makes it possible to rotate the thumb so that the tip of the thumb can oppose the tip of each finger in turn. The thumbs and fingers possess broad fingertips. In addition, the human thumb has three muscles that are not found in the chimpanzee thumb, which can be seen in Figure 16–23. This thumb is well adapted for a precision grip.

There are no stone tools associated with fossil remains of *A. afarensis*. The hand bones of this species show many apelike features such as a short thumb with a narrow metacarpal and curved phalanges in the other fingers. In contrast with the hand skeleton of *A. afarensis*, the hand of the later *A. robustus* is consistent with a precision grip. The precision grip is a requirement for toolmaking. The thumb is well developed and includes an area where the flexor pollicis longus muscle, a distinctive human anatomical feature, inserts. In contrast to the fingers of modern apes, the fingers of *A. robustus* are short and straight.

The humanlike anatomy of the *A. robustus* hand plus the presence of stone tools at the australopithecine site of Swartkrans suggests that the later australopithecines made tools, as did members of the genus *Homo*. Yet tools may have played very different roles in the two populations. The importance of tool technology to human evolution is discussed in the next chapter.

[17]R. L. Susman, "Fossil Evidence for Early Hominid Tool Use," *Science*, 265 (1994), 1570–1573.

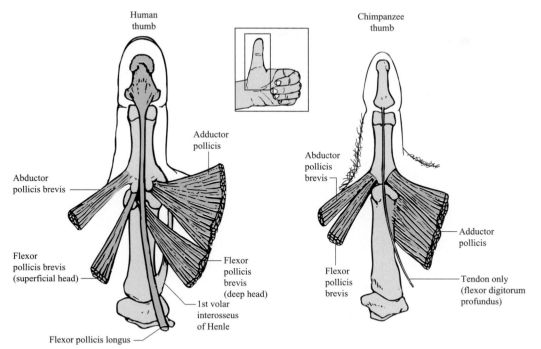

FIGURE 16–23 *Muscles of the thumb.* In this diagram we are looking at the bottom of the human and chimpanzee thumb. We can observe the various muscles that cross over the joint between the metacarpal and proximal phalanges (i.e., the phalanges closest to the palm). When we compare the anatomy of the two thumbs, we observe the following: (1) Humans possess a deep head of the flexor pollicis brevis muscle; chimpanzees do not. (2) Humans possess a first volar interosseous muscle of Henle; chimpanzees do not. (1) Humans have a flexor pollicis longus muscle. This muscle lies in a bony groove formed by a pair of small sesamoid bones located at the joint between the metacarpal and proximal phalanges. Chimpanzees have only a tendon that mimics this muscle. The sesamoid bones that form a bony groove are absent.

Australopithecine Dentition

Most known australopithecine fossils are isolated teeth and jaw fragments with teeth. In general, australopithecine dentition is very hominid-like. Yet the early australopithecines show many nonhominid features, while the robust australopithecines evolved rather specialized dentition. Like weight and stature, the dentition suggests a greater degree of sexual dimorphism than found in later hominids.

THE DENTITION OF *AUSTRALOPITHECUS AFARENSIS* AND *AUSTRALOPITHECUS ANAMENSIS* The dentition of *A. afarensis* resembles in many ways that of the apes. The dental arcade is intermediate in shape between that of modern humans and apes (Figure 16–24, Figure

16–C in the color insert: "Hominid Fossils"). The posterior teeth lie in a fairly straight line except for the third molar which is positioned inward. The upper incisors are relatively large and project forward. The canines project above the tooth row and are conical in shape, in contrast to the spatulate shape of the modern human canine. A small diastema frequently occurs between the upper canine and premolar.

The anterior lower premolar is of special interest. As we saw in Chapter 13, the ape premolar is sectorial, consisting of a single cusp that hones against the upper canine, while the modern human premolar is bicuspid (Figure 16–25). The tooth in *A. afarensis* appears to be a transitional tooth between the apes and modern humans, showing a slight development of the second cusp. The teeth exhibit a significant degree

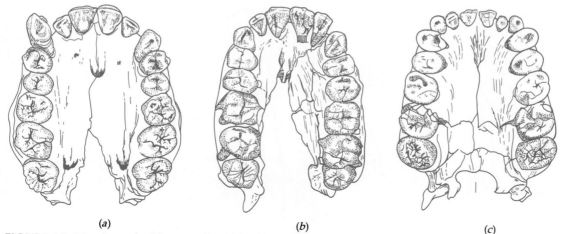

(a) (b) (c)

FIGURE 16–24 *Australopithecine dentition.* Upper dentition of *(a) Australopithecus afarensis* (AL 200-1a), *(b) Australopithecus africanus* (Sts 52b), and *(c) Australopithecus boisei* (OH 5). From Clark Spencer Larsen, Robert M. Martter, and Daniel L. Gebo, *Human Origins: The Fossil Record,* 2d ed., pp. 49, 59, and 66. Copyright ©1985, 1991 by Waveland Press, Inc., Prospect Heights, Ill. Reprinted with permission of the publisher.

of sexual dimorphism, the male upper canine being larger than that of the female.

In many ways the earlier dental and cranial remains of *A. anamensis* from Kanapoi show a number of similarities with the Miocene apes (Figure 16–A in the color insert: "Hominid Fossils"). For example, the jaw exhibits a shallow palate and large canines and the skull fragment displays a small ear opening similar to those of living African apes. On the other hand the canines have long vertical roots, they are implanted vertically in the jaw, and the tooth enamel is thick as is characteristic of the later hominids.

The apelike character of early australopithecine dentition is no longer seen in the later *A. africanus.* Now the dentition is basically humanlike, although the teeth are relatively larger than those of later *Homo.* The dentition of the robust australopithecines, however, shows many specialized features. These include thickened tooth enamel and an expansion in the size of the surface area of the premolars and molars. These and other changes may be related to a specialized diet consisting of tough, fibrous materials.

DECIDUOUS DENTITION The australopithecine fossils include dentition from infants and juveniles including the "Taung baby," the

first australopithecine to be discovered. This jaw contains a complete set of deciduous teeth and first adult molars in the process of erupting. In modern humans, these features would characterize the dentition of a 6-year-old child.

FIGURE 16–25 *Australopithecine premolar.* The anterior lower premolar from *A. afarensis* is compared with the premolars from a chimpanzee and a modern human. The human premolar is characterized by two cusps, A and B, while the chimpanzee sectorial premolar has only one cusp. Note that the premolar of *A. afarensis* is intermediate with a small development of cusp B.

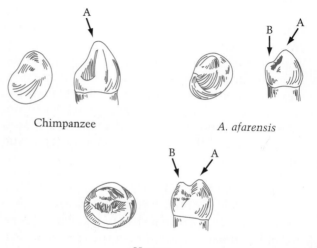

Chimpanzee   *A. afarensis*

Human

Many anthropologists see in the Taung dentition evidence of a long childhood period in the australopithecines. A feature of modern humans is a lengthened childhood period as compared to that of apes. This prolonged maturation is related to the development of learned behavior as a major mode of hominid adaptation.

Recent analyses of australopithecine, ape, and human dentition contradict the idea that the length of australopithecine childhood was more like the human pattern than the ape pattern. In one study, the development of australopithecine dental crowns and roots was plotted against development standards of both modern humans and apes. The dental pattern of the gracile australopithecines best fit the ape pattern. For example, in the apes the canine erupts after the eruption of the first molars, in contrast to the earlier eruption of the canine in contemporary humans. In the australopithecines the eruption of the canine is delayed, as it is in apes. This fact suggests that these forms had a relatively short maturation period, similar to those of chimpanzees and gorillas today.[18] On the other hand, the robust australopithecine dental pattern does not appear to resemble closely the dentition of either humans or apes.

Other paleoanthropologists have analyzed the development of tooth enamel, and their analyses suggest that enamel formed more rapidly in the early fossil hominids than it does in recent humans. Thus, the australopithecine molars appear to have formed and erupted more rapidly than those of contemporary humans.[19]

New medical technology, in particular the computerized axial tomography (CAT) scan, has been used to visualize the skull of the juvenile australopithecine from Taung. Investigators scanned the Taung skull and compared it with scans of both a human and a chimpanzee at the same stage of first-molar eruption. The scans revealed that the australopithecine dentition growth and eruption pattern more closely resembled that of a 3- to 4-year-old chimpanzee than that of a 5- to 7-year-old human.[20] Studies of bone growth in the Taung facial skeleton show a pattern similar to that of the chimpanzee.[21] All these studies suggest that the prolongation of childhood may be a relatively late development in hominid evolution.

The Australopithecine Brain

An important part of hominid evolution is the story of the development of the brain. Brains are not normally preserved in the fossil record. Brain size, and some very general features of brain anatomy, however, are reflected in the size and structure of the cranium or brain case.

The size of the brain can be estimated by measuring the volume or cranial capacity of the brain case. Cranial capacities of known australopithecine craniums vary from 400 to 530 cubic centimeters (Table 16–4). These cranial capacities reflect a small brain as compared to that of modern *H. sapiens*, which averages about 1350 cubic centimeters. In general the smallest australopithecine cranial capacities belong to *A. afarensis*, while the largest are found in robust specimens.

Some insights into australopithecine mentality might be revealed by an analysis of the structure of the brain. As we saw in Chapter 13, it is possible to make an endocranial cast that represents the shape and features of the inside of the brain case. Several natural endocranial casts have also survived. These casts provide some information about the pattern of convolutions and the location of grooves on the surface of the brain. Although this line of research is controversial, the australopithecine brain appears to exhibit a simpler pattern of convolutions with fewer grooves than are found in the modern human brain. It is, however, very difficult to make behavioral interpretations of this evidence.

[18]B. H. Smith, "Dental Development in *Australopithecus* and Early *Homo*," *Nature*, 323 (1986), 327–330.

[19]A. D. Beynon and B. A. Wood, "Patterns and Rates of Enamel Growth in the Molar Teeth of Early Hominids," *Nature*, 326 (1987), 493–496.

[20]G. C. Conroy and M. W. Vannier, "Dental Development of the Taung Skull from Computerized Tomography," *Nature*, 329 (1987), 625–627.

[21]T. G. Bromage, "Taung Facial Remodeling: A Growth and Development Study," in P. V. Tobias (ed.), *Hominid Evolution: Past, Present and Future* (New York: Liss, 1985), 239–245.

TABLE 16–4

AUSTRALOPITHECINE CRANIAL CAPACITIES

SPECIES	SPECIMEN	SITE	CRANIAL CAPACITY (CUBIC CENTIMETERS)
A. afarensis	AL 333-45	Hadar	500
A. afarensis	AL 162-28	Hadar	400
A. africanus	Sts 5	Sterkfontein	485
A. africanus	Sts 60	Sterkfontein	428
A. africanus	MLD 37/38	Makapansgat	435
A. aethiopicus	WT 17000	West Lake Turkana	410
A. robustus	SK 1585	Swartkrans	530
A. boisei	OH 5	Olduvai Gorge	530
A. boisei	KNM-ER 406	Koobi Fora	510
A. boisei	KNM-ER 13750	Koobi Fora	475
A. boisei	KNM-ER 407	Koobi Fora	506

ERECT BIPEDALISM AND THE BRAIN The athlete working out in a gym produces a great deal of heat which is generated by the muscles. The evaporation of sweat from the skin is one way that the human body keeps itself cool. Too great a rise in body temperature can lead to dysfunction and, ultimately, death. Although it is not as obvious, the brain also produces heat. In a large-brained animal, such as a human, the prevention of overheating of the brain is vital.

When the body temperature reaches a certain point, blood vessels just beneath the skin of the face and scalp dilate, bringing more blood to the skin where it is cooled by sweating. (It is interesting to note that humans have the greatest sweating capacity of any animal and that the density of sweat glands on the forehead is especially high.) This blood, now cooled, flows to the head and enters the brain case by way of small veins passing through small holes, or **foramina,** in the skull. Once in the brain case, the relatively cool blood flows through the brain, helping to keep it cool.

Paleoanthropologist Dean Falk examined many modern human and ape skulls, looking for these foramina.[22] She established that the skulls of modern African apes have very few, while modern humans have a large number of foram-

ina in the skull. Falk next looked for these foramina in fossil skulls. She discovered that while the skulls of A. robustus had very few, those of A. africanus had a significant number, although they were fewer than the number found in Homo.

Evidence suggests that the robust australopithecines may have lived in wooded areas. Being primarily vegetarians, they probably would have spent much of their daylight hours in shade and did not face major problems of exposure to solar radiation. The gracile australopithecines, on the other hand, very likely lived on the more open savanna and had to face the problems of heat overload.

Like other diurnal savanna mammals, the early hominids evolved mechanisms to prevent heat overload. Although the gracile australopithecines had relatively small brains, the mechanism for cooling the brain that evolved acted as a preadaptation for expansion of the brain in Homo. The foramina are present to a degree in A. africanus, and their number increases dramatically in Homo from about 2 million years ago. The increase in the number of these holes correlates with the increase in the size of the brain.

Because of the role that erect bipedalism plays in cooling the body, which was discussed earlier, and the development of a cooling mechanism for the brain, hominids are capable of being more active in the day when many competitors are rest-

[22]D. Falk, "Brain Evolution in Homo: The 'Radiator' Theory," Behavioral and Brain Sciences, 13 (1990), 333–381.

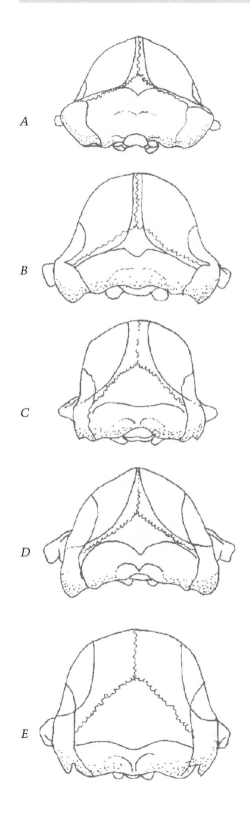

A

B

C

D

E

FIGURE 16–26 *Development of crests on australopithecine skulls.* The relatively small size of the brain case and the relatively large size of the muscles of the jaw and neck may result in the development of crests to allow adequate surface area for the attachment of these muscles. The nuchal muscle of the neck attaches to the nuchal crest at the back of the skull. The temporalis muscle of the jaw attaches to the sagittal crest along the top of the skull. These two crests may meet and fuse to form a compound temporo-nuchal crest. Cresting can be seen in these occipital views of the skulls of *(A)* chimpanzee, *(B) A. afarensis* (AL 333-45), *(C) A. africanus* (Sts 5), *(D) A. boisei* (KNM-ER 406), and *(E) H. habilis* (KNM-ER 1813), an early member of the genus *Homo* (Chapter 17).

ing in the shade of trees. They are also able to survive on less water and therefore to exploit fairly dry and open habitats in contrast to the apes.

The Australopithecine Skull

The structure of the australopithecine skull is a reflection of the relatively small cranium associated with a large dentition and powerful chewing apparatus. The skull of *A. afarensis* shows a marked **prognathism** (projecting forward) of the lower part of the facial skeleton. Air spaces, normally present within some bones of the skull, are enlarged **(pneumatized),** which reduces the weight of the skull. The temporalis muscle, an important muscle in chewing, is large. Its expansion is reflected in the development of a **temporo-nuchal crest** that provides an expanded surface area for attachment of the muscle to the skull (Figure 16–26).

The cranium of *A. africanus* is somewhat larger than that of *A. afarensis.* The skull of *A. africanus* is less heavily pneumatized, and the temporal and nuchal lines do not meet to form the temporal-nuchal crest. The face is somewhat shorter, because of a reduction in the size of the anterior dentition, and has a very characteristic concave, or "dish-shaped," profile. The nasal bones are relatively flat, and the forehead, behind the moderately large brow ridges, is low and flat. The top view shows a very marked **postorbital constriction.** When the skull is viewed from the rear, the lowest part of it is the point of greatest width.

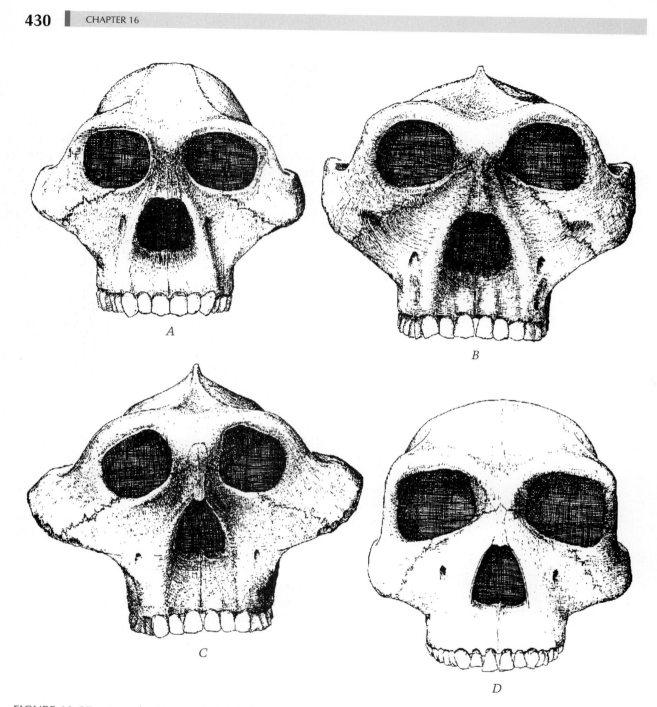

FIGURE 16–27 *Australopithecine facial skeletons.* Idealized composite drawings of *(A) A. africanus, (B) A. robustus, (C) A. boisei,* and *(D) Homo habilis,* an early member of the genus *Homo* (Chapter 17).

The increase in size of the posterior dentition in *A. africanus* is related to a more heavily built mandible. In these forms chewing created powerful stresses on the bones of the skull, and bony struts developed to withstand these stresses. For example, two bony columns, called **anterior pillars,** occur on both sides of the nasal aperture in *A. africanus* (Figure 16–27).

The robust australopithecines are characterized by a specialized chewing apparatus that includes large premolars and molars associated with a thick, deep mandible. Many features of the skull are related to the development of powerful chewing muscles that resulted in powerful forces being placed on the posterior teeth. The zygomatic arch is long and powerfully built for the attachment of the masseter muscle. It flares away from the skull to accommodate the temporalis muscle that passes between it and the side of the skull. A small anterior sagittal crest appears on top of the skull in most specimens for attachment of the powerful temporalis muscle.

Australopithecine Ecology

As is true for all animal populations, hominid evolution represents a continuous adaption to their ecological niches. Evolutionary modifications are often responses to changes in the environment or a response to competition with other populations. A challenge of paleontological studies is the great difficulty in determining the environmental factors associated with populations that are exclusively known from fossilized bones. Yet fossils do occur in a context along with the fossils of other animals and plants, archaeological material, and geological features. This allows us to develop some hypotheses regarding the lifeways of ancient populations.

LATE PALEOCENE ENVIRONMENTS   Paleoanthropologists search for environmental factors that help explain evolutionary change. Specifically, we are looking for possible explanations for the emergence of the various australopithecine species and for the origins of the genus *Homo*. It is significant that east Africa, an area associated with australopithecines and early *Homo* populations, is also an area that experienced major physical changes from Late Eocene through Late Pliocene times. Major episodes of faulting, warping, uplifting, and volcanic activity dramatically changed the east African landscape. The escarpments and gorges of the East African Rift System were formed. New mountains and highland areas formed, and river systems, lakes, and deltas were created, changed,

and destroyed. Associated with many of these geological changes were profound changes in climate.

Elizabeth Vrba refers to a major cooling event that took place approximately 2.5 million years ago.[23] This was a global climate change associated with the first widespread glaciation of the North Pole. This cooling event is associated with the spread of arid and open habitats in east and south Africa.

From the analyses of known dates for various fossil finds, it appears that this cooling event is associated with the appearance of new hominid species. These include the robust australopithecines and the genus *Homo*. It is really not known if the cooling event was the main factor that brought about the origins of the two lineages or whether they had already evolved before 2.5 million years ago and the cooling event was responsible for their rapid evolution into new forms.

The robust australopithecines are clearly adapted for a diet of tough, fibrous material such as that found in open grassland habitats. Specific anatomical adaptations for a grassland diet include thickened tooth enamel, expansion in size of the surface area of the premolars and molars, and an increase in the mass of the chewing muscles as seen in the robust and flaring zygomatic arch and the development of a sagittal crest. These anatomical changes parallel those of other mammals that feed on such material.

Analysis of the surfaces of the posterior teeth by the electron scanning microscope confirms this hypothesis. Richard Kay and Frederick Grine note that the wear pattern on the molars of the robust forms resembles those of living primates that eat hard food items. In contrast, the wear pattern on the molars of the gracile forms resembles more closely the pattern found on living primates that consume leaves and fruits.[24]

[23]E. S. Vrba, "Late Pliocene Climatic Events and Hominid Evolution," in F. E. Grine (ed.), *Evolutionary History of the "Robust" Australopithecines* (New York: Aldine de Gruyter, 1988), 405–426.

[24]R. F. Kay and F. E. Grine, "Tooth Morphology, Wear and Diet in *Australopithecus* and *Paranthropus* from Southern Africa," in F. E. Grine (ed.), *Evolutionary History of the "Robust" Australopithecines* (New York: Aldine de Gruyter, 1988), 427–447.

TABLE 16–5

PLIO-PLEISTOCENE HOMINID HABITAT, RESOURCE, GEOGRAPHICAL PREFERENCE*

HABITAT, RESOURCE, OR CONTEXT	A.r./A.b.	A.b.	H.h./A.b.
Montane forest†	x		
Gallery forest/riparian woodland‡		x	x
Closed habitat		x	
Closed/mesic§		x	
Groves of trees			x
Dambo (wet grassland)			x
Open savanna			x
Open/xeric‖	x	x	
Riverine		x	
Stream channel margins		x	x
Fresh water			x

*A.r. refers to *Australopithecus robustus*; A.b. to *Australopithecus boisei*; H.h. to *Homo habilis*.
†Mountain forests.
‡Forests and woodlands along rivers.
§Associated with a moderate amount of moisture.
‖Associated with a small amount of moisture.
Source: Adapted from N. E. Sikes, "Early Hominid Habitat Preferences in East Africa: Paleosol Carbon Isotopic Evidence," *Journal of Human Evolution*, 27 (1994) 25–45.

Several reconstructions of the paleohabitats associated with early hominid remains show many situations other than open grasslands. Table 16–5 lists the results of several of these studies. Nancy E. Sikes tells us that "available paleoenvironmental evidence from Plio-Pleistocene hominid fossil and archaeological localities in Africa . . . portrays a diversity of vegetation communities similar to today's topical savanna mosaic, from swamps to treeless or wooded grasslands, woodland, gallery forest, and montane forest. Very few early hominid localities are reconstructed as open grasslands."[25] Perhaps the robust australopithecines exploited the grasslands for food but retreated to more forest habitats for protection from carnivores and from ultraviolet radiation at other times.

As we saw in an earlier section, the evidence for tool using among the robust australopithecines is not clear but certainly remains a

possibility. In contrast to tool use by members of the genus *Homo*, the robust australopithecines could have used wood and even stone tools for digging up tubers and other materials that often grow underground in the savannas. Generally, we can think of the robust australopithecines as very specialized forms adapted to very demanding habitats.

The evidence for the extinction of the australopithecines is not clear. The youngest known australopithecine is SK 3 from Swartkrans, South Africa. This specimen of *A. robustus* dates from about 900,000 B.P. There is some evidence for another period of cooling at about this time, but the evidence for this event is not very clear. The fate of *A. boisei* from east Africa is uncertain since fossil evidence from between 1.2 million and 900,000 B.P. is scarce in that region.

Australopithecus and the Species Problem

Paleoanthropologists have observed a significant amount of diversity among the australopithecines whenever a fossil population is represented by many specimens. The question then arises: Does this variable assembly of specimens represent one highly variable species or does it represent several different species?

Some paleoanthropologists argue that the range of variation among the australopithecines may have been greater than that found among contemporary hominoids. For example, the degree of sexual dimorphism may have been considerably greater than the differences between the average male and female measurements.

The specimens from Hadar and Laetoli provide a good example of this dilemma. Many paleoanthropologists see these fossils as representing a single species, *A. afarensis*. The smaller specimens, such as "Lucy," would represent females, while the larger, more robust material, represented by AL 444-2, would represent males. If there is only one species present at this time, then *A. afarensis* could be the common stock from which the later australopithecines and *Homo* evolved. This viewpoint has led to an evolutionary scheme whereby *A. afarensis* is seen evolving into two branches, one leading to *A. africanus* and *Homo* and the other leading to

---

[25]N. E. Sikes, "Early Hominid Habitat Preferences in East Africa: Paleosol Carbon Isotopic Evidence," *Journal of Human Evolution*, 27 (1994), 26.

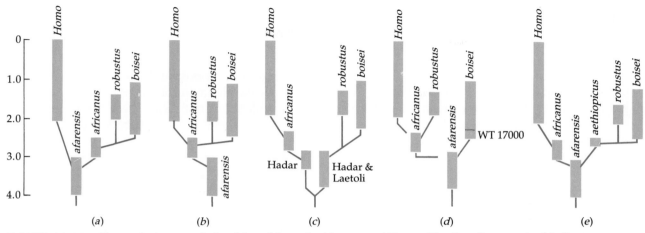

FIGURE 16–28 *The evolutionary relationships of* Australopithecus *and* Homo. The five diagrams in this figure represent different ideas about the relationship among the species of *Australopithecus* and the relationships between *Australopithecus* and *Homo*. The last two diagrams (*d* and *e*), which include the "Black Skull," are currently considered to be the most likely hominid phylogenies. The position of *A. ramidus* is still too tentative to place in these diagrams, although it might be directly ancestral to *A. afarensis*.

A. robustus and *A. boisei*. (Other variations of this scheme have also been proposed.)

Other paleoanthropologists see the Hadar and Laetoli populations as presenting two different species. One population shows robust features that would later lead to the robust australopithecines; the other population includes "Lucy" and leads to *A. africanus* and *Homo*. (Again, other variations on these themes have been suggested.) Several of these hypotheses are diagrammed in Figure 16–28.

A NOTE TO THE STUDENT While in the 1980s the general tendency among paleoanthropologists has been to see the existence of a relatively few number of variable species, today many scholars are proposing that this variation is best explained on the basis of the existence of multiple species. In fact, many new hominid species have been recently proposed; in the next two chapters we will see some examples of this within the genus *Homo*. It now appears that there may have been many more species of early non-*Homo* species of hominid than earlier believed, and that the early history of the Hominidae may have been marked by several evolutionary lines, perhaps the result of a modest adaptive radiation.

Students who are studying paleoanthropology for the first time are likely to be confused and

frustrated by the many interpretations of the fossil record. Yet one of the things that makes paleoanthropology so exciting is the constant discovery of new fossils and new techniques of investigation that lead to constant reevaluation of the data and development of new hypotheses.

During the past decade, several skillful, competent paleoanthropologists have proposed schemes that attempt to explain the evolutionary relationships among these early fossil forms. As time goes on, as new fossils are uncovered, and as new philosophies emerge, new hypotheses will be created. Through the scientific approach, we shall slowly come closer and closer to a true understanding of our evolutionary history, as surely as our early ancestors slowly evolved into new and more advanced forms and, ultimately, into modern human beings.

Summary

Four of the most significant features of the Hominidae are erect bipedalism, the manufacturing of tools, reduction in the size of the dentition, and the enlargement of the brain. The australopithecines are clearly erect bipeds as evidenced by their postcranial skeletons and the footprints preserved at Laetoli. Although the earliest australopithecines were erect bipeds, they are characterized by some features such as relatively long arms and long curved fingers and toes that suggest some proficiency in moving around in the trees.

There is no direct evidence that australopithecines manufactured tools. The earliest known stone tools date from about 2.6 to 2.4 million years ago. Many researchers attribute the tools exclusively to *Homo*. However, the fact that some stone tools may predate the origin of *Homo* and the fact that the australopithecine hand was quite capable of manufacturing tools, lends credibility to the idea that australopithecines made crude stone tools. They also very likely manufactured objects of perishable materials.

The dentition pattern of *A. afarensis* is, in many ways, intermediate between that of the apes and that of humans. For example, in *A. afarensis*, the dental arcade is intermediate in shape between that of modern humans and apes, the canines project above the tooth row, and a small diastema frequently occurs between the upper canine and premolar. The anterior lower premolar appears to be a transitional tooth between the apes and modern humans, showing a slight development of the second cusp. The dentition of the earlier *A. anamensis* shows even more similarities to the Miocene apes.

The dentition of *A. africanus* is basically humanlike, although the teeth are relatively larger than those of later *Homo*. The dentition of the robust australopithecines, however, shows many specialized features. These include thickened tooth enamel and an expansion in the size of the surface area of the premolars and molars. These and other changes may be related to a specialized diet consisting of tough, fibrous materials.

While the australopithecines resemble the later hominids with regard to their locomotor pattern, their brain size was comparatively small. The australopithecine cranial capacity ranged from 400 to 530 cubic centimeters. This number is similar to that of the larger apes and significantly smaller than the 1350-cubic-centimeter average for modern *H. sapiens*.

Although the fossils are associated with closed, wet habitats, the robust australopithecines are clearly adapted for a diet of tough, fibrous material such as that found in open grassland habitats. Specific anatomical adaptations include thickened tooth enamel, expansion in size of the surface area of the premolars and molars, and an increase in the mass of chewing muscles as seen in the robust and flaring zygomatic arch and the development of a sagittal crest. Although the evidence is not clear, these hominids could have used tools to dig up tubers and similar underground vegetation.

Paleoanthropologists have proposed several schemes to explain the evolutionary relationships among the several species of australopithecines. The two major schemes center on the role of *A. afarensis*. Some see *A. afarensis* as the ancestor of all later australopithecines and the genus *Homo*, while others see the fossils from Hadar and Laetoli as representing two species, one giving rise to *A. africanus* and *Homo* and the other evolving into the robust australopithecine populations.

STUDY QUESTIONS

1. Why were the fossils from Aramis originally assigned to the species *Australopithecus ramidus* and then reassigned to the species *Ardipithecus ramidus*?

2. Describe the geographical distribution of australopithecine sites. What is the range of dates for these sites?

3. What evidence suggests that the australopithecines were erect bipeds? How did the locomotor pattern of *A. afarensis* differ from that of *H. sapiens*?

4. Did the australopithecines use and manufacture tools? Describe the anatomical and archaeological evidence. If they did, how could the use of tools differ in the australopithecines compared with *Homo*?

5. The architecture of the skull is, in part, a reflection of the dentition and the jaw. In the robust australopithecines, what are some of the skull features that can be associated with the large posterior dentition of these hominids?

6. Some paleoanthropologists consider *A. afarensis* an intermediate between the Miocene hominoids and the hominids. What are some of the apelike characteristics of the skeleton of *A. afarensis*?

HOMINID FOSSILS

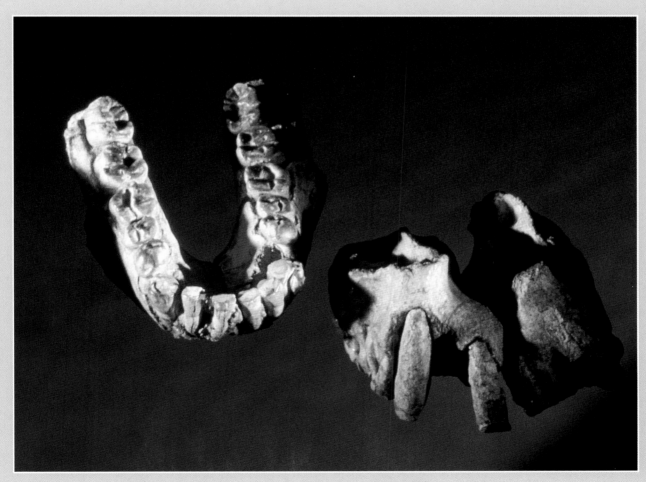

FIGURE 16-A *(left)* A mandible (KNM-KP 29281) and *(right)* maxilla (KNM-KP 29283) of *Australopithecus anamensis* from the site of Kanapoi, Kenya.

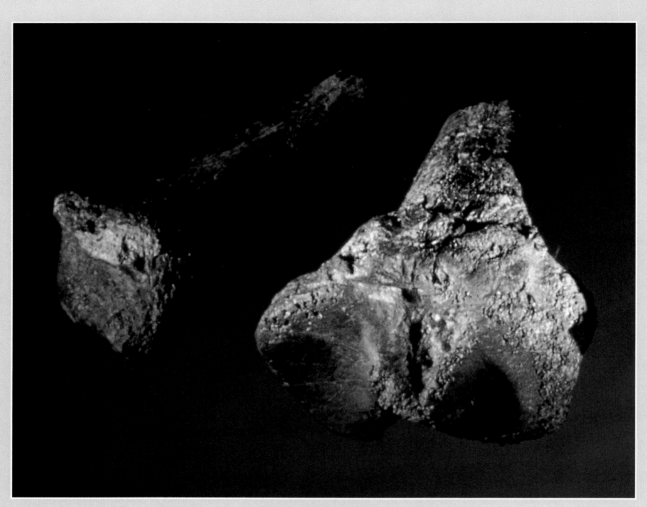

FIGURE 16-B Two pieces of a right tibia of *Australopithecus anamensis* from the site of Kanapoi, Kenya. The section on the right is part of the knee while the section on the left articulates with the foot.

FIGURE 16-C   The upper jaw and palate of *Australopithecus afarensis*, AL 200-1, from Hadar, Ethiopia.

FIGURE 16-D A skull of *Homo erectus*, KNM-ER 3733, from Koobi Fora, East Lake Turkana, Kenya.

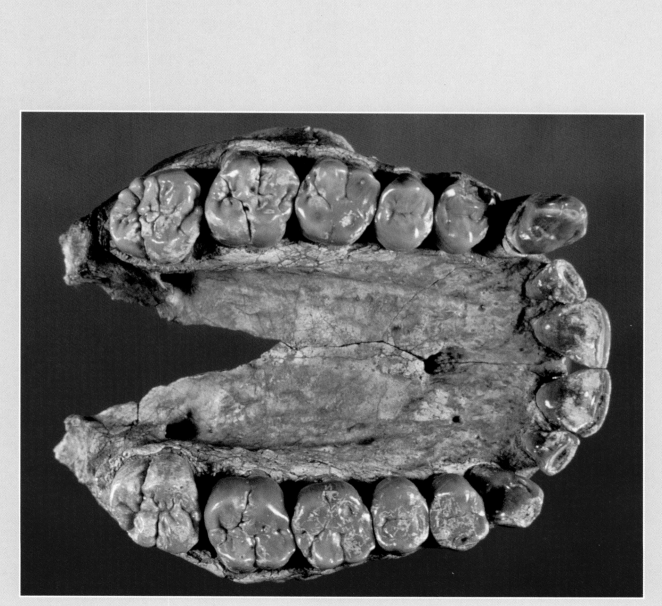

FIGURE 16-C The upper jaw and palate of *Australopithecus afarensis*, AL 200-1, from Hadar, Ethiopia.

FIGURE 16-D A skull of *Homo erectus*, KNM-ER 3733, from Koobi Fora, East Lake Turkana, Kenya.

7. What are the major differences between *A. africanus* and the robust australopithecines?

8. What are the six australopithecine species discussed in this chapter? What are the relationships among these populations in time, space, and evolutionary ties?

SUGGESTED READINGS

Conroy, G. C. *Primate Evolution.* New York: Norton, 1990. This book presents a detailed and well-organized introduction to the australopithecines.

Dart, R. A. *Adventures with the Missing Link.* New York: Viking, 1959. This is Raymond Dart's autobiographical account of his work with the australopithecines of south Africa.

Day, M. *Guide to Fossil Man,* 4th ed. Chicago: University of Chicago Press, 1986. This guide consists of entries detailing important fossil finds.

Delson, E. (ed.). *Ancestors: The Hard Evidence.* New York: Liss, 1985. This volume is a collection of presentations made at a symposium held at the American Museum of Natural History in 1984 that summarize our knowledge of the fossil record at that point in time.

Grine, F. E. (ed.). *Evolutionary History of the Robust Australopithecines.* New York: Aldine, 1988. This book presents a collection of essays on various aspects of the robust australopithecines.

Johanson, D. C., and M. A. Edey. *Lucy: The Beginnings of Humankind.* New York: Simon and Schuster, 1981. This is a fascinating behind-the-scenes account of paleoanthropology. The book focuses on the fossil nicknamed "Lucy" and the change in thinking about human evolution that this find has prompted in many circles.

Reader, J. *Missing Links: The Hunt for Earliest Man,* rev. ed. Boston: Little, Brown, 1989. This book tells the story of the hunt for and discovery of many important fossil hominids.

Willis, D. *The Hominid Gang.* New York: Viking, 1989. This easy-to-read book describes the lives and work of the paleoanthropologists responsible for our knowledge of the australopithecines.

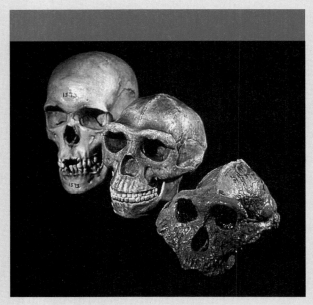

Homo erectus skull (center) between modern *Homo sapiens* skull (left) and australopithecine skull (right).

Homo erectus *may well be the most interesting and the most important of the fossil hominids. It is the species of the genus* Homo *immediately preceding ourselves, the first hominid species to show a recognizably human adaptive pattern, the first hominid to successfully inhabit regions outside of Africa, and the first hominid to, as Louis Leakey put it, "make tools according to a set and regular pattern."*[1]

Milfred H. Wolpoff and A. Nkini

[1]M. H. Wolpoff and A. Nkini, "Early and Early Middle Pleistocene Hominids from Asia and Africa," in E. Delson (ed.), *Ancestors: The Hard Evidence* (New York: Liss, 1985), 202.

CHAPTER

17

HOMO HABILIS
AND *HOMO ERECTUS*

All modern human beings belong to the genus *Homo, Homo* being the Latin word for "human being." While anthropologists use the term *human* in many of their discussions, *human* is not a technical term. We will leave the question of what it is to be human to the philosophers and cultural anthropologists.

However, the origins of our "humanity" lie in the origins and evolution of the genus *Homo.* What then are the essential characteristics that define this genus? Since hominid adaptations are often behavioral, we must look beyond the fossil record and examine the archaeological record as well. This chapter will examine both the paleontology and archaeology of those members of the genus *Homo* that arose before the evolution of our own species, *Homo sapiens.*

THE EVOLUTION OF THE GENUS *HOMO*

A major problem faced by paleoanthropologists is the identification of the earliest members of the genus *Homo*. Since *Homo* most likely evolved directly from *Australopithecus*, early specimens of *Homo* retain many features of the earlier genus. Many Early Pleistocene fossils show interesting yet puzzling combinations of features, making it extremely difficult to assign a particular specimen to one or another of the two genera.

The earliest members of the genus *Homo* have been placed in the species *Homo habilis*, although some paleoanthropologists see enough variation in the fossil record to warrant the creation of additional species. *Homo habilis* is followed by *Homo erectus*, a very successful group that migrated out of Africa to inhabit major portions of Europe and Asia. These species are the subjects of this chapter.

The Origins of the Genus Homo

As we saw in the previous chapter, the climate of earth cooled about 2.5 million years ago. This was associated with drier climates, more open habitats, and the development of marked seasons. Following this time we see in the fossil record many new species of australopithecines: *A. africanus*, *A. robustus*, and *A. boisei*. We also find the earliest members of the genus *Homo*. A temporal bone from the Chemeron Formation of Kenya may be the oldest known member of the genus *Homo*. First described in 1967, this small part of a cranium has recently been dated at about 2.4 million B.P.[2]

We do not know whether the origin of this new genus was a response to the change in climate or whether the lineage leading to *Homo* had already evolved and the climatic changes merely shaped its continuing evolution. Members of the genus *Homo* coexisted with the australopithecines until the latter became extinct some 900,000 years ago.

It is reasonable to conclude that the genus *Homo* evolved from an australopithecine. From the chronologies of the australopithecines this ancestor was probably not a robust australopithecine. *Homo* most likely arose from *A. afarensis*, *A. africanus*, or another yet undiscovered population. Figure 16–28 diagrams some suggested affiliations between *Australopithecus* and *Homo*.

MORPHOLOGY OF THE GENUS *HOMO*
Homo and *Australopithecus* both share many features that unite them in the family Hominidae. How, then, do these two genera differ?

Table 17–1 compares the two hominid genera. Compared with *Australopithecus*, *Homo* teeth and jaws are small. The zygomatic arch is smaller, and the sagittal crest never develops on the brain case. The cranial capacity of *Homo* exceeds the range of cranial capacities in *Australopithecus*. Australopithecine cranial capacities generally fall between 400 and 530 cubic centimeters, while the various known fossil representatives of *Homo* range between about 500 and 1750 cubic centimeters (Table 17–2). The lower values are found in the earlier species.

Several postcranial bones and bone fragments are known from both genera, with most of them representing the leg. Although separate *Homo* and *Australopithecus* patterns can be identified, the distinctions between the two morphological patterns are primarily differences in proportions and details of structure. Members of both genera were erect bipeds.

CLASSIFICATION OF THE GENUS *HOMO*
Traditionally *Homo* encompasses three distinct species, although some paleoanthropologists place some early specimens in other species. The earliest well-known species of the genus *Homo* is *Homo habilis* ("handy human being"). The fossils from Koobi Fora and Olduvai Gorge in east Africa show a great deal of variation. Most paleoanthropologists see this as variation within the species. Others, however, believe that some of the variation is best explained in terms of more than one species. For example, Bernard Wood places many specimens from Koobi Fora in the species *Homo rudolfensis*.[3]

---

[2]A. Hill et al., "Earliest *Homo*," *Nature*, 355 (1992), 719–722.

[3]B. Wood, "Origin and Evolution of the Genus *Homo*," *Nature*, 355 (1992), 783–790.

TABLE 17–1

THE GENERA *AUSTRALOPITHECUS* AND *HOMO* COMPARED

AUSTRALOPITHECUS	HOMO
Cranial capacity of 400–530 cubic centimeters.	Cranial capacity of 500–2300 cubic centimeters.
Bones of brain case thin.	Bones of brain case very thick to thin.
Crests may develop on brain case.	Crests never develop on brain case.
Point of maximum width of brain case near bottom.	Point of maximum width of brain case bottom to top.
Moderate to large brow ridge.	Large to slight brow ridge.
Marked postorbital constriction.	Moderate to slight postorbital constriction.
Flaring of zygomatic arch.	Zygomatic arch not flared.
Facial skeleton large relative to size of brain case.	Facial skeleton small relative to size of brain case.
Facial skeleton often dish-shaped.	Facial skeleton never dish-shaped.
Suture between nasal and frontal bones upside-down V.	Suture between nasal and frontal bones horizontal.
Anterior pillars alongside nasal aperture.	No anterior pillars.
Relatively large prognathous jaw.	Jaw less massive.
Lack of chin.	Chin may develop.
Premolars and molars large to extremely large.	Smaller premolars and molars.
Thin postcranial bones.	Thick to thin postcranial bones.

The next species to appear is *Homo erectus* ("erect human being"), although some paleoanthropologists place the early African *H. erectus* fossils in still another species, *Homo ergaster.* The one living member of the genus is *Homo sapiens* ("wise human being").

We can view the evolution of *Homo* in many ways. Some paleoanthropologists see it as a continuum in which arbitrary divisions define the three species; others see this evolution as an example of punctuated equilibrium (Chapter 6). In the latter view, each species is seen as relatively stable over fairly long periods, with short periods of relatively rapid change occurring at the boundaries between the species. Because many regions and many time intervals are not represented in the fossil record, we must wait until more fossil hominids are discovered before we can learn which hypothesis is closer to the actual situation.

Homo habilis

The first specimen of *H. habilis* was discovered by the Leakeys in 1960 at Olduvai Gorge. The original specimen consists of a damaged mandible and parts of the brain case of a juvenile; later a mandible and cranial bones of an adult were recovered. In 1964 these specimens and others were placed in the newly defined species. The *H. habilis* finds from Olduvai Gorge date from 2 to 1.7 million B.P.

In 1986 Tim White discovered another specimen of *H. habilis* at Olduvai Gorge (see color insert "Excavations at Dik Dik Hill, Olduvai Gorge"). This find is significant because it includes not only parts of the skull but also bones of the right arm and leg that belong to the same individual. For the first time, cranial and postcranial remains attributed to *H. habilis* were found in association. The association, however, is puzzling. Aspects of the skull appear to be rather *Homo*-like, yet some of the postcranial bones resemble those of the australopithecines. This find dates to about 1.8 million B.P.

Several hominid fossils were recovered from Koobi Fora, East Lake Turkana, between 1969 and 1976. One of these, KNM-ER 1470, is shown in Figure 17–1. These fossils date between 2 and 1.6 million B.P. The material from Koobi Fora, however, shows well-defined variation and can be divided into a large and a small series. The large specimens, which include KNM-ER 1470,

TABLE 17–2

CRANIAL CAPACITIES OF *HOMO*

SPECIES	SPECIMEN	SITE	CRANIAL CAPACITY (CUBIC CENTIMETERS)
H. habilis	OH 7	Olduvai Gorge	674
H. habilis	OH 16	Olduvai Gorge	638
H. habilis	OH 24	Olduvai Gorge	594
H. habilis	KNM-ER 1470	East Lake Turkana	752
H. habilis	KNM-ER 1813	East Lake Turkana	509
H. erectus	OH 9	Olduvai Gorge	1067
H. erectus	KNM-ER 3733	East Lake Turkana	850
H. erectus	WT 15000	West Lake Turkana	900
H. erectus	Skull III	Zhoukoudian	918
H. erectus	Skull X	Zhoukoudian	1225
H. erectus	Skull XI	Zhoukoudian	1015
H. sapiens	Kabwe	Kabwe	1285
H. sapiens	Steinheim	Steinheim	1100
H. sapiens	Swanscombe	Swanscombe	1325
H. sapiens	Neandertal	Neander Valley	1525
H. sapiens	La Chapelle	La Chapelle-aux-Saints	1625
H. sapiens	Cro-Magnon	Cro-Magnon	1600

have a relatively large brain case with a cranial capacity of about 750 cubic centimeters. The face is broad and flat, teeth and jaws are large, and it exhibits a slight brow ridge.

The small specimens have smaller cranial capacities; the cranial capacity of KMN-ER 1813 is approximately 510 cubic centimeters (Figure 17–2). They have smaller faces and jaws, smaller teeth, and more prominent brow ridges. Opinion varies on whether these forms represent a single variable species or two distinct species. Those who take the latter view have suggested that they be placed in the species *Homo rudolfensis*. A possible *H. habilis* from Sterkfontein, South Africa, is estimated to have lived between 2 and 1.5 million years ago.

THE MORPHOLOGY OF *HOMO HABILIS*
The genus *Homo* is characterized by several major evolutionary trends that contrast with the australopithecines. First, the *Homo* dental pattern shows a relative decrease in the size of the molars and premolars as compared with the size of the incisors and canines. In *H. habilis* the front teeth are approximately the same size as those of *Australopithecus*, but the premolars and molars show the beginning of size reduction.

Most cranial remains of *H. habilis* are relatively incomplete, but estimates of cranial capacity average above 500 cubic centimeters, and it may reach as high as 750 cubic centimeters. In these estimates we see the beginning of the expansion of brain size that characterizes the genus.

The bones of the cranium are thinner, and the cranium is more delicate and rounded than that of the australopithecines. The cranium lacks developed muscular crests and prominent anterior pillars. In many ways the *H. habilis* cranium is also more delicate and rounded than the cranium of the later *H. erectus*. There is variation in the dimensions of the facial skeletons among the known specimens. Some specimens retain some features found in the australopithecine face such as facial and mandibular bone characteristics related to powerful chewing.

Another feature of the genus *Homo* is a general increase in body size. Determining stature from the length of the femur, paleoanthropologists estimate that *H. habilis* from Olduvai Gorge (OH 62) stood approximately 1 to 1.25 meters (3.3 to 4.1 feet) tall and was similar in size to *A. afarensis*. This suggests that the evolution of large body size in *Homo* took place at a later stage. The limb proportions of *H. habilis* resemble those of *A.*

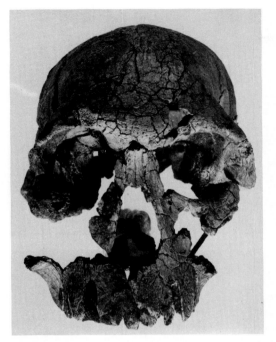

FIGURE 17–1 Homo habilis *(KNM-ER 1470) from Lake Turkana.*

FIGURE 17–2 *Cast of the skull of* Homo habilis *(KNM-ER 1813) from Lake Turkana.*

afarensis, suggesting that *H. habilis* possessed long, powerful arms. Yet other features of the postcranial skeleton are relatively modern.

Perhaps it is best to think of *H. habilis* as a transitional species that lived between 2 and 1.5 million years ago. Although members of this species are the earliest individuals to be classified into *Homo,* as transitional forms they exhibit older australopithecine features in combination with newly evolved traits that became characteristic of *Homo.* One explanation for the variation in the facial skeleton among the known specimens is that it represents a greater degree of sexual dimorphism than is found in later species. On the other hand, more than one species may have existed at this time.

Summary

Australopithecine incisors and canines are relatively small, while the premolars and molars are relatively large; this correlates with the massiveness of the jaw, the flaring of the zygomatic arch, and the development of a small sagittal crest. The dentition of *Homo* is smaller, as is the jaw; the zygomatic arch is reduced in size, and the sagittal crest never develops on the brain case. The cranial capacity of the known fossils of *Homo* range between about 500 and 1750 cubic centimeters, in contrast with the australopithecine cranial capacities of 400 to 530 cubic centimeters.

The earliest specimen of *Homo* appears to be a 2.4-million-year-old fossil from Kenya. It has not been assigned to a specific species. The earliest named species of the genus *Homo* is *H. habilis,* known from specimens found at Olduvai Gorge and East Lake Turkana in east Africa and Sterkfontein in South Africa; they lived from about 2 to 1.5 million years ago. The front teeth of *H. habilis* are approximately the same size as those of *Australopithecus,* but the premolars and molars show the beginning of size reduction. Estimates of cranial capacity average between about 500 and 750 cubic centimeters. The bones of the cranium are thin, and the cranium in general is delicate and rounded. Paleoanthropologists estimate that *H. habilis* from Olduvai Gorge was approximately 1 to 1.25 meters (3.3 to 4.1 feet) tall and was similar in size to *A. afarensis;* the limb proportions resemble those of *A. afarensis,* suggesting that *H. habilis* possessed long, powerful arms. It is best to think of *Homo habilis* as a transitional species exhibiting older australopithecine features in combination with newly evolved traits of the genus *Homo.*

HOMO ERECTUS

The earliest specimens of *H. erectus* date from about 1.8 million years ago. These early specimens resemble *H. habilis.* Fossil materials of both *Homo* and *Australopithecus* have been found in the same level of the same site at East Lake Turkana. Here the remains of the robust australopithecine KNM-ER 406 (Figure 16–12) are found with those of the *H. erectus* KNM-ER 3733 (Figure 17–3, Figure 16–D in the color insert: "Hominid Fossils"). These finds date to between 1.6 and 1.3 million years ago.

At some unknown point in time, some *H. erectus* populations left the tropical and subtropical regions of Africa, which had been the hominid homeland, and wandered northward into more temperate and subarctic habitats. By the beginning of the Middle Pleistocene, about 700,000 years ago, *Australopithecus* and *H. habilis* had long since been extinct, and members of the species *H. erectus* were the only hominids occupying the earth.

The Discoveries of *Homo erectus*

The first discoveries of *H. erectus* were made in the 1890s. As each new find appeared, it was placed in a new species and often in a new genus as well; some generic names were "*Pithecanthropus,*" "*Sinanthropus,*" and "*Atlanthropus.*" Most paleoanthropologists today consider all these forms to be variants of the single species *H. erectus.* Fossils that most paleoanthropologists

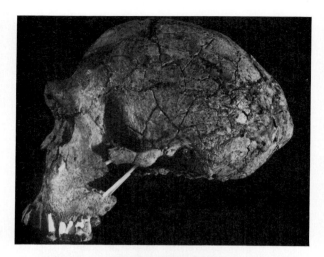

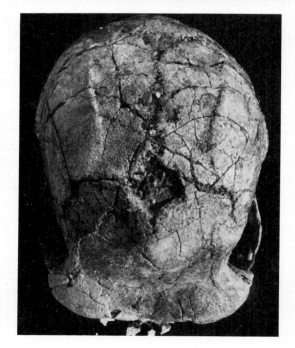

FIGURE 17–3 Homo erectus *(KNM-ER 3733) from Lake Turkana.* Side, front, and top views.

place within the species *H. erectus* have been found in Java, China, central Asia, and Africa.

HOMO ERECTUS FROM JAVA   Eugene Dubois, a nineteenth-century Dutch anatomist, believed that Asia was the place of human origin. To prove his point, he traveled to the Dutch East Indies (now Indonesia), and there, in 1890 at Kedung Brubus, he discovered a hominid jaw fragment. Dubois continued his work; in 1891 he discovered a small skullcap at Trinil, Java. A year later, he found a femur from a hominid that walked bipedally (Figure 17–4). The original name given to the material found by Dubois, *"Pithecanthropus erectus,"* refers to this erect posture. Dubois's material is part of the Trinil fauna, which characterizes the Kabuh Beds of Java. These beds have been dated to the First Glacial, approximately 700,000 to 500,000 B.P.

Dubois's work in Java and the discovery of a "primitive" cranium associated with a relatively modern femur excited the anthropological community. Soon paleoanthropologists traveled to Java to search for the remains of early hominids. Additional specimens of *H. erectus* were found at Sangiran, Modjokerto, Ngandong, and Sambungmachan.

The notion that Asia was the homeland of *Homo* weakened with the discovery of African *H. habilis* and *H. erectus* fossils dating to between 2 and 1.6 million years B.P. Until recently, the oldest Asian *Homo* fossils were generally thought to be less than 1 million years old. Then, in 1994, Carl Swishen and Garniss Curtis, using a new dating method, redated the Java finds from Sangiran and Mojokerto to 1.8 and 1.6 million

B.P., respectively.[4] These new dates reopen the question of the homeland of modern humans.

HOMO ERECTUS FROM CHINA   In 1927 a molar tooth was discovered in a cave near the village of Zhoukoudian, near Beijing, China. This tooth was placed in a new species, *"Sinanthropus pekinensis."* The next 10 years saw the recovery of over a dozen skulls and almost 150 teeth. These fossils were lost at the time of the Japanese invasion of China during World War II (see Box 17–1). Except for two teeth from the first excavation, all we have today of the original material are meticulous descriptions and excellent casts. Since 1979, new excavations have been conducted at Zhoukoudian. Abundant stone tools and remains of nonhominid animals have been found, but *H. erectus* material has been fragmentary.

The fossils from Zhoukoudian show a degree of variability and sexual dimorphism greater than that found among modern peoples. The skulls are often considered to represent "typical" *H. erectus* forms (Figure 17–5). Cranial capacities of the Zhoukoudian population, based on the analysis of five of the skulls, show a range from 915 to 1225 cubic centimeters.

The dating of the Zhoukoudian fossils is extremely difficult since we have no chronometric dates. The fossils are usually considered to be of Middle Pleistocene age, approximately 400,000

---

[4]C. C. Swishen, III, G. H. Curtis, T. Jacob, A. G. Getty, A. Suprijo, and Widiasmoro, "Age of the Earliest Known Hominids in Java, Indonesia," *Science*, 263 (1994), 1118–1121.

FIGURE 17–4   *The femur of* Homo erectus *from Java.*

BOX 17–1

THE DISAPPEARANCE OF THE ZHOUKOUDIAN FOSSILS

The discoveries of *Homo erectus* fossils at Zhoukoudian, China, caused great excitement among anthropologists, paleontologists, and the public. The fossils represented a wealth of information about prehistoric humans and their culture.

The invasion of China by Japan at the beginning of World War II created difficulties for the project, and the excavations were suspended in 1937. The fossils continued to be studied at the Peking Union Medical College, however, for at this time the United States was not at war with Japan and the Japanese invaders were respecting foreign interests in China. The project participants, though, expecting an eventual conflict between Japan and the United States, were concerned about the safety of the fossils.

In late November 1941, the fossils from Zhoukoudian were carefully packed into two redwood crates and placed in the college vault. From the vault they were transported by car to the Marine headquarters in Beijing, where they were transferred to regulation footlockers. These footlockers were then transported by train to Camp Holcomb, 140 miles away, where they were stored. They were to remain in the barracks until the arrival of the USS *President Harrison,* which would transport the fossils to the United States for the duration of the war.

The Japanese attacked Pearl Harbor on December 7, 1941; in China, lying east of the international date line, it was Monday morning, December 8. The Japanese immediately took over the Peking Union Medical College and began searching for the fossils.

The fossils, however, were no longer at the college, having been moved to Camp Holcomb. The Japanese took over the camp; there were no casualties. The Americans at the camp were placed under arrest and led away from the camp— the fossils were never seen again.

Many hypotheses have been proposed about the fate of the Zhoukoudian fossils. Some believe that they were simply destroyed by the Japanese invaders, who may not have understood their value. Others believe that they were transported to Japan, southeast Asia, or Taiwan. They may even have eventually arrived in the United States. Whatever the case may be, in spite of many attempts to discover their fate, to this day the mystery of the fossils' disappearance remains unsolved.

Exacting measurements and descriptions of the fossils were published, and fine plaster casts were made. Yet many modern techniques of analysis, such as the use of x-rays and CAT scans on fossil material, did not exist in the 1930s. The rediscovery of the fossils would provide the scientific community with important new knowledge for the understanding of human evolution.

References: For detailed information on the disappearance of the Zhoukoudian fossils and the attempts to recover them, see C. G. Janus, *The Search for Peking Man* (New York: Macmillan, 1975); and H. L. Shapiro, *Peking Man* (New York: Simon and Schuster, 1974).

years old. They were found in an archaeological context associated with the remains of butchered animals, including insectivores, bats, rabbits, rodents, carnivores, deer, and rhinoceroses. Also found were many stone chopper tools and evidence of fire in the form of ashes and charcoal.

Several other sites have been excavated in China. In 1965 a skull was recovered in Lant'ien County, Shensi Province, that might be older than the fossils from Zhoukoudian. Dated at approximately 800,000 to 730,000 B.P., it may be the oldest *H. erectus* find in China. The skull has a small cranial capacity, which is estimated at 780 cubic centimeters. Some bones of the skull are thicker than those of any other *H. erectus* yet discovered. Other sites include Hexian, Gongwangling, Chenjiawo, Yuanmou, Yunxi, Yunxian, Xichuan, and Nanzhao.

HOMO ERECTUS FROM CENTRAL ASIA   In 1991 a mandible was described at a scientific meeting held to commemorate the 100th anniversary of the discovery of the first *H. erectus*

FIGURE 17–5   Homo erectus *from Zhoukoudian, China. (a)* Side view of male skull; *(b)* top view of reconstructed skull; *(c)* front view of reconstructed skull.

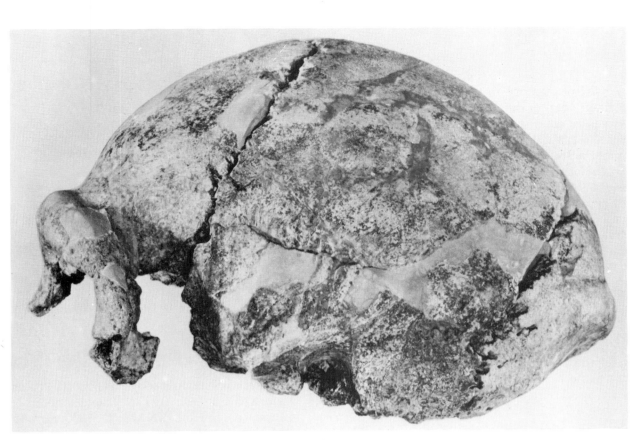

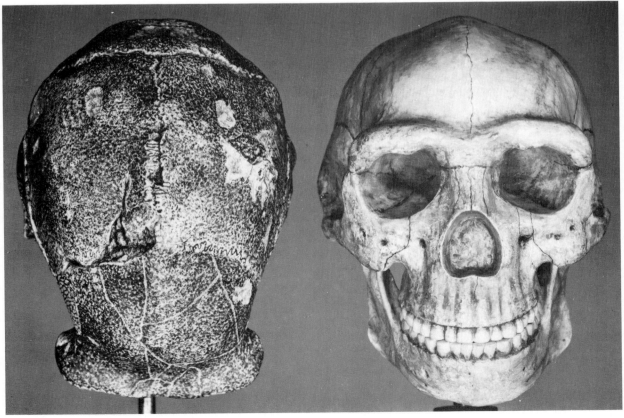

(a)

(b)   (c)

in Java. The newly discovered jaw was found at the site of Dmanisi in the Republic of Georgia, formerly part of the Soviet Union. The well-preserved *H. erectus* mandible contains a complete set of teeth and resembles closely the *H. erectus* material from Africa.[5]

The basalt layer immediately underlying the bed in which the fossil was found has been dated by potassium-argon dating to 1.8 million B.P. The fossil bed was also dated by geomagnetic dating and falls within the Olduvai subchron which is dated at between 1.95 and 1.77 million B.P. These dates make the Dmanisi mandible the oldest hominid found in Eurasia. It very likely represents one of the earliest hominid populations to have migrated out of Africa.

HOMO ERECTUS FROM AFRICA   We will refer to the African hominids that lived during the same time as the Asian *H. erectus* by the same species name. An increasing number of paleontologists, however, see enough anatomical difference between the Asian and African forms to call them by different names. In this scheme the African hominids are labelled *Homo ergaster* while the Asian fossils retain the name *Homo erectus.*

Several fossils that can be attributed to *Homo erectus* are known from Olduvai Gorge. The first to be discovered (OH 9) was found by Louis Leakey in 1960 and consists of a partial cranium; it was found at the top of Bed II and is about 1.25 million years old (Figure 17–6). OH 9 is one of the largest-known *H. erectus* skulls. Other, younger fossils include a small, fragmented, and rather incomplete skull (OH 12), partial mandibles, and a few postcranial bones.

What is perhaps the oldest *H. erectus* comes from East Lake Turkana. A femur (KNM-ER 1481A) and a pelvis (KNM-ER 3228) discovered beneath the KBS tuff (Chapter 16) suggest the presence of *H. erectus* before 1.8 million B.P. Many *H. erectus* fossils have been recovered at East Lake Turkana, including a very complete skull (KNM-ER 3733), pictured in Figure 17–3,

FIGURE 17–6   *Cast of the skull of* Homo erectus (*OH 9*) *from Olduvai Gorge.*

which is from an individual who lived about 1.8 million years ago.

A very exciting find was made in 1984 on the western side of Lake Turkana, dated at about 1.6 million B.P. This find, KNM-WT 15000, from the site of Nariokotome, consists of an almost complete skeleton of a subadult male *H. erectus* close to 12 years old (Figure 17–7 and 17–8). It is estimated that "Turkana boy," if he had lived, would have reached about 183 centimeters (6 feet) in height. Until this discovery, it was generally believed that *H. erectus* populations were composed of relatively short individuals as compared with many modern *H. sapiens* populations, with males not exceeding about 168 centimeters (5 feet 6 inches) in height.

In the early excavations at Swartkrans, in South Africa, some bones were found that differed from those of the australopithecines; first named "*Telanthropus capensis,*" many now consider them to be *H. erectus*. Unfortunately, the remains are fragmentary.

Other, less well-known fossils are from north Africa. The oldest north African material, from Ternifine, Algeria, dates from the Mindel Glacial, about 700,000 to 500,000 years ago. This material consists of three mandibles, a piece of skull, and a few teeth, all of which show many similarities to the *H. erectus* specimens from Zhoukoudian. Additional material is known from Sidi Abderrahman and Thomas Quarries, also in Algeria. Some of the more important finds of *H. erectus* are pictured in Figure 17–9.

[5]L. Gabunia and A. Vekua, "A Plio-Pleistocene Hominid from Dmanisi, East Georgia, Caucasus," *Nature*, 373 (1995), 509–512.

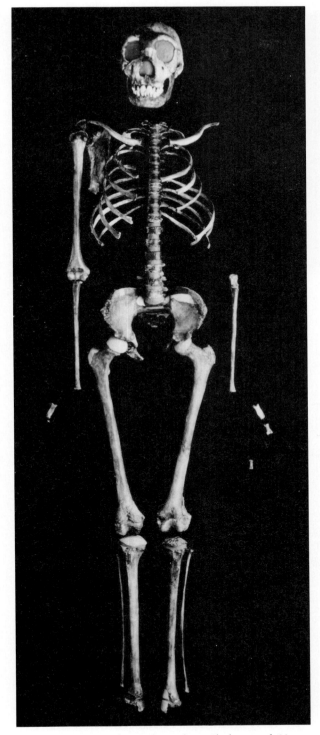

FIGURE 17–7   *Lake Turkana boy.* Skeleton of *Homo erectus* (WT 15000) from West Turkana.

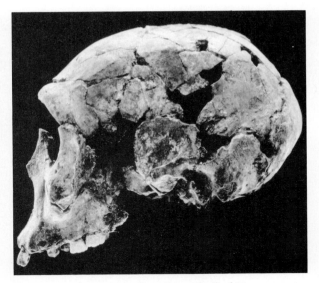

FIGURE 17–8   *Lake Turkana boy.* Skull of *Homo erectus* (WT 15000) from West Turkana.

HOMO ERECTUS FROM EUROPE   Did *H. erectus* ever occupy Europe? Before 1995 we would have said that the earliest hominids occupied Europe between 524,000 and 478,000 years ago. A fragmentary fossil tibia and a tooth that may be as old as this come from Boxgrove, England. A mandible found near the village of Mauer, near Heidelberg, Germany, may be about the same age (Chapter 18). Recently discovered fossils, including the fragmentary remains of at least four hominids and artifacts found in the limestone cavern of Gran Dolina in the Atapuerca Mountains of Spain, may be considerably older than 780,000 B.P.[6]

The classification of the Boxgrove and Heidelberg fossils is problematic. Some paleoanthropologists see them as being archaic *H. sapiens*, while others see them as European representatives of *H. erectus*. The Gran Dolina hominids are equally problematic. While they are too early and do not display enough characteristics of *H. sapiens* to be called archaic *H. sapiens*, some paleoanthropologists suggest that they are not *H.*

[6]E. Carbonell, et al., "Lower Pleistocene Hominids and Artifacts from Atapuerca-TD6 (Spain)," *Science,* 269 (1995), 826–830; J. M. Pares and A. Perez-Gonzalez, "Paleomagnetic Age for Hominid Fossils at Atapuerca Archaeological Site, Spring," *Science,* 269 (1995), 830–832.

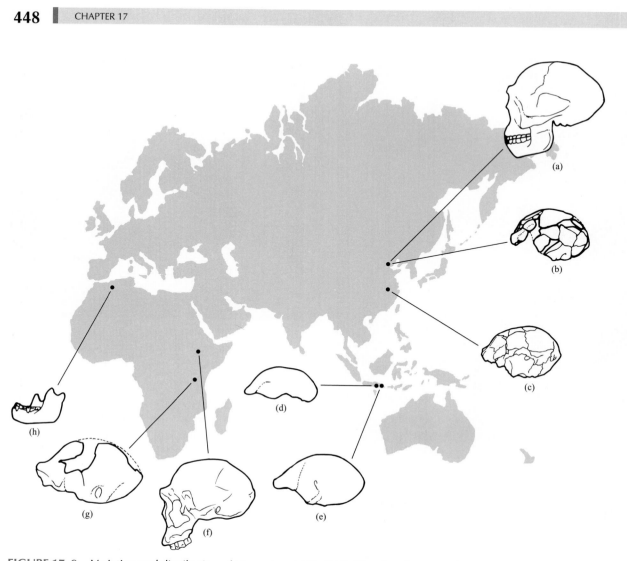

FIGURE 17–9 *Variation and distribution of* H. erectus. *(a)* Skull XII, Zhoukoudian, People's Republic of China; *(b)* Skull XI, Zhoukoudian, People's Republic of China; *(c)* Hexian, People's Republic of China; *(d)* "Pithecanthropus erectus" II, Java; *(e)* "Pithecanthropus erectus," Java; *(f)* KNM-ER 3733, Lake Turkana, Kenya; *(g)* OH 9, Olduvai Gorge, Tanzania; *(h)* Ternifine II, Algeria.

erectus or *H. ergaster*. Eudald Carbonell, one of the excavators of the site, believes that the finds might merit an entirely new species.[7]

The artifacts found with the fossils at Gran Dolina are cruder than African artifacts of the same time period elsewhere. In fact, they resemble Asian *H. erectus* tools.

The accuracy of the paleomagnetic dates has been questioned by some investigators. If the dates prove to be accurate, who were these early Europeans? One scenario is that they were ancestors of the Heidelberg people who, in turn, were ancestors of the Neandertals.

The Morphology of *Homo erectus*

The early specimens of *H. erectus* resemble *H. habilis*, the species from which *H. erectus* probably evolved. Toward the latter part of the Middle Pleistocene many individuals began to show features associated with *H. sapiens*; there appears to be no sharp dividing line between *H. erectus* and *H. sapiens*. In describing the mor-

[7]J. C. Gutin, "Remains in Spain Now Reign as Oldest Europeans," *Science*, 269 (1995), 754–755.

phology of *H. erectus,* we will discuss fossils that, for the most part, do not show *H. habilis-* or *H. sapiens*-like characteristics. Many of the features of the *H. erectus* skull that are discussed in this section are illustrated in Figure 17–10. They may also be observed in the photographs in Figure 17–5 through 17–8 and Figure 16–D in the color insert: "Hominid Fossils").

THE MORPHOLOGY OF THE *HOMO EREC-TUS* SKULL   The cranial capacity of *H. erectus* averages about 1000 cubic centimeters and generally ranges between about 750 and 1250 cubic centimeters; there is a general increase in cranial capacity over time (Table 17–2). The size of the brain case of most specimens falls within the lower range of variation of modern *H. sapiens.* The distinctive shape of the *H. erectus* cranium betrays major differences in the development of various parts of the brain housed within it.

Most specimens of *H. erectus* have cranial bones that are thick when compared with the thin cranial bones of *H. sapiens.* The brow ridges are thick and continuous, and behind the brow ridges is a pronounced postorbital constriction. The forehead is low and relatively flat, or **platy-cephalic.** Along the midline at the top of the brain case in some specimens is a bony ridge, the **sagittal keel.** Unlike the sagittal crest found in the robust australopithecines, the sagittal keel is a thickening of bone along the top of the cranium. The profile of the cranium as seen from the side clearly shows the angularity of the occipital; above this angularity is a horizontal bar of bone, the **occipital torus.** In the rear view, the greatest width of the skull is relatively low. The facial skeleton of *H. erectus* is comparatively large and broad, with large orbits and nasal openings. The brow ridge extends as a bar of bone across the nasal root and both orbits.

The genus *Homo* is characterized by a reduction in the size of the dentition through time. It is not surprising, therefore, that the teeth of *H. erectus* are smaller than those of *Australopithecus* and larger than those of *H. sapiens.* In general, the dentition in *H. erectus* and that in *H. sapiens* appear very similar. Looking down upon the tooth row, we see that it diverges toward the back, with the greatest distance between the teeth occurring between the third molars. In *H. sapiens,* the greatest distance is between the sec-

ond molars because the ends of the tooth row turn slightly inward. In *H. erectus* the first molar is the largest tooth in the mouth, while in *H. sapiens* the second or third molar is the largest. The *H. erectus* molars often show fine wrinkling, or **crenulation,** around the base.

The reduction in size of the molars and premolars and the contrast in relative tooth size between *H. erectus* and the australopithecines suggest that the incisors and canines were more involved in the processing of food in *H. erectus* than they were in the australopithecines. This may be related to major changes in diet, with an increasing emphasis on meat, and to new ways of preparing food for eating, which were made possible by the development of cooking and more effective tools.

The mandible lacks a chin but does have a **mandibular torus,** which is a thickening of bone on the inside of the mandible. In the side view, we can observe several small openings in the jaw; through these **mental foramina** nerves and blood vessels pass through the bone to the living tissues of the facial muscles and skin. Modern humans usually have a single mental foramen on each side of the jaw; *H. erectus* has several.

THE POSTCRANIAL SKELETON OF *HOMO ERECTUS*   Although the number of postcranial bones is few, several parts of the postcranial anatomy, especially the femur, have been studied. Externally, the *H. erectus* femur resembles that of *H. sapiens,* but x-rays reveal that the outer wall of the shaft of the femur is twice as thick as that of *H. sapiens.* Although other relatively minor differences exist in the postcranial skeletons of the two species, both *H. erectus* and *H. sapiens* show an identical or very similar form of erect bipedalism. While the size of *H. habilis* remained relatively small, the "Turkana boy" *H. erectus* skeleton (KNM-WT 15000) suggests a stature similar to that of *H. sapiens.* Thus it appears that the evolution of large body size, characteristic of *Homo,* took place during the transition from *H. habilis* to *H. erectus.*

New Dates and New Debates

Many paleoanthropologists see the role of *H. erectus* in hominid evolution as follows: The genus *Australopithecus* gave rise to the genus

A

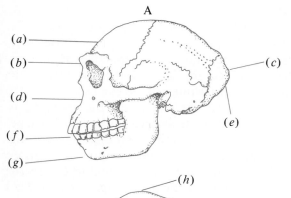

B

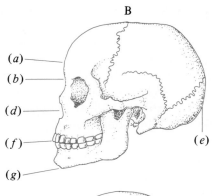

(a)
(b)
(d)
(f)
(g)

(a)
(b)
(c)
(e)

(d)

(f)
(e)

(g)

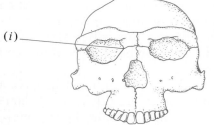

(h)

(i)

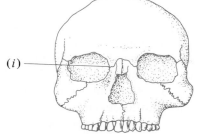

(i)

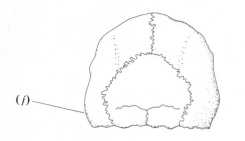

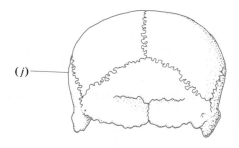

(j)

(j)

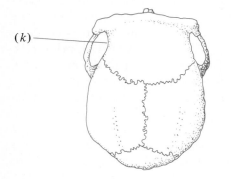

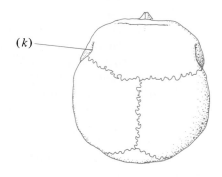

(k)

(k)

FIGURE 17–10 *A comparison of the skulls of (A)* Homo erectus *and (B) modern* Homo sapiens.

H. erectus	Modern H. sapiens
(a) Low, flat forehead	Vertical forehead
(b) Prominent brow ridges extending as a bar	Brow ridges slight or absent
(c) Occipital torus	
(d) Relatively large facial skeleton with large orbits and large nasal opening	Relatively small facial skeleton
(e) Angular occipital	Rounded occipital
(f) Relatively large teeth	Relatively small teeth
(g) Large mandible	Small mandible
(h) Sagittal keel	
(i) Horizontal nasal frontal suture-	Nasal-frontal suture upside-down V
(j) Widest point low on brain case	Widest point high on brain case
(k) Pronounced postorbital construction	Slight postorbital construction

Homo in Africa about 2.5 million years ago. The earliest named representatives of the genus *Homo* belong to the species *H. habilis* which, in turn, gave rise to *H. erectus* some 1.8 to 1.6 million years ago. *Homo erectus* remained exclusively in Africa for hundreds of thousands of years. Then, about 1 million years ago, in part because of the invention of advanced stone tools such as the hand axe, some *H. erectus* populations migrated out of Africa and spread into Asia and Europe.

This view is being challenged by the new dates determined for *H. erectus* fossils from Java. The new dates suggest that the fossils in Java are as old as the oldest fossils in Africa.

One new scenario is that some *H. erectus* populations moved out of Africa about 2 million years ago and established new populations in Asia and eventually in Europe. Another idea is that perhaps a pre-*H. erectus* population—*H. habilis* or even *Australopithecus*—moved out of Africa before 2 million B.P. and independently gave rise to *H. erectus* populations in Africa and Asia. However, no *H. habilis* or australopithecine fossils have been found outside Africa to date.

If the new older dates for *H. erectus* in Java prove to be accurate, then Dubois's nineteenth-century contention that Asia was the cradle of humanity once again becomes a viable hypothesis. At this time, however, we are still left wondering about the nature of the relationship between the African and the Asian *H. erectus*

populations. Since both Asian and African populations show evolutionary trends leading to *H. sapiens*, which group gave rise to modern *H. sapiens*, or did they both? Some further ideas on this will be presented in Chapter 19.

Summary

The first fossil to be attributed to *H. erectus* was discovered in 1891 at Trinil, Java. Since then, several additional specimens have been recovered from that island. In the 1920s and 1930s, over a dozen skulls and almost 150 teeth were discovered in a cave near the village of Zhoukoudian, near Beijing, China. Since then, several other sites have been excavated in China. African examples of *H. erectus* are from Olduvai Gorge, East Lake Turkana, Swartkrans, and several sites in north Africa. WT 15000, or "Turkana boy," from East Lake Turkana, is an almost complete skeleton of a subadult *H. erectus*. A recent discovery of *H. erectus* is the mandible from the Republic of Georgia.

The cranial capacity of *H. erectus* averages about 1000 cubic centimeters and generally ranges between about 750 and 1250 cubic centimeters; the cranial bones are thick, as are the brow ridges. The forehead is low and platycephalic, and along the midline at the top of the brain case is a bony ridge, the sagittal keel. The profile of the cranium shows the angularity of the occipital, above which is a horizontal bar of bone, the occipital torus. The facial skeleton is comparatively large and broad, with large orbits and nasal openings. The teeth are smaller than those of *Australopithecus* and larger than those of *H. sapiens*. The mandible lacks a chin but does have a mandibular torus, as well as multiple mental foramina on each side of the mandible.

While most paleoanthropologists see *H. erectus* evolving in Africa and then moving into other areas, the recent redating of two Javanese finds places doubt on this scenario. At 1.8 and 1.6 million years old, these fossils are as old as any African finds. This raises questions as to how the African and Asian populations were related and what relationship they had with later *H. sapiens*.

THE CULTURE OF *HOMO HABILIS* AND *HOMO ERECTUS*

Earlier we saw that behavioral adaptability provides important ways by which humans cope with the requirements of their varied habitats. When did learned behavior begin to be the dominant means of coping with the environment? The evidence for the change from predominantly innate adaptations to cultural adjustments is even more fragmentary than the fossil evidence of physical evolution.

Early hominids very likely made tools of perishable materials such as wood and hides long before they learned to work stone; even chimpanzees make tools out of sticks. It is not until about 2½ million years ago that stone tools begin to appear in archaeological sites. With the appearance of stone tools a stage of cultural development called the **Paleolithic** begins. *Paleo* means "old" and *lithic* means "stone"; the Paleolithic is the "Old Stone Age." The people of these cultures continued to make tools out of perishable materials, but they also chipped away at stone. As time went on, they manufactured an increasing variety of durable stone tools.

The **Lower Paleolithic** begins with the manufacture of the first stone tools, some 2.6 million years ago. Most paleoanthropologists attribute these earliest tools to *H. habilis*; later Lower Paleolithic cultures characterize *H. erectus*. The **Middle Paleolithic** refers to the stone tools of the Neandertals and their contemporaries. Finally,

the **Upper Paleolithic** includes the stone tools of anatomically modern peoples. Some evidence of the behavior of *H. habilis* and *H. erectus* is seen in the archaeological record, which is the subject of this section.

Interpreting the Archaeological Evidence

Artifacts are the physical remains of human activities. A carefully chipped arrowpoint and a highly decorated piece of pottery are in themselves works of art worthy of our admiration. Besides their artistic merit, however, artifacts make up the evidence from which human behavior can be deduced. In this context, a broken piece of flint or a hole in the ground can be as critical in the interpretation of prehistoric behavior as the finest work of prehistoric art.

We use a number of terms in describing archaeological evidence. An archaeological **site** is any location where manufactured objects are found. All the artifacts from a given site make up an **assemblage,** which, in turn, can be divided into a series of **industries.** Each industry contains all the artifacts made from one type of material, for example, a **lithic (stone) industry** and a **bone industry.** Because stone is preserved better than materials such as bone and wood, most ancient sites contain only a lithic industry. Nevertheless, we must constantly keep in mind that all hominids probably used some combination of bone, wood, horn, and other perishable material as well. When similar assemblages occur in many sites, we speak of an **archaeological culture.** Such a culture is usually named after the site where it was first seen. The Oldowan culture, for example, is named after Olduvai Gorge.

An artifact that appears to have been made for a specific function is a **tool;** examples of tools are clubs, spears, scrapers, burins, carrying devices, and hammerstones. However, many natural objects can be used without further modification; such objects, called **utilized material,** include anvils, hammerstones, and utilized flakes. The word **debitage** refers to the waste and nonutilized material produced during tool manufacture. Unmodified rocks brought to a site by human agency that show no signs of use are termed **manuports.**

A **core** is a nodule of rock from which pieces, or **flakes,** are removed. The individual flakes can be further altered by **retouch,** the further removal of tiny flakes, to create **flake tools.** Two types of flake tools are the **scraper,** a flake with a scraping edge on the end or side, and the **burin,** a tool with a thick point. The remaining core can be fashioned into a **core tool,** such as a **hand ax.** A cutting edge is created by flaking on one or both ends; the little flakes are produced by hitting a **hammerstone** against the core. The edge itself is often jagged, but it is quite effective in butchering animals.

Interpreting the archaeological record is often extremely difficult. Ideally, we would like to know the functions of each artifact type. Usually we must, however, be content merely to describe its shape or to place it in one of several standardized categories such as chopper or scraper. The archaeologist must be careful not to interpret these categories as proven functions. A scraper, for example, may have functioned as a knife rather than as an instrument for scraping flesh off a hide.

The Culture of Early *Homo*

If both *Australopithecus* and *Homo* were present in the Pliocene and Early Pleistocene, which one made the tools that have been recovered? The australopithecines may have manufactured some tools, and given the toolmaking abilities of modern chimpanzees, this should not seem surprising.

We may hypothesize that the differentiation of the two genera most likely lay in the progressive development of toolmaking and changes in subsistence patterns in *Homo*. It then follows that the bulk of the archaeological material recovered most likely represents the activities of *Homo*. If this is the case, the presence of an australopithecine in such a context may suggest that the relationship between *Homo* and *Australopithecus* was essentially antagonistic. However, evidence suggests that the robust australopithecines may also have been capable of manufacturing stone tools.

The artifacts of this early period have been found over large geographical areas. They were so simple that they probably developed independently at several different locations. During the long time involved, and considering how very slowly culture evolved, similar types of tools spread out over great expanses. These early artifacts lack the standardization of the later assemblages. Some of the variability is accounted for by evolution over time and differences in the type of stone used. The most important fact is that much of the variation between assemblages indicates differences in behavior. We would expect to find that a collection of artifacts at a butchering site would differ from a collection at a site where stone tools were manufactured.

THE ARCHAEOLOGY OF OLDUVAI GORGE

The oldest known archaeological remains are stone artifacts from the Gona River region of Ethiopia dated at between 2.6 and 2.5 million B.P. Even so, the best known early archaeological assemblages are probably those of Olduvai Gorge. Oldowan tools are assigned to the cultural stage called the Lower Paleolithic, or the Lower Old Stone Age.

An interesting site at Olduvai is the FLK site in Upper Bed I (Figure 17–11). The site contains about 2500 artifacts and 60,000 bones! One find consists of the disarticulated remains of *Deinotherium,* an extinct species of elephant. Of the 123 recovered artifacts associated with the elephant, all but five can be classified as tools; most of these are choppers.

The DK site from Bed I is older than 1.75 million B.P.; like most sites of this period, this site was located close to water. Many crocodile bones have been found, as well as bones from extinct forms of tortoise, cattle, pig, elephant, hippopotamus, horse, and giraffe; all these animals must have played some role in the early hominid diet. The DK lithic industry includes several tool types, among them various forms of choppers (Figure 17–12 and Table 17–3).

The tools known as choppers are made from flat stones shaped by the tumbling effects of stream water. Once collected, a hammerstone is used to create a core with a sharp edge. The resulting tool can be used for many functions such as chopping and cutting; the flakes knocked off the core can be used as knives and puncturing tools.

Paleoanthropologists assume that objects are tools if certain conditions are met. They look for regularity in shape among the objects and whether the objects are found in association with things they may have been used on, such as

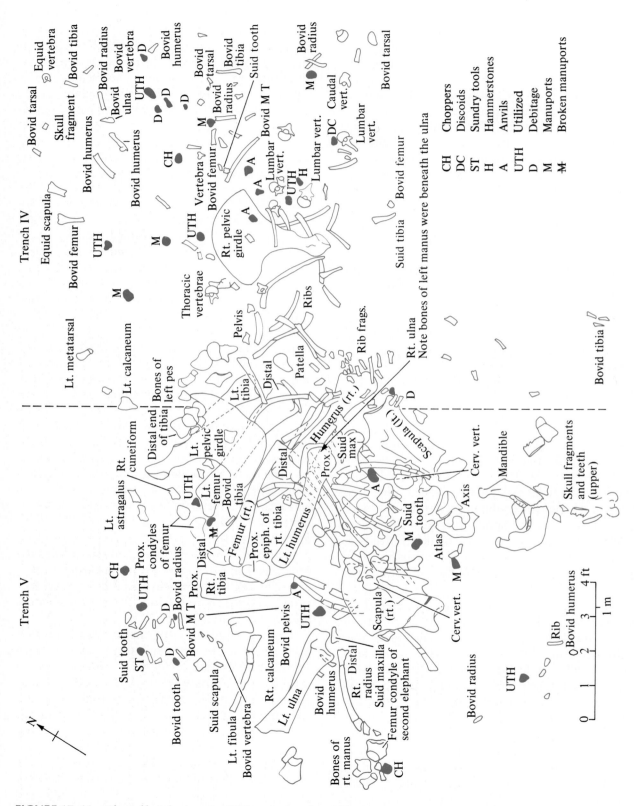

FIGURE 17–11 *Plan of butchering site, FLK north, Level 6, Olduvai Gorge.*

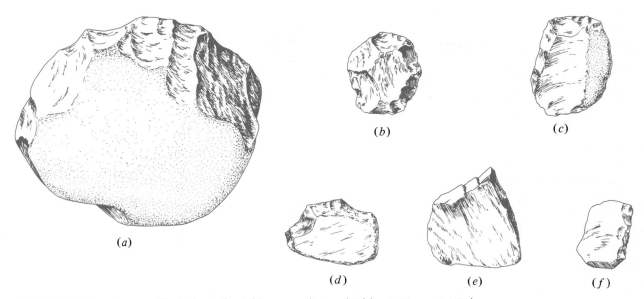

FIGURE 17–12 *Stone artifacts from the Oldowan culture of Olduvai Gorge. (a)* Side chopper; *(b)* discoid; *(c)* end scraper; *(d)* side scraper; *(e)* burin; *(f)* utilized flake.

butchered animals. Also, tools are often found far from where the material to make them is located. Many stones from FLK and DK display these features and are therefore considered to be tools.

The tools described above are characteristic of what is known as the *Oldowan culture.* This assemblage of tools is widespread during this time throughout eastern and southern Africa. Later in time (Middle and Upper Bed II at Olduvai Gorge),

we find a group of tools labeled "Developed Oldowan." This assemblage includes new tool types such as the **awl, cleaver,** and crude hand ax.

One of the most interesting features at Olduvai Gorge is the stone circle of the DK site (Figure 17–13). This circle, about 3.7 to 4.3 meters (12 to 14 feet) in diameter, is formed of basalt blocks loosely piled up to just under 30 centimeters (1 foot) high. Associated small piles of stones may have been supports for branches, while the circle itself may have been a base to support a living structure made of brush. If this stone circle is the support of some type of hut, it would represent the earliest known human habitation structure. Other interpretations, however, have been made. The circle may simply be the result of fractured basalt forced up from an underlying layer of lava by the radiating roots of an ancient tree.

THE ARCHAEOLOGY OF LAKE TURKANA

Another region of east Africa that has been extensively studied is the Koobi Fora area of East Lake Turkana (Figure 17–14). Several different kinds of sites have been identified in this region.

One type of site is that in which a single large animal is found associated with stone artifacts. The HAS site, for example, consists of a hippopotamus lying in a stream channel that was

TABLE 17–3

STONE INDUSTRY FROM DK, OLDUVAI GORGE

	NUMBER	%	NUMBER	%
Tools			154	12.9
Choppers	47	3.9		
Scrapers	30	2.5		
Burins	3	0.3		
Others	74	6.2		
Utilized material			187	15.6
Anvils	3	0.3		
Hammerstones	48	4.0		
Flakes	37	3.1		
Others	99	8.3		
Debitage			857	71.5

Source: M. D. Leakey, *Olduvai Gorge, Vol 3, Excavations in Beds I and II, 1969–1963* (Cambridge, England: Cambridge University Press, 1971), 39.

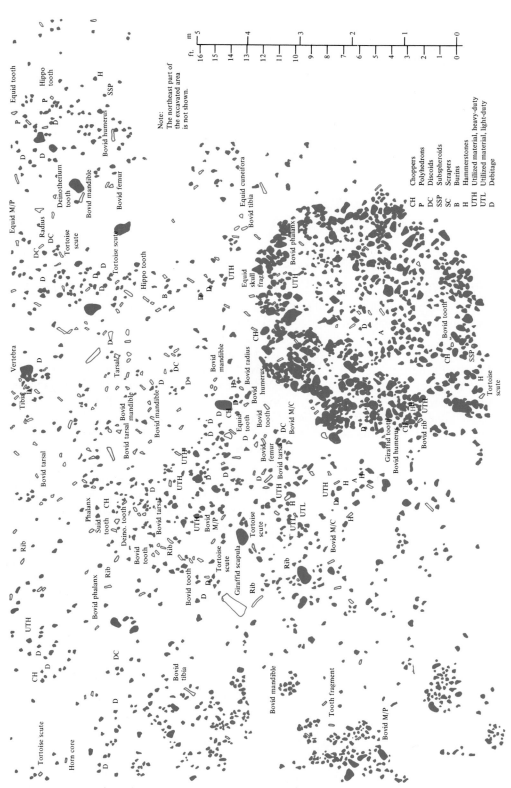

FIGURE 17–13 *Plan of the stone circle, site DK, Olduvai Gorge.*

FIGURE 17–14   *Site at East Lake Turkana.* Paleoanthropologists Richard Leakey and Kamoya Kimeu examine a fossil jaw.

once part of a delta system. The HAS site is about 1.6 million years old. Paleoanthropologists believe that hominids found the animal already dead and that they used the site for scavenging. Scattered among the animal bones and on the nearby bank are 119 artifacts, most of which are small, sharp flakes that could be held between the fingers and used as knives to carve up the carcass (Figure 17–15).

Different human activities take place in different locations, and different activities are associated with different tools. The KBS site at Koobi Fora presents a behavioral picture very different from that seen at the HAS site. The KBS site contains hundreds of stone artifacts, along with bones from many animal species: pig, gazelle, waterbuck, giraffe, hippopotamus. The site was once the sandy bed of a stream, and perhaps a small group of hominids regularly gathered there to cut up small pieces of game. The large variety of animals represented suggests that the hominids transported game to this central location.

The Culture of *Homo erectus*

Although *H. erectus* is poorly represented in the fossil record, their behavior is well represented

in the archaeological record. The artifacts found in Java, China, and elsewhere in Asia are not as finely made as the material from Europe and Africa, which may be partly the result of an absence of suitable raw materials, such as flint (Box 17–2). Nevertheless, the artifacts from Zhoukoudian do include large choppers quite like the more advanced Oldowan tools. In Europe, north Africa, and southwestern Asia as far east as Pakistan, the well-known hand ax tradition developed (Figure 17–16).

THE ACHEULEAN TRADITION   The culture of *H. erectus* spans the latter part of the Lower Paleolithic. The most frequent cultural manifestation of the Lower Paleolithic is the *Acheulean tradition*, characterized by several highly diagnostic tool types, including the hand ax (Figure 2–4). A hand ax is produced by striking a core, a large flake of flint, or similar material with either a hammerstone or a **bone hammer,** thus removing a flake; the blank is turned over repeatedly so that flakes are removed from both sides. The resulting hand ax may have been used for butchering an animal, working wood, cracking bones, digging for roots, and many other purposes.

Throughout this period, archaeologists can trace the development of finer technological con-

FIGURE 17–15 *The use of flake tools.* Archaeologists Kathy Schick and Ray Dezzani are shown using a stone flake to cut through the thick skin of an elephant that died of natural causes.

BOX 17–2

THE VIRTUES OF BAMBOO

Anthropologists have observed that the tools manufactured by *Homo erectus* show different levels of manufacturing sophistication in different areas of the world. In the 1930s Harvard archaeologist Hallam Movius discovered that the stone tools found on one side of an imaginary line running across northern India were more crudely made than stone tools found on the other side. This line is known as the **Movius line**.

The stone tools found east of the Movius line in eastern and southeastern Asia are less finely made and less standardized than tools of similar age found west of the line. An example of the more symmetrical western tools are those of the Acheulean tradition mentioned in the text. The simplicity and lack of variety of eastern and southeastern stone tools was seen as an indication of the backwardness of the people who lived in these regions.

Today there is another explanation: the *Homo erectus* populations that lived east of the Movius line had a resource that suited their needs for most purposes better than stone. That resource was bamboo.

Paleoanthropologist Geoffrey G. Pope reconstructed the habitats that existed during the time of *Homo erectus.* He found that areas east of the Movius line were forested with high concentrations of bamboo. The areas west of the line consisted primarily of open grassland habitats where stone may have been an easily available and effective resource for tool manufacture.

In many ways bamboo is easier to work than stone. It is also a very versatile material. Pope tells us that "there are few useful tools that can-

not be constructed from bamboo. Cooking and storage containers, knives, spears, heavy and light projectile points, elaborate traps, ropes, fasteners, clothing, and even entire villages can be manufactured from bamboo."[1] The crude stone tools might have been used to manufacture bamboo tools.

Pope believes that bamboo substituted for more advanced stone tools. The crude nature of the stone tools east of the Movius line is not an indication of the cultural or biological backwardness of the *Homo erectus* populations in this area. While this seems logical to us, bamboo tools are perishable. No bamboo tools have survived that date back to *Homo erectus* times.

Source: G. G. Pope, "Bamboo and Human Evolution," *Natural History* (October 1989), 49–56.
[1]Ibid., 53.

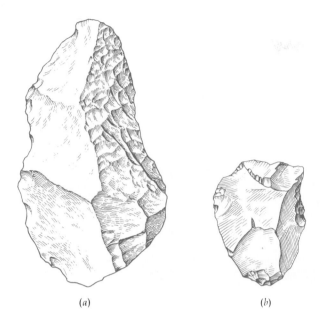

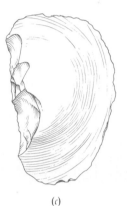

FIGURE 17–16 *Tools of* H. erectus. *(a)* Abbevillean hand ax from Olduvai Gorge; *(b)* chopping tools from Zhoukoudian; *(c)* cleaverlike tool from Zhoukoudian.

trol in the manufacturing of hand axes. The earlier types were produced with hammerstones, and the flakes removed were large and thick; this resulted in a finished product that was large and had a ragged cutting edge. Later, the use of hammers of bone or other similar material produced thinner and more regular flakes; this resulted in a thinner tool with a fairly straight cutting edge.

While hand axes are often considered diagnostic of the Lower Paleolithic, they make up only a small percentage of all the tool types from Lower Paleolithic sites; in fact, some sites lack hand axes altogether. Cores were also transformed into hammers and choppers, while the flakes were made into a variety of tools such as scrapers, awls, and knives.

THE FIRST USE OF FIRE   Archaeologists debate the earliest date for the controlled use of fire. The earliest suggested date is 1.5 million years ago, a date that is based on the analysis of baked sediments from Koobi Fora and Chesowanja in Kenya.[8] Some believe that the sediments were burned at a temperature consistent with that of an open campfire but not consistent

with that of a natural brush fire. Fire was very likely being used in a controlled manner about a million years later at Zhoukoudian.[9]

Homo erectus probably used fire for warmth. Members of this species, having spread outward from the more tropical zones where they originated, lived in some fairly cold climates. In addition, fire could have acted as a gathering point for the group, thus increasing social solidarity and ritualism.

Through cooking, food is made more digestible. Although the hominids of the time would not have realized it, fire also kills parasites and disease organisms and can detoxify food. So cooking could have significantly increased the health of the groups that used fire in this way. In addition, cooked meat, under many circumstances, remains edible longer than uncooked meat; cooking is therefore a means of preservation.

HABITATIONS   The site of Terra Amata, in the city of Nice in southern France, is approximately 400,000 years old. When excavated in 1966, this site, once a part of the beach, was interpreted as containing several dwellings. If this interpretation is correct, the huts measure 6 by 12 meters (20 by 40 feet) and are characterized by

[8]S. James, "Hominid Use of Fire in the Lower and Middle Pleistocene," *Current Anthropology,* 30 (1989), 1–11; A. Sillen and C. K. Brain, "Old Flame: Burned Bones Provide Evidence of an Early Use of Fire," *Natural History* (April, 1990), 6–10.

[9]L. Binford and N. M. Stone, "Zhoukoudian: A Closer Look," *Current Anthropology,* 27 (1986), 453–476.

BOX 17–3

TOOLS FOR CLAWS

Sometime around 2.6 to 2.5 million years ago certain hominid populations began to make simple stone tools. These tools, in part, substituted for the strong jaws, long claws, powerful tusks, heavy feet, and strong muscles of various other animals. But these stone tools did more than that. They began hominids on a path toward greatly expanded habitats and an increasing ability to alter and even destroy habitats. Kathy D. Schick and Nicholas Toth, in their book *Making Silent Stones Speak: Human Evolution and the Dawn of Technology,* point out that stone cutting tools would have allowed early hominids to quickly butcher thick-skinned animals and carry pieces to a place where the meat would be safe from other animals.

Cutting tools would also allow them to cut through the dense skin and gain access to the meat soon after the animal died. Scavengers usually must wait until the dead animal has decayed somewhat before they can penetrate the thick skin to get at the meat.

Anvils and stone hammers would give relatively easy access to bone marrow. Digging sticks would enhance the ability to retrieve deeply buried roots. These and other tools could be used to make numerous food resources available that were not available to hominid populations that lacked this technology.

Nonhuman carnivores and scavengers are usually specialized to efficiently exploit a few specific food resources. On the other hand,

hominids, with their tool kits, could exploit many resources in many different habitats. This enabled them to expand their range and numbers at the expense of other animal populations.

The following illustration shows how tools substituted for biological equipment of other animals and thereby allowed hominids to exploit many new resources. It also illustrates how technology permitted the hominids to enter new ecological niches and to compete with other animals for the same resources.

Reference: K. D. Schick and N. Toth, *Making Silent Stones Speak: Human evolution and the Dawn of Technology* (New York: Simon and Schuster, 1993), 183–186.

a. Stone flake. Analog: Carnivore flesh-cutting carnassial teeth.

c. Digging stick. Analog: Bushpig snout and tusks; elephant and aardvark feet.

e. Carrying devices and containers: wooden skewer, bark tray, ostrich and tortoise shell, skin bag. Analog: animal stomach.

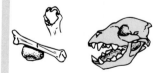

b. Hammer and anvil. Analog: Hyena bone-crushing teeth and jaws.

d. Missiles, clubs, spear. Analog: Carnivore canines and claws, antelope horns.

f. Hammer and anvil. Analog: Baboon nut-cracking cheek teeth.

g. Fire. Analog: Herbivore jaws and teeth, stomach with microorganisms to aid in consumption and digestion.

oval floors. A study of what some interpret as postholes, stone supports, and hearths suggest that the huts were made of saplings or branches. The site has traditionally been associated with *H. erectus*; however, some investigators believe that the artifacts were actually produced by archaic *H. sapiens.*

Archaeologist Paola Villa studied Terra Amata. He discovered that about 40 percent of the cores and flakes could be put together to reconstruct the original stones from which they had been manufactured. Surprisingly, these pieces came from different stratigraphic levels. A specific tool was manufactured at a specific point in time, but the pieces of the tool were widely distributed at what first appear to be different time levels. This fact suggests that there has been a significant disturbance at Terra Amata and that natural processes have moved artifacts made at a singular point in time into levels that seem to represent different points in time. Perhaps, then, the spatial arrangements of stones and postholes originally interpreted as dwellings are the result of natural disturbances and not of human activity.[10] Further analysis of the site and the discovery of new sites are needed to provide a clearer picture of the shelters occupied by *H. erectus.*

Homo erectus probably made use of a variety of dwelling types. Some of these dwellings may have been in the open or up against a cliff, perhaps under a cliff overhang. Few habitations were constructed in caves, contrary to the popular notion of *H. erectus* individuals as cave dwellers. Because of the good preservation of cave sites, archaeologists have tended to concentrate on their excavation.

HUNTING, SCAVENGING, AND GATHERING The classic description of early hominid subsistence patterns was that *A. africanus* may have occasionally hunted small game and that *H. erectus* and perhaps *H. habilis* were big-game hunters. Today, new finds and reanalyses of previously found fossils and artifacts place some doubt on this traditional interpretation. Also, much of the reconstruction of ancient lifestyles has traditionally been made based on analogies with modern hunter-gatherers. The validity of this practice has been questioned in recent years. For example, in relationship to subsistence, the division of labor between males and females may not have been the same in the past as it is today.

Not so long ago, tools found in association with bones that have cut marks on them were assumed to have been used by hominids for hunting, killing, and butchering the animals represented by the bones. Detailed microscopic studies of bones, however, tell a different story

(Figure 17–17). Paleoanthropologist Pat Shipman has studied cut marks on bones associated with tools and has found several interesting facts.[11]

First, many bones that had been processed by hominids have carnivore tooth marks in addition to cut marks from tools. In some cases the cut marks overlay the tooth marks, suggesting that the prey animal had already been killed by a carnivore before it was butchered. Second, Shipman found that tool cut marks are often not near joints but occur on the shafts of bones. This suggests that the hominids did not have the whole carcass to butcher. Perhaps they cut off meat that remained after carnivores had left the scene or had been chased off. Hominids could have also eaten the marrow.

The debate over the traditional "*H. erectus,* the hunter" hypothesis can be illustrated in terms of competing interpretations of the site of Ambrona. Although some paleoanthropologists believe that this site is the result of the activities of archaic *H. sapiens,* F. Clark Howell has excavated what he considers to be a hunting camp of *H. erectus* at Ambrona. Howell has recovered the bones of the now-extinct mammoth *Elephas antiquus,* along with those of smaller elephant species, deer, horse, and aurochs. Although no bones of *Homo* have been recovered, the animals were found dismembered, and the bones were scattered over the site.

In association with the animal bones at Ambrona were more than 100 stone tools. Howell believes that a couple of *H. erectus* bands, using fire, joined in running the animals into what was then boggy marshland. Once the animals became stuck in the soft ground, the hunters simply waited until they became exhausted from their fruitless struggle to free themselves. Then, with wood spears the hunters killed the animals, and with stone tools they butchered their prey.

The hunting hypothesis has been questioned on several points. The animal bones at Ambrona and those at another Spanish site, Torralba, have been found in areas frequented by carnivores that may have been responsible for the accumulation of at least some of the bones. Although tools are present, the bones show little clear evidence of

[10]P. Villa, "Conjoinable Pieces and Site Formation," *American Antiquity,* 47 (1982), 276–290.

[11]P. Shipman, "Scavenging or Hunting in Early Hominids: Theoretical Frameworks and Tests," *American Anthropologist,* 88 (1986), 27–43.

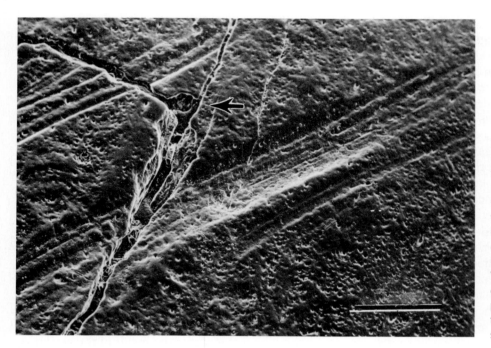

FIGURE 17–17 *Evidence of butchering.* This photograph, taken by a scanning electron microscope, shows cut marks made with a stone tool on the surface of a fossilized bone. The cut marks are seen crossing a weathering crack (indicated by the arrow). Within the groove of each cut mark are many fine, parallel striations, features typical of such marks. The scale bar is 0.5 mm long.

having been processed by these tools. Only sixteen stone-tool cut marks were found on fourteen of the many bones analyzed, but even these marks show no consistent pattern characteristic of butchering.[12]

Also, many marks on the bones previously classified as stone-tool marks may be due to other causes such as soil abrasion and the action of tree roots. According to this analysis, hunting activity seems an unlikely explanation for the association of tools and bones at Ambrona and Torralba. If these and other *H. erectus* sites are not actually hunting sites, then the conclusions made about the ability of *H. erectus* to act cooperatively and in the well-organized manner needed to hunt large game are also of questionable merit. Complicating matters is the contention that Ambrona might actually be an archaic *H. sapiens* site. If this is true, then early members of *H. sapiens* also might not have been efficient hunters.

It is likely that *H. habilis* and perhaps *H. erectus* were predominantly scavengers and gatherers of wild plants. They may have done some hunting, but many anthropologists now believe that hunting did not become a major part of any human subsistence pattern until the emergence of modern *H. sapiens.*

Scavenging and hunting are two quite different activities. However, all nonprimate mammalian scavengers also hunt, and this may have also been the case among early hominids. In searching for dead animals that still have some food value, animals that are primarily scavengers have to cover larger ranges than those that are primarily hunters. On the other hand, scavenging does not require as much speed as hunting, but scavenging is aided by endurance. Shipman points out that human bipedalism is not the best locomotor pattern for speed, but it is an efficient method of movement in terms of endurance. Bipedalism may have evolved, at least in part, in response to selective pressures involved in a scavenging lifestyle. However, since bipedalism evolved well before the use of stone tools, Shipman's analysis of stone-tool cut marks on bones cannot shed light on the question of the scavenging behavior of our earliest ancestors.

[12]P. Shipman and J. Rose, "Evidence of Butchery and Hominid Activities at Torralba and Ambrona: An Evaluation Using Microscope Techniques," *Journal of Archaeological Science,* 10 (1983), 467.

Summary

Humans adjust to their habitats largely in terms of cultural behavior. Cultural behavior may be inferred from the archaeological record.

The oldest known archaeological material dates from between 2.6 and 2.5 million B.P. from the Gona River region of Ethiopia; other important east African archaeological sites include Olduvai Gorge and East Lake Turkana. While both *Australopithecus* and *Homo* were for the most part contemporary at these sites, it is assumed that the development of technology was largely an adjustment of *Homo* and that the artifacts recovered represent the behavior of this genus. Early east African sites are places where people butchered animals and places where people lived and manufactured tools.

Homo erectus is associated with the hand-ax traditions such as the Acheulean. The sites of *H. erectus* also contain evidence of the use of fire. The degree to which *H. erectus* depended on hunting for subsistence is debated. In the early 1980s and before, most anthropologists believed that hunting was a major behavior of *H. erectus*. Today, many researchers believe that gathering wild vegetation and scavenging for meat and marrow were more important methods of obtaining food.

STUDY QUESTIONS

1. What was the first named species within the genus *Homo?* Where has it been found and what are its features?
2. How can the variability among the various *H. erectus* finds be explained?
3. Compare the anatomical characteristics of the genera *Homo* and *Australopithecus*.
4. What was the distribution of *H. erectus?* Briefly describe the finds made in each major geographical area.
5. How did the Acheulean tradition differ from the Oldowan?
6. What were some of the things that, among hominids, *H. erectus* accomplished first?
7. When did the controlled use of fire first occur? What are some of the uses that fire served during the Pleistocene?
8. What evidence exists to justify the idea that *H. erectus* was primarily a gatherer of wild plant material and a scavenger of already killed animals as opposed to an efficient big-game hunter?

SUGGESTED READINGS

The following handbooks list individual fossils along with pertinent information:

Day, M. *Guide to Fossil Man: A Handbook of Human Paleontology*, 4th ed. Chicago: University of Chicago Press, 1986.
Larsen, C. P., R. M. Matter, and D. L. Gebo. *Human Origins: The Fossil Record*, 2d ed. Prospect Heights, Ill.: Waveland, 1991.

Also recommended are the following:

Fagan, B. *The Journey from Eden: Peopling the Prehistoric World*. New York: Thames Hudson, 1990. This book is a general survey of prehistory.
Klein, R. G. *The Human Career: Human Biological and Cultural Origins*. Chicago: University of Chicago Press, 1989. This is a comprehensive and readable book detailing current research in paleontology and archaeology.
Lanpo, J., and H. Weiwen. *The Story of Peking Man*. Beijing: Foreign Languages Press, 1990. This translation of a book written by two Chinese paleoanthropologists describes the history, discoveries, and current research at Zhoukoudian.
Reader, J. *Missing Links: The Hunt for Earliest Man*, rev. ed. Boston: Little, Brown, 1989. This book tells the story of the hunt for and discovery of many important fossil hominids.
Rightmire, C. P. *The Evolution of Homo erectus*. Cambridge, England: Cambridge University Press, 1990. This book is a fairly technological analysis of selected specimens of *H. erectus*, with a discussion of the species' role in human evolution.
Shapiro, H. L. *Peking Man*. New York: Simon and Schuster, 1974. This is the story of the discovery, nature, and loss of the *H. erectus* fossils from Zhoukoudian, China.
Schick, K. D., and N. Toth. *Making Silent Stones Speak: Human Evolution and the Dawn of Technology*. New York: Simon and Schuster, 1993. This is a readable and insightful account of the role of early stone technology in the evolution of the hominids.

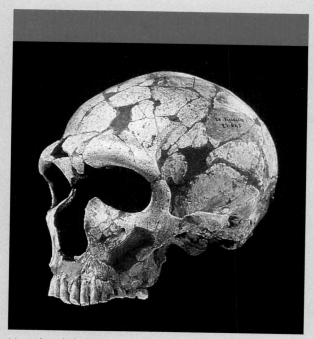

Neandertal skull from La Ferrassie, France.

The origin of anatomically modern humans has long been an issue in paleoanthropology, tied up as it is with the fate of everyone's favorite caricature of cavemen, the Neanderthals. Anatomically speaking, the evolutionary shift from some kind of Homo erectus *ancestor to* Homo sapiens *involved the decrease of skeletal and dental robusticity, modification of certain functional—particularly locomotor—anatomy, and an increase in cranial volume. Behaviorally, the transition brought with it a more finely crafted tool technology, more efficient foraging strategies, and artistic expression.*[1]

Roger Lewin

[1]R. Lewin, *Human Evolution: An Illustrated Introduction*, 3d ed. (Boston: Blackwell Scientific, 1993), 149.

CHAPTER

THE EARLIEST *HOMO SAPIENS* AND THE NEANDERTALS

18

Anthropologists generally divide the genus *Homo* into three species: *H. habilis, H. erectus,* and *H. sapiens.* It is important to remember, however, that nature does not classify; humans do. In empirical terms, no abrupt changes immediately lead to clear or absolute distinctions between species that have evolved from one another.

The classification itself is not important. The significance of current debates lies in the realization that evolution from one morphological pattern to another was continually taking place. Although some researchers do not see the emergence of the *H. sapiens* pattern until between 250,000 and 100,000 years ago, others see the first glimpse of this pattern as early as 500,000 B.P.

THE TRANSITION TO *HOMO SAPIENS*

During the later part of the Middle Pleistocene, fossil hominids appear that exhibit to varying degrees characteristics found more commonly in later forms. Few hominid fossils exist from this period, and the dates are generally unreliable. Paleoanthropologists disagree as to the affiliation of these specimens; to some they are later variants of the species *H. erectus*, while to others they are early members of the species *H. sapiens*.

Labeling an organism as "human" is by and large highly subjective. Yet many scholars have suggested that the most important criterion might be mental ability. We see a general increase in the size of the brain in the hominids of the Late Middle Pleistocene. Their mental abilities may have been approaching those of modern peoples. Although there was also a gradual reduction in facial size, some transitional forms looked like *H. erectus* with a large cranium.

The Discoveries of Early Archaic *Homo sapiens*

Evidence of early archaic *H. sapiens* has been found in Africa, Europe, and Asia. Throughout this large geographical area the specimens are fairly similar; yet analysis of the archaeological remains shows the development of many adaptations to local habitats.

THE EARLY ARCHAIC *HOMO SAPIENS* FROM AFRICA   Several well-preserved fossils were recovered between 1921 and 1925 at Kabwe (Broken Hill), Zambia, as part of a mining operation; the cave was subsequently destroyed. The fossils include a nearly complete skull (Figure 18–1), an upper jaw, a pelvis, femur, tibia, and humerus; however, the postcranial material may not be contemporary with the cranium. The dating of the fossils is difficult—they may be 250,000 years old—but a considerably more recent date of 125,000 B.P. has also been suggested. The Kabwe cranium has a large cranial capacity of 1280 cubic centimeters, but it possesses massive brow ridges, probably among the thickest of any known Pleistocene hominid. It has a very long

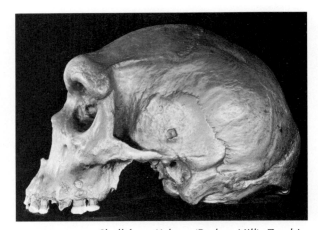

FIGURE 18–1   *Skull from Kabwe (Broken Hill), Zambia.*

and broad facial skeleton with a sloping forehead. The Kabwe individual when alive was in need of a dentist. Dental caries (cavities) are thought to be a consequence of refined sugar found in modern diets, yet the Kabwe teeth possessed dental caries and an abscess (infection) in the jaw.

In 1973 paleontologists discovered a partial cranium in a site near Lake Ndutu, near the western end of Olduvai Gorge. The beds probably date from about 400,000 years ago, but, as with most of the finds from the Middle Pleistocene, the dating is far from secure. Some features of the cranium bear a resemblance to *H. erectus*: the cranial capacity of approximately 1100 cubic centimeters and the thickness of the cranial bones. Many other details of the cranium suggest a relationship with the later archaic *H. sapiens*: the lack of a sagittal keel and the shape of the cranium.

The Kabwe and Lake Ndutu fossils, and other African fossils from the Middle Pleistocene, support the hypothesis that an early population of *H. sapiens* appeared during the later part of the Middle Pleistocene. The retention of some *H. erectus* features shows that these specimens likely represent transitional populations between *H. erectus* and *H. sapiens*.

THE EARLY ARCHAIC *HOMO SAPIENS* FROM ASIA AND EUROPE   Representatives of early archaic *H. sapiens* are also known from other parts of the world. A well-preserved cranium was recovered in 1978 from Dali, in Shaanxi Province, China. The Dali skull is typical of archaic *H. sapiens*. Its cranial capacity of 1120 cubic centimeters falls within the range of modern humans. The skull and facial features, however, resemble those of earlier hominids. These archaic characteristics include a sloping forehead and large brow ridges. The skull also has a small face that is flatter than those found in other areas of the world. Some paleoanthropologists point to this feature as evidence of the existence of features found in modern Chinese back in time. The Dali skull is about 200,000 to 100,000 years old.

A skull found in 1980 in Lontandong Cave, Hexian County, is the first cranium to be discovered in eastern or southeastern China. It dates to between 280,000 and 240,000 B.P. Although it resembles the *H. erectus* skulls from Zhoukoudian in some attributes, such as a less marked postorbital constriction, it appears to be more modern.

Two fossil skulls, recovered in 1989 and 1990 in Yunxian, are considered to be 350,000 years old or younger based upon the analysis of other fossil animals. These two skulls, unfortunately crushed, are classified as *H. erectus*, yet they show many resemblances, primarily in the face, to modern *H. sapiens* (Figure 18–2). These fossils play a major role in the controversy over the ori-

gins of modern humans that will be discussed in the next chapter.

Near the end of 1993 a human tibia, and in 1995 a tooth, were discovered at Boxgrove, England.[2] Both ends of the very robust limb bone are missing. The fossils appear to represent hominids living during a warm interglacial that has been dated by faunal analysis to between 524,000 and 478,000 B.P. Although very little can be determined about the individual from a tibia shaft, the find does place hominids in England at this early time. The site of Boxgrove has been excavated over the past 10 years and has yielded much archaeological material and the remains of butchered animals. Further excavation is planned in order to try to uncover additional hominid skeletal remains.

The Boxgrove fossils and the roughly contemporary Mauer mandible represent the oldest hominids from Europe (Figure 18–3). The Mauer mandible, also known as the Heidelberg jaw, was found in 1907 in a site near the village of Mauer, which is located a short distance from the city of Heidelberg, Germany. The mandible was found associated with stone tools similar to those de-

---

[2]M. B. Roberts, C. B. Stringer, and S. A. Parfitt, "A Hominid Tibia from Middle Pleistocene Sediments at Boxgrove, UK," *Nature*, 369 (1994), 311–313.

FIGURE 18–2 *Skull from Yunxian, China.*

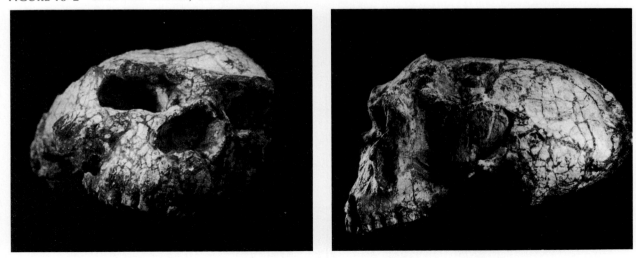

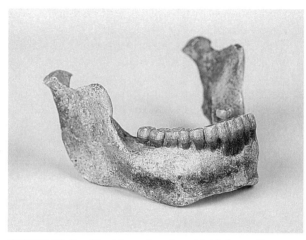

FIGURE 18–3   *The Mauer jaw from Heidelberg, Germany.*

scribed by Jacques Boucher de Crévecoeur de Perthes in 1838 (Figure 2–4). The mandible is large and robust, yet the teeth are not particularly large. Although some paleoanthropologists consider the mandible to represent a European *H. erectus*, others see it as an early archaic *H. sapiens.*

In the mid-1960s, a few broken teeth and an occipital were found near the village of Vértesszöllös, not far from Budapest, Hungary. The skull is represented only by the occipital region, which is less angular and more rounded than that in *H. erectus*. It dates to between 475,000 and 250,000 B.P. The reconstructed skull has a cranial capacity of 1400 cubic centimeters, which is indicative of *H. sapiens*. Yet other features, such as the thickness of the bones, suggest *H. erectus* affiliations.

Several other finds are known from Europe, including a very complete skull from Petralona in northern Greece. It might be older than 200,000 B.P. and shows a mixture of *H. erectus* and *H. sapiens* characteristics. Several fossils have been uncovered in Arago Cave, in the Pyrenees Mountains of France.

LATER TRANSITIONAL ARCHAIC *HOMO SAPIENS*   Two of the best known later archaic *H. sapiens* from Europe are those from Steinheim and from Swanscombe. The skull from Steinheim was found near Stuttgart, Germany, in 1933 and is dated to about 240,000 to 200,000 B.P. (Figure 18–4). The remains from Swanscombe, England, are of approximately the same age. This latter find consists of an occipital, discovered in 1935; a left parietal, discovered in 1936; and a right parietal, discovered 19 years later. All of these belong to the same individual.

The most complete of the two finds is the one from Steinheim. The skull possesses many fea-

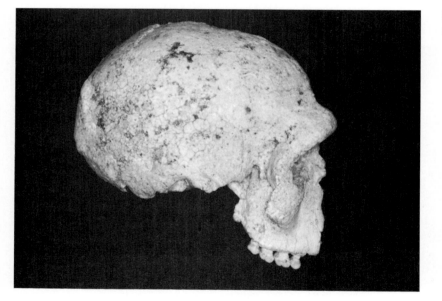

FIGURE 18–4   *Fossil from Steinheim, Germany.*

tures that are reminiscent of *H. erectus*, including a low, sloping forehead and large brow ridges. Yet in other ways, the Steinheim skull resembles that of the later *H. sapiens*, especially the Neandertal subspecies. For example, the facial skeleton is relatively small, the face and upper jaw are not prognathous, and the teeth are relatively small. The place of greatest width of the skull is higher than in the typical *H. erectus*.

Other hominid remains are known from the Second Interglacial, but knowledge of the material is limited. Four skull fragments and a molar tooth were discovered at the site of Bilzingsleben, Germany, which dates from 228,000 B.P. A skull recovered at Salé, Morocco, shows some basic characteristics of *H. erectus*; its cranial capacity is between 930 and 960 cubic centimeters. The mandible from Montmaurin, France, dates from the Second Interglacial or Early Riss; in many ways, it is intermediate between the Mauer mandible and those of the later Neandertals.

Summary

The fossil material of the earliest archaic *H. sapiens* is scattered and often incomplete, and it is associated with rather poorly documented dates. Several finds show characteristics of *H. sapiens* along with those of *H. erectus*, and paleoanthropologists differ as to their specific designation; some are considered *H. erectus*, while others are classified as archaic *H. sapiens*. The early archaic *H. sapiens* are known from Africa, Europe, and Asia. They include fossils from Zambia and Tanzania, China, England, Hungary, and Greece. The later transitional *H. sapiens* are known from England, Germany, France, and Morocco.

THE NEANDERTALS

Just as the distinction between species is not absolute, the status of fossils or fossil populations within species is often unclear. People prefer firm answers to questions. Yet in paleontology, pat answers are not possible; hypotheses compete for acceptance. In recent years, the debate over the role of a population of predominantly European hominids from the last Pleistocene glacial has shared center stage with other paleontological issues. Some paleoanthropologists believe that this population, called the Neandertals, evolved into modern Europeans. According to this view, Neandertals are placed in the species *H. sapiens* and are given the subspecies name *H. sapiens neandertalensis*. Humans of the last 250,000 years or so that display anatomical characteristics closer to those of contemporary humans are labeled *H. sapiens sapiens*.

Other paleoanthropologists do not consider the Neandertals to be *H. sapiens*; they place them in a separate species, *H. neandertalensis*. These people consider Neandertals to have been a highly specialized population biologically and culturally different from *H. sapiens*. Other hypotheses represent intermediate positions between these two ideas. Because of the debate that surrounds them, and because they are the best known population from the early part of the last glaciation, we will discuss the Neandertals in detail.

Whether or not the Neandertals are direct ancestors of modern *Homo sapiens*, they are fascinating and important hominid populations. Erik Trinkaus and Pat Shipman tell us:

> Seeing Neandertals in context, in the broad sweep of human evolution, is a valuable perspective. But we must not forget that they were neither "new and improved" versions of *Homo erectus* nor crude prototypes of modern *Homo sapiens*. They were themselves; they were Neandertals—one of the more distinctive, successful, and intriguing groups of humans that ever enriched our family history.[3]

The Discoveries of the Neandertals

The first Neandertal finds were made in the late 1820s through the 1840s. They were not recognized as prehistoric hominids and subsequently received little systematic examination. The discovery of a Neandertal in 1856 in the Neander Valley near Dusseldorf, Germany, marked the beginning of a controversy that persisted well into the present century.

Europeans of the Victorian age were totally unprepared to accept the Neander Valley fossils as the remains of one of their ancestors. At the time of the discovery, Darwin's *On the Origin of Species* was 3 years in the future, and none of the fossil populations mentioned in the preceding chapters had been discovered. The thought that this primitive-looking creature could have been related to modern people was repugnant to all but a few scholars. The alternatives offered were, by today's standards, incredible. One Englishman considered the creature to be a "half-crazed, half-idiotic [type of man] with murderous propensities." Others considered it to be a freak, a stupid Roman legionnaire, or a victim of water on the brain.

Then, in 1886 two skeletons were removed from a cave in Belgium near the town of Spy.

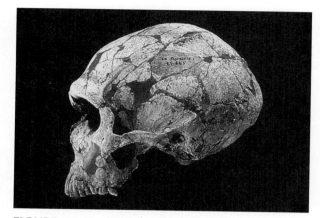

FIGURE 18–5 *Neandertal skull from La Ferrassie, France.*

With the discovery of still more Neandertals, such as those at La Chapelle-aux-Saints (see Box 18–2), Le Moustier, La Quina, and La Ferrassie (Figure 18–5), all discovered in France in 1908 and 1909, the Neandertal pattern of features began to emerge.

The greatest concentration of Neandertal fossils found to date comes from central France. As Figure 18–6 shows, fossils that display the Neandertal pattern to varying degrees are distributed from as far west as Portugal to as far east as Uzbekistan.

Today, the remains of about 400 Neandertal individuals have been collected. Although their place in human evolution is still problematic, they are no longer defined in the outlandish terms of the Victorians.

The label "Neandertal" refers generally to European populations that lived during the last Pleistocene glacial (the Würm), from about 120,000 to about 35,000 B.P. Within this time span, all European hominid fossils found to date display to varying degrees a distinct combination of skeletal features. This morphological pattern distinguishes Neandertals from the populations from which they evolved and into which they may have later evolved.

The Neandertal pattern is also found in western Asia, including Israel, Iraq, Russia, and Uzbekistan. In some of these places the Neandertals are contemporary with *H. sapiens sapiens*. The Neandertal range may have extended beyond Europe and western Asia. Although some paleoanthropologists consider some African and

---

[3]E. Trinkaus and P. Shipman, *The Neandertals: Changing the Image of Mankind* (New York: Knopf, 1992), 419.

BOX 18–2

LA CHAPELLE-AUX-SAINTS

One of the great misfortunes of paleoanthropology is that one of the earliest reasonably complete skeletons of a Neandertal was discovered at La Chapelle-aux-Saints, France, in 1908. The bones, discovered as part of a burial, were sent to Paris, where the entire skeleton was reconstructed (see accompanying Figure).

Between 1911 and 1913, Marcellin Boule described La Chapelle-aux-Saints as representing a brutish population whose members walked with a shuffling and slouched gait. These descriptions colored people's perception of Neandertals for decades, as Boule and Henri V. Valois's description of the La Chapelle-aux-Saints specimen shows:

> We are impressed by its bestial appearance or rather by the general effect of its simian [apelike] characters. The brain-box, elongated in form, is much depressed; the orbital arches are enormous; the forehead is very receding; the occipital region very projecting and much depressed; the face is long and projects forward; the orbits are

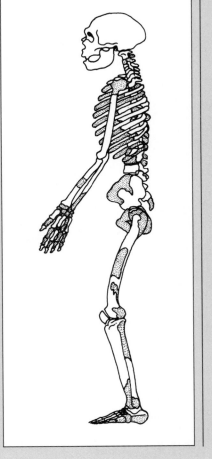

enormous; the nose, separated from the forehead by a deep depression, is short and broad; owing to the prolongation of the malar bones, the upper jaws form a kind of muzzle; the lower jaw is strong and thick; the chin is rudimentary.[1]

The above description was published in 1957, several years after it was discovered that the fossil from La Chapelle-aux-Saints was that of an old man with a severe case of arthritis of the jaw, spine, and, possibly, the legs. In addition, this find is not representative of the population and appears rather extreme even by Neandertal standards. It is a good example of sampling error in the fossil record. Yet this one individual has been called the "classic" Neandertal. Although Boule and Vallois's list of traits is generally correct, their interpretations of Neandertal as bestial and apelike are not.

---

[1]M. Boule and H. V. Vallois, *Fossil Men* (New York: Dryden, 1957), 214. Printed with permission of Holt, Rinehart, and Winston, Inc.

Far Eastern finds to represent the Neandertal pattern, the evidence for this is not convincing.

The Morphology of the Neandertals

With slouched posture a Neandertal man clothed in a leopard skin and carrying a crude wood club walks toward his cave. He stops, appearing dazed and confused, for he is lost. The cave he stands before is not his.

This portrait of a "caveman" that would make Forrest Gump look like a genius is a common way of picturing Neandertals. In fact, healthy Neandertals were not slouching or bent at the knee, nor were they necessarily any less intelligent than modern peoples. Anatomically, people called Neandertals displayed several unique physical characteristics. Yet transported to the present time and dressed in modern clothing, Neandertals might not elicit a second glance.

THE NEANDERTAL SKULL   If brought to life and dressed in modern clothing, Neandertals might be thought of as being only slightly strange. Yet details of their anatomy do contrast in several important ways with the anatomy of modern hu-

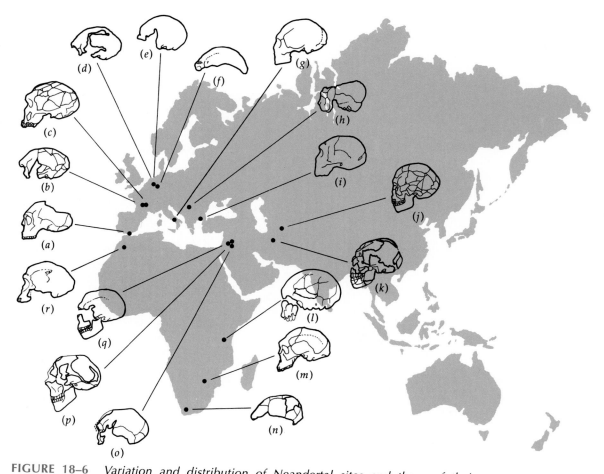

FIGURE 18–6 *Variation and distribution of Neandertal sites and those of their contemporaries and near contemporaries.* *(a)* Gibraltar; *(b)* La Quina, France; *(c)* La Ferrassie, France; *(d)* Neandertal, Germany; *(e)* Spy I, Belgium; *(f)* Spy II, Belgium; *(g)* Monte Circeo, Italy; *(h)* Krapina, Yugoslavia; *(i)* Petralona, Greece; *(j)* Teschik Tasch child, Uzbekistan; *(k)* Shanidar 1, Iraq; *(l)* LH 18, Laetoli, Tanzania; *(m)* Kabwe (Broken Hill), Zambia; *(n)* Saldanha, South Africa; *(o)* Skhūl IX, Israel; *(p)* Skhūl IV, Israel; *(q)* Tabūn, Israel; *(r)* Jebel Irhoud, Morocco.

mans. For instance, the skull shows many unique features (Figures 18–7 and 18–8 and Table 18–1).

Neandertals are "flat-headed" or platycephalic. The distance from the top of the head to the level of the eye sockets is less than that in modern *H. sapiens.* However, the massive skull encases a large brain. In fact, the average cranial capacity of all known Neandertals is a little larger than the average capacity of contemporary *H. sapiens.* It ranges between about 1300 and 1750 cubic centimeters, with an average of about 1400 cubic centimeters. This fact has led certain mod-

ern scholars to speculate on the possibility of superintelligent Neandertals. The slightly greater average cranial capacity, however, is more likely due to sampling error or to the fact that the musculature of the Neandertals was heavier than that of modern humans, requiring a larger surface area for the attachment of facial and cranial muscles.

In most mammals, the base of the skull, called the **basicranium,** is relatively flat, and a line from the roof of the mouth to the back of the skull is fairly straight. The basicrania of *H.*

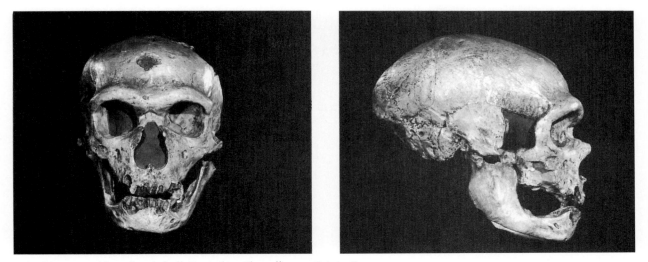

FIGURE 18–7 *Neandertal skull.* Cast of La Chapelle-aux-Saints, France.

sapiens sapiens and *H. erectus* are bent. The Neandertals, which are an enigma in many ways, display a basicranium that is more like the general mammalian pattern, straighter than the pattern found in *H. sapiens sapiens* and *H. erectus.* The possible consequences of the shape of the base of the cranium for the production of speech is discussed later in this chapter.

The face of modern *H. sapiens* is flat compared with the Neandertal face; that is, the nasal region of the face is more in line with the forehead. In Neandertals this region projects forward. Also, the nasal region is smaller in modern *H. sapiens* than in Neandertals.

The forward-projecting face of the Neandertal may be due in part to the Neandertal's greatly enlarged facial sinuses and the positioning of the teeth. A **facial sinus** is a hollow, air-filled space in the bones of the front of the skull. The teeth project forward. From the side view one sees a gap between the last molar and the edge of the ascending branch of the mandible. The larger sinuses are also characteristic of earlier hominids such as Arago, Steinheim, and Petralona, but the

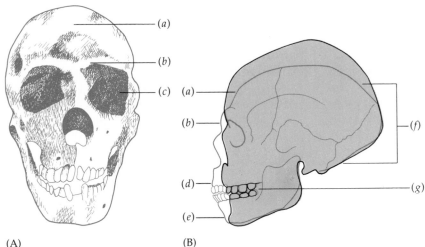

(A)   (B)

FIGURE 18–8 *The Neandertal skull.* *(A)* Front view (Shanidar 1); *(B)* side view (reconstruction of La Chapelle-aux-Saints) with silhouette of *H. sapiens sapiens.* *(a)* Platycephalic appearance; *(b)* large, continuous brow ridge; *(c)* large orbits; *(d)* forward-projecting face; *(e)* lack of chin; *(f)* occipital "bun"; *(g)* gap between last molar and ascending branch of mandible.

TABLE 18–1

NEANDERTALS (*HOMO SAPIENS NEANDERTALENSIS*) AND MODERN HUMANS (*HOMO SAPIENS SAPIENS*) COMPARED

NEANDERTALS	MODERN HUMANS
Flat-headed (platycephalic) brain case	Higher and rounder brain case
Cranial capacity of 1300–1750 cubic centimeters	Cranial capacity of 900–2300 cubic centimeters
Well-developed brow ridges with continuous shelf of bone	Brow ridges moderate to absent; never a continuous shelf of bone
Backward extension of occiput into a "bun"	Rounded occiput; no "bun"
Relatively flat basicrania	Bent basicrania
Maximum skull breadth at about midpoint (viewed from rear)	Maximum skull breadth higher on skull (viewed from rear)
Forward projection of face	Flatter face (nose and teeth more in line with eye sockets)
Variably developed chin	Well-developed chin
Relatively large incisors	Relatively small incisors
Taurodontism (molars and premolars with enlarged pulp cavities and fused roots)	No taurodontism
Bones thinner than in *H. erectus*	Bones thinner than in Neandertals
Sockets for femurs further back	Sockets for femurs further forward
Dorsal groove on side of outer border of scapula (in about 60% of specimens)	Ventral groove on side of outer border of scapula (in most specimens)
Long bones more curved with large areas for muscle attachments	Long bones straighter with smaller articular surfaces
More powerful muscles to flex fingers	Less powerful grip

forward dentition pattern of the Neandertal is rare in other hominids.

Compared with the Neandertal face, the modern human face is small, as are the eye sockets; the front of the upper jaw and the mandible are also small. Neandertals, with their forward projection of the jaw, have sufficient room behind the dental arcade for an internal buttress reminiscent of the simian shelf of apes. There is no room for a simian shelf on the relatively delicate mandible of a modern human (Figure 18–9). Instead, the modern human has a strong **chin,** a bony projection of the lower part of the mandible. Neandertals show varying development of a chin; in some it is completely absent, while in others it is slightly developed.

Several interesting features of the Neandertal skull are seen from the side and back views. The maximum breadth of the Neandertal skull is higher than that in *H. erectus* but lower than that in modern populations; this gives the skull a "barrel" shape when seen from behind. In the side view, the great length of the skull can be

seen. The backward projection of the occipital region forms what is called a "bun."

The foramen magnum is the hole in the base of the skull through which the spinal cord passes. Yoel Rak reports that in Neandertal children, including a recently found 10-month-old infant, the foramen magnum is oval in contrast to the round opening in modern children.[4] The significance of this difference is unknown.

Many Neandertal specimens show signs of arthritis in the **temporomandibular joint,** where the mandible articulates with the rest of the skull. The presence of arthritis may be an indication of excessive strain on the joint. Could it be that the Neandertals used their teeth as tools? There is some evidence for this in the wear patterns on teeth, which suggest that Neandertals used their teeth for such tasks as softening skins.

Neandertal incisors are, on the average, larger than those of modern populations, and some-

---

[4]R. Lipkin, "Neandertal Tot Enters Human-Origins Debate," *Science News*, 145 (1994), 5.

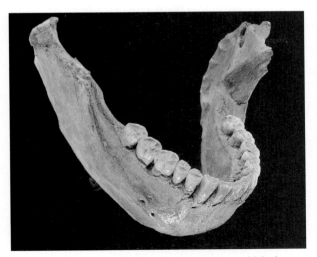

FIGURE 18–9 *A Neandertal mandible.* Mandible from a female Neandertal from Tabūn, Israel.

times they are as large as those of *H. erectus.* The molars and premolars are no larger than those of modern *H. sapiens,* and the third molar sometimes is very small.

HOW CAN WE EXPLAIN THE NEANDERTAL FACIAL CONFIGURATION?

Until the mid-1980s, the most frequently mentioned selective agent used to explain the Neandertal face was cold. One suggestion proposed that the forward projection of the face was a means of keeping the nasal cavities away from the brain, which is sensitive to low temperatures. One function of the nasal cavities is to warm the air that is moving through the head to the lungs; for people living in extremely cold climates, maximum warming means a minimum chance of damaging the brain. In addition to the projecting face, the nasal cavities in Neandertals are very large, providing a greater surface area for the warming of the air.

Although the Neandertal face may have served well for cold adaptation, this hypothesis does not provide a complete explanation for the Neandertal face. For one thing, the Neandertal facial morphology is found in populations that existed before the onset of the Würm Glacial and during the glacial itself in latitudes not affected by the drops in temperature.

Yoel Rak has proposed an explanation for the Neandertal facial configuration in terms of biomechanics of the skull.[5] The Neandertal has a robust face with large canines and incisors. The structure of the Neandertal face may have been an adaptation to withstand the considerable stresses that developed between the upper and lower teeth. The front teeth of the Neandertals often show considerable wear, indicating that, like some Eskimos, they used their front teeth to chew hides and other nonfood materials.

We should not expect a single cause for a complex anatomical pattern. Rak concludes that "the unique Neandertal facial configuration is more probably the result of a combination of factors; a highly complex interaction of forces from the chewing apparatus, a response to climatic conditions and a variety of other factors as yet undetermined."[6]

THE NEANDERTAL POSTCRANIAL SKELETON

Compared with the modern human skeleton, the Neandertal skeleton is generally more robust and the musculature is heavier. Neandertals, who averaged a little over 152 centimeters (5 feet) tall, are generally shorter than most modern humans. Neandertals possess massive limb bones compared with the thin limb bones of modern humans. The long bones are generally curved, with larger areas for the attachment of muscles. The morphology of the finger bones indicates that Neandertals were capable of a more powerful grip than that of modern humans. Taken together, the entire Neandertal postcranial pattern is one that allowed for great power while permitting fine control of the body. Anthropologist F. Clark Howell suggests that a Neandertal "would have been a formidable opponent in a college wrestling tournament."[7]

The Neandertal scapula is characterized by a deep groove on the back surface. This suggests strong development of the teres minor muscle that extends from the scapula to the upper end of the humerus (Figure 18–10). In modern humans a groove is usually found on the inside (rib side) of the scapula. The Neandertal pattern indicates a powerful teres minor muscle, which

[5]Y. Rak, "The Neandertals: A New Look at an Old Face," *Journal of Human Evolution,* 15 (1986), 151–164.
[6]Ibid., 157.
[7]F. C. Howell, *Early Man* (New York: Time-Life, 1965), 126.

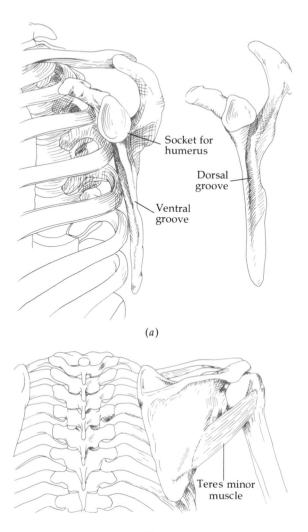

(a)

(b)

FIGURE 18–10 *The Neandertal scapula.* (a) Side view of the left scapula of Shanidar 1 (right) and of a modern *H. sapiens* (left). The ventral-groove pattern is found in 80 percent of modern humans and is related to the development of a shoulder muscle, the teres minor, which connects the upper arm to the scapula by attaching to a small portion of the dorsal surface of the scapula. In more than 60 percent of the Neandertal scapulas, we see a single, large groove on the dorsal side of the outer border. All of the outer edge and part of the dorsal surface provided attachment for the teres minor muscle, indicating that it was well developed. (b) When the teres minor muscle contracts, it pulls the humerus in toward the scapula, thus strengthening the shoulder joint. At the same time, it turns the upper arm, forearm, and hand outward. (From "The Neandertals," by E. Trinkaus and W. W. Howells. Copyright © 1979 by Scientific American, Inc. All rights reserved.)

functions to rotate the humerus outward while helping to keep the head of the humerus in its socket during movement. A powerful teres minor muscle working to balance other arm muscles that pull the arm down allows for powerful throwing and pounding activities while permitting fine control of movement.

Although Neandertals have often been portrayed as bowed over with their heads hung forward, capable only of an "apelike" walk, this description has no basis in fact—Neandertals were completely bipedal. However, scholars disagree whether or not Neandertal posture and locomotion were identical to those of modern humans. Like other parts of the Neandertal skeleton, and in contrast with those of modern humans, the pelvic bones are quite robust. There is an exception to this generalization in the upper portion of the pubis which is thinner and longer in Neandertals. The consequence of this feature for locomotion and posture has not been resolved.

Origin of the Neandertals

The robust appearance, low cranium, and prominent brow ridges suggest that the Neandertals evolved through transitional forms from *H. erectus* populations. When this pattern first began to show itself is a highly debated topic in physical anthropology.

In 1995 it was announced that fossils that might be older than 780,000 years have been found at the site of Gran Dolina, in the Atapuerca Mountains of Spain. This date was established by use of the geomagnetic reversal time scale (Chapter 14). If this date is correct, these would represent the earliest known European inhabitants (Chapter 17). To some researchers the Atapuerca fossils might have been ancestors of the Heidelberg people who lived in Europe about 500,000 years ago and who may have been ancestors to a line that led to Neandertals (Figure 18–3).

In the early 1990s, partial skulls that display elements of the Neandertal patterns were discovered in the Atapuerca Mountains of Spain, the same region where the earliest European fossils were found.[8]

---

[8]J. L. Arsuaga et al., "Three New Human Skulls from the Sima de los Huesos Middle Pleistocene Site in Sierra de Atapuerca, Spain," *Nature*, 362 (1993), 534–537.

However, clearer indications of this pattern appear approximately 130,000 years ago and are manifest in fossils such as those from Fontéchevade. A fragmentary skull found at Biache in northeastern France is platycephalic and has an occipital bun. Another French find, from La Chaise, shows the typical Neandertal dental pattern. From Saccopastore, near Rome, two skulls, dated at about 90,000 B.P., display almost the full Neandertal pattern. Nevertheless, the Saccopastore occipital is more rounded and less projecting, and the cranial capacity of 1300 cubic centimeters is at the lowest limit for Neandertals. The Saccopastore, Biache, and La Chaise may be considered early Neandertals.

One of the earliest sites to yield skeletons that display what might be the complete Neandertal pattern is Krapina, in Yugoslavia, which contained fragmentary remains of at least forty-five individuals and perhaps many more. Unfortunately, the site was first excavated by dynamite. Dynamite and bones are not compatible, and so the remains of the individuals are highly fragmentary. The site might be as much as 120,000 years old.

Careful analysis of the Krapina fossils shows a population with massive brow ridges, cranial capacities up to 1450 cubic centimeters, and the typical Neandertal pelvic pattern. From about 70,000 years ago to between 40,000 and 35,000 years ago, the Neandertal pattern, which had taken tens of thousands of years to develop, remained relatively stable (Table 18–2).

Other Neandertals

We have been discussing only the Neandertals from northern, western, and southern Europe, but the Neandertal complex of characteristics also existed in other areas. Two subadult children were unearthed in western Asia, one at Kiik-Koba, in the Russian Crimea, and the other at Teshik Tash, in Uzbekistan, near the Afghanistan border. These finds resemble western European Neandertals, but the remains from Teshik Tash do not show the same degree of forward projection of the face as do western populations. Also, the long bones are relatively thin and lack the curvature seen in most of the western European Neandertal fossils. However, these differences may represent normal variation within the Neandertal population.

An interesting progression of fossils comes from Israel. Working at the sites of Tabūn and Skhūl on Mount Carmel, Dorothy Garrod found populations that displayed a surprising range of variation. Some specimens reflect the essential Steinheim features, others show more modern characteristics, and still others exhibit a mixture of more modern and Neandertal features. Skhūl is dated at 119,000 B.P. by thermoluminescence dating (Chapter 14). Not enough of the Neandertal complex of traits is present in these individuals for many paleoanthropologists to justify calling them Neandertals (Figure 18–11).

From Shanidar Cave, Iraq, come the remains of eight individuals. Besides showing the Nean-

TABLE 18–2

POSSIBLE ORIGIN OF NEANDERTALS

AGE (YEARS AGO)	FOSSILS (FROM EUROPE)	COMMENT
35,000–40,000	*Homo sapiens sapiens*	"Disappearance" of Neandertals
35,000–70,000	La Quina, Le Moustier, La Chapelle-aux-Saints, La Ferrassie, Spy I	Neandertal pattern well developed and stable
70,000–120,000	Krapina, Saccopastore	Perhaps the first to show complete Neandertal pattern
90,000–130,000	Biache, La Chaise, Fontéchevade	Clear indications of Neandertal pattern
200,000	Arago, Ehringsdorf	Show some characteristics of the later Neandertals
200,000–240,000	Swanscombe, Steinheim	Beginning to show more of the Neandertal pattern
300,000	Atapuerca	Displays some elements of the Neandertal pattern

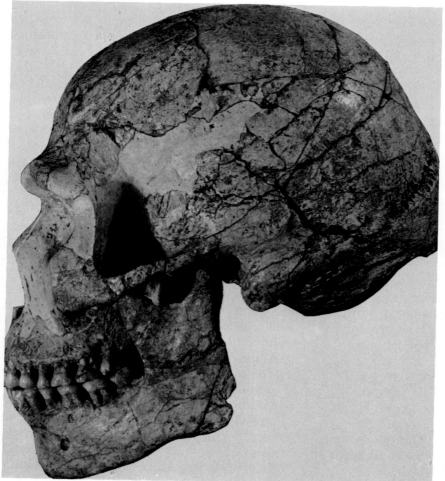

FIGURE 18–11   *Skull V, Skhūl, Mount Carmel, Israel.*

dertal pattern with some more modern over-tones, many of the Shanidar individuals are interesting for cultural reasons. From this cave, dated about 46,000 B.P., comes evidence of burial with flowers and, perhaps, the first known incident of successful surgery. We explore the evidence in Box 18–3.

About 35,000 years ago the Neandertals disappear as a recognizable type in the fossil record. Writers have envisioned more modern peoples moving into the regions occupied by Neandertals and killing them off, but there is no empirical evidence that this occurred. Others attribute the disappearance of Neandertal fossils to the evolution of the Neandertals into anatomically modern *H. sapiens.* These competing hypotheses will be discussed further in the next chapter in the context of the origins of modern *H. sapiens sapiens.*

Summary

We cannot say exactly when fossils classified as *H. sapiens* first appeared; the precise point in time is a relative and arbitrary matter. The best known archaic *H. sapiens* population is the Neandertals, a predominantly European population dating from about 120,000 to 35,000 years ago. Some researchers believe that the Neandertals evolved into *H. sapiens sapiens* in Europe; others think they were a side branch of human evolution that did not contribute to the gene pool of contemporary peoples. There is increasing evidence that people with more modern anatomical characteristics than the Neandertals were evolving in Africa more than 200,000 years ago.

Neandertals are found in Europe and western Asia, including Israel, Iraq, Russia, and Uzbekistan. Some investigators have classified finds outside this area as Neandertal, but most contemporary paleoanthropologists do not agree with this assessment. In other areas of the world there were other populations of *H. sapiens*, including perhaps the earliest *H. sapiens sapiens* in Africa.

Neandertals are platycephalic, with a massive skull encasing a large brain. The forehead is sloping, and the well-developed brow ridges fuse over the nose and form a continuous shelf of bone above the orbits. The far-forward position of the dentition and the enlarged facial sinuses are associated with a forward-projecting nasal region. The maximum breadth of the Neandertal skull is lower than that in modern populations, giving the skull a "barrel" shape. In the side view, the backward projection of the occipital region forms a bun. The postcranial bones are robust, and the long bones curved; the relatively large areas for muscle attachment suggest a powerfully built musculature.

About 35,000 years ago the Neandertals "disappeared" as a recognizable subspecies. By this time *H. sapiens sapiens* was the only type of hominid existing on earth.

NEANDERTAL LANGUAGE AND CULTURE

As we saw in Chapter 12, monkeys and apes are capable of rudimentary cultural behavior. The great apes also may be capable of a certain amount of nonoral linguistic behavior. Yet it was in the hominid line that cultural behavior and language became the primary means of adaptation.

The Brain and Language in Prehistoric Populations

The dramatic increase in the genetic potential for cultural and linguistic adjustments correlates with several evolutionary adaptations beginning more than 1.5 million years ago. Starting at about 1.6 million B.P., brain size began to increase over

and beyond that which can be explained by an increase in body size. This process, known as encephalization (Chapter 13), corresponds with the development, by *H. erectus*, of the hand ax. Oldowan tools had been made earlier, but hand axes are more sophisticated tools with complex properties.

In order for hominids to produce complex tools, several anatomical and neural changes were necessary. Some researchers point to evidence suggesting that from 1.6 million to about 300,000 B.P., the brain not only was increasing in size but also was becoming neurally reorganized in a way that increased its ability to process information in an abstract (symbolic) way. This symbolism allowed complex information to be stored, relationships to be derived, and information to be efficiently retrieved and communicated to others.

In addition to the evolution of the brain's new "data management" system, other neural reorganizations were occurring. In modern people, a "bump," usually located on the left hemisphere of the frontal lobe of the cerebral cortex, controls the muscles for speech. This area of the brain, known as **Broca's area,** may have been present as early as 1.8 million B.P. in KNM-ER 1470 (Figure 17–1), a specimen of *Homo habilis*. The presence of Broca's area does not necessarily mean that *H. habilis* could speak, or at least not in a modern sense.

The other neural and anatomical features needed for fully developed language and speech may not have evolved this early. It is not possible to know exactly when the reorganization of the brain reached its modern state; many investigators believe this may have occurred about 300,000 years ago. Until recently, the anatomical evidence for the earliest speech was almost totally lacking. After all, most of the structures used in producing speech are soft tissues such as the tongue, lips, soft palate, and vocal chords, which are not fossilized.

LOOK WHO'S TALKING   If the brain's reorganization was basically modern by about 300,000 or more years ago, and if this reorganization was a prerequisite for full language abilities, then who were the first people to speak in a modern way? There are two lines of anatomical evidence

BOX 18–3

SHANIDAR 1 AND PALEOPATHOLOGY

Paleopathology is the study of diseases and injuries in fossil specimens. About 17 percent of the Neandertal bones from Shanidar have a joint disease called calcium pyrophosphate deposition disease.[1] Although fossilized bones are usually all that remains of an ancient organism, soft-tissue diseases and injuries can sometimes be inferred from the evidence found in fossilized bones. One of the nine Shanidar finds, Shanidar 1, is a good example of what a paleopathologist can conclude from a fossil specimen.

> Shanidar 1 was one of the most severely traumatized Pleistocene hominids for whom we have evidence. He suffered multiple fractures involving the cranium, right humerus, and right fifth metatarsal, and the right knee, ankle, and first tarsometatarsal joint show degenerative joint disease that was probably trauma related.[2]

In addition to the injuries listed above, Shanidar 1 was blind in the left eye, as inferred from a crushed orbit. Because of injuries, his right arm, clavicle, and scapula had never fully grown. The humerus had apparently been cut off slightly above the elbow, and healing of the bone indicates that the individ-

ual survived this ordeal. If this was an intentional procedure to remove a withered arm, then it is the earliest known evidence of successful surgery. An unusually great amount of wear on Shanidar 1's front teeth suggests that the teeth were used for grasping in place of the right arm. In addition, analysis of the skull shows that the top right side was damaged and had healed before his death.

There are several possible explanations of Shanidar 1's infirmness. One scenario is offered by Erik Trinkaus:

> Shanidar 1 sustained a massive crushing injury to the right side of the body, primarily in the region of the arm and shoulder. A crushing injury, such as a rock fall, is more likely than an incised wound because an incised wound of this degree would probably have been associated with fatal hemorrhaging. A soft tissue injury would account for the evidence of infection (os-

teomyelitis) in the clavicle. The fractures of the distal humeral diaphysis and olecranon fossa region would have occurred at the same time, and the pseudoarthrosis/amputation would have developed subsequently. The small size of the right arm bones could be the product of hypoplasia or atrophy, depending upon when the injury occurred; either interpretation of the small size of the bones is consistent with a prolonged period of survival.

The fracture of the right fifth metatarsal probably occurred at the same time as the injury to the right arm. The extensive degenerative joint disease of the right lower limb and the abnormal curvature of the left tibial diaphysis were probably secondary to the trauma, resulting in part from soft tissue injury and in part from abnormal locomotion due to the injury.

In this interpretation, the cranial injuries would be seen as secondary to the crushing trauma to the right side of the body. They may have occurred at the same time from the individual falling away

The normal (top) and abnormal (bottom) humeri of Shanidar 1. The middle section of the normal humerus was restored in plaster and should be somewhat longer, making the abnormal humerus about 10 percent shorter than the normal one.

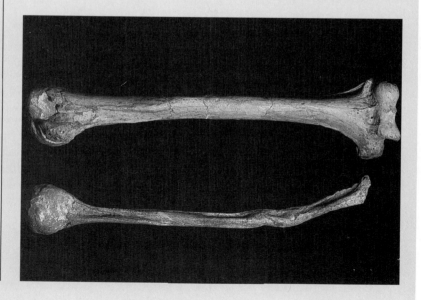

from the blow to the right side and striking a hard object, or they may have happened later as a result of the individual's inability to get around easily.[3]

Trinkaus offers other possibilities as well.[4] What is obvious is that this individual had major debilitating injuries and lived to a relatively old age; he died a few years younger than the average life expectancy for Americans at the end of the nineteenth century. Shanidar 1 may not have been able to contribute directly to the food supply of his community, yet his longevity perhaps attests to other functions he was able to provide. By analogy with contemporary societies, we may surmise that his wisdom and experience were valued by the community and contributed to the survival of his society.

---

[1]B. M. Rothschild, "Oldest Bone Diseases," *Nature*, 349 (1991), 288.
[2]E. Trinkaus, *The Shanidar Neandertals* (New York: Academic, 1983), 401.
[3]Ibid., 409–410.
[4]Ibid., 410–411.

---

that provide us with clues about speaking abilities; both are controversial.

One type of evidence for speech comes from examination of the shape of the basicranium, the floor of the brain case. A straight basicranium suggests that the larynx (voice box) is positioned high in the neck; such a vocal tract would be unable to produce many human speech sounds (Figure 18–12a). In modern humans, the basicranium is flexed, or bent, indicating a larynx low in the neck; this creates an acoustic situation favorable for speech sounds (Figure 18–12e). The australopithecine basicranium is straight and is similar to the ones in modern apes. The basicranium of *H. erectus* is more flexed than the australopithecine basicranium but not quite as bent as that in a modern adult human skull. This may mean that the position of the larynx, and hence the shape of the vocal tract, may have approached the modern configuration as early as 1.6 million B.P. Note that this date corresponds with the dates for the beginning of increased encephalization and the evidence for the presence of Broca's area in the brain.

According to some reconstruction, the Neandertal basicranium is straighter than that of the modern human or *H. erectus*, and this has led to computer models of the Neandertal vocal apparatus indicating that Neandertals could not pronounce certain vowel sounds such as a, i, and u. Even if this is true, Neandertal's lack of articulate speech, in the modern sense, would not necessarily mean that more modern humans living at the same time as or before Neandertals could not speak as we do. After all, since *H. erectus* has a quite modern basicranium, Neandertals are seen by some as not being typical of *H. sapiens.*

Each point in the debate over the Neandertals' speaking ability can be argued from opposite directions. A new reconstruction of the La Chapelle-aux-Saints skull suggests to some paleoanthropologists that the basicranium was not as straight as previously thought. These investigators believe that the Neandertal basicranium falls within the range of some *H. sapiens sapiens* populations.

The second anatomical indication for speech is found in the analysis of the hyoid bone. The hyoid bone is a delicate bone in the neck that anchors muscles connected to the jaw, larynx, and tongue (Figure 18–13). This bone is so fragile that we have only one fossil specimen, that of a 60,000-year-old Neandertal found in Kebara Cave in Israel.

For some researchers the Kebara hyoid contradicts the basicranial data on Neandertals. It is seen by some as being almost identical in size, shape, and position in the neck to the hyoids of contemporary humans and thus indicates that the Neandertals *could* talk like modern humans.

However, some anthropologists do not accept the Kebara hyoid as being reliable evidence of the Neandertals' ability to speak. Although the Neandertal hyoid is very similar to that of modern humans, a single bone out of context of the skele-

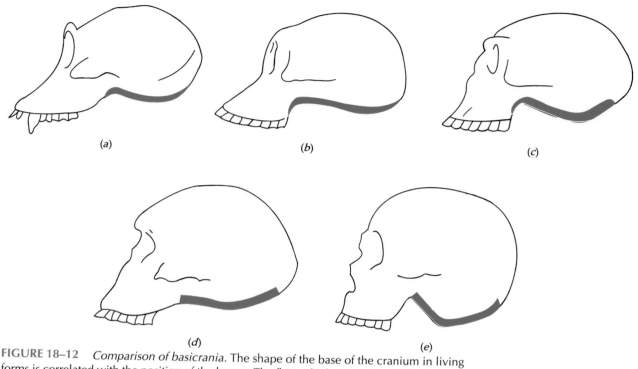

FIGURE 18–12 *Comparison of basicrania.* The shape of the base of the cranium in living forms is correlated with the position of the larynx. The flatter the basicranium, the higher the larynx in the neck. In turn, the position of the larynx in the throat influences the type of vocalizations that can be produced. The figure shows a series of composite representations of *(a)* the chimpanzee, *(b) Australopithecus africanus, (c) Homo erectus, (d)* Neandertal, and *(e) Homo sapiens sapiens.* (Skulls are not drawn to scale.)

ton from which it came says little about Neandertal speech abilities. What is critical is the placement of the bone. If the Neandertal hyoid was positioned differently than in modern humans, the Neandertals would not have been able to produce all of the same sounds. A study of the hyoids of thirty mammalian genera suggests that the size and shape of the hyoid is not correlated with its placement. So the similar size and shape of the Neandertal and modern hyoid do not mean that it was situated in exactly the same place in the throat as it is in the modern human body.

Our discussion of the origin of speech points to a basic problem in reconstructing any type of ancient behavior. The exact origins of all ancient patterns or capabilities are difficult to determine because of small sample sizes and the lack of crucial data. Yet it is evident that from australopithecines to modern people there was a gradual progression in linguistic and general mental abilities.

The Culture of the Neandertals

The cultural tradition associated most frequently with Neandertals is the Mousterian, named after the rock shelter of Le Moustier in France. Some non-Neandertals are also found in association with Mousterian assemblages, and non-Mousterian cultural traditions existed during the time of the Neandertals. Just as the skeletal remains of the Neandertals reflect a wide range of morphological variation, the cultural material shows variability in tool types. Also, with the Neandertals the first concrete evidence of a concern about the supernatural emerges.

THE TOOLS OF NEANDERTALS   The Mousterian is a Middle Paleolithic cultural tradition. It is a continuation and refinement of the Acheulean tradition. It is characterized by an increase in the number and variety of flake tools and an ultimate deemphasis of the hand ax. For example, in some early Neandertal sites, hand axes make up as much as 40 percent of the stone tools, whereas in later assemblages, they drop to less than 8 percent. In some Mousterian sites bone tools are predominant.

Many Mousterian stone tools were made by chipping away at a core that was prepared by removing small flakes. The core was then struck to remove larger flakes that could be further worked to create cutting, drilling, and scraping tools.

The sites of the Middle Paleolithic show great variability in tool types and their frequencies (Figure 18–14). Several different lithic industries can be defined. This variability has been explained by François Bordes and his students in terms of differing cultural traditions and movements of populations.

Lewis and Sally Binford have interpreted this variability in another way.[9] They note that human behavior is patterned in space; that is, different human activities take place in different places, and different human activities are associated with different tool types. Thus, activities taking place in a classroom differ from those taking place in a cafeteria, an office, or a library. Tools associated with the classroom include chalk and erasers, maps, and bulletin boards, while those associated with the cafeteria include plates and eating utensils.

The Binfords see the Mousterian as a single cultural tradition, with the different kinds of sites associated with different activities. For example, the typical Mousterian may represent butchering activities, while the Mousterian of Acheulean tradition may represent the activities of bone and wood tool manufacture.

WERE NEANDERTALS "CAVEMEN"? Humans are not by nature cave-dwelling animals, as caves are dark, often damp, and quite uncomfortable. People did inhabit the mouths of caves, but not the deep interiors. In fact, most often

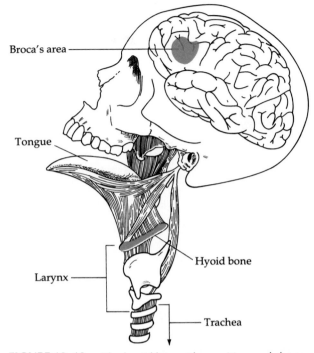

FIGURE 18–13 *The hyoid bone.* The position and shape of the hyoid bone is an important indicator of the potential for speech. The hyoid bone anchors muscles connected to the jaw, larynx, and tongue. Broca's area of the brain controls these muscles as they function to produce speech sounds.

what are called "caves" are not caves at all but rock shelters or rock overhangs.

Rock shelters are among the best places where fossils and artifacts can be found. In many areas, the cycle of wetting and drying out occurs less frequently in rock shelters than in open sites, and hence the chance of rapid deterioration is reduced. Because of the buildup of garbage and the flaking off of material from the roof and floor, caves often provide the researcher with a well-preserved stratigraphy. Since preservation is somewhat better in caves than in open sites, caves have been extensively investigated for signs of humans, and most Neandertal sites have been found in this context.

Neandertals also may have spent a great deal of their time in open-air sites, but these have not been preserved as often as rock shelters have. This is an example of how differential preserva-

---

[9]L. R. Binford and S. R. Binford, "A Preliminary Analysis of Functional Variability in the Mousterian of Levallois Facies," in J. D. Clark and F. C. Howell (eds.), *Recent Studies in Paleoanthropology* (Washington, D.C.: American Anthropological Association, 1966), 238–295.

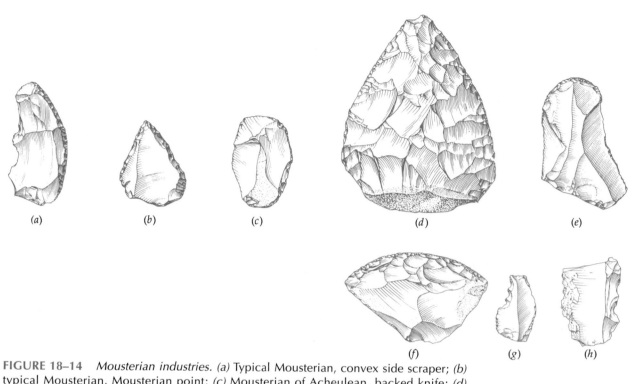

FIGURE 18–14 *Mousterian industries.* (a) Typical Mousterian, convex side scraper; (b) typical Mousterian, Mousterian point; (c) Mousterian of Acheulean, backed knife; (d) Mousterian of Acheulean, hand ax; (e) Mousterian of Acheulean, end scraper; (f) Quina-type Mousterian, traverse scraper; (g) and (h) denticulate Mousterian, denticulate tools.

tion influences the data. However, some open-air sites are known; among the most famous is Molodova I, in the western part of the Ukraine. At this site, mammoth bones served as the support for animal hides that created a house with an inside area 5.4 meters (18 feet) in diameter. Fifteen hearths have been found in the floor of this ancient home.

Some groups of Neandertals probably were more settled than others. Like modern hunter-gatherers, most groups moved from time to time in search of new sources of food. While on the move, and when staying in one place for a short time, they would probably have made huts and windbreaks out of grass, leaves, and sticks. These structures are normally not preserved in the archaeological record.

THE WORLD VIEW OF THE NEANDERTALS

While paleoanthropologists can reconstruct diet and technology with a great deal of confidence,

the reconstruction of religion and philosophy is a great deal more conjectural. From the rich finds of Neandertal cultures some generalities can be made about their world view of life.

As far as is known, Neandertals were the first to systematically and perhaps ritually bury their dead (Figure 18–15). In one cave, an adolescent boy appears to have been carefully buried in a sleeping position. He rests on his right side, with his knees bent and his head positioned on his forearm. In his grave are stone tools and animal remains that may have been meant to aid him in a supposed next world.

The data have led some paleoanthropologists to the conclusion that Neandertals had an awareness not only of the uniqueness of each individual but also of the importance of the individual to society and of society to the individual. The burial of the dead emphasizes both the worth of the individual and preparation for a next life. The burial together of families, or at least members

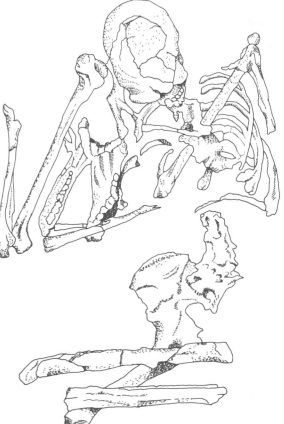

FIGURE 18–15 *Neandertal burial.* An adult male burial from Mount Carmel. The body was buried with the jawbones of a great wild boar.

of a group, indicates relationships strong enough for people who were together during life to wish to remain together in death in the afterworld. Many rituals today reinforce group solidarity by providing a common goal and communal activities; they also provide a united way for society to face the unknown. Perhaps rituals served similar purposes among the Neandertals.

A possible bear cult of the Neandertals has puzzled investigators for years. The very fact that these people may have hunted the gigantic cave bear presents the first mystery, as the larger bears of this species stood more than 3.7 meters (12 feet) tall and had long and deadly claws and perhaps a disposition to match. Many other, less dangerous prey could have been hunted; it does not appear that the Neandertals had to hunt the

bear to survive. So the suggestion has been made that either the bear had some religious or magical meaning associated with it or killing the bear represented a test of manhood. At Drachenloch, Switzerland, a subterranean "vault" was found lined with stones and containing the skulls of several cave bears. At the same site was the skull of one bear with the leg bone of another bear stuck through its cheek; the skull was resting on the bones of a third bear. Other sites have been interpreted as revealing evidence of ritualistic practices involving the cave bear.

The whole idea of a Neandertal "cult of the cave bear" has been questioned in recent years. From a study of cut marks on bones found in association with Neandertals, Lewis Binford concludes that Neandertals were not even big-game hunters.[10] The cut mark pattern is similar to that expected from scavenging, not from hunting. In addition, Philip Chase and Harold Dibble point out that the excavation at Drachenloch was not carefully conducted and that the interpretation of its meaning was exaggerated. The stone vault was probably a natural collection of rocks. This, along with the fact that there were no butchering marks on any of the bears found in association with the rocks, places doubt on the "hunting for ritualistic use" hypothesis. The interpretation of other sites as reflecting ritualistic activity has also been questioned.[11]

NEANDERTAL LIFESTYLES   Lewis Binford has provided other speculations about Neandertal lifestyles.[12] While some anthropologists picture the everyday life of the Neandertals as being similar to that of modern hunter-gatherers, Binford believes that Neandertals lived differently than any *H. sapiens sapiens* population. From his study of sites at Combe-Grenal in southwestern France, he concludes that male and female Neandertals lived in separate areas, that males contributed little in the way of food to their mates and offspring,

---

[10]L. Binford, "Ancestral Lifeways," *Anthroquest*, 32 (1985), 15–20.
[11]P. Chase and H. Dibble, "Middle Paleolithic Symbolism: A Review of Current Evidence and Interpretation," *Journal of Anthropological Archeology*, 6 (1987), 263–296.
[12]J. Fischman, "Hard Evidence," *Discover* (February 1992), 44–51.

and that Neandertals showed little ability for linguistic displacement, that is, planning for the future (Chapter 12).

Binford bases his conclusions on archaeological evidence. For example, at Combe-Grenal he identifies two areas. The "nest areas" contain simple stone tools made from material obtained close by. Other areas, 2.7 to 3 meters (9 to 30 feet) away from each nest area, contain more elaborate stone tools, such as scrapers, that were made from materials obtained from sites about 3.2 kilometers (2 miles) away. On the basis of this and other evidence, Binford suggests that the nest areas might have been where women and children lived and that the more distant areas represent activities of men.

In neither area is there much in the way of animal remains, used for food, that had to be transported from a distance to the site. This suggests to Binford that men may have gone off to hunt or scavenge and ate most of the meat where it was found, but that they lacked the ability to plan and to bring meat back to a home base. The exceptions are the crania that contained the brain, "the stone age equivalent of canned food,"[13] and marrow bones that are found at Combe-Grenal. Perhaps these were too difficult to process in the field and were brought back to a place where it was safer to work on them. Women, who did not hunt or scavenge, ate and fed their children foodstuffs gathered from around the nest sites. However, according to Binford, men occasionally shared a little animal food with women and children, as evidenced by bone fragments found in the nest sites.

Even Binford admits that his ideas are highly speculative. Also, we cannot make generalizations about all Neandertals on the basis of a single site. The fact remains that the Neandertals are still one of the most mysterious populations of the genus *Homo*.

Summary

About 1.6 million years ago, the human capacity for cultural behavior began a dramatic climb. As the brain increased in size, tools became more sophisticated than tools in previous times. The brain not only was increasing in size but also was evolving in a way that made it able to manage more complex information.

The principal information management system was language. Some investigators believe that some form of language ability, similar to our own, may have evolved as early as 300,000 years ago. When people could talk in a modern sense is a debated issue, but a fossil hyoid bone indicates that Neandertals may have been able to produce all the speech sounds that modern people can produce.

Neandertals used a variety of tools made of stone, bone, shell, and possibly wood. Their cultural tradition is called the Mousterian, although it is not confined to them. This tradition continued the use of hand axes, but the number and variety of flake tools increased throughout the Neandertal period. Neandertals lived in both rock shelters and open-air sites, but never caves, and although some groups were probably more settled than others, most groups were probably nomadic.

Neandertals seem to show a consciousness that we can recognize as "human." They appear to have buried their dead and may have placed artifacts and flowers in the graves. They maintained sick and injured individuals; some evidence indicates that they performed surgery. Some anthropologists, however, such as Lewis Binford, believe that the Neandertals may have differed in many ways from modern *H. sapiens sapiens*. Men and women may have lived basically separate lives, and Neandertals may have not had the insights to exploit invisible or distant resources to the same extent as modern people.

STUDY QUESTIONS

1. What are some of the fossils that are considered to be early archaic *Homo sapiens*? What are some of the characteristics of these fossils?
2. Describe two later transitional archaic *Homo sapiens*.
3. Where have Neandertal fossils been discovered? What are the dates of Neandertal sites?
4. What are some of the major anatomical differences between Neandertals and modern humans?

---

[13]Ibid., 50.

5. Summarize what is known about the origins of the Neandertals.
6. About 1.8 million years ago, a rapid increase in the genetic potential for cultural and linguistic abilities seems to have begun. What might have been some of the reasons for this phenomenon?
7. What type of evidence is used to construct models on the potential for language and speech abilities in fossil populations?
8. Compare and contrast the cultural manifestations of *H. erectus* with those of the Neandertals.
9. Discuss assumptions that have been made about the Neandertals' world view.

SUGGESTED READINGS

The following handbooks list individual fossils along with pertinent information:

Day, M. *Guide to Fossil Man: A Handbook of Human Paleontology*, 4th ed. Chicago: University of Chicago Press, 1986.

Larsen, C. S., R. M. Matter, and D. L. Gebo. *Human Origins: The Fossil Record*, 2d ed. Prospect Heights, Ill.: Waveland, 1991.

Also recommended are the following:

Reader, J. *Missing Links: The Hunt for Earliest Man*, rev. ed. Boston: Little, Brown, 1989. This book tells the story of the hunt for and discovery of many important fossil hominids.

Mellars, P. *The Neanderthal Legacy: An Archaeological Perspective.* Princeton, N.J.: Princeton University Press, 1995. This book is an overview of western European Neandertal material culture, subsistence patterns, and society.

Solecki, R. S. *Shanidar: The First Flower People.* New York: Knopf, 1971. This is the story of Solecki's excavation of the Neandertals in Iraq.

Trinkaus, E. *The Shanidar Neandertals.* New York: Academic, 1983. This is a book detailing the finds of nine early eastern Neandertals. The final chapter gives an overview of the evolution of the Neandertals.

Trinkaus, E., and P. Shipman. *The Neandertals: Changing the Image of Mankind.* New York: Knopf, 1992. This is a survey of perceptions and attitudes about the Neandertals from the time of their discovery until today.

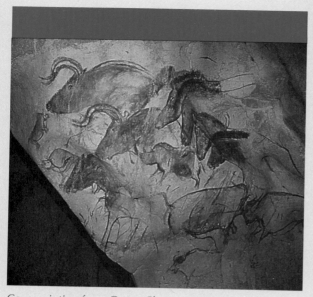

Cave painting from Grotte Chauvet, France. Pictured are horses, bison, a rhinoceros, an elephant, and wild cattle.

Few topics in anthropology have generated more interest and debate over the past few years than the biological and behavioural origins of fully "modern" human populations. The debates have arisen partly from new discoveries and the application of new dating methods, and partly from the use of more sophisticated approaches to the modelling of human evolutionary processes, both in terms of biological evolution, and the associated (and inevitably interrelated) patterns of cultural change.[1]

Paul Mellars and Chris Stringer

[1]P. Mellars and C. Stringer (eds.), *The Human Revolution* (Princeton, N. J.: Princeton University Press, 1989), ix.

CHAPTER 19

MODERN
HOMO SAPIENS

Anthropocentrism is the belief that humans are the most important elements in the universe and that everything else exists for human use and fancy. As was discussed in Chapter 2, this belief runs counter to modern scientific thought. Yet since the nineteenth century, scientists have continued to debate what it is to be a modern human being. These discussions often seem to be anthropocentric or, if we may coin a new term, *sapiencentric*.

As an example, some scholars see the origins of creative thought and behavior, such as that seen in pictorial art, as occurring only after the origins of modern humans—*H. sapiens sapiens*. Although the Neandertals and their contemporaries do not appear to have expressed themselves through pictorial art, they may have developed other creative outlets such as storytelling. We just do not know!

As we will see shortly, anatomically modern peoples may have originated at the same time as or even before the time of the Neandertals, yet *H. sapiens sapiens* did not develop pictorial art until about 30,000 years ago. Why? Perhaps art and other new behaviors originated because of changes in the environment or as the result of cultural exchanges and not because of any physical or mental changes. This chapter will focus on what it means to be modern and will examine the debate over modern human origins and evolution.

HOMO SAPIENS SAPIENS

Life has been described as opportunistic. The first living organisms evolved more than 3.8 billion years ago. At first, the total weight of all living organisms, the biomass, was almost insignificant. As time went on, and as living organisms diversified and spread into new niches, their biomass increased.

The growth in the biomass, or population, of hominids was at first limited. They were confined to one continent, and their ability to exploit resources was limited. By the time modern *Homo sapiens* had evolved, hominids had expanded out of Africa into Europe and Asia. Modern peoples, now equipped with tools and skills to survive in a wide range of habitats, migrated to major islands and island chains and into North and South America.

With new land and ever-increasing technological prowess, the biomass of humans increased almost geometrically. From what was a small early hominid population in Africa some 5 million years ago, humans today number almost 6 billion and some humans are planning the colonization of the moon. This chapter discusses the origin of

FIGURE 19–1 *Variation and distribution of* Homo sapiens sapiens. *(a)* Upper Cave 101, Zhoukoudian, People's Republic of China; *(b)* Tepexpan, Mexico; *(c)* Niah Cave, Borneo; *(d)* Wadjak, Java; *(e)* Talgai, Australia; *(f)* Omo, Ethiopia; *(g)* Omo, Ethiopia; *(h)* Lothagam Hill, Kenya; *(i)* Fish Hoek, South Africa; *(j)* Cape Flats, Cape Peninsula, South Africa; *(k)* Asselar, Mali; *(l)* Afalou, Algeria; *(m)* Cro-Magnon, France; *(n)* Combe Capelle, France; *(o)* Oberkassel, Germany; *(p)* Predmost, Czechoslovakia, *(q)* Jebel Qafzeh IX, Israel.

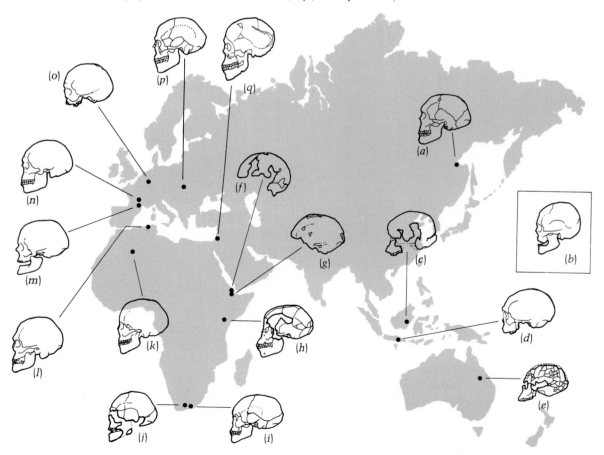

modern humans, their cultural achievements, and their expansion throughout the world.

The Distribution of Fossil *Homo sapiens sapiens* in the Old World

Today, modern *H. sapiens* populations are distributed widely throughout the world. This section will survey the earliest appearances of modern *H. sapiens* in the Old World (Figure 19–1).

ASIA   Two early modern hominids from Israel, one from Jebel Qafzeh and the other from Tabūn, place anatomically modern humans well back into the Neandertal time range (Figure 19–2). The Jebel Qafzeh fossil has been dated by electron spin resonance dating to between 115,000 and 96,000 B.P. The dating of Tabūn is less certain, but it is probably older than 100,000 B.P.

Although many paleoanthropologists are coming to the conclusion that Jebel Qafzeh and Tabūn are about 100,000 years old, the earliest reliable dates for modern *H. sapiens* in eastern Asia are much more recent. One of these early dates is associated with an anatomically modern human from Niah Cave, in North Borneo; the fossil has been dated by radiocarbon dating at about 41,500 B.P. The adult female found in the cave is delicately built; the skull lacks brow ridges, the forehead is high, and the back of the head is rounded. The Niah Cave individual resembles modern populations of New Guinea.

Many finds have been made in China, but perhaps the best known is a series of skulls from the Upper Cave of Zhoukoudian. The skulls are all modern, but they are interesting in that each one differs in some respects from the others, providing a good example of intrapopulation variability. One skull shows a forward-jutting zygomatic arch and **shovel-shaped incisors** similar to those of present Asian populations. Shovel-shaped incisors are incisors that have a scooped-out shape on the tongue side of the tooth. These skulls also resemble closely many American Indian skulls.

EUROPE   Early modern humans are often seen in terms of a population called Cro-Magnon, which lived about 28,000 years ago or later. Discovered in 1868 in a rock shelter in southwest-

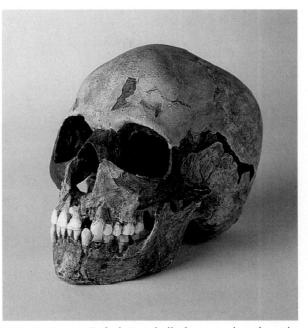

FIGURE 19–2   *Qafzeh II, a skull of a young boy, from the cave of Jabel Qafzeh, Israel.*

ern France, several partial skeletons became the prototype of modern *H. sapiens.* Early scholars envisioned Cro-Magnon people as light-skinned, beardless, upright individuals who invaded Europe and destroyed the bestial Neandertals. In general, Cro-Magnon people are characterized by broad, small faces with high foreheads and prominent chins and cranial capacities as high as 1590 cubic centimeters (Figure 19–3). Their height has been estimated at between 163 and 183 centimeters (5 feet 4 inches and 6 feet), but their skin color and amount of body hair can only be surmised.

In other parts of Europe even older fossil populations of modern people existed. At the 38,000-year-old site of Mladeč in Czechoslovakia paleontologists found a cranium that was quite robust yet basically modern in appearance. It, and other finds in eastern, central, and southern Europe, show modern features; yet these specimens also retain some Neandertal characteristics, such as robustness and brow ridges, that are intermediate in size between the Neandertals and modern humans.

AFRICA   The oldest sub-Saharan fossils that show modern characteristics are fragmentary

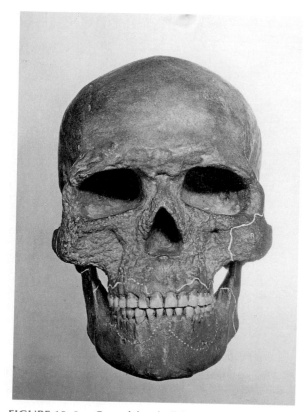

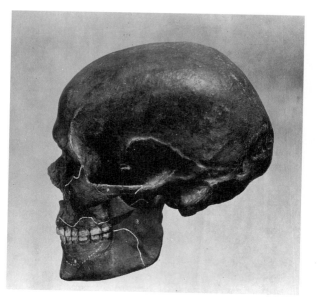

FIGURE 19–3   *Cast of the skull from Cro-Magnon, France.*

finds from the Klasies River Mouth in South Africa. This material is about 120,000 years old as dated by electron spin resonance dating. Also in South Africa, finds from Border Cave that have many modern features have been dated to between 115,000 to 100,000 B.P. The dating from both sites, however, has been questioned, as has the degree to which they exhibit modern features. Other African fossils, such as Omo I from Ethiopia, dated at 130,000 B.P., are quite modern in appearance (Figure 19–4). Still other early African hominids show a mixture of archaic and modern features.

The Anatomy of *Homo sapiens sapiens*

Modern humans have a distinctly round head that contains a large brain which averages 1350 cubic centimeters. From front to back, the cranial arch, or vault, is short but high. The occipital bone is delicate. Compared with that of ear-

lier hominids, the modern human face is small, as are the eye sockets; the front of the upper jaw and the mandible are also small. The modern human has a strong **chin,** a bony projection of the lower part of the mandible. Compared with the earlier hominid skeletons, the modern human skeleton is generally less robust and the musculature is lighter.

Ideas on the Origin of *Homo sapiens sapiens*

Competing hypotheses have been suggested to explain the origin of modern humans. In the late 1980s, a provocative idea received a great deal of attention from the popular media as well as from anthropologists. It is called the "Mitochondrial Eve" hypothesis.

THE STORY OF "MITOCHONDRIAL EVE"
The "mitochondrial" in "Mitochondrial Eve's"

name refers to mitochondrial DNA (mtDNA). Mitochondrial DNA is found in the cytoplasm of the cell and, in humans, codes for only thirteen proteins (Chapter 4). An individuals' mtDNA is inherited exclusively from the mother's sex cell. Since there is no recombination of the two parents' mtDNA, the only difference in a child's mtDNA and that of its mother or grandmother or great-grandmother, or any other direct female relative, is due to mutation. Alan Wilson, Rebecca Cann, and Mark Stoneking propose that the mtDNA of all modern populations can be traced back to an African woman who lived about 200,000 years ago. She became known as "Mitochondrial Eve."[2] Wilson, Cann, and Stoneking based their date on comparisons of differences in mtDNA in contemporary populations. By assuming a mutation rate of 2 percent per million years, they believe that current variation in mtDNA suggests a common ancestor that lived about 200,000 years ago.

[2]R. L. Cann, M. Stoneking, and A. C. Wilson, "Mitochondrial DNA and Human Evolution," *Nature*, 325 (1987), 31–36.

FIGURE 19–4 *Omo I skull, Kibish Formation, Ethiopia*

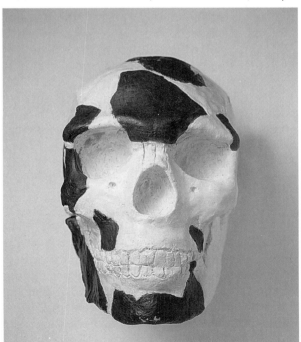

A study published in 1995 reported on the analysis of a section of the Y chromosome of humans, chimpanzees, gorillas, and orangutans. The researchers calculated a mutation rate based on the supposed time that pairs of each of the above species had a common ancestor and differences in the area of the Y chromosome under study. On the basis of this mutation rate they propose that *Homo sapiens sapiens* originated 275,000 years ago. However, even the investigators consider their findings to be tentative.[3]

CRITICISMS OF THE "EVE" HYPOTHESIS
Led by Milford Wolpoff, paleoanthropologists have pointed out that in order for the geneticists' model to work, the only thing affecting the differences in the structure of mitochondrial DNA would be random mutation. However, any genes entering the gene pool of "Eve's" descendants from other populations would create a different degree of variation than would be expected if random mutation was the only cause for such variation. There *were* people before "Eve"; so, if all modern people are the descendants of "Eve's" gene pool only, then all people not of her line would have died off without breeding with any of "Eve's" descendants.

Some anthropologists also see flaws in the geneticists' techniques for calculating mutation rates and in some basic assumptions they make about evolution. They point out that the same data used in the original studies that established an African origin can also be used to generate phylogenetic trees that show non-African origins.

Like other scientific controversies, the debate between proponents and opponents of the "Mitochondrial Eve" hypothesis illustrates the self-correcting nature of science. As the research used to compile the data for a hypothesis is constantly repeated and reanalyzed, the new research either validates the old hypothesis or invalidates it. The construction of specific phylogenetic trees showing an African origin for modern *H. sapiens sapiens* is now questioned, but the research did il-

[3]Dorit, R. L., H. Akashi, and W. Gilbert, "Absence of Polymorphism at the ZFY Locus on the Human Y Chromosome," *Science*, 268 (1995), 1183–1185.

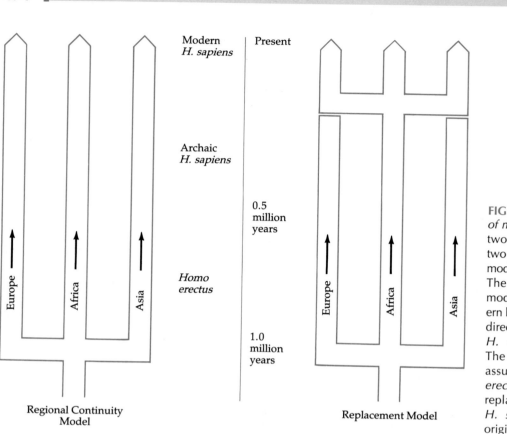

Regional Continuity Model

Replacement Model

FIGURE 19–5 *The origins of modern humans.* These two diagrams represent two views of the origins of modern *H. sapiens sapiens.* The regional continuity model assumes that modern human populations are direct descendants of local *H. erectus* populations. The replacement model assumes that local *H. erectus* populations were replaced by migrations of *H. sapiens sapiens* that originated in Africa.

lustrate that there is greater mtDNA variation in African populations. This reinforces the idea, inferred from the fossil record, that hominids, including the australopithecines, have existed in Africa longer than on any other continent.

THE REPLACEMENT MODEL   The "Mitochondrial Eve" hypothesis was a line of evidence for what is called the **replacement model** for the origins of modern *H. sapiens.* According to the replacement model, which anthropologist William Howells calls the "Noah's Ark" hypothesis, modern humans are seen as having evolved in Africa and radiated out of this area, replacing the Neandertals and other hominid populations (Figure 19–5). In this model Neandertals are often labeled *H. neandertalensis* and therefore are not even considered to be *H. sapiens.* Physical variation in modern populations would have evolved only after the proposed 200-thousand-year-ago origin of modern humans. In Africa, *H. erectus* evolved

into an archaic form of *H. sapiens* and then into modern *H. sapiens.* In other areas of the world *H. erectus* evolved into different forms of archaic *H. sapiens,* such as the Neandertals, and these forms became extinct.

One type of evidence that supports this hypothesis is the presence of what appear to be anatomically modern humans 120,000 years ago at the Klasies River Mouth in South Africa, 130,000 years ago at Omo, and between 115,000 and 92,000 years ago at Jebel Qafzeh in Israel. These dates, however, are not certain.

THE REGIONAL CONTINUITY MODEL   The **regional continuity model,** also known as the multiregional model, assumes multiple origins of modern *H. sapiens* from existing local populations (Figure 19–5). Each local population of archaic humans gave rise to a population of modern *H. sapiens;* for example, Neandertals gave rise to modern European populations. This is not to say that each regional archaic population evolved in total isolation. On the contrary, enough gene flow between these populations would have had to occur to result in a single subspecies, *H. sapiens sapiens*. Also, although Neandertals and other archaic populations in Africa and Asia are seen as evolving in place, regional continuity proponents envision migration between populations. This gene flow and similar selective forces in the different regions are seen as reasons for parallel evolution in the direction of modern humanity.

According to this model, modern-population differences in physical characteristics are deeply rooted. Even with gene flow, some local archaic features would be retained in contemporary populations. Proponents of the regional continuity model believe that modern *H. sapiens'* last common ancestor existed 1 million to perhaps 1.8 million years ago.

The evidence for the regional continuity model is what appears to be a continuity of anatomical features in most areas of the world, the presence of Neandertal characteristics in modern populations, the appearance of modern *H. sapiens* in most parts of the world at about the same time, and the continuity of tool types in many areas of the world. The regional continuity proponents are not convinced of the accuracy of the early *H. sapiens sapiens* dates.

There are also several intermediate models of the evolution of modern *H. sapiens* that combine the ideas of the replacement and regional continuity models. These intermediate models assume different degrees of inbreeding between archaic hominids and *H. sapiens sapiens* populations. As more fossils are found, and perhaps if statistical analyses of molecular data are refined, one valid picture of the evolution of modern humans may emerge.

The Migrations of *Homo sapiens sapiens* to Australia and the New World

There is evidence of modern-looking populations in Africa as early as 130,000 years ago, in Asia somewhat after that, and in Europe at 38,000 B.P. and perhaps earlier. Except for the mysterious Kow Swamp fossils to be discussed shortly, all hominids in Australia and the New World are modern in appearance. No australopithecine, *H. habilis*, or typical *H. erectus* populations have been found.

AUSTRALIA   People reached New Guinea and nearby islands from the mainland of southeast Asia by crossing over land connections formed by the lowering of ocean levels associated with glacials. Australia was never connected by land to the mainland of Asia, yet according to recent research humans may have reached Australia more than 60,000 years ago. The early migrants to Australia must have used some form of watercraft to move across the 80 or more kilometers (50 or more miles) of sea separating Australia from Asia. They have left artifacts that may be more than 60,000 years old.[4]

Many of the finds from southeast Asia resemble the modern Australian aborigines. The Wadjak skulls from Java, discovered in 1890, show large brow ridges, a receding forehead, a deep nasal root, and large teeth (Figure 19–6). A find from Lake Mungo in New South Wales, dated at 25,500 B.P., represents the oldest skeletal remains in Australia and is also the earliest evidence of cremation burial anywhere in the world. Large

---

[4]V. Morell, "The Earliest Art Becomes Older—More Common," *Science,* 267 (1995), 1908–1909.

FIGURE 19–6   *Skull from Wadjak, Java.*

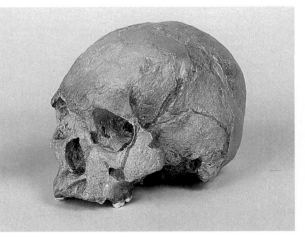

fragments of bone remain after cremation. The remains of the Lake Mungo individual, whose bones had been broken and placed in a depression, are those of a person of fully modern appearance.

One of the mysteries of prehistory concerns a second population from Australia. This population, from Kow Swamp, in the state of Victoria, displays a low, retreating forehead, large brow ridges, and other features reminiscent of *H. erectus*. The surprising thing is that the Kow Swamp finds are dated to between 14,000 and 9500 B.P., hundreds of thousands of years after the *H. erectus* pattern ceased to be recognizable elsewhere in the world. Since forty burials have been excavated, we cannot attribute this to sampling error.

THE EFFECT OF ISOLATION ON EVOLUTION How could the Kow Swamp fossils retain so many features of *H. erectus* tens of thousands of years after the *H. sapiens* pattern had been established elsewhere in the world? In a survey of the fossil record we find many other examples of *H. erectus* features being maintained, although none as recent as Kow Swamp. For instance, the Solo fossils, on the island of Java, consist of eleven fragmentary skulls and two tibiae that have never been dated accurately, but they may be more recent than 35,000 B.P. Along with fossils from Saldanha in South Africa, which have been dated to just before 40,000 B.P., the Solo fossils show an affinity to *H. erectus.*

It is probably no coincidence that these more conservative specimens represent populations that lived on islands (Australia and Java) or in areas geologically isolated, at least partially, by features of landscape. That is, *H. erectus* features persisted longest in those populations that were most isolated from the larger hominid gene pool since isolated groups would have contributed less and drawn less from the common human gene pool.

THE NEW WORLD Most anthropologists believe that the Americas were populated by Asian big-game hunters who followed their prey across the Bering Strait to North America. American aborigines show similarities to Asian populations in body build, head shape, eye and skin color, hair type, dentition, presence of the Diego blood antigen, and many other physical characteristics. They also share many features of their languages.

When did the first migrants arrive in the New World? Today, on a clear day, the shore of Siberia is visible from Cape Prince of Wales, Alaska. At times in the past Siberia and Alaska were connected by a landmass, as much as 2000 kilometers (1243 miles) from north to south, called **Beringia.** Beringia was exposed by drops in sea level during the Pleistocene, which occurred because of large amounts of water trapped in glacial ice.

Current geological and biological evidence suggests that Beringia existed at 80,000 B.P. or before and remained until about 35,000 years ago. Before 80,000 B.P., North America and Asia had not been connected for about 15 million years. A warm period from 35,000 to 27,000 years ago flooded Beringia. During this time people may have crossed the open water during the winter when the channel froze or may have even used simple watercraft. From approximately 27,000 to 11,000 years ago Beringia again provided a wide grassy plain to those moving between Asia and North America. This plain was exposed as dry land for the last time about 11,000 years ago.

The firmest dates for the first presence of people in the New World are about 11,000 B.P., but dates up to 27,900 years ago have been suggested. Most of the evidence for the early presence of humans in the New World is archaeological rather than paleontological; we will discuss this archaeological evidence in a later section of this chapter.

There is little skeletal evidence of early hominids in the New World. An electron spin resonance date of 15,400 B.P. has been determined for human bones found in Kansas. If this date is correct, the remains would be the oldest yet found in the Americas. Fossils with dates of about 11,000 to 10,000 years old have been recovered in North, Central, and South America. All fossil hominids found in the Americas possess Asian characteristics and also appear similar to contemporary American Indian populations.

BOX 19–1

TEETH AND TONGUES: NATIVE AMERICAN ANCESTRY

Archaeological and genetic evidence suggests that the ancestors of Native Americans reached the New World over a land bridge called Beringia, which connected Asia and North America. This hypothesis is supported by linguistic and dental evidence.

Linguists group the approximately 600 Native American languages spoken today into three language families: the Eskimo-Aleut (spoken in far northern Alaska, Canada, and Greenland), the Na-Dene (spoken in parts of Alaska and northwest and north central Canada and in the American Southwest and northern Mexico), and the Amerind (spoken in all other areas of the New World). The linguistic evidence suggests that there were three separate migrations into the New World. Each of the three New World families is more closely related to different Old World language families than the three are to one another.[1] The first migration appears to have consisted of people who spoke a language ancestral to the Amerind languages. Next, the ancestors of Na-Dene entered the New World, and the last to arrive were the Eskimo-Aleut people.[2]

This threefold linguistic division of the aboriginal peoples of the New World is further supported by the study of some 200,000 prehistoric teeth.[3] The dental samples can be divided into three groups that parallel the linguistic groups. The dental criteria used are the number of roots characteristic of the lower first molar and of the upper first premolar and incisor shoveling. The table below shows the three dental groups and their corresponding linguistic groups.

---

[1]M. Ruhlen, "Voices from the Past," *Natural History,* 96 (March 1987), 6–10.
[2]Ibid., 10.
[3]C. G. Turner, II, "Telltale Teeth," *Natural History,* 96 (January 1987), 6–10.

DENTAL CATEGORIES AND LINGUISTIC GROUPS

	FIRST DENTAL GROUP	SECOND DENTAL GROUP	THIRD DENTAL GROUP
Lower first molar with three roots	Highest frequency, 27–41%	Lowest frequency, 6–11%	Intermediate, 10–22%
Roots of upper first premolar	High frequency, single rooted	High frequency, multirooted	Intermediate
Strong incisor shoveling	Lowest frequency, 60–70%	Highest frequency, 90–100%	Intermediate, 80–90%
Corresponding linguistic group	Eskimo-Aleut	Amerind	Na-Dene

Why would people migrate across what had been the ocean bottom? The land connection was not a sandy sterile area, as might be suspected from its previous state of submersion, nor was it an ice-covered plain. Instead, Beringia was a combination of tundra, marsh, and grassland. It was home to large herds of mammoth, caribou, bison, and other animals, making it perhaps an even better place to hunt than present-day Alaska. So, quite possibly, Siberian hunters followed game over the land, ultimately reaching Alaska. Since Beringia existed for thousands of years at a time, the migration from Asia to North America could have been a very slow one.

Summary

We cannot say exactly when fossils classified as *H. sapiens sapiens* first appeared; the precise point in time is a relative and arbitrary matter. However, the earliest *H. sapiens sapiens* may be from Africa at about 130,000 years ago. The "Mitochondrial Eve" hypothesis proposes an even earlier date for an African origin of modern humans. Modern *H. sapiens sapiens* may have been present in Asia as early as 115,000 years ago and in Australia and Europe about 60,000 and 38,000 years ago, respectively. The only hominid populations found in Australia and the New World are classified as *H. sapiens sapiens*. Firm dates for people in the New World go back to only about 11,500 years ago, although considerably older dates have been proposed.

Two models have been proposed to account for the appearance and spread of *H. sapiens*. According to the replacement model, modern *H. sapiens sapiens* evolved in a limited area, such as in Africa or Asia, and then moved into other areas of the world, completely replacing the Neandertals and other non-*H. sapiens sapiens* populations. On the other hand, proponents of the regional continuity model believe that the Neandertals contributed to the origin of modern Europeans while other populations evolved into *H. sapiens sapiens* in other geographical areas. Intermediate models see different degrees of interbreeding between archaic hominids and *H. sapiens sapiens* populations. By about 35,000 years ago, *H. sapiens sapiens* was the only type of hominid existing on earth.

THE CULTURE OF *HOMO SAPIENS SAPIENS*

Upper Paleolithic peoples developed a level of cultural complexity that had never before existed, a level exceeding that of most twentieth-century hunting-gathering peoples. The cultural traditions associated with the Upper Paleolithic are found throughout Europe, northern Asia, the Middle East, and northern Africa. Human cultural achievements appear most complex, however, on the northern plains of Europe and eastern Asia and in southwestern France.

The idea that Europe and eastern Asia developed more elaborate and varied technological inventories than the rest of the world might be because more research has been done in these regions. This section deals with the technological developments of the Upper Paleolithic, the

nature of people's relationship to their habitats, and finally, people's aesthetic and religious achievements.

Upper Paleolithic Technology

The Upper Paleolithic is often defined in terms of the **blade.** Blades are not unique to this period, but the high frequency of their use is.

Blades are flakes with roughly parallel sides and extremely sharp edges which are generally about twice as long as they are wide. They are manufactured from carefully prepared cores, and they can be made quickly and in great numbers. The manufacture of blades represents an efficient use of natural resources—in this case, flint. François Bordes points out that the Upper Paleolithic blade technique could produce 305 to 1219 centimeters (10 to 40 feet) of cutting edge from a pound of flint, whereas the early Mousterian technique could produce only 102 centimeters (40 inches).[5]

From the basic blade, a variety of highly specialized tools can be manufactured. Unlike humans of the Lower Paleolithic, who used the general-purpose hand ax, humans of the Upper Paleolithic used tools designed for specific purposes. The primary function of many of these tools was to make other tools.

Bone, along with antler, horn, and ivory, became a very common raw material. Bone has many advantages over stone; for example, it does not break as easily. The widespread use of bone, ivory, and antler was a result of the development of the **burin,** which had a chisel-like point that did not break under pressure. Some later Upper Paleolithic cultures became very dependent on bone implements, and stone points practically disappeared.

A major reason for the success of Upper Paleolithic populations was the development of new projectile weapons. These were **compound tools,** that is, tools composed of several parts. Hafting appears in the archaeological record; the ax is no

---

[5]F. Bordes, *The Old Stone Age* (New York: McGraw-Hill, 1968).

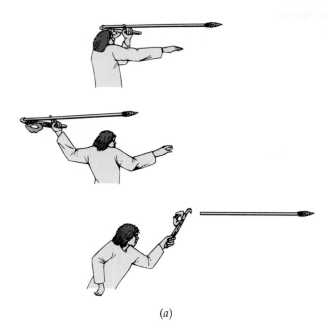

(a)

(b)

FIGURE 19–7   *The spear thrower. (a)* The hook of the spear thrower is inserted into the base of the spear and, using the spear thrower, the spear is thrown. *(b)* A spear thrower from the Magdalenian site of Enlène, France, showing two headless ibexes embracing. The handle is missing.

longer a hand ax, but an ax with a handle. Spears were made with bone points hafted to a shaft. The spear was often used with an atlatl or spear thrower. The spear thrower functions to increase the distance the spear can be thrown and the force of its penetration into an animal's body (Figure 19–7). Harpoons consisted of a barbed

bone point that detached from the shaft after entering the animal, yet the point remained tied to the shaft by a cord; the shaft dragging behind the animal would impede its flight. The shaft could be retrieved and used again. In glacial climates, long pieces of wood were rare, and the shafts were valuable; the points were easily made from antler or bone. Later in the period, the bow and arrow appeared. Several types of fishing gear, such as barbed fishhooks and fish spears, also are known.

Another innovation of the Upper Paleolithic is the eyed needle that first appeared about 25,000 years ago (Figure 19–8). They were usually made of bone or ivory. Many presume that the needle was used to make waterproof tailored clothing similar to that commonly worn by contemporary people living in high northern latitudes. Evidence of European Upper Paleolithic clothing also comes from images of clothed humans found in some cave paintings, evidence of clothing seen in sculptures, beads that were probably sewn on shirts and pants, and the presence of stone tools that appear to have been used for working hides.

The impression of woven material made in wet clay reveals the existence of weaving 27,000 to 25,000 years ago. Woven materials may have been used for clothing or flexible baskets.[6]

Upper Paleolithic Cultural Traditions

Upper Paleolithic tool technologies of Europe are often divided into five traditions which are, from earliest to most recent, the Châteperronian, Aurignacian, Gravettian, Solutrean, and Magdalenian. Much of the archaeological evidence of these traditions comes from France. We will briefly survey how these traditions manifested themselves in France.

The Châteperronian (also called the Lower Perigordian) is in many ways a transitional combination of industries. Beginning about 32,000 years ago, it contains many tools that are characteristic of the Mousterian tradition of the Ne-

---

[6]Bower, B., "Stone Age Fabric Leaves Swatch Marks," *Science News,* 147 (May 6, 1995), 276.

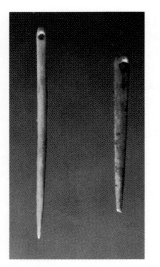

FIGURE 19–8 *Upper Paleolithic eyed needles.* Eyed needles were first manufactured about 25,000 years ago. They were usually made of bone or ivory.

andertals. Yet mixed with these older tool types are tools that are found in the next tradition, the Aurignacian. The Aurignacian is associated only with modern peoples such as the Cro-Magnon. Beginning about 28,000 years ago, these people began making tools of bone and antler.

Bone becomes a very important material for the manufacture of tools as seen in the Gravettian tradition (also called the Upper Perigordian) beginning about 25,000 years ago. They made bone awls, punches, and points. The Solutrean, beginning about 20,000 years ago, took flint working to a high level of sophistication and were replaced about 17,000 to 16,000 years ago by the Magdalenians who at first made very poorly crafted stone tools. Although the Magdalenians were not the best stone toolmakers, they excelled in the use of bone and antler. They also developed Upper Paleolithic art to its peak,

FIGURE 19–9 *Upper Paleolithic tool types. (a)* Aurignacian, scraper on retouched blade; *(b)* Aurignacian, Aurignacian blade; *(c)* Solutrean, laurel-leaf point; *(d)* Solutrean, borer end scraper; *(e)* Perigordian, burin; *(f)* Perigordian, denticulated backed bladelet; *(g)* Magdalenian, backed bladelet; *(h)* Magdalenian, shouldered point.

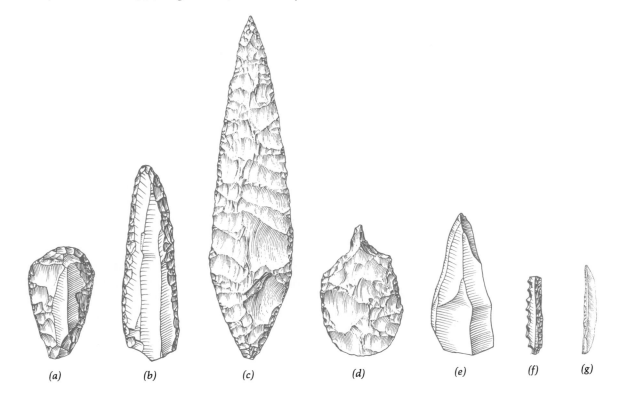

(a) *(b)* *(c)* *(d)* *(e)* *(f)* *(g)*

as we will discuss shortly. Figure 19–9 illustrates some Upper Paleolithic tool types.

NON-EUROPEAN UPPER PALEOLITHIC CULTURES   European-type assemblages are found in the Middle East, India, east Africa, the Crimea, and Siberia. On the other hand, some African traditions differed from those in Europe and maintained the hand ax as the most commonly found tool. The retention of the hand ax in some parts of Africa was not an indication of backwardness but an adjustment to forest conditions; the hand ax has a long history of development in some parts of Africa.

Recently it has been suggested that some people living in Africa as long as 90,000 years ago developed certain tool types, such as bone harpoon points, that would not be seen in Europe until 14,000 B.P. At Katanda in Zaire archaeologists found barbed and unbarbed bone points. These points may have been hafted to a wood shaft and used to spear fish. The Katanda people also used materials such as ocher pigment and stones brought in from distant localities. They may have developed a semi-settled lifestyle based on fishing tens of thousands of years before people did in other parts of the world.[7]

In east and southeast Asia, simple chopping tools were used until the end of the Paleolithic. According to one suggestion, this was the result of reliance on materials other than stone, such as bamboo, for tool manufacture (see Box 17–2).

Similarly, chopping tools and crude flake tools made up most of the stone artifacts of the natives of Australia. When the first inhabitants reached the continent about 60,000 to 40,000 years ago, they found an environment where the largest animal was the kangaroo. Australia also lacked the types of raw materials needed for producing good blade tools. Although they did have resources of bone and wood and made a variety of tools out of these materials, their overall technology was restricted by the lack of resources and by their isolation from ideas that were developing elsewhere.

---

[7] J. E. Yellen et al., "A Middle Stone Age Worked Bone Industry from Katanda, Upper Semliki Valley, Zaire," *Science*, 268 (1995), 553–556.

Human Relationship to the Environment

The development of the Upper Paleolithic must be seen in relation to the nature of the environment during that time. The period comprises the latter part of the last glaciation, the Würm. Northern and western Europe were essentially a **tundra,** a land frozen solid throughout most of the year but thawing slightly during the summer. A proliferation of plant life in the summer was capable of supporting large herds of animal life. The tundra of Canada today teems with animal life, such as the moose and caribou. The Pleistocene European tundra was a low-latitude tundra, receiving more solar radiation than that received by the Canadian tundra today, and thus could support a fantastic mass of herd animals.

Upper Paleolithic peoples hunted the large herd animals, often specializing in one or two types, in contrast to the scavenging or perhaps more individualistic hunting techniques of the Neandertals. This shift in orientation toward cooperative hunting of herd animals with improved projectile technology may have been responsible for the development of the Upper Paleolithic complex. Among the more important animals hunted were reindeer, ibex, horse, and bison; fish, especially salmon, were also important.

Unfortunately, growing mastery in the utilization of these natural resources may have disrupted ecological balances. During the Late Pleistocene, more than fifty genera of large mammals became extinct. Yet the extinction of large animals was not accompanied by the extinction of many smaller animals or plants, and the analysis of the record has shown no evidence of droughts in most areas. Most extinctions can be correlated with the movements of people into a specific area. It seems very possible that human technology and social efficiency had developed to a point at which the environment could have been endangered.

The Upper Paleolithic of Europe occurred during a time of great cold, and people developed the technology to survive in such an environment. As mentioned earlier, the archaeological record contains bone needles which were used to make elaborately decorated clothing. In one case, two skeletons were found near the city of Vladimir, Russia, that had been buried in shirts covered with about 300 sewn-on ivory beads. (The position of the beads permitted reconstruction of the clothing.) Each individual wore a pullover shirt with a round neck, a pair of trousers, boots, and some type of head covering.

Humans in a cold environment also need housing. In southwestern France they used rock shelters, but many open-air settlements have also been found. Settlements in this area were built in the river valleys, somewhat protected from the cold of the plateau.

Art of the Upper Paleolithic

The Upper Paleolithic is associated with a variety of artistic methods and styles. Paintings and engravings can be seen developing from early forms to the colorful and skillful renderings of the Magdalenian peoples. Realistic, stylized, and geometric modes were used.

Paleolithic art also found its expression in the modeling of clay; sculpturing in rock, bone, ivory, and antler; and painting and engraving on large surfaces, such as cave walls, as well as on small objects. Utensils were decorated, but perhaps the most interesting works are the statues and cave paintings.

Some of the most famous statuaries are the female statues, called **Venus figurines,** which were carved in the round from a variety of materials. Although only a few centimeters high, the figures have extremely exaggerated breasts and buttocks and very stylized heads, hands, and feet (Figure 19–10). Perhaps they represent pregnant women. Upper Paleolithic artists also made models of animals, including the famous set of statues of a bison, a bull, a cow, and a calf found deep in a cave in France. The earliest Upper Paleolithic sculpture dates to about 32,000 B.P. In Europe, painting was a later development.

Upper Paleolithic cave art is found in France, Spain, Italy, the South Urals, Australia, and other parts of the world. Dates of older than 30,000 years have been proposed for some European cave art.

The search for the origins of modern behaviors such as art has centered on Europe. Re-

FIGURE 19–10 *Venus figurine.* The Venus of Willendorf, from Austria, 11.1 centimeters (4.3 inches) high.

cently, however, earlier evidence of complex behavior has been observed in another part of the world. Early migrants to Australia may have decorated rock shelters and cliff faces at a very early time. Stone flake tools as well as pigments that could have been used for painting have been found in strata dated at 60,000 years ago by thermoluminescence and other dating methods. This date is earlier than any previously suggested date for cave art; it is also earlier than previously proposed dates for the peopling of Australia. Further study is necessary to confirm this date.[8]

The subject matter of cave art, for the most part, is animals, although humans also are depicted. These were hunting peoples, and we might suppose that the art expressed their rela-

---

[8]V. Morell, op. cit.

FIGURE 19–11 *Cave art.* Painted reindeer from the Dordogne, France.

tionship to the fauna that supported them (Figure 19–11). Several hypotheses have been suggested to explain the meaning of cave art.[9]

Some researchers believe that most representations of nature served magical purposes. This conclusion is based upon several facts. First, some cave paintings are found in almost inaccessible areas of caves. Perhaps rituals, not open to the majority of the people, were performed using the paintings and engravings. For example, some modern societies believe that if a person harms an image of an animal or person, the act will have a similar effect on the real animal or person. This is called **imitative magic.** An Upper Paleolithic shaman may have performed similar rituals so that the animal depicted would be weakened and would therefore be easier to capture and kill.

Other investigators see no evidence of imitative magic. They suggest that the cave may have acted as a meeting place where people shared information on hunting. A recently discovered cave, Grotte Chauvet, contains hundreds of animal images, none of which are of food animals (Box 19–2). So at least for the people who created these images, the art seems to have no relation to hunting, magical or otherwise. Still other caves contain ancient footprints of men, women, and children. This suggests that entire groups, not just specific individuals such as shamans, visited the galleries. Perhaps the artworks served primarily aesthetic purposes.

[9]M. Conkey, *On the Origin of Paleolithic Art: A Review of Some Cultural Thoughts* in E. Trinkaus (ed.), *Mousterian Legacy* (Oxford: British Archaeological Reports, International Series, 164, 1983), 201–227.

BOX 19–2

UPPER PALEOLITHIC CAVE ART

Until 1995 the most spectacular of the approximately 300 caves known to contain Upper Paleolithic paintings was Lascaux Cave in France. In 1942 the Lascaux cave paintings were accidentally discovered by four boys searching for hidden treasure. One of the boys, Jacques Marsal, was so impressed by the cave's 80 multicolored paintings and 1500 engravings that as an adult he became the curator of the cave, one of France's major tourist attractions. Marsal held this position until his death in 1989. Because of the deterioration of the paintings due to problems created by tourism, however, the cave is now closed to the public. In its place, a full-scale replica of the main hall, dubbed

Lascaux II, has been built by the French government.

In January 1995 the French government announced that Jean-Marie Chauvet and other explorers had found an underground limestone cavern that contained about 300 Upper Paleolithic paintings and engravings. The cavern, known as Grotte Chauvet, located near the town of Vallon-Pont-d'Arc, is about five times larger than the cave at Lascaux, with four larger chambers yet to be explored.

The cave at Vallon-Pont-d'Arc appears to be undisturbed and is interesting in several ways. Many large animal groupings are portrayed. In other caves animals are usually depicted individually. Hyenas, bears, lions, owls, and a panther are depicted here; they are less common in other Paleolithic caves. In other caves, the animals

pictured are usually not carnivores, but herbivores which are generally harmless to people. Grotte Chauvet also contains about forty rhinoceros paintings. Both carnivores and rhinoceroses were not food animals. Archaeologists are attempting to explain why they, and not food animals such as reindeer, are depicted on the cave walls.

The cave's explorers also found ancient human footprints, tracings of human hands, brushes, pigments, pieces of flint, evidence of the use of controlled fire, and the skeletal remains of bears. Geometric shapes such as dots and bars are found associated with the paintings. In addition to human-made images, the cave contained a bear skull that appears to have been carefully placed on a stone slab. Was the slab an altar of some type? Some investigators have characterized the cave as a sacred place. Yet perhaps what looks sacred to a modern Westerner was something entirely different to the people who used and decorated the cave. The cave was occupied an estimated 30,000 years ago, but accurate dating has yet to be completed.

Paintings of a bear (top) and panther (right) from Grotte Chauvet, France. (See also p. 488.)

Reference: J. Pfeiffer, "The Emergence of Modern Humans," *Mosaic,* 21 (1990), 20; M. Simons, "In a French Cave: Wildlife Scenes from a Long-Gone World," *The New York Times Science Section* (January 24, 1995), B10; B. Bower, "French Cave Yields Stone Age Art Gallery," *Science News,* 147 (January 28, 1995), 52–53; and J. Fischman, "Painted Puzzles Line the Walls of an Ancient Cave," *Science,* 267 (1995), 614; A. Marshack, "Images of the Ice Age," *Archaeology,* 48 (July/August 1995), 28–39.

The decoding of the meaning of ancient pictures and other symbols may prove to be illusive. If archaeologists 20,000 years from now were to find evidence of late-twentieth-century objects, would they be able to determine what these objects mean to us today? A logo representing a company performing tune-ups on automobiles might be interpreted as an important religious symbol. One thing does seem likely. The people who made the paintings were attempting to develop symbolic and descriptive ways to transmit and store information. This would later be manifest in the development of writing systems.

Archaeology of the New World

Early inhabitants of the New World entered Alaska from Asia. Once in Alaska, where did the earliest inhabitants of the New World go? Glacial ice covered southern Alaska, much of Canada, and the northwestern United States. An ice-free route, however, was open during most of the Pleistocene through central Alaska and the eastern foothills of the Rocky Mountains and along the Pacific coast. Like Beringia, these routes provided large game for migrating hunters.

Most likely the migrants entered the New World in very small groups. Since there was no competition for food from other human groups, the first populations in the New World increased rapidly in size and range. According to some estimates, the founding population in America could theoretically have been as small as twenty-five people. Such calculations are interesting, but they are not direct evidence of what actually occurred. Some evidence does exist that people moved across Beringia more than once (Box 19–1). Each migration may have been very small, but every time a new group entered the New World, its members would have brought with them a new influx of genes and gene combinations.

In the last 30 years, dates of over 100,000 years have been proposed for New World sites based on archaeological evidence. In the last few years, reanalysis of these dates has shown that none of these sites can conclusively be said to be older than 11,500 B.P. One of the many candidates for a pre-11,500-year-old date is Meadow-croft Rockshelter in Pennsylvania. The site contains flakes, a projectile point, and other tools from a level that has been dated by radiocarbon dating to 16,000 to 11,000 B.P. A possible basket fragment comes from an even lower level and is dated at 19,000 ± 2400 years. The dates have been questioned because of possible contamination of the site by naturally occurring coal. The coal is derived from ancient trees and has lost all of its radioactive carbon. The nonradioactive carbon from these trees, dissolved in water, may have mixed with the carbon in the basket and other organic material in the level. If this occurred, the older carbon would make the artifacts appear older than they really are.

Another possible early site is Orogrande Cave in southern New Mexico, dated at 27,000 B.P. The evidence includes what archaeologist Richard MacNeish believes is a human palm print on a piece of fire-baked clay. Other archaeologists are not yet convinced of the antiquity of the print or even that it was made by a human. Recently dates of 18,000 to 12,260 B.P. have been suggested for sites in the Mojave Desert of California and the Petrified Forest of Arizona. While finds from Kansas, Pennsylvania, New Mexico, California, Arizona, and other areas of the New World suggest the possibility of pre-11,500-B.P. dates for humans in the New World, archaeological finds from Clovis, New Mexico, provide the oldest agreed-upon dates for people in the New World. The finds from Clovis and surrounding sites date from 11,500 to 11,000 B.P.

FOLSOM AND CLOVIS POINTS   Just as fossils are not found in the chronological order in which they were deposited, neither are artifacts. In 1926 a cowboy discovered "arrowheads" near the town of Folsom, New Mexico; these and similar artifacts are called Folsom points. These artifacts are associated with a type of bison that had been extinct for about 10,000 years (Figure 19–12). In the light of current speculation on early dates for the first Americans, 10,000 years ago might not seem startling; yet in the 1920s the belief was that humans had not been in North America anywhere near this long.

In 1932 another important "arrowhead" find was made in New Mexico when blade tools were

FIGURE 19–12 *Folsom point.* A Folsom point in association with ribs of extinct bison, Folsom, New Mexico.

discovered near the town of Clovis; these Clovis points are larger than the later Folsom points. The term "arrowhead" is placed in quotation marks because neither the Folsom nor the Clovis points are really arrowheads, nor are they spearheads; they were used to tip lances. A lance is a weapon that is held and repeatedly thrust into the quarry. On the other hand, a spear is made to be thrown, not held, and often has barbs to keep it from falling out of the prey animal.

Both the Folsom and Clovis points are **fluted;** that is, each type has a rounded groove in the shaft of the point (Figure 19–13). This furrow made hafting of the wood lance shaft to its point easier. Fluted points are not found in other parts of the world and are assumed to be an American invention. Clovis and Folsom assemblages are the most common tool types found between about 11,500 and 9000 B.P. Clovis and similar points have been found in all fifty states except Hawaii, and from the Arctic to South America.

FORAGING ACTIVITIES OF THE FOLSOM AND CLOVIS PEOPLES   The Clovis and Folsom people were primarily hunters of large game. The Clovis people, whose remains first appeared in the western United States, hunted mammoths and appear to have followed the herds eastward, ultimately reaching the north-

east coast. However, the mammoth declined to the point of extinction, perhaps because of overhunting, and in the Great Plains and the Rocky Mountain valley the Folsom tradition replaced that of the Clovis people. Bison was the mainstay of the Folsom hunters.

We have emphasized hunting, but gathering activities were also important. The problem is that while the bones of hunted animals may persist for tens of thousands of years in the archaeological record, the remains of vegetable products are much less likely to leave traces. Also, many important sites were excavated before the development of modern techniques, such as pollen analysis. Even so, some evidence does exist, and it suggests that hunting peoples set up seasonal camps in grasslands where they exploited plant resources. The more extensive use of vegetable (and aquatic) resources seems not to have begun until sometime after 10,000 years ago, as was the case in the Old World. We turn to this recent period of time in the next and final section.

Summary

The Upper Paleolithic traditions generally represent an increase in the percentage of blade tools over time; sometimes these blades were hafted to ax or spear handles. In addition to stone tools, tools of bone, antler, horn, and ivory became more varied and complex than those of earlier

FIGURE 19–13 *Artifacts from the New World.* (a) Clovis point; (b) Folsom point.

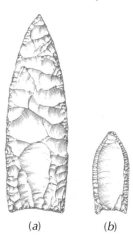

(a)   (b)

times. *Homo sapiens sapiens* may have been the first big-game hunters.

In the Upper Paleolithic, artistic development showed mastery of both painting and sculpting and use of complex symbols. Large cave paintings were expertly executed in western Europe and east to the Urals as well as in Australia; small objects were also decorated, and numerous small statues were produced. The art may have been created for its own sake, or it may have had ritual or other symbolic significance.

The earliest established New World lithic industries are the Folsom and Clovis which have been dated to about 11,500 and 9000 B.P. These unique fluted points are not found in other parts of the world. The Clovis people were hunters of mammoth, while the later Folsom hunters relied on bison.

POST-PLEISTOCENE *HOMO SAPIENS*

The transition to *Homo sapiens* of the Upper Paleolithic represents a substantial change in form and in technological capabilities. Yet the general mode of subsistence remained basically the same throughout this period. Gathering wild vegetables, hunting wild game, and collecting products of the seas, lakes, and rivers provided for the nutritional needs of all Paleolithic populations.

Also during the Paleolithic, the functioning group remained small, generally about twenty-five individuals, although certain lush local environments allowed larger populations. About 10,000 years ago, the nature of people's relationships to their environments, and the social and cultural components of their beings, began to take on new perspectives. This included an increase in population densities, which culminated in the formation of cities; the utilization of new sources of food and work energy; and the development of those social institutions that became the elements of civilization. These factors have been looked upon by some as the greatest developments of human evolution, and by others as the beginning of the end for the human species.

The Pleistocene ended about 10,000 years ago with the end of the last glaciation. A few thousand years before, human populations in some parts of the world entered a period of rapid sociocultural change. Paleolithic cultures were replaced by other types of cultures and, ultimately, modern agricultural and industrial societies.

The Mesolithic: Transition from Hunting-Gathering to Farming

The change from a hunting-gathering existence to a farming economy did not occur overnight nor did it occur everywhere. However, the dependence on group living, along with the biological and technological developments of all human evolution, created a potential for new systems of subsistence. This potential began to be expressed at an increased pace in the period between the retreat of the last glaciers and the advent of agricultural communities, a cultural stage known as the **Mesolithic.**

During the Mesolithic, societies began to utilize the land around them more intensively. The last part of the Upper Paleolithic was characterized by enormous herds of large mammals in the grasslands of Eurasia. About 12,000 years ago, however, climatic changes began to occur which ultimately converted these grasslands into forests. With the advance of the forests came the disappearance of the herds; they were replaced by less abundant and more elusive animals, such as elk, red deer, and wild pigs.

"MAN'S BEST FRIEND"   In the United States today there are about 50 million domesticated dogs. Some of these dogs fulfill utilitarian functions: guide dogs, guard dogs, police dogs and hunting dogs. Most dogs, however, are pets and companions. Dogs are so much a part of our culture that there is now a Dog Genome Project similar to the Human Genome Project discussed in Chapter 4. A goal of this project is to learn how the different breeds of dog evolved.[10]

Domestic dogs derived from gray wolves who can still breed with domesticated dogs (Figure 19–14). In fact, most experts classify dogs in the same species, *Canis lupus*, as wolves, placing dogs in the subspecies *Canis lupus familiaris*.

[10]R. Mestel, "Ascent of the Dog," *Discover* (October 1994), 90–98.

(a)

(b)

FIGURE 19–14   *Domestication of the dog.* Domesticated dogs, such as this German shepherd *(b)* were bred from the gray wolf *(a).*

Why were dogs domesticated? There are many ideas on this. One scenario is that in areas where forestation had occurred, hunters had to play hide-and-seek with well-hidden animals. The domestication of the dog may have been the result of the increased pressures of hunting in dense, dark forests. As discussed in the chapters on primates and the fossil record, the development of a refined visual sense in primates was accompanied by a decrease in the sense of smell. The wolf's nose seems to have been employed by people to sniff out nonvisible prey. By 14,000 to 10,000 years ago, the wolf had already been domesticated in such widespread places as southwestern Asia, Japan, Iran, England, Illinois, and Idaho.

AQUATIC AND VEGETABLE RESOURCES Along with changes in hunting patterns came an intense exploitation of aquatic resources, and Mesolithic sites are often found near seas, lakes, and rivers. A characteristic type of site is the **shell midden,** a large mound composed of shells, which provides evidence of the emphasis on shellfish as a food resource. Fishing was an important activity, and remains of boats and nets from this period have been recovered. Waterfowl also made up an important part of the diet in many areas.

In addition, people began to exploit intensively the plant resources of their habitats. Much of this exploitation was made possible by the de-velopment of a technology for processing vegetable foods that cannot be eaten in their natural state; for example, the milling stone and the mortar and pestle were used to break up seeds and nuts. Storage and container vessels found in Mesolithic sites allowed for easy handling of small and pulverized foods (Figure 19–15). Farming developed out of this utilization of plant resources.

THE ORIGINS OF DOMESTICATION **Do-mestication** involves the control of the reproductive cycle of plants and animals. Through the use of farming techniques, people could plant and harvest large quantities of food in specific areas; in time, they selected the best food-producing plants to breed. Domestication thus led to selection initiated by humans, which over the centuries has created new varieties of plants. Many theories have been proposed regarding the origins of plant domestication, but the important point to note is that domestication probably was not a deliberate invention. It most likely arose from an intensive utilization of and dependence upon plant material, a pattern that developed out of Mesolithic economies.

Anthropologists Joy McCorriston and Frank Hole believe that the first plant domestication occurred around the margins of evaporating lakes in the Jordan Valley of Jordan and Israel. This event has been dated at about 10,300 years

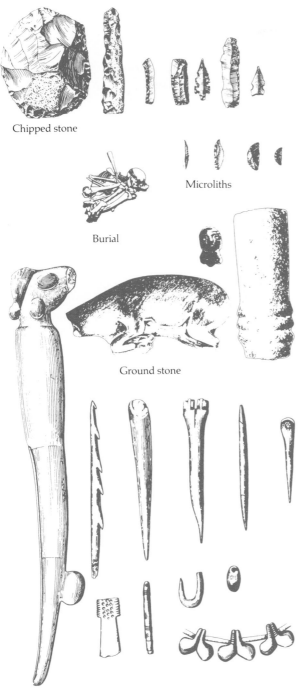

Chipped stone

Microliths

Burial

Ground stone

Bone

FIGURE 19–15 *Mesolithic artifacts.* Various artifacts from the Mesolithic of Palestine (Natufian), ca. 8000 ± 500 B.C.

tication occurred independently in the Near East and the New World, and perhaps in southeast Asia and west Africa as well.

Although the development of farming has been seen as the great revolution leading to modern civilization, we must emphasize that farming was a revolution in potential only. Many hunting-gathering peoples rejected farming because it would have brought about a decline in their standard of living. For example, even in a semiarid region during a drought, the food supply of the San of South Africa is reliable and plentiful. The farming and pastoral communities are the ones that suffer the most in such times.

The Neolithic: The Farming "Revolution"

Ultimately, in some areas over a period of thousands of years, and sometimes very quickly, food production came to dominate hunting and gathering in many parts of the world. With farming came the development of a new way of life—life in the village. This stage of human history is called the **Neolithic.**

The Neolithic was a time of great change in both technology and social organization. By producing food in one place rather than searching for it, societies developed a more settled pattern of existence. Farming meant that more food could be acquired in less space, and as a result, population densities increased. This led to the interaction of greater numbers of people and thus brought about a greater exchange of ideas and an increase in innovation, which is dependent on such exchanges.

The Neolithic was characterized by the elaboration of tools for food preparation: querns, milling stones, mortars, and pestles. Pottery, used only rarely by nonfarming peoples, became refined and varied, and the techniques of weav-

ago.[11] In addition to its development in this Near East location, plant and animal domestication developed in areas of Mexico and Peru. Domes-

[11] J. McCorriston and F. Hole, "The Ecology of Seasonal Stress and the Origins of Agriculture in the Near East," *American Anthropologist,* 93 (1991), 46–69.

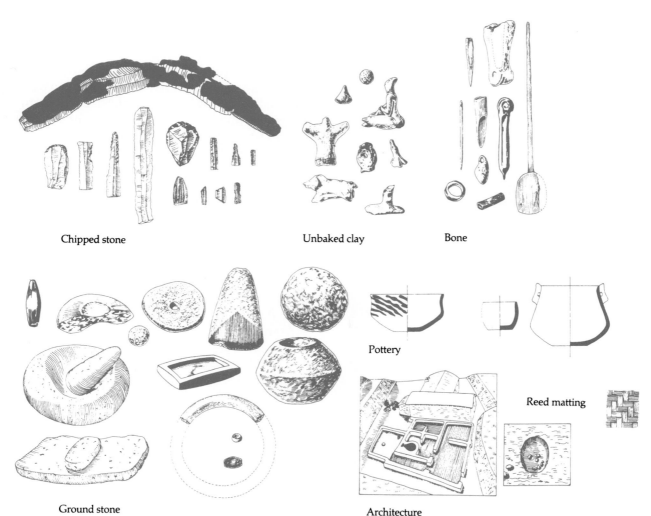

Chipped stone

Unbaked clay

Bone

Pottery

Reed matting

Ground stone

Architecture

FIGURE 19–16 *Neolithic artifacts.* Various artifacts from the Neolithic of Jarmo, Iraq, ca. 6750 ± 200 B.C.

ing and spinning cloth were developed (Figure 19–16).

Most Neolithic villages were small, self-sufficient farming communities. During the Neolithic, however, many technological and social systems were being developed that would later be important in the first civilizations. This can be seen at the settlement of Çatal Hüyük in Turkey, which dates from 8500 to 7700 B.P.

At Çatal Hüyük timber, obsidian, marble, stalactite, and shell were all imported, and skillfully made artifacts attest to the development of occupational specialization. Wooden bowls and boxes, jewelry, bone awls, daggers, spearheads,

lance heads, arrowheads, ladles, spoons, spatulas, hooks and pins, obsidian mirrors, and other beautifully made objects contributed to a rich material inventory. The residents at Çatal Hüyük lived in plastered mud-brick houses which were contiguous with one another; they entered them from the roof. Murals painted on the walls depicted animals, hunters, and dancers, and statues portrayed gods and goddesses, as well as cattle.

The Rise of Civilization

There are many thoughts on the origins of civilization, but one of the major factors involved was the increase in population (Table 19–1). Techniques such as irrigation and flood control made agriculture possible in special areas such as the floodplain of the Tigris and Euphrates rivers, and this supported large populations. Once populations reached a certain number, that number depending on environmental and social variables, the older patterns of social organization broke down and new ones developed. In the older systems, each individual participated in food production, and all members maintained a similar standard of living; kinship served as the cornerstone of social organization. These patterns were replaced by the occupational division of labor, class systems, political and religious hierarchies, public works such as road and public-building construction, codes of law, markets, new forms of warfare, and urban centers. Allied with these important sociological traits were material traits such as monumental architecture, the development of science, and, in many cases, metallurgy and writing systems.

The earliest civilization, Sumer, developed in the Middle East about 5500 years ago. During this period, known as the **Bronze Age** of the Old World, people first developed the art of metallurgy. Civilizations also arose in other parts of the Old World: first in Egypt, China, and India, and later in Europe and sub-Saharan Africa. In addition, civilization developed independently in the New World—in Mexico, Peru, and adjacent areas.

Because of increased food supplies and the increased number of children that a family could take care of, populations increased rapidly with the development of the Neolithic and Bronze Age cultures. A couple living in a mobile society can usually deal with only one infant at a time because the mother has to carry the infant everywhere and the child normally nurses until 5 years of age or later. Until the infant walks and is weaned, a second child would be a great burden. In contrast, a farming couple can usually support a large family with babies born only a year apart. Even today, it is not unusual for an Amish farming family in the United States to have ten or more children; these children become valued farmworkers.

In the Old World, the Bronze Age was followed by the **Iron Age.** This period saw the rise and fall of great empires and a shift of power from the Middle East to Greece and Rome and then to western Europe. The 1700s marked the beginning of the **Industrial Age,** which led directly to the modern civilizations of today.

TABLE 19–1			
HUMAN POPULATION GROWTH			
YEARS AGO (FROM 1995)	YEARS ELAPSED*	WORLD POPULATION (THOUSANDS)	COMMENT
1,000,000		125	
300,000	700,000	1,000	
10,000	290,000	5,320	Domestication begins
6,000	4,000	86,500	
2,000	4,000	133,000	
242	1,758	728,000	Industrialization
92	150	1,610,000	Medical "revolution"
42	50	2,400,000	
32	10	3,000,000	
0 (the present)	32	5,700,000	
Year 2000	5	6,300,000	
Year 2100	100	10,400,000	

*Note that (1) it took 700,000 years to reach the first million from a population of 125,000; (2) it took only 45 years (1950 to 1995) for an increase of about 3.3 billion to occur; (3) it is estimated that between 1995 and 2100 about 4.7 billion people will be added to the world population.
Source: Adapted from Edward S. Deevey, Jr., "The Human Population," *Scientific American* (September 1960). Copyright © 1960 by Scientific American, Inc. All rights reserved. Data for projection for the years 2000 and 2100 are reported in G. Tyler Miller, Jr., *Living in the Environment,* 6th ed. (Belmont, Calif.: Wadsworth, 1990), p. 2.

Summary

Humans were exclusively foragers and scavengers for the vast majority of prehistory. About 10,000 years ago, domestication of plants and animals became a subsistence option for the people in the Near East. Plant and animal domestication spread widely throughout the Old World; it was independently developed in the New World. In most parts of the world, the foraging way of life was gradually replaced by farming. A few foraging societies, however, still exist.

In the places where farming and raising animals occurred, settlement patterns changed from nomadic to settled and population size increased dramatically. Ultimately, the kinship-based organization of society was supplemented by government control. Cities arose to produce goods, to distribute these goods and farm products, and to ship excesses to other societies. Cities also served as religious and political centers. Writing, mathematics, science, and metallurgy became features of most developing civilizations. In addition, animals were "drafted" to do farmwork, such as pulling ploughs. Eventually, beginning in the eighteenth century, human and animal power was joined by machine power, and the Industrial Age was born.

STUDY QUESTIONS

1. Where and at what time does *H. sapiens sapiens* appear in the fossil record?
2. How do the replacement model and the regional continuity model of the origin of *H. sapiens sapiens* differ from each other? What is the evolutionary role of the Neandertals in each of these models?
3. How did people get to the New World? When did the peopling of the New World occur?
4. Discuss the cultural innovations of the Upper Paleolithic.
5. What do the terms *Mesolithic* and *Neolithic* refer to? What characterizes each of these cultural stages?
6. In what area of the world and when did plant domestication first originate? Where else did it independently develop?
7. How did the first civilizations differ from the Neolithic farming societies?

SUGGESTED READINGS

Brace, C. L. *The Stages of Human Evolution,* 5th ed. New York: Prentice-Hall, 1995. This edition of a book first published in 1967 is a detailed inventory of hominid fossils with chapters on evolutionary theory.

Fagan, B. *The Journey from Eden: Peopling the Prehistoric World.* New York: Thames Hudson, 1990. This book is a general survey of prehistory.

Gowlett, J. *Ascent to Civilization: The Archaeology of Early Humans,* 2d ed. New York: McGraw-Hill, 1992.

Lamberg-Karlovsky, C. C., and J. A. Sabloff. *Ancient Civilizations: The Near East and Mesoamerica.* Prospect Heights, Ill.: Waveland, 1987.

Mellars, P., and C. Stringer (eds.). *The Human Revolution: Behavioural and Biological Perspectives on the Origins of Modern Humans.* Princeton, N. J.: Princeton University Press, 1990. This is an encyclopedic volume on the emergence of modern humans from primarily the replacement-model point of view.

Smith, F. H., and F. Spencer. *The Origins of Modern Humans.* New York: Liss, 1984. This is an excellent book on the topic mentioned in its title.

Trinkaus, E. (ed.). *The Emergence of Modern Humans: Biocultural Adaptations in the Late Pleistocene.* Cambridge, England: Cambridge University Press, 1989. This book contains nine essays on the appearance of modern humans throughout the world as well as the relationship of modern humans to other forms such as Neandertals. This book basically takes the regional continuity approach.

Wenke, R. J. *Patterns in Prehistory: Humankind's First Three Million Years,* 3d ed. New York: Oxford University Press, 1989.

Williams, S. *Fantastic Archaeology: The Wild Side of North American Prehistory.* Philadelphia: University of Pennsylvania Press, 1991. This book explores the misinterpretations of North American archaeological data as well as outright hoaxes, followed by an up-to-date summary of the prehistory of the Americas.

The earth as a container.

We travel together, passengers on a little spaceship, dependent on its vulnerable resources of air,
water, and soil . . . preserved from annihilation
only by the care, the work, and the love we give
our fragile craft.

Adlai E. Stevenson (1900–1965)

EPILOGUE

The amount of cultural change that has occurred in the past 10,000 years has been phenomenal. Any adult in a modern industrial society could list numerous technological innovations and social changes that have taken place in their own lifetime. It is not possible to notice biological evolutionary changes in such a short period of time. Yet humans are still evolving. All of the factors that influence evolution—mutation, sampling error, migration, non-random mating, and natural selection—are still operating on human populations.

Domestication of plants and animals created new conditions that affected the human gene pool. More recently, urbanization and industrialization have produced conditions, such as the use of medical x-rays, that, among other effects, increased mutation rates. A whole array of other factors such as weapons of modern warfare, the depletion of the ozone layer, acid rain, and the reduction of biological diversity could affect future human evolution.

THE INDUSTRIAL REVOLUTION

Up until about 5000 years ago, the major source of energy for *Homo sapiens* was the muscles of their own bodies. With the advent of agricultural societies, draft animals, such as oxen, did some of the work. It was not until the 1700s that machines began to take over some of the jobs of people and animals. The use of machines ushered in the Industrial Age, and with it an enormous amount of change.

Since 1750 the world population has multiplied 7½ times, from about 725 million to about 5.7 billion in 1995. Where agrarian societies were about 90 percent rural, many industrial societies are now more than 80 percent urban. Many other changes that have occurred in the past 250 years are listed in Table E–1. The first section of this Epilogue discusses some of these changes and their consequences.

Urbanization

Cities first arose about 5000 years ago, but they were small and represented nuclei for predominantly rural agricultural societies. **Urbanization** refers to the proportionate rise in the number of people living in cities in comparison to the number living in rural areas. Although early urban centers were economically important, major urbanization did not occur in any part of the world until the end of the nineteenth century. Urbanization is correlated with the rise of industrialism since the economic changes caused by industrialism led to the migration of rural populations to the cities.

An **urbanized society** is one in which a majority of the population live in cities. Kingsley Davis states, "Before 1850 no society could be described as predominantly urbanized, and by 1900 only one, Great Britain, could be so regarded."[1]

Today, the story has changed. Up to 80 percent of the people in the world's more developed countries live in cities, and 41 percent of the entire world population lives in cities. If the rate of urbanization remains constant, by the year 2020 about 62 percent of the world's population will be living in urban areas of 2500 people or more.[2] Figure E–1 shows population projections for the thirteen largest cities in the world in the year 2000.

Most people who write about the consequences of urbanization do not realize how recent urbanization is. One school of thought maintains that urbanization is a natural consequence of human evolution. Undoubtedly, humans do have a degree of preadaptation to city life. In many ways, the city has allowed for the expression of social systems that are not possible in rural or hunting-gathering societies. Nevertheless, it would be a mistake to say that humans have evolved or are evolving a high selective fitness for city life.

For most of human evolutionary history, natural selection operated on scavenging or hunting-gathering societies. In the last 10,000 years, selective pressures associated with farming have had their effect, as can be seen in the relationship of sickle-cell anemia to farming (Chapter 6). Urbanization, on the other hand, is a phenomenon chiefly of the twentieth century. Some parts of the world have been urban for four to five generations, but urbanization for most of the world has been much more recent. Consequently, a close fit to urban life has not had sufficient time to evolve. Also, the nature of urban habitats has changed greatly even in this short time.

Mutations occur, natural selection works, and drift and nonrandom mating operate in urban situations. Therefore, evolution is occurring in cities, but this evolution may be different from that taking place in agricultural areas. Evolutionary forces produce one of two basic results: survival (adaptation) or extinction; thus far, extinction has been the most frequent outcome of evolution.

It is premature to say how the conditions of urbanization will affect humankind. In the next few pages, we will present some of the data and

---

[1]K. Davis, "The Urbanization of the Human Population," *Scientific American*, 213 (September 1965), 41.

[2]G. T. Miller, Jr., *Living in the Environment*, 6th ed. (Belmont, Calif.: Wadsworth, 1990), 187.

TABLE E–1

THE PAST TWO-AND-A-HALF CENTURIES OF CHANGE

1. The largest urban communities of the industrial era are nearly twenty times the size of the largest of the agrarian era.

2. Women in industrial societies give birth to only about a third as many children as women in preindustrial societies.

3. Life expectancy at birth is almost three times greater in advanced industrial societies than it was in agrarian societies.

4. The family, for the first time in history, is no longer a significant productive unit in the economy.

5. The role and status of women in the economy and in society at large have changed substantially.

6. The role and status of youth have also changed, and youth cultures have become a significant factor in the life of industrial societies.

7. The average per capita production and consumption of goods and services in advanced industrial societies is at least ten times greater than in traditional agrarian societies.

8. The division of labor is vastly more complex.

9. Hereditary monarchical government has disappeared in industrial societies, except in ceremonial and symbolic survival, and the proprietary theory of the state has vanished entirely.

10. The functions and powers of government have been vastly enlarged.

11. Free public educational systems have been established and illiteracy has been largely eliminated in industrial societies.

12. New ideologies have spread widely (notably socialism, capitalism, nationalism, and pragmatism), while older ones inherited from the agrarian era have been substantially altered or have declined in influence.

13. The speed of travel has increased 100 times, and the speed of communication 10 million times, rendering the entire planet, in effect, smaller than England in the agrarian era.

14. A global culture has begun to emerge, as evidenced in styles of dress, music, language, technology, and organizational patterns (e.g., factories, public schools).

15. Global political institutions (e.g., the United Nations, the World Court) have been established for the first time.

16. Several societies have acquired the capacity to obliterate the entire human population.

Source: Adapted from G. Lenski, P. Nolan, and J. Lenski, *Human Societies: An Introduction to Macrosociology* (New York: McGraw-Hill, 1995), 270–271. Used with permission of McGraw-Hill, Inc.

ideas about the effects of both urbanization and industrialization on human evolution. Since all industrial societies today are highly urbanized, the term **industrial society** will be used to denote societies consisting of largely urban populations that engage in manufacturing, commerce, and services.

INDUSTRIAL SOCIETIES AND MUTATION

With industrialism came the use and development of physical and chemical materials that are known or suspected to cause mutation; among these are chemicals added to foods, some used in medicines, and many used for insect control. These mutagens, along with induced radiation, were discussed in Chapter 5. The long-term effects of the increase in mutagenic substances on human evolution are unknown, but an increase in the mutation rate might increase the genetic load of industrial populations. This, along with the fact that some persons with genetic diseases can today survive to reproduce, could lower the general viability of a population.

While any increase in deleterious mutations within a population will cause human suffering, the benefits of the substances causing mutation may outweigh the suffering. When used properly, some mutagens, such as x-rays, have lengthened lives. Thus, many things that can be harmful in one sense are beneficial in others. As Curt Stern says, "When, in prehistoric times, fire was made to serve human purposes it introduced a new danger which, in spite of extensive safe-guards, still kills and maims many people every year."[3] Although mutagenic substances are not directly analogous to fire, further research is needed to

---

[3]C. Stern, *Principles of Human Genetics*, 3d ed. (San Francisco: Freeman, 1973), 632.

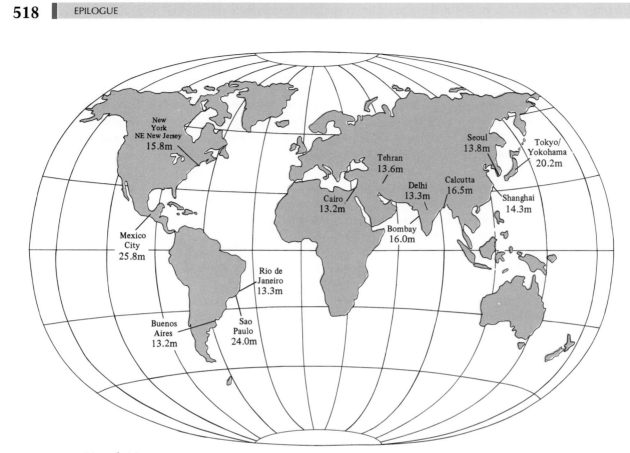

FIGURE E–1 *Rise of cities.*

determine whether mutagens in the industrial environment will, overall, be advantageous or destructive to our future.

INDUSTRIAL SOCIETIES AND SAMPLING ERROR

Sampling error is a phenomenon of small population size. As we discussed in earlier chapters, genetic drift occurs easily in societies consisting of small bands; yet demonstrating that genetic drift occurs in large urban centers would be difficult. The founder effect is also limited in industrial societies. For example, when small groups left the cities to establish communes in the 1960s, they did not remain closed; new people entered and some of the original "settlers" left.

INDUSTRIAL SOCIETIES AND MATING PATTERNS

Industrial societies are characterized by both physical and social mobility. In the past

150 years, the invention of trains, automobiles, and aircraft has increased the ease with which people can travel long distances. Such movement is important in industrial societies, since jobs often become available at distant locations. In the last few decades, for example, numerous engineers were needed in areas where the aerospace and automotive industries were developing, and so many engineers moved to those areas. Also, international trade, tourism, and overseas military operations bring people from diverse areas together.

L. L. Cavalli-Sforza and W. F. Bodmer have listed the following genetic consequences of much mobility: First, because of intergroup mating, hybrid groups have tended to develop from populations that were once widely separated (Figure E–2). Second, a general decrease has taken place in genetic isolates, with an accompanying decrease in inbreeding. Third, the number of het-

(a)

(b)

FIGURE E–2 *"Racial" hybrids.* Warfare often brings widely separated populations together for more than conflict. For instance, thousands of children were born during the Vietnam War as a result of relationships between American soldiers and Vietnamese civilians. *(a)* African-American/ Vietnamese hybrid and *(b)* American-"white"/Vietnamese hybrid.

erozygotes may increase when genetic isolates break down. Fourth, mating that can now take place in a larger group may become more selective and, hence, increase the probability of assortative mating.[4]

Once people become settled in an area, mates are often chosen from within a very close radius. A high percentage of the urban marriages in the last 40 years have been between people who lived very close to each other before they were married. The important factor is that the population density of a large city can be very high. For example, London has a population density of about 4027 people per square kilometer (10,429 per square mile).[5] Manhattan has a density of 26,261 people per square kilometer (68,015 per square mile).[6] So even within a small distance many potential mates are available in a large city. Also, because of mobility, the people who live close to one another in a large city may have diverse origins. Compared with members of hunting-gathering societies, most urbanites choose their mates from among people living closer to them. Even so, the chances of marrying someone of a different ethnic background are, of course, much greater.

INDUSTRIAL SOCIETIES AND DIFFERENTIAL FERTILITY   Each environmental or cultural shift brings new selective pressures and new fitness values for the potential genotypes of a population. The processes of industrialism and urbanization have created many selective situa-

[4]L. L. Cavalli-Sforza and W. F. Bodmer, *The Genetics of Human Populations* (San Francisco: Freeman, 1971), 784–785.
[5]*The World Almanac and Book of Facts, 1995* (New York: World Almanac, 1994), 840.
[6]*Statistical Abstract of the U.S.*, 110th ed. (Washington, D.C.: U.S. Bureau of the Census, 1990), 35.

tions not found in farming or hunting-gathering societies. We will discuss only two of these: the spread of disease and pollution.

Throughout most of human history, people lived in small groups on sparsely populated continents. If a small hunting camp was infected by a viral disease, most of the members who contracted the disease either died or recovered before coming into contact with another group. Since disease organisms are parasites that must move from host to host in order to propagate, the rapid growth of populations has eased the spread of certain types of disease.

In crowded circumstances, disease travels very rapidly from one person to the next, as can be seen in the rapid spread of flu epidemics around the world in recent times. Another example is the geometric rise in the cases of acquired immune deficiency syndrome (AIDS). In 1992 about 10 million people worldwide were infected with the AIDS virus. That number is expected to reach 40 million by the year 2000.[7]

Pollution of various types, such as air, water, thermal, and noise pollution, may also be bringing about differential mortality in industrial societies. Hunter-gatherers who move camps usually leave their garbage behind, but as people began to build cities, the amount and persistence of filth increased along with the population.

The first urban centers had many kinds of pollution. As early as 5000 years ago, when crude oil was being burned as a fuel, air pollution had started to ravage urbanites' lungs. In 1167 the army of Frederick Barbarossa found that the air of Rome "had become densely laden with pestilence and death." British kings of the Middle Ages decreed that polluting the air by burning coal was punishable by death, but the Industrial Age ushered in new toxins for the atmosphere.

More recently, the automobile has created a brownish haze over many cities throughout the world (Figure E–3). The ingredients in this smog can cause breathing difficulties, chest pains, coughing, and nausea. Some of these substances are known to cause degeneration of the optic nerve, hearing impairment, skin disease, eye ir-

ritation, asthma attacks, bronchitis and emphysema, and headaches. Many substances found in smog are known to be cancer-producing agents. Smog also damages crops, forests, and wildlife.

The high population density in cities also has created problems of water pollution. The methods used to provide food for these large populations have created soils saturated with insecticides, which eventually find their way into lakes, rivers, and oceans. Nuclear power plants spill boiling water into the ocean, causing thermal pollution.

As has been stressed in previous chapters, the precise effects of pollutants on human evolution are unknown. We do know that smog kills or contributes to the death of an increasing number of people. Most likely, pollutants affect some people more severely than others. Selective pressures are often very subtle, and a shift of even a fraction of a percent in the fitness value of a genotype may lead to a major shift in gene frequencies over the generations.

Consequences of Industrialism: The Earth at Risk

Smog and water pollution are only two of many environmental concerns. Although modern technology has made many peoples' lives easier and longer, it has also put the entire planet at risk of destruction. Four consequences of the industrial revolution that are particularly menacing are the weapons of modern warfare, the depletion of the ozone layer, acid rain, and the reduction of biological diversity.

NUCLEAR, CHEMICAL, AND BIOLOGICAL WARFARE   In December 1987 the United States and the Soviet Union agreed to destroy 2611 nuclear warheads carrying missiles, eliminating all intermediate-range missiles. In 1991 it was announced that there would be a reduction in short-range nuclear weapons and other military cutbacks. In 1994 the Ukrainian president agreed to destroy all nuclear warheads that Ukraine inherited as a result of the breakup of the Soviet Union. Yet the world is still left with thousands of megatons of nuclear power. As of 1994, more than 25 countries had or were developing nuclear

[7]E. Eckholm, "AIDS Fatalities Steady in U.S., Accelerates Worldwide," *New York Times* (June 28, 1992), E5.

FIGURE E–3 *Smog.*

weapons. New and even more devastating weapons are being developed by the United States and other countries.

Concern also exists about chemical weapons. The American Chemical Association estimates that the United States has 5000 times the amount of nerve gas needed to eliminate every person on earth.[8] More than 24 other countries are actually working on or developing chemical weapons or have already stockpiled them.

---

[8]G. Garelick, "Toward a Nerve-Gas Arms Race," *Time*, 131 (January 11, 1988), 28.

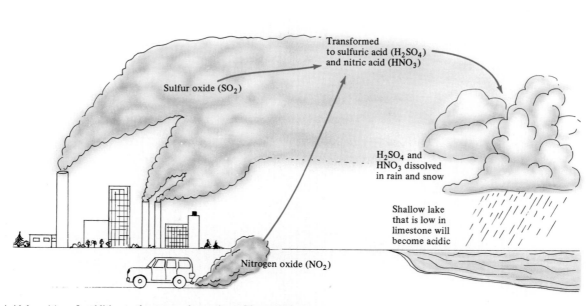

Acid deposition: In addition to the process shown above, SO_2 and NO_2 can combine with ammonia gas and other materials in the atmosphere and fall to the ground as sulfate and nitrate salts.

FIGURE E–4 *Acid rain.*

A third tool of war is biological weapons. Current research attempts to use genetic engineering and other methods to create deadly viruses, bacteria, parasites, and venoms. Although a 1972 treaty, ratified by 103 nations, bans the use and production of biological weapons, research goes on.

The use of nuclear, chemical, and biological weapons could threaten the survival of the human species. Any of these destructive agents could cause environmental damage that would render the earth uninhabitable.

THE DEPLETION OF THE OZONE LAYER

Ozone, a molecule composed of three oxygen atoms (O_3), forms in the **stratosphere,** the area of the atmosphere 20 to 50 kilometers (12 to 30 miles) above the earth's surface. The ozone layer encircles the earth and absorbs 99 percent of the ultraviolet radiation from the sun. High amounts of ultraviolet interrupt normal cell activity, and so without this protection, most life on earth would cease.

In recent years, evidence has mounted that the ozone layer is thinning because of industrial activities, in particular the use of chloroflurocar-

bons (CFCs), a class of chemicals used as refrigerants, in plastic foams, and in some spray cans. Natural factors such as volcanic eruptions and the 11-year solar cycle also increase or decrease the amount of ozone. Currently, the depletion of ozone is increasing the frequency of skin cancer in humans. Each 1 percent deletion of ozone may increase skin cancer by about 6 percent. NASA's ozone-measuring satellite indicates that globally ozone is decreasing 2.3 percent per decade. In the northern midlatitudes (roughly between Seattle and New Orleans) ozone losses are between 4 and 5 percent per decade.[9]

In addition, depletion of ozone could eventually decrease certain food crops, affect food chains, and cause changes in world climatic patterns. If the depletion goes unchecked, it could ultimately threaten all life on earth. Meanwhile, many scientists and politicians are working on a worldwide ban on CFCs and other ozone-destroying chemicals by 1999.

---

[9]R. A. Kerr, "Ozone Destruction Worsens," *Science*, 252 (April 12, 1991), 204.

ACID RAIN   Some industrial plants, such as those that burn fossil fuel, release sulfur dioxide into the atmosphere; and automobile exhaust contains nitrogen oxides which also enter the atmosphere. Sulfur dioxide and nitrogen oxides are carried back to the earth in rain; they oxidize to form sulfuric acid and nitric acid, respectively. **Acid rain,** as this precipitate is called, has acidified lakes to the point where life can no longer exist. In Canada alone, aquatic life has been depleted or threatened in at least 48,000 lakes, mainly because of U.S. industry (Figure E–4). Acid rain has changed environments, sometimes drastically, and therefore has created new selective pressures on humans by destroying food, water, and other resources.

THE REDUCTION OF BIOLOGICAL DIVERSITY   The rain forests contain about half of the earth's species, yet by 1990, human activities had led to a 55 percent reduction of rain forests. By the year 2035, the remaining rain forests will be gone or greatly disturbed. What does this mean to humans? A partial list of the effects of the loss of the world's rain forests includes reduction in atmospheric oxygen which is created by green plants, loss of plants used in making medicines, loss of fuel plants, loss of as many as 20,000 food plants, possible transformation of tropics into deserts, major changes in world climates, and crop failures due to the extinction of insects that formerly pollinated the crops.

The Control of Population

Many of the world's current problems are directly related to the enormous increase in population. At its present rate of growth the human species could eventually crowd everything else off the earth (Figure E–5). Of course, before that could happen, widespread disease, mass starvation, and other catastrophic events would come into play. In the late 1980s and early 1990s, up to 40 million people per year died from a lack of food or from normally nonfatal infections worsened by deficiencies in food resources.

Many world governments have begun to tackle the problem of population growth. In 1994 delegates from about 180 countries met in Cairo

FIGURE E–5 *People crowd Broadway in New York City after the Bicentennial parade.*

for the United Nations International Conference on Population and Development. After 9 days of heated debate, the members endorsed a plan to reduce the rate of population growth.[10]

One of the main elements in this plan is the education of women. In general, as the educational level of women increases, the fertility rate decreases. The Cairo conference suggested that governments institute policies to raise the literacy and educational levels among women in third world countries. The conference also called for world governments to work toward policies that would give equal access to women in jobs, obtaining credit, receiving inheritances, and owning property. Women so empowered will likely choose to have fewer children than women whose lives revolve exclusively around domestic concerns.

Many ecologists consider the Cairo plan to be too weak. Some countries have adopted much more severe measures to reduce their populations, including mandating sterilization for males who have fathered a specified number of children or imposing economic or other social punishments on people who have what is defined by the country in question as too many children (Figure E–6). Family-planning programs reduced the world's population by about 130 million people between the years 1978 and 1983. However, the funds for family-planning programs in many parts of the world have been cut in recent years.

Population reduction policies have not had the predicted effect. The peak population growth rate of about 2 percent annually was registered in the mid-1960s. It is now down to about 1.8 percent. However, the world population still climbed to about 5.7 billion in 1995, and it will reach approximately 6.3 billion in the year 2000. Two factors account for the increase: people are living longer, and nearly 34 percent of the world's population is below the age of 15. At an annual growth rate of 1.8 percent, the world population will double in 39 years.

Along with population control, people must learn to use resources better and recycle those that are scarce. Also, they must use their technological knowledge to prevent, not to create, environmental deterioration.

Summary

With industrialization came problems foreign to foragers. Many products and by-products of factories included mutagens and carcinogens. Industrial cities were often polluted and characterized by disease and crime. The need for more space and resources to support the growth of populations led (and continues to lead) to significant environmental disruptions. In addition, the weapons of modern warfare and the consequences of recent technologies have led to increased environmental destruction. These factors, as well as new patterns of mating and migration, have created selective pressures on urban and industrial societies that are very different from those that characterized the first 4 million years of hominid evolution.

WHAT CAN WE SAY ABOUT THE FUTURE?

Ever since modern evolutionary theory originated, people have wondered what is in store for the human species in the future. Some have said that people will lose all their hair and develop hooves or that people's legs will degenerate from lack of use. The type of thinking behind these hypotheses not only is illogical but could be counterproductive in the search for solutions to contemporary problems.

This pattern of thought is similar to the nineteenth-century Lamarckian theory of evolution. The assumption is that when something becomes unnecessary, it will disappear, and when something becomes necessary, it will appear. Thus, one might reason that body hair will totally disappear because clothes can take its place. This type of thinking becomes dangerous when it is applied to something like smog. Some maintain that smog is not all that bad because eventually people will evolve lungs that can cope with it.

---

[10]W. Roush, "Population: A View from Cairo," *Science*, 265 (1994), 1164–1167.

FIGURE E–6 *The homeless.*

Evolution does not proceed by way of necessity or lack of necessity. A trait appears only if there is genetic potential for it and only if that potential is expressed. The chance that any particular new trait will appear, and appear at the right time and in the right place, is infinitesimally small.

Similarly, a trait disappears only if it is selected against or if it diminishes because of random genetic drift. If it is selectively neutral, there will be no reason for it to vanish. Hair will not become more scarce unless the *lack* of hair has a selective advantage over the retention of hair. Lungs will not adapt to smog unless mutations occur that allow this to happen. However, there is no reason to believe that this will happen. Considering the ingredients of smog at high concentrations, extinction is a greater possibility.

Science provides no crystal balls. The anthropologist or other researcher cannot describe what the human form will be like in the future, nor can anyone predict random change or the effects that unknown environmental conditions of the future will have on the genetic material. Nevertheless, there are some absolutes—existence or nonexistence, for instance. Since we do know some of the requirements that can support life and some of the conditions that can bring about extinction, we can—and should—examine *H. sapiens'* chances for survival.

For the human species to continue, policy makers must realize that certain conditions are necessary for survival. First, certain resources are nonreplenishable, for example, fossil fuels (such as coal and oil) and natural gases (such as helium). Humans depend on these resources and have no guarantee of a substitute should they run out.

Second, the earth is, in effect, a container with the ground acting as the bottom and the atmosphere acting as the sides and lid. Pollution is pumped into the ground, water, and air, where it often becomes trapped. Humans reside in that container, and they require that healthful conditions exist within it.

Third, the earth has a finite amount of space. Humans cannot occupy all that space, since the things they depend on for food and environmental stability must also have room to exist.

Learning from Our Mistakes

Continued media and educational discussions about population problems and massive pollution of bodies of water, as well as other potentially destructive occurrences, have focused at least some political concern on environmental programs. Yet concern is not enough. Culture—learned, patterned, transmittable behavior—is humankind's major tool for survival. The next years will test just how good a tool it is. For what is needed, if humans are not to go the way of the dinosaurs, is a willingness to change basic beliefs and behaviors that have proved to be nonadaptive. Ideas that place humans above nature must be replaced with ideas that see people as a *part* of nature. Rather than subdue the world around us, we should intelligently interact with the environment. Rather than reproduce ourselves into situations of increasing starvation, disease, and general degradation, we should use reproductive restraint.

We must also avoid the trap of thinking that technology will always save us; as we saw in Chapter 1, the misuse of modern technology *is* one cause of the ecological crisis. We must learn to be more selective in the types of technology we use and develop. Why not put our money and effort into technologies such as solid-waste recycling, nonpolluting machinery, and efficient and nondisruptive energy sources instead of innovations that lead to the darkening of our lungs, the poisoning of our food, air, and water, and the possible dehumanizing of the human species?

In your daily life you can help restore the quality of the environment by doing such things as choosing a simpler lifestyle. In this light, G. Tyler Miller, Jr., offers the following suggestions:

Choose a simpler life-style by reducing resource consumption and waste and pollution production. Do this by distinguishing between your true needs and wants and using trade-offs. For every high-energy use, high-waste, or highly polluting thing you do (buying a car, living or working in an air conditioned building), give up a number of other things. Such a life-style will be less expensive and should bring you joy as you learn how to break through the plastic, technological barriers that artificially separate most of us from other people, from other parts of nature, and from our true selves.[11]

Above all, we must not fall into a gloom-and-doom trap. In many respects, the next 50 or so years may be the most exciting in human history. Each of us can be a "hero" by virtue of our own involvement in the social and technological revolution that has already begun. Apathy will be the worst enemy of the struggle to prove that we can efficiently interact with nature.

APPLICATION OF ANTHROPOLOGICAL KNOWLEDGE

The knowledge gained through anthropological investigation is not purely academic. The study of genetics has aided in building theories of inheritance which have been important in recognizing, treating, and—through counseling—preventing genetic disease. In this light, research into genetics and general evolutionary theory has awakened people to the dangers of increasing the genetic load by arresting a disease without curing it. We have also developed hypotheses on the long-range evolutionary effects of artificially increased mutation rates, which are a result of human-caused environmental contamination by radiation and chemicals.

Studies of human variation have put differences among people into an empirical perspective instead of one based on social and biological myths. These studies have very definitely affected policy making as well as the ideas held by the educated public. In fact, the works of an early anthropologist, Franz Boas, were extensively cited in the historic 1954 U.S. Supreme Court decision that legally ended racial segregation in the United States. Anthropological studies have

---

[11]G. T. Miller, Jr., *Living in the Environment*, 6th ed. (Belmont, Calif.: Wadsworth, 1990), 615.

shown that the tendency of some groups within our society to score lower on IQ tests is due to social deprivation and environmental deterioration, and to cultural bias in the tests themselves, rather than to supposed innate differences. This has been realized by some educators and administrators. We hope that the implementation of policies aimed at correcting these situations will increase the standard of living for everyone.

Anthropology is an ecological discipline, and one of its main contributions has been the investigation of relationships between humans and their environment. From these studies, it has become clear that people, like all animals, must maintain a proper balance with nature. The great potential of people for cultural behavior provides adaptive flexibility, but it is limited; if this potential is used carelessly, it could create a sterile environment.

The studies of humans' closest relatives, the primates, and of evolutionary history have provided a multidimensional picture of human nature. Through these anthropological studies, many current biological and social problems, such as those that arise in urban situations, are

put into understandable perspectives from which solutions can be sought.

Anthropology and You—A Personal Note to the Student

Most of you are probably taking an anthropology course because it is a general education requirement or because you chose it as an elective. For you, we hope that this course has provided perspectives and information that have been enriching. Some of you, however, may have become interested in pursuing anthropology further, and you may even be interested in anthropology as a career.

Traditionally, anthropologists with M.A.s and Ph.D.s have worked almost exclusively as teachers, researchers, curators, and writers attached to colleges, universities, and museums. Although the number of jobs in these areas has been decreasing, we believe that a B.A. in anthropology is a valuable liberal arts degree. H. Russell Bernard and Willis E. Sibley found that a B.A. degree in anthropology "if it is combined with appropriate personal training [provides] . . . an ex-

TABLE E–2

FIELDS OR GRADUATE PROGRAMS THAT MAY BE ENTERED WITH A B.A. DEGREE IN ANTHROPOLOGY*

1. Health assistance occupations
2. Physical therapy
3. Occupational therapy
4. Speech pathology and audiology
5. Medical or dental technology
6. Dietetics
7. Sanitary control
8. Public health
9. Environmental health
10. Public administration
11. City management
12. Hospital administration
13. Government agency work
14. Personnel management
15. Counseling and helping occupations
16. Advertising
17. Market research
18. Journalism
19. Radio and TV
20. Public relations
21. Purchasing
22. Sales
23. Library work
24. City planning
25. Business management
26. Systems analysis
27. Recreation
28. Teaching
29. Museum work
30. Police work
31. Science writing
32. Extension and community development
33. Law
34. Federal and international overseas agency work
35. Travel work

*Listed are some fields for which a B.A. in anthropology would provide excellent preparation. Many of these fields also require an advanced degree (such as a master's degree) in the specific field or certification in the field.
Source: H. R. Bernard and W. E. Sibley, *Anthropology and Jobs* (Washington, D.C.: American Anthropological Association, 1975).

cellent competitive position for careers in many fields."[12] Table E–2 lists some of the careers that students with a B.A. or an M.A. degree in anthropology may be able to enter. Several sources of information on anthropology as a career, as well as on the uses of anthropology in nonanthropological fields, may be found in the Suggested Readings.

STUDY QUESTIONS

1. What factors differentiate urban from rural life?
2. What are some of the problems caused by the enormous increase in population in the last 250 years?
3. What are some of the major problems facing people as they "prepare" for the twenty-first century?
4. In your opinion, what should be done to improve the quality of human life?

SUGGESTED READINGS

Bodley, J. H. *Anthropology and Contemporary Human Problems*, 2d ed. Palo Alto, Calif.: Mayfield, 1985. This book considers current problems such as natural resource depletion, war, hunger, and popula-

tion growth, and it attempts to put them into an anthropological perspective.

Brown, L. B., et al. *State of the World 1995*. New York: Norton, 1995. This book reports on world ecological and economic conditions. A new volume is published each year, so look for the most current edition.

Flavin, C. *Reassessing Nuclear Power: The Fallout from Chernobyl*. Washington, D.C.: Worldwatch Institute, 1987. This is a 91-page booklet that reports on the decline in interest in the development of nuclear power after the Chernobyl disaster.

Miller, G. T., Jr. *Living in the Environment*, 9th ed. Belmont, Calif.: Wadsworth, 1996. This is an excellent and comprehensive text that outlines environmental problems and presents possible solutions. Thousands of references are listed.

Shrivastava, P. *Bhopal: Anatomy of a Crisis*. New York: Ballenger, 1987. This report explores the causes and consequences of the world's worst industrial accident.

The following sources provide information on anthropology as a career or on the uses of anthropology in nonanthropological fields. All are published by the American Anthropological Association, 1703 New Hampshire Avenue NW, Washington, D.C., 20009.

American Anthropological Association. *Getting a Job Outside the Academy*, 1982.
American Anthropological Association. *Guide to Departments of Anthropology* (published annually).
Givens, D. *Federal Job Opportunities for Anthropologists*, 1986.
Givens, D. *State Employment Opportunities for Anthropologists*, 1986.
Goldschmidt, W. (ed.). *The Uses of Anthropology*, 1979.
Trotter, R. *Anthropology for Tomorrow*, 1988.

---

[12]H. R. Bernard and W. E. Sibley, *Anthropology and Jobs* (Washington, D.C.: American Anthropological Association, 1975), 1–2.

APPENDIX

AN INTRODUCTION TO SKELETAL ANATOMY AND THE ANATOMY OF THE BRAIN

Important evidence for evolution is found in anatomy. Because of the interest of anthropologists in the skeletons of living primates, the fossil record, and human burials, physical anthropologists have become specialists in the skeleton. Skeletal evidence is also used in studies of growth and development and in forensic anthropology.

Various aspects of the skeleton are discussed in several chapters of this text. Because different readers may study these chapters in different orders, a general introduction to skeletal anatomy is presented in this appendix so that it can be used with any chapter.

In order to understand the primate skeleton, it is important to constantly refer to the drawings and to locate on them the bones and features that are being discussed. Important bones and features that can be seen in the drawings in this appendix appear in bold type. This is a general discussion designed to provide the reader with tools necessary for understanding the text. More detailed discussions of skeletal anatomy may be found in the Suggested Readings at the end of this appendix.

SKELETAL ANATOMY OF PRIMATES

The Postcranial Skeleton

The postcranial skeleton is that part of the skeleton behind the skull or below the skull in bipedal animals such as humans; it is all the skeleton except the skull. The axis of the skeleton is the spine, or **vertebral column,** which consists of a series of interlocking vertebrae. The vertebrae differ in morphology in various regions of the spine. The vertebrae in these regions may be identified as **cervical, thoracic, lumbar, sacral, and coccygeal.** The term *articulation* refers to the coming together of two bones at a joint. All **ribs** articulate with the vertebrae, and most of the ribs articulate in front with the **sternum.**

The forelimbs and hindlimbs are connected to the spine at the **shoulder girdle** and the **pelvis,** respectively. The shoulder girdle consists of two bones, the **clavicle** (collarbone), which articulates with the sternum, and the **scapula** (shoulder blade). The scapula articulates with the clavicle and the **humerus,** the bone of the upper arm.

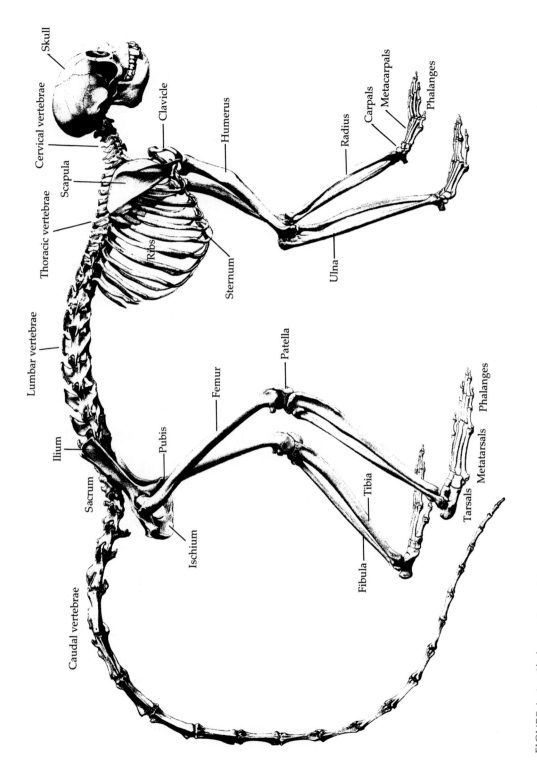

FIGURE A–1 *Skeleton of an Old World monkey, Miopithecus talapoin.*

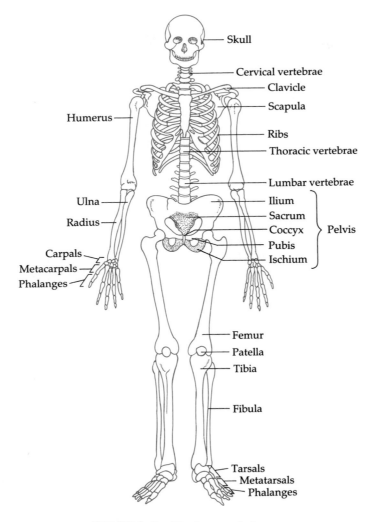

Skull

Cervical vertebrae

Clavicle

Scapula

Humerus

Ribs

Thoracic vertebrae

Lumbar vertebrae

Ulna

Ilium

Radius

Sacrum

Coccyx

Pubis

Ischium

Pelvis

Carpals

Metacarpals

Phalanges

Femur

Patella

Tibia

Fibula

Tarsals

Metatarsals

Phalanges

FIGURE A–2   *The human skeleton.*

The articulations of the clavicle with the scapula and the scapula with the humerus are close together, providing for movement and flexibility in the shoulder. The humerus articulates with the scapula as a ball in a socket.

The lower arm consists of a pair of bones, the **radius** and the **ulna.** The radius articulates with the humerus in such a way that it can rotate around an axis; in so doing, the wrist and hand rotate. The wrist consists of eight bones, the **carpals;** the palm region of the hand contains the five **metacarpals.** The bones of the fingers are the **phalanges,** two in the thumb and three in each finger. (However, there has been a reduction in the number of bones in the fingers in some primates, such as the potto, spider monkeys, and colobus monkeys.)

The hindlimbs articulate with the spine by means of the pelvis. The pelvis itself is composed of three units: a pair of **innominate** bones and the sacrum. The latter is made up of fused sacral vertebrae. Each innominate in the adult is divided into three regions corresponding to what are three separate bones in the fetus. These regions are the **ilium,** the **ischium,** and the **pubis.**

The bone of the upper leg is the **femur.** The lower leg, like the lower arm, consists of two bones, the **tibia** and the **fibula;** unlike the lower arm, the lower leg does not rotate. The small **patella** is commonly called the kneecap. The ankle consists of the seven **tarsals;** the arch of the foot, five **metatarsals;** and the toes of the **phalanges,** two in the big toe and three in each of the others.

The Skull

The skull consists of twenty-eight separate bones plus the teeth. The skull has two major parts: the **mandible,** or lower jaw, and the **cranium.** The skull may also be partitioned into a **facial skeleton** and the **cranium,** or **brain case.** The facial skeleton includes the mandible and the skeleton of the upper jaw, along with the regions of the nose and eyes.

THE BRAIN CASE The brain is housed in the brain case, or cranium. The brain case is made up of several separate bones. As we can see from the top or side, the bones of the cranium come together at immovable joints called *sutures.* The part of the skull surrounding the sides and top of the brain is the **calvarium,** which is composed of the **frontal, parietals, temporals,** and **occipital.**

The cranial base is the floor of the brain case. It consists of the ethmoid and sphenoid, plus parts of the occipital, temporals, and frontal bones. A large hole, the **foramen magnum,** is found in the occipital bone. The spinal cord passes through this opening and enters and merges with the brain. On either side of the foramen magnum are two rounded surfaces, the **occipital condyles,** which fit into a pair of depressions on the top of the uppermost vertebra. This is how the skull articulates with the spine. Finally, the auditory bulla, a balloonlike structure, houses the middle ear.

THE FACIAL SKELETON AND MANDIBLE The skeletal supports for the senses of smell, sight, hearing, and taste, and the skeletal apparatus for chewing, are all parts of the facial skeleton. The facial skeleton is composed of a number of small bones. It can be divided into several regions, including the nasal cavity, upper jaw, and mandible.

The upper jaw is made up of two pairs of bones, the **premaxillae** and **maxillae.** The top of the nose is formed by the **nasal bones.** Within the nose itself the inner surface of the nasal cavity is covered with membranes containing the receptors for the sense of smell. These membranes sit on a series of thin, convoluted bony plates, the turbinals and nasal conchae, which may be extensive in animals with a keen sense of smell.

The mandible, or lower jaw, is composed of two halves fused in the middle in many primates. The **horizontal ramus** contains the teeth. Behind the molars the **vertical ramus** rises at an angle and ends in a rounded surface, the **mandibular condyle,** which articulates with the rest of the skull. To the front of the vertical ramus is a projection, the **coronoid process.** There are four types of teeth embedded in the mandible: the **incisors, canines, premolars,** and **molars.** In addition, the facial skeleton includes the lacrimals,

FIGURE A–3 *Divisions of the skull.*

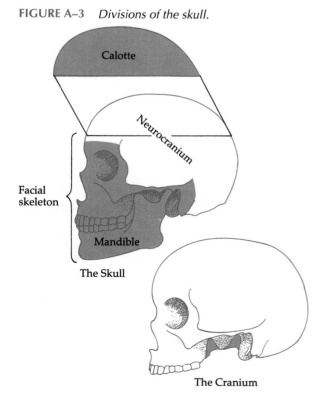

Calotte

Neurocranium

Facial skeleton

Mandible

The Skull

The Cranium

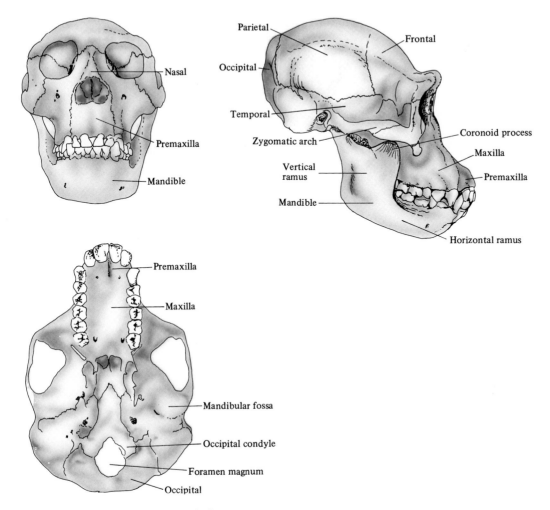

Parietal

Occipital

Temporal

Zygomatic arch

Vertical ramus

Mandible

Nasal

Premaxilla

Mandible

Frontal

Coronoid process

Maxilla

Premaxilla

Horizontal ramus

Premaxilla

Maxilla

Mandibular fossa

Occipital condyle

Foramen magnum

Occipital

FIGURE A–4   *The chimpanzee skull.*

palatine, vomer, and **zygomatics,** as well as part of the frontal.

THE ANATOMY OF THE HUMAN BRAIN

We may identify several structures that are parts of the brain. The major parts of the human brain that appear below in bold type are identified in the figures.

The **brainstem** is involved with certain body functions that are essential to life, such as the regulation of breathing and heartbeat. Attached to the brainstem is a major structure of the hind-brain, the **cerebellum.** The cerebellum has a number of functions, including those that are basic to movement of the body: balance, body position, and position in space.

In the center of the brain, immediately above the brainstem, is a group of cells that make up the limbic system. Like the brainstem and cerebellum, the limbic system is involved with basic functions of the body. It regulates body temperature, blood pressure, blood sugar levels, and more. Sexual desire and self-protection through fight or flight, emotional reactions critical to the

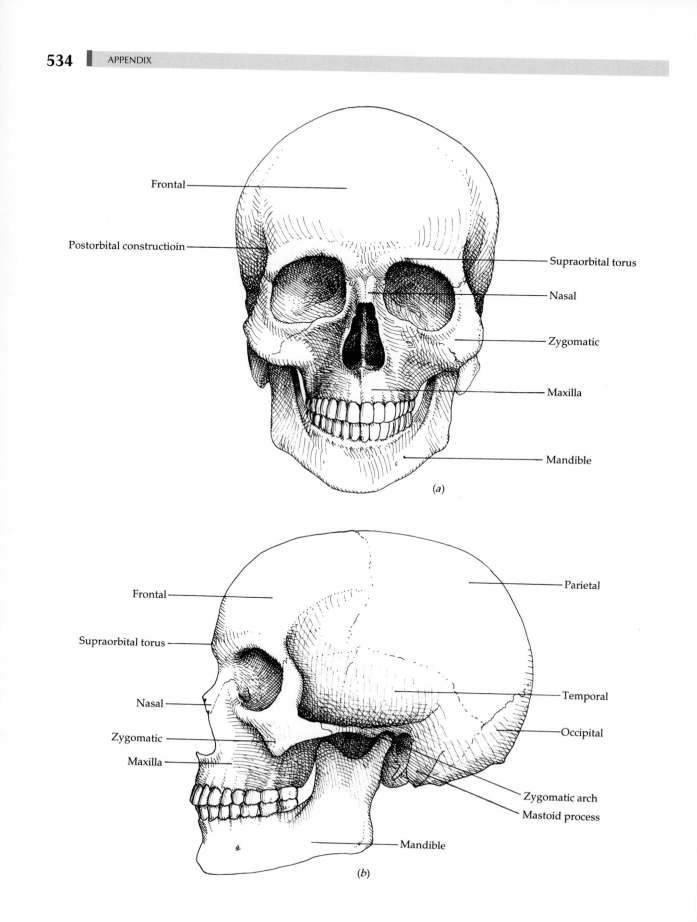

Frontal

Postorbital constructioin

Supraorbital torus

Nasal

Zygomatic

Maxilla

Mandible

(a)

Parietal

Frontal

Supraorbital torus

Nasal

Zygomatic

Maxilla

Temporal

Occipital

Zygomatic arch

Mastoid process

Mandible

(b)

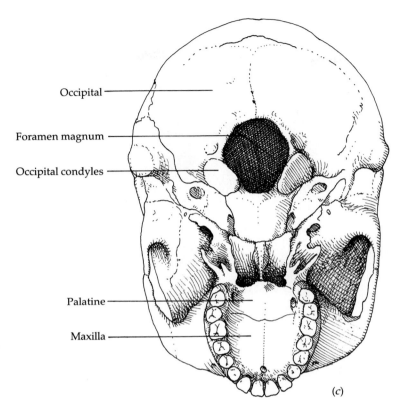

Occipital

Foramen magnum

Occipital condyles

Palatine

Maxilla

(c)

FIGURE A–5 *The human skull.*

survival of the individual, lie within the limbic system.

A critical part of the limbic system is a structure known as the **hypothalamus.** The hypothalamus regulates hunger, thirst, sleeping, waking, body temperature, chemical balances, heart rate, sexual activity, and emotions. It also plays a major role in the regulation of hormones through control of the **pituitary gland.** The pituitary gland regulates the estrous cycle and reproductive behavior.

The Cerebrum

The most prominent structure of the human brain is the **cerebrum,** which is so large that it covers and obscures many structures of the brain. The cerebrum is divided into two halves, or hemispheres; the right hemisphere controls the left side of the body, and the left controls the right side of the body. The two halves are connected by nerve fibers that make up the **corpus callosum.**

The human cerebrum is covered by the **cerebral cortex,** a layer about 3 millimeters (0.125 inch) thick. The human cortex is intricately folded into a series of rounded ridges, or convolutions, separated from one another by fissures. The convolutions serve to increase the surface area of

FIGURE A–6 *The human mandible.*

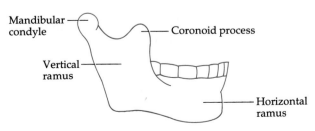

Mandibular condyle

Coronoid process

Vertical ramus

Horizontal ramus

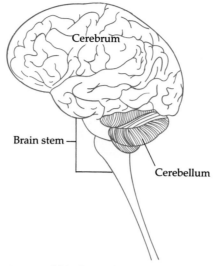

Main Parts of the Brain

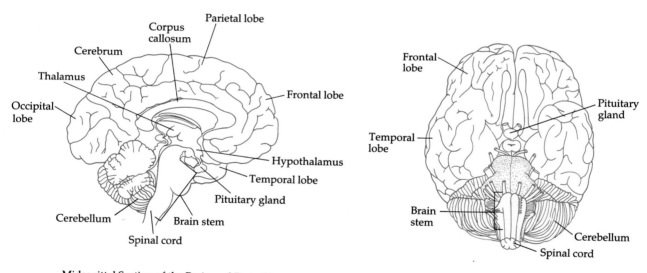

Midsagittal Section of the Brain and Brain Stem

Ventral View of the Brain

FIGURE A–7   *The human brain.*

the cerebral hemispheres since a convoluted surface has a greater surface area than a smooth surface.

Each hemisphere is divided into four lobes by deep grooves, and each lobe is named after the bone of the skull that overlays the lobe. The functions of the cortex in the various lobes have been determined by studies of electrical stimulation of

the area, observations of persons with specific brain damage, and animal experimentation. The **temporal lobes** deal with perception and memory, and a section of the temporal lobe, the **auditory cortex,** is responsible for hearing. The **occipital lobes** handle the sense of sight; the cortex in this area is often called the visual cortex. The **parietal lobes** receive sensory information from the body.

The largest parts of the cerebrum are the **frontal lobes,** which deal with purposeful behavior.

While the two cerebral hemispheres look alike, there are many subtle differences. In general, the left side deals more with language than the right side does; the right is involved more with spatial abilities.

SUGGESTED READINGS

Aiello, L., and C. Dean. *An Introduction to Human Evolutionary Anatomy.* London: Academic, 1990. This is a very detailed description of human anatomy from an evolutionary perspective.

Steele, D. G., and C. A. Bramblett. *The Anatomy and Biology of the Human Skeleton.* College Station, Tex.: Texas A&M University Press, 1988. This book features a large number of excellent photographs of human bones carefully labeled.

Swindler, D., and C. D. Wood. *An Atlas of Primate Gross Anatomy.* Melbourne, Fla.: Krieger, 1982. This book contains a series of detailed line drawings illustrating the comparative anatomy of the baboon, chimpanzee, and human.

White, T. D., and P. A. Folkens. *Human Osteology.* San Diego, Calif.: Academic, 1991. This book is a detailed discussion of the human skeleton for the paleoanthropologist.

GLOSSARY

abductor A muscle that moves a part of the body away from the midline of the body.

ABO blood-type system A blood-type system that consists of two basic antigens, A and B. Blood-type O is the absence of both antigens.

acclimatory adjustment Reversible physiological adjustments to stressful environments.

accretion Growth by virtue of an increase in intercellular materials.

acid rain Rain that carries acids that pollute water systems and soils.

acrocentric chromosome Chromosome in which the centromere is near one end, resulting in arms of very unequal length.

adaptation Changes in gene frequencies resulting from selective pressures being placed upon a population by environmental factors; results in a greater fitness of the population to its ecological niche.

adaptive radiation The evolution of a single population into a number of different species.

adenine One of the bases found in DNA and RNA.

adenosine triphosphate (ATP) The main fuel of cells. ATP is manufactured by the mitochondria.

adjustment The ability of humans to survive in stressful environments by nongenetic means.

adolescent growth spurt A rapid increase in stature and other dimensions of the body that occur during puberty.

adult The period in an individual's life cycle after the eruption of the permanent teeth.

agglutination A clumping together of red blood cells in the presence of an antibody.

aging The uninterrupted process of normal development that leads to a progressive decline in physiological function and ultimately to death.

agonistic behavior Behavior that involves fighting, threats, and fleeing.

albinism A recessive abnormality leading to little or no production of the skin pigment melanin.

allantois Sac within the amniote egg in which waste products produced by the embryo are deposited.

allele An alternate form of a gene.

Allen's rule Among endotherms, populations of the same species living near the equator tend to have body parts that protrude more and to have longer limbs than populations farther away from the equator.

allogrooming Grooming another animal.

allometric growth Pattern of growth whereby different parts of the body grow at different rates with respect to each other.

allopatric species Species occupying mutually exclusive geographic areas.

alpha chain One of the two polypeptide chains making up the globin unit of the hemoglobin molecule.

alpha-feto protein (AFP) A compound, produced by the fetus, that enters the mother's blood through the placenta. Excessive amounts of AFP may indicate neural tube defects or other fetal abnormalities.

altruistic act A behavior characterized by self-sacrifice that benefits others.

alveoli   Small air sacs located in the lungs, which are richly endowed with blood capillaries. Oxygen is absorbed by the blood in the alveoli.

amino acid   A type of molecule that forms the basic building block of proteins.

amino acid racemization   Chronometric dating method based on change in the three-dimensional structure of an amino acid from one form to its mirror image over time.

amniocentesis   A medical technique in which amniotic fluid is removed for study of the fetus.

amnion   A fluid-filled sac, formed from embryonic tissue, that contains the embryo in the amniote egg.

amniote egg   An egg with a shell and several internal membranes, which made reproduction on land possible.

amniotic fluid   The fluid surrounding the fetus.

analogies   Anatomical structures that serve similar functions.

anterior pillars   Bony columns located on both sides of the nasal aperture, which help withstand the stresses of chewing.

anthropocentricity   The belief that humans are the most important elements in the universe.

anthropoid   A member of the suborder Anthropoidea; includes the New World monkeys, Old World monkeys, apes, and humans.

anthropological linguistics   The study of language in cross-cultural perspective; the origin and evolution of language.

anthropology   The broad-scope scientific study of people from all periods of time and in all areas of the world. Anthropology focuses on both biological and cultural characteristics and variation as well as on biological and cultural evolution.

anthropometry   The study of measurements of the human body.

antibody   A protein manufactured by the body to neutralize or destroy an antigen.

antigen   A substance that stimulates the production or mobilization of antibodies. An antigen can be a foreign protein, toxin, bacteria, or other substance.

ape   A common term that includes the lesser apes (the gibbons and siamang) and the great apes (the orangutan, chimpanzee, bonobo, and gorilla).

applied anthropology   A branch of anthropology devoted to applying anthropological theory to practical problems.

arbitrary   A characteristic of language. A word, or other unit of sound, has no real connection to the thing it refers to; the meanings of the arbitrary elements of a language must be learned.

arboreal   Living in trees.

arboreal quadrupedalism   A form of quadrupedalism in which the animal walks along a branch grasping with both hands and feet.

archaeological culture   A series of similar assemblages that occur in many sites.

archaeology   The scientific study of past and current cultures through the analysis of artifacts and the context in which they are found.

archetype   The divine plan or blueprint for a species or higher taxonomic category.

areolar area   The dark area surrounding the nipple of the breast.

argon 40/argon 39 (^{40}Ar/^{39}Ar) dating   Radiometric dating method in which the material is radiated so that the nonradioactive ^{39}K is transformed into ^{39}Ar. The argon gas is then extracted and the amounts of ^{40}Ar and ^{39}Ar are measured.

artifact   Any physical remains of human activity.

artificial gene   A gene made in a laboratory and used in place of a defective or undesirable gene.

assemblage   All the artifacts from a given site.

assortative mating   Preference for or avoidance of certain people as mates for physical or social reasons.

asymmetry of function (lateralization)   The phenomenon in which the two hemispheres of the brain specialize in regard to different functions.

atom   A building block of matter.

auditory bulla   A flat or inflated structure that forms in the floor of the skull and houses the middle ear.

autapomorphic feature   A feature that is unique to a particular species.

autogrooming   Self-grooming.

autosome   A chromosome other than a sex chromosome.

awl   A type of tool used to puncture a hole in a soft material such as wood or skin.

back cross   The process of crossing a hybrid with its homozygous recessive parent.

balanced polymorphism   Maintenance of two or more alleles in a gene pool as the result of heterozygous advantage.

band   Among geladas, a social group consisting of a number of harems and all-male units.

band   Among humans, the basic social unit of hunting and gathering peoples, which typically consists of about thirty-five to fifty members.

basal metabolic rate   The measure of the total energy utilized by the body to maintain those body processes necessary for life; the minimum level of heat produced by the body at rest.

base   A subunit of a nucleotide that makes up DNA and RNA molecules: adenine, cytosine, guanine, thymine, uracil.

basicranium   The floor of the brain case.

behavioral adjustment   Survival in stressful environments made possible by cultural means, primarily technology.

behavioral thermoregulation   Using behavior, such as avoiding or seeking sources of heat, to regulate body temperature.

Bergmann's rule   Within the same species of endotherms, populations with less bulk are found near the equator, while those with greater bulk are found farther from the equator.

Beringia   The landmass, some 2000 kilometers (1243 miles) from north to south, that connected Siberia and Alaska during the glacials.

beta chain   One of the two polypeptide chains that make up the globin unit of the hemoglobin molecule.

biacromial width   A measurement of the width of the shoulders.

bilaterally symmetrical   A situation where, when cut down the middle, the two halves formed are generally mirror images of each other.

bilophodont   Refers to a form of molar found in Old World monkeys and consisting of four cusps with a small constriction separating them into two pairs.

binocular field   The visual field produced by overlapping of the separate visual fields from each eye when the eyes are located on the front of the face.

binomen   A two-part name given to a species; the first name is also the name of the genus. An example of a binomen is *Homo sapiens.*

binomial nomenclature   A system of naming species that uses a double name such as *Homo sapiens.* The first name alone names the genus; both names used together name the species.

biological environment   The living elements surrounding the organism.

biological evolution   Change in the frequencies of alleles within a gene pool of a population over time.

bipedalism   See **erect bipedalism.**

bitrochanteric width   A measurement of hip width.

blade   Flakes with roughly parallel sides and extremely sharp edges; blades are frequently found in Upper Paleolithic sites.

blending theory   An early, incorrect idea that the inherited characteristics of offspring are intermediate between maternal and paternal genetic characteristics.

bone age   A standard age based upon the appearance of centers of ossification and fusion of growth plates.

bone breccia   Cave fill consisting of masses of bone cemented together with calcium carbonate that has dissolved out of limestone.

bone hammer   A bone used as a hammer in the removal of flakes from a core in the manufacture of stone tools.

bone industry   All of the bone artifacts from a particular site.

bottlenecking   (see population bottlenecking).

brachiation   Hand-over-hand locomotion along a branch with the body suspended underneath the branch by the arms.

branch running and walking   A form of quadrupedalism in which the animal walks along a branch grasping with both hands and feet.

breast bud   An elevation of the breast as a small mound; the earliest sign of puberty in the female.

Broca's area   A small area in the human brain that controls the production of speech.

Bronze Age   The stage of cultural history that includes the earliest civilizations and the development of metallurgy.

brow ridge   Ridge of bone above the eye sockets.

burin   A stone tool with a chisel-like point used for engraving or manufacturing bone tools.

calendrical system   A system of measuring time based on natural recurring units of time, such as the revolutions of the earth around the sun; it records the number of such units that have elapsed with reference to a specific point in time.

call system   A system of vocalized sounds in which one grades into another.

carbohydrates   Organic compounds composed of carbon, oxygen, and hydrogen; includes the sugars and starches.

carnivore   An animal that eats primarily meat.

carrier   A person who possesses a recessive allele in the heterozygous condition.

cast   A representation of an organism created when a substance fills in a mold.

cataract   Opacity of the eye lens, often inherited as a dominant. The type may vary according to the action of a modifying gene.

catarrhine nose   Nose in which nostrils open downward and are separated by a narrow nasal septum; found in Old World monkeys, apes, and humans.

catastrophism   Idea that the earth has experienced a series of catastrophic destructions and creations and that fossil forms found in each layer of the earth are bounded by creation and destruction events.

cebid   A member of the family Cebidae; the New World monkeys excluding the marmosets and tamarins.

cell   The smallest unit able to perform all the activities collectively called life. All living organisms are either one cell or composed of several cells.

centriole   A pair of small bodies found near the nucleus of the cell from which the spindle is formed.

centromere   A structure in the chromosome holding the two chromatids together; during cell division it is the site of attachment for the spindle fibers.

cephalic index   The breadth of the head relative to its length.

cerebral cortex   The "gray matter" of the brain; the center of conscious evaluation, planning, skill, speech, and other higher mental activities.

cheek pouch   Pocket in the cheek that opens into the mouth; some Old World monkeys store food in the cheek pouch.

cheek teeth The premolars and molars.

chin   A bony projection of the lower border of the outside of the mandible.

chondrodystrophic dwarfism   Form of dwarfism in which the individual's head and trunk are of normal size but the limbs are quite short; inherited as a dominant.

chordate   A member of the phylum Chordata; chordates are characterized by the presence of a notochord, dorsal hollow single nerve cord, and gill slits at some point in the life cycle.

chorion   A membrane derived from the amnion that lies just beneath the shell in the amniote egg and acts as a surface for oxygen absorption.

chorionic villus biopsy   A method of analyzing the embryo by sampling the tissue of the placenta surrounding the developing embryo.

chromatid   One of the two strands of a replicated chromosome. Two chromatids are joined together by a centromere.

chromosomal aberration   Abnormal chromosome number or chromosome structure.

chromosome   A body containing the hereditary material which is found in the nucleus of the cell.

chronological age   Period of time since birth.

chronometric dates   Dates that refer to a specific point or range of time. Chronometric dates are not necessarily exact dates, and they are often expressed as a probability.

chron   A large division of a geomagnetic time scale which shows primarily a single polarity.

chronospecies   Arbitrarily defined divisions of an evolutionary line.

clade   A group of species with a common evolutionary ancestry.

cladistics   A theory of classification that differentiates between shared ancestral and shared derived features.

cladogram   A graphic representation of the species (or other taxa) being studied, based upon cladistic analysis.

class   Major division of a phylum, consisting of closely related orders.

classification   A system of organizing data.

cleaver   A large core tool with a straight, sharp edge at one end.

clinal distribution   A distribution of frequencies showing a systematic gradation over space; also called continuous variation.

cline   Continuous change in a trait or trait frequency over space or time.

cloning   The process of asexual reproduction in an otherwise multicellular animal.

codominance   The situation in which, in the heterozygous condition, both alleles are expressed in the phenotype.

codon   A sequence of three bases on the DNA molecule that codes for a specific amino acid or other genetic function.

communication   Occurs when a stimulus or message is transmitted and received; in relation to animal life, when one animal transmits information to another animal.

community   Among chimpanzees, a large group of animals that, through fission and fusion, is composed of a series of constantly changing smaller units including the all-male party, family, unit, nursery unit, consortship, and gathering.

comparative cytogenetics   The comparative study of the heredity mechanisms within the cell.

competition   The situation in which two populations occupy the same or parts of the same niche.

complementary pair   A set of two nucleotides, each on a different polynucleotide chain, that are attracted to each other by a chemical bond. In DNA, adenine and thymine, and cytosine and guanine, form complementary pairs.

compound tool   A tool composed of several parts, for example, a harpoon.

computerized tomography   A technology used in medicine that permits visualization of the interior of an organism's body.

conduction   The movement of heat from one object to another by direct contact.

cones   Cells of the retina of the eye; each of the three types of cones is sensitive to a specific wavelength of light, thereby producing color vision.

consanguineous mating   Mating between biological relatives.

consort pair   A temporary alliance between a male and an estrus female.

constitutive heterochromatin   Chromosomal material thought not to contain any actual genes.

continuous variation   A distribution of frequencies showing a systematic gradation over space; also called clinal distribution.

control   In the scientific method, a situation in

which a comparison can be made between a specific situation and a second situation that differs, ideally, in only one aspect from the first.

convection Movement of heat from an object to the surrounding fluid, either gas or liquid; heat causes the fluid to move away from the object.

convergence Nonhomologous similarities in different evolutionary lines; the result of similarities in selective pressures.

coprolite Fossilized fecal material.

core A nodule of rock from which flakes are removed.

core area Sections within the home range of a primate population that may contain a concentration of food, a source of water, and a good resting place or sleeping trees, and in which most of the troop's time is spent.

core tool A tool manufactured by the removal of flakes from a core.

cranial capacity The volume of the brain case of the skull.

creation-science The idea that scientific evidence can be and has been gathered for creation as depicted in the Bible. Mainstream scientists and the Supreme Court discount any scientific value of creation-science statements.

crenulation A fine wrinkling found around the base of a tooth.

critical temperature The temperature at which the body must begin to resist a lowering of body temperature; occurs in the nude human body at approximately 31°C (87.8°F).

cross-cousin preference marriage Marriage between a person and his or her cross-cousin (father's sister's child or mother's brother's child).

crossing-over The phenomenon whereby sections of homologous chromosomes are interchanged during meiosis.

cultural anthropology The study of the learned patterns of behavior and knowledge characteristic of a society and of how they vary.

cultural determinism The idea that except for reflexes all behavior is the result of learning.

cultural environment The products of human endeavor, including technology and social institutions.

culture Learned, nonrandom, systematic behavior and knowledge that can be transmitted from generation to generation.

culture-bound The state or quality of having relevance only to the members of a specific cultural group.

cusp A point on a tooth.

cytogenetics The study of the heredity mechanisms within the cell.

cytology The study of the biology of the cell.

cytoplasm Material within the cell between the plasma membrane and the nuclear membrane.

cytosine One of the bases found in the DNA and RNA molecule.

debitage Waste and nonutilized material produced in the process of tool manufacture.

deciduous teeth The first set of teeth that develop in mammals; also known as the baby or milk teeth.

deletion A chromosomal aberration in which a chromosome breaks and a segment is not included in the second-generation cell. The genetic material on the deleted section is lost.

deme The local breeding population; the smallest reproductive population.

dendrite A branchlike projection from a cell.

dendrochronology Tree-ring dating.

dental age A standard age based upon the time of eruption of particular teeth.

dental arcade The tooth row as seen from above.

dental comb A structure formed by the front teeth of the lower jaw projecting forward almost horizontally; found in prosimians.

dental formula Formal designation of the types and numbers of teeth. The dental formula 2.1.2.3/2.1.2.3 indicates that in one-half of the upper jaw and lower jaw there are two incisors, one canine, two premolars, and three molars.

deoxyribonucleic acid (DNA) A nucleic acid that controls the structure of proteins and hence determines inherited characteristics; genes are portions of the DNA molecule that fulfill specific functions.

deoxyribose A five-carbon sugar found in the DNA molecule.

development The process whereby cells differentiate into different and specialized units.

developmental adjustments Alterations in the pattern of growth and development resulting from environmental influence.

diabetes Failure of the body to produce insulin, which controls sugar metabolism; has a complex genetic basis influenced by environmental factors.

diaphragm A muscle that lies beneath the lungs. When the diaphragm contracts, the volume of the lungs increases, causing a lowering of pressure within the lungs and movement of air from the outside into the lungs. When the diaphragm relaxes, air is expelled from the lungs.

diaphysis The shaft of a long bone.

diastema A space between teeth.

diphyodonty Having two sets of teeth, the deciduous and the permanent teeth.

discontinuous variation Distribution of alleles, allele combinations, or any traits characterized by little or no gradation in frequencies between adjacent regions.

discrete A characteristic of language. Signals, such as words, represent discrete entities or experiences; a discrete signal does not blend with other signals.

displacement (behavior) The situation in which one animal can cause another to move away from food, a sitting place, and so on.

displacement (language) A characteristic of language. The ability to communicate about events at times and places other than when they occur; enables a person to talk and think about things not directly in front of him or her.

distance curve A graph showing the total height (or other measurement) of an individual on a series of dates.

diurnal Active during daylight hours.

dizygotic twins Fraternal twins; twins derived from separate zygotes.

DNA hybridization A method of comparing DNA from different species by forming hybrid DNA.

domestication The control of the reproductive cycle of plants and animals.

dominance (behavior) Behavior in which one animal displaces another and takes preference in terms of sitting place, food, and estrus females.

dominance (genetic) When in the heterozygous genotype only one allele is expressed in the phenotype, that allele is said to be dominant.

dominance hierarchy A system of social ranking based upon the relative dominance of the animals within a social group.

dorsal Toward the top or back of an animal.

Down's syndrome Condition characterized by a peculiarity of eyefolds, malformation of the heart and other organs, stubby hands and feet, short stature, and mental retardation; result of an extra chromosome 21.

dryomorphs Group of Miocene hominoids from the Early and Middle Miocene of east Africa and Eurasia, including members of the genus *Dryopithecus*.

duplication Chromosomal aberration in which a section of a chromosome is repeated.

dyspnea Difficult or painful breathing.

ecological isolation Form of reproductive isolation in which two closely related species are separated by what is often a slight difference in the niches they occupy.

ecological niche The specific microhabitat in which a particular population lives and the way that population exploits this microhabitat.

ecology The study of the relationship of organisms or groups of organisms to their environment.

ectotherm An animal that derives most of its body heat from external heat sources.

ectotympanic A bony element within the middle ear that supports the tympanic membrane or eardrum.

edema Retention of water in the tissues of the body.

effector An enzyme produced by one of the structural genes that binds with the repressor and prevents it from binding to the operator.

electron spin resonance A chronometric dating technique based upon the behavior of electrons in crystals exposed to naturally occurring radioactivity; used to date limestone, coral, shell, teeth, and other materials.

electrophoresis A method for separating proteins in an electric field.

Ellis–van Creveld syndrome A rare recessive abnormality characterized by dwarfism, extra fingers, and malformations of the heart; it has a high incidence among the Amish.

embryology The branch of biology that studies the formation and development of the embryo.

empirical Received through the senses (sight, touch, smell, hearing, taste), either directly or through extensions of the senses (such as a microscope).

encephalization quotient (EQ) A number reflecting the increase in brain size over and beyond that explainable by an increase in body size.

endocranial cast A cast of the inside of the brain case.

endocrine glands Organs that produce hormones.

endotherm An animal whose body heat is regulated by internal physiological mechanisms.

environment Everything external to the organism.

epidermal ridges Fine ridges in the skin on the hand and foot which are richly endowed with nerve endings and are responsible for the highly developed sense of touch; responsible for the fingerprint pattern.

epidermis The outermost layer of the skin.

epiphyses Secondary centers of ossification near the ends of long bones.

epoch A unit of geological time; a division of a period.

era A major division of geological time defined by major geological events and delineated by the kinds of animal and plant life it contains. Humans evolved in the Cenozoic era.

erect bipedalism A form of locomotion found in humans in which the body is maintained in an upright posture on two legs while moving by means of a heel-toe stride.

ergonomics The study of scientific data on the

human body and the application of such data to problems of design.

erythroblastosis fetalis   A hemolytic disease affecting unborn or newborn infants caused by destruction of the infant's Rh+ blood by the mother's anti-Rh antibodies.

erythrocyte   Red blood cell. Cell found in blood which lacks a nucleus and contains the red pigment hemoglobin.

estrogen   Hormone produced in the ovary.

estrus   Time period during which the female is sexually receptive.

ethmoturbinals   Bony plates, occurring as pairs, that are found within the nasal region of the skull and support the nasal membranes.

eugenics   The study of the methods that can improve the inherited qualities of a species.

eukaryote   Cell with a nucleus that contains nDNA.

eutherian mammal   A placental mammal.

evaporation   Transformation of a liquid into a gas utilizing energy.

evolution   See **biological evolution.**

exogamy   Outbreeding in human groups. A male in many societies must find a wife in a neighboring band.

exon   The sequences in the DNA molecule that code for the amino acid sequences of corresponding proteins.

extensor   A muscle that straightens out the bones about a joint.

extinction   The disappearance of a population.

facial sinus   A hollow, air-filled space in the bones of the front of the skull.

familial hypercholesterolemia   A rare, dominant abnormality controlled by a multiple-allele series of at least four alleles. The disease is caused by a defective protein and can result in extremely high levels of cholesterol in the blood.

family   Major division of an order, consisting of closely related genera.

fetal hemoglobin (HbF)   A normal variant of hemoglobin, consisting of two alpha and two gamma polypeptide chains found in the fetus and early infant; it is gradually replaced by hemoglobin A.

fetalization hypothesis   A theory of evolutionary change which holds that organisms in a group maintain younger characteristics of ancestral groups while becoming sexually mature during what was previously an infantile or juvenile stage of development; also, the retarded development of specific characteristics.

fission-fusion society   Constantly changing form of social organization whereby large groups undergo fission into smaller units and small units fuse into larger units in response to the activity of the group and the season of the year.

fission-track dating   The determination of a chronometric date by counting the proportion of atoms of a radioactive isotope such as uranium 238 that have decayed leaving visible tracks in a mineral relative to the total number of atoms of the isotope.

fitness   Measure of how well an individual or population is adapted to a specific ecological niche.

flake   A small piece of stone removed from a core when the core is struck by a hammerstone or bone hammer.

flake tool   A tool manufactured from a flake.

fluted   Referring to fluted points where a rounded groove has been made in the shaft of the point, most likely to facilitate hafting.

folivore   An animal that eats primarily leaves.

folk taxonomy   Classification of some class of phenomena based on cultural tradition.

food chain   A sequence of sources of energy in which each source is dependent on another source.

food sharing   The act of allowing animals other than those who acquired the food to have some of that food.

foramen magnum   A large opening in the occipital bone at the base of the skull through which the spinal cord passes.

foramina   Small holes found in bone that permit the passage of nerves and blood vessels.

forebrain   The anterior of three swellings in the hollow nerve cord of the primitive vertebrate brain formed by a thickening of the wall of the nerve cord.

forensic anthropology   Application of the techniques of osteology and skeletal identification to legal problems.

fossil   Remains or traces of any ancient organism.

founder principle   Situation in which a founding population does not represent a random sample of the original population; a form of sampling error.

four-chambered heart   A heart that is divided into two sets of pumping chambers effectively separating oxygenated blood from the lungs from deoxygenated blood from the body.

fovea   A depression within the macula of the retina of the eye which contains a single layer of cones with no overlapping blood vessels; region of greatest visual acuity.

frugivore   An animal that eats primarily fruits.

gamete   A sex cell produced by meiosis that contains one copy of a chromosome set (twenty-three chromosomes in humans). In a bisexual animal the sex cell is either a sperm or an ovum.

gametic mortality Form of reproductive isolation in which sperm are immobilized and destroyed before fertilization can take place.

gene A section of DNA that has a specific function.

gene flow The process in which alleles from one population are introduced into another population.

gene pool The sum of all alleles carried by the members of a population.

gene therapy A genetic-engineering method in which a gene is altered and then inserted into a cell to correct an inherited abnormality.

generalized species Species that can survive in a variety of ecological niches.

generalized trait A trait used for many functions.

genetic counselor A medical professional who advises prospective parents or a person affected by a genetic disease of the probability of having a child with a genetic problem.

genetic determinism The idea that all behavior, including very specific behavior, is biologically based, in contrast to cultural determinism.

genetic drift The situation in a small population in which the allelic frequencies of the F_1 generation differ from those of the parental generation as a result of sampling error.

genetic engineering The artificial manipulation of genetic material to create specific characteristics in individuals.

genetic equilibrium A hypothetical state in which a population is not evolving because the allele frequencies remain constant over time.

genetic load The totality of deleterious alleles in a population.

genetics The study of the mechanisms of heredity and biological variation.

genome All of the genes carried by a single gamete.

genome imprinting The phenomenon whereby an allele may have a different effect on the offspring depending on the sex of the contributing parent.

genotype The genetic constitution of an individual.

genus A group of closely related species.

geographical isolation Form of reproductive isolation in which members of a population become separated from another population through geographical barriers that prevent the interchange of genes between the separated populations.

geographical race A major division of humankind into large geographical areas in which people resemble one another more closely than they resemble people in different geographical areas.

geomagnetic reversal time scale (GRTS) A chart showing the sequence of normal and reversed polarity.

gestation The period of time from conception to birth.

gill bar Skeletal element supporting the gill slit in nonvertebrate chordates and some vertebrates.

gill pouches Structures forming in the early human embryo that are thought to be homologous to the gill slits of other chordates.

gill slits Structures that filter out food particles in nonvertebrate chordates and are used for breathing in some vertebrates.

glacial Period of expansion of glacial ice.

globin A constituent of the hemoglobin molecule; consists of two alpha and two beta polypeptide chains.

Gloger's rule Within the same species of warm-blooded animals, there is a tendency to find more heavily pigmented forms near the equator and lighter forms farther away from the equator.

glucose-6-phosphate dehydrogenase (G6PD) deficiency Lack of an enzyme of the red blood cell inherited as an X-linked recessive. Afflicted individuals develop severe anemia when in contact with the fava bean or certain antimalarial drugs.

gluteus maximus In humans, the largest muscle of the human body; acts to extend the leg in running and climbing.

gluteus medius Muscle of the pelvis that in monkeys and apes acts as an extensor but in humans acts as an abductor.

gluteus minimus Muscle of the pelvis that in monkeys and apes acts as an extensor but in humans acts as an abductor.

gout Abnormal uric acid metabolism inherited as a dominant with variation expression.

grammar A set of rules used to make up words and then combine them into larger utterances such as phrases and sentences.

great apes The orangutan from Asia and the chimpanzee, bonobo, and gorilla from Africa.

grooming In primates, the activity of going through the fur with hand or teeth to remove insects, dirt, twigs, dead skin, and so on; also used as a display of affection.

grooming cluster A small group of closely related females that engage in a high degree of grooming.

ground running and walking A form of quadrupedalism that takes place on the ground as opposed to in the trees.

growth Increase in the size or mass of an organism.

growth hormone A hormone produced by the pituitary gland; essential for normal growth.

growth plate Narrow growth zone between the epiphysis and diaphysis of a bone.

guanine One of the bases found in DNA and RNA molecules.

habitat   The place in which a particular animal lives.

half-life   The time required for one-half of the atoms of a radioactive isotope to decay.

hammerstone   A stone used to remove flakes from a core by striking the hammerstone against the core.

hand ax   Large core tool with a sharp cutting edge, blunted at one end so it can be held in the hand.

hard palate   The bony roof of the mouth which separates the mouth from the nasal cavity, permitting the animal to breathe and chew at the same time.

Hardy-Weinberg equilibrium   A mathematical model of genetic equilibrium: $p^2 + 2pq + q^2 = 1$.

harem   A subunit of a larger social group consisting of a male associated with two or more females.

heel-toe stride   Method of progression characteristic of humans where the heel strikes the ground first; the person pushes off on the big toe.

heliocentric   A sun-centered model of the universe.

heme   A constituent of the hemoglobin molecule; each heme unit contains an atom of iron.

hemochorial placenta   Type of placenta found in most higher primates in which materials pass between the maternal and fetal bloodstreams through a single vessel wall.

hemoglobin   Red pigment in red blood cells that carries oxygen to and carbon dioxide from body tissues.

hemoglobin A   Normal adult hemoglobin whose globin unit consists of two alpha and two beta chains.

hemoglobin A$_2$ A normal variant of hemoglobin A consisting of two alpha and two delta polypeptide chains which is found in small quantities in normal human blood.

hemoglobin C   An abnormal variant of hemoglobin A differing from it in having a single amino acid substitution on the beta chain at the same position as the substitution producing hemoglobin S.

hemoglobin F   A normal variant of hemoglobin, also known as fetal hemoglobin, that consists of two alpha and two gamma polypeptide chains and is found in the fetus and early infant; it is gradually replaced by hemoglobin A.

hemoglobin S   An abnormal variant of hemoglobin A differing from it in having a single amino acid substitution on the beta chain; known as sickle hemoglobin.

hemolytic disease   Disease involving the destruction of blood cells.

hemophilia   A recessive X-linked trait characterized by excessive bleeding due to a faulty clotting mechanism.

herd   Among geladas, a large social unit consisting of several bands that come together under very good grazing conditions.

heterodont dentition   Dentition characterized by regional differentiation of teeth by function.

heterozygosity   The quality of being heterozygous.

heterozygous   Having two different alleles of a particular gene.

high-altitude hypoxia   Low oxygen pressure occurring at high altitude.

high-altitude (mountain) sickness   Shortness of breath, physical and mental fatigue, rapid pulse rate, and headaches experienced by persons not acclimatized to high altitudes.

higher taxa   Taxa above the genus level, such as family, order, class, phylum, and kingdom.

hindbrain   The posterior of three swellings in the hollow nerve cord of the primitive vertebrate brain formed by a thickening of the wall of the nerve cord.

home base   A location to which males and females return in human societies.

home range   The area occupied by an animal or animal group.

homeothermic   The ability to control body temperature and maintain a high body temperature through physiological means.

hominid   A member of the family Hominidae, which includes modern humans and species of the genera *Homo*, *Australopithecus* and *Ardipithecus*, found in the fossil record.

hominoid   A member of the superfamily Hominoidea, which includes the apes and humans.

homodont dentition   Situation in which all teeth are basically the same in structure although they may differ in size, as is found in reptiles.

homologous chromosomes   Chromosomes of the same pair containing the same genes but not necessarily the same alleles.

homology   A similarity due to inheritance from a common ancestor.

homoplasy   A similarity that is not homologous. Homoplasy can arise from parallelism, convergence, and chance.

homozygous   Having two like alleles of a particular gene; homozygous dominant when the allele is dominant and homozygous recessive when the allele is recessive.

homozygous dominant   Having two dominant alleles of the same gene.

homozygous recessive   Having two recessive alleles of the same gene.

hormones   Complex molecules produced by the endocrine glands that regulate many bodily functions and processes.

human factors research   See **ergonomics**

humerofemoral index   Index that gives the relative

proportion of the humerus and femur (length of humerus × 100/length of femur).

hybrid The result of a cross or mating between two different kinds of parents.

hybrid inviability Form of reproductive isolation in which a mating between two species gives rise to a hybrid that is fertile but which nevertheless does not leave any offspring.

hybrid sterility Form of reproductive isolation in which a hybrid of two species is sterile.

hydraulic behavior The transport and dispersal of bones in water.

hypercalcemia High levels of calcium in blood caused by excessive amounts of vitamin D; sluggish nerve reflexes and calcification of soft tissues.

hyperplasia Growth by virtue of increase in the total number of cells resulting from mitosis.

hypertrophy Growth by virtue of increase in the size of cells.

hyperventilation Increased breathing rate producing a high level of oxygen in the lungs.

hypothermia Lowered body temperature induced by cold stress.

hypothesis An educated guess about the relationship of one variable to another.

imitative magic A type of magic based upon the belief that one can affect an actual entity such as a person or animal by manipulating the image of that entity.

immunological comparison Method of molecular biology that compares molecules by use of antigen-antibody reactions.

immunological distance (ID) A measure of the strength of an antigen-antibody reaction which is indicative of the evolutionary distance separating the populations being studied.

immutable Unchanging.

inclusive fitness An individual's own fitness plus his or her effect on the fitness of any relative.

incomplete penetrance The situation in which an allele that is expected to be expressed is not always expressed.

independent assortment A Mendelian principle stating that differing traits are inherited independently of each other. It applies only to genes on different chromosomes.

index fossil A paleospecies that had a very wide geographical distribution but existed for a relatively short period of time, either becoming extinct or evolving into something else.

induced mutation Mutation caused by human-made conditions.

Industrial Age A cultural stage characterized by the first use of complex machinery, factories, urbanization, and other economic and general social changes from a strictly agricultural society.

industrial melanism Phenotypic change toward darker coloration in industrial areas.

industrial society A society consisting of largely urban populations that engage in manufacturing, commerce, and services.

industry All artifacts in a site made from the same material, such as bone industry.

infantile That period in an individual's life cycle from birth to the eruption of the first permanent teeth.

insectivore An animal that eats primarily insects; also a member of the mammalian order Insectivora.

interglacial Period of warming between two glacials.

intermediate expression The situation whereby a heterozygous genotype is associated with a phenotype that is more-or-less intermediate between the phenotypes controlled by the two homozygous genotypes.

intermembral index The length of the humerus and radius relative to the length of the femur and tibia.

intron DNA sequence in a eukaryotic gene that is not translated into a protein.

inversion Form of chromosome aberration in which parts of a chromosome break and reunite in reversed order. No genetic material is lost or gained, but the positions of the involved alleles are altered.

Iron Age A cultural stage characterized by the use of iron as the main metal.

ischial callosities A thickening of the skin overlying a posterior section of the pelvis (ischial tuberosity), found in Old World monkeys and some apes.

isotopes Atoms of the same element but of different atomic weight.

juvenile That period in an individual's life cycle lasting from the eruption of the first to the eruption of the last permanent teeth.

karyotype The standardized classification and arrangement of photographed chromosomes.

kin selection A process whereby an individual's genes are selected for by virtue of that individual's increasing the chances that his or her kin's genes will be propagated into the next generation.

kingdom A major division of living organisms. All organisms are placed in one of five kingdoms: Monera, Protista, Fungi, Planti, and Animalia.

Klinefelter's syndrome A sex chromosome count of XXY; phenotypically male, tall stature, sterile.

knuckle walking Semierect quadrupedalism, found in chimpanzees and gorillas, with upper parts of the body supported by knuckles as opposed to palms.

kwashiorkor   A form of protein-caloric malnutrition brought about by a protein-deficient diet containing a reasonable supply of low-quality carbohydrates.

lactation   Act of female mammal producing milk.

lesser apes   The gibbons and siamang of Asia.

lethals   Defects that cause premature death.

leukocyte   A white blood cell; cell in blood that functions to destroy foreign substances.

lexicon   In linguistics, the total number of meaningful units (such as words and affixes) of a language.

lexigram   A symbol that represents a word.

life expectancy   How long a person can, on the average, expect to live.

life span   The theoretical genetically determined maximum age.

linguistics   The scientific study of language.

linkage   Association of genes on the same chromosome.

lipids   Class of compounds that includes fats, oils, and waxes.

lithic (stone) industry   All artifacts in a site that are made of stone.

lithosphere   The hard outer layer of the earth.

local race   Distinctive, partially isolated groups, usually remnants of once-larger units and large local races with a greater degree of gene flow occurring between them.

Lower Paleolithic   A cultural stage beginning with the manufacture of the first stone tools.

lumbar curve   A curve that forms in the lumbar region of the spine in humans.

macroevolution   Large-scale evolution; the evolution of new species and higher taxa.

macula   The central area of the retina consisting of only cones.

mammals   Members of the class Mammalia, a class of the subphylum Vertebrata, which are characterized by a constant level of activity independent of external temperature and by mammary glands, hair or fur, heterodonty, and other features.

mammary glands   Glands found in mammalian females that produce milk.

mandible   The bone of the lower jaw; contains the lower dentition.

mandibular symphysis   The area where the two halves of the mandible join together.

mandibular torus   A thickening of bone on the inside of the mandible.

manuport   An unmodified, natural rock, brought to a site by human agency, which shows no sign of alteration.

marasmus   A form of protein-caloric malnutrition caused by a diet deficient in both protein and carbohydrates.

marsupial   A member of the infraclass Metatheria of the class Mammalia; young are born at a relatively less developed stage than in placental mammals. After birth young attach to a mammary gland in the pouch or skin fold where they continue to grow and develop.

masseter   A muscle of chewing that arises on the mandible and inserts on the zygomatic arch of the skull.

maximum parsimony principle   The principle that the most accurate phylogenetic tree is one based on the fewest changes in the genetic code.

mechanical isolation   Form of reproductive isolation that occurs because of an incompatibility in the structures of the male and female sex organs.

meiosis   Form of cell division occurring in specialized tissues in the testes and ovary that leads to the production of gametes or sex cells.

melanin   Brown-black pigment found in the skin, eyes, and hair.

melanocyte   Specialized skin cell that produces the pigment melanin.

menarche   First menstruation.

mental foramen   A small opening in the mandible through which blood vessels and nerves pass.

Mesolithic   A cultural stage characterized by generalized hunting and gathering.

messenger RNA (mRNA)   Form of RNA that copies the DNA code in the nucleus and transports it to the ribosome.

metacentric chromosome   Chromosome in which the centromere appears roughly in the center and the two arms are roughly the same length.

microenvironment   A specific set of physical, biological, and cultural factors immediately surrounding an organism.

microevolution   Small-scale evolution; genetic changes within a population over time.

microhabitat   A very specific habitat in which a population is found.

microrace   Arbitrary division of large local races.

midbrain   The middle of the three swellings in the hollow nerve cord of the primitive vertebrate brain formed by a thickening of the wall of the nerve cord.

Middle Paleolithic   Referring to the stone tools of the Neandertals and their contemporaries.

mitochondria   Bodies found in the cytoplasm that convert the energy in the chemical bonds of organic molecules into ATP.

mitochondrial DNA (mtDNA)   A double-stranded

loop of DNA found within the mitochondria; there can be as few as 1 or as many as 100 mitochondria per cell, and each mitochondrion possesses between four and ten mtDNA loops.

mitosis Form of cell division in which one-celled organisms divide and body cells divide in growth and replacement.

model A representation of a phenomenon on which tests can be conducted and from which predictions can be made.

modifying gene A gene that alters the expression of another gene.

mold A cavity left in firm sediments by the decayed body of an organism.

molecular biology The comparative study of molecules.

molecule Two or more atoms linked by a chemical bond.

monkey Any member of the superfamily Ceboidea (New World monkeys) or Cercopithecoidea (Old World monkeys).

monocausal explanation Attributing more than one cause to the explanation of a phenomenon.

monogamous family A social group, found among lesser apes and other primates, consisting of a single mated pair and their young offspring.

monotreme A member of the subclass Prototheria of the class Mammalia; an egg-laying mammal.

monozygotic twins Identical twins; derived from a single zygote.

morphology The study of structure.

mounting A behavioral pattern whereby one animal jumps on the posterior area of a second animal as part of the act of copulation or as part of dominance behavior.

Movius line An imaginary line running across northern India.

multicausal explanation Attributing more than one cause to the existence of a phenomenon.

multimale group A social unit consisting of many adult males and adult females.

multiple-allele series A situation in which a gene has more than two alleles.

mutation An alteration of the genetic material.

natural selection Differential fertility and mortality of genotypes within a population.

negative eugenics Method of eliminating deleterious alleles from the gene pool by encouraging persons with such alleles not to reproduce.

neocortex Gray covering on the cerebrum of some vertebrates; site of higher mental processes.

Neolithic A cultural stage marked by established farming.

New World semibrachiation Locomotor pattern involving extensive use of hands and prehensile tail to suspend and propel the body in species otherwise quadrupedal.

niche See **ecological niche.**

nocturnal Active at night.

nondisjunction An error of meiosis in which the members of a pair of chromosomes move to the same pole rather than moving to opposite poles.

norm The most frequent behavior that the members of a group show in a specific situation.

notochord A cartilaginous rod that runs along the back (dorsal) of all chordates at some point in their life cycle.

nuchal crest Flange of bone in the occipital region of the skull which serves as the attachment of the nuchal musculature of the back of the neck.

nuchal muscle The muscle in the back of the neck that functions to hold the head up. In primates with heavy facial skeletons, the large nuchal muscle attaches to a nuchal crest.

nuclear DNA (nDNA) DNA found within the nucleus of the cell.

nuclear membrane A structure that binds the nucleus within the cell.

nucleic acid The largest of the molecules found in living organisms; it is composed of chains of nucleotides.

nucleotide The basic building block of nucleic acids; a nucleotide is composed of a five-carbon sugar (either ribose or deoxyribose), a phosphate, and a base.

nucleus A structure containing the chromosome which is found in the cell.

obesity A condition where a person's weight is 20 percent greater than a sex- and age-specific weight-for-height standard.

occipital condyles Two rounded projections on either side of the foramen magnum which fit into a pair of sockets on the top of the spine, thus articulating the skull with the spine.

occipital torus A horizontal bar of bone seen above the angularity in the occipital.

Old World semibrachiation Locomotor pattern involving extensive use of hands in leaping in a basically quadrupedal animal.

olfactory Referring to the sense of smell.

omnivorous Eating both meat and vegetable food.

one-male group A social unit consisting of a single male associated with several females.

ontogeny The processes of growth and development of the individual from conception to death.

ontology The study of ontogeny.

oogenesis The production of ova.

open A characteristic of language referring to its expansionary nature, which enables people to coin new labels for new concepts and objects.

operator A site in the operon to which a repressor can bind, shutting off transcription of structural genes in the operon.

operon A group of genes all controlled by the same regulatory gene.

opposable thumb Anatomical arrangement in which the fleshy tip of the thumb can touch the fleshy tip of all the other fingers.

order Major division of a class, consisting of closely related families.

orthognathous Describes a face that is relatively vertical as opposed to being prognathous.

orthograde Vertical in posture.

ossification Process of bone formation.

osteodontokeratic culture An archaeological culture based upon tools made of bone, teeth, and horn.

osteology The study of bones.

outgroup Species used in a cladistic analysis that are closely related to the species being studied and are used to differentiate between shared derived and ancestral derived features.

ovulation The point during the femal reproductive cycle, usually the midpoint, when the mature ovum breaks through the wall of the ovary.

ovum A female gamete or sex cell.

ozone A molecule composed of three oxygen atoms (O_3). Atmospheric ozone shields organisms from excessive ultraviolet radiation.

paleoanthropology Scientific study of fossils and artifacts and the context in which they are found.

paleoecology The study of the relationship of extinct organisms or groups of organisms to their environments.

Paleolithic A type of culture called the Old Stone Age.

paleontology The study of fossils.

paleopathology The study of injuries and disease in prehistoric populations.

paleospecies A group of similar fossils whose range of morphological variation does not exceed the range of variation of a closely related living species.

palynology The study of fossil pollen.

pangenesis An early, inaccurate idea that the acquired characteristics of parents are transmitted to their offspring.

parallelism Homoplastic similarities found in related species that did not exist in the common ancestor; however, the common ancestor provided initial commonalities that gave direction to the evolution of the similarities.

partial pressure The pressure exerted by a particular gas in the atmosphere.

pedigree A reconstruction of past matings in a family expressed as a diagram.

penetrance The degree to which an allele is expressed in the phenotype.

pentadactylism Possessing five digits on the hand and/or foot.

peptide bone A link between amino acids in a protein.

pericentric inversion A type of inversion in which two breaks occur in a chromosome, one on either side of the centromere, and the centerpiece is turned around and rejoined with the two outside pieces.

period A unit of geological time; a division of an era.

peripheralization Process whereby an adolescent animal encounters aggressive behavior from adults and gradually moves away from the group over time.

permanent estrus display Fixed anatomical features of the adult human female, such as large buttocks, that mimic the cyclic anatomical features of estrus monkeys and apes, such as a swollen sexual skin.

permanent teeth The second set of teeth that erupts in mammals; humans have thirty-two permanent teeth.

phenotype The observable and measurable characteristics of an organism.

phenylketonuria (PKU) A genetic disease, inherited as a recessive, brought about by the absence of the enzyme responsible for conversion of the amino acid phenylalanine to tyrosine; phenylalanine accumulates in the blood and then breaks down into by-products that cause severe mental retardation in addition to other symptoms.

phenylthiocarbamide (PTC) An artificially created substance whose main use is in tests detecting the ability to taste it; ability to taste PTC is inherited as a dominant.

phosphate unit A unit of the nucleic acid molecule consisting of a phosphate and four oxygen atoms.

phyletic gradualism model The idea that evolution is a slow process with gradual transformation of one population into another.

phylogenetic tree A graphic representation of evolutionary relationships among species.

phylogeny The evolutionary history of a population or taxon.

phylum Major division of a kingdom, consisting of closely related classes; represents a basic body plan.

physical anthropology A branch of anthropology concerned with human biology and evolution.

physical environment The inanimate elements surrounding an organism.

phytoliths   Microscopic pieces of silica that form within plants; the distinctive shapes of phytoliths found in different plants permit their identification when observed embedded in fossil teeth.

placenta   An organ that develops from fetal membranes and functions to pass oxygen, nutrients, and other substances to and waste material from the fetus.

placental mammal   A member of the infraclass Eutheria of the class Mammalia; mammals that form a placenta.

plasma   Liquid portion of the blood containing salts, sugars, fats, amino acids, hormones, plasma proteins, and so on.

plasma membrane   A structure that binds the cell but allows for the entry and exit of certain substances.

plate tectonics   The theory that the surface of the earth is divided into a number of plates that move in relationship to each other. Some of these plates carry the continents.

platelets   Cell fragments in the blood that function in blood clotting.

platycephlalic   Having a low, relatively flat forehead.

platyrrhine nose   Nose in which nostrils open sideways and are usually separated by a broad nasal septum; characteristic of the New World monkeys.

play   Energetic and repetitive activity engaged in primarily by infants and juveniles.

play group   A group of juveniles within a larger social unit that engage in play behavior.

pleiotropy   Situation in which a single allele may affect an entire series of traits.

pliomorphs   Group of small Miocene hominoids from the Middle Miocene of Europe and China, including the genera *Pliopithecus* in Europe and *Laccopithecus* in Asia.

pneumatized   The presence of air spaces within some bones of the skull.

point mutation   An error at a particular point on the DNA molecule.

polar body   A cell that develops in oogenesis; it contains little cytoplasm and does not develop into a mature ovum.

polygenic   The result of the interaction of several genes.

polymorphism   The presence of several distinct forms of a gene or phenotypic trait within a population with a frequency greater than 1 percent.

polypeptide   Chain of amino acids.

polyphyodonty   The continuous replacement of teeth such as is found in reptiles.

population bottlenecking   A form of genetic drift in which a population has been significantly re-duced in size for some reason such as a natural disaster. The reduction in size is accompanied by a reduction in variability in successive populations.

populationist   The viewpoint that only individuals have reality and that the type is illusory; since no two individuals are exactly alike, variation underlies all existence.

positive eugenics   Method of increasing the frequency of desirable traits by encouraging reproduction by individuals with these traits.

postmating mechanism   Any form of reproductive isolation that occurs after mating.

postorbital bar   A feature of the skull formed by an upward extension of the zygomatic arch and a downward extension of the frontal bone that supports the eye.

postorbital constriction   As seen from top view, a marked constriction in the skull immediately behind the orbits and brow ridge.

postorbital septum   A bony partition behind the eye which isolates the eye from the muscles of the jaw and forms a bony eye socket or orbit in which the eye lies.

potassium-argon dating   Chronometric dating technique based on the rate of decay of potassium 40 to argon 40.

power grip   A grip in which an object is held between the fingers and the palm with the thumb reinforcing the fingers.

preadaptation   The situation in which a new structure or behavior that evolved in one niche is by chance also suited, in some cases better suited, to a new niche.

precision grip   A grip in which an object is held between one or more fingers with the thumb fully opposed to the fingertips.

prehensile tail   A tail found in some New World monkeys that has the ability to grasp.

premating mechanism   A form of reproductive isolation that prevents mating from occurring.

prenatal   That period of an indvidual's life cycle from conception to birth.

presenting   A behavior involving a subordinate primate showing his or her anal region to a dominant animal.

preservation potential   The probability of a bone's being preserved after death.

primary center of ossification   Area of first appearance of bone within the cartilage model of a long bone.

primatology   The study of primates.

prognathism   A jutting forward of the facial skeleton and jaws.

prokaryote A cell, more primitive than a eukaryote, having no nucleus. Prokaryotes include bacteria and blue-green algae.

pronograde Posture in which the body is held parallel to the ground.

prosimians Members of the suborder Prosimii; includes the living Madagascar lemuriformes and the lorises, potto, angwantibo, and galagos.

protein Long chains of amino acids joined together by peptide bonds (a polypeptide chain).

protein-caloric malnutrition A class of malnutrition that includes kwashiorkor and marasmus.

protoculture The simplest or beginning aspects of culture as seen in some nonhuman primates.

prototherian mammal A mammal belonging to the subclass Prototheria; a monotreme or egg-laying mammal.

provisionized colony Groups of free-ranging primates that have become accustomed to humans because of the establishment of feeding stations.

puberty An event in the life cycle that includes rapid increase in stature, development of sex organs, and the development of secondary sexual characteristics.

pubic symphysis The area of the pelvis at which the two innominates join.

punctuated equilibrium A model of evolution characterized by an uneven tempo of change.

purine Base found in nucleic acids which consists of two connected rings of carbon and nitrogen; in DNA and RNA, adenine and guanine.

pyrimidine Base found in nucleic acids which consists of a single ring of carbon and nitrogen; in DNA, thymine and cytosine; in RNA, uracil and cytosine.

quadrumanous Locomotor pattern found among orangutans which often suspend themselves under branches and move slowly using both forelimbs and hindlimbs.

quadrupedalism Locomotion using four limbs.

race A division of a species; a subspecies.

radiation Electromagnetic energy given off by an object.

radioactivity The phenomenon whereby an unstable atom radioactively decays into another type of atom and in the process emits energy and/or particles.

radiocarbon dating A method of chronometric dating based on the decay of carbon 14.

radiometric dating techniques Chronometric dating methods based upon the decay of radioactive materials; examples are radiocarbon and potassium-argon dating.

ramamorphs Group of Miocene hominoids from the Middle Miocene of east Africa and Eurasia, including members of the genera *Sivapithecus* and *Gigantopithecus.*

range See **home range.**

recessive An allele expressed only in the homozygous recessive condition.

recombinant DNA A technique for transferring genetic material from one organism to another.

recombination A mechanism of meiosis responsible for each gamete's uniqueness. As the chromosomes line up in metaphase, they can combine into several configurations.

red blood cell See **erythrocyte.**

regional continuity model The hypothesis stating that modern *H. sapiens* had multiple origins from existing local populations; each local population of archaic humans gave rise to a population of modern *H. sapiens.*

regulatory gene A segment of DNA that functions to initiate or block the function of another gene.

relative fitness (RF) The fitness of a genotype compared to the fitness of another genotype in the same gene system. Relative fitness is measured on a scale of 0 to 1.

reliable Predictable.

replacement model The hypothesis stating that modern *H. sapiens* evolved in Africa and radiated out of this area, replacing archaic hominid populations.

repressor protein The product of a regulator gene that blocks the function of another gene.

reproductive isolating mechanism A mechanism that prevents reproduction from occurring between two populations.

reproductive population A group of organisms capable of successful reproduction.

reproductive risk A measure expressed in terms of the number of zygotes needed from a mating pair to produce two offspring that will in turn reproduce.

reptiles Members of the class Reptilia; terrestrial vertebrates that include the lizards, snakes, and turtles.

residual volume The amount of air still remaining in the lungs after the most forceful expiration.

restriction enzyme Enzyme used to "cut" the DNA molecule at specific sites; used in recombinant DNA technology.

retina The layer of cells in the back of the eye that contains the rods and cones, which are sensitive to light.

retinoblastoma A cancer of the retina of the eye in children, inherited as a dominant.

retouch Further refinement in the manufacture of stone tools by the removal of additional small flakes.

Rh blood-type system A blood-type system consisting of two major alleles. A mating between an Rh⁻ mother and an Rh⁺ father may produce the hemolytic disease erythroblastosis fetalis in the infant.

rhinarium The moist, naked area surrounding the nostrils in most mammals; absent in most primates.

ribonucleic acid (RNA) A type of nucleic acid based upon the sugar ribose; exists in cells as messenger RNA and transfer RNA.

ribose A five-carbon sugar found in RNA.

ribosome Small, spherical body within the cytoplasm of the cell in which protein synthesis takes place.

rods Cells of the retina of the eye that are sensitive to the presence or absence of light; function in black-and-white vision.

sagittal crest Ridge of bone along the midline of the top of the skull which serves for the attachment of the temporalis muscle.

sagittal keel A bony ridge formed by a thickening of bone along the top of the skull; characteristic of *H. erectus*.

sampling error In population genetics, the transmission of a nonrepresentative sample of the gene pool over space or time as a result of chance.

Scala naturae A rank-order sequence of contemporary animals that falsely suggests an evolutionary sequence.

scent marking Marking territory by urinating or defecating or by rubbing scent glands against trees or other objects.

science A way of learning about the world by applying the principles of scientific thinking, which includes making empirical observations, proposing hypotheses to explain these observations, and testing these hypotheses in valid and reliable ways; also refers to the organized body of knowledge that results from scientific study.

scraper A tool manufactured from a flake that has a scraping edge on the end or side.

seasonal isolation Form of reproductive isolation in which the breeding seasons of two closely related populations do not exactly correspond.

secondary center of ossification Area of ossification, usually near the end of a long bone.

secondary sexual characteristic Physical feature other than the genitalia that distinguishes males from females after puberty.

sectorial premolar Unicuspid first lower premolar with a shearing edge.

secular trend The tendency over the last hundred or so years for each succeeding generation to mature earlier and become, on the average, larger.

sediment Material that is suspended in water; in still water it settles at the bottom.

sedimentary beds Beds or layers of sediments called strata.

sedimentation The accumulation of geological or organic material deposited by air, water, or ice.

segregation In the formation of sex cells, the process in which paired hereditary factors separate, forming sex cells that contain either one or the other factor.

selective agent Any factor that brings about differences in fertility and mortality.

selective coefficient A numerical expression of the strength of a selective force operating on a specific genotype.

selective pressure Pressure placed by a selective agent upon certain individuals within the population that results in the change of allele frequencies in the next generation.

serum Plasma after the clotting material has settled out.

sex chromosomes The X and Y chromosomes. Males usually have one X and one Y chromosome; females usually have two X chromosomes.

sex-controlled trait Trait that is expressed differently in males and females.

sex-limited trait Trait that is expressed in only one of the sexes.

sexual dimorphism Differences in structure between males and females of the same species.

sexual division of labor Situation in which males and females in a society perform different tasks. In hunting and gathering societies males usually hunt while females usually gather wild vegetable food.

sexual isolation Form of reproductive isolation in which one or both sexes of a species initiate mating behavior that does not act as a stimulus to the opposite sex of a closely related species.

sexual skin Found in the female of some primate species; skin in anal region that turns bright pink or red and may swell when the animal is in estrus.

shared ancestral (symplesiomorphic) features Compared with shared derived features, a homology that did not appear as recently and is therefore shared by a larger group of species.

shared derived (synapomorphic) features A recently appearing homology shared by a relatively small group of closely related taxa.

sharing cluster Among chimpanzees, a temporary group that forms after hunting to eat the meat.

shell midden A large mound composed of shells, which provides evidence of the emphasis on shellfish as a food resource.

shovel-shaped inciors Incisors with a scooped-out shape on the tongue side of the tooth.

sickle-cell anemia Disorder in individuals homozygous for hemoglobin S in which red blood cells develop a sickle shape, clogging capillaries and resulting in anemia, heart failure, and so on.

sickle-cell trait The condition of being heterozygous for hemoglobin A and S although the individual usually shows no abnormal symptoms.

sign A nonarbitrary indicator of something else, as footprints are a sign that someone was present and smoke is a sign of fire.

simian shelf A bony buttress on the inner surface of the foremost part of the ape mandible, functioning to reinforce the mandible.

single-crystal fusion A form of potassium-argon dating that uses a laser to melt individual crystals to release the argon.

site A location where artifacts are found.

social Darwinism The application of the principles of biological evolutionary theory to an analysis of social phenomena.

social intelligence The knowledge and images originating in an individual's brain that are transferred by speech (and in the last 5000 years, writing) to the brains of others.

society A group of interacting people who share a geographical region, a sense of common identity, and a common culture.

sociobiology The study of the biological control of social behavior.

sociocultural anthropology A branch of anthropology dealing with variations in patterns of social interaction and differences in cultural behavior.

sonogram The image produced by ultrasound equipment.

specialized species A species closely fitted to a specific niche and able to tolerate little change in that niche.

specialized trait Structure used primarily for one function.

speciation An evolutionary process said to occur when two previous subspecies (of the same species) are no longer capable of successful interbreeding; they then become two different species.

species The largest natural population whose members are able to reproduce successfully among themselves but not with members of other species.

sperm Male gamete or sex cell.

spermatogenesis Sperm production.

spontaneous generation An old and incorrect idea that complex life forms could be spontaneously created from nonliving material.

spontaneous mutation Mutations that occur spontaneously, that is, in response to the usual conditions within the body or environment.

standard deviation A statistical measurement of the amount of variation in a series of determinations; the probability of the real number falling within plus or minus one standard deviation is 67 percent.

stereoscopic vision Visual perception of depth due to overlapping visual fields and various neurological features.

strata Layers of sedimentary rocks.

stratigraphy The investigation of the composition of the layers of the earth used in relative dating; based on the principle of superposition.

stratosphere That part of the atmosphere 20 to 50 kilometers (12 to 31 miles) above the earth's surface where ozone forms.

structural gene A segment of DNA that codes for a polypeptide other than a regulator.

subchron A small subdivision within a chron.

subcutaneous fat The fat deposited under the skin.

subera A division of an era. The Cenozoic is divided into two suberas, the Tertiary and the Quaternary.

submetacentric chromosome Chromosome in which the centromere lies to one side of the center, producing arms of unequal length.

subspecies Interfertile groups within a species that display significant differentiation among themselves.

superposition Principle that under stable conditions strata on the bottom of a deposit were laid down first and hence are older than the layers on top.

suspensory behavior Form of locomotion and posture whereby animals suspend themselves underneath a branch.

sweating The production of a fluid, sweat, by the sweat glands of the skin; the evaporation of sweat from the skin leads to cooling of the body.

symbol Something that can represent something distant from it in time and space.

sympatric species Different species living in the same area but prevented from successfully reproducing by a reproductive isolating mechanism.

symphyseal face The surface of the pubis where one pubis joins the other at the pubic symphysis.

symplesiomorphic feature See **shared ancestral feature.**

synapomorphic feature See **shared derived feature.**

syndrome A complex of symptoms related to a single cause.

synthetic theory of evolution   The theory of evolution that fuses Darwin's concept of natural selection with information from the fields of genetics, mathematics, embryology, paleontology, animal behavior, and other disciplines.

tactile pads   The tips of the fingers and toes of primates; areas richly endowed by tactile nerve endings sensitive to touch.

taphonomy   The study of the processes of burial and fossilization.

taxon   A group of organisms at any level of the taxonomic hierarchy. The major taxa are the species and genus and the higher taxa, family, order, class, phylum, and kingdom.

taxonomy   The theory of classification.

Tay-Sachs disease   Deficiency in an enzyme of lipid metabolism inherited as a recessive; causes death in early childhood.

tectonic plate   A segment of the lithosphere.

telocentric chromosome   Chromosome in which the centromere is located at the very end of the chromosome.

temporalis   A muscle of chewing which arises on the jaw and inserts on the side of the skull.

temporomandibular joint   The joint formed at the point of articulation of the mandible and the base of the skull.

temporonuchal crest   A crest on the back of the skull, forming on the occipital and temporal bones.

termite stick   Tool made and used by chimpanzees to collect termites for food.

terrestrial quadrupedalism   A form of quadrupedalism in which the animal walks on the ground using the hands and feet; the palms of the hand are flat on the ground.

territory   The area a group defends against other members of its own species.

testosterone   A male sex hormone.

thalassemia   Absence or reduction of alpha- or beta-chain synthesis in hemoglobin; in the homozygous condition (thalassemia major) a high frequency of hemoglobin F and fatal anemia occurs; in the heterozygous condition (thalassemia minor) it is highly variable but usually has mild symptoms.

theory   A step in the scientific method in which a statement is generated on the basis of highly confirmed hypotheses and used to generalize about conditions not yet tested.

theory of acquired characteristics   Concept, popularized by Lamarck, that traits gained during a lifetime can then be passed on to the next generation by genetic means; considered invalid today.

therian mammal   A mammal belonging to the subclass Theria; the live-bearing mammals, including the marsupials and placental mammals.

thermoluminescence dating   A chronometric dating method based on the observation that when some materials are heated, they give off a flash of light. The intensity of the light is proportional to the amount of radiation the sample has been exposed to and the length of time since the sample was heated.

threat gesture   A physical activity that serves to threaten another animal. Some threat gestures are staring, shaking a branch, and lunging toward another animal.

thymine   One of the bases found in RNA.

toilet claw   A claw found on the second toe of prosimians that functions in grooming.

tool   An object that appears to have been used for a specific purpose.

trait   One aspect of the phenotype.

transfer RNA (tRNA)   Within the ribosome, a form of RNA that transports amino acids into the positions coded in the mRNA.

translocation   Form of chromosomal mutation in which segments of chromosomes become detached and reunite with other nonhomologous chromosomes.

tree-ring dating   Chronometric dating method that determines the age of a wood sample by counting the number of annual growth rings.

troop   A multimale group found among baboons and other primates.

true brachiation   Hand-over-hand locomotion along a branch with the body suspended underneath the branch by the arms.

true-breeding   Showing the same traits without exception over many generations.

tuff   Geological formation composed of compressed volcanic ash.

tundra   A type of landscape where the ground is frozen solid throughout most of the year but thaws slightly during the summer.

Turner's syndrome   Genetic disease characterized by forty-five chromosomes with a sex chromosome count of X−; phenotypically female, but sterile.

twin studies   Comparisons of monozygotic twins to dizygotic twins for the purpose of estimating the degree of environmental versus genetic influence operating on a specific trait.

tympanic membrane   The eardrum.

typological   The viewpoint that basic variation of a type is illusory and that only fixed ideal types are real; two fossils that differ from each other in certain respects represent two types and, hence, are two different species.

ultrasound   A method of taking a picture of the fetus using sound waves.

unconformity   The surface of a stratum that represents a break in the stratigraphic sequence.

uniformitarianism   Principle stating that physical forces working today to alter the earth were also in force and working in the same way in former times.

Upper Paleolithic   Referring to the stone tools of anatomically modern peoples.

uracil   One of the bases found in RNA.

urbanization   The proportionate rise in the number of people living in cities in comparison to those living in rural areas.

urbanized society   A society in which a majority of people live in cities.

utilized material   Pieces of stone that have been used without modification.

variable   Any property that may be displayed in different values.

vasoconstriction   Constriction of the capillaries in the skin in response to cold temperatures, which prevents much of the warm blood from reaching the surface of the body where heat could be lost.

vasodilation   Opening up of the capillaries of the skin in response to warm temperatures, increasing the flow of blood to the surface of the body and thereby increasing the loss of body heat.

velocity curve   A curve illustrating the velocity or rate of growth over time by plotting the degree of growth per unit of time.

ventral   The front or bottom side of an animal.

Venus figurines   Small Upper Paleolithic statues chracterized by exaggerated breasts and buttocks and very stylized heads, hands, and feet.

vertebrate   A member of the subphylum Vertebrate; possesses a bony spine or vertebral column.

vertical clinging and leaping   A method of locomotion in which the animal clings vertically to a branch and moves between branches by leaping vertically from one to another. The animal moves on the ground by hopping or moves bipedally.

white blood cell   See **leukocyte.**

X chromosome   The larger of the two sex chromosomes. Females usually possess two X chromosomes; males usually possess one X and one Y chromosome.

X-linked   Refers to genes on the X chromosome.

Y chromosome   The smaller of the two sex chromosomes. Females usually possess no Y chromosome; males usually possess one X and one Y chromosome.

Y-5 pattern   Pattern found on molars with five cusps separated by grooves, reminiscent of the letter Y.

Y-linked   Refers to genes on the Y chromosome.

yolk sac   A sac containing yolk which is formed from embryonic tissue in the amniote egg.

zygomatic arch   The "cheekbone"; an arch of bone on the side of the skull.

zygote   A fertilized ovum.

zygotic mortality   Form of reproductive isolation in which fertilization occurs but development stops soon after.

GLOSSARY OF PRIMATE HIGHER TAXA

Extinct taxa are indicated by †.

Adapidae† Family of Eocene prosimians found in North America, Asia, Europe, and possibly Africa; may be related to lemurs and lorises.

Adapinae† Subfamily of the Adapidae found in Europe and Asia.

Alouattinae Subfamily of the Cebidae; includes the howler monkeys.

Anthropoidea Suborder of the order Primates; includes the New World monkeys, Old World monkeys, apes, and humans.

Aotinae Subfamily of the Cebidae; includes the owl monkeys.

Callitrichidae A family of New World monkeys consisting of the marmosets and tamarins.

Catarrhini Infraorder of the order Primates that includes the superorders Cercopithecoidea and Hominoidea.

Cebidae A family of New World monkeys that includes the squirrel, spider, howler, and capuchin monkeys, among others.

Cebinae Subfamily of the Cebidae; includes the capuchin and squirrel monkeys.

Ceboidea A superfamily of the suborder Anthropoidea; includes all the New World monkeys, consisting of the families Callitrichidae and Cebidae.

Cercopithecidae Family of the superfamily Cercopithecoidea; includes the Old World monkeys.

Cercopithecinae Subfamily of the family Cercopithecidae; includes Old World monkeys that are omnivorous and possess cheek pouches, such as the macaques, baboons, guenons, and mangabeys.

Cercopithecoidea Superfamily of the suborder Anthropoidea; consists of the Old World monkeys.

Colobinae A subfamily of family Cercopithecidae; Old World monkeys that are specialized leaf eaters, possessing a complex stomach and lacking cheek pouches, such as the langurs and colobus monkeys.

Daubentoniidae Family of Madagascar prosimians consisting of the aye-aye.

Hominidae Family of the superfamily Hominoidea; includes humans.

Hominoidea Superfamily of the suborder Anthropoidea; includes the apes and humans.

Hylobatidae Family of the superfamily Hominoidea; the lesser apes consisting of the gibbons and siamang.

Indriidae Family of Madagascar prosimians which includes the indri, sifaka, and avahi.

Lemuridae A Madagascar prosimian family that includes the lemurs.

Lorisidae Prosimian family that includes the loris, potto, angwantibo, and galago.

Notharctinae† Subfamily of the Adapidae, found primarily in North America.

Omomyidae† Family of Eocene and Oligocene primates, showing some resemblance to the tarsiers, found in North America, Europe, Asia, and Africa.

Oreopithecidae† A specialized hominoid from the Late Miocene of Europe.

Parapithecidae† Family of several Late Eocene and Early Oligocene antrhopoid genera from the Fayum; includes *Apidium*.

Panidae Family within the superfamily Hominoidea that consists of the chimpanzee, bonobo, and gorilla.

Parapithecoidea† Suborder of the order Primates that contains the family Parapithecidae.

Pithecinae Subfamily of the Cebidae; includes the titis, sakis, and uakaris.

Platyrrhini Infraorder of the order Primates that includes the New World monkeys and various new world fossil taxa.

Plesiopithecidae† Family within the superfamily Plesiopithecoidea; contains the genus *Plesiopithecus*, from the Oligocene of the Fayum, Egypt.

Plesiopithecoidea† Superfamily within the suborder Prosimii; contains the genus *Plesiopithecus*, from the Oligocene of the Fayum, Egypt.

Pongidae Family within the superfamily Hominoidea that consists of the orangutan.

Primates Order of the class Mammalia that includes the living prosimians, tarsiers, New World monkeys, Old World monkeys, lesser apes, great apes, and humans.

Proconsulidae† Miocene hominoids from Africa.

Propliopithecidae† Family of the infraorder Catarrhini from the Middle Oligocene to Late Miocene of Africa and Europe; they may have given rise to the Old World monkeys and the hominoids.

Prosimii Suborder of the order Primates that includes the living Madagascar lemuriforms and the lorises, potto, angwantibo, and galagos.

Tarsiidae Family of the suborder Tarsioidea that consists of the tarsiers.

Tarsioidea Suborder of the primates consisting of the tarsiers.

Victoriapithecidae† Family of Early and Middle Miocene Old World monkeys from north and east Africa.

PHOTO CREDITS

Chapter 1 Opening   S. Salgado/Magnum.
Figure 1–1, 1–4   Peter Menzel.
Figure 1–2   Jan Collsioo/Gamma Liaison.
Figure 1–3   International Development Research Center, Gary Toomey.
Figure 1–5   Peter Weit/Sygma.
Figure 1–6   Copyright © 1994 Tim D. White/Brill Atlanta.
Figure 1–10   Patrick Durand/Sygma.

Chapter 2 Opening   Neg. #326814, Department of Library Services, American Museum of Natural History.
Figure 2–2, 2–5   National Portrait Gallery, London.
Figure 2–3   Ansel Adams/Magnum.
Figure 2–4   Photograph by Dodie Stoneburner.
Figure 2–7   Brown Brothers.
Figure 2–8   Culver Pictures.

Chapter 3 Opening   Field Museum of Natural History.
Figure 3–4   Irven DeVore/Anthro-Photo.
Figure 3–9   Dr. Jon Synder/Phototake.

Chapter 4 Opening   Photo Researchers.
Figure 4–1   Courtesy of SmithKline Beecham Clinical Labs, Van Nuys, California.
Figure 4–4   (a) Courtesy of SmithKline Beecham Clinical Labs, Van Nuys, California. (b) Courtesy of The National Foundation, March of Dimes.
Figure 4–11   (b) Russell & Son, Queen Victoria and her family, 1894. Gernsheim Collection, Harry Ransom Humanities Research Center, The University of Texas at Austin.

Figure 4–18   Courtesy of Patricia Farnsworth, Ph.D., UMD-NJ Medical School.
Figure 4–19   Photograph by Philip L. Stein.

Chapter 4 Color Insert:
Figure 4–A   Ray Simmons/Photo Researchers.
Figure 4–B   Michael Abbey/Photo Researchers.
Figure 4–C   Omikron/Science Source/Photo Researchers.
Figure 4–D   Dan McCoy/Rainbow.

Chapter 5 Opening   Mark Chester/Photo Researchers.

Chapter 6 Opening   (a) Andrew Rakoczy/Photo Researchers. (b) Carl Frank/Photo Researchers.
Figure 6–3   From the experiments of Dr. H. B. D. Kettlewell, University of Oxford. Used with permission of Dr. H. B. D. Kettlewell.

Chapter 7 Opening   (Top) Everett Collection; (center) Archive Photos; (bottom) Steve Granitz/Retna.
Figure 7–8   Courtesy of J. M. Tanner, Institute of Child Health, University of London.
Figure 7–9   Courtesy of Larry S. Luke, School of Dentistry, University of California, Los Angeles.
Figure 7–18   (a) Steve Mains/Stock Boston; (b) Sygma.

Chapter 8 Opening   Jean-Claude Lejeune/Stock Boston.
Figure 8–1   Photograph by Philip L. Stein.
Figure 8–2   (a) Neg. #231604/R. MacMillan, Department of Library Services, American Museum of Natural History. (b) Mark M. Lawrence/Stock Market.

Figure 8–6 *(a)* Anthropological Archives, Smithsonian Institution Photo 3084; *(b)* Gaye Hilsenrath/Picture Cube.

Figure 8–7 *(a)* Culver Pictures; *(b)* The Bettmann Archive/Bettmann Newsphotos; *(c)* Culver Pictures.

Chapter 8 Color Insert
Figure 8–A Irven DeVore/Anthro-Photo.
Figure 8–B Tronick/Anthro-Photo.
Figure 8–C Victor Englebert/Photo Researchers.
Figure 8-D George Holton/Photo Researchers.
Figure 8–E Anthro-Photo.
Figure 8–F Mike Yamashita/Woodfin Camp & Associates.
Figure 8-G Halpern/Anthro-Photo.
Figure 8–H George Holton/Photo Researchers.
Figure 8–I Michael McCoy/Photo Researchers.
Figure 8–J Jack Fields/Photo Researchers.
Figure 8–K Paolo Koch/Photo Researchers.
Figure 8–L Farell Grehan/Photo Researchers.
Figure 8–M Daniel Zirinoky/Photo Researchers.
Figure 8–N Rapho Division/Photo Researchers.
Figure 8–O Emil Muench, ASPA/Photo Researchers.

Chapter 9 Opening Culver Pictures.
Figure 9–1 Culver Pictures.
Figure 9–12 Zoological Society of San Diego.
Figure 9–13 Ron Garrison, Zoological Society of San Diego.

Chapter 10 Opening A. W. Ambler, National Audubon Society/Photo Researchers.
Figure 10–4 Photograph by Dodie Stoneburner.
Figure 10–9, 10–10 Courtesy of Prof. Bernhard Meier, Ruhr-Universität Bochum.
Figure 10–11, 10–13, 10–20, 10–22, 10–28. Ron Garrison/Zoological Society of San Diego.
Figure 10–12, 10–15, 10–16, 10–17, 10–18, 10–21, 10–26, 10–29, 10–30, Box 10–1, Box 10–3 Zoological Society of San Diego.
Figure 10–19 R. Van Nostrand/Zoological Society of San Diego.
Figure 10–23 Photograph by John M. Bishop.
Figure 10–24 Eric & David Hosking/Photo Researchers.
Figure 10–27 F. D. Schmidt/Zoological Society of San Diego.
Box 10–2 AP/Wide World Photos.

Chapter 10 Color Insert:
Figure 10–A, 10–B Courtesy of Prof. Bernhard Meier, Ruhr-Universität Bochum.
Figure 10–C Norman Myers/Bruce Coleman.

Figure 10–D, 10–F, 10–G, 10–H Ron Garrison/Zoological Society of San Diego.
Figure 10–E Wayne McGuire, Anthro-Photo.
Figure 10–I F. Gohier/Photo Researchers.

Chapter 11 Opening Daniel Hrdy/Anthro-Photo.
Figure 11–1, 11–3, Box 11–2 Ron Garrison/Zoological Society of San Diego.
Figure 11–2 Zig Lesczynski/Animals Animals.
Figure 11–4, 11–5 Richard Wrangham/Anthro-Photo.
Figure 11–8, Box 11–1 Irven DeVore/Anthro-Photo.
Figure 11–9 B. Smuts/Anthro-Photo.
Figure 11–10, 11–12 Copyright © National Geographic Society.
Figure 11–11 Tom McHugh/Photo Researchers.
Figure 11–13 Courtesy of Geza Teleki.
Box 11–4 Courtesy of Takayoshi Kano, Primate Research Institute, Kyoto University, Japan.

Chapter 12 Opening Kal Muller, Woodfin Camp.
Figure 12–1, 12–3 Marjorie Shostak/Anthro-Photo.
Figure 12–2 James Malcolm/Anthro-Photo.
Figure 12–4 Irven DeVore/Anthro-Photo.
Figure 12–5 Mel Konner/Anthro-Photo.
Figure 12–6 From D. L. Chaney and R. M. Seyfarth, *How Monkeys See the World.* Copyright © 1990 by The University of Chicago Press. Used with permission of The University of Chicago Press.
Figure 12–7 Photo courtesy of R. A. and B. T. Gardner.
Figure 12–8 Courtesy of Roger S. Fouts.
Figure 12–9 GSU/Yerkes Language Research Center.
Figure 12–10 Dr. Ronald H. Cohn/The Gorilla Foundation.
Figure 12–12, 12–13 Courtesy of Masao Kawai, Japan Monkey Centre, Kyoto University, Japan.

Chapter 12 Color Insert
Figures 12–A through 12–C Robert C. Bailey.

Chapter 13 Opening Culver Pictures.
Figure 13–1, 13–3, 13–4 Zoological Society of San Diego.
Figure 13–2 Ron Garrison/Zoological Society of San Diego.
Figure 13–12 Photographs by Robert N. Frankle and Rebecca L. Stein.
Figure 13–13, 13–19 Photographs by Dodie Stoneburner.
Figure 13–21 Courtesy of Jeffrey H. Schwartz, University of Pittsburgh.
Figure 13–28 Courtesy of J. J. Yunis.

Chapter 14 Opening James L. Amos/Photo Researchers.

Figure 14–1   Sygma.
Figure 14–2   Neg. #315485, 325097, 125158, Courtesy Department of Library Services, American Museum of Natural History.
Figure 14–4   Photograph by Rick Freed.
Figure 14–6   From John Buettner-Janusch, *Origins of Man*, 1966. Used with permission of John Wiley & Sons, Inc.
Box 14–2   E. M. Fulda/American Museum of Natural History.
Box 14–3   Breck P. Kent/Earth Scenes.

Chapter 14 Color Insert
Figures 14–A through 14–H   Institute of Human Origins.

Chapter 15 Opening   From John G. Fleagle, *Primate Adaptations and Evolution*, 1988, Academic Press.
Figure 15–4   Denver Museum of Natural History.
Figure 15–6, 15–7   Courtesy of Elwyn L. Simons and the Peabody Museum of Natural History, Yale University, New Haven, CT.
Figure 15–9   Courtesy of Russell Ciochon, University of Iowa.
Figure 15–10   Courtesy of T. Setoguchi and A. L. Rosenberger.
Figure 15–11   National Geographic Society.
Figure 15–12, 15–13   The Natural History Museum, London.
Figure 15–17   W. Sacco/Anthro-Photo.
Figure 15–19   Courtesy of and Copyright © Eric Delson.
Figure 15–20   Bobbie Brown/Anthro-Photo.

Chapter 16 Opening   David Brill/National Geographic Society.
Figure 16–1   Copyright © 1994 Time D. White/Brill Atlanta.
Figure 16–4, 16–6, 16–7   Courtesy of the Transvaal Museum.
Figure 16–5   Alun R. Hughes by permission of Professor Philip V. Tobias.
Figure 16–8   Alun R. Hughes, Paleoanthropology Research Unit, University of the Witwatersrand.
Figure 16–10   National Geographic Society, courtesy of Hugo Van Lawick.
Figure 16–11   National Geographic Society.
Figure 16–12   Courtesy of R. E. F. Leakey, National Museums of Kenya.
Figure 16–13   Photo by Alan Walker/National Museums of Kenya.
Figure 16–14   Institute of Human Origins.

Figure 16–15   Don Johanson/Institute of Human Origins.
Figure 16–16   Photo by T. White.
Figure 16–17   Andrew Hill/Anthro-Photo.
Figure 16–22   Courtesy of the Transvaal Museum, Pretoria, photo by J. F. Thackeray.

Chapter 16 Color Insert:
Figure 16–A, 16–B   Kenneth Garrett/National Geographic Image Collection.
Figure 16–C   Donald C. Johanson/Institute of Human Origins.
Figure 16–D   David L. Brill/National Geographic Society and the National Museums of Kenya.

Chapter 17 Opening   Carl W. Harmon/National Geographic Image Collection.
Figure 17–1, 17–3   Courtesy of R. E. F. Leakey, National Museums of Kenya.
Figure 17–2, 17–6   Natural History Museum, London.
Figure 17–4   Courtesy of Michael H. Day.
Figure 17–5   Neg. #336185, 336412, and 410816, Courtesy Department of Library Services, American Museum of Natural History.
Figure 17–7   David L. Brill/National Geographic Society and the National Museums of Kenya.
Figure 17–8   David L. Brill/National Museums of Kenya.
Figure 17–14   Alan Walker/Anthro-Photo.
Figure 17–15   Courtesy of Kathy D. Schick and Nicholas Toth, CRAFT Research Center, Indiana University. From Schick and Toth, *Making Silent Stones Speak*, 1993, pages 167.
Figure 17–17   Courtesy of Pat Shipman.

Chapter 18 Opening   David L. Brill photo of Musee de l'Homme, Paris Artifact/Brill Atlantic.
Figure 18–1, 18–7   Neg. #410816, 327423, and 327424. Courtesy Department of Library Services, American Museum of Natural History.
Figure 18–3   Natural History Museum, London.
Figure 18–4   Courtesy of Milford H. Wolpoff.
Figure 18–5   David L. Brill photo of Musee de l'Homme, Paris Artifact/Brill Atlantic.
Figure 18–9   David L. Brill/Brill Atlantic.
Figure 18–11   From the collection of the Peabody Museum, Harvard. Courtesy of Erik Trinkaus.
Box 18–3   Copyright © Erik Trinkaus. Used with permission of Erik Trinkaus.

Chapter 19 Opening   Jean Clottes/Ministere de al Culture/Sygma.
Figure 19–2, 19–4, 19–6   Natural History Museum, London.

Figure 19–3 Department of Library Services, American Museum of Natural History.

Figure 19–7 *(b)* Collection Phototheque du Musee de l'Homme, Paris.

Figure 19–8 Professor Randall White, New York University.

Figure 19–10, 19–11 Neg. #326474 and 15038. Courtesy Department of Library Services, American Museum of Natural History.

Figure 19–12 Denver Museum of Natural History.

Figure 19–14 *(a)* Joe McDonald/Animals Animals; *(b)* Ralph A. Reinhold/Animals Animals.

Box 19–2 Jean Clottes/Ministere de al Culture/Sygma.

Epilogue Opening NASA.

Figure E–2 Catherine Karnow/Woodfin Camp & Associates.

Figure E–3 Elliott Erwitt, Magnum.

Figure E–4 Ray Ellis/Photo Researchers.

Figure E–6 Rashid Jalukder/UNESCO.

ILLUSTRATION CREDITS

Figure 1–9   From *Science of Biology* by Paul Weisz. Copyright © 1963 by McGraw-Hill, Inc. Used with permission of McGraw-Hill, Inc.

Figure 1–11   From *Fundamentals of Biology*, 3d ed., by Eugene P. Odum. Copyright 1971 by W. B. Saunders Company. Used with permission of W. B. Saunders Company and Eugene P. Odum.

Figure 2–9   From *Biological Anthropology: A Text–Workbook Approach*, by Stephen Gabow and Leslie Fleming. Copyright © 1991 by Kendall/Hunt Publishing Company. Used with permission.

Box 3–2   From *Bodyspace: Anthropometry, Ergonomics and Design* by Stephen Pleasant (Philadelphia: Taylor Francis, 1986). Used with permission of Stephen Pleasant.

Figure 4–3   From *Principles of Human Genetics*, 3d edition by Curt Stern. Copyright © 1973 by Curt Stern. Reprinted with permission of W. H. Freeman and Company.

Figure 4–10   From M. C. G. Israëls, et al., "Haemophilia in the Female," *The Lancet*, 260 (1951). Used with permission of M. C. G. Israëls.

Figure 4–14   From *The Nature of Life* by J. H. Postlethweite and J. L. Hopson. Copyright © 1989 by McGraw-Hill, Inc. Used with permission of McGraw-Hill, Inc.

Figure 4–15, 4–17   From *Biology* by J. H. Postlethweite, J. L. Hopson, and R. C. Veres. Copyright © 1991 by McGraw-Hill, Inc. Used with permission of McGraw-Hill, Inc.

Figure 4–16   Figure from *An Introduction to Human Genetics*, 4th ed., by Eldon Sutton. Copyright © 1988 by Harcourt Brace & Company, reproduced by permission of the publisher.

Figure 4–20   Reprinted with permission from NIH/CEPH Collaborative Mapping Group, "A Comprehensive Genetic Linkage Map of the Human Genome," *Science*, 258 (1992), 82. Copyright © 1992 American Association for the Advancement of Science.

Figure 5–2   *(a)* From J. G. Carlson, "Analysis of X-ray Induced Single Breaks in Neuroblast Chromosomes of the Grasshopper," *Proceedings of The National Academy of Sciences*, 27 (1941). Used with permission of The National Academy of Sciences and J. G. Carlson. *(b)* From C. E. Purdom, *Genetic Effects of Radiation*. Copyright © 1963 by Academic Press, Inc. Used with permission of Academic Press, Inc., and C. E. Purdom.

Figure 6–1   Based on data from A. H. Booth, "Observations on the Natural History of the Olive Colobus Monkeys, *Procolobus verus* (van Beneden), "*Proceedings of the Zoological Society of London*, 1929 (1957). Used with permission of The Zoological Society of London.

Figure 6–5   Data from C. A. Clarke, "Blood Groups and Disease," *Progesss in Medical Genetics*, vol. 1, Grune and Stratton, 1961. By permission of Grune and Stratton and C. A. Clarke.

Figure 6–6   From John Buettner-Janusch, *Origins of Man*. Copyright © 1966 by John Wiley & Sons, Inc. Used with permission of John Wiley & Sons, Inc.

563

Figure 6–11 From *The Nature of Life* by J. H. Postlethweite and J. L. Hopson. Copyright © 1989 by McGraw-Hill, Inc. Used with permission of McGraw-Hill, Inc.

Figure 6–12, 6–13 From David Lack, *Darwin's Finches*, 1947. Reprinted with the permission of Cambridge University Press.

Figure 7–1 Amos Rapoport, *House Form and Culture*, Copyright © 1969, p. 99. Reprinted by permission of Prentice-Hall, Inc., Englewood Cliffs, New Jersey.

Figure 7–3 From "Barometric Pressure and Oxygen Pressure at High Altitude," in G. E. Folk, *Introduction to Environmental Physiology* (Philadelphia: Lea and Febiger, 1966).

Figure 7–4 From A. Hurtado, "Animals in High Altitudes: Resident Man," in D. B. Dill (ed.), *Handbook of Physiology: Adaptation to the Environment*, 1964. Courtesy of The American Physiological Society and Alberto Hurtado.

Figure 7–5 From J. A. Harris, et al., *The Measurement of Man*. University of Minnesota Press, Minneapolis. Copyright © 1930 by the University of Minnesota.

Figure 7–6, 7–7 From W. M. Krogman, *The Human Skeleton in Forensic Medicine*, 2d ed., 1962. Courtesy of Charles C. Thomas, Publisher, Springfield, Illinois.

Figure 7–11 From B. M. Gilbert and T. W. McKern, "A Method for Aging the Female Os Pubis," *American Journal of Physical Anthropology*, 38 (1973). Copyright © 1973 Alan R. Liss, Inc. Reprinted by permission of Wiley–Liss, a division of John Wiley & Sons, Inc.

Figure 7–13, 7–14, 7–15 From J. M. Tanner, *Growth at Adolescence*, 2d ed. (Oxford: Blackwell Scientific Publications, 1962). Used with permission of Blackwell Scientific Publications.

Figure 7–16 From A. R. Friancho and P. T. Baker, "Altitude and Growth: a Study of the Patterns of Physical Growth of a High Altitude Peruvian Quechua Population," *American Journal of Physical Anthropology*, 32 (1970), p. 290. Courtesy of The Wistar Institute Press.

Figure 7–17 Courtesy of Open Books and Harvard University Press.

Figure 7–19 Data from tables in H. V. Meredity, "Findings from Asia, Australia, Europe, and North America on Secular Change in Mean Height of Children, Youths, and Young Adults," *American Journal of Physical Anthropology*, 44 (1976), 315–326. Original data published in R. E. Roth and M. Harris, *The Physical Condition of Children Attending Public Schools in New South Wales* (Sydney: Department of Public Instruction, 1908), and D. L. Jones, W. Hemphill, and E. S. A. Meyers, *Height, Weight and Other Physical Characteristics of New South Wales Children: Part I, Children Age Five Years and Over* (Sydney: New South Wales Department of Health, 1973).

Figure 8–3, 8–5 From A. E. Mourant, A. C. Kopeć, and K. Domaniewski-Sobczak, *The Distribution of the Human Blood Groups and Other Polymorphisms*, 2d ed. (London: Oxford University Press, 1976). Used with permission of Oxford University Press.

Figure 8–4 From E. Sunderland, "Hair-Colour Variation in the United Kingdom," *Annuals of Human Genetics*, 21 (1955–56). Used by permission of Cambridge University Press.

Figure 8–8 From *The Kinds of Mankind* by Morton Klass and Hal Hellman (J. B. Lippincott). Copyright © 1971 by Morton Klass and Hal Hellman.

Figure 8–9 Adapted from L. L. Cavalli-Sforza, et al., "Reconstruction of Human Evolution: Bringing Together Genetic, Archaeological, and Linguistic Data," *Proceedings of the National Academy of Sciences*, 85 (1988), 6002–6006. Courtesy of L. L. Cavalli-Sforza.

Figure 8–10 From *Intelligence: Statistical Concepts of Its Nature* by L. J. Bischof. Copyright © 1954 by Doubleday & Company, Inc. Used with permission of Random House, Inc.

Box 8–1 From D. H. Ubelaker, "Skeletal Evidence for Kneeling in Prehistoric Ecuador," *American Journal of Physical Anthropology*, 51 (1979), 683. Used with permission of The Wistar Institute Press.

Figure 9–2, 9–9 Figure from *Life: An Introduction to Biology*, 2d ed., George G. Simpson and William S. Beck. Copyright © 1957, 1965, by Harcourt Brace Jovanovich, Inc., and reproduced with their permission.

Figure 9–10 From A. S. Romer, *The Vertebrate Body*. Copyright © 1959 by A. S. Romer. Used with permission of The University of Chicago Press and A. S. Romer.

Figure 9–11 (b) From W. E. LeGros Clark, *The Antecedents of Man*, 1959 by Edinburgh University Press. By permission of Quadrangle/The New York Times Book Co.

Figure 9–14 Reprinted with permission from M. J. Novacek, "Mammalian Phylogeny: Shaking the Tree," *Nature*, 356 (12 March 1992), 121–125.

Copyright © 1992 American Association for the Advancement of Science.

Box 9–1   Reprinted by permission of the publishers from *The Diversity of Life* by Edward O. Wilson, Cambridge, Mass.: The Belnap Press of Harvard University Press. Copyright © 1992 by Edward O. Wilson.

Box 9–2   Reprinted with permission from J. G. M. Thewissen, S. T. Hussain, and M. Arif, "Fossil Evidence for the Origin of Aquatic Locomotion in Archaeocete Whales," *Science*, 263 (1994), 210–212. Copyright © 1992 American Association for the Advancement of Science.

Box 9–3   From J. H. Ostrom, "Osteology of *Deinonychus antirrhopus*, an Unusual Theropod from the Lower Cretaceous of Montana," *Bulletin of the Peabody Museum of Natural History*, 30 (1969). Used with permission of the Peabody Museum of Natural History and John H. Ostrom.

Figure 10–2   From W. E. LeGros Clark, *The Antecedents of Man*, 1959 by Edinburgh University Press. By permission of Quadrangle/The New York Times Book Co.

Figure 10–5   From Adolph H. Schultz, *The Life of Primates*. Copyright © 1969 by Adolph H. Schultz. Used with permission of Universe Books, Weidenfeld, and A. H. Schultz.

Figure 10–6   From E. C. Amoroso, "Placentation," in *Marshall's Physiology of Reproduction*, 3d ed., vol. 2, 1952. Used with permission of Longmans, Green & Co. and E. C. Amoroso.

Figure 10–7   From G. J. Romanes, *Darwin, and after Darwin* (Chicago: Open Court, 1892). After Hackel.

Figure 10–8, 10–14, 10–25   From C. F. Hockett, *Man's Place in Nature*. Copyright © 1973 by McGraw-Hill, Inc. Used with permission of McGraw-Hill, Inc., and C. F. Hockett.

Figure 11–6, 11–7   Figure from *Primate Behavior: Field Studies of Monkeys and Apes* by Irven DeVore. Copyright © 1965 by Holt, Rinehart and Winston, Inc. Reprinted by permission of Holt, Rinehart and Winston, Inc. and by Irven DeVore.

Figure 12–11   From D. L. Chaney and R. M. Seyfarth, *How Monkeys See the World*. Copyright © 1990 by The University of Chicago Press. Used with permission of The University of Chicago Press.

Box 12–2   F. S. Szalay and R. K. Costello, "Evolution of Permanent Estrus Displays in Hominids," *Journal of Human Evolution*, 20 (1991), 439–464. Courtesy of F. S. Szalay.

Figure 13–6, 13–7   From Adolph H. Schultz, *The Life of Primates*. Copyright © 1969 by Adolph H. Schultz. Used with permission of Universe Books, Weidenfeld, and A. H. Schultz.

Figure 13–8   From John Buettner-Janusch, *Origins of Man*, 1966. Used with permission of John Wiley & Sons, Inc.

Figure 13–9   Reprinted from Adolph H. Schultz, "The Skeleton of the Trunk and Limbs of Higher Primates," *Human Biology*, 2 (1930). Copyright © 1930 by Warwick and York, Inc. Used with permission of Wayne State University Press.

Figure 13–10   Neg. #320654, Department of Library Services, American Museum of Natural History.

Figure 13–14   From Robert D. Martin, *Primate Origins and Evolution*. Copyright © 1990 by R. D. Martin. Reprinted/reproduced by permission of Princeton University Press.

Figure 13–15, 13–16   Figure from *Life: An Introduction to Biology*, 2d ed., George G. Simpson and William S. Beck. Copyright © 1957, 1965, by Harcourt Brace Jovanovich, Inc., and reproduced with permission.

Figure 13–17   Reprinted with permission of Macmillan Publishing Co., Inc. from W. Penfield and T. Rasmussen, *The Cerebral Cortex of Man*. Copyright © 1950 by Macmillan Publishing Co., Inc.

Figure 13–18   Adapted from R. G. Tague and C. O. Lovejoy, "The obstetric pelvis of A.L. 288–1 (Lucy)," *Journal of Human Evolution*, 15 (1986), 237–255. Reprinted with permission of Academic Press.

Figure 13–20, 13–25, 13–26   L. Aiello and C. Dean, *An Introduction to Human Evolutionary Biology* (San Diego: Academic Press, 1990). Illustration by Jo Cameron. Reprinted with permission of Leslie Aiello and Academic Press.

Figure 13–22, 13–24   From Daris R. Swindler, *Dentition of Living Primates* (San Diego: Academic Press, 1976). Reprinted with permission of Daris R. Swindler and Academic Press.

Figure 13–29   J. J. Yunis, J. R. Sawyer, and K. Dunham, "The Striking Resemblance of High-Resolution G-Banded Chromosomes of Man and Chimpanzees," *Science*, 208 (1980), 1145–1149. Copyright © 1980 by the AAAS.

Figure 13–31   From Morris Goodman, Alejo E. Romero-Herrera, Howard Dene, John Czelusniak, and Richard E. Tashian, "Amino Acid Sequence Evidence on the Phylogeny of Primates and Other Eutherians," in Morris Goodmand (ed.), *Macromolecular Sequences in Systematic and Evolutionary Biology* (New York: Plenum, 1982).

Figure 14–3 From Pat Shipman, *Life History of a Fossil* (Cambridge, Mass.: Harvard University Press, 1981), 14. Copyright © 1981 by the President and Fellows of Harvard University. Reprinted by permission of Harvard University Press.

Figure 14–5 From Glenn Ll. Isaac, "Early Hominids in Action: A Commentary on the Contribution of Archaeology to Understanding the Fossil Record in East Africa," *Yearbook of Physical Anthropology*, 19 (1975). Reproduced by permission of John Wiley & Sons, Inc.

Figure 14–8 From M. D. Leakey, *Olduvai Gorge*, vol. 3, *Excavations in Beds I and II, 1960–1963* (Cambridge: Cambridge University Press, 1971).

Figure 14–13 Adapted from W. Brian Harland, et al., *A Geologic Time Scale 1989*, 1990. Reprinted with the permission of Cambridge University Press and W. Brian Harland.

Figure 14–14 Adapted from *The Nature of Life* by J. H. Postlethweite and J. L. Hopson. Copyright © 1989 by McGraw-Hill, Inc. Used with permission of McGraw-Hill, Inc.

Figure 14–15 From W. Kenneth Hamblin, *The Earth's Dynamic System*, 2d ed., 1978. Burgess Publishing Co.

Figure 14–16 From *Man in Prehistory*, 2d ed., by Chester S. Chard. Copyright © 1975 by McGraw-Hill, Inc. Used with permission of McGraw-Hill, Inc.

Figure 15–2 From E. Simons and D. Russell, "Notes on the Cranial Anatomy of *Necrolemur*," *Breviora*, 127 (1960). Museum of Comparative Zoology, Harvard University. Copyright © President and Fellows of Harvard College.

Figure 15–3 Reprinted with permission of Macmillan Publishing Co., Inc., from E. L. Simons, *Primate Evolution*. Copyright © 1972 by Elwyn L. Simons.

Figure 15–5 Based upon J. G. Fleagle, et al., "Age of the Earliest African Anthropoid," *Science*, 234 (1986), 1247–1249. Copyright © 1986 by the AAAS.

Figure 15–8, Box 15–2 John G. Fleagle, *Primate Adaptations and Evolution* (San Diego: Academic, 1988). Drawing by Stephen Nash. Reproduced by permission of John G. Fleagle and Academic Press.

Figure 15–14 From A. C. Walker and M. Pickford, "New Postcranial Fossils of *Proconsul africanus* and *Proconsul nyanzae*," in Russell L. Ciochon and Robert S. Corrucini, *New Interpretations of Ape and Human Ancestry* (New York: Plenum, 1983), 325–351. Reprinted with permission of Plenum and Alan C. Walker.

Figure 15–15 From R. L. Bernor, "Geochronology and Zoogeographic Relationships of Miocene Hominoidea," in Russel L. Ciochon and Robert S. Corrucini, *New Interpretations of Ape and Human Ancestry* (New York: Plenum, 1983). Reprinted with permission of Plenum and Dr. Bernor.

Box 15–4 Reprinted with permission from F. S. Szalay and A. Berzi, "Cranial Anatomy of Oreopithecus," *Science*, 180 (1973), 184. Copyright © 1973 American Association for the Advancement of Science. Courtesy of F. S. Szalay.

Figure 16–2, 16–19 From S. Jones, et al. (eds.), *The Cambridge Encyclopedia of Human Evolution* (Cambridge: Cambridge University Press, 1992), 232, 237. Copyright © Cambridge University Press 1992. Reprinted with permission of Cambridge University Press.

Figure 16–3 Courtesy of C. K. Brain, Transvaal Museum.

Figure 16–9 From F. Brown, "Development of Pliocene and Pleistocene Chronology of the Turkana Basin, East Africa, and Its Relation to Other Sites," in R. S. Corruccini and R. L. Ciochon (eds.), *Integrative Paths to the Past: Paleoanthropological Advances in Honor of F. Clark Howell* (Englewood Cliffs, N. J.: Prentice-Hall, 1994), 300. Reprinted with permission of Prentice-Hall.

Figure 16–18 From W. E. LeGros Clark, *History of the Primates*, 5th ed. Copyright © 1949, 1965, by the Trustees of the British Museum (Natural History). Used with permissions of The University of Chicago Press.

Figure 16–20, 16–25 Drawings by Luba Dmytryk Gudz from *Lucy: The Beginnings of Humankind*. Copyright © 1981 by Donald C. Johanson and Maitland A. Edey.

Figure 16–21 From *Osteodontokeratic Culture of Australopithecus prometheus*, Transvaal Museum Memoir No. 10, 1957. Used with the permission of the Transvaal Museum, Republic of South Africa.

Figure 16–23 Reprinted with permission from R. L. Susman, "Fossil Evidence for Early Hominid Tool Use," *Science*, 265 (1994), 1572. Copyright © 1994 American Association for the Advancement of Science. Randall L. Susman, Univ. at Stony Brook.

Figure 16–24 From Clark Spencer Larsen, Robert M. Matter, and Daniel L. Gebo, *Human Origins: The Fossil Record*, 2d ed., 49, 59, and 66. Copyright © 1985, 1991 by Waveland Press, Inc., Prospect Heights, Ill. Reprinted with permission of publisher.

Figure 16–26 Tim D. White, Donald C. Johanson, and William H. Kimbel, "*Australopithecus africanus:* Its Phylogenetic Position Reconsidered," *South African Journal of Science,* 77 (October 1981).

Figure 16–27 From Yoel Rak, *The Australopithecine Face* (New York: Academic Press, 1983). Reproduced by permission of Yoel Rak and Academic Press.

Figure 17–11, 17–12, 17–13 From M. D. Leakey, *Olduvai Gorge,* vol. 3, *Excavations in Beds I and II, 1960–1963* (Cambridge: Cambridge University Press, 1971). Reprinted with the permission of Cambridge University Press.

Figure 17–16 From François Bordes, *The Old Stone Age.* Copyright © 1968 by François Bordes. Used with permission of McGraw-Hill, Inc.

Box 17–1 Courtesy of Kathy D. Schick and Nicholas Toth, CRAFT Research Center, Indiana University. From Schick and Toth, *Making Silent Stones Speak,* 1993, 167, 184–185.

Figure 18–14 From François Bordes, *The Old Stone Age.* Copyright © 1968 by François Bordes. Used with permission of McGraw-Hill, Inc.

Figure 18–15 From Grahame Clarke, *The Stone Age Hunters,* 1967. Used with permission of Thames and Hudson, Ltd.

Box 18–2 From M. Boule and H. V. Vallois, *Fossil Men,* 1957. Used with permission of Holt, Rinehart and Winston.

Figure 19–7 *(a)* From C. J. Jolly and R. White, *Physical Anthropology and Archaeology,* 5th ed. Copyright © 1995 by McGraw-Hill, Inc. Used with permission of McGraw-Hill, Inc.

Figure 19–9, 19–13 From François Bordes, *The Old Stone Age.* Copyright © 1968 by François Bordes. Used with permission of McGraw-Hill, Inc.

Figure 19–15, 19–16 From *Prehistoric Men* by Robert Braidwood. Copyright © 1967, 1975 by McGraw-Hill, Inc. Reprinted by permission of McGraw-Hill, Inc.

Figure A–1 Courtesy Department of Library Services, American Museum of Natural History.

Figure A–2 Reprinted from D. R. Brothwell, *Digging Up Bones,* third edition. Copyright © 1981 by D. R. Brothwell. Used by permission of the publisher, Cornell University Press.

INDEX